ICT Ethics and Security in the 21st Century:

New Developments and Applications

Marian Quigley
Monash University, Australia

Senior Editorial Director:	Kristin Klinger
Director of Book Publications:	Julia Mosemann
Editorial Director:	Lindsay Johnston
Acquisitions Editor:	Erika Carter
Development Editor:	Mike Killian
Production Coordinator:	Jamie Snavely
Typesetters:	Keith Glazewski & Natalie Pronio
Cover Design:	Nick Newcomer

Published in the United States of America by
Information Science Reference (an imprint of IGI Global)
701 E. Chocolate Avenue
Hershey PA 17033
Tel: 717-533-8845
Fax: 717-533-8661
E-mail: cust@igi-global.com
Web site: http://www.igi-global.com/reference

Library of Congress Cataloging-in-Publication Data

ICT ethics and security in the 21st century: new developments and
applications / Marian Quigley, editor.
   p. cm.
 Includes bibliographical references and index.
 Summary: "This book examines a range of major issues concerning ICT ethics
and security in the 21st century and provides perspectives on contemporary
ethical and security issues from leading international scholars"--Provided by
publisher.
 ISBN 978-1-60960-573-5 (hbk.) -- ISBN 978-1-60960-574-2 (ebook) 1.
Information technology--Moral and ethical aspects. 2. Information technology-
-Social aspects. 3. Information technology--Security measures. 4. Computer
security. I. Quigley, Marian.
 T58.5.I2256 2011
 303.48'33--dc22
                         2010040621

British Cataloguing in Publication Data
A Cataloguing in Publication record for this book is available from the British Library.

All work contributed to this book is new, previously-unpublished material. The views expressed in this book are those of the authors, but not necessarily of the publisher.

Table of Contents

Foreword xiii

Preface xv

Acknowledgment xx

Section 1
Online Ethics

Chapter 1
Understanding Trust in Virtual Communities: Revisited 1
Qing Zou, McGill University, Canada
Eun G. Park, McGill University, Canada

Chapter 2
Social Networks and Students' Ethical Behavior 27
Lori N. K. Leonard, University of Tulsa, USA
Tracy S. Manly, University of Tulsa, USA

Chapter 3
The Ethics of Security of Personal Information upon Facebook 46
Shona Leitch, Deakin University, Australia
Matthew Warren, Deakin University, Australia

Chapter 4
Copyright and Ethical Issues in Emerging Models for the Digital Media Reporting of Sports
News in Australia 66
Mary Wyburn, University of Sydney, Australia

Section 2
Ethical Concerns in the Handling and Delivery of Health and Safety Information

Chapter 5
The Protocols of Privileged Information Handling in an E-Health Context: Australia 87
Juanita Fernando, Monash University, Australia

Chapter 6
The Changing World of ICT and Health: Crossing the Digital Divide 111
Prajesh Chhanabhai, University of Otago, New Zealand
Alec Holt, University of Otago, New Zealand

Chapter 7
The Socio-Ethical Considerations Surrounding Government Mandated Location-Based
Services during Emergencies: An Australian Case Study 129
Anas Aloudat, University of Wollongong, Australia
Katina Michael, University of Wollongong, Australia

Section 3
Ethics and Security in Organisations

Chapter 8
Monitoring Employee Actions in the Workplace: Good Business Practice or Unethical
Behaviour? 156
Cliona McParland, Dublin City University, Ireland
Regina Connolly, Dublin City University, Ireland

Chapter 9
Policy and Issues in Deploying Automated Plagiarism Detection Systems in Academic
Communities: A Case Study of VeriGuide 172
Chi Hong Cheong, The Chinese University of Hong Kong, Hong Kong
Tak Pang Lau, The Chinese University of Hong Kong, Hong Kong
Irwin King, The Chinese University of Hong Kong, Hong Kong

Chapter 10
Security Technologies and Policies in Organisations 196
Nickolas J. G. Falkner, The University of Adelaide, Australia

Chapter 11
Critical Infrastructure Protection: An Ethical Choice 214
Graeme Pye, Deakin University, Australia
Matthew Warren, Deakin University, Australia
William Hutchinson, Edith Cowan University, Australia

Chapter 12

Effective Infrastructure Protection through Virtualization 231

    Dennis C. Guster, St. Cloud State University, USA

    Olivia F. Lee, St. Cloud State University, USA

Chapter 13

Firewall Rulebase Management: Tools and Techniques 254

    Michael J. Chapple, University of Notre Dame, USA

    Aaron Striegel, University of Notre Dame, USA

    Charles R. Crowell, University of Notre Dame, USA

Chapter 14

Integration of COBIT, Balanced Scorecard and SSE-CMM as an Organizational &

Strategic Information Security Management (ISM) Framework 277

    James E. Goldman, Purdue University, USA

    Suchit Ahuja, Purdue University, USA

Compilation of References 310

About the Contributors 343

Index 350

Detailed Table of Contents

Foreword xiii

Preface xv

Acknowledgment xx

Section 1
Online Ethics

The chapters in this section primarily focus on ethical issues concerning the use of the Internet. These include: the establishment of trust in virtual communities, the education of students in using social networking systems, and personal information and its security on these systems. The last chapter in this section focuses on copyright issues concerning the digital media reporting of Australian sport.

Chapter 1

Understanding Trust in Virtual Communities: Revisited 1
Qing Zou, McGill University, Canada
Eun G. Park, McGill University, Canada

Trust is an essential component in interpersonal and commercial relationships. The anonymity and lack of physical presence which characterize online communication within virtual communities may impede or compromise the establishment of trust between parties. Consequently, the authors argue for the need for increased research into the nature of trust and trust building.

Chapter 2

Social Networks and Students' Ethical Behavior 27
Lori N. K. Leonard, University of Tulsa, USA
Tracy S. Manly, University of Tulsa, USA

The impersonal nature of the Internet may alter young people's ethical behaviour, promoting their over provision of personal information or their inappropriate behaviour or conversations. Focusing primarily on college students, the authors emphasise the need for their education concerning the proper use of social networking systems. They propose that such an education should be founded upon four classical ethical theories: utilitarianism, distributive justice, rights theory, and virtue ethics.

Chapter 3

The Ethics of Security of Personal Information upon Facebook 46

Shona Leitch, Deakin University, Australia
Matthew Warren, Deakin University, Australia

With a particular focus on the social networking site, Facebook, this chapter examines the ethical issues associated with personal information and its security. Following a discussion of a number of examples of breaches of security, the authors propose a model that evaluates Facebook security and risks. They conclude that the potential for identity theft and unethical behaviour on Facebook is often greater than on other social networking sites.

Chapter 4

Copyright and Ethical Issues in Emerging Models for the Digital Media Reporting of Sports
News in Australia 66

Mary Wyburn, University of Sydney, Australia

This chapter is concerned with copyright and ethical issues arising from the digital media reporting of sports news. Although the chapter focuses on the conflict between sports and media organization in Australia, it has wider, international implications. Following on from issues raised at a 2009 Senate enquiry, the author highlights the need for amendments to the copyright law or the establishment of an industry code of conduct.

Section 2
Ethical Concerns in the Handling and Delivery of Health and Safety Information

This section focuses on the problems and possible solutions concerning the electronic management and exchange of patient health information using ICT, as well as the difficulty of access to health information by the public in underdeveloped countries. The last chapter in this section uses an Australian case study to highlight the socio-ethical concerns regarding the use of mobile applications in emergency management.

Chapter 5

The Protocols of Privileged Information Handling in an Ehealth Context: Australia 87

Juanita Fernando, Medicine, Nursing & Health Sciences, Monash University, Australia

The author utilizes two case studies to highlight the problems associated with the implementation of an e-health system in Australia. These include time-poor clinicians, the complexity of legal health privacy frameworks, budgetary constraints, fragmentation, computer demands and disciplinary silos. The author claims that the resulting avoidance techniques by e-health clinicians are linked to adverse patient health outcomes.

Chapter 6

The Changing World of ICT and Health: Crossing the Digital Divide.................................. 111

Prajesh Chhanabhai, University of Otago, New Zealand

Alec Holt, University of Otago, New Zealand

The authors argue that whilst the heath consumer in developed nations have been empowered by the growth of technology and the resulting increased access to health information, those in underdeveloped countries may have become further disadvantaged. Consequently, the gap between information-rich and information- poor may have widened. The chapter examines the range of communication techniques used by developing countries, suggesting that mobile phones may offer a better solution than a sole reliance on the Internet.

Chapter 7

The Socio-Ethical Considerations Surrounding Government Mandated Location-Based

Services during Emergencies: An Australian Case Study... 129

Anas Aloudat, University of Wollongong, Australia

Katina Michael, University of Wollongong, Australia

This chapter focuses on the management of the 2009 Victorian bushfires in Australia. Despite the Australian government's utilization of mobile applications including mobile alerts and location services, 173 deaths resulted. The authors emphasise the potential for breaches in privacy, security and trust inherent in the use of these technologies, arguing that these need to be addressed prior to the widespread adoption of these services.

Section 3
Ethics and Security in Organisations

Chapters in this section deal with security methods for critical infrastructures and organizations and the ethical nature of these security choices. Ethical codes of behaviour within organizations are also examined.

Chapter 8

Monitoring Employee Actions in the Workplace: Good Business Practice or Unethical

Behaviour? 156

Cliona McParland, Dublin City University, Ireland

Regina Connolly, Dublin City University, Ireland

The ethical impact of electronic monitoring in the workplace is examined in this chapter. Managers' motivations for undertaking surveillance of its employees are discussed and employees' concerns about privacy are examined. The authors note that while European laws favour the rights of the employee, no hierarchy of privacy or ethical concerns has yet been established.

Chapter 9

Policy and Issues in Deploying Automated Plagiarism Detection Systems in Academic
Communities: A Case Study of VeriGuide 172

    Chi Hong Cheong, The Chinese University of Hong Kong, Hong Kong
    Tak Pang Lau, The Chinese University of Hong Kong, Hong Kong
    Irwin King, The Chinese University of Hong Kong, Hong Kong

This chapter discusses the growing problem of student plagiarism within universities which has accompanied the rise of the Internet. It examines the policy and issues encountered by the Chinese University of Hong Kong in its implementation of the automated plagiarism detection system, Veriguide. The authors conclude that student education should accompany any technological system adopted to combat plagiarism.

Chapter 10

Security Technologies and Policies in Organisations 196

    Nickolas J. G. Falkner, The University of Adelaide, Australia

The author proposes a hybrid ethical approach to the establishment of a code of ethics for organizations. Teleological, deontological and virtue-oriented aspects of the ethics associated with ICT security policy are discussed in order to provide a theoretical basis for such a code. The chapter also provides a set of case studies and general rules as an ethical basis for security policies.

Chapter 11

Critical Infrastructure Protection: An Ethical Choice 214

    Graeme Pye, Deakin University, Australia
    Matthew Warren, Deakin University, Australia
    William Hutchinson, Edith Cowan University, Australia

This chapter investigates the ethical choices associated with the management of threats to critical infrastructure systems during times of disaster. It utilizes the example of the protection of the security of a water supply infrastructure and the case study of an Australian community threatened by bushfire.

Chapter 12

Effective Infrastructure Protection through Virtualization 231

    Dennis C. Guster, St. Cloud State University, USA
    Olivia F. Lee, St. Cloud State University, USA

The chapter examines the protection of computer infrastructure in the face of a range of disasters including natural disaster, equipment failure and security breaches. The authors argue that the virtualization of hosts offers a better means of protection for computer infrastructure which, as well as being easier to manage, can be easily restored following a natural disaster.

Chapter 13

Firewall Rulebase Management: Tools and Techniques 254

Michael J. Chapple, University of Notre Dame, USA

Aaron Striegel, University of Notre Dame, USA

Charles R. Crowell, University of Notre Dame, USA

The authors focus on the firewall-one of the foundational network components for modern day computer security–and the need to maintain its maximum security effectiveness in the face of changing security threats and enterprise application needs. They provide a general model for the auditing and analysis of installed firewalls and insight for the proactive identification of rules with a high likelihood of becoming orphaned in the future.

Chapter 14

Integration of COBIT, Balanced Scorecard and SSE-CMM as an Organizational &

Strategic Information Security Management (ISM) Framework 277

James E. Goldman, Purdue University, USA

Suchit Ahuja, Purdue University, USA

The authors propose an organizational security strategy which involves the integration of a number of popular approaches: COBIT, Balanced Scorecard and CMM. They argue that this will provide a more comprehensive evaluation instrument that better aligns the business with its IT and information security strategies.

Compilation of References 310

About the Contributors 343

Index 350

Foreword

If the topic of ICT Ethics and Security in the 21st century is about anything at all, surely it is about change and all the challenges associated with change. To quote Italian philosopher Niccolo Machiavelli, "it must be considered that there is nothing more difficult to carry out, nor more doubtful of success, nor more dangerous to handle, than to initiate a new order of things." Yet 500 years on, although technology has advanced in unimaginable ways since Machiavelli, we still wrestle with the same intrinsic challenges of how to change the "order of things." We might justifiably ask what we really know about change, and in particular, what we know about making changes in the context of ICT ethics and security . Can we measure change? If so, what unit of measurement do we use? Productivity, compliance, user satisfaction, ethical acceptability? All of them?

However, we have learnt some things about ICT ethics and security. For instance, we know that introducing new technologies is likely to lead to changed behaviors either positive or negative, changes in legislation eventually, opportunities for those who would subvert the law, if not ethical values, and so on. We might also reflect on what we know about the preferred types of vehicle we choose to facilitate or mandate change. Traditionally, we have used strategies such as legislation, policy, standards, computerized business rules, as well as more socially oriented approaches, such as training and engagement tactics. But are they effective strategies, how viable are they in the long term, how far away are we from realizing the goal of controlling change in ICT security, and what role can ethics play in determining change for the good of all parties concerned?

ICT Ethics and Security in the 21st Century: New Developments and Applications has three sections, the first of which deals with online ethics. In the five years since Dr Quigley published her last book in this area, there have been many new developments in the online world. For example, with Web 2.0, we are really only now beginning to understand the implications of this way of interacting via the Web. Already, this has had a profound effect on many of us in terms of how we communicate with those around us, not least the younger among us, and so it is vitally important that the scientific community research and report on this significant area of change. In this section, we look at scientific research and discussion on virtual communities, social networking, plagiarism, and copyright.

Section two deals with ethical concerns in health and safety. The health arena is an obvious area in which the dual challenges of ethics and security come to the fore. For example, whilst we all quite rightly put great trust in our doctors and nurses to make appropriate medical decisions and evaluations on our behalf, are we equally justified in assuming that their computer knowledge is mature enough to safeguard and maintain our health information? This section also reports on how mobile/wireless technology is revolutionizing how health information is shared and how safety outcomes can be improved.

In the last section, ethics and security in organizations is examined. Organizations face challenges across the whole spectrum of issues in ICT ethics and security, and so in the section, we observe a maturing environment in which innovations in employee surveillance, ethical policy writing, standards, virtualization, computerized rules, and critical infrastructure are impacting the business.

This book explores current topics in ICT ethics and security that demonstrate both the challenges and the progress being made in this ever pervasive world of change that we live in. Each chapter is a snapshot of work being done in a particular area. Individually, they describe state of the art research being conducted in a specific domain; collectively, they start to address those intrinsic challenges of how to "change the order of things." Never before have such challenges been more immediate or consequential. ICT Ethics and Security in the 21st Century: New Developments and Applications is required reading for those seriously interested in how ICT is affecting us all.

Donald C. McDermid
August 2010

Donald C. McDermid, *BSc (hons) Comp Sc, Dip Adult Ed, MBA, PhD is an Associate Professor at the School of Computer and Security Science, Edith Cowan University, Western Australia. Donald has published over 40 academic papers in journals and at conferences and two books including a recent book on ICT ethics. His research interests are in the area of governance and change management-particularly in how IT can support change in health, where, compared to other sectors, change has been relatively slow to be embraced. A member of the Australian Computer Society and a committee member of the Health Informatics Society of Australia, he is passionate about raising the reputation of the ICT profession in Australia.*

REFERENCES

Machiavelli, N. (2004). *The Prince*. London, UK: Penguin.

Preface

The fifteenth and sixteenth centuries are celebrated for the voyages of discovery that proved the world is round. The eighteenth century saw the first proclamations of universal human rights. The twentieth century's conquest of space made it possible for a human being to look at our planet from a point not on it, and so to see it, literally, as one world. Now the twenty-first century faces the task of developing a suitable form of government for that single world. It is a daunting moral and intellectual challenge, but one we cannot refuse to take up. The future of the world depends on how well we meet it. (Singer, 2004, p.219)

As the renowned ethicist and academic, Peter Singer points out, what may have once been considered as local or national issues are now understood to be global. For example, the growing understanding that greenhouse gas emissions alter the world climate and affect everyone on the planet has generated international forums to attempt to find global solutions. On an economic level, too, a national disaster, particularly in a first world country, can have a worldwide and long lasting effect-as demonstrated by the US financial crisis of 2007. Similarly, technological development and its uses have global implications. Hence, whilst the contributors to *ICT Ethics and Security in the 21st Century: New Developments and Applications* may primarily focus on national case studies or examples, these too, either explicitly or implicitly, have global significance.

Singer also stresses the need for world governance–a scenario made more relevant and pressing by the borderless nature of the Internet. And of course, global governance requires an underlying, mutually agreed upon and universal code of ethics and legislation. The recent dispute between the Google Corporation and Chinese authorities has illustrated both the difficulties of achieving such a consensus as well as those associated with local or national regulation of the Internet.

ICT Ethics and Security in the 21st Century: New Developments and Applications highlights both the ongoing nature of some of the issues discussed in my earlier edited volume (Quigley, 2005), as well as new ethical dilemmas and security challenges posed by the rise of more recent technologies. Contributors to this volume address similar challenges to those of the 2005 text-issues such as the digital divide, threats to privacy and organisational security measures-albeit in differing contexts.

The development of Web 2.0 technologies in particular has refocused longstanding debates concerning issues such as copyright, defamation, privacy, and the protection of minors. However, it is the uses to which technology is put, rather than the technology itself which needs scrutiny. As the creator of the first website, Sir Tim Berners–Lee has noted, "This is humanity which is communicating over the Web, just as it's communicating over so many other different media ... we have to, first of all, make it a universal medium, and secondly we have to work to make sure that it supports the sort of society that we want to build on top of it" (Berners-Lee, 2005).

During the last five years, new technologies have developed apace and have been taken up by users at breathtaking speed. Web 2.0 technologies have enabled the Internet to become interactive so that the reader/consumer has now also become a writer/producer. This is exemplified by the development of social networking services (SNSs) such as MySpace, Twitter and Facebook. Individual computer users now write and upload personal diary entries or blogs for public view and upload their home videos for all to share on YouTube. They may expand their network of 'friends' via Facebook or assume a virtual identity for participation in a virtual world such as *Second Life* or in order to play 'massively multiplayer online role-playing games' (MMORPGs) such as the immensely popular *World of Warcraft* (WoW). Students and researchers may choose to contribute entries as well as consult the online encyclopaedia, *Wikipedia*.

The speed of the take up rate of these technologies is illustrated by the recent claim made by its founders that in the six years since its inception, the number of Facebook users has grown to 500 million or 1 in 14 of the world's population. However, access to ICTs is still by no means universal, whilst for those with access, security, and privacy concerns remain. For example, the threat to patients' privacy is one of the concerns highlighted by researchers in the growing area of e-health.

The need for an ethical education and the acceptance of individual moral responsibility in the proper use of technology is also addressed by a number of contributors to this volume. Trust is an essential element between members of virtual communities and young people in particular need to be educated in the proper use of social networking sites so that no one is subjected to defamation or personal vilification. In addition, methods to address the growing problem of plagiarism amongst student populations should include education concerning copyright as well as technological solutions.

Together with the ethical and security problems concerning online sites which are addressed here, other contributors highlight how the advancements in mobile technologies and the widespread use of mobile phones have opened up their potential as a communication device in emergency situations-provided they are properly used-and as a more economical alternative for providing access to health information in developing countries.

The need to maintain and update the security of critical infrastructures upon which essential community services depend, as well as that of computer systems within organisations also comprise a significant section of this text. As the authors note, however, security decisions go hand in hand with ethical choices, and organisations need to establish and abide by a system of ethical codes.

ICT Ethics and Security in the 21st Century: New Developments and Applications brings together a selection of relevant current research being undertaken in this important field of study. It comprises a valuable resource for ICT researchers, educators, students and professionals, and both employers and employees of large organisations searching for resolutions to the everyday ethical and security dilemmas with which we must grapple in our highly globalised and technologised world.

ORGANISATION OF THE BOOK

The book is divided into three sections:

- **Section 1:** Online Ethics (Chapters 1- 5)
- **Section 2:** Ethical Concerns in the Handling and Delivery of Health and Safety Information (Chapters 6 - 8) and
- **Section 3:** Ethics and Security in Organisations (Chapters 9 - 14).

Section 1: Online Ethics

Chapter 1: '*Understanding Trust in Virtual Communities: Revisited*' by Qing Zou & Eun G. Park, School of Information Studies, McGill University, Canada. The authors highlight trust and trust building as essential elements in communication within virtual communities, particularly as, unlike traditional communities, they have their own unique characteristics such as anonymity and lack of physical presence. Focusing on social rather than technical aspects of trust, this chapter examines different types of trust and the associated issues and challenges.

Chapter 2: '*Social Networks and Students' Ethical Behaviour*' by Lori N. K. Leonard & Tracy S. Manly, University of Tulsa, USA. This chapter focuses on social networking sites in order to examine the changing ethical structure of students when using technology. The authors also suggest ways to teach ethics in light of this change and include a discussion of four classical ethical theories that should be considered when discussing or teaching social networking.

Chapter 3: '*The Ethics of Security of Personal Information upon Facebook*' by Shona Leitch and Matthew Warren, School of Information Systems, Deakin University, Australia. The authors examine the ethical issues associated with personal information as well as the security of that information on social networking systems, with a particular emphasis on Facebook. They discuss a number of examples where personal information has been breached and put forward a model that evaluates the security and risks and proposes a framework that relates to the use of information within Facebook.

Chapter 4: '*Copyright and Ethical Issues in Emerging Models for the Digital Media Reporting of Sports News in Australia*' by Mary Wyburn, University of Sydney, Australia. This chapter addresses the copyright and ethical issues concerning the emerging models for the digital reporting of sports news in Australia. It also highlights their wider international implications. In particular, it explores the use by news organisations of a defence in copyright law that provides protection against an infringement action for the reporting of news and the use by sports organisations of journalist accreditation to limit, by way of contract, the uses made of copyright material generated at sports events.

Chapter 5: '*The Protocols of Privileged Information Handling in an E-Health Context: Australia*' by Dr Juanita Fernando, Medicine, Nursing & Health Sciences, Monash University, Australia. Utilizing the findings from two case studies, the author emphasizes the need for a review by health authorities of real-life workplace privacy and security before setting new privileged information handling protocols as the foundation of a new national e-health scheme.

Section 2: Ethical Concerns in the Handling and Delivery of Health and Safety Information

Chapter 6: '*The Changing World of ICT and Health: Crossing the Digital Divide*' by Prajesh Chhanabhai & Alec Holt, University of Otago, New Zealand. The authors argue that, whilst technology has empowered the healthcare consumer, at the same time, it has contributed to the widening of the digital divide. This chapter examines how developing countries have tackled this problem by using varying communication techniques to share health information. The authors suggest that mobile phone technology may provide better access to health information than the Internet in these countries.

Chapter 7: '*The Socio-Ethical Considerations Surrounding Government Mandated Location-Based Services during Emergencies: An Australian Case Study*' by Anas Aloudat and Katina Michael, School of Information Systems and Technology, University of Wollongong, Australia. The chapter presents a case study on how modern technologies, namely mobile applications, are changing the landscape of emergency management in Australia. Through an examination of the 2009 Victorian bushfires, the authors discuss the ethical considerations associated with the adoption of mobile technologies for emergency management.

Chapter 8: '*Monitoring Employee Actions in the Workplace: Good Business Practice or Unethical Behaviour?*' by Cliona McParland & Dr. Regina Connolly, Dublin City University, Ireland. This chapter examines some of the major issues concerning workplace surveillance in a computer-mediated work environment, including managers' motivations and employee concerns about threats to their privacy. The ethical impact of monitoring in the workplace is examined, addressing whether management's ability to monitor employee actions in the workplace represents good business practice or constitutes an invasion of privacy.

Section 3: Ethics and Security in Organisations

Chapter 9: '*Policy and Issues in Deploying Automated Plagiarism Detection Systems in Academic Communities: A Case Study of Veriguide*' by Chi Hong Cheong, Tak Pang Lau, and Irwin King, Department of Computer Science and Engineering, The Chinese University of Hong Kong.

The authors note that as the Internet has contributed to a growth in student plagiarism, educational institutions are seeking technological solutions to combat it. The chapter examines the policy and issues encountered by the Chinese University of Hong Kong in its implementation of the automated plagiarism detection system, Veriguide.

Chapter 10: '*Security and Policies in Organisations*' by Nickolas J. G. Falkner, The University of Adelaide, Australia. In attempting to find a well-established code of ethics that binds the organisation as a whole, the author proposes a hybrid ethical approach that can be adapted to any business–one which is flexible, extensible and practical. The chapter provides a set of case studies and general rules as an ethical basis for the development and implementation of security policies. Teleological, deontological, and virtue-oriented aspects of the ethics surrounding organisational ICT security policy are discussed in order to provide a more theoretical basis for an ethical organisation.

Chapter 11: '*Critical Infrastructure Protection: An Ethical Choice*' by Graeme Pye and Matthew Warren, Deakin University, Australia and William Hutchinson, Edith Cowan University, Australia. Focusing on Australia and utilising the case study of a community threatened by bushfire, the chapter investigates the ethical choices that arise with regard to managing threats to critical infrastructure systems during times of disaster, which may impinge upon the availability and quality of the resources that critical infrastructure systems supply to the community.

Chapter 12: '*Effective Infrastructure Protection through Virtualization*' by Dennis C. Guster and Olivia F. Lee, St. Cloud State University, Minnesota, USA. Protection of an organisation's computer infrastructure in order to maintain continuity of operations involves a number of different concerns, including: managing natural disasters, equipment failure, security breaches, poor data management, inadequate design, and complex/impractical design. The authors argue that the virtualization of hosts offers a better means of protection for computer infrastructure which, as well as being easier to manage, can be easily restored following a natural disaster.

Chapter 13: '*Firewall Rulebase Management: Tools and Techniques*' by Michael J. Chapple and Aaron Striegel, Department of Computer Science and Engineering, University of Notre Dame, USA and Charles R. Crowell, Department of Psychology, University of Notre Dame, USA. This chapter examines the problem of how to keep the firewall-one of the foundational network components for modern day computer security-at maximum security effectiveness in the face of changing security threats and enterprise application needs. It provides a general model for the auditing and analysis of installed firewalls and insight for the proactive identification of rules with a high likelihood of becoming orphaned in the future.

Chapter 14: '*Integration of COBIT, Balanced Scorecard and SSE-CMM as an Organizational & Strategic Information Security Management (ISM) Framework*' by James E. Goldman & Suchit Ahuja, Purdue University, USA. The authors propose an integrated framework comprising Control Objectives for Information Technology (COBIT) and Balanced Scorecard (BSC) frameworks, in conjunction with Systems Security Engineering Capability Maturity Model (SSE-CMM), arguing that it provides a more comprehensive mechanism for strategic information security management: one that is fully aligned with business, IT and information security strategies.

Marian Quigley
August 2010

REFERENCES

Lawson, M. (2010). Berners-Lee on the read/write web. *BBC News*. Retrieved July 30, 2010, from http://news.bbc.co.uk/2/hi/technology/4132752.stm

Quigley, M. (2005). *Information security and ethics: Social and organizational issues*. Hershey, PA: IRM Press.

Singer, P. (2004). *One world: The ethics of globalisation*. Melbourne, Australia: Text Publishing.

Acknowledgment

I wish to thank all of the contributors to this volume as well as those whose work, for various reasons, did not make it into print this time.

My grateful appreciation is also extended to all of the chapter reviewers and the Editorial Advisory Board members for their valuable assistance to me and for their considered responses and advice to the authors.

I am grateful to the Foreword Author, Donald McDermid for his interest in the project, and particularly to Mehdi Khosrow-Pour and the publishing team at IGI Global for making this project possible.

This book is dedicated to my late parents, Thomas and Dorothy Fenton who always had such faith in me.

Marian Quigley
Monash University, Australia
August 2010

Section 1
Online Ethics

Chapter 1
Understanding Trust in Virtual Communities:
Revisited

Qing Zou
McGill University, Canada

Eun G. Park
McGill University, Canada

ABSTRACT

With people participating in various virtual communities in everyday life, trust building between participants is significant and indispensable in order to maintain communication in both traditional and virtual communities. In particular, virtual communities provide a platform or network through which members can communicate with faster and more simultaneous interactions in invisible ways. Since the importance of trust in virtual communities has been widely recognized, trust as a complex, multi-faceted, and context-dependent concept has been examined by many researchers in several disciplines. In this chapter, the authors aim to examine the definitions and characteristics of trust in the context of virtual communities and discuss terms relevant to the concept of trust. Different types of trust are investigated. Issues, challenges and future research directions revolving around trust are discussed. In examining the concept of trust, this chapter focuses on social rather than technical aspects of trust and trust building in virtual communities.

INTRODUCTION

With the widespread use of the Internet and the rise of social computing in recent years, people

DOI: 10.4018/978-1-60960-573-5.ch001

are becoming more engaged by participating in various virtual communities in everyday life. Unlike traditional communities, virtual communities have their own unique characteristics such as anonymity and lack of physical presence. Virtual communities are not confined to specific geographical locations. This makes it possible for people who share similar values, interests, experiences, and knowledge and have similar beliefs and personal views, to come together, although their background and motivations may differ. People can interact with other members of a virtual community anywhere at any time. People can also be involved in multiple virtual communities and communicate with members of other virtual communities simultaneously. In doing so, trust and trust building between participants become significant and indispensable in order to maintain communication in both traditional and virtual communities. In particular, virtual communities provide a platform or network for members to communicate through faster and simultaneous interactions in a variety of ways. Although the importance of the concept of trust in virtual communities has been widely accepted, it still remains a complex, multifaceted and context-dependent concept (Kelton, Fleischmann, & Wallace, 2008; Stabb, Bhargava, Lilien, Rosenthal, Winslett, & Sloman, 2004).

In this chapter, firstly we examine the terms *community* and *virtual community* and describe their characteristics. Then, we examine the definitions and characteristics of the term *trust* in the context of virtual communities and review relevant issues related to the concept of trust. Different types of trust and trust building are also investigated. Major research issues, challenges, and further research directions revolving around the term *trust* are discussed. In examining the concept of trust, this chapter focuses on the social aspects rather than the technical side of the terms.

BACKGROUND

Community

There have been several definitions of the term *community*, which reflects the fact that there may be difficulties and confusion in defining the term (Bhattacharyya, 2004). Since a community seemingly refers to geographic proximity and the characteristics of defining *community* are similar to those of *group* (Christenson, Frendley, & Robinson, 1994), the term *community* is used interchangeably with the term *group*. Let us first examine the term *group* in order to understand the term *community*. Brandon and Hollingshead (2007) define the term *group* as "an entity comprised of people having interdependent goals, who are acquainted, interact with one another and have a sense of belonging associated with their membership" (p.106). Wilson and Ryder (1996) also agree that groups become communities, "when they interact with each other and stay together long enough to form a set of habits and conventions, and when they come to depend upon each other for accomplishment of certain ends" (p. 801).

Turning to the term *community*, it is defined as "a constructed arena where multiple people with shared interests interact with each other" (Dehnart, 1999, A standard definition of community, para. 5). In comparing these definitions, we see that three components are shared: people, interaction, and a sense of belonging. In other words, community is composed of people who join as members, they socially interact, and their members have a set of shared denominators as their social identification or a sense of belonging to the community (Christenson et al., 1994). This third component is considered important since people need to have a sense of belonging by occupying a mutual and collective interest or intention to form a community. In line with this notion, the following definitions emphasize a sense of sharing, by saying that community is "any social configuration that possesses shared identity and norms" (Bahattacharyya, 2004, p. 12), or "a social organization of people who share knowledge, value and goals" (Jonassen, Peck, & Wilson, 1999, p. 118). To see whether the characteristics of the term *community* may apply to another term, *virtual community*, we now examine how differently or similarly people act in the virtual community.

Virtual Community

With the development of the Internet - also called virtual space, online space or cyberspace - people began to interact with each other through the medium. Rheingold (1993) defines the term virtual community as "social aggregations that emerge from the Net which is loosely interconnected computer networks, when sufficient people carry on those public discussions... to form webs of personal relationships in cyberspace" (p. 5). More specifically, Ridings, Gefen, and Arinze (2002) state that "virtual communities can be defined as groups of people with common interests and practices that communicate regularly and for some duration in an organized way over the Internet through a common... mechanism" (p. 273). In comparison with virtual communities, traditional communities tend to depend on a typical sense of location and relationships among their members and are generally bound to regional and physical proximity. Unlike traditional communities, virtual communities can work across and beyond space, time and physical organizational boundaries (Lipnack & Stamps, 1997; Mowshowitz, 1997). That is why virtual communities are considered a natural extension of traditional communities through a new medium in an online or virtual context (Ostwald, 1997).

Virtual communities have the same three components as the term community: people as members, social interaction, and a sense of belonging. Whittacher, Issaces, and O'Day (1997, p. 29) describe that (1) "[m]embers of virtual communities have a shared goal, interest, need, or activity that provides the primary reason for belonging to community"; (2) "[m]embers engage in repeated, active participation and often, intense interactions, strong emotional ties and shared activities occurring between participants"; (3) "[m]embers also have access to share resources

and there are policies for determining access to those resources"; and (4) "[r]eciprocity of information, support and services between members is considered significant". They also emphasize that there is a shared context of social conventions, language, and protocols (Whittacher et al., 1997).

Regarding the specific differences of virtual communities from traditional communities, Dehnart (1999) describes the following noticeable changes: "media is becoming an arbiter, not just a creator, of community; communities can be entirely dependent upon technology for their survival; the identities of community members is [*sic*] becoming more ambiguous; communication is becoming less direct, requiring more proactive interaction among members of a community; and passive or anonymous participation is becoming standard" (Changing notions of community, para. 1). Among the three components mentioned above, Owston (1998) emphasizes that a virtual community is most of all "a group of people who regularly interact online and share common goals, ideals, or values" (p. 60). If a traditional community is a meeting place, virtual communities, rather than being places, exist as social networks (Wellman & Gulia, 1999). Ward (1999) supports this point by asserting that "the spirit of community or communion that is found among networks of people is far more important than having a sense of place" (p. 98). People not only interact but also "learn from each others' work, and provide knowledge and information resources to the group related to certain agreed-upon topics of shared interest" (Hunter, 2002, p. 96). Therefore, social interactions in virtual communities can be considered as processes of transforming technology to meet people's needs. In addition, since members easily enter and leave a virtual community and their commitment to shared ideas and values in virtual communities could be ephemeral, the anonymity of members might impose different senses of identity in virtual communities.

As new technologies and communication tools emerge, communication methods change by reducing barriers of time and space that may hinder communication. Traditional face-to-face communication occurs only with people interacting simultaneously at the same location. Unlike traditional forms of communication, with computer-mediated communication tools and new network technologies, people can use video conferencing, a messenger program or an Internet phone (e.g. MSN, Skype, etc.). These communication tools allow users to communicate anytime, anywhere, simultaneously and ubiquitously. All of these technologies have a profound impact on the way people interact with each other and think of a community. New technology makes the creation of new or disguised identities possible. In particular, recent years have seen the proliferation of social networking and computing tools, such as Bulletin Board Systems (BBS), Internet Relay Chat (IRC), email listservs, Instant Messaging (IM), Really Simple Syndication (RSS) feeds, blogs, wikis, Facebook, Second Life, YouTube, Flicker, and Twitter, and accordingly members' social interactions also vary. As a result, new types of communication also emerge in virtual communities. So far the most common interactions remain mainly on text-based systems. Members' interactions are dichotomized into either synchronous or asynchronous types. Synchronous interactions can be found in IM, IRC, and Second Life, in which people communicate with each other in a more real-time sense. Asynchronous interactions and communications take place over a period of time in BBS, email listservs, blogs and social network web sites. For instance, while two individuals comment on a post in a blog, over time or (often) almost at the same time, they may become aware of other replies. Although those replies do not need real-time attention, this function is made possible by underlying systems. To take another example, in Facebook, most interactions are asynchronous, such as updating status and writing on other members' walls. More and more systems support both types of interactions, which allow people to choose how they will interact with other members.

To consider social interaction in depth, researchers have made efforts in conceptualizing how people interact within virtual communities. In particular, some models and theories have been proposed for member relations in virtual communities. Short, Williams, and Christie (1976) propose a social presence theory. The theory defines social presence as the "degree of salience of the other person in the interaction and the consequent salience of the interpersonal relationships" (p. 65). They define social presence as a quality of the medium itself and hypothesize that "communications media vary in their degree of [s]ocial [p] resence, and that these variations are important in determining the way individuals interact" (Short et al., 1976, p. 65). More specifically, Swinth and Blascovich (2002) state "social presence can be thought of as whether or not there are social cues that signify the presence of others within some interactional context" (p. 319). In another model, Reduced Social Cues (Hiltz & Turoff, 1978; Kiesle, 1986; Sproull & Kiesler, 1991) are introduced where nonverbal, visual, status and position cues are largely missing in an online context, personal identities are becoming ambiguous, and communication occurs in a social vacuum. They explain that cues indicate a person's social identity in virtual communities (Nass & Brave, 2005; Sproull & Kiesler, 1991; Tajfel & Turner, 1986). While some cues are in many ways missing, other cues might exist and may possibly be easier to change as well (Sproull & Kiesler, 1991). For example, online avatars have become very popular in some virtual communities. They represent some cues of community members. However, an avatar can be created, modified, and erased in a moment. In the reduced social cues approach, de-individuation means a state in which people lose their individuality, because group members do not feel they stand out as individuals and individuals act as if they are submerged in the group (Festinger, Pepitone, & Newcomb, 1952). This kind of impersonal view has been challenged by many studies on member relationships in virtual communities. The medium or underlying technology that supports a virtual community cannot predict its members' behavior. In spite of lacking nonverbal and social cues, personal relationships can still be further developed and fostered within virtual communities (Lea & Spears, 1991; Spears & Lea, 1992). Regarding social interaction in virtual communities, the formation of social interaction and member communication is becoming more dependent upon the social context of virtual communities and the way to utilize the medium with members' needs (Jarvenpaa, Shaw, & Staples, 2004; Spears, Lea, Corneliessen, Postmes, & Ter Haar, 2003). Both the medium and members of virtual communities have an impact in shaping the complexity and quality of member relationships in the communities.

Then why do people join virtual communities? People gather and use virtual communities for different purposes and reasons. Some people want to share the common sense of community, others are just looking for various types of information, and others may be in a virtual community for several more reasons. Rheingold (1993) states that virtual communities have two main functions for members, although there may be more: one is to act as a meeting or gathering place and the other is to act as a tool for members' use. The most frequently reported reason is to find information. Virtual communities bring together people with the same interests from all over the world. By searching or browsing a certain topic, people might get a breadth and depth of information from many virtual communities. This goes beyond a simple factual exchange, as search engines are powerful enough to find factual information. Knowledge exchange and information sharing are among the main reasons people use virtual communities (Constant, Sproull, & Kiesler, 1996; Ridings & Gefen, 2004; Wasko & Faraj, 2000). People also join virtual communities for recreational purposes, such as to play games. In Eastern Asian countries, many people play "Go," a popular Chinese game, in virtual communities. Chess lovers play chess,

share experience, and improve skills with many unknown players from virtual communities. It is quite easy for game lovers to find numerous game sites in virtual communities (e.g. Computer, Xbox, PlayStation, Wii, etc.). Members socialize and make new friends easily within those virtual communities. Social support is another reason people join a virtual community (Sproull & Faraj, 1997). People with similar issues regarding health concerns or real estate problems join together in virtual communities to share their personal stories and past experience. For example, Radin (2006) studies an online breast cancer community sponsored by a nonprofit organization in Canada that consisted of members from New Zealand, Hong Kong, and Europe. Therefore, through their different purposes, virtual communities can be categorized into four categories: (1) transaction communities, (2) interest communities, (3) relationship communities, and (4) fantasy communities (Armstrong & Hagel, 1996). Lu, Zhao, & Wang (2008) add one more type: mixed communities. Transaction communities "mainly focus on the transaction needs and from which people could get trading information"; In interest communities, "people share interest or expertise on a specific topic [and] gather together to communicate with each other"; Relationship communities refer to a space where "people with similar experience could come together and form meaningful interpersonal relationships"; And fantasy communities "usually refer to online games and in which people could come together get fantastic experience" (Lu et al., 2008, p. 1).

In summary, the unique characteristics of virtual communities mean that they are irrelevant of physical location, system-, technology- and medium-dependent, and social context-dependent. Members are relatively invisible or anonymous and they amass lower logistical and social costs (Sproull & Faraj, 1997). Knowledge exchange and information sharing seem to be closely related to virtual communities (Constant et al. 1996; Wasko & Faraj 2000). In comparison with traditional communities, the characteristics of virtual communities may bring some issues and challenges to the communities themselves. Considering social interaction and the sustainable membership of a community, the issue of trust in virtual communities cannot be avoided. The more we understand trust, the better we understand the concept *community*.

TRUST

Definitions and Characteristics

Although a great amount of literature pertains to trust in the traditional sense of communities, "the findings of some of these studies transcend the distinction of traditional or virtual context" and the extant literature is an important source for understanding trust in virtual communties (Connolly, 2008, p. 260). Since the concept *trust* is complex, researchers have tried to define the term from interdisciplinary points of view, including sociology, philosophy, psychology, economics, political science, and others. Researchers tend to present several perspectives on trust because of the complexity and confusion revolving around trust. The three views of trust are indentified by Brenkert (1998): attitudinal, predictability, and voluntarist. Among these, an attitudinal definition is given by Mayer, Davis, and Schoorman (1995) and agreed upon by the majority. They state that "trust is the willingness of a party to be vulnerable to the actions of another party based on the expectation that the other will perform a particular action important to the trustor, irrespective of the ability to monitor or control that other party" (p. 712). The predictability view of trust "stresses the importance of expectations about the behavioral predictability of the other party" (Connolly, 2008, p. 260). The voluntarist view of trust is that individuals voluntarily make themselves vulnerable and believe in another party's goodwill and harmlessness (Connolly, 2008). Simply put,

trust has aspects of an attitude, an attribution, an expectation, a feeling or belief, an intension, and a trait (Hoffman, Lee, Woods, Shadbolt, Miler, & Bradshaw, 2009).

Various aspects of trust intertwine with each other. Govier (1997) points out that trust is fundamentally "an attitude, based on beliefs and feelings and implying expectations and dispositions" (p. 4). From this statement, trust is an attitude and likely to involve beliefs, feelings, and expectations. When people trust, they tend to expect kind and benevolent behaviors and actions toward themselves. Nevertheless, people might do terrible things to each other and thus take risks to believe and trust. Specifically, Govier (1997, p. 6) describes the detailed features regarding the attitude of trust:

1. Expectations of benign, not harmful, behavior based on beliefs about the trusted person's motivation and competence;
2. An attribution or assumption of general integrity on the part of the other, a sense that the trusted person is a good person;
3. A willingness to rely or depend on the trusted person, an acceptance of risk and vulnerability, and
4. A general disposition to interpret the trusted person's actions favorably.

Similarly, Gefen (2000) states that trust demonstrates the confidence in the trustees' *benevolence*, *ability*, *integrity*, and *predictability* in uncertain circumstances. Seen through these features, trust exists implicitly in many parts of our daily lives and our social world (Govier, 1997). Although people often are unaware of the trust processes, as Baier (1986) describes, "[m]ost of us notice a given form of trust most easily after its sudden demise or severe injury. We inhabit a climate of trust as we inhabit an atmosphere and notice it as we notice air, only when it becomes scarce or polluted" (p. 234). For example, people usually extend their trust to airline pilots, even when they have not met them, because people trust the regulations and the system that ensures that those pilots can be trusted to do their job. Trust is based on the trustor's relevant experience and knowledge of others, and thus it is not just a game of chance (Jøsang, 1996). The willingness to rely or depend on the trusted person and to assume risk and vulnerability is vital to trust. Similar to the definition of trust given above by Mayer et al. (1995), Chopra and Wallace (2003) stress three elements: "a trustee to whom the trust is directed, confidence that the trust will be upheld, and a willingness to act on that confidence" (p. 2) and define that "trust is the willingness to rely on a specific other, based on confidence that one's trust will lead to lead to positive outcomes" (p. 3).

Trust is also context dependent. Grabner-Kräuter, Kaluscha, & Fladnitzer (2006) stress that context characteristics is one of three perspectives (context characteristics, trustor properties, and characteristics of the trusted object) in defining trust. Relationships and interactions between trustor and context, between trustee and context, among trustor, trustee, and context are acknowledged and addressed in many definitions of trust. Across disciplines there is agreement that people trust others in the context of their specific roles. Govier (1997) supports this fact by saying that "trust is not a binary choice between all and nothing. We may trust or distrust to various degrees… trust and distrust are often relativized to specific roles or contexts" (p. 5). Govier (1997) also points out that "trust on the whole does not mean trust in every context" (p. 5), since trust is not likely to be extended to other areas or specialties. For instance, we trust our physician with health-related matters. We trust our mechanics to fix our cars, but not our teachers on this matter.

Interestingly, people tend to trust, based not on complete but incomplete knowledge, experience, and capabilities (Govier, 1997), only because people may not be able to get a complete picture of everything. Nevertheless, as Luhmann (1979) notes, people tend to judge, trust and assume that the outcomes will be beneficial. In this way, people assume that trust can broaden our possibilities and reduce complexity of communication and social interactions. Since people have information about every aspect of life, even incomplete, and people tend to generalize from their experience, the outcome of any interaction still remains predictable (although people are not like machines following rules). However, people do not trust blindly. They know something about the people or situation they trust.

Therefore, trust is highly subject to a degree of belief about agents, not as an object property of an agent (McKnight & Chervany, 1996). The degree of such belief ranges from total trust to total distrust. For instance, there might be a situation in which an agent does not have an opinion of other agents' trustworthiness or is ignorant of others' trustworthiness. However, an agent will still make a trusting action, based on anticipation of a subjective judgment regarding the other agent (Abdul-Rahman & Hailes, 2000).

Trust is also created inductively, as Govier (1997, p. 8) remarks:

The attitude of trust presupposes inductively grounded beliefs and confident expectations that go further than strict induction world warrant. So it presupposes something we well know: we are creatures who reason inductively, and we have a tendency to extend our confidence beyond the evidence.

Since people trust inductively, based on their beliefs, Govier (1997) goes on to point out that "the attitude of trust presupposes inductively grounded beliefs and confident expectations … We build more trust on the trust we have … Trust is possible because we are inductive creatures who extend induction to provide ourselves with confident expectations about the future. Many of these expectations are about other people" (p. 8). The trust of other people is possible because people inductively extend their beliefs and responses to others, based upon their sense of themselves, position in the world and their values. This fact implies that trust is dynamic and value-added as additional experiences and evidence may increase or decrease the degree of trust in others later on (Abdul-Rahman & Hailes, 2000).

Trust as a complex concept is likely to be composed of many attributes. Grandison and Sloman (2000) identify the attributes of trust as the following: reliability, dependability, honesty, truthfulness, security, competence, and timeliness (p. 3). As some researchers agree, they also point out that these attributes are dependent on the environment, where trust resides with people (Grandison & Sloman, 2000, p. 3). Mayer et al.'s study includes three factors of perceived trustworthiness as ability, benevolence, and integrity (1995). Trust is also closely related to two conditions: risk and dependence (Rousseau, Stikin, Burt, & Camerer, 1998). Chopra and Wallace (2003) categorize a range of perspectives into the following areas: nature of trust, elements of trust, preconditions (dependence and risk), dimensions, trustworthiness (what attributes are desired of a potential recipient of trust), influences (what factors influence trust), and processes (how does trust build and evolve). Among all of these, we only focus on antecedent, risk, and dependence that are crucial to trust building processes and examine them in a more detailed manner. Antecedents are conditions that lead to trust and support trust building. In different contexts, researchers have identified context-dependent and more common antecedents. Mayer et al. (1995) summarize that trust antecedents appearing in literature generally fall into three major categories: ability, benevolence, and integrity. In virtual communities, most of all, information technology factors are greatly considered as antecedents to trust.

Risk has also been studied in many disciplines. Risk and uncertainty exist in every aspect of our lives because our ability to gather and handle information is limited. Economist Knight (1921) makes his famous distinction between risk (randomness

with knowable probabilities) and uncertainty (randomness with unknowable probabilities). More specifically, risk refers to "situations in which the outcome of an event is unknown, but the decision-maker knows the range of possible outcomes and the probabilities of each" (Klein, 2009, p. 326). Kahneman and Tversky (1979) propose Prospect Theory to explain the framing effects that human is likely to be risk aversion for gains and risk proness for losses by incorporating psychological mechanisms. Although the importance of risk in understanding trust has long been recognized (Luhmann, 1988), there is no consensus on risk and its relationship with trust. Importantly, researchers agree that complete certainty will not lead to trust and trust does not need to be involved in such circumstances. Mayer, et al. (1995) argue that trust would lead to risk taking and perceived risk moderates the relationship between trust and risk taking. Risk occurs when we do not have complete information about the situation we are in; if we take certain actions, the outcome may be unpredictable in such a way that the outcome is harmful to us. As a result, risk may lead to trust and trust building. Mayer, et al. (1995) address that "it is unclear whether risk is an antecedent to trust, is trust, or is an outcome of trust" (p. 711). We should note that not all risk taking or the presence of risk is related to trust. The relationship between risk and trust is complex. Risk is necessary for the formation of trust (Chen & Dhillon, 2003). Pavlou (2003) finds that risk is not a causal predictor of trust and is not an antecedent to trust; on the other hand, trust is an antecedent of perceived risk.

Dependence refers to one party relying on others to achieve a desired result. Dependence can be categorized into shallow dependence, shallow inter-dependence, deep dependence, and deep inter-dependence (Sheppard, & Sherman, 1998). Shallow dependence "occur[s] when one's outcomes are contingent upon the action of another" (p. 424). In shallow inter-dependence, both parties must effectively coordinate behavior in order to achieve desired goals (p. 424). In deep dependence, "a trustee's behavior is often outside the trustor purview" (p. 425). Deep interdependence is characterized by shared values and norms. Sheppard and Sherman (1998) remark that "trust is the acceptance of the risks associated with the type and depth of the inter-dependence inherent in a given relationship" (p. 425). The distinction between confidence and trust depends on perception and attribution and our ability to distinguish between dangers and risks (Luhmann, 1988). In a situation of confidence, people do not consider alternatives, while in a situation of trust, people choose one action over others in spite of the possibility of being disappointed by that action (Luhmann, 1988). Trust and confidence can lead to disappointment. In the case of confidence, people will "react to disappointment by external attribution" (Luhmann, 1988, p. 97). In the case of trust, people will "have to consider an internal attribution and eventually regret trusting choice" (Luhmann, 1988, p. 98).

We see that trust is considered a dynamic and social phenomenon. Trust evolves all the time. The characteristics of trust can be summarized as the following: (1) it exists as a subjective degree of trust; (2) it is established in a certain context; (3) it involves expectations of future outcomes; (4) it is not necessarily transitive (Abdul-Rahaman & Hailes, 2000); (5) trust might be based on prior experiences, and (6) trust might not be always beneficial. Viewed from different perspectives, there might be more characteristics of trust in different contexts.

Types of Trust

Unlike traditional communities, virtual communities do not have face-to-face contact and their visual cues are different. To understand trust better, some researchers have tried to identify the types of trust in virtual communities.

Lewis (1999) classifies trust into two types: deep trust and swift trust. Deep trust refers to not just an acknowledgement between two agents but trusting interpersonal relationships built on mutual appreciation. Swift trust, also called scatter trust (Govier, 1997) or thin trust (Putnam, 2000), refers to "a more generalized decision to give most people the benefit of the doubt" (Radin, 2006, p. 593). Some researchers identify trust as consisting of three dimensions in an intertwined mode: ability, benevolence, and integrity (Mayer et al., 1995; Gefen & Straub, 2004). Ability refers to skills or competencies that allow an individual to be perceived as competent in a certain area, such as a mutual interest or hobby, in virtual communities. Benevolence means that others care about and treat the trustor well. Integrity is the expectation that the trustee will act in accordance with social norms or principles that the trustor accepts.

In order to produce an acceptable typology, McKnight and Chervany (2001) analyze numerous definitions of trust from various fields, including psychology, social psychology, sociology, economics, political science, management, and communications. They identify two kinds of trust: construct type and referent type. The construct type of trust refers to "what type of construct trust is" (p. 7025), while the referent type of trust "refers to the object of trust" (p. 7025). McKnight and Chervany (1996) categorize trust into three different types: (1) *interpersonal trust,* (2) *system trust* or *impersonal trust* and (3) *dispositional trust.* Interpersonal trust refers to direct trust between two or more people (or groups) in a specific context. System trust or impersonal trust refers to trust that is not founded upon any personal attributes or states but rather upon the perceived properties of a system or institution. Luhmann (1988) states "[a] system – economic, legal, or political – requires trust as an input condition. Without trust it cannot stimulate supportive activities in situations of uncertainty or risk" (p. 103). In the modern world, our societies build not only on interpersonal trust but also on system trust. Take the monetary system as an example: we may not trust what other people say about the value of money, but we do trust the banking system, which ensures the value of money. Another example would be the legal system. We do not trust other people but trust the legal system to ensure the justice of our society. In comparison with interpersonal trust, system trust "is incomparably easier to acquire than personal trust.... [B]ut, [o]n the other hand, it is incomparably more difficult to control" (Luhmann, 1979, p. 50). System trust implies that people depend on the system. In other words, people trust the information processed by others as the elements of the system and within the system only. System trust is closely related to impersonal structure. McKnight, Cumming, and Chervany (1998) suggest that two types of impersonal trust can be differentiated as: structural assurances and situational normality" (p. 478). Structural assurances include safeguards such as regulations, guarantees, or contracts (Shapiro, 1987; Zucker, 1986). Situational normality may include one's own role and others' roles in the situation (Baier, 1986). System trust is based on the perception that things appear normal (Baier, 1986) or in "proper order" (Lewis & Weigert, 1985, p. 974).

Dispositional trust is based on the personality attributes of the trusting party (McKnight & Chervany, 1996). Dispositional trust is a pervasive attitude toward others that exhibits a basic trust or general inclination to display faith in humanity (McKnight & Chervany, 1996). Dispositional trust is sometimes called "basic trust that... describes the general trusting attitude of the trustor" (Abdul-Rahman & Hailes, 2000, p. 3). It can be considered independent of any context. Therefore, there is no consensus in relation to dispositional versus situational trust. While dispositional trust is assuming that other people are always trustworthy, irrespective of whether people are good or bad, "one will obtain better outcomes by trusting them- hence, one should trust them" (McKnight & Chervany, 1996, p. 38). In virtual communities, people tend to depend on technology and media more than in traditional communities. Even the

identity of members is very difficult to obtain and trust because of members' easy appearance and disguise.

Similarly, in classifying trust some researchers suggest that trust may be broadly categorized into three layers: dispositional, learnt, and situational trust (Dibben, Morris, & Lean, 2000; Giffin, 1967; Worchel, 1979). Dispositional trust refers to "the personal trait or disposition of an individual to be trusting or not" (Dibben, et al., 2000, p. 56). Dispositional trust here may be slightly different from that discussed above. Learnt trust is an individual's general tendency to trust. Situational trust is dependent on situational cues such as context or information available (Worchel, 1979).

Regarding trust building, some researchers categorize trust differently. Sarker, Valacich, & Sarker (2003) identify personality-based (that develops because of a person's trusting nature), institutional-based (this is a function of an individual's belief in institutional norms/procedures), and cognitive-based trust (that develops from social cues and impressions that an individual receives from the other). In another categorization, Lewicki and Bunker (1996) extend that trust is developed in transitional stages into three types of trust: calculus-based trust, identification-based trust, and knowledge-based trust. Calculus-based trust refers to trust that exists between individuals in the early stage of a relationship. This form of trust is grounded "not only in the fear of punishment for violating the trust but also in the rewards to be derived from preserving it" (Lewicki & Wiethoff, 2000, p. 88). Knowledge-based trust exists between two parties based on the predictability of the other party. Identification-based trust exists where the parties understand, appreciate and share one another's wants and needs.

To assess interpersonal trust, McAllister (1995) divides interpersonal trust into affect-based trust and cognition-based trust. In his study, cognition-based trust is defined as choosing "whom we will trust in which respects and under what circumstances, and we base the choice on what we take do be 'good reasons,' constituting evidence of trustworthiness" (Lewis & Wiegert, 1985, p. 970). Affect-based trust consists of the emotional bonds between individuals (Lewis & Wiegert, 1985). Some researchers stress affective (e.g., caring, emotional connection) elements along with the cognitive elements of trust (Kanawattanachai & Yoo, 2007). Emotional states have an effect on trust. Emotions may change the ability, benevolence, and integrity of the trusting individual in some way cognitively (Dunn & Scheweitzer, 2005). Trusting actions appear to be sudden and dramatic (Murnighan, Malhotra, & Weber, 2004). In the meantime, emotional attachments may cause a trusting individual to take a sudden risk and have irrational trust (Rawlins, 2009; Weber, Malhotra, and Murnighan, 2005). As we have seen in the several different types of trust from multiple perspectives, it is apparent that many factors are involved in identifying, grouping and assessing trust and we need to take a holistic approach in understanding trust and trust building.

Trust Building in Virtual Communities

When trust is considered in the particular setting of virtual communities, many researchers question whether the findings of trust and trust building in traditional communities can be applied to virtual communities, since there are differences in trust building in the two communities (Castelfranchi & Tan, 2001; Herring, 2002; Kollock, 1999).

Returning to the three types of trust (i.e. interpersonal trust, system trust, and dispositional trust), building trust in virtual communities mostly involves interpersonal trust (McKnight & Chervany, 1996; McKnight & Chervany, 2001; Ridings et al., 2002). Trust is built through social interactions among individual members and/or between members and the entire community. Most importantly, we need to pay attention to the fact that achieving trust in virtual communities is strongly dependent upon the technological

medium of the Internet and built-in web systems and tools. In addition, as emerging social networking sites make social interaction over the Internet much easier than before, virtual communities start to leverage social networking technology. With the advancement of security technology, security measures may protect communities from attacks and unwarranted access. When no risk is involved, trust becomes redundant so that over-emphasizing security may lead to a climate of distrust (Kramer, 1999). Therefore, trust in virtual communities depends highly on system trust or impersonal trust, as social interaction activities are possible only though the capabilities of the technological medium and supporting systems. In line with this notion, the trust of members is likened to trusting a technological medium (including a remote agent, medium, and the technology in general) rather than members themselves, particularly when the true identity of members is not necessarily revealed to others (Burauska & Asldama, 2008).

The approach of considering trust building as a process has been elaborated through theoretical models. Zucker (1986) proposes three different modes of trust production. They are characteristic-based, process-based, and institutional-based trust building mechanisms. Characteristic-based trust is produced based on personal characteristics such as ethnic background, religion, age, sex, etc. The major mechanism for the production of this type of trust is through a sense of shared commonality with other parties. Process-based trust is produced based on social exchanges between individuals and organizations. The exchanges may be obtained directly from previous successful experiences in building trust and indirectly from established reputation, brands, etc. Institutional-based trust is produced through a third party and is tied to broad societal institutions and on intermediary mechanisms (Zucker, 1986).

When comparing types of trust, among deep trust and swift trust swift trust seems more important at the early stage of building trust. For long-term trust, cognition-based trust is followed by affect-based trust (McAllister, 1995). Among three stages of trust building (i.e. calculus-based, knowledge-based and identification-base), the calculus-based distrust holds high negative expectations in impersonally interacting compared to others. The identification-based distrust has more negative emotional attachment than others and holds high confidence in negative expectations regarding others (Lewicki & Bunker, 1996; Lewicki & Wiethoff, 2000). In addition, the violation of trust is likely to be an emotional event for the trustor (Lewicki & Bundker, 1996; Morrison & Robinson, 1997). When parties are unable to conform to expectations, trust is violated. However, not every violation may change the trust between trustors and trustees. Frequent or severe violates of trust are likely to change the trusting relationship. Lewicki and Wiethoff (2000) discuss that violations of calculus-based trust are likely to encourage calculus-based distrust. Violations of identification-based trust have a greater effect on the parties' emotional well-being. Violations of identification-based trust are likely to end the relationship itself, if they are not properly addressed. To repair such a violation, parties must first communicate in an attempt to identify and understand the breach, and then explicitly recommit themselves to their trusting relationship (Lewicki & Wiethoff, 2000). Nooteboom criticizes (2002) that it is unlikely that knowledge-based trust will secede from the calculus-based trust because knowledge is required when forming calculus-based trust.

Empirically, some researchers propose several frameworks: a conceptual framework of trust where antecedents link to outcomes (Shankar, Urban, & Sultan, 2002; Lu, Zhao, & Wang, 2009) and trust antecedents with cognitive, affective, interpersonal, and social factors (Kramer, 1999). Among them, Gefen, Karahanna and Straub (2003) identify five categories of constructing trust antecedents: (1) knowledge-based trust, which focuses on trust building through ongoing interactions; (2) institution-based trust, which refers to relying upon an impersonal structure or third party to build trust (this corresponds to impersonal trust or system trust); (3) calculative-based trust, which deals with rational assessments of ongoing relationships; (4) cognition-based trust, which refers to trust building through impressions rather than repeated personal interactions over a longer period of time, and lastly (5) personality-based trust, which refers to individual personalities that influence trust building. The above categories and antecedents facilitate overall trust building and may influence the initial decision to trust.

In addition, the differences between offline and online interactions may influence the formation of trust. In virtual communities, interactions occur through a technological medium, which may potentially eliminate or reduce some important factors for trust building. Some antecedent conditions are compromised in virtual communities. Lack of authority to govern interactions, anonymity, and ease of joining, leaving, or lurking impose on trust building. Although lacking social and other traditional cues facilitates trust building, interactions within virtual communities are filled with other cues that might be interpreted as indices of trust (de Laat, 2005). For example, account name, email address, avatar, login time, and login frequency might be valuable cues to the information about individual members. In communicating with each other, most interactions are text-based, since people use language and write letters to convey meaning. Different people might have their own patterns, such as using specific words, spelling, or abbreviations. Different styles and forms of writing may reveal who the individuals are and give us a sense of how they interact with others.

As various factors contribute to trust building, the concept of trust is directly or indirectly related to several relevant terms as well, including authority, identity, authenticity, shared values, commitment, reputation, etc. "Trust involves beliefs about the intentions of the authority" (Tyler & Lind, 1992, p. 142) and authorities are "the subset of people or information perceived to be credible"

(Rieh & Danielson, 2007, p.313). People come to trust because they believe that the authority can be trusted to try to behave fairly (Tyler & Lind, 1992). Authority is influenced by one's thoughts and institutional affiliation and at the same time, influences on people's actions (Wilson, 1983).

Lynch (2001) considers identity as related to trust and anonymity and pseudonymity as closely related to identity and trust building in virtual communities. Although account name, email address, and other cues including writing style and content may be sources for identity, those cues have limited reliability. They might be changed and not be persistent. It is becoming increasingly popular for members to have links to their personal web sites and weblogs in signature files (Donath, 1998). Some members may reveal their MSN or Facebook account to others during interactions. This may result in linking to more permanent online identities or even real identities. The authenticity of the identity is directly related to the authenticity of the cues associated with the identity. It is impractical to verify all the information on identity for members in virtual communities. On the other hand, authenticity of identity is tied to the authoritative identity for authorizing sources. In other words, authenticity is associated with a third-party authority. However, because identity alone cannot lead to trust, communications and interactions among members of virtual communities often lead to a sense of belonging and shared values, which often evoke social trust (Porter, 2004; Siegrist, Cvetkovich, & Gutscher, 2001). Commitment is also seen as a mandatory factor in maintaining trust (Hunt & Morgan, 1994). Reputation and a trusted third party have a strong influence on a member's initiative to participate in interactions and trust building (Kollock, 1999; Jarvenpaa, Tractinsky, & Vitale, 2000).

To better understand the relationships between trust and other concepts, a credibility assessment model may be applied to virtual communities (Hilligoss & Rieh, 2008). The proposed model consists of three levels of credibility judgments: construct,

heuristics, and interaction. "The construct level pertains to how a person constructs, conceptualizes, or defines credibility.... The heuristics level involves general rules of thumb used to make judgments of credibility.... The interaction level refers to credibility judgments based on specific source or content cues" (Hilligoss & Rieh, 2008, p. 1473). This model shows that the three levels are interlinked and credibility is relative to the social context in information seeking and credibility judgments (Hilligoss & Rieh, 2008, p. 1482).

In summary, as virtual communities are distinctive from traditional communities in many ways, building trust in virtual communities also may differ. With the development of technology in recent years, new virtual communities are emerging and changing all the time in given contexts. Newly created web tools and technological systems become significant in building trust as those tools support communication and innovatively create member interaction. As seen in this section, many studies show that there are several types of trust and trust building. Importantly, as trust building is considered a process through social interaction in virtual communities, several factors in building trust are involved. Trust building is clearly critical in virtual communities and is still being discussed.

ISSUES AND DISCUSSION

As trust and trust building in virtual communities have heterogeneous and multifaceted aspects, literature about the two terms brings notable and valuable issues to research communities. Although many issues have been studied, more comprehensive studies are needed to further explore these topics theoretically and/or empirically in depth. Key research issues that we discuss in this section can be grouped into the following five issues:

1. Examining the nature and role of trust in perspectives consisting of trustor, trustee, and context;

2. Studying kinds of factors that affect virtual communities in the given context;

3. Examining concepts such as distrust, anti-trust, trust repair, and especially, the negative side of trust;

4. Investigating trust from a multi-dimensional perspective; and

5. Exploring the identity of members and other personal traits that may affect trust building in a virtual community.

Most of all, considering that trust and trust building is highly dependent on situational contexts (Granovetter, 1985), research on examining the specific context is one of the major issues in a certain type of virtual community. As e-commerce-related virtual communities in recent years are growing at an exponential rate, e-commerce-related virtual communities become "a new form of e-business medium" (Wu & Tsang, 2008, p. 115). Various communities (i.e. e-Bay, Amazon, PayPal, etc.) provide a valuable key to understanding electronic commerce and digital economy (Ridings et al., 2002). Since members benefit by acquiring electronic resources, the power to search for information is significant in expediting e-trading efficiently, speedily, and at greatly reduced transaction costs. Lu, Zhao, and Wang (2008) point out that important factors to forming this kind of virtual community include familiarity, structural assurances, and perceived similarity to others in building trust between members' capabilities.

Trust building in virtual communities is a complex process and it is affected by several factors. One issue in this matter is examining explicit and implicit factors in the given context of the communities. Trust and trust building in one type of virtual community may be different in another type. It is agreed that antecedent conditions of trust in one type of virtual community may be different from another kind. As types of trust vary, different types of social interaction also have an impact on trust formation. Different types

of available information may not cultivate trust in the same way. Types of information sought and exchanged in social interaction may be scrutinized in different types of communities. For example, to understand radical virtual communities (i.e. terrorist communities), some factors may have been taken for granted that should have had more attention (i.e. ethnicity, race, culture, etc.), since virtual communities reflect the real world, and trust and trust building need to be put into a wide context. Yan (2009) finds out that children and adolescents have limited knowledge and limited resources to develop their understanding on the complexity and potential harm of the Internet. Unsurprisingly, we could spot private information on social networking sites such as Facebook. That information may lead to potential harm. According to Wolak, Finkelhor, & Mitchell (2004), trust is developed between sex predators and victims through communications on the Internet and may eventually lead to face-to-face meetings and sexual activities.

Contexts, cultures and personal traits are all important factors. Trust may have different influences, depending on genders and cultures. According to Hofstede (1980), gender is an important dimension of culture. Buchan, Croson, and Solnick (2008) study trust and gender through behavior and beliefs in the investment game. They find that the relationship between expected return and trusting behavior is stronger among men than women. Connolly and Bannister (2007) compare antecedents of consumer trust in online shopping in Ireland and the United States and find that culture does play a role in relation to trust. Other researchers also confirm that trust may affect people in different cultures differently (Kim, 2007; Turel, Yuan, & Connelly). Stepanikova, Mollborn, Cook, Thom, and Kramer (2006) find through a study of patients that racial/ethnic/language-based differences are reflected in a patient's trust in a physician based on their perception of a physician's behaviors. Factors such as the average age of members in virtual communities and information technology artifacts used in virtual communities may affect trust as well.

To understand trust better, distrust has been a focus of trust research and become one of the most significant issues. Regarding distrust, there are two perspectives. Some researchers argue that distrust and trust are two distinct concepts, not two ends of one continuum (Lewicki, McAllister, & Bies, 1998; McKnight & Choudhury, 2006), while others take the opposite view that trust and distrust are the opposite ends of the same continuum (Schoorman, Mayer, & Davis, 2007). Importantly, there is a dimension between trust and distrust, in which people neither trust nor distrust. Hardin (2002) suggests there are asymmetries between trust and distrust because they have "asymmetric grounds both motivational and epistemological" and they have "substantially asymmetric implications for behavior and for society" (p. 90). Distrust usually arises when a breach of trust happens and a trust building process may lead to either trust or distrust. Distrust seems to be related to strong negative emotions. The importance of distrust has been recognized not only in e-commerce but also in other areas. For example, in e-commerce, vendors or online shops, whether they are legitimate or illegitimate, try to diminish distrust and foster trust. In virtual learning communities, distrust may have negative effects and discourage people from learning. Like trust, distrust may be related to gains or losses depending on different circumstances. Additionally, trust is not always positive and beneficial. In some senses, cyber bullying is a breach of trust and may lead to distrust. Mishna, Saini & Solomon (2009) suggest that cyber bullying occurs within the context of students' social groups and relationships. They have categorized cyber bulling into three types: posting, coercing and "backstabbing" and masquerading. Surprisingly, they have found that many students cyber bully their friends. When cyber bullying happens, students are unlikely to disclose it to parents. The reasons may be very complex when students decide to take risks to trust or distrust. As long as distrust

exists as a distinct and corresponding concept of trust, further research may reveal the antecedents of distrust and the relation of distrust and trust. Further studies on this issue need to be conducted.

As mentioned in the previous section, trust has been recognized as a multidimensional and multi-faceted construct. Mitchell & Zigurs (2009) list more than twenty theories in literature of trust in virtual teams, such as social identity theory, social impact theory, media richness theory, etc. Putnam (1993) states "trust is an essential component of social capital" (p. 170). In other words, in social capital theory, trust is treated as a variable (Khodyakov, 2007). Some researchers recognize trust as an essential factor for collaborative behavior (Gambetta, 1988). Others suggest that trust is a conscious or rational choice (Hardin, 1992; Williamson, 1993). Lewis & Weigert (1985) define trust as the "undertaking of a risk in the course of action on the confident expectation that all persons involved in the action will act competently and dutifully" (p. 971).

Another perspective on obtaining trust is seeing it as a process. Trust building could be considered as stages of development since trust is built gradually as people interact with each other. Trust building is a continuous process and requires positive refinements (Ofuonye, Beatty, Reay, Dick, & Miller, 2008). Trust could be conceptualized as a psychological state in terms of an individual's disposition and interrelated internal cognitive and affective processes (Kramer, 1999) so that it may operate as a moderator after examining recent trust studies in organizational settings (Dirks & Ferrin, 2001). They further suggest that trust has an important impact on attitudinal and behavioral outcomes as well as on management. To some extent, virtual communities are loosely connected organizations. Some findings such as those on organizational settings may be applied directly to virtual communities. In general, various aspects in looking at trust from social, cognitive, affective and contextual perspectives need to be taken into account to develop a comprehensive theory on trust and trust building. Definitions and theories built upon one discipline alone may reveal a partial picture of trust and trust building. Studying multiple factors from multi-disciplines is an interesting area for further research and will add a new dimension to the existing theories and models.

Lastly, the identity of community members is significant. As web tools and technology are highly significant in virtual communities, it may be tricky and complicated to recognize community members' real identities through anonymous identification or online aliases. Therefore, confirming identities and gaining authority members are ongoing and noteworthy research issues. People might be at greater risk if they reveal the web addresses of their personal web sites, wikis, blogs, or Facebook accounts, because it may be possible to determine their real identities through gathered information from those sources in a limited setting. In some virtual communities, online identity and off-line identity might be tangled or mixed together so that building trust through identities can be very complex. Different types of visual cues are emerging in virtual communities. This kind of visual cue is different from face-to-face environments and an important source of identification. Song and Kim (2006) investigate the effect of subjective norms, social comparison, and social identity on intention to use an avatar service in virtual communities. New virtual communities, like ones on Second Life, have even brought largely text-based social interactions to 3D level. Examining trust building needs to be revisited in those new types of virtual communities.

In summary, we agree that in an online environment, trust is based on beliefs in the trustworthiness of a trustee, which is composed of three distinct dimensions (that are mostly agreed upon): integrity, ability, and benevolence (McKnight & Choudhury, 2002). It is important to examine the factors, dimensions, and major issues in a virtual community when reconsidering the construct of trust in the virtual context.

Questions such as whether each dimension and factor is equally important and whether other factors or new dimensions exist can lead to a deeper understanding of trust.

FUTURE RESEARCH DIRECTIONS

Numerous aspects and issues need to be further examined, including the five key issues discussed above. In this section, we highlight some additional future research avenues, although this list is not complete.

First, we suggest that the focus should be on a further investigation of the characteristics and factors of trust in virtual communities. Previous studies reveal that there are different types of virtual communities and different factors of trust building that affect virtual communities. With the development of new technology, it is quick and simple to stay connected with other people. For example, smart phones or other mobile devices are convenient for people to be in and out of virtual communities in a much easier way. A person's real identity may be unknown, but his or her current location may be tracked by the use of mobile phone technology. However, these technologies may be available only to some members. All of these factors may have an impact on the operation of a virtual community. Regarding this, we ask some research questions that need to be investigated further: How do virtual communities get created? What activities and dynamics are actually going on in virtual communities? What factors cause virtual communities to merge, collapse and disappear? How do new technologies interact with the activities of virtual communities? Finally, what methods are appropriate for conducting this research to answer these questions? Given the multi-faceted phenomenon of virtual communities, it seems necessary to take a holistic approach with multi-faceted and multi-dimensional components. As virtual communities are social hubs, studies on members' information searching and sharing behaviors and interaction between members and member relations may also shed light on more elusive issues such as group norms, community attachment, commitment, trust, and trust development.

Second, time is an inevitable factor among many of the factors in trust and trust building in virtual communities. One study of particular interest finds that although old or experienced members have gradually developed trust in the community over time, the importance of trust decreases with experience (Gefen, Karahanna, & Straub, 2003). Or new members of a virtual community may behave differently from old members. Some longitudinal studies in limited laboratory settings demonstrate that trust changes over time (Serino, Furner, & Smatt, 2005). In regards to this matter, more studies need to explore the relationship of time and other factors in trust building in real settings. The result of these studies may also be applied to different types of virtual communities as well as offline communities.

Third, swift trust is formed in virtual communities with members who may only have limited information about the communities and other members. Some studies suggest swift trust is based on stereotypical impressions from categorical information and communication behaviors such as members' characteristic patterns of communication behavior (Jarvenpaa & Leidner, 1998). Regarding the swift trust issue, some questions arise, such as: Is swift trust dependent on types of virtual communities? What factors may affect long-term trust to be built from swift trust? Is there a relationship between swift trust and technology in building trust?

Finally, it is necessary to pay more attention to the violation of trust and trust repair. After trust has been violated or damaged, people in communities repair violated trust in order to re-build it. Understanding trust repairing processes will add valuable insight. Regarding this matter, some research questions arise, such as: how is trust violated? How is trust repaired and rebuilt? What factors have an impact on the trust reparation process? What conditions of strategies are effective in repairing violated trust?

We would like to emphasize that the studies on trust and trust building need to be conducted not only with empirical data but also in theory. We expect that longitudinal studies on trust in virtual communities will produce important outcomes for the field and continue to draw the attention of researchers in the future.

CONCLUSION

Trust exists in every aspect of our society in both traditional and virtual communities. Trust as a multi-dimensional concept has been examined regarding its definition, nature, characteristics, types and factors in different approaches. It is not surprising to see that there are various models of trust and trust building. As virtual communities are built for many purposes, the importance of understanding trust and trust building has practical and theoretical implications on many aspects of our society. Trust and trust building might be more complicated with the development of new technology as well as with the emergence of various virtual communities. In the near future we hope there will be more technical solutions for trust management and some concerns of trust may be solved. Nevertheless, social aspects of virtual communities remain a similarly important issue and accordingly, trust building will continue to be a focus of research on virtual communities.

REFERENCES

Abdul-Rahman, A., & Hailes, S. (2000). Support trust in virtual communities. In *Proceedings of the 33rd Hawaii International on System Science, Maui, Hawaii, USA*, (pp. 1769-1777).

Armstrong, A., & Hagel, J. (1996). The real value of online communities. *Harvard Business Review, 74*(3), 134–141.

Baier, A. (1986). Trust and antitrust. *Ethics, 96,* 231–260. doi:10.1086/292745

Bhattacharyya, J. (2004). Theorizing community development. *Journal of the Community Development Society, 34*(2), 5–34. doi:10.1080/15575330409490110

Brandon, D. P., & Hollingshead, A. B. (2007). Characterizing online groups. In Joinson, A. N., McKenna, K. Y. A., Postmes, T., & Reips, U. D. (Eds.), *The Oxford handbook of Internet psychology* (pp. 105–119). Oxford, UK/ New York, NY: Oxford University Press.

Brenkert, G. (1998). Trust, business and business ethics: An introduction. *Business Ethics Quarterly, 8*(2), 195–203.

Buchan, N. R., Croson, R., & Solnick, S. J. (2008). Trust and gender: An examination of behavior, biases, and beliefs in the investment game. *Journal of Economic Behavior & Organization, 68*(3-4), 466–476. doi:10.1016/j.jebo.2007.10.006

Burauskas, G., & Aldama, J. I. (2008). *Trust in virtual community.* Unpublished master thesis, Lunds University, Lund, Sweden.

Castelfranchi, C., & Tan, Y. H. (2001). *Trust and deception in virtual societies.* Dordrecht, The Netherlands: Kluwer Academic Publishers.

Chen, S. C., & Dhillon, G. S. (2003). Interpreting dimensions of consumer in e-commerce. *Information Technology Management, 4*(2-3), 303–318. doi:10.1023/A:1022962631249

Chopra, K., & Wallace, W. A. (2003). Trust in electronic environments. In *Proceedings of the 36th Annual Hawaii international Conference on System Sciences (Hicss '03) - Track 9 - Volume 9* (January 06 - 09, 2003). HICSS. IEEE Computer Society, Washington, DC, 331.1.

Christenson, J., Fendley, K., & Robinson, J. (1994). Community development. In J. Christenson, & J. Robinson (Eds.). *Community development in perspective* (pp. 3-25). Ames, IO: Iowa State University.

Connolly, R. (2008). Trust and the virtual environment: Research and methodological considerations. *International Journal of Networking and Virtual Organisation, 5*(3/4), 259–274. doi:10.1504/IJNVO.2008.018823

Connolly, R., & Bannister, F. (2007). Consumer trust in Internet shopping in Ireland: Towards the development of a more effective trust measurement instrument. *Journal of Information Technology, 22*(2), 102–118. doi:10.1057/palgrave. jit.2000071

Constant, D., Sproull, L., & Kiesler, S. (1996). The kindness of strangers: The usefulness of electronic weak ties for technical advice. *Organization Science, 7*(2), 119–135. doi:10.1287/orsc.7.2.119

De Laat, P. B. (2005). Trusting virtual trust. *Ethics and Information Technology, 7*(3), 167–180. doi:10.1007/s10676-006-0002-6

Dehnart, A. (1999). *Digital neighborhoods.* Retrieved January 12, 2010, from http://www. andydehnart.com/writing/articles/digital_neighborhoods/

Dibben, M. R., Morris, S. E., & Lean, M. E. J. (2000). Situational trust and co-operative partnerships between physicians and their patients: A theoretical explanation transferable from business practice. *QJM, 93*(1), 55–61. doi:10.1093/qjmed/93.1.55

Dirks, K. T., & Ferrin, D. L. (2001). The role of trust in organizational settings. *Organization Science, 12*(4), 450–467. doi:10.1287/orsc.12.4.450.10640

Donath, J. (1998). Identity and deception in the virtual community. In Smith, M., & Kollock, P. (Eds.), *Communities in cyberspace* (pp. 29–59). London, UK: Rutledge.

Dunn, J., & Schweitzer, M. (2005). Feeling and believing: The influence of emotion on trust. *Journal of Personality and Social Psychology, 88*, 736–748. doi:10.1037/0022-3514.88.5.736

Festinger, L., Pepitone, A., & Newcomb, T. (1952). Some consequences of deindividuation in a group. *Journal of Abnormal and Social Psychology, 47*, 382–389. doi:10.1037/h0057906

Gambetta, D. (1988). Can we trust trust? In Gambetta, D. (Ed.), *Trust: Making and breaking cooperative relationships* (pp. 213–237). New York, NY: Basil Blackwell.

Gefen, D. (2000). E-commerce: The role of familiarity and trust. *Omega: The International Journal of Management Science, 28*(6), 725–737. doi:10.1016/S0305-0483(00)00021-9

Gefen, D., Karahanna, E., & Straub, D. W. (2003). Trust and TAM in online shopping. *Management Information Systems Quarterly, 27*(1), 51–83.

Gefen, D., & Straub, D. W. (2004). Consumer trust in B2C e-commerce and the importance of social presence: Experiments in e-products and e-services. *Omega: The International Journal of Management Science, 32*(6), 407–424. doi:10.1016/j.omega.2004.01.006

Giffin, K. (1967). The contribution of studies of source credibility to a theory of interpersonal trust in the communication process. *Psychological Bulletin, 68*(2), 104–120. doi:10.1037/h0024833

Govier, T. (1997). *Social trust and human communities*. Montreal, Canada: McGill-Queen's University Press.

Grabner-Kräuter, S., Kaluscha, E. A., & Fladnitzer, M. (2006). Perspectives of online trust and similar constructs: A conceptual clarification. In *Proceedings of the 8th International Conference on Electronic Commerce: The New e-commerce: Innovations For Conquering Current Barriers, Obstacles and Limitations To Conducting Successful Business on the internet* (Fredericton, New Brunswick, Canada, August 13 - 16, 2006). (pp. 235-243). ICEC '06, Vol. 156. New York, NY: ACM. doi: 10.1145/1151454.1151496

Grandison, T., & Sloman, M. (2000). A survey of trust in Internet applications. In *IEEE Communications Surveys and Tutorials, 3*(4), 2-16.

Granovetter, M. S. (1985). Economic action and social structure: The problem of embeddedness. *American Journal of Sociology, 91*(3), 481–510. doi:10.1086/228311

Hardin, R. (1992). The street-level epistemology of trust. *Analyse & Kritik, 14*, 152–176.

Herring, S. C. (2002). Computer mediated communication on the Internet. *Annual Review of Information Science & Technology, 36*, 109–168. doi:10.1002/aris.1440360104

Hilligoss, B., & Rieh, S. Y. (2008). Developing a unifying framework of credibility assessment: Construct, heuristics, and interaction in context. *Information Processing & Management, 44*(4), 1467–1484. doi:10.1016/j.ipm.2007.10.001

Hiltz, S. R., & Turoff, M. (1978). *The network nation: Human communication via computer*. Reading, MA: Addison-Wesley.

Hoffman, R. R., Lee, J. D., Woods, D. D., Shadbolt, N., Miler, J., & Bradshaw, J. M. (2009). The dynamics of trust in cyberdomain. *IEEE Intelligent Systems, 24*(6), 5–11. doi:10.1109/MIS.2009.124

Hofstede, G. (1980). *Culture's consequences: International differences in work-related values*. Newbury Park, CA: Sage.

Hunt, S. D., & Morgan, R. M. (1994). Relationship marketing in the era of network competition. *Marketing Management, 3*(1), 18–28.

Hunter, B. (2002). Learning in the virtual community depends upon changes in local communities. In Renninger, K. A., & Shumar, W. (Eds.), *Building virtual communities: Learning and change in cyberspace* (pp. 96–126). Cambridge, UK: Cambridge University Press. doi:10.1017/CBO9780511606373.009

Jarvenpaa, S. L., & Leidner, D. E. (1998). Communication and trust in global virtual teams. *Journal of Computer-Mediated Communication 3*(4). Retrieved on February 20, 2010, from http://jcmc.indiana.edu/vol3/issue4/jarvenpaa.html

Jarvenpaa, S. L., Shaw, T. R., & Staples, D. S. (2004). Toward contextualized theories of trust: The role of trust in global virtual teams. *Information Systems Research, 15*(3), 250–267. doi:10.1287/isre.1040.0028

Jarvenpaa, S. L., Tractinsky, N., & Vitale, M. (2000). Consumer trust in an Internet store. *Information Technology Management, 1*(1-2), 45–71. doi:10.1023/A:1019104520776

Jonassen, D. H., Peck, K. L., & Wilson, B. G. (1999). *Learning with technology: A constructivist perspective*. Upper Saddle River, NJ: Merrill.

Jøsang, A. (1996). The right type of trust for distributed systems. New Security Paradigms Workshop, In *Proceedings of the 1996 Workshop on New Security Paradigms*, Lake Arrowhead, California, United States, (pp. 119-131).

Kahneman, D., & Tversky, A. (1979). Prospect theory: An analysis of decisions under risk. *Econometrica, 47*, 313–327. doi:10.2307/1914185

Kanawattanachai, P., & Yoo, Y. (2007). The impact of knowledge coordination on virtual team performance over time. *Management Information Systems Quarterly, 31*(4), 783–808.

Kelton, K., Fleischmann, K. R., & Wallace, W. A. (2008). Trust in digital information. *Journal of the American Society for Information Science and Technology, 59*(3), 363–374. doi:10.1002/asi.20722

Khodyakov, D. (2007). Trust as a process: A three-dimensional approach. *Sociology, 41*(1), 115–132.. doi:10.1177/0038038507072285

Kiesler, S. (1986). Thinking ahead: The hidden messages in computer networks. *Harvard Business Review*, (January-February): 46–60.

Kim, D. J. (2008). Self-perception-based versus transference-based trust determinants in computer-mediated transactions: A cross-cultural comparison study. *Journal of Management Information Systems, 24*(4), 13–45. doi:10.2753/MIS0742-1222240401

Klein, P. G. (2009). Risk, uncertainty, and economic organization. In J. G. Hülsmann, & S. Kinsella (Eds.), *Property, freedom, & society: Essays in honor of Hans-Hermann Hoppe* (pp. 325-338). Auburn, AL: Ludwig von Mises Institute. Retrieved on May 1st, 2010, from http://mises.org/daily/3779

Knight, F. H. (1921). *Risk, uncertainty, and profit*. New York, NY: Kelley and Millman, Inc.

Kollock, P. (1999). The production of trust in online markets. In Lawler, E. J., Macy, M., Thyne, S., & Walker, H. A. (Eds.), *Advanced in group process, 16* (pp. 99–123). Greenwich, CT: JAI Press.

Kramer, R. M. (1999). Trust and distrust in organizations: Emerging perspectives, enduring questions. *Annual Review of Psychology, 50*, 569–598. doi:10.1146/annurev.psych.50.1.569

Lea, M., & Spears, R. (1991). Computer-mediated communication, de-individuation and group decision-making. [Special Issue: Computer-supported cooperative work and groupware.]. *International Journal of Man-Machine Studies, 34*, 283–301. doi:10.1016/0020-7373(91)90045-9

Lewicki, R. J., & Bunker, B. B. (1996). Developing and maintaining trust in work relationships. In Kramer, R. M., & Tyler, T. R. (Eds.), *Trust in organization: Frontiers of theory and research* (pp. 114–139). Thousand Oaks, CA: Sage.

Lewicki, R. J., McAllister, D. J., & Bies, R. J. (1998). Trust and distrust: New relationships and realities. *Academy of Management Review, 23*(3), 438–458. doi:10.2307/259288

Lewicki, R. J., & Wiethoff, C. (2000). Trust, trust development, and trust repair. In Deutsch, M., & Coleman, P. T. (Eds.), *The handbook of conflict resolution: Theory and practice* (pp. 86–107). San Francisco, CA: Jossey-Bass.

Lewis, J. D. (1999). *Trusted partner: How companies build mutual trust and win together.* New York, NY: Simon & Schuter.

Lewis, J. D., & Weigert, A. J. (1985). Trust as a social reality. *Social Forces, 63*(4), 967–985. doi:10.2307/2578601

Lipnack, J., & Stamps, J. (1997). *Virtual teams.* New York, NY: John Wiley and Sons, Inc.

Lu, Y., Zhao, L., & Wang, B. (2008). Exploring factors affecting trust and purchase behavior in virtual communities. *IEEE Symposium on Advanced Management of Information for Globalized Enterprises, 2008. AMIGE, 2008,* (pp. 1-5).

Lu, Y., Zhao, L., & Wang, B. (2009). (in press). From virtual community members to C2C e-commerce buyers: Trust in virtual communities and its effect on consumers' purchase intention. *Electronic Commerce Research and Applications.* doi:.doi:10.1016/j.elerap.2009.07.003

Luhmann, N. (1979). *Trust and power.* Toronto, Canada: John Wiley.

Luhmann, N. (1988). Familiarity, confidence, trust: Problems and alternatives. In Gamebetta, D. (Ed.), *Trust: Marking and breaking cooperative relations* (pp. 94–107). New York, NY: Basil Blackwell.

Lynch, C. (2001). When documents deceive: Trust and provenance as new factors for information retrieval in a tangled web. *Journal of the American Society for Information and Technology, 52*(1), 12–17. doi:10.1002/1532-2890(2000)52:1<12::AID-ASI1062>3.0.CO;2-V

Mayer, R. C., Davis, J. H., & Schoorman, F. D. (1995). An integrative model of organization trust. *Academy of Management Review, 20*(3), 709–734. doi:10.2307/258792

McAlister, D. J. (1995). Affect- and cognition-based trust as foundations for interpersonal cooperation in organizations. *Academy of Management Review, 38*(1), 24–59. doi:10.2307/256727

McKnight, D. H., & Chervany, N. L. (1996). *The meanings of trust* (Technical Report 94004). Carlson School of Management, University of Minnesota, retrieved on February 1st, 2010, from http://misrc.umn.edu/wpaper/WorkingPapers/9604.pdf

McKnight, D. H., & Chervany, N. L. (2001). Conceptualizing trust: A typology and e-commerce customer relationships model. *Hawaii International Conference on System Sciences, 7,* Los Alamitos, CA, USA: IEEE Computer Society. (pp. 7022-7031).

McKnight, D. H., & Chervany, N. L. (2002). What trust means in e-commerce customer relationships: An interdisciplinary conceptual typology. *International Journal of Electronic Commerce, 6*(2), 35–59.

McKnight, D. H., & Chervany, N. L. (2006). Distrust and trust in B2C e-commerce: Do they differ? In *Proceedings of the Eighth International Conference on Electronic Commerce* (pp. 482-491). Fredericton, New Brunswick: Association for Computing Machinery.

McKnight, D. H., Cummings, L. L., & Chervany, N. L. (1998). Initial trust formation in new organizational relationships. *Academy of Management Review, 23*(3), 473–490. doi:10.2307/259290

Mishna, F., Saini, M., & Solomon, S. (2009). Ongoing and online: Children and youth's perceptions of cyber bullying. *Children and Youth Services Review*, *31*, 1222–1228. doi:10.1016/j.childyouth.2009.05.004

Mitchell, A., & Zigurs, I. (2009). Trust in virtual teams: Solved or still a mystery? *The Data Base for Advances in Information Systems*, *40*(3), 61–83.

Morrison, E. W., & Robinson, S. L. (1997). When employees feel betrayed: A model of how psychological contract violation develops. *Academy of Management Review*, *22*, 226–256. doi:10.2307/259230

Mowshowitz, A. (1997). Virtual organization-introduction to the special section. *Communications of the ACM*, *40*(9), 30–37. doi:10.1145/260750.260759

Murnighan, J. K., Malhotra, D., & Weber, J. M. (2004). Paradoxes of trust: Empirical and theoretical departures from a traditional model. In Kramer, R. M., & Cook, K. S. (Eds.), *Trust and distrust in organizations: Emerging perspectives, enduring questions* (pp. 293–326). New York, NY: Russell Sage Foundation.

Nass, C., & Brave, S. (2005). *Wired for speech*. Cambridge, MA: MIT Press.

Nooteboom, B. (2002). *Trust: Forms, foundations, functions, failures and figures*. Cheltenham, UK/Northampton, MA: Edward Elgar.

Ofuonye, E., Beatty, P., Reay, I., Dick, S., & Miller, J. (2008). How do we build trust into e-commerce websites? *IEEE Software*, *25*(5), 7–9. doi:10.1109/MS.2008.136

Ostwald, M. J. (1997). Virtual urban futures. In Holmes, D. (Ed.), *Virtual politics: Identity & community in cyberspace* (pp. 125–144). London, UK: Sage.

Owston, R. (1998). *Making the link: Teacher professional development on the Internet*. Portsmouth, NH: Heinemann.

Pavlou, P. A. (2003). Consumer acceptance of electronic commerce: Integrating trust and risk with the technology acceptance model. *International Journal of Electronic Commerce*, *7*(3), 69–103.

Porter, C. E. (2004). A typology of virtual communities: A multi-disciplinary foundation for future research. *Journal of Computer-Mediated Communication*, *10*(1). Retrieved October 26, 2009, from http://jcmc.indiana.edu/vol10/issue1/porter.html

Putnam, R. (1993). *Making democracy work: Civic tradition in modern Italy*. Princeton, NJ: Princeton University Press.

Putnam, R. (2000). *Bowling alone: The collapse and revival of American community*. New York, NY: Simon and Schuster.

Radin, P. (2006). To me, it's my life: Medical communication, trust, and activism in cyberspace. *Social Science & Medicine*, *62*, 591–601. doi:10.1016/j.socscimed.2005.06.022

Rawlins, B. (2009). Irrational trust. Retrieved on May 1st, 2010, from http://www.instituteforpr.org/essential_knowledge/detail/irrational_trust_rawlins/

Rheingold, H. (1993). *The virtual community: Homesteading on the electronic frontier*. Reading, MA: Addison-Wesley.

Ridings, C. M., & Gefen, D. (2004). Virtual community attraction: Why people hang out online. *Journal of Computer-Mediated Communication*, *10*(1). Retrieved on January 12, 2010 from http://jcmc.indiana.edu/vol10/issue1/ridings_gefen.html

Ridings, C. M., Gefen, D., & Arinze, B. (2002). Some antecedents and effects of trust in virtual communities. *The Journal of Strategic Information Systems*, *11*, 271–295. doi:10.1016/S0963-8687(02)00021-5

Rieh, S. Y., & Danielson, D. R. (2007). Credibility: A multidisciplinary framework. *Annual Review of Information Science & Technology, 41*, 307–364. doi:10.1002/aris.2007.1440410114

Rousseau, D., Sitkin, S., Burt, R., & Camerer, C. (1998). Not so different after all: A cross-discipline view of trust. *Academy of Management Review, 23*(3), 393–404.

Sarker, S., Valacich, J. S., & Sarker, S. (2003). Virtual team trust: Instrument development and validation. *Information Resources Management Journal, 16*(2), 35–55. doi:10.4018/irmj.2003040103

Schoorman, F. D., Mayer, R. C., & Davis, J. H. (2007). An integrative model of organizational trust: Past, present and future. *Academy of Management Review, 32*, 344–354.

Serino, C., Furner, C. P., & Smatt, C. M. (2005). Making it personal: How personalization affects trust over time. *Proceedings of the Hawaii International Conference on System Sciences (ICIS)*, Waikoloa, HI.

Shankar, V., Urban, G. L., & Sultan, F. (2002). Online trust: A stakeholder perspective, concepts, implications, and future directions. *The Journal of Strategic Information Systems, 11*(3-4), 325–344. doi:10.1016/S0963-8687(02)00022-7

Shapiro, S. P. (1987). The social control of impersonal trust. *American Journal of Sociology, 93*(3), 623–658. doi:10.1086/228791

Sheppard, B. H., & Sherman, D. M. (1998). The grammars of trust: A model and general implications. *Academy of Management Review, 23*(3), 422–437. doi:10.2307/259287

Short, J., Williams, E., & Christie, B. (1976). *The social psychology of telecommunications*. New York, NY: John Wiley.

Siegrist, M., Cvetkovich, G. T., & Gutscher, H. (2001). Shared values, social trust, and the perception of geographic cancer clusters. *Risk Analysis, 21*(6), 1047–1054. doi:10.1111/0272-4332.216173

Song, J., & Kim, Y. J. (2006). Social influence process in the acceptance of a virtual community service. *Information Systems Frontiers, 8*(3), 241–252. doi:10.1007/s10796-006-8782-0

Spears, R., & Lea, M. (1992). Social influence and the influence of the social in computer mediated communication. In Lea, M. (Ed.), *Contexts of computer-mediated communication* (pp. 30–65). Hemel Hempstead, UK: Harvester Wheatsheaf.

Spears, R., Lea, M., Corneliessen, R. A., Postemes, T., & Ter Harr, W. (2002). Computer-mediated communication as a channel for social resistance: The strategic side of SIDE. *Small Group Research, 33*(5), 555–574. doi:10.1177/104649602237170

Sproull, L., & Faraj, S. (1997). Atheism, sex and databases: The net as a social technology. In Kiesler, S. (Ed.), *Culture of the Internet* (pp. 35–51). Mahwah, NJ: Lawrence Erlbaum Associates.

Sproull, L., & Kiesler, S. (1991). Computers, networks and work. *Scientific American*, (September): 84–91.

Stabb, S., Bhargava, B., Lilien, L., Rosenthal, A., Winslett, M., & Sloman, M. (2004). The pudding of trust. *IEEE Intelligent Systems, 19*(5), 74–88. doi:10.1109/MIS.2004.52

Stepanikova, I., Mollborn, S., Cook, K. S., Thom, D. H., & Kramer, R. M. (2006). Patients' race, ethnicity, language, and trust in a physician. *Journal of Health and Social Behavior, 47*(4), 390–405. doi:10.1177/002214650604700406

Swinth, K. R., & Blascovich, J. (2002). Perceiving and responding to others: Human-human and human-computer social interaction in collaborative virtual environments. *Proceedings of the 5th Annual International workshop on PRESENCE.* Porto, Portugal.

Tajfel, H., & Turner, J. C. (1986). *The social identity of intergroup relations.* Chicago, IL: Nelson-Hall.

Turel, O., Yuan, Y., & Connelly, C. E. (2008). In justice we trust: Predicting user acceptance of e-customer services. *Journal of Management Information Systems, 24*(4), 123–151. doi:10.2753/MIS0742-1222240405

Tyler, T. R., & Lind, E. A. (1992). A relational model of authority in group. *Advances in Experimental Social Psychology, 25,* 115–192. doi:10.1016/S0065-2601(08)60283-X

Ward, K. J. (1999). The cyber-ethnographic and the emergence of the virtually new community. *Journal of Information Technology, 14,* 95–105. doi:10.1080/026839699344773

Wasko, M. M., & Faraj, S. (2000). It is what one does: Why people participate and help others in electronic communities of practice. *The Journal of Strategic Information Systems, 9,* 155–173. doi:10.1016/S0963-8687(00)00045-7

Weber, J. M., Malhotra, D., & Murnighan, J. K. (2005). Normal acts of irrational trust, motivated attributions, and the process of trust development. In Staw, B. M., & Kramer, R. M. (Eds.), *Research in organizational behavior* (pp. 75–102). New York, NY: Elsevier.

Wellman, B., & Gulia, M. (1999). Net surfers don't ride alone. In Wellman, B. (Ed.), *Networks in the global village* (pp. 331–366). Boulder, CO: Westview Press.

Whittaker, S., Isaacs, E., & O'day, V. (1997). Widening the net: Workshop report on the theory and practice of physical and network communities. *SIGCHI Bulletin, 18*(1), 27-32.

Williamson, O. E. (1993). Calculativeness, trust, and economic organization. *The Journal of Law & Economics, 36,* 453–486. doi:10.1086/467284

Wilson, B., & Ryder, M. (1996). Dynamic learning communities: An alternative to designed instruction. In M. Simonson (Ed.) *Proceedings of selected research and development presentations* (pp. 800-809). Washington, D. C.: Association for Educational Communications and Technology. Retrieved on January 20, 2010, from http://carbon.ucdenver.edu/~mryder/dlc.html

Wilson, P. (1983). *Second-hand knowledge: An inquiry into cognitive authority.* Westport, CT: Greenwood Press.

Wolak, J., Finkelhor, D., & Mitchell, K. J. (2004). Internet-initiated sex crimes against minors: Implications for prevention based on findings from a national study. *The Journal of Adolescent Health, 35*(5), 424–433. doi:10.1016/j.jadohealth.2004.05.006

Worchel, P. (1979). Trust and distrust. In Austin, W. G., & Worchel, P. (Eds.), *Social psychology of intergroup relations* (pp. 174–187). Monterey, CA: Broks/Cole.

Wu, J. J., & Tsang, A. S. L. (2008). Factors affecting members trust belief and behaviour intention in virtual communities. *Behaviour & Information Technology, 27*(2), 115–125. doi:10.1080/01449290600961910

Yan, Z. (2009). Limited knowledge and limited resources: Children's and adolescents' understanding of the Internet. *Journal of Applied Developmental Psychology, 30,* 103–115. doi:10.1016/j.appdev.2008.10.012

Zand, D. E. (1972). Trust and managerial problem solving. *Administrative Science Quarterly, 17*(2), 229–239. doi:10.2307/2393957

Zucker, L. G. (1986). Production of trust: Institutional sources of economic structure. In Staw, B. M., & Cummings, L. L. (Eds.), *Research in organizational behavior* (pp. 53–111). Greenwich, CT: JAI Press.

ADDITIONAL READING

Ba, S. (2001). Establishing online trust through a community responsibility system. *Decision Support Systems, 31*(4), 323–336. doi:10.1016/S0167-9236(00)00144-5

Bachmann, R., & Zaheer, A. (Eds.). (2006). *Handbook of Trust Research*. Cheltenham, UK: Edward Elgar.

Benbasat, I., Gefen, D., & Pavlou, P. A. (2010). Introduction to the Special Issue on Novel Perspectives on Trust in Information Systems. *Management Information Systems Quarterly, 34*(2), 367–371.

Dyer, J. H., & Chu, W. (2003). The role of trustworthiness in reducing transaction costs and improving performance: empirical evidence from the United States, Japan, and Korea. *Organization Science, 14*(1), 57–68. doi:10.1287/orsc.14.1.57.12806

Fukuyama, F. (1995). *Trust - The social virtues and the creation of prosperity*. London: Penguin.

Gefen, D., Benbasat, I., & Pavlou, P. A. (2008). A Research Agenda for Trust in Online Environments. *Journal of Management Information Systems, 24*(4), 275–286. doi:10.2753/MIS0742-1222240411

Gill, H., Boies, K., Finegan, J. E., & McNally, J. (2005). Antecedents of trust: Establishing a boundary condition for the relation between propensity to trust and intention to trust. *Journal of Business and Psychology, 19*, 287–302. doi:10.1007/s10869-004-2229-8

Golembiewski, R. T., & McConkie, M. (1975). The centrality of interpersonal trust in group processes. In Cooper, C. L. (Ed.), *Theories of Group Processes* (pp. 131–185). New York, NY: Wiley & Sons.

Grabner-Kräuter, S., & Kaluscha, E. A. (2003). Empirical research in on-line trust: a review and critical assessment. *International Journal of Human-Computer Studies, 58*, 783–812. doi:10.1016/S1071-5819(03)00043-0

Jones, Q. (1997). Virtual-Communities, virtual settlements & cyber-archaeology: A theoretical outline. *Journal of Computer-Mediated Communication, 3*(3). Retrieved October 29, 2009, from http://jcmc.indiana.edu/vol3/issue3/jones.html

Kanawattanachai, P., & Yoo, Y. (2002). Dynamic nature of trust in virtual teams. *Strategic Information Systems, 11*, 187–213. doi:10.1016/S0963-8687(02)00019-7

Kramer, R. M. (2006). *Organizational trust: a reader*. New York: Oxford University Press.

Kramer, R. M., & Cook, K. S. (Eds.). (2007). *Trust and Distrust in Organizations: Dilemmas and Approaches*. London: Sage.

Kramer, R. M., & Tyler, T. R. (Eds.). (1996). *Trust in Organizations. Frontiers of Theory and Research*. Thousand Oaks, CA: Sage.

Marková, I., & Gillespie, A. (Eds.). (2007). *Trust and distrust: Socio-cultural perspectives*. Greenwich, CT: Information Age Publishing, Inc.

McKnight, D. H., & Chervany, N. L. (2001). Trust and distrust definitions: One bite at a time. In Falcone, R., Singh, M., & Tan, Y.-H. (Eds.), *Trust in cyber-societies* (pp. 27–54). Berlin, Heidelberg: Springer-Verlag. doi:10.1007/3-540-45547-7_3

Porter, C. E., & Donthu, N. (2008). Cultivating Trust and Harvesting Value in Virtual Communities. *Management Science, 54*(1), 113–128. doi:10.1287/mnsc.1070.0765

Preece, J., & Maloney-Krichmar, D. (2003). Online communities: Focusing on sociability and usability. In Jacko, J., & Sears, A. (Eds.), *Handbook of Human-Computer Interaction* (pp. 596–620). Mahwah, NJ: Lawrence Erlbaum.

Spears, R., Lea, M., & Lee, S. (1990). Deindividuation and group polarisation in computer mediated communication. *The British Journal of Social Psychology, 29*, 121–134.

Uslaner, E. (2002). *The moral foundations of trust.* New York: Cambridge University Press.

Vance, A., Elie-dit-cosaque, C., & Straub, D.W. (2008). Examining trust in information technology artifacts: The effects of system quality and culture. *Journal of Management Information Systems, 24*(4), 73–100. doi:10.2753/MIS0742-1222240403

Wasko, M. M., & Faraj, S. (2005). Why should I share? Examining social capital and knowledge contribution in electronic networks of practice. *Management Information Systems Quarterly, 29*(1), 35–58.

Zahedi, F. M., & Song, J. (2008). Dynamics of trust revision: Using health infomediaries. *Journal of Management Information Systems, 24*(4), 225–248. doi:10.2753/MIS0742-1222240409

KEY TERMS AND DEFINITIONS

Antecedent: Conditions or factors to support trust building.

Identity: Representation or identification to be distinguished from the other party.

Online Community: An online community is a virtual community that exists online, mainly on the Internet, where its members with similar interests, experience, or shared values take part in social interactions such as share information, knowledge, and experience with other members.

Trust: One party is willing to believe that the other party's behaviors should accord with the expectation or social norms of the party held.

Trust Building: Trust formation or trust development during mutual communication and interaction of participants.

Virtual Community: A virtual community is a social aggregation in which individuals with similar interests, experience, or shared values regularly interact and interconnect with each other, regardless of geographic boundaries, through a specific medium.

Chapter 2
Social Networks and Students' Ethical Behavior

Lori N. K. Leonard
University of Tulsa, USA

Tracy S. Manly
University of Tulsa, USA

ABSTRACT

Social networking sites are prevalent among young adults. College students in particular are utilizing these sites to keep in contact with friends and to make new friends. However, with the positives of social networking, there are also negatives. Students can provide too much personal information online, engage in inappropriate conversations, scrutinize other students, ridicule peers, and so forth. Because of the impersonal environment that technology creates, an individual's normal behavior can change which leads to a change in his/her basic ethical structure. The purpose of this chapter is to provide a discussion of the changing ethical structure of students, as well as an examination of the ways to teach ethics, given those changes. The chapter also includes a discussion of four classical ethical theories that should be considered when discussing or teaching social networking. Future research directions are also given.

INTRODUCTION

The ethical choices made by individuals are strongly influenced by the person's environment. What one decides to wear to class or eat in the cafeteria is influenced by roommates and peers. Whether one gossips is influenced by friendships and acquaintances. Wanting to belong and have friendships is a part of student life. This need for belonging is even more intent when social networking environments are considered (Dwyer, Hiltz, & Passerini, 2007). The social environment encountered by current traditional college students (that have been termed, "wired from birth") differs vastly from that faced by those in previous generations. The ability to be connected at all times blurs the line between professional and personal time, given that every moment in time can be captured

DOI: 10.4018/978-1-60960-573-5.ch002

and recorded on the network (Kumar, Novak, & Tomkins, 2006) and that those connections can extend beyond geographical boundaries (Maran, 2009). In some significant ways, this phenomenon also affects the ethical decisions and behaviors of students in the current generation (Gross & Acquisti, 2005). Universities, especially business colleges, are amplifying ethics coverage in the curriculum. Ethics is often integrated into existing business discipline courses, such as accounting, finance, management information systems, and marketing. Additionally, Universities are being to develop stand-alone courses. Many of the current stand-alone courses are being offered at the graduate level. Regardless of the course, the approach to teaching business ethics may also need to be modified to address the current social environment facing students. For example, many younger adults will post virtually any personal information or photo to Facebook (Barnes, 2006), including phone number and address as well as indecent photos. Students willingly watch the misfortunes of others on a YouTube video when they would be unlikely to tolerate similar behavior if witnessed personally. Given these changes in the environment, how ethics is addressed in the curriculum must change.

The concern is that a student's basic ethical structure is being altered by technological advancements. This can be explained by looking at the six components of one's basic ethical structure: consequences, likelihood of effect, relatedness, reach of result, society's opinion, and time to consequences. Each of these categories needs to be addressed to examine the effect of readily available online applications on them. This chapter examines how the environment of social networks and constant connectedness influences the components of a student's basic ethical structure. It also proposes ways to teach in this changing ethical environment by presenting four ethical theories (utilitarianism, distributive justice, rights theory, and virtue ethics) that should be considered when teaching ethics to students. In many cases, just

making students aware of the ethical concerns is enough. In other cases, specific steps have to be taken to modify the students' intended actions by making them aware of the consequences of the action or the effect on others. The chapter will, therefore, provide a discussion of the changing ethical structure of students and an examination of the ways to teach ethics given those changes.

BACKGROUND

Fifty-five percent of online Americans between the ages of 12-17 use at least one online social networking site (Lenhart & Madden, 2007), and seventy-five percent of online young adults between the ages of 18-24 have a profile on a social networking site (Lenhart, 2009) and this number is increasing every day. Social networking sites, such as Facebook, MySpace, LinkedIn and Twitter, allow individuals to build relationships with other individuals who share a common interest, whether it is personal or professional (DiMicco, et al, 2008). Users can create a profile and build a personal network, while breaking down barriers of time, distance, and culture (Maran, 2009; Reynolds, 2010). The common interest is often the simple desire to interact with other individuals. For teens, girls primarily use social networking sites to reinforce existing relationships, where as boys use social networking sites to flirt and make new friends (Lenhart & Madden, 2007). Teens and young adults utilize social networking sites to keep up with friends, make plans with friends, make new friends, and so forth (Lenhart, 2009). Regardless of the reason, social networking has become an integral part of young adults' daily lives. For example, when the author's morning business class was asked how many of them had checked their MySpace or Facebook prior to attending class, nearly all raised their hand. Yet, when asked whether they had checked their email before class, only a third raised their hand. Twenty-two percent of American youths visit social networking sites several times a day (Lenhart & Madden, 2007) and this number is continuing to grow. In fact, social networking has become just as important as the cell phone; young adults cannot envision daily life without either and both have become part of the student's status symbol.

Being an integral part of life, lines become blurred as to what information should be shared and with whom, and how one should behave or react when inappropriate information is shared. With poor social networking behavior as wide ranging as cyberstalking and cyberbullying to blackmail, young adults must be educated as to the ethical obligations one has while on a social networking site. Cyberstalking is threatening behavior directed towards a person using the Internet (Reynolds, 2010). This primarily occurs in adult age groups. Cyberstalking can lead to great anguish for the person being stalked because of threatening e-mail, excessive phone calls, and so forth. Cyberbullying is the humiliation, harassment, or threatening of another person via the Internet (Reynolds, 2010). This primarily occurs in student age groups. Cyberbullying can become so overwhelming for young adults that some commit suicide as a result. These are very common examples of how innocently supplied information via a social networking site can go wrong. Another common example is the uploading of inappropriate material, such as videos that depict violence or obscenity (Reynolds, 2010). While most social networking sites prohibit such conduct, it is very hard to police. Therefore, these inappropriate postings can inadvertently advocate questionable behavior in young adults, such as underage drinking and drug use.

Education may provide a solution, however. De Souza and Dick (2009) found that children who are taught the importance of privacy are less likely to reveal sensitive information online. They also found information disclosure of MySpace users to be driven by peer pressure, website interface design (having a box to fill-in), and signaling (how they want to be perceived). They found

that MySpace pages seem to be used to form the young adult's "identity" or how he wants to be perceived. When there is a need to form an "identity", people begin to behave differently. Because there is no way to verify that the posted information is legitimate, young adults can make their "identity" freely. This can result in falsified information, or worse.

Ethical decisions are complex and often include substantial uncertainty. However, social networking is making the decision process even more difficult, or presumably easier if the individual doesn't see that there is an ethical decision to be made. The next section provides a summary of student ideas regarding social networking, followed by ways to address the changes in ethical structure that are occurring as a result of social networking. Lastly, ways to teach ethics in this changing technological environment are presented.

STUDENT IDEAS ABOUT SOCIAL NETWORKING

Current students from the millennial generation (born 1984-2002) perceive the use of technology differently than their professors and prospective employers from earlier generations (silent generation (born 1927-1945), baby boomers (1946-1964), generation X (1965-1983)) (Jonas-Dwyer & Pospisil, 2004). Therefore, professors must first understand current students' perspectives regarding social networking before they can teach proper ethical conduct. Millennials are used to technology being integrated in day-to-day activities; they use instant messaging and text messaging as a natural communication or socialization mechanism. They also can multi-process by using the computer, talking on the phone, listening to music, and doing homework all at the same time (Brown, 2000). The millennial generation expects a learning environment different from previous generations, and universities must modify how they teach to reach this audience. In particular, millennials are

Table 1. Social networking perceived advantages

- *"Easier to keep in contact with family and friends who live far away."*
- *"I get to keep up with friends I normally wouldn't have without it."*
- *"They allow people to reconnect with old friends, allow employers to find potential employees, and allow corporations to keep employees actively involved in what's going on with the company."*
- *"I can see how they facilitate the maintenance of distant/work relationships."*
- *"Impress friends"*
- *"I can keep in touch with people I meet at conferences, friends, and classmates. We can share what we are up to via photographs."*
- *"Networking with others in similar job positions or with similar interests and/or hobbies."*
- *"Easy communication and interaction with people."*
- *"I am able to keep up with people I don't see very often but don't talk to enough to warrant a call just to catch up."*
- *"The ability to show off the number of inside jokes you have."*
- *"I can connect and remain connected with people that are otherwise difficult to maintain relationships with."*
- *"Network with former grads for career opportunities."*

looking for a learning environment where the instructor is the leader or role model, where they are challenged in the classroom, where they can work on school projects with their friends (i.e. social interaction), where they can have fun and find humor in learning, where they are treated with respect, and where there is flexibility (i.e. students engaged in many activities beyond the classroom, allowed to choose communications methods, and so forth) (Jonas-Dwyer & Pospisil, 2004). Therefore, it becomes a balancing act of catering to the "new technologically savvy generation" (Jonas-Dwyer & Pospisil, 2004) while still delivering the more traditional requirements of University study.

In order to gather initial thoughts regarding social networking among students, current business students were informally queried about their ideas related to social networking. Before gathering data, the researchers' first pilot tested the questions on a small group of students. After making needed clarifications, a sample of students was selected to participate. Current students were utilized because they represent the majority of Web users and are more apt to be online than any other age category (Hsu & Chiu, 2004). Forty-four students from three business courses completed a short questionnaire. The group of students included both graduate and undergraduate students, enrolled in a junior level course. The students all attend the same university, a private institution from the Midwestern region of the United States. The students were informed

that participation was completely voluntary and that the information would be recorded, but no individual would be identified. General questions were first gathered regarding participation in various social networking tools, such as Facebook, MySpace, LinkedIn, Twitter, Personal blog, and other. Questions for the social networking tools were with regards to use, how often accessed, and time spent using each. Additionally, the students were requested to provide information regarding the (perceived) advantage of social networking tools, whether employers should check the social networking pages of current and prospective employees, whether employees should be surfing social networks during work hours and on company-issued computers, and whether there is a distinction between personal and professional information shared through social networking.

Some of the student comments received on the questionnaires are shown in Tables 1 through 4 and are discussed below. The students' queried used Facebook more than any other social networking site followed by the professional networking site, LinkedIn. Over half of the Facebook users log in daily or multiple times per day, with some spending more than 14 hours per week on Facebook.

Perceived Advantages of Social Networking

When asked about the perceived advantages of social networking, the most common response was

Table 2. Social networking and employer monitoring

Question – Should employers routinely check the social networking profiles of current employees? Prospective Employees?		
	Yes	**No**
Current Employees	• *"The person is representing the company and if they are friends on facebook... check away!"* • *"They should probably check periodically to see if there is anything inappropriate that deals with the company."* • *"They only have the right if you are advertising that you are their employee."* • *"Yes, especially if the employee is in a high visibility position as they are ambassadors representing the company."* • *"I want to say no but if people make their information public to everyone (which I don't) then employers have the right to see it to and probably should use it as another tool to see how employees and candidates really are."* • *"On many of these sites, you can display the company you work for, and employers should know how you are portraying the company."*	• *"...should not be searching for relationship or other personal data, as these things are not relevant to most companies."* • *"People should not be punished for what happens on these sites, so why check them?"* • *"...their personal life may not necessarily reflect their work abilities or habits."* • *"No. Invasion of privacy. Acceptable if befriended though."* • *"A person's personal life shouldn't affect the perception of the employer of its employee."* • *"It should be private life that is separated from work."* • *"I think these are part of the employees' personal life and is no business of their employers. It should be ok for employees to 'let down' a little without having to worry about how their employer may view their profile and its contents."* • *"Once hired, it's not their business."*
Prospective Employees	• *"Can give you an idea of the person."* • *"The definitely should check before hiring someone."* • *"Helps to show what kind of character a prospective employee has."* • *"Yes. Because I believe it can describe a person's lifestyle."* • *"Helps to assure you know candidate although it may allow employer to access data not allowed to ask."*	• *"They shouldn't. These profiles are private for both current and prospective employees."* • *No, because much of the information on the profiles are viewed as private (depending on the person and their personal beliefs)."* • *"Depends on industry. Would say no 90% of the time."*

the ability to keep up with friends and relatives. Table 1 provides example responses from students regarding what they perceive as being the reason to utilize a social networking site. While keeping in touch with friends and family is a good use for social networking and probably the most common, a few students also noted the ability to find potential employers and employees. With the ability to meet potential employers comes the ability for the potential employers to view information about those potential employees. This is a case where ethics' education can help the students to understand that what they are posting could be viewed poorly by their current or future employer. Many students also commented about the ease of communications and "inside jokes". Inside jokes can lead to ethical concerns for a student, especially when those inside jokes lead to harm for another. This perceived advantage is just one example of

the changing nature of a student's basic ethical structure. Why would "inside jokes" ever be considered an advantage? Ethics education must focus on the perceived advantages to understand the changing nature of students and how best to reach them in the traditional classroom setting. Another issue to consider is trust. Online trust is something that must be built (Myskja, 2008); however, it appears that trust is given away fairly freely in social networking. More education needs to be focused on what and when to trust in such environments.

Social Networking and Employer Monitoring

Responses about whether employers should check the social networking pages of current and prospective employees were mixed. Table

2 provides example responses from students regarding whether employers should be allowed to check the social networking profiles of current and prospective employees. Reasons given for allowing employers to check current employees centered on employees being representatives of the company and the company being obligated to ensure that the company name is being represented in the best light. Reasons given for why employers should not be checking current employees' social networking sites dealt with privacy and separation of personal and work life. Privacy is a hotly debated topic when the Internet is involved, and having students' mention "privacy" was not unexpected. What was not gathered in the questionnaire was whether the student, as an employee, would willingly "friend" another employee in a social network. Responses might be different if the students knew they would want to "friend" their employer.

On the other hand, many students felt prospective employees should have their sites checked. They felt that one's character can be gauged from these sites and it helps to understand the prospective employee's lifestyle. In other words, before one is hired, many students felt the social networking sites should be open game. Very few reasons were given as why not to check, and those reasons primarily dealt with maintaining privacy for the prospective employee, similar to responses regarding those currently employed. This is another area where ethics education is needed. What a student places on the social networking site today will be relevant when a person decides to seek different employment.

Social Networking Activities at Work

Student attitudes about using social networks during work hours and on company-issued computers were also mixed. Table 3 provides example responses from students regarding whether employees should have access to social networking sites at work and on company technology after hours. There were very strong feelings regarding this issue, and as previously mentioned, people are using social networking sites to project who they are or how they want to be perceived. Therefore, the use of social networking sites constantly is second nature to them. Many students indicated that social networking can be used for business purposes and therefore would need to be accessed while at work. Students also indicated that employees should be allowed to access social networking sites while on a break or for a limited amount of time, as long as productivity is not affected. This is an indication of the addictive nature of social networking, and also an indication of the lack of separation between work hours and personal hours. Productivity was also cited as a reason for not allowing the use of social networking sites during work hours. Social networking sites can result in reduced employee productivity. This goes back to the need of the millennial generation to have fun and socialize with friends (Jonas-Dwyer & Pospisil, 2004) regardless of the environment in which they are in. More education is needed for students to understand the productivity needs of an organization versus the personal needs of the employee.

After work hours, most students believed it was okay to utilize company laptops and smartphones to access social networking sites because they were on their own time. One student even indicated that he did not see the use as being harmful in any way to the company. A few students did not believe browsing and posting to social networking sites were the best use of company resources even after hours. Most students do not realize that companies have policies and procedures regarding the use of computer technology owned by the company. Education is again needed so that students will understand the ethical issues involved before they are employed.

Table 3. Social networking activities at work

	Yes	No
Question – Should employees have access to social networking sites at work? What about on company-issued laptops (or smartphones) after hours?		
At work	• *"Yes – if they are using them for business purposes."* • *"Depends on the job. A recruiter or sales rep, definitely. Otherwise, maybe not."* • *"Yes, I believe if you are on a break or after hours you should be ok."* • *"I find no harm if employees have access to social networking sites at work or after work hours."* • *"Yes, for a limited amount of time."* • *"People take breaks at work and should be able to explore those sites if they want."* • *"I believe, depending o the job position, that social networking can be very positive and companies should encourage not limit their use."* • *"As long as productivity doesn't get affected by habitual use."* • *"Yes, many times I communicate to contacts through there."* • *"Social networking sites are becoming a major source for business related publicity/advertising."*	• *"...these sites are often huge distractions."* • *"Not at work."* • *"They shouldn't have access to networking sites irrelevant to work."* • *"During work hours is probably not a good idea because it limits productivity."* • *"Because of may company privacy laws and restrictions, I would not advocate using these services on work devices."* • *"No, it's personal."*
After hrs on laptops / smartphones	• *"This is their free time."* • *"After hours it seems like it would be okay."* • *"As long as service is being used responsibly."* • *"I can't see that it would harm the company."*	• *"Even though it's after hours, I don't think it's the best way to use the equipment."* • *"After hours on company equipment shouldn't be allowed."*

Perceived Personal vs. Professional Behavior

Lastly, the comments from students about the distinction between personal and professional behavior show different ideas. Table 4 provides example responses from students regarding whether there is a distinction between personal and professional information shared through social networking. Many students strongly believe that personal social networking sites should not include professional information, and that there should be separate sites designed by employees, one for personal and one for professional. It was also cited that there are social networking sites specifically designed for professional information, such as LinkedIn. Most students who believe there is currently not a distinction between personal and professional information on social networking sites believes there should be. However, the students recognize it can be difficult to make the distinction. This goes back to a previous comment regarding identification of "friends". Once an employee "friends" fellow employees or even the employer on a social networking site, it may not matter whether the company name is mentioned. The lines will become blurred between personal and professional.

SOCIAL NETWORKING'S EFFECT ON ONE'S ETHICAL STRUCTURE

Given the previous discussion of student perceptions of social networking, it is important to consider how one's ethical structure can be affected by this social media outlet. An individual's basic ethical structure consists of six components. This section will discuss each of those six components and the potential effects of social networking.

Table 4. Social networking: Personal vs. professional information

Question – Is there a distinction between personal and professional information shared through social networking?		
	Yes	**No**
Distinction between Personal and Professional	• *"Yes, I don't believe professional information should be shared through social networking. It is unsafe and inappropriate."* • *"There is a distinction between personal and professional information and there should be. Trade secrets and other proprietary information should never be shared."* • *"When you go work, what you do should not be typically shared on networking sites. Operational security is practiced in larger firms, government and sensitive jobs."* • *"There is a distinction – but I welcome more viewing – a potential employer can get to know me better."* • *"Some social networks are more professionally oriented than others, i.e. LinkedIn."* • *"Yes, there are things that the company might not want you to share with your friends and there are things you don't want your company to know about you."* • *"Many users create multiple profiles, one home and one work, so that they can limit their conversations to particular audiences."*	• *"No, but there should be. An employee's personal life should not affect his/her job. If what a person does in their time off doesn't affect their work, it should be none of the employer's business."* • *"I don't think a distinction is made. There probably should be so that everything an individual says or posts is not attributed to the company as well."* • *"No. Employers will view it either way."* • *"All the information on social networks can be public information, so it becomes both personal and professional information."* • *"People should always think twice before sharing information!"* • *"Not really (a distinction). Should be a distinction for security and legal reasons."*

An individual's basic ethical structure consists of the following components: consequences, likelihood of effect, relatedness, reach of result, society's opinion, and time to consequences (Haag and Cummings, 2010). *Consequences* are the amount of benefit or harm that will result from a particular decision. Consequences to an action are easily identified when in a traditional, face-to-face setting. For example, if two individuals are arguing face-to-face, the argument can quickly escalate into a physical altercation (i.e., punches being thrown). There are clear consequences to these actions. However, when individuals argue via a social networking site, it can be quite different. First, the argument has no direct consequences; no punches are going to be thrown (physically). Therefore, the individuals feel more free in terms of what they can say (type) in this setting. The feeling is more of "you can't touch me". Without clear consequences in the individual's mind, more hurt can occur than a punch to the face. Putting thoughts into typed words is ever lasting. In an-

other example, imagine that an individual finds a hurtful video of a complete stranger. Instead of realizing that the video is harmful and does hurt someone, he forwards a link to the video to all of his friends. Again, the person forwarding the message perceives no consequence of his action. In reality, the consequence is being felt by the individual in the video. Just because the viewer has never met this person before does not mean that someone is not being affected. Social networking makes the individual feel absent from the situation, but the situation still exists. This issue relates to the questionnaire comment regarding the perceived advantage of "inside jokes". Clearly, not knowing the consequence of the joke plays a part in the continuance of that joke.

Likelihood of effect is the consideration of whether a harm or benefit will occur because of the actions taken. Is there really a consideration made as to the effects of one's actions in a social network? Social networks allow one to post comments freely without considering the effects. In a traditional setting, hurtful comments said face-to-face are easily assessed. One person can tell from the other's facial expressions and body language whether he has invoked an emotional result. He will know immediately whether the comment has been harmful. Now take that same example to a social networking site. An individual can post a hurtful comment about another individual on Facebook but not have the consideration of the true effect of those actions. Hurtful comments may ensue from the other individual but there is no true sense of the effects of the action. Therefore, this type of behavior continues because neither party can feel or see the hurt caused on the other.

Relatedness is the premise that one will identify with the person who will receive benefit or suffer as a result of the action. Students' post and view personal information. In some instances, hurtful postings occur, yet students often do not come to the aid of their peers. In a traditional setting, if a friend were being verbally abused, one would come to his aid. The harm from the comments would be visible and most people would want to relieve that pain. At a minimum, even if someone did not aid the victim as the comments were occurring, he would offer comfort afterwards. With social networking, the cycle of pain escalates by more people viewing the message or posting and referring it to others to view it as well. Instead of coming to another's aid, the suffering increases because of the disconnected emotions. The people forwarding the posting cannot identify with the person who is suffering because in most cases they do not know him or have very little connection with him. The ethical component of this type of choice needs to be brought to light for current students if this cycle is to be changed, and given that our questionnaire indicated that lines can often be blurred between personal and professional in a social network setting, the relatedness can become very identifiable if the right (or wrong) person comes across the hurtful information.

Reach of result is how many people will be affected by the decision made. Reach of result may be the most important of all six components. With social networking, the network is far reaching. In a traditional social setting, actions can occur with a short reach. Those involved in the event will know of the incident; those people may tell their friends; and so forth. However, eventually the reach ends. With social networking the reach is limitless. One might say that the reach still only affects the people being hurt. However, those are not the only individuals being affected by the actions. Everyone else who is viewing the actions is being affected. The reality is that anyone connected to the actions could potentially change their future actions based on this event. Will the individuals learn from the decisions made and behave more ethically as a result, or will the individuals take the decisions to be norm and behave as their example peers have? More must be done to educate individuals as to the reach of decisions in social networks.

Society's opinion is how one perceives his decision will be viewed by society. Society's opinion should play a large role in one's ethical decisions. How one's intended actions are being perceived should affect the ultimate decision made. This rings true in a traditional setting. In the classroom, for example, students are very aware of society's opinion (and instructors' opinions) on cheating. Therefore, the student's actions are affected by that opinion. With social networking, there seems to be a lack of societal influence. It is common knowledge that anything can be posted in these environments. What might be shocking to a few is completely acceptable to many others. The social networking sites have become the individual's voice, and that voice comes with a no-holds-barred kind of attitude. For example, posting what some may view as inappropriate photos, others view as self-expression. However, that self-expression should consider society's perception, especially if one wishes to seek future employment in that society. This is especially true since social networking sites are viewed when prospective employees are researched prior to a job interview (as was indicated in the questionnaire findings).

Time to consequences refers to the amount of time that transpires before the effects of the decision are felt. The harm caused by social networking decisions can be immediate for those who are being harmed, yet the consequences on the one doing the harm can take much longer. Going back to the previous example regarding the fist fight, the physical hurt occurs immediately and the consequences (i.e. arrest, other legal action, or so forth) also occur almost immediately. However, when this same argument occurs via a social networking site, consequences can take much longer. Regardless of the harm the comments/postings have caused, it will take time to pull together enough evidence to result in the same consequences as the physical altercation. Even if the comments are just as harmful as the fist, it is difficult to prove the harm and therefore the individual believes he can do as he wishes without much of a consequence for his+- actions on a social networking site. While this may be true, it is not ethically sound.

Regardless of one's sense of ethics, these six aspects will play a part in the decision made. They can be taken individually as to influences, but in reality, there will be overlap. The ethical components will all have varying degrees of influence on the individual's decision.

TEACHING IN A CHANGING ETHICAL ENVIRONMENT

Given the multitude of ways that social networking can affect an individual's behavior, University education is a place to start to reverse this trend. Perceived importance has been found to significantly influence whether an employee will misuse the Internet (Liao, et al., 2009). Therefore, much can be done to increase the awareness (perceived importance) of the social networking impact on one's ethical structure. First, courses dedicated to ethics education must be added to the col-

lege curriculum. Many universities have already begun to do this, but others must follow suit. A dedicated course will increase student awareness of the importance of a strong ethical structure, and it will allow for more time to be dedicated to ethics. Many current textbooks do have an ethics' chapter, but that chapter is placed late in the book. This means that ethics may or may not be covered during the semester, depending on time management, and if it is covered, only one to two class discussions are devoted to the topic. A separate, dedicated course to ethics will give the topic the proper coverage and stress the importance of the topic to students.

Second, social networking must be specifically addressed in the ethics' courses. Many ethics' textbooks fail to discuss social networking. While basic ethical principles are presented, the changing face of technology and communication is being neglected. Course textbooks have to include this topic, and until that happens, college faculties must take the initiative to develop their own material to teach on the topic.

Additionally, on-campus student activities and student groups should focus on social networking and ethical awareness. This can include the use of well-educated speakers in ethics and social networking, and real-world examples of the potential pitfalls of social networking that have created public uproar, such as cyberbullying that has led to suicide. These can be very powerful. In the best situation, real-world examples with the use of guest speakers would be utilized in the classroom as well.

In terms of social networking issues to be addressed in the curriculum, instructors should begin with the basic ethical structure, providing specific examples of how social networking actions should be affected by that structure. One way that these issues can be identified and examined for impact is through the use of classical ethical theories. Professors can help students develop a foundation for ethical decision making by introducing and explaining classical ethical theories that have influenced moral philosophy for years. There are four ethical theories covered in many contemporary business ethics' textbooks and this section views social networks in light of each one. Several textbooks and the chapters related to ethical theory exist. Some of those textbooks are: *Business Ethics: A Real World Approach* by Andrew Ghillyer (Chapter 1 – Understanding Ethics); *Business Ethics: Decision-Making for Personal Integrity and Social Responsibility* by Laura P. Hartman and Joseph DesJardins (Chapter 3 – Philosophical Ethics and Business); *Business Ethics: Ethical Decision Making and Cases* by O.C. Ferrell, John Fraedrich, and Linda Ferrell (Chapter 6 – Individual Factors and Moral Philosophies and Values); *Business Ethics* by Richard T. DeGeorge (Section 2 (Chapters 2 through 6) – Moral Reasoning in Business); and *An Introduction to Business Ethics* by Joseph Desjardins (Chapter 2 – Ethical Theory and Business).

Of the theories most often addressed in business ethics' textbooks, four are presented below with their application to the environment of social networks. Two of the theories, utilitarianism and distributive justice, have an orientation of teleology. Teleology refers to the end or purpose. Thus, these theories determine the most ethical choice by assessing the outcome of the decision or behavior. The other two theories presented, rights theory and virtue ethics, represent theories based on deontology. Deontology refers to decision making that focuses on principles or rules to be applied in lieu of examining the consequences of the decision.

Utilitarianism

Utilitarianism is most closely associated with the work and writings of philosopher John Stuart Mill (1806-1873). Utilitarianism holds that the most ethical act is the one that provides the greatest good for the greatest number. Right and wrong are determined by the consequences of the action; thus, utilitarianism is deemed to be a consequentialist approach. This theory has great appeal in business as it provides for a traditional cost-benefit type of analysis.

An important part of applying utilitarian thinking to the atmosphere of social networks is in allowing the students to identify the relevant stakeholders. Often, in this environment, the student perceives that his messages affect him and him alone. However, simple illustrations from instructors can demonstrate this is not the case. Other stakeholders that should be considered include the recipients of the messages and those who might be referenced in the postings. Students may have to be reminded of the "reach" of their messages. Finally, the point should be made that outsiders often view individuals as representatives of certain organizations. While they are students, each individual is associated with his or her University and even clubs and groups to which they belongs. After graduation, individuals are often thought to represent the company for which they work. This issue is related to the students' perceptions (in the questionnaire) regarding the lack of separation between personal and professional information on social networking sites that was previously discussed.

Potential benefits and harms need to be considered for all of the stakeholders. From the viewpoint of the University or company, profiles from employees in social networks have the potential benefit of providing increased exposure and believable word-of-mouth publicity. However, inappropriate language, comments or pictures can be detrimental to the public perception of an entire group. While it would be nice to assume that those outside the organization would separate the comments of an individual from the whole, this is not always the case. Some outsiders will perceive the opinions of one member as representative of the attitudes of the club or company. This could be damaging to the public relations of the company.

From the perspective of the peers and friends of the individual, they receive the benefit of having current information and updates. As noted earlier, this is the greatest perceived advantage of participating in social networks. However, those in the social networks are subject to having pictures and information posted about them without their consent or knowledge. It is important to stress that each individual should monitor his own behavior as if everything he does could or would be made public. In the current era of quick dissemination of material through social networks, this is a reality. This affects teenagers even before their college days. Teens share confidential information with someone they trust only to find it widely shared.

Lastly, the individual needs to consider the potential advantages and disadvantages of social networks, especially when deciding the amount of personal information to share on these sites. Being involved allows closer contact and up-to-date information on a wide circle of family, friends and acquaintances. This networking can provide both personal satisfaction and the possibility of business opportunities. However, when sound judgment is not employed in determining the level of disclosure, students may open themselves up to personal costs that include loss of relationships, loss of reputation, and even loss of employment opportunities.

Utilitarianism is a relevant and useful ethical theory that allows professors to open the discussion about social networks. Students can explore the stakeholder groups and create their own lists of potential benefits and harms in a systematic way. Professors can provide examples and ask students to share from their personal experiences to enrich the discussion and broaden the students' thinking.

Distributive Justice

Distributive justice originates from the thinking and writing of John Rawls (1921-2002). This theory is similar to utilitarianism as it focuses on the outcome of the decision in order to determine the most ethical choice. Rawls' theory suggests that the individuals will make the fairest decision when they do so from behind a "veil of ignorance".

When using this rationale, those affected by the decision must determine the best outcome without knowing their place in the situation. They do not know if they are gifted or not, wealthy or poor, strong or disabled in some way. The decision must be made such that it benefits the whole of society and that each person would agree without knowing his position. As described in Hartman and Desjardins (2008, p. 81), "He contends that our decisions *ought* to be made in such a way, and our social institutions *ought* to be organized in such a way, that they would prove acceptable to us *no matter whose point of view we take.*"

This theory can be useful in encouraging students to think analytically about their participation in social networks. What type of comments, pictures and material should be posted on social networks? Professors can encourage students to explore this question from behind the "veil of ignorance". Who are the affected parties? Would each of them agree on an answer without knowing which role they will play? In considering this ethical theory, professors may also want to raise question regarding the amount of time spent on social networks. How would this time be otherwise spent? If the time is spent during office or work hours, employers have a stake in this behavior as well. How would the students feel if they were in the employer's role and then learned that employees were spending one to two hours a day on these sites? If the students were responsible for paying the employees for their time at work, even when they were being unproductive, they would understand more of the effect. Of course this can be illustrated very easily also by referring to common occurrences in class, such as students arriving ten or more minutes late to class. Would the students like to wait on the instructor for ten minutes and then the instructor keep them ten minutes past class time in order to make it up? Of course, they would not and they would not want to pay employees for personal activities. These points could be used to influence how the student's basic ethical structure is framed in the future.

Rights Theory

Rights theory falls in the category of deontology in that it focuses on the *means* of making an ethical decision and not on the outcome of the decision. The focus is on creating rules that can be followed to result in ethical behavior. Immanuel Kant (1724-1804) is the best known philosopher in this realm. His categorical imperative states that we should act only in a way that we could will our act to become universal law. Further, he also states that we should treat all people as ends in and of themselves and not just as a means to an end. He strongly believes that one rule to follow is "to respect each human being".

When applying rights theory to behavior in social networks, the focus switches from identification of stakeholders to the individual student. How can respect for each person and the categorical imperative be applied to social networks? Respect for each person and only acting in a way that would also be acceptable for everyone to act require consideration from the student about what information and images to post. Should I upload this picture of several people from a party without asking them? Would it be acceptable if everyone did this? Would I want others to upload similar types of photos of me without my permission? Is it okay to forward sensitive personal information from a friend? Would it be acceptable if everyone did this? A good example of this would be posting a picture of a group of friends' drinking alcohol. Regardless of the intention of the photo or the amount of alcohol consumed (both factors that cannot be determined from the posting), the perception is established. Individuals will form perceptions from this photo and current, and future, employers and fellow employees could be part of the "network of friends" that can view this photo. Therefore, even if only one individual posted the photo, the "reach" is extensive and there are "consequences" to others in the photo.

Virtue Ethics

Virtue ethics began with the thinking and writing of Aristotle (384 BC – 322 BC). Virtue ethics is deontological in nature because it pertains to the means of decision making, not the ends or outcome of the decision. However, virtue ethics differs from rights theory because it focuses on what kind of person one should be instead of on what types of actions a person should take. If approaching an ethical dilemma, one should ask, "What would a person of virtue do?" Aristotelian moral virtues include courage, self-control, generosity, magnificence, high-mindedness, gentleness, friendliness, truthfulness, wittiness and modesty.

Teaching virtue ethics allows professors the opportunity to discuss the development of character with students. Much of each student's character is formed before college, but as adults, college students can be proactive in determining the character they wish to carry into their professional lives. In the context of social networks, virtue ethics requires students to consider, "How would a virtuous person behave in this environment?" Virtues such as truthfulness play a big role in deciding what information to post in social networks. More subtle virtues such as modesty and gentleness are also worth consideration. Even the virtue of self-control comes into play when considering the time devoted to social networks. The way an individual would like to be perceived may not be the reality of who he is. Being truthful about one's background, religion, job position, and so forth may be difficult but necessary to accurately represent one. For example, posting that one is a medical professional could be problematic once others seek medical advice from that person. This is an excellent example of "reach" and "consequences" because inaccurate medical advice can be passed on and ultimately hurt a multitude of individuals. Getting past how students would like to be perceived could be a challenge, yet it must be addressed. Another example pertains to the amount of time students are devoting to social networking each day. Students often get caught up in the online socializing aspect and forget their many other obligations, such as studying, preparing homework, meeting with teams for project work, or even showing up for their employment responsibilities. Education in this area can focus on how a virtuous person would behave, ultimately showing that there must be a balance between work and play.

FUTURE RESEARCH DIRECTIONS

Future research should focus on establishing curriculum in the aforementioned "teaching" section and on testing the ethical approaches outlined above in a University setting. For example, the utilitarianism approach could be used to stress the potential benefits and harms of social networking. Using example scenarios, the students can be placed into everyday, realistic social networking situations. By placing the students into common situations, the students may more readily visualize the consequences and reach of their actions by being led to discover the "benefits vs. harms". This will also tie the approach to the basic ethical structure discussed previously. Another example would be to test the distributive justice approach. This approach could also utilize scenarios. In the scenarios, students would be instructed to make a decision that would benefit the whole society and that each person in the group would agree to. This would force students to hear differing opinions and would ultimately result in changes to their ethical structure. Researchers should develop the relevant scenarios and corresponding questionnaires that will aid in the analysis of each approach. Not only could this be used during in-class instruction, it could also be used in projects. Students could be assigned to work through a situation and develop an appropriate response based on the principles outlined in the approach being studied. Both would provide a huge benefit to students regarding understanding the ethical

issues involved in social networking. It would also be a huge stepping-stone for instructors' to learn about students' understanding of ethics in social networking.

Each of the four ethical theories can, therefore, be tested over time to determine which approach or combination of approaches is having the most impact on the student's ethical structure. Once the approach(es) has been identified, additional scenarios should be added to classroom discussion to fully cover all realms of the ethical structure, making sure students understand their ethical obligation when social networking.

CONCLUSION

The use of social networking sites is not going to decrease in the foreseeable future. More people are going to join each year until something better appears. Also, one's basic ethical structure is likely to change for better or worse as a result of this technology. Therefore, social networking and ethics have to coincide. By discussing with students their ethical influences and how social networking has blurred those influences, behavior can improve. Also, introducing ethical theories and applications of those theories in the class setting can help to frame a student's ethical decision making.

Just as with all new technologies, society has to adapt to the changes. Understanding proper ethical behavior on social networking sites is an example of an adaptation faculty can teach. Learning how to apply basic ethical theories through scenario assessment can help equip young adults to be more prepared for what is to come in the future.

REFERENCES

Barnes, S. B. (2006). A privacy paradox: Social networking in the United States. *First Monday*, *11*(9), 1–15.

Brown, J. (2000). Growing up digital: How the Web changes work, education, and the ways people learn. *CHANGE.*

De Souza, Z., & Dick, G. N. (2009). Disclosure of information by children in social networking–not just a case of you show me yours and I'll show you mine. *International Journal of Information Management, 29,* 255–261. doi:10.1016/j.ijinfomgt.2009.03.006

DeGeorge, R. (2010). *Business ethics* (7th ed.). Upper Saddle River, NJ: Pearson Education Inc.

DesJardins, J. (2009). *An introduction to business ethics* (3rd ed.). New York, NY: McGraw-Hill.

DiMicco, J., Millen, D. R., Geyer, W., Dugan, C., Brownholtz, B., & Muller, M. (2008). Motivations for social networking at work. *Proceedings of the ACM Conference on Computer Supported Cooperative Work.* New York, NY: ACM.

Dwyer, C., Hiltz, S. R., & Passerini, K. (2007). Trust and privacy concern within social networking sites: A comparison of Facebook and MySpace. *Proceedings of the Americas Conference on Information Systems.* New York, NY: ACM.

Ferrell, O. C., Fraedrich, J., & Ferrell, L. (2008). *Business ethics: Ethical decision making and cases.* Boston, MA: Houghton Mifflin Company.

Ghillyer, A. (2008). *Business ethics: A real world approach.* New York, NY: McGraw-Hill Irwin.

Gross, R., & Acquisti, A. (2005). Information revelation and privacy in online social networks. *Proceedings of the ACM Workshop on Privacy in the Electronic Society* (pp. 71-80). New York, NY: ACM.

Haag, S., & Cummings, M. (2010). *Management Information Systems for the information age* (8th ed.). New York, NY: McGraw-Hill Irwin.

Hartman, L., & DesJardins, J. (2008). *Business ethics: Decision-making for personal integrity and social responsibility.* New York, NY: McGraw-Hill Irwin.

Hsu, M. H., & Chiu, C. M. (2004). Internet self-efficacy and electronic service acceptance. *Decision Support Systems, 38,* 369–381. doi:10.1016/j.dss.2003.08.001

Jonas-Dwyer, D., & Pospisil, R. (2004). The millennial effect: Implications for academic development. *Proceedings of the HERDSA Conference* (pp. 194-207).

Kumar, R., Novak, J., & Tomkins, A. (2006). Structure and evolution of online social networks. *Proceedings of the ACM SIGKDD International Conference on Knowledge Discovery and Data Mining* (pp. 611-617). New York, NY: ACM.

Lenhart, A. (2009). *Social networks grow: Friending mom and dad.* Pew Internet & American Life Project. Retrieved January 19, 2010, from http://pewresearch.org/pubs/1079/social-networks-grow

Lenhart, A., & Madden, M. (2007). *Social networking websites and teens: An overview.* Pew Internet & American Life Project. Retrieved January 19, 2010, from http://www.pewinternet.org/Reports/2007/Social-Networking-Websites-and-Teens.aspx

Liao, Q., Luo, X., Gurung, A., & Li, L. (2009). Workplace management and employee misuse: Does punishment matter? *Journal of Computer Information Systems,* 49–59.

Maran, C. M. (2009). Parallel life on social network: A study. *The IUP Journal of Management Research, 8*(12), 7–30.

Myskja, B. K. (2008). The categorical imperative and the ethics of trust. *Ethics and Information Technology, 10,* 213–220. doi:10.1007/s10676-008-9173-7

Reynolds, G. W. (2010). *Ethics in Information Technology* (3rd ed.). Boston, MA: Course Technology.

ADDITIONAL READING

AACSB. (2004). Ethics Education in Business Schools. Report of the Ethics Education Task Force. Retrieved January 12, 2010, from http://www.aacsb.edu/resource_centers/EthicsEdu/EthicsEdu-in-B-Schools.pdf

Acquisti, A., & Groww, R. (2006). Imagined communities: awareness, information sharing, and privacy on the Facebook. *Lecture Notes in Computer Science*, *4258*, 36–58. doi:10.1007/11957454_3

AP-AOL Instant Messaging Trends Survey Reveals Popularity of Mobile Instant Messaging. (2007). Retrieved January 12, 2010, from http://corp.aol.com/press-releases/2007/11/ap-aol-instant-messaging-trends-survey-reveals-popularity-mobile-instant-mess

Arthur, D., Sherman, C., Appel, D., & Moore, L. (2006). Why young consumers adopt interactive technologies. *Young Consumers*, *7*(3), 33–38. doi:10.1108/17473610610705354

Barnes, N. D., & Barnes, F. R. (2009). Equipping your organization for the social networking game. *Information & Management*, *43*(6), 28–33.

Brandenburg, C. (2008). The newest way to screen job applicants: a social networker's nightmare. *Federal Communications Law Journal*, *60*(3), 597–626.

Brown, S. A. (2008). Household technology adoption, use, and impacts: past, present, and future. *Information Systems Frontiers*, *10*, 397–402. doi:10.1007/s10796-008-9098-z

Cheung, C. M. K., & Lee, M. K. O. (2010). A theoretical model of intentional social action in online social networks. *Decision Support Systems*, *49*(1), 24–30. doi:10.1016/j.dss.2009.12.006

Chi, L., Chan, W. K., Seow, G., & Tam, K. (2009). Transplanting social capital to the online world: insights from two experimental studies. *Journal of Organizational Computing and Electronic Commerce*, *19*(3), 214–236. doi:10.1080/10919390903041931

Christ, R. E., Berges, J. S., & Trevino, S. C. (2007). Social networking sites: to monitor or not to monitor users and their content? *Intellectual Property & Technology Law Journal*, *19*(7), 13–17.

de Laat, P. B. (2008). Online diaries: Reflections on trust, privacy, and exhibitionism. *Ethics and Information Technology*, *10*(1), 57–69. doi:10.1007/s10676-008-9155-9

Donelan, H., Herman, C., Kear, K., & Kirkup, G. (2009). Patterns of online networking for women's career development. *Gender in Management*, *24*(2), 92–111. doi:10.1108/17542410910938790

Ferrell, O. C. (2005). *A Framework for Understanding Organizational Ethics*. In R. A. Perterson & O.C.

Ferrell, O. C., & Ferrell, L. (2008). A Decision Making Framework for Business Education. In Swanson, D. L., & Fisher, D. G. (Eds.), *Advancing Business Ethics Education*. Information Age Publishing.

Ferrell (Eds.), *Business Ethics: New Challenges for Business Schools and Corporate Leaders*, Armonk, New York: M.E. Sharpe.

Harrison, R., & Thomas, M. (2009). Identity in online communities: social networking sites and language learning. *International Journal of Emerging Technologies and Society*, *7*(2), 109–124.

Hoffman, D. L., Novak, T. P., & Venkatesh, A. (2004). Has the Internet become indispensable? *Communications of the ACM*, *47*(7), 37–42. doi:10.1145/1005817.1005818

Howard, B. (2008). Analyzing online social networks. *Communications of the ACM, 51*(11), 14–16. doi:10.1145/1400214.1400220

Howe, N., & Strauss, W. (2000). *Millennials Rising: the Next Great Generation.* New York: Vintage.

Howe, N., & Strauss, W. (2006). *Millennials and Pop Culture: Strategies for a New Generation of Consumers.* Great Falls, VA: LifeCourse Associates.

Howe, N., & Strauss, W. (2007). *Millennials Go to College Surveys and Analysis: From Boomer to Gen-X Parents, 2006 College and Parent Surveys.* Great Falls, VA: LifeCourse Associates.

Howe, N., & Strauss, W. (2007). *Millennials Go to College: Strategies for a New Generation on Campus.* Great Falls, VA: LifeCourse Associates.

Ioannides, Y. M., & Soetevent, A. R. (2007). Social networking and individual outcomes beyond the mean field case. *Journal of Economic Behavior & Organization, 64*(3/4), 369–390. doi:10.1016/j.jebo.2006.06.017

Josephson Institute. (2008). 2008 Report Card on the Ethics of American Youth. Retrieved January 12, 2010, from http://charactercounts.org/programs/reportcard/index.html

Kaplan, A. M., & Haenlein, M. (2009). The fairyland of Second Life: Virtual social worlds and how to use them. *Business Horizons, 52,* 563–572. doi:10.1016/j.bushor.2009.07.002

Kaplan, A. M., & Haenlein, M. (2010). Users of the world, unite! The challenges and opportunities of social media. *Business Horizons, 53,* 59–68. doi:10.1016/j.bushor.2009.09.003

Kluemper, D. H., & Rosen, P. A. (2009). Future employment selection methods: evaluating social networking web sites. *Journal of Managerial Psychology, 24*(6), 567–580. doi:10.1108/02683940910974134

Kraut, R., Patterson, M., Lundmark, V., Kiesler, S., Mukophadhyay, T., & Scherlis, W. (1998). Internet paradox: a social technology that reduces social involvement and psychological well-being? *The American Psychologist, 53*(9), 1017–1031. doi:10.1037/0003-066X.53.9.1017

Kwai, R., & Wagner, C. (2008). Weblogging: A study of social computing and its impact on organizations. *Decision Support Systems, 45*(2), 242–250. doi:10.1016/j.dss.2007.02.004

Leader-Chivee, L., Hamilton, B. A., & Cowan, E. (2008). Networking the way to success: online social networks for workplace and competitive advantage. *People and Strategy, 31*(4), 40–46.

Lehavot, K. (2009). "MySpace" or yours? The ethical dilemma of graduate students' personal lives on the Internet. *Ethics & Behavior, 19*(2), 129–141. doi:10.1080/10508420902772728

Lenhart, A. (2009). Adults and Social Network Websites. Pew Internet & American Life Project. Retrieved January 12, 2010, from http://www.pewinternet.org/Reports/2009/Adults-and-Social-Network-Websites.aspx

Marshall, K. P. (1999). Has technology introduced new ethical problems? *Journal of Business Ethics, 19*(1), 81–90. doi:10.1023/A:1006154023743

McMahon, J. M., & Cohen, R. (2009). Lost in cyberspace: ethical decision making in the online environment. *Ethics and Information Technology, 11,* 1–17. doi:10.1007/s10676-008-9165-7

Messinger, P. R., Stroulia, E., Lyons, K., Bone, M., Niu, R. H., Smirnov, K., & Perelgut, S. (2009). Virtual worlds – past, present, and future: new directions in social computing. *Decision Support Systems, 47,* 204–228. doi:10.1016/j.dss.2009.02.014

Needham, A. (2008). Word of mouth, youth and their brands. *Young Consumers, 9*(1), 60–62. doi:10.1108/17473610810857327

Orenstein, P. (2009). Growing Up on Facebook. *The New York Times*. Retrieved January 12, 2010, from http://www.nytimes.com/2009/03/15/magazine/15wwln-lede-t.html

Pew Research Center for the People & the Press. (2007). Social networking websites and teens: an overview. Retrieved January 12, 2010, from http://www.pewinternet.org/PPF/r/198/report_display.asp

Salter, M., & Bryden, C. (2009). I can see you: harassment and stalking on the Internet. *Information & Communications Technology Law*, *18*(2), 99–122. doi:10.1080/13600830902812830

Shao, G. (2009). Understanding the appeal of user-generated media: a uses and gratification perspective. *Internet Research*, *19*(1), 7–25. doi:10.1108/10662240910927795

Sledgianowski, D., & Kulviwat, S. (2009). Using social network sites: the effects of playfulness, critical mass and trust in a hedonic context. *Journal of Computer Information Systems*, *49*(4), 74–83.

Sprague, R. (2007). Googling Job Applicants: Incorporating Personal Information into Hiring Decisions. *The Labor Lawyer*, *23*(1), 19–40.

Svantesson, D. (2009). The right of reputation in the Internet era. *International Review of Law Computers & Technology*, *23*(3), 169–177. doi:10.1080/13600860903262230

Thelwall, M. (2008). No place for news in social network web sites? *Online Information Review*, *32*(6), 726–744. doi:10.1108/14684520810923908

Thelwall, M. (2008). Social networks, gender, and friending: an analysis of MySpace member profiles. *Journal of the American Society for Information Science and Technology*, *59*(8), 1321–1330. doi:10.1002/asi.20835

Thelwall, M., & Wilkinson, D. (n.d.). Public dialogs in social network sites: what is their purpose? *Journal of the American Society for Information Science and Technology*, *61*(2), 392–404.

Tobin, H. (2008). Is Facebook making our kids violent? *Review - Institute of Public Affairs*, *60*(4), 25.

Valkenburg, P. M., Peter, J., & Schouten, A. P. (2006). Friend networking sites and their relationship to adolescents' well-being and social self-esteem. *Cyberpsychology & Behavior*, *9*(5), 584–590. doi:10.1089/cpb.2006.9.584

Willett, R. (2009). "As soon as you get on Bebo you just go mad": young consumers and the discursive construction of teenagers online. *Young Consumers*, *10*(4), 283–296. doi:10.1108/17473610911007120

Zhang, J., & Daugherty, T. (2009). Third-person effect and social networking: implications for online marketing and word-of-mouth communication. *American Journal of Business*, *24*(2), 53–63.

KEY TERMS AND DEFINITIONS

Consequences: The amount of benefit or harm that will result from a particular decision.

Distributive Justice: Philosophy that encourages decision making from behind the "veil of ignorance" about one's relative position.

Likelihood of Effect: The probability that benefit or harm will result from the decision made.

Relatedness: How much one identifies with the person(s) who is receiving the benefit or harm.

Reach of Result: How many people who will be affected by the decision made.

Rights Theory: Ethical theory that focuses on individual rights and rules that can be followed to protect those rights.

Society's Opinion: How one perceives their decision will be viewed by society.

Time to Consequences: How long it will take for the benefit or harm to occur.

Utilitarianism: Theory which says that the most ethical decision is the one that results in the greatest good for the greatest number.

Virtue Ethics: Ethical reasoning based upon virtues of character rather than rules or outcomes.

Chapter 3
The Ethics of Security of Personal Information upon Facebook

Shona Leitch
Deakin University, Australia

Matthew Warren
Deakin University, Australia

ABSTRACT

Social networking systems are an ever evolving and developing means of social interaction which is not only being used to disseminate information to family, friends and colleagues, but as a way of meeting and interacting with "strangers" through the advent of a large number of social applications. Social networking systems, as well as being a way for those people who are isolated to interact with other people, can also have a huge social and personal impact on some users, for example, harassment via a social networking site resulting in suicide. This personal information (not just factual data), including the thoughts and feelings of individuals, can be used by others through social applications to cause emotional and psychological distress. The level of security for all this personal information on social networking systems such as Facebook will be examined in the chapter, as well as the possible threats and ethical issues that could impact users. This chapter will discuss a number of examples where personal information has been breached and will put forward a model that evaluates the security and risks and proposes a framework that relates to the use of information within Facebook.

INTRODUCTION

Information access, anytime, anywhere, any place is one of the features of the twenty first century. The widespread global adoption of Electronic Business and faster Internet connections through broadband provides access to business and commerce from a networked desktop computer.

The initial focus of the Internet was the distribution of information in a static manner but over time, the Internet has developed into Web 2.0. The Web is no longer a collection of static

DOI: 10.4018/978-1-60960-573-5.ch003

Figure 1. The Difference between Web 1.0 and Web 2.0

Web 1.0   Web 2.0
DoubleClick --> Google AdSense
Ofoto --> Flickr
Akamai --> BitTorrent
mp3.com --> Napster
Britannica Online --> Wikipedia
personal websites --> blogging
evite --> upcoming.org and EVDB
domain name speculation --> search engine optimization
page views --> cost per click
screen scraping --> web services
publishing --> participation
content management systems --> wikis
directories (taxonomy) --> tagging ("folksonomy")
stickiness --> syndication

pages of HTML that describe something in the world. Increasingly, the Web is the world where everything and everyone in the world casts an "information shadow," an aura of data which, when captured and processed intelligently, offers extraordinary opportunity and mind-bending implications (O'Reilly & Battelle, 2009).

The difference between Web 1.0 and Web 2.0 is shown in Figure 1. In essence, the difference in development and usage relates to the move from static information to dynamic information and this transformation is encapsulated as Web 2.0. A major issue for successful Web 2.0 applications is the involvement of users to add value (Serrano and Torres, 2010).

The emergence of Web 2.0 and related Internet sites such as Facebook has had a major impact upon the Internet in recent years. One of the interesting aspects of Facebook is the use of third party applications and the interactions that this allows. This means that individual Facebook pages now act as a web page, blog, instant messenger, email system and the use of third party applications allows for real time functionality (DiMicco & Millen, 2007; Shuen, 2008).

The rise in popularity of Facebook has meant issues surrounding its security and its ethical use have become more important and this chapter will explore many of these issues.

BACKGROUND: THE HISTORY OF SOCIAL NETWORKING

Social networking sites (SNSs) are virtual spaces where people congregate to discuss ideas, share information and communicate (Raacke & Bonds-Raacke, 2008). SNSs have become increasingly popular and are being used on a daily basis by millions of users across the globe.

The first accepted SNS was SixDegrees.com which was launched in 1997 and allowed users to create a profile, list their friends and view their details. It closed as a business in 2000. This may be due to the limited functionality of the early sites or the fact that it was still early in the evolution of the Internet and many people may not have had a large number of friends who were also Internet users to connect with via a SNS. Cyworld was launched in 1999. This was a Korean virtual world site which was morphed into a SNS in 2001 (Kim & Yun, 2007).

In the early part of the millennium, a new wave of SNSs were released which included Ryze, Friendster and LinkedIn. Only LinkedIn achieved a good deal of success. The others (which include many more) failed to achieve mass popularity. This has been in part, blamed on the fact that these SNSs felt they could support each other and did not need to compete against each other (Festa, 2003). This mistake meant that the sites failed to evolve to meet the needs and expectations of users.

From 2003 onwards, many of the SNSs which are still used in 2010 were developed. MySpace in particular, picked up many users after the failure of Friendster by encouraging music bands, music promoters and music lovers to join. This niche market allowed MySpace to expand quickly, however it may also be a part of the explanation of the popularity of Facebook which does not have a music focus. One other notable policy of MySpace was to allow minors to have profiles, however, this decision also led to a number of legal actions regarding sexual contact between adults and minors (Consumer Affairs, 2006). This was the beginning of a number of security concerns that affected MySpace.

Facebook was also initially developed for a niche group of users by only allowing users with a .edu email address to register. Its purpose was to allow communication, collaboration and networking amongst US college students. In 2005, other groups of individuals such as high school students were allowed to join, ending in Facebook being open to anyone with a valid email address in 2006. Facebook has travelled a different route to MySpace as it has no focus on any particular niche of users (beyond the initial niche group on its inception). This, along with its heavy focus on the use of "applications" (such as games, groups and personalisation options) has given it mass popularity among a wide demographic. There are still many sites which bring together users with particular interests and hobbies, however the

most successful SNSs appear to be those that are organised around people rather than their interests. The introduction of web capable mobile devices has also fuelled the increase in popularity. The uptake of devices such as the iPhone and especially created mobile software versions of Facebook has kept its popularity high.

The reasons for the popularity of SNSs are varied but include (Ellison et al, 2007):

* To communicate and keep in touch with friends (as a way of supporting pre-existing friendships);
* To make new friends and social relationships;
* To promote oneself.

There are many different SNSs using different technologies and attracting users based on individual preferences and interests. Some of the most widely used SNSs are:

* **Facebook:** Facebook was created in 2004 as a means for US college students to communicate with friends within their campus of study (Dwyer et al, 2007). Until September 2005, Facebook.com was not eligible to be used by anyone not holding a .edu email address;
* **MySpace:** Noted as being created in 2003 (although the history of its inception is in doubt), MySpace was created as a way create or join groups, post photos or videos, post "bulletins," and write personal blogs (Wilson, 2007);
* **Bebo:** Started in 2005, Bebo is an acronym for "Blog Early, Blog Often". Despite initial success, Bebo has been outperformed by MySpace and Facebook and AOL announced in 2010 that they planned to sell the site or close it down (Letzing, 2010);
* **LinkedIn:** Founded in 2002, LinkedIn is a professional networking site with a strong emphasis on business networking;

Figure 2. Breakdown of the use of SNSs by age (Pew Internet, 2008)

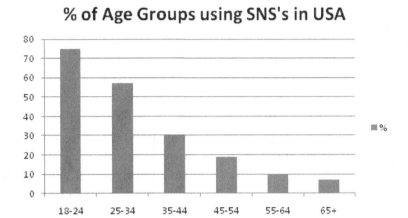

Twitter: One of the newer SNSs, founded in 2006, Twitter allows for social networking along with micro blogging and has been termed as the "SMS of the Internet" (D'Monte, 2009).

Whilst SNSs have a variety of different features and technical options, most have two major components: a list of "friends" and a profile page. Profile pages are unique to each individual and a place where "you can type oneself into being" (Sunden, 2003). Usually, the initial signup process involves answering an array of questions which may include: name, age, location information, interests, work history, education background and a profile photo.

Social networking is a social environment (Stafford et al, 2004) and has taken the use of media to a new level (beyond content media and communication media). It moves far beyond a simplistic way of communicating such as the use of email and with this complexity has come many more issues and concerns and consequently, a great deal of research into areas such as, group computer mediated communication (CMC), group structure and power, the security of individuals and organisational structure and work productivity issues.

SNSs are unique in their demographic breakdown. Whilst it is common in the media to advertise the popularity of social networking with teenagers, they are clearly being used by a wide range of different age groups with the fastest growing age group on Facebook being women over the age of 55 (Smith, 2009).

From statistical data obtained from the Pew Internet and American Life Project Survey delivered in December 2008, it is clear that SNSs are not dominated by one particular gender (50% split) or race: 33% of white Americans, 43% of Black Americans and 48% of Hispanic Americans have a SNS profile. The number of users is also balanced in other categories such as educational level, household income and whether they are based in a suburban or rural area (Pew Internet, 2008; Lenhart, 2009a).

One of the concerns over such a dramatic uptake of SNSs relates to the privacy and security of information contained within these sites. Research has shown that (Lenhart, 2009b):

- 60% of adult social network users restrict access to their profiles so that it is only accessible to their immediate friends;
- 36% of social network users allow anyone to see their online profile;

Table 1. Information shared by SNS users (Dwyer et al, 2007)

	Photograph of yourself	Real Name	Home Town	Email Address	Relationship status	Sexual Orientation
Facebook	98.6%	100%	92.8%	94.2%	73.9%	78.3%
MySpace	100%	66.7%	91.7%	39.6%	89.6%	75%

- 43% of adults think it would be pretty easy for someone to find out who they are from their profile; 23% of teens say it would be pretty easy.

It is often discussed and warnings issued to Internet users concerning hoaxes and scams that may target financial records, request bogus payments and so on. However, this cautiousness seems to be less concerning for users on SNSs (especially teenage users) (George, 2006) who believe that if there is no financial incentive for criminals, then the risk of their information being misused is limited. This, however, is a fallacy, as shown in an early study on SNSs by Gross and Acquisti (2005) which found that the personal information displayed by 4,000 college students on Facebook such as their birth town and date of birth would make it relatively easy for someone to obtain their social security number.

In a study by Dwyer et al (2007), 117 subjects were asked about the type of information they included on their profile on the SNS they used (Table 1).

It is clear from this that Facebook users generally include more personal information on their profile than MySpace users. This may be related to Facebook's policies of including your real name (or risk having your profile cancelled), it may also be due to the fact that, prior to 2005, Facebook was a "closed" SNS with only college students having access and therefore it fostered a greater sense of trust.

The amount of information a user discloses on a SNS seems to be related in part to how much they trust the site which they are using. Mayer et al (1995) define trust as "the willingness of a party to be vulnerable to the actions of another party based on the expectation that the other will perform a particular action important to the trustor, irrespective of the ability to monitor or control that other party" (p.71) and it is considered especially important for online interactions (Coppola et al, 2004). Dwyer et al (2007) found that Facebook users were more trusting than the users of MySpace and were therefore prepared to share more information about themselves on the site. This may be due to the number of different security settings and options available on Facebook regarding who can view data, photos, profile updates and so on. It should also be noted that it is common for individuals to post misleading information either deliberately or to create a more interesting "persona" for themselves.

The most popular SNSs in terms of registered users are MySpace and Facebook. As Facebook has the fastest growing user base with the most diverse demographic (age, gender, use (business and social) and race), the authors have focused on it in relation to the discussion of security and privacy in SNSs.

BACKGROUND TO THE FACEBOOK SOCIAL NETWORKING SITE

The global use of the Internet has developed in recent years and impacts all aspects of society from business and education to social activities.

Table 2. Global Internet Usage (InternetWorld, 2009)

Region	Number (millions of users)	% Regional Penetration
Asia	704.2	18.5
Europe	402.4	50.1
North America	251.7	73.9
Latin America/Caribbean	175.8	30
Africa	65.9	6.7
Middle East	48	23.7
Oceania/Australia	20.8	60.1
World Average		24.7

The global impact of the Internet can be shown by Table 2.

The environment of increasing numbers of Internet users and a faster Internet, allowed for Web 2.0 to be devolved (Shuen, 2008) and one of the leading Web 2.0 applications in terms of global impact is Facebook. Facebook's inception took place in 2004 and in February 2010 Facebook announced it had reached its 400 millionth registered user (Schonfeld, 2010). Facebook is a social utility that helps people communicate more efficiently with their friends, family and co-workers. The Facebook environment means that anyone can sign up for Facebook and interact with the people they know in a trusted environment (Facebook, 2009a). Facebook has had a global impact. In 2010, there were more than 350,000 active applications currently on the Facebook platform; more than 250 applications have more than one million monthly active users and more than 65 million active users currently accessing Facebook through their mobile devices (Facebook, 2009b). In 2010, the growth of Facebook continued with more than 100 million users accessing Facebook through mobile devices (Facebook, 2010).

FACEBOOK SECURITY AND PRIVACY EXAMPLES

In a SNS context, there are of a number of key security and privacy issues. These are (Boyd, 2008; Dwyer et al, 2007; Shin, 2010):

- **Security:** In SNSs, security refers to users' perception of security, that is, perceived security which is defined as the extent to which a user believes that using a SNS application will be risk-free.
- **Privacy:** In a SNS context Privacy can be defined as control over the flow of one's personal information, including the transfer and exchange of that information. Privacy within SNS is often not expected or is undefined.
- **Trust:** Trust in SNS is defined as the willingness of a party to be vulnerable to the actions of another party based on the expectation that the other will perform a particular action important to the trustor, irrespective of the ability to monitor or control that other party. In SNS, trust is a critical determinant of sharing information and developing new relationships.

Nancy (2009) has taken the view that dealing with Social Networking risks (including security) is a management issue and therefore can be dealt with by Organisational Policy. Nancy proposes a policy strategy for reducing organisational web-related risks. This strategy includes:

1. ***Conduct a legal review of your corporate website.*** Organisations should not take chances with online posting of their content. An organisation should assign a member of their legal team or another responsible individual to review all website content including but not limited to text, white papers, book excerpts, surveys, news articles, photos, videos, cartoons and links to external sites.

Avoid copyright infringement claims by securing the written permission of copyright holders before publishing third party content on your business site. Avoid defamation claims by eliminating negative comments about competitors and their products.

2. *Establish a written Internet policy.* Effective organisational web management begins with a clear and comprehensive Internet policy that focuses on content, use, and other key issues such as security.

3. *Address personal Web use*. Notify employees that the company's Internet system is a business tool that is intended primarily for authorized commerce, communication, research and other business- related purposes. Spell out exactly how much personal Web surfing is allowed, when and for what purposes. Address video snacking such as viewing online videos during breaks as part of the organisational Web use policy.

4. *Review and update all company policies*. While developing the organisational Web policy, take time to review and update all the company's employment policies. Notify employees that all employment policies apply to the Internet, regardless of whether employees are surfing at work or posting content at home on their own personal websites.

5. *Provide formal Internet policy training*. Educate employees about Web-related risks and rules, policies and procedures. Require all employees to sign and date an acknowledgment form, confirming that they have participated in formal Internet policy training. Retain all employee acknowledgement forms.

6. *Inform employees that Web content and usage rules apply,* regardless of whether employees are viewing, forwarding, downloading, uploading, transmitting screen shots, copying files, storing files, or otherwise engaged in Internet-related activity.

7. *Notify employees that they are prohibited from using company computer resources to create, view, print*, copy, download, upload, transmit, file or forward content that is offensive or otherwise in violation of any company rule or policy.

8. *Prohibit employees from mentioning (in words or images) the company*, its people, products, services, secrets, suppliers or customers on personal or third-party websites without first securing written permission from management.

9. *Prohibit employees from identifying themselves as employees of the company,* in words or images, on personal or third-party websites, including LinkedIn and other SNSs designed for business people, without first securing written permission from management.

10. *Prohibit employees from posting business e-mail addresses on personal and third-party websites,* including business-related SNSs, without first securing written permission from management.

11. *Inform employees that they have no reasonable expectation of privacy when using the company's Internet system*. Explain to staff why you monitor the organisation's Internet, how monitoring works, what management is looking for, why policy compliance is mandatory, and what type of penalties await policy violators.

12. *Don't forget the company intranet*. All user policy and training to make clear the fact that Internet rules and all other employment policies, including but not limited to electronic usage and content rules, apply to the organization's internal intranet system, too.

13. *Discipline policy violators.* If monitoring unearths a violation, act immediately to discipline the violator.

The Nancy framework offers a managerial or compliant focused approach in which to deal with SNS issues from a policy viewpoint. The framework is flawed because you cannot change behaviour through policies or punishment. The framework does not deal with attitudes of younger staff usages of SNS or the fact that many organisations are making a strategic decision to develop their new business models based upon SNS systems.

.There have been a number of real life examples highlighting security and ethical issues. In the next part of the chapter we discuss some real life examples. These examples relate to a number of different countries and highlight the global nature and impact of SNS systems.

INFORMATION LOSS

Individuals often do not understand the implications of making certain information public through social networking systems such as Facebook. Research on companies by the Society of Corporate Compliance and Ethics and the Healthcare Compliance Association revealed that about 24% of the companies had disciplined their employees for inappropriate behaviour on SNSs (such as Facebook) that caused embarrassment for the organisation (Whitney, 2009). For example, pictures uploaded by a finance industry employee disclosed the truth of that person faking a sick day and the disclosure of that information via Facebook resulted in that employee losing their job (McCarthy, 2008).

Research shows that SNSs are leaking personal identity information to third parties including data aggregators, which track and aggregate user viewing habits for targeted ad-serving purposes. One of the user implications is of having tracking cookies associated with user identity information from their profile. This makes tracking the user movement across several websites. Although user identity is not directly available to third-parties

who track through IP (Internet Protocol) addresses, these IP addresses can be easily related to a particular user, disclosing personal information through the SNSs (Vijayan, 2009). The leakage of personal information to third parties implies that they not only learn about the viewing habits of some users but can also associate a specific person to the viewing habits (Krishnamurthy & Wills, 2009).

Third parties receive user information not only from their tracking cookies but also from the user's unique identifier through the HTTP headers. Another way for third parties to obtain user information is through objects contained in servers or request URLs that appear as belonging to the social network site but in reality belong to third-parties (Vijayan, 2009).

A majority of users have their social networking identity information linked to tracking cookies. This implies that personal identity information is available to aggregators. The question remains, do these aggregators record this information? Personal information may also available be through secondary leakage through external applications (Krishnamurthy & Wills, 2009).

In Australia, new laws introduced by the Attorney General of Australia have changed the legal situation of crimes associated with the use of SNSs. The Attorney General has now set jail terms of up to ten years for individuals using networking sites such as Facebook to steal identities without having to wait for them to obtain money as a part of the fraud (Hildebrand, 2009). This stance by the Australian Government clearly indicates the severity and rampant nature of identity theft on SNSs. The premise of these sites is the sharing of personal information with a group of "friends". Unfortunately, as sites such as Facebook have expanded, many users now have friends that are not known to them in "real life" (users have never met them in person). This change in the nature of the use of Facebook has meant that for those criminals seeking personal information in order for financial gain, it has become much easier. Many users of Facebook under utilise the privacy and security options available to them and simply fail to consider the importance of the information they are sharing (Strater & Richter, 2007).

Viral wall messages, phishing and malware spam advertising by third party applications have all been linked to security and privacy breaches involving SNSs. Identity theft worms are common and have been spreading throughout Facebook, enticing users, for example, to click links commenting, "find out what other users are saying about you" which spreads the worm through the Facebook messaging capabilities (Dimmel, 2008).

VIRUSES, MALWARES AND TROJAN ATTACKS

SNSs enable viruses, Malwares and Trojans to thrive on their ability to access personal information and cause password attacks leading to a breach of network. SNSs also open the gates for cybercriminals and sexual predators and this is likely to become a major issue for the future.

Increased use of SNSs such as Facebook increase the chance of malware or peer phishing attacks that can potentially cause serious damage to organizational data security (Socialman, 2009). For example, there were concerns over a data leak after a hacker broke into the 'Top Friends' application on Facebook' making users' private information visible (Goldie, 2008).

THIRD PARTY APPLICATIONS

Facebook uses a large number of third party applications as a part of its platform. These are provided for entertainment, education and social purposes. However, Facebook does not control the third-party applications and websites supported through its platform. Publicly available information is made available to these third-party applications and websites once a user begins to

use them. Additional user information is only sent upon user authorisation. Before approving third-party applications or websites, Facebook ensures their agreement to Facebook terms of user information and takes technical measures to ensure that only authorised information is delivered to third-party vendors.

Facebook users have the option of altering their privacy settings or limiting the user information available through selectively changing 'everyone' settings. They can also use application settings, to block specific applications from accessing user information or limit the accessible information that may be shared by friends. Facebook does not guarantee third party vendors will follow Facebook rules and advises users to read through each third party's privacy and security policies (Facebook, 2009c).

In September 2009, an online Facebook poll entitled, "Should Obama be killed?" was posted. Little chance or time was spared before the United States Secret Service was called upon to investigate this possible threat and to trace the creator of the poll. Whilst it proved to be a childish prank, it has brought attention to another range of issues related to the privacy and security aspects of SNSs, such as (Ostrow, 2009):

- Should SNSs take more care and responsibility in policing themselves and the content posted by their members?
- Is there a limit to the self expression of users?
- Do government and law enforcement have a role in policing these sites? This poses real issues as governments and law enforcements agencies only have national jurisdiction and cannot control or monitor SNSs in a global context.

The first point raises considerable difficulty as the poll in question was posted through a third party application and therefore not directly controlled by Facebook. It is these third party applications which are going to make social networking much more difficult to control and "police" in future years, due to the fact that Facebook does not have direct control over these third party organisations.

ORGANISATIONAL IMPACT

Corporate organisations use SNSs for different reasons. An important use is as a marketing tool to increase the organisation's business profile. Individuals within the company generally create a company profile on Facebook as a way of informally communicating with customers, sharing information, promoting products, getting informal product feedback and building brand loyalties (New York Times, 2008). Companies also use SNSs to recruit employees. Organisations such as Microsoft and Starbucks use SNSs such as Facebook to search for potential candidates. Goldman, Sachs and Deloitte run their own alumni networks for hiring back former employees and strengthening their alumni-come-possible clients (King, 2006).

Small and medium businesses are using social networking websites to obtain strategic information in terms of growing or gaining a competitive advantage. For example, a small trucking company explains in a post on a social networking website the difficulties in getting a loan. Soon, a number of people responded, giving advice and suggesting websites the trucking company should visit. Some of them were loan officers trying to gain business for their financial organizations rather than users offering unbiased assistance (CMS Wire, 2010). Accepting the importance of social media, companies have formulated policies to regulate employee use of social networking. Telstra, for example, has developed a 3R's policy on the use of social media engagement. The 3R's – Representing, Responsibility and Respect outline the boundaries to Telstra employees when (in relation to) social networking (Telstra, 2009). Employers have identified a few areas of concern related to employee's use of SNSs during office hours. Some concerns voiced included perceived loss in staff productivity, data leakage from staff gossiping freely in an open environment and Malware and Phishing scams practiced by cyber criminals (Cluley, 2009).

According to a survey by Morse Consultancy of 1,460 UK office workers, more than 50% of UK's office staff actively use SNSs for their personal use during office hours resulting in a waste of 40 minutes a week. The estimated loss from this is approximately 1.38 billion pounds (Morse, 2009). Data leakage through SNSs is also a growing phenomenon. Organisations, unwittingly or deliberately, post confidential information about a product road map, confidential financial information or even derogatory comments about the company management in a blog or a SNS (M86Security, 2009).

SNSs such as Facebook are now a popular medium for cyber criminals to spread viruses and malwares. The Orkut worm in 2007 is an example of such malpractice (M86Security, 2009). These viruses jeopardise a company's network, exposing the company to huge risks of being hacked, becoming victims of data theft or even bringing down the network. The availability of personal information makes phishing an easy possibility (M86Security 2009). Organisations are increasing their potential risk to cyber incidents such as viruses and frauds. This problem is likely to continue to grow.

THE RIGHT TO PRIVACY?

As mentioned previously, organisations have concerns about Facebook and its usage. These concerns also relate to individuals and their right to privacy as well as the privacy of the organization itself. Employers can monitor current and potential employees through SNSs including Facebook and some colleges and schools keep track of their students' posts on networking sites.

Police can use online information for investigation and tracking (Jones et al, 2008).

Facebook's Beacon service tracks the activities of its members on more than forty four participating websites and sends reports of these activities to the user's Facebook friends. Beacon is considered to be tracking both Facebook members and non members on Facebook and its partner websites. This information can be used for more intrusive marketing practices (Havenstein et.al, 2007). The service was removed following an online petition of 50,000 Facebook users (Story, 2007).

Facebook users can restrict certain information from being viewed by friends but as soon as a user joins a network or group, their profile is open to view for all other members whether they are in the users' friend list or not (Sophos, 2007) but users are often unaware of these features. In 2009, Facebook changed its privacy settings, including the control over who can see individual messages posted on Facebook (BBC, 2009). This means that Facebook users can amend their access rights on information they post so that specific individuals may view postings but not photos.

The Canadian Privacy Commissioner recently revealed privacy gaps in Facebook's operation. These gaps included information regarding user account deletion, disclosure of information to third parties and holding user information indefinitely. The Commissioner also recommended steps to improve them to ensure better protection of user information. The recommendations called for greater transparency of the policies for sharing information with third parties and an information retention policy for deactivated accounts (Hayden, 2009).

There are a number of key issues surrounding privacy in SNSs; one of these is the candidness of SNSs to communicate to users what information is private and what is public. This is clearly laid out in Facebook's policy documents, however, it is likely very few of the 400 million users have taken the time to read them in detail and change their settings accordingly. Another issue is trusting

that those that have access to any personal information (such as those on a friend's list) will treat personal information, in the form of birth dates, status updates and photos in an ethical manner and not disseminate or use the information in an unethical fashion. Again, this relies on individuals and their conscience. However, it is prudent of users of such SNSs to take responsibility for their own actions (many Facebook posts criticise Facebook regarding breaches of information) and make sure that they check their privacy settings, only make available information that they are comfortable with sharing and only add people to the "friend lists" who are actually friends or known to the user - as was the original purpose of Facebook, rather than the more recent use of adding as many "friends" as possible.

THE IMPACT OF PUBLIC OPINION: AN AUSTRALIAN CASE

In Australia, the murder of Trinity Bates in Queensland in February 2010, saw a flurry of Internet and especially Facebook pages being set up. Some were tribute sites to mourn the loss of a child, others were hate sites set up by web vigilantes against the man accused of the murder. The Queensland Premier sent an open letter to Facebook's CEO asking "what it will do to block the 'sickening' hijacking of Internet memorials?" (Herald Sun, 2010). Whilst the Queensland Premier was concerned mainly about the users posting Internet pornography and other inappropriate material on the memorial sites, of as much concern is the ethical issue surrounding the use of Facebook to vilify and pre-judge the accused defendant. The man charged with the murder has been named in the mainstream press but the vigilantes went further, posting much more personal information such as addresses and information about the defendant's family members.

Facebook answered the letter by releasing a statement from its US based director of communications and public policy. Defending Facebook's monitoring systems, the response stated that users could draw attention to offensive content by clicking on a "report" button beneath any post on the SNS. This answer has done little to placate people who feel their grief has been compounded by the actions of a few, however they fail to understand or to realise the lack of control and limited monitoring that takes place on many SNSs (The Australian, 2010a).

The comments on the vigilante sites may have major consequences for legal trials and could lead to them being aborted. This could mean that jury selection could be put at risk because the process of innocence until proven guilty could be compromised. In terms of the Trinity Bates example, how could someone have a fair trial in Queensland, when public opinion has already found a person guilty?" (The Australian, 2010b).

It appears that governments are struggling to deal with new media and are playing catch-up with methods of dealing with the issue. This incident has clearly highlighted, not simply the lack of security and monitoring on SNSs but the ethical issues surrounding the free speech on which such sites are based. The fact that such software could severely impact our judicial system, a fundamental core of society, means that this is an issue of great importance to all societies.

Facebook currently has a low user to staff ratio with only 1000 staff across the world, therefore there are simply not enough resources to manage all the information that has been uploaded and posted in real time (The Australian, 2010b).

The solution to this situation is complicated. One option may be to employ more staff and put structures and boundaries in place to clearly define what is considered an acceptable Facebook group. In doing this, however, we are then fundamentally changing the core of Facebook and allowing a third party (government or public opinion) to decide what is or is not acceptable to society. A more successful long term strategy would be to improve education and self regulation of such

sites but success is dependent upon the reliance of most people to act in a responsible manner and set their own rules and boundaries. As a result of the Trinity Bates case, the Australian Federal Government has announced that they will create an online ombudsman to deal with concerns regarding SNSs and inappropriate content (The Australian, 2010c).

ONLINE HARASSMENT

Most of Facebook's members use the SNS to connect with friends, colleagues, family and even to make new friends but there have been a number of cases where Facebook has been used for unethical purposes, such as online harassment - sometimes with dire consequences.

In theory, prisoners or criminals could use Facebook as a tool to harass, taunt and terrorise their victims. Prisoners generally only get supervised Internet access for educational reasons but they are finding more ways to access Facebook, most notably with the increased commonness of web active mobile phones. They have even been recruiting friends and family members to update their pages for them, which means it could be out of the control of the appropriate prison authorities. Barry Mizen, whose 16-year-old son Jimmy was murdered in 2008 in the UK, says his family endured months of personal attacks via Facebook after his son's killer, Jake Fahri, was convicted and sentenced to life in prison in March 2009 (BBC, 2010).

The sheer number of people using SNSs makes it difficult to monitor misuse, both for law-enforcement officials and site administrators. Tim Sparapani (Facebook's Director of Public Policy) estimates that Facebook users spend 18 billion minutes on the site each day. "We have 400 million active users and a tiny, tiny staff. We need to find novel ways to handle that kind of crushing amount of activity. It's the burden of being so immensely popular," (Time, 2010). Some victims' advocates believe that as well as offenders losing civil liberties when they are found guilty of a crime, they should also lose their "cyber liberties" (Time, 2010). Facebook currently bans people who have been convicted of sexually based offences but has no specific policy for those convicted of other sorts of crimes. "Policing" of this policy is difficult and therefore a number of countries and states have been required to establish their own legislation. The US state of Illinois has made it illegal for sex offenders to use social networks and if they are found to be using a SNS, they can be charged with a felony offence. In the UK, however, plans to do something similar have been thwarted as it was believed such laws would breach human rights laws and policies (Skinner, 2009). The issue arose when it was revealed that the police would be asked to share sex offenders' details and email addresses with social network administrators.

As Facebook is a US based organisation, the organisation has to conform with US law; the US Federal Communications Decency Act clearly states that Web sites owners aren't responsible for harassment undertaken by the web sites users (Davis, 2009). This fact does little to calm the users who are becoming increasingly frustrated with the lack of concern regarding personal privacy and protection against defamation, abuse and the theft of information.

FACEBOOK SECURITY ISSUES FRAMEWORK

The authors have developed a Security Framework in relation to Facebook (Leitch & Warren, 2009). This model was originally developed to look at the security issues in relation to Second Life, a virtual environment (Lee & Warren, 2007) and was redesigned so that it assesses the security issues and threats particular to Facebook. The model was amended based upon analysis of security incidents reported in the business and academic press. The following section discusses Facebook security breaches and highlights how this relates to the framework.

The authors acknowledge that the modified framework may not be exhaustive in identifying all the different security dimensions. It is also important to note that the security dimensions are not listed according to any order of importance. The Facebook Security Framework can be found in Table 3.

SOLUTIONS AND RECOMMENDATIONS

The Facebook Security Framework helps to identify and analyse the impact that different security and privacy threats could have upon an organisation. The framework can be used to look at a particular problem: for example, what is the potential of fraud via Facebook? and then analyse the scenario from the different viewpoints reflected by the framework.

The ongoing aim of the research is to update the Facebook Security Framework to reflect the ever changing threats that Facebook will face. The Framework can then be used to analyse new, emerging issues relating to Facebook.

FUTURE RESEARCH DIRECTIONS

The next stage of the future research is to compare the security issues and risks associated with SNSs such as Facebook and determine where common problems and solutions occur. It is envisaged that a large component of this future research will be to undertake a detailed psychological and sociological study on the users of SNSs (especially in an Australian context) in order to identify the reasons behind the lack of concern over personal security and the disclosure of information and to assess the means by which these risks and possible solutions can be more effectively disseminated to

Table 3. Facebook security framework (Leitch & Warren, 2009)

Security Threat Dimension	Nature of issue	Implication
I. Privacy & Confidentiality	• Information exchanged and transmitted between third party applications and Facebook applications may not be private. Text chat, voice chat and private instant message between users may not be encrypted. • Third Party applications may be used to record an online conversation between users without the expressed consent of users. • Facebook users may accidently alter their privacy settings and unintentionally release their information.	• Organisations will need to develop guidelines and policies to determine what information may/may not be discussed in Facebook, and how stakeholders will be notified if they are being monitored. • Facebook users would need to be educated about the privacy issues in relation to Facebook. • Companies such as Telstra have established guidelines that restrict employees from discussing commercial-in-confidence information within Social Media Sites. • Facebook would need to ensure that users are educated about the privacy issues in relation to Facebook.
II. Authentication & Identity Theft	- Verifying the identity of a Facebook user could be an issue. Identity theft is possible if social engineering techniques or by the use of key logging software. - Some third party applications may require credit card registration for identity verification or alternative payment systems, e.g.in the Battlestations application you can purchase *ochos* using your credit card and spend *ochos* during the game.	- Difficulty in verifying identify due to limited Facebook authentication, e.g. user name and password and Facebook request a mobile phone number in certain circumstance, e.g. being able to quickly reply to messages. - Difficulties in ensuring security since applications are third party. Educate Facebook users about using secure socket layer technology (SSL secure socket layer technology (SSL secure socket layer (SSL) applications.
III. Intellectual Property Theft	- Theft of Intellectual Property in existing copyrighted materials, e.g. video, music.	- Difficulties in ensuring that video and audio content streamed in Facebook do not breach existing copyright laws.
IV. Vandalism, Harassment & Stalking	- Stalking of friends and harassment is a potential issue.	- Facebook users can exclude and block potential friends. Any incident can be reported to Facebook for further investigations.
V. Defamation & Disparagement	- Deception, spreading false and misleading information rumour mongering. - Libel, defamation and slandering. - Disparagement remarks real world products.	- Dealing with negative comments, is something that an individual user can resolve, e.g. delete comment or remove friend. If the situation is serious then the matter can be reported to Facebook. There is a developing trend of media reporting Facebook entries. - Balancing freedom of speech and censorship in Facebook. - Ensuring that culturally sensitive issues and actions that affect the stability of societies are addressed in Facebook.
VI. Spam & Cybersquatting	- Unsolicited emails and messages that may contain viruses or malware.	- A major dilemma for Facebook is the growth of spam. The potential risks relate to identify theft and the issues associated with third party software.
VII. Payment and Transaction Integrity	- As mentioned before, some third party applications may require credit card registration for identity verification or alternative payment systems, e.g.in the Battlestations application you can purchase *ochos* using your credit card and spend *ochos* during the game.	- Difficulties in ensuring security since applications are third party. Educate Facebook users about using secure socket layer technology (SSL secure socket layer technology (SSL secure socket layer (SSL) applications.
VIII. Malwares and Computer Virus	- Unsolicited emails and messages that may contain viruses or malware.	- Educating Facebook users about the potential threat associated with malware and viruses being sent via Facebook, e.g. having an updated virus and spyware checker.

users in order to limit the continued security and ethical concerns related to SNSs.

The future research directions will also relate to the mapping of new security and privacy threats that relate to the Framework and the impacts that this could cause: for example, what would be the impact of a new phishing attack method upon Facebook?

CONCLUSION

This chapter has introduced the concept of SNSs by providing a brief history of their development, purpose and expanding usage by all demographics. Facebook's increasing popularity has also highlighted a number of associated security and privacy issues and threats, particularly in the area of personal identity and information disclosure. The outcome of the research is that the same security and privacy threats that exist within the general Internet community also relate to Facebook. In many cases, these risks are greater due to the sheer number of Facebook users as well as the fact that they place their trust in the safeguarding of their personal information in their Facebook friends' hands. This has meant that the potential impact for identify theft and other unethical behaviour is even greater than that generally seen in the Internet community.

This chapter contributes to practice and research by providing an overview of security issues concerning Facebook and highlighting that future research should focus on understanding and developing policies for the safety and security of information on SNSs.

REFERENCES

M86Security. (2009). *Social networking: The pros, the cons and the solution*. Retrieved November 20th, 2010, from http://www.m86security.com/documents/pdfs/white_papers/business/WP_SocialNetworking.pdf

BBC. (2009). *Facebook gives users more control of privacy*. Retrieved March 30th, 2010, from http://news.bbc.co.uk/2/hi/technology/8404284.stm

BBC. (2010). *The prisoners causing trouble on Facebook*. Retrieved March 30th, 2010, from http://news.bbc.co.uk/2/hi/uk_news/8496658.stm

Boyd, D. (2008). Facebook's privacy trainwreck: Exposure, invasion, and social convergence. *Convergence, 14*(1), 13–20.

Cluley, G. (2009). Denying staff access to SNSs will only drive them to find a way round the ban, social network: The business case. *IEEE Engineering and technology, 4*(10).

Consumer Affairs. (2006). *Connecticut opens MySpace.com probe*. Retrieved July 12th, 2010, from http://www.consumeraffairs.com/news04/2006/02/myspace.html

Coppola, N., Hiltz, S. R., & Rotter, N. (2004). Building trust in virtual teams. *IEEE Transactions on Professional Communication, 47*(2), 95–104. doi:10.1109/TPC.2004.828203

D'Monte, L. (2009). Swine flu's tweet tweet causes online flutter. *Business Standard*. Retrieved January 18th, 2010, from http://www.business-standard.com/india/news/swine-flu%5Cs-tweet-tweet-causes-online-flutter/356604/

Davis, W. (2009). Facebook harassment suit could spur cyberbullying laws. *The Daily Online Examiner*. Retrieved November 25th, 2009, from http://www.mediapost.com/publications/index.cfm?fa=Articles.showArticle&art_aid=114854

DiMicco, J. M., & Millen, D. R. (2007). Identity management: Multiple presentations of self in Facebook. *Proceedings of the 2007 International ACM conference on Supporting group work, Florida, USA.*

Dimmel, B. (2008). *Identity theft worm hits Facebook*. Retrieved October 18th, 2009, from http://www.infopackets.com/news/security/2008/20081208_identity_theft_worm_hits_facebook.htm

Dwyer, C., Hiltz, S., & Passerini, K. (2007). Trust and privacy concern within social networking sites: A comparison of Facebook and MySpace. *Proceedings of the Thirteenth Americas Conference on Information Systems,* Keystone, Colorado August 09 -12, 2007.

Ellison, N., Steinfield, C., & Lampe, C. (2007). The benefits of Facebook friends: Exploring the relationship between college students' use of online social networks and social capital. *Journal of Computer-Mediated Communication, 12*(3). Retrieved July 30th, 2007, from http://jcmc.indiana.edu/vol12/issue4/ellison.html

Facebook. (2009a). *Facebook facts.* Retrieved September 25th, 2009, from http://www.facebook.com/press/info.php?factsheet

Facebook. (2009b). *Facebook statistics.* Retrieved September 25th, 2009, from http://www.facebook.com/press/info.php?statistics

Facebook. (2009c). *Facebook site governance: Facebook's privacy policy–full version.* Retrieved on November 7th, 2009, from http://www.facebook.com/note.php?note_id=%20322194465300

Facebook. (2010). *Facebook statistics.* Retrieved June 6th, 2010, from http://www.facebook.com/press/info.php?statistics

Festa, P. (2003). Investors snub Friendster in patent grab. *CNet News.* Retrieved July 7th, 2010, from http://news.com.com/2100-1032_3-5106136.html

Goldie, L. (2008). Facebook to discuss security with ICO after data leak. *New Media age.* Retrieved November 21st, 2009, from http://www.nma.co.uk/news/facebook-to-discuss-security-with-ico-after-private-data-leak/38591.article

Gross, R., & Acquisti, A. (2005). Information revelation and privacy in online social networks. [Alexandria, VA: ACM.]. *Proceedings of WPES, 05,* 71–80.

Havenstein, H., Vijayan, J., & Perez, J. (2007, December, 10). Facebook fiasco may lead to closer look at online privacy issues. *Computerworld.*

Hayden, A. (2009). *Facebook needs to improve privacy practices, investigation finds.* Office of the Privacy commissioner for Canada. Retrieved November 24th, 2009, from http://www.priv.gc.ca/media/nr-c/2009/nr-c_090716_e.cfm

Herald Sun. (2010). Governments powerless to stop Facebook vandalism, says IT expert. Retrieved February 28th, 2010, from http://www.heraldsun.com.au/.../governments-powerless-to-stop-facebook-vandalism-says-it-expert/story-e6frf7jx-1225834291255

Hildebrand, J. (2009). *Facebook identity theft enough for jail.* Retrieved July 20th, 2010, from http://www.news.com.au/story/0,27574,25764253-421,00.html

InternetWorld. (2009a). *Global internet statistics.* Retrieved September 25th, 2009, from http://www.internetworldstats.com/stats.htm

Jones, S., Millermaier, S., Goya-Martinez, M., & Schuler, J. (2008). Whose space is MySpace? A content analysis of Myspace profiles. *First Monday, 13*(9). Retrieved September 25th, 2009, from http://www.uic.edu/htbin/cgiwrap/bin/ojs/index.php/fm/article/view/2202/2024

Kim, K.-H., & Yun, H. (2007). Cying for me, Cying for us: Relational dialectics in a Korean social network site. *Journal of Computer-Mediated Communication, 13*(1).

King, R. (2006). Social networks: Execs use them too. *Business Week.* Retrieved September 15th, 2009, from http://www.businessweek.com/technology/content/sep2006/tc20060911_414136.htm

Krishnamurthy, B., & Wills, C. (2009). On the leakage of personally identifiable information via online social networks. *Proceedings of ACM Workshop on Online Social Networks*, Barcelona, Spain.

Lee, C., & Warren, M. (2007). Security issues within virtual worlds such as Second Life. *Proceedings of the 5th Australian Information Security Management Conference*, Edith Cowan University, Western Australia.

Leitch, S., & Warren, M. (2009). Security issues challenging Facebook. *Proceedings of the 8th Australian Information Security Management Conference*, Perth, Australia.

Lenhart, A. (2009a). *Adults and social network sites*. Pew Internet & American Life Project. Retrieved July 3rd, 2010, from http://www.pewinternet.org/~/media//Files/Reports/2009/PIP_Adult_social_networking_data_memo_FINAL.pdf

Lenhart, A. (2009b). *Social networks grow: Friending Mom and Dad*. Pew Internet & American Life Project. Retrieved July 10th, 2010, from http://pewresearch.org/pubs/1079/social-networks-grow

Letzing, J. (2010). AOL pulls plug on Bebo social networking effort. *The Wall Street Journal*. Retrieved July 6th, 2010, from http://www.marketwatch.com/story/aol-pulls-plug-on-bebo-social-networking-effort-2010-04-06

Mayer, R. C., Davis, J. H., & Schoorman, F. D. (1995). An integrative model of organizational trust. *Academy of Management Review, 20*(3), 709–734. doi:10.2307/258792

McCarthy, C. (2008). You, there. Step back from the webcam. *Cnet News*, Retrieved November 20th, 2010, from http://news.cnet.com/8301-13577_3-9853908-36.html

Morse. (2009). *Press Release: Twitter and social networks cost UK businesses*. Retrieved January 10th, 2010, from http://www.morse.com/press_20.htm

Nancy, F. (2009). *The e-policy handbook: Rules and best practices to safely manage your company's e-mail, blogs, social networking, and other electronic communication tools*. USA: American Management Association.

New York Times. (2008). How to use social networking sites for marketing and PR. Retrieved November 22nd, 2009, from http://www.nytimes.com/allbusiness/AB11702023_primary.html

O'Reilly, T., & Battelle, J. (2009). Web squared: Web 2.0 five years on. *Proceedings of Web 2.0 Summit*, San Francisco, USA.

Ostrow, A. (2009). *Obama assassination poll on Facebook was created by a minor*. Retrieved October 1st, 2009, from http://mashable.com/2009/10/01/kill-obama-poll/

Pew Internet. (2008). *Dataset: Cloud computing, politics and adult social networking*. Pew Internet & American Life Project. Retrieved July 1st, 2010, from http://www.pewinternet.org/Shared-Content/Data-Sets/2008/May-2008--Cloud-computing-politics-and-adult-social-networking.aspx

Raacke, J., & Bonds-Raacke, J. (2008). MySpace and Facebook: Applying the uses and gratifications theory to exploring friend-networking sites. *Cyberpsychology & Behavior, 11*(2), 169–174. doi:10.1089/cpb.2007.0056

Schonfeld, E. (2010). Facebook closing in on 500 million visitors a month (ComScore). *TechCrunch*. Retrieved June 18th, 2010, from http://techcrunch.com/2010/04/21/facebook-500-million-visitors-comscore

Serrano, N., & Torres, J. (2010). *IEEE Software, May/ June*. USA: IEEE Computer Society.

Shin, D. (2010). The effects of trust, security and privacy in social networking: A security-based approach to understand the pattern of adoption. *Interacting with Computers, 3*(5).

Shuen, A. (2008). *Web 2.0: A strategy guide.* O'Reilly Media, Inc.

Smith, J. (2009). *Fastest growing demographic on Facebook: Women over 55.* Retrieved February 12th, 2010, from http://www.insidefacebook. com/2009/02/02/fastest-growing-demographic-on-facebook-women-over-55/

Socialman. (2009). Allowing staff to use Orkut? Better take care. *Social Unwire India.* Retrieved November 20th, 2009, from http://www.social. unwireindia.com/2009/07/allowing-staff-to-use-orkut-better-take-cover

Sophos. (2007). *Press release: Facebook members bare all on networks.* Retrieved November 20th, 2009, from http://www.sophos.com/pressoffice/ news/articles/2007/10/facebook-network.html

Stafford, T. F., Stafford, M. R., & Schkade, L. L. (2004). Determining uses and gratifications for the internet. *Decision Sciences, 35,* 259–288. doi:10.1111/j.00117315.2004.02524.x

Story, L. (2007, December 6). Apologetic, Facebook changes ad program. *New York Times.* USA.

Strater, K., & Richter, H. (2007). Examining privacy and disclosure in a social networking community. *ACM International Conference Proceeding Series, 229.* Pittsburgh, USA.

Sunden, J. (2003). *Material virtualities.* New York, NY: Peter Lang.

Telstra (2009). *Social media policy–Telstra's 3R's of social media engagement.* Telstra, Australia. Retrieved November 20th, 2009, from http:// www.telstra.com.au/abouttelstra/media/docs/ social-media-company-policy_final_150409.pdf

The Australian. (2010a). *Bligh hits out at sick net sites.* Retrieved February 28th, 2010, from http://www.theaustralian.com.au/politics/state-politics/bligh-hits-out-at-sick-net-sites/story-e6frgczx-1225834063831

The Australian. (2010b). *Facebook vandal complaints futile.* Retrieved from http://www.theaustralian.com.au/australian-it/facebook-vandal-complaints-futile/story-e6frgakx-1225834303404, Accessed 28th February, 2010

The Australian. (2010c). *Online ombudsman for Facebook woes.* Retrieved February 20th, 2010, from http://www.theaustralian.com.au/australian-it/online-ombudsman-for-facebook-woes/story-e6frgakx-1225834756343

Time Magazine. (2010). *How prisoners harass their victims using Facebook.* Retrieved October 15th, 2009, from http://www.time. com/time/business/article/0,8599,1964916,00. html#ixzz0gb2oD8Ge

Vijayan, J. (2009). *Social networking sites leaking personal information to third parties.* Retrieved November 10th, 2009, from http://www. networkworld.com/news/2009/092409-social-networking-sites-leaking-personal.html

Whitney, L. (2009). *Employers grappling with social network use.* Retrieved November 20th, 2009, from http://news.cnet.com/8301-10797_3-10360849-235.html

Wilson, J. (2007). MySpace, your space, or our space? *New Frontiers in Electronic Evidence . Oregon Law Review, 86,* 1201.

Wire, C. M. S. (2010). *Social media is good and bad for business.* Retrieved January 10th, 2010, from http://www.cmswire.com/cms/document-management/smb-tech-rollup-social-media-is-good-and-bad-for-business-with-security-top-of-mind-006711.php

ADDITIONAL READING

Baird, T. (2009). *The Truth About Facebook - Privacy Settings Every Facebook User Should Know, and Much More - The Facts You Should Know*. Emereo Pty Ltd.

Funk, T. (2008). *Web 2.0 and Beyond: Understanding the New Online Business Models, Trends, and Technologies*. Praeger.

Holtzman, D. (2006). *Privacy Lost: How Technology Is Endangering Your Privacy*. Jossey-Bass.

Liebowitz, J. (2007). *Social Networking: The Essence of Innovation*. The Scarecrow Press.

Matwyshyn, A. (2009). *Harboring Data: Information Security, Law, and the Corporation*. Stanford Law Books.

Mills, J. (2008). *Privacy: The Lost Right*. Oxford University Press.

Myron, M. (2009). *What Is Privacy?: Investigating the meaning of privacy in Facebook and the social consequences of this*. VDM Verlag.

Nissenbaum, H. (2009). *Privacy in Context: Technology, Policy, and the Integrity of Social Life*. Stanford Law Books.

Oqvist, K. (2009). *Virtual Shadows - Your Privacy in the Information Society*. British Informatics Society Ltd.

Sankar, K., & Bouchard, S. (2009). *Enterprise Web 2.0 Fundamentals*. CISCO Press.

Shariff, S., & Churchill, A. (2009). Truths and Myths of Cyber-bullying: International Perspectives on Stakeholder Responsibility and Children's Safety . *Peter Lang Publishing, ISBN-10, 1433104660*.

Shun, A. (2008). *Web 2.0: A Strategy Guide: Business thinking and strategies behind successful Web 2.0 implementations*. O'Reilly Media.

Solove, D. (2006). *The Digital Person: Technology and Privacy in the Information Age*. NYU Press.

Solove, D. (2008). *The Future of Reputation: Gossip, Rumour, and Privacy on the Internet*. Yale University Press.

Solove, D. (2009). *Understanding Privacy*. Harvard University Press.

Stamp, M. (2005). *Information Security: Principles and Practice*. Wiley.

Whiteman, M., & Mattford, H. (2007). *Principles of Information Security*. Course Technology.

Whiteman, M., & Mattford, H. (2010). *Management of Information Security*. Course Technology.

Zandt, D. (2010). *Share This!: How You Will Change the World with Social Networking*. Berrett-Koehler Publishers.

Zittrain, J. (2009). *The Future of the Internet--And How to Stop It*. Yale University Press.

KEY TERMS AND DEFINITIONS

Facebook: Online system to allow exchange of information between agreed parties.

Internet: An interconnected system of networks that connects computers around the world via the TCP/IP protocol.

Malware: Malicious software that interferes with normal computer functions.

Risk: The possibility of suffering harm or loss; danger.

Security: Something that gives or assures safety, as: (a) Measures adopted by a government to prevent espionage, sabotage, or attack; (b) Measures adopted, as by a business or homeowner, to prevent a crime.

Social Networking: A term to describe websites that allow people to join a social network and exchange information with their online friends.

SNS: Social Networking Site.

Threat: An indication of impending danger or harm.

Trojan Horse: A computer program hidden in another program to do damage when the software is activated, e.g. Malware hidden in pirated software.

Web 1.0: Web pages from earlier Web applications, the information is static.

Web 2.0: Web pages from current Web applications, the information is dynamic and interactive.

Chapter 4

Copyright and Ethical Issues in Emerging Models for the Digital Media Reporting of Sports News in Australia

Mary Wyburn
University of Sydney, Australia

ABSTRACT

The chapter examines the copyright and ethical issues raised by emerging models for the digital media reporting of sports news in Australia. In particular, it explores the use by news organisations of a defence in copyright law that provides protection against an infringement action for the reporting of news and the use by sports organisations of journalist accreditation to limit, by way of contract, the uses made of copyright material generated at sports events. It briefly outlines some proposed responses to these issues, including amending copyright law or establishing an industry code of conduct for the accreditation of news organisations accessing and reporting on sports events in the digital media. These matters were raised in a 2009 Senate inquiry. The inquiry attracted submissions from international news organisations concerned that a more restricted access regime established by sports organisations in Australia might influence the terms negotiated in other countries. The conflicts arising in this industry sector are a small part of a much larger international landscape in which new digital communications technologies are offering greater business opportunities but at the same time challenging existing commercial relationships.

INTRODUCTION

This chapter looks at the copyright and ethical issues raised by emerging models for the digital media reporting of sports news in Australia. A

2009 Senate committee report highlighted the conflicting stakeholder interests affected by these developments (Senate Standing Committee on Environment, Communications and the Arts (ECA), *The Reporting of Sports News and the Emergence of Digital Media Report*, May 2009). The committee recommended sports and news

DOI: 10.4018/978-1-60960-573-5.ch004

media organisations negotiate an agreement on the issues or failing this, the government take measures to establish an industry code of conduct.

Interest in the committee's consideration of these issues is not limited to Australia. The conflict between sports and news organisations is a small part of a much larger international picture, in which new digital communications technologies offer increased opportunities but also increased risks to established sports and media businesses. The popular sports like football (in all its versions) and cricket, have developed international profiles alongside the truly international sporting events of the Olympic and Commonwealth Games. Sports events are now the subject of digital piracy, involving the use of television signals, high-speed broadband and streaming technology (Mellis, 2008; NetResults, 2008) and often operating in a context where broadcasting regulation has not yet reached (DBCDE, 2009). At the same time as sports organisations are challenged by new communications technologies, established news media are struggling to contain the unauthorised use of their news content by search engines (Sinclair, 2010) and other information aggregators, as well as by bloggers, while they develop sustainable new business models (Perez-Pena, 2009). In this international context, precedents set in one country may influence the bargains being made in other jurisdictions, so there is international interest in how Australia is working towards solutions in this area.

BACKGROUND

Stakeholders in the Reporting of Sports News

Developing communications technologies are providing new ways for sports organisations to commercialise their sporting events. There are new ways for consumers to experience the events (subscription television, internet streaming, web

blogging, mobile phone), new markets for the products being developed (web sites catering for fans, social networking sites) and new methods of advertising (virtual advertising (Deutsch, 2000)). These developments mean sports organisations are able to grant rights to an increasing range of new communications platforms (for example, mobile phones) and as to particular aspects of their sports events (for example, match statistics (West Australian Newspapers Ltd, 2009)). If any of these rights are to be granted exclusively, sports organisations must deny access to others. So, for example, Hutchison Telecoms has sponsored the Australian test cricket team through Cricket Australia (Hutchison Telecoms, 2009). This arrangement gives it exclusive rights in relation to mobile phone distribution of live match footage.

There are also other interests at stake. Another commercial interest is that of the news media organisations. The commercial media in its many forms (the press (newspapers, online newspapers, magazines), radio and television) vigorously seeks content to attract a readership or audience and sports coverage is very popular. The readership in turn attracts advertisers who want to reach that audience and are willing to pay the media organisations to do so. Some of the media not only publish their own coverage of sports but they also sell their sports news products to other media organisations that are unable or unwilling to send journalists to report directly on the sports events (syndication). News agencies have developed with their main role being the supply of news product to third parties. Some media, primarily the television broadcasters, are interested in sports events mainly for their value as entertainment, attracting audiences and thereby attracting advertisers. They will generally pay for rights to broadcast the entire event, often with some form of exclusivity (ECA, 2009).

There is an associated public interest at stake in the news gathering activities of media organisations. News media play an important public interest role by reporting news and opinions to the general public. Certain sections of the public closely follow the news about a range of sports (both national and international) and the media provides detailed commentaries on the events, as well as more personality-based human interest stories on the individual athletes. Some of the commercial sports competitions are associated with international events that attract the attention of a wider audience than the domestic competitions (for example, the World Cups in soccer and rugby). In these cases there is a wider public interest attracted because the competing teams represent their countries, rather than merely their local clubs.

A public interest wider than merely supplying information to sports followers is also present. Considerable public funds are used to support state and national athletes, teams and sports events and there is public interest in how these funds are used. There is also public interest in media coverage of issues such as drugs or violence in sport. Public health issues and issues of social inclusion are also part of the overall picture of the public interest in sport (ECA, 2009). The social significance of some sporting events is evidenced by provisions in Australian broadcasting legislation (*Broadcasting Services Act 1992* (Cwlth)) that ensure certain key sports events of national and cultural significance are available by way of free-to-air broadcast, rather than merely by subscription; referred to as anti-siphoning laws (Craufurd Smith and Bottcher, 2002; DBCDE, 2009). News organisations assert that they bring an independent view of the news they cover. Some news organisations contrast their own independent perspective with what they see as the biased nature of some of the news sourced from sports organisations, which they characterise as more like publicity rather than news (ECA, 2009).

Like the operations of sports organisations, the business models for news media organisations have undergone considerable recent change. For several years the media have been utilising the internet as a platform for their products. Initially it was merely an additional outlet for their print, television and radio products. More recently it has developed into a significant platform in its own right. The internet allows media organisations to make available a valuable archive of electronic news product that can be offered for a fee to subscribers or to other casual users. But the main shift of emphasis has been in the developing online readership. Products are now generated for this particular market. At first the online readership was consuming mostly free product but there has been a trend towards making valuable products available only on a fee basis.

The news media are making available the material generated at sports events by their journalists as part of their expanding online product range. In the past, the sports news images (photographs and video) and accompanying commentaries, had a relatively short shelf life in the newspaper, magazine or broadcast. Consumers now expect sports news to be available more rapidly and updated more frequently. There is also potential for those same images and text to have commercial value for an extended period. Indeed, in some instances, the passage of time will significantly increase the value of these sometimes iconic images, as they are later recognised as playing an important historical role. Some news organisations have established web sites dedicated to sports news on which appear photo and video galleries (ECA, 2009).

While sports organisations recognise the importance of sport as news and the public interest involved in sport as news, they view some of the developing activities of the news media organisations as a commercialisation of their events without their consent and without the sports organisations sharing in the proceeds generated. In the past, the main income for sports events came from the broadcast rights. When this was the case, the line between that operation and news coverage of the event was relatively clear. Now the online content of the news media looks very much like the material that sports organisations would license to others, often on the basis of some element of exclusivity. For example, the news media may provide updated information on sports events as well as galleries of photographic images. The online audio-visual elements that have grown in popularity mimic a short version broadcast, especially if the audio-visual clips cherry pick the key events such as race finishes or tries scored. Understandably, sports organisations have begun to more vigorously seek to control these commercial uses of material generated at their events.

In addition to news organisations, there are a number of other commercial businesses interested in tapping into sports events in order to generate income. These include mobile phone operators and internet service providers. While not strictly media organisations, these carriers have recently become involved in providing sports content to their subscribers.

Developments in communications technology have led to a fundamental shift in the relationship between sports and news organisations and how they view the ownership of intellectual property generated around sports events. In the past, the sports organisations were reliant on the news organisations for generating a good part of the public interest in their sports events. However, with the development of new business models, particularly using digital and internet technologies, sports organisations are now far less dependent on the news media for the success of their events. They can now offer information and products generated around the sports events more directly to the public.

Among the rights being asserted more vigorously by sports organisations are intellectual property rights, in particular copyright. This has brought them into conflict with other rights holders, especially news organisations. News organisations have ownership of the intellectual property generated by their employed journalists and they often contract for ownership with their freelance journalists. They rely on special defences in copyright law that protect from infringement

action the reporting of news. Because the sports events are generally held in venues they own or lease, sports organisations can control, by way of contract, the terms on which third parties have access to the event. For example, the sports organisations may accredit journalists from news organisations to attend and report on their events. Sports organisations have begun to use their right to control access to sports events to impose contract terms that seek to limit the use of material generated by journalists and other third parties at their events.

News media organisations have responded to these developments in various ways. Some have sufficient commercial influence in the marketplace to convince the sports organisations to negotiate a different set of terms of access. Other smaller players in the marketplace have called for changes to copyright legislation or other legislative amendments to protect the right of news media to access sports events.

Senate Inquiry

A 2009 Senate committee report has recommended a negotiated agreement be reached between the sports and media organisations but failing this, the government should take measures to establish an industry code of conduct (ECA, 2009). The inquiry was held because of two earlier disputes about the accreditation of journalists for sporting events, one involving football and the other cricket.

In 2007 the Australian Football League (AFL) granted one organisation (Slattery Media Group) exclusive rights to manage AFL photography (ECA, 2009). Subsequently, under its 2008 accreditation agreement with journalists, the AFL sought to limit the supply by journalists of photographic images of AFL events to third parties. There was disagreement about the precise nature of the contractual limitation. The AFL claimed it was merely trying to limit the on sale of photographic images so they did not go to non-news reporting agencies and that its 2008 terms were the same as its 2007 terms (ECA, 2009). News agencies like The Associated Press, whose business is to supply material to third parties, claimed the proposed terms would limit any sale of images to third parties. They tried unsuccessfully to negotiate a modification of the terms (ECA, 2009).

Football was not the only sport in dispute over journalist accreditation. In 2007, prior to the cricket test between Australia and Sri Lanka, Cricket Australia (CA) apparently offered some media organisations accreditation terms including a provision to the effect that all intellectual property rights in images taken at match venues would be owned by CA (ECA, 2009). The proposed accreditation terms also placed limits on the frequency of website updates (for example, no updating from the venue "more than six times per hour" (ECA, 2009, para. [3.43]). In 2008 CA's contract terms sought even further rights to control the distribution of match images by news agencies to non-sports websites, magazines and mobile phone operators. There was some uncertainty about the exact contract terms, as they appeared in side letters rather than the main contracts (ECA, 2009).

Submissions to the Senate inquiry indicate these issues are not only relevant domestically. Attempts by Australian sports organisations to seek more control over the images and commentary generated by their events, reflect similar developments overseas, for example, in relation to the 2006 Federation Internationale de Football Association (FIFA) World Cup, the 2007 Rugby World Cup and the 2008 Indian Premier League (cricket) (Getty Images, 2009). The receipt of submissions from significant overseas news media organisations and industry coalitions (for example, The Associated Press, the World Association of Newspapers, Thomson Reuters and the News Media Coalition) and the contribution to the Senate committee hearings of these organisations, indicate they see precedents being set in Australia as having relevance in the wider international context. Concerns were expressed by news organisations

that the Australian contract terms being offered and negotiated were more restrictive than those offered overseas and they would therefore set an unfavourable precedent, as well as make it more difficult for Australian news organisations to negotiate less restrictive terms of access and use from overseas sports organisations (ECA, 2009).

What the Australian sports organisations were seeking was stricter limits on the reporting by news organisations of their sports on the new communications platforms such as internet websites and mobile phones. The sports organisations were concerned the news organisations were relying on the *Copyright Act 1968* (Cwlth) free defence of fair dealing for the reporting of news, when they were in fact commercialising the sports event without sharing any of the benefits with the sports organisations. They argued the defence was so general in its terms, it would be necessary for them to bring costly and time consuming litigation to enforce their copyright against the news organisations (ECA, 2009). If the fair dealing news reporting exception could be relied upon to excuse the website and mobile phone uses of the intellectual property material generated at the sports event (for example, the communication of images and audio-visual material discussed above), it had the potential to significantly reduce the value for which the sports organisations could sell these rights to third parties. It would also affect the broadcast rights which had up to now been the key source of income for several of the major sports.

For their part, the news organisations were concerned the sports organisations were using the contract terms by which news media gain access to the sports venues, to impose inappropriate limits on the subsequent use of images and other material generated at the sports events. The news organisations wanted to be free to use the new media platforms being accessed by consumers. They pressed their claim that the restrictions proposed by the sports organisations would be detrimental to the public interest in access to news.

This chapter briefly explores the protection of an event by copyright and then examines the legal and ethical aspects of the news media's reliance on the fair dealing for news reporting exception to copyright infringement to enable free use of images and other copyright material generated at sports events subsequently communicated through new media platforms. It also examines attempts by the sports organisations to impose contract terms to limit such use of the news reporting fair dealing exception. The chapter then briefly outlines some of the proposed responses to these issues, such as amendment to copyright law or establishing an industry code of conduct for the accreditation of news organisations accessing and reporting on sports events in the digital media.

SPORTS NEWS REPORTING AND DIGITAL MEDIA

Copyright and Ownership of Sports Events

Before examining the question of the reliance by news media on the news reporting fair dealing defence to report sports news on the new communications platforms, it is useful to first briefly look at what aspects of sports events attract copyright.

There is no protection for a sporting event per se under Australian intellectual property law. A 1937 Australian case about horse racing established that such events are not protected unless they fall within one of the recognised heads of intellectual property law. In *Victoria Park Racing and Recreation Grounds Company Ltd v Taylor* the plaintiff conducted horse races at a racecourse on fenced land it owned in a suburb of Sydney. The defendant, Taylor, owned adjacent land. An observation platform was built on Taylor's land from which a radio broadcaster (the Commonwealth Broadcasting Corporation Ltd) broadcast by way of a commentary telephoned to a radio station, details of the plaintiff's races, as well as

race information from the plaintiff's notice boards (starters, scratchings, barrier positions, results). The plaintiff was unsuccessful in its claim for an injunction to prevent the broadcasting of the races based on the law of nuisance and on intellectual property law. In relation to the intellectual property claim, the court could not find any property right in a 'spectacle.' The established categories of intellectual property, for example, patents, trade marks, designs, were "dealt with in English law as special heads of protected interests and not under a wide generalisation" (*Victoria Park Racing and Recreation Grounds Company Ltd v Taylor*, Dixon J, p. 509). In relation to the copyright claimed in the material on the notice boards, the court found there was no copyright in the mere statement of facts appearing on the notice boards. Without any broadcasting regulations then in place preventing such conduct, in the court's view the solution for the plaintiff was to build a higher fence.

British sports organisations were in the same position at this time. In 1944 a number of British sporting organisations combined to form the Association for the Protection of Copyright in Sports but it was unsuccessful in its lobbying for the introduction of copyright in sporting events (Blais, J, 1992, p. 515).

However, there are some jurisdictions that offer protection for sporting spectacles. In the United States, wider relief has been granted based on the law of "... unfair competition, unjust enrichment, interference with contractual relations and quasi-property rights in news reports ..." in the case of sports events like the baseball games in *Pittsburgh Athletic Co. v KQV Broadcasting Co.* 24 F. Supp. 490 (1938) referred to by Blais (1992, p. 520). Protection is more direct in Brazil. Brazilian law gives sports organisations "the right to authorize or prohibit the fixation, broadcast or retransmission of public sporting events for which a fee is charged for admittance" (Blais, 1992, p. 537). The legislation provides for the athletes and their coaches to receive a share of the royalty income (Blais, 1992, p. 537). The right operates for sixty years from the event (Blais, 1992, p. 537). Blais (1992) suggests it would be appropriate to revisit the issue of copyright protection for televised sports events, in light of "a constantly evolving communications landscape" and their position as "a commercially important aspect of the entertainment industries" (Blais, 1992, p. 539). One submission to the ECA called for legislative amendment to expressly provide copyright protection for sporting events (ECA, 2009).

Although there is no protection for a sporting event per se under Australian copyright law, particular aspects of an event may be the subject of copyright protection. Images from the event captured by photography constitute artistic works under copyright law. Written commentary on the event will constitute a literary work. A sporting event may be the subject of a broadcast (radio or television), in which case it will be protected by copyright as part of the broadcast. If the event is recorded on film or as an audio recording (sound recording), it will be protected under these categories of copyright subject matter. Australia has certain performers protection rights but "a performance of a sporting activity" is expressly taken not to be a performance for these purposes (*Copyright Act 1968* (Cwlth), s 248A(2)(c)). Australian copyright legislation protects this range of copyright material generated around a sporting event by granting the owner of copyright exclusive rights in various ways the material is exploited, including reproduction (of images, sound and video) and communicating the material (making it available online and electronically transmitting it) to the public (*Copyright Act 1968* (Cwlth), ss 31, 85-88).

The copyright ownership of news reporting has been controversial in Australia over a long period. Like the matters raised in the inquiry, previous conflicts over the issue reflect earlier attempts by various interests to gain control of the commercialisation of news outputs as developing information communication technologies created new ways of exploiting them. The earlier conflicts had been between news media proprietors and their employed and freelance journalists. The ECA showed a third party, the sports organisations, was now involved.

Under the Copyright Act the ownership of copyright news material constituting literary, dramatic or artistic works was originally split between the news proprietors and their employed journalists. Under the default rules of ownership in the copyright legislation, if no contrary contract terms were agreed, the news proprietors had ownership of the copyright for the purposes of publication in their newspapers and periodicals. The employed journalists retained copyright ownership for other purposes. With the expansion of photocopying technology in the 1970s and 1980s and the appearance of the commercial media monitor (of print and broadcast material) and then later the development of electronic technologies for databases, the proprietors sought by way of contract and by urging legislative reform, to acquire ownership of these new copyright uses. This led to a Copyright Law Review Committee reference (*Report on Journalists' Copyright*, 1994) and ultimately resulted in changes to the ownership provisions introduced in 1998 (*Copyright Act 1968* (Cwlth), s35(4)). Now, subject to contract provisions to the contrary, news media proprietors have copyright ownership for these new technology uses of the output of their employed journalists. The employed journalists retain copyright rights for book publication and hardcopy facsimile reproduction. In the case of freelance journalists, they will be the first owner of copyright but they can contract otherwise.

Copyright and the Free Exception for News Reporting

It was not only copyright ownership that was being fought over during this earlier period. The developing photocopying and media monitoring uses of copyright news material also gave rise to conflicts about the operation of the free fair dealing exception for the reporting of news.

Australian copyright legislation has a range of exceptions that permit certain uses of copyright material that would otherwise constitute an infringement. Some of the exceptions are free (no remuneration is paid to the copyright owner) and some operate as a statutory licence under which remuneration goes to the copyright owner. Important amongst these provisions are the various free fair dealings with copyright material. Unlike the general open-ended fair use exception to copyright infringement in the United States copyright legislation (*Copyright Act 1976* (US), s 107) which provides an inclusive list of free fair uses, the Australian provisions are a closed list of fair dealings. Some consideration has been given to the adoption in Australia of an open-ended fair use exception, in particular when Australia was amending its intellectual property legislation to implement its obligations under the *Australia-United States Free Trade Agreement* (Attorney-General's Department, 2005). Some changes to the exceptions were made as a response to the review that was conducted, including the addition of a fair dealing for parody or satire. The fair dealing exceptions include fair dealing for research or study (ss 40, 103C), criticism or review (ss 41, 103A), parody or satire (ss 41A, 103AA) and the reporting of news (ss 42, 103B) (*Copyright Act 1968* (Cwlth)).

The exception for reporting of news (s 42) provides:

1. A fair dealing with a literary, dramatic, musical or artistic work, or with an adaptation of a literary, dramatic or musical work, does not constitute an infringement of the copyright in the work if:
   a. it is for the purpose of, or is associated with, the reporting of news in a newspaper, magazine or similar periodical and a sufficient acknowledgement of the work is made; or
   b. it is for the purpose of, or is associated with, the reporting of news by means of a communication or in a cinematograph film.

2. The playing of a musical work in the course of reporting news by means of a communication or in a cinematograph film is not a fair dealing with the work for the purpose of this section if the playing of the work does not form part of the news being reported.

A similar exception (s 103B) applies when the use is of one of the copyright subject matters other than works (sound recordings, cinematograph film and broadcasts (sound and television)). It provides:

1. A fair dealing with an audio-visual item does not constitute an infringement of the copyright in the item or in any work or other audio-visual item included in the item if:
   a. it is for the purpose of, or is associated with, the reporting of news in a newspaper, magazine or similar periodical and a sufficient acknowledgement of the first-mentioned audio-visual item is made: or
   b. it is for the purpose of, or is associated with, the reporting of news by means of a communication or in a cinematograph film.

The news reporting fair dealing exception, like the other fair dealing exceptions, requires the dealing to be fair and that it be for the requisite purpose. Beyond these conditions, no specific guidelines are provided in the legislation (for example, by way of percentage or number of words). The application of the exception is a question of judgment in the particular circumstances, ultimately decided in the case of a dispute, by the court. The exception's underlying public interest in the freedom of news reporting is obvious but there is case law in Australia reflecting conflict over its boundaries.

In *De Garis v Neville Jeffress Pidler Pty Ltd* a media monitoring organisation copying newspaper articles for its clients, sought to rely upon various exceptions including the news reporting fair dealing provision, to defend a copyright infringement claim made against it. It was unsuccessful in relation to the news reporting exception. The court referred to dictionary definitions of news. It recognised that news could encompass matters beyond current events. However, here it was not an instance of reporting by way of the newspaper or magazine outlets required by the section and in any case the copying for commercial supply of whole works, without permission and without remuneration to the authors, could not be regarded as fair (*De Garis v Neville Jeffress Pidler Pty Ltd*).

The news reporting fair dealing defence has been raised in the context of the broadcast of a spectacle, the City of Sydney New Year's Eve fireworks for 2000. In December 1999, Nine Network Australia Pty Ltd (Nine), which had acquired exclusive rights to record and televise the fireworks, sought interlocutory (interim) injunctions to prevent the Australian Broadcasting Corporation, a public broadcaster, from televising the fireworks (*Nine Network Australia Pty Ltd v Australian Broadcasting Corporation*). Nine's application, based on a claim of copyright in various aspects of the fireworks (artistic works: drawings, sculptures, works of artistic craftsmanship and a dramatic work: the script for the fireworks display accompanied by music), was rejected. There were a number of questions about whether copyright subsisted in aspects of the spectacle as argued for by Nine but in the court's view the Australian Broadcasting Corporation had a strong argument it would able to rely on the news reporting fair dealing defence to any copyright infringement claim. The court acknowledged the public interest in the national broadcaster being able to broadcast parts of the New Year's Eve celebrations. Even so, the court was sensitive to the limits of the defence and the question of what amounts to news, including how extensive the coverage of the event could be and still remain news reporting. It recognised that news can be reported in an amusing and entertaining fashion (the hosts of the public broadcast included television personalities known for their comedy work) and still constitute news. In the circumstances, including a delay in initiating the action, the court decided to refuse the application (*Nine Network Australia Pty Ltd v Australian Broadcasting Corporation*).

As with all fair dealing defences, the individual circumstances must be examined but in some cases a line has been drawn between the reporting of news which falls within the exception and mere entertainment, which does not. The case of *TCN Channel Nine Pty Ltd v Network Ten Pty Ltd* shows that drawing this line may be a difficult exercise. The case involved a late night chat show broadcast on one television network, using excerpts from various sources, including a competitor network's broadcasts. The first network sought to rely on various defences, including the news reporting fair dealing defence. For some excerpts the defence was applied but some were held to fall on the wrong side of the line between news and entertainment (*Nine Network Australia Pty Ltd v Australian Broadcasting Corporation*).

The *TCN Channel Nine Case* was an example of one media organisation broadcasting excerpts from another media organisation. There has been Australian case law more directly addressing this issue in the context of reporting sports news. The cases are only at the interlocutory stage of the proceedings and therefore do not explore the legal issues in detail, so their value as legal precedents is low but they nevertheless illustrate the business and legal issues arising in this context.

In *Thoroughvision Pty Ltd v Sky Channel Pty Ltd* the applicant (TVN) owned copyright in the film of thoroughbred horse races in the state of Victoria and it was also the exclusive licensee for film of the Sydney races. TVN broadcasts the film live on its own subscription television channel (for Totalisator Agency Boards (TABs), hotels and clubs) and via Foxtel's subscription television service. It also broadcasts replays of the films on its programmes such as Racing Review. Channel

Seven is sub-licensed by TVN to broadcast on free-to-air television some of the Victorian race films and the Sydney films. Seven also has a licence from the Victorian Racing Club (VRC) to include in its television broadcasts certain of the VRC race meetings, but by agreement, copyright in the broadcasts and films of the races is owned by the VRC. Sky Channel, a subscription television channel, on a number of occasions in October 2005, reproduced and re-broadcast excerpts of varying lengths (from 20 to 30 seconds) from the previous day's broadcasts of races by Seven, as part of Sky's Racing Retro programme. The excerpts were mainly of the race finishes. TVN and Seven sought interlocutory injunctions against Sky, arguing it had infringed their copyright in the Victorian and Sydney race films and in Seven's broadcast of certain race meetings, by way of reproduction and communication to the public. Sky denied any use of the Victorian or Sydney film. In relation to the broadcast material it did use (excerpts from Seven's broadcasts), it argued that what it took did not amount to a substantial part of the broadcast and therefore did not constitute infringement of copyright. Alternatively, if the material did amount to a substantial part, Sky argued it could rely upon the fair dealing defence for reporting news (s 103B) to avoid a finding of copyright infringement (*Thoroughvision Pty Ltd v Sky Channel Pty Ltd*).

Weighing up the evidence as it stood at the interlocutory stage, the court was not prepared to grant interlocutory injunctions against Sky. However, some interesting points relevant to the ECA inquiry were raised by the court. The court doubted that Seven's activities would suffer from Sky's use of the excerpts. In its view the value of Seven's broadcast was its "immediacy or 'live' aspect" and Sky's programme occurred eighteen hours later, so in effect Sky was using the excerpts as "archival footage" (*Thoroughvision Pty Ltd v Sky Channel Pty Ltd*). However, at the same time the delay meant the importance of the excerpts of the race finishes as news was "severely limited if

it has not evaporated altogether" (*Thoroughvision Pty Ltd v Sky Channel Pty Ltd*). Nevertheless the court recognised the excerpts might still retain their quality as news for a smaller group of race followers. The court also pointed out that competing free-to-air television stations made "similar use of such excerpts" from Seven's race broadcasts in their news bulletins and Seven had not objected to the practice (*Thoroughvision Pty Ltd v Sky Channel Pty Ltd*). The court mentioned its concern that one of the motives behind the proceedings was to protect TVN's rival programme Racing Review. If TVN succeeded, the court considered this would reduce viewer choice and would arguably be contrary to the public interest. The court rejected the application for interlocutory relief but ordered a "speedy trial of the action" (*Thoroughvision Pty Ltd v Sky Channel Pty Ltd*).

In another interlocutory application, *Telstra Corporation Pty Ltd v Premier Media Group Pty Ltd*, the applicant (Telstra), a retail internet supplier and mobile phone service operator, obtained the exclusive licence for communication via the internet and mobile phone of the broadcast and film of the National Rugby League (NRL) football matches. Under the licence, Telstra could communicate footage of the matches (full matches and unlimited highlights) but not earlier than twenty four hours after the match concluded. Limited highlights (of not more than five minutes) could be communicated within the twenty four hour period. Premier Media produced sports channels for broadcast by subscription television operators. It also produced audio-visual content for websites and mobile phones (Fox Sports News). The Fox Sports News was made up of highlights broadcast on the Fox Sports channel news and included material from the NRL matches, with a new commentary added to the original broadcast material. The highlights were available on the internet about forty eight hours after the matches and remained available for about forty eight hours. For the purposes of the interlocutory proceedings, the excerpts of NRL matches were agreed by the parties to be two minutes long. The excerpts contained the key parts of the games, including the tries, in the order in which they occurred. The evidence indicated that Premier Media was the exclusive licensee for the pay television rights in the NRL matches. One of its two owners, Publishing and Broadcasting Ltd, held the free-to-air broadcast rights to NRL games. The other, News Ltd, through a subsidiary, was joint owner of the NRL.

Telstra argued that it had paid the NRL for exclusive rights for internet and mobile phone communication of NRL matches and this was being undermined by the actions of Premier Media. Telstra, as exclusive licensee, sought interlocutory relief in respect of Premier Media's alleged infringement of copyright in the film or television broadcast of the NRL matches. For the purposes of the interlocutory application the parties agreed to limit the issue to whether Premier Media could rely on the fair dealing for reporting news exception to copyright infringement (*Copyright Act 1968* (Cwlth), s 103B). Telstra argued Premier Media could not rely on the defence. In respect of whether it was a fair dealing, it argued that "long established conventions" between free-to-air and pay television broadcasters permitting some reuse of one another's broadcasts as part of news reporting, did not apply to internet and telephony platforms (*Telstra Corporation Pty Ltd v Premier Media Group Pty Ltd*).

The court did not grant the interlocutory injunction. It was not persuaded at this early stage of the proceedings that a distinction could be drawn between what had developed as accepted practices in free-to-air and pay television on the one hand and internet and telephony on the other. In the court's view the uses of the match broadcasts made by Premier Media (sequential highlights with voiceover of one or two minutes) "would not be seen as necessarily entirely out of order in pay television and free-to-air television" (*Telstra Corporation Pty Ltd v Premier Media Group Pty Ltd*). It would be for the court at the full hearing to determine whether the defence applied and it

would then be "a question of judgment and impression which takes into account the public interest inherent in s 103B…" (*Telstra Corporation Pty Ltd v Premier Media Group Pty Ltd*). The court made some interesting observations about the s 103B defence but it must be borne in mind these were merely comments and not findings for the purposes of the proceedings. One point noted by the court was that this was not a case where the parties had attempted to contract out of the benefit of s 103B as between themselves. Another point was that, while for the purposes of the interlocutory application the parties agreed the match highlights were "newsworthy," the court did not see news as necessarily being "exhausted" after twenty four hours (*Telstra Corporation Pty Ltd v Premier Media Group Pty Ltd*). The NRL competition involved games from Friday to Monday evening and match highlights could still constitute news beyond twenty four hours because "[n]ot everyone works from Monday to Friday, with Saturday and Sunday off, with full access to their newspapers and televisions" (*Telstra Corporation Pty Ltd v Premier Media Group Pty Ltd*).

Copyright and Contract Terms for Accrediting Sports Journalists

For some news organisations, especially the news agencies, the problem is less about the scope of the fair dealing for news reporting defence and more to do with attempts to impose new contract terms, as part of the accreditation of journalists seeking access to sports events. They told the Senate inquiry they were concerned about the terms dealing with the ownership of copyright material generated at sports events, the effect of which was a contracting out of the news reporting fair dealing exception. The larger news organisations indicated to the committee that so far they had been able to negotiate appropriate accreditation terms (ECA, 2009).

The law of contract can have several effects on the operation of copyright in the context of the reporting of sports news.

Contract terms may be used to decide the ownership of copyright. For the most part, copyright legislation provides only a general framework for ownership of copyright material. The author and other relevant parties are free to agree to terms that differ from the set of default ownership rules in the act. The author is usually the first owner of a copyright work and this would include freelance journalists. Such journalists may contract with news organisations to sell the copyright or to grant them a licence over certain uses of the material. Employed journalists have a split ownership (discussed above) under which journalists retain only the book rights for their works and rights in hardcopy facsimiles made from paper editions, although contractual arrangements may provide for a different ownership picture. The submissions to the ECA indicated that some sports organisations were seeking to impose contract terms under which ownership of copyright material created at the sports events would rest with the sporting organisation (The Associated Press, 2009). This would be a contractual override of the default ownership provisions in the copyright legislation.

It has long been recognised that contract terms may operate to limit the creation of unauthorised copyright material where an event is being conducted by someone who can control the terms on which others enter an enclosed area where the event is taking place. In a 1917 English case, the organisers of the Ladies' Kennel Show granted "sole photographic rights" to one organisation but they were unable to prevent photographs taken at the show being published in the defendant's journal (*Sports and General Press Agency Ltd v 'Our Dogs' Publishing Co. Ltd*). The court was of the view that if the organisers wanted to restrict photography at the event, they should have done so by way of contract terms limiting the conditions of entry to the show.

The Senate inquiry submissions also indicated some sports organisations were using the journalist accreditation contract provisions to limit the extent of news reporting of their events. For example, the submissions described contractual provisions limiting the number of photographs from a particular game and length of video footage from news conferences and interviews held at the sports venue that could be posted online (The Associated Press, 2009). In this way the sports organisations were setting the parameters of the use and thereby seeking to override what would otherwise be a case by case determination of what amounted to a fair dealing for the reporting of news. This would avoid the uncertainty of the fair dealing provisions. While there may have been arguments about what constitutes news under the fair dealing exception, the contract terms in the accreditation agreements set particular time limits in order to distinguish current event-type news from other longer term uses of the material. If the contract limits were overreached, the sports organisations could seek relief by way of injunctions and damages for breach of the agreed terms. The fair dealing exception for news reporting would still operate but its effect would be limited by the contractual obligations of the news organisations and the contract remedies available to the sports organisations.

The ability of parties to contract out of the legislated exceptions to copyright infringement is a controversial issue and it has been considered both here and overseas. It is a particularly important issue in the context of the use by rights owners of technological protection measures to prevent unauthorised access and use of copyright material and the legislative measures introduced to prohibit the marketing and use of circumvention devices that override the technological protection measures (*Copyright Act 1968* (Cwlth) Part V, Division 2A, ss 116AK-116D)). While there are some exceptions to copyright infringement where the legislation expressly prevents contracting out (for example, copies made as part of the technical process of running a computer, back-up copies of software and copies of software made to correct errors or for security testing: s 47H), this is not the case with the fair dealing exceptions, although an earlier review committee report was in favour of prohibiting the contracting out of the fair dealing provisions (Copyright Law Review Committee *Copyright and Contract*, 2002).

Ethical Issues

In its consideration of the issues, the ECA had its sights firmly fixed on the commercial competition between sports and news media organisations over the products being developed for the new communications platforms. For the most part, the ECA did not consider in detail the ethical issues, although it did touch on a couple of wider policy matters. One of these was the failure of the news media to use the new technologies to extend their coverage to sports other than the relatively small number of major commercial sports. Another was the bargaining imbalance that existed for some parties in the process of negotiating accreditation for access to sports events.

There are a number of ethical issues raised in this context. From the perspective of the commercial stakeholders, one of these is the use of a free copyright exception to avoid licensing the rights for essentially commercial uses of material generated at the sports event. Another is the use of control over access, combined with contract terms, to contract out of the application of a free copyright exception. From the public interest perspective, there is the issue of providing for free use of copyright material for news reporting but without having any balancing obligation to provide news reporting for the less commercially significant sports.

There was no discussion in the ECA about the role of copyright material generated by the spectators or the sports men and women competing in the event. This raises both legal and ethical issues. The on the spot photographic and audio-visual mate-

rial generated by the public has only just begun to be tapped by the news media but this material is generated by the public without regard to any of the professional and ethical restraints placed on the work of professional journalists. Some sports organisations, especially those involved in the Olympics and Commonwealth Games, have much more experience in contracting for limits on a spectator's conduct within the event venue. However, with the advent of social networking platforms such as Facebook and Twitter, there are now numerous internet sites carrying images and audio-visual material from sports events.

Solutions and Recommendations

What were the suggested solutions to the uncertainties of the news reporting fair dealing exception in copyright law?

The sports organisations were pressing for more specific regulation than is currently available under the reporting of news fair dealing exception. Among the suggestions were more detailed guidelines and definitions in copyright law (legislation or regulations) in order to clarify the application of the exception to the new digital platforms or such guidelines could appear in "non-binding explanatory advice issued by government" (ECA, 2009, para. [4.18]). The news organisations were generally in favour of retaining the current fair dealing defence. For instance, the ECA referred to conventions that had developed in the television industry around the reporting of news fair dealing defence. Under a "3 x 3 x 3 television protocol" broadcasters could re-broadcast as part of their television news reports, excerpts from the broadcasts of others but not beyond the accepted limits of three minutes "at three hourly intervals" and "not more than three times in a twenty four hour period" (ECA, 2009, para. [2.14]). The ECA (2009, para. [4.22]) was of the view that the fair dealing exceptions needed to be flexible enough to be able to address new technologies as they developed and any detailed guidelines relating to specific technologies would "be superseded and become irrelevant over time."

What were the suggested solutions to the attempt by some sports organisations to use contract to obtain copyright ownership or to limit the use of the news reporting fair dealing exception?

The Associated Press (2009) suggested copyright legislation should be amended to invalidate any contracting out of the fair dealing exceptions. It also suggested a "guaranteed right of access for news media at sporting and related events" be introduced (The Associated Press, 2009, para. [4.9]) but this proposal was insufficiently detailed for the ECA to consider it further (ECA, 2009).

As far as the copyright issues were concerned, the ECA (2009, para. [5.14]) was of the view that "[t]his is not primarily a copyright issue" and that "[c]opyright laws are of no relevance to the issues raised in this inquiry" about how the work of sports journalists "is used or re-used." The ECA was not convinced of the case for copyright reform. If there were copyright issues at stake, for example, uses falling outside the fair dealing exception for news reporting, then litigation was available to have these matters determined. The ECA (2009, para. [5.23]) recommended against parliament amending copyright law to clarify the application of the fair dealing exception for news reporting, "unless future specific case law outcomes appear to warrant it" but recommended government "consider and respond to" the Copyright Law Review Committee report on copyright and contract (ECA, 2009, para. [5.25]).

The ECA saw the journalist access and accreditation issues as the most important ones, as they related to the freedom of the press to report on sports news. Some submissions were in favour of the development of an industry code of conduct to address the issue of the negotiation and content of accreditation agreements.

Industry codes are seen as more economically efficient ("more flexible" and "less intrusive") than detailed legislative regulation (ACCC, 2005, p. 2). They are currently relevant in two contexts

in Australian copyright law. There is a voluntary *Code of Conduct for Copyright Collecting Societies*, established in 2002. All of the main copyright collecting societies have agreed to its terms. The other copyright context in which industry codes arise, is that of liability for secondary infringement (authorisation). One of the factors to be taken into account when a court is considering liability for infringement by way of authorising the infringing act, is "whether the person took any reasonable steps to prevent or avoid the doing of the act, including whether the person complied with any relevant industry codes of practice" (*Copyright Act 1968* (Cwlth), ss 36(1A)(c), 101(1A)(c)). This provision is particularly important in respect of the controversial issue of the liability of internet service providers for copyright infringement occurring on their networks as part of peer-to-peer file sharing but so far the negotiations for the establishment of an industry code in this context have been unsuccessful.

There are three code options available under Australian trade practices law. The first option is a voluntary code agreed to by industry participants, such as the copyright collecting society code mentioned above. Such a code may be endorsed by the trade practices regulator, the Australian Competition and Consumer Commission (ACCC) where the ACCC regards the code as of "a high quality" (ECA, 2009, para. [4.30]). The second and third options are prescribed codes under s 51AE of the *Competition and Consumer Act 2010* (Cwlth) (formerly the *Trade Practices Act 1974* (Cwlth)), one voluntary and one mandatory. Under a prescribed voluntary industry code, industry participants may choose whether or not to become a signatory to the code and be bound by its terms. There are no such codes presently operating (ECA, 2009). The third option is a prescribed mandatory industry code of conduct which obliges all industry participants to comply with its terms (ECA, 2009). An example of this type of code is the Franchising Code. Non-compliance with a prescribed code is a breach of s 51AD. Action in relation to the breach may be taken by the ACCC and a private action can also be brought by other code participants (ECA, 2009). The government department with general oversight of prescribed industry codes is the Federal Treasury (ECA, 2009).

Industry codes of practice (for example, the Commercial Television Industry Code of Practice) have also been developed under the *Broadcasting Services Act 1992* (Cwlth) (s 123) by broadcasting industry participants, in consultation with the Australian Communications and Media Authority (ACMA). ACMA is a statutory authority with responsibility for regulating areas such as broadcasting and telecommunications and which operates within the portfolio of the Department of Broadband, Communications and the Digital Economy (ACMA, 2010).

The ECA considered it was preferable for the relevant industry participants to come to negotiated arrangements rather than have an industry code imposed on them. Although a mandatory code was being called for by The Associated Press and supported by some other submissions, the committee noted that "many stakeholders remain optimistic that current disagreements may be able to be worked out through less intrusive mechanisms" (ECA, 2009, para. [4.42]). It recommended that "stakeholders negotiate media access to sporting events based on the principle that all bona fide journalists, including photojournalists and news agencies, should be able to access sporting events regardless of their technological platform" but where such negotiations were unsuccessful, "the Minister consider initiating the process for consideration of a code under Section 51AE of the Trade Practices Act" (ECA, 2009, paras. [5.38]-[5.39]).

In its report, the ECA emphasised the public interest issues involved in this commercial dispute between industry participants. It encouraged the federal government to "take into account the opportunities and challenges presented by digital media to sports organisations' current and future revenue prospects and options" and recommended the then current inquiry into sports (Crawford

Review) "pay particular attention to the capacity of sports to invest in digital innovation" (ECA, 2009, para. [5.21]). In the Crawford Report, released in November 2009, the Independent Sports Panel (IDP) (2009, p. 137) was of the view that a "balance" was needed between the commercial interests of the sports organisations and "reasonable access to content for news reporting" by the news media. However, the IDP (2009, p. 137), like the ECA, was not persuaded of the need for government intervention at this stage and preferred the sports and media organisations to work towards "mutually beneficial arrangements."

A voluntary code of practice agreed between a number of key sports and news media organisations, was launched in March 2010 (*Code of Practice for Sports News Reporting (Text, photography and data) 2010)*.

FUTURE RESEARCH DIRECTIONS

Developments in digital media have brought opportunities for both sports and news media organisations, not only to extend their current offerings but also to create new products for these markets. However, the new communications platforms have significantly changed the previous relations between the two industry players. There is considerable scope for further research into the copyright and ethical aspects of the relationships developing as part of the new digital media.

One aspect of this is the special role news organisations play in the public interest by ensuring access to news. But this special position is more difficult to maintain with the plethora of new information outlets facilitated by the internet. News and news reporting, as it is experienced on the new digital information platforms, is changing the nature of news. For the ECA, sports news was not just news about the match but included tragic events such as crowd injuries and political issues such as race in sport. It noted the importance of visual images in conveying the news (ECA, 2009).

The ECA (2009, para. [5.14]) in its report recognised that with the expanding role of the internet in communicating news, it was also important to maintain "historical news information" and so news on the internet could no longer be regarded as merely "transitory." How long is it before an event is no longer regarded as news? How much of the wealth of digital archival material available on the internet can legitimately be regarded as news to which the public should have access?

Another aspect needing further inquiry relates to the contractual overriding of the copyright exceptions. The developing digital communications environment has challenged copyright law on a number of fronts, the most public of which has been the downloading of copies of copyright music and film through peer-to-peer file sharing networks. Issues such as the contractual overriding of exceptions to copyright infringement have until now mainly involved individual users who are seeking to rely on the fair dealing for research or study or criticism or review exceptions (the closest things to a personal use exception under Australian copyright law) and the public information institutions such as libraries. The same mechanism (contractual override of statutory exceptions) is now being used by sports organisations against commercial media organisations. Should public interest exceptions be able to be contracted out of or are some alternative mechanisms required to provide a balance of the commercial and public interests at stake?

One issue not fully explored by the ECA was the potential impact of competition law. Rather than each benefiting from the business of the other, as occurred in the past, sports and news media organisations now find themselves more often in competition for audiences and the associated advertising income. But if sports organisations need to exclusively license the new communications platforms of the internet and mobile phone, how can this be done? If the sports organisations are the sole source of access and information about important sports events, are they legitimately able to use their control to affect the operation of other businesses in the downstream markets reliant on obtaining this information? Some downstream players, such as the large media outlets, have so far been able to negotiate access terms but what about the smaller players, such as rural and remote news outlets?

Another area for future research relates to the proposed solutions so far offered, such as legislating for access or alternatively codes of conduct that may be developed voluntarily or imposed as part of a mandatory industry framework.

CONCLUSION

The developing digital communications marketplace has seen the blurring of the traditional boundary between sports news and sports entertainment. At the same time technological developments have led to significant changes in consumer expectations of when and how they access all sorts of information, including sports news.

Sports and news organisations are each claiming the other is entering their traditional domain. From the point of view of sports organisations, the news organisations appear to be using material generated at their sporting events for entertainment rather than strictly news reporting and this use as entertainment should be licensed on a commercial basis. The response of the news media is that their expanded offerings utilise the new communications platforms but they are still in the business of news and there are public interest issues at stake. In the past, what often differentiated the two uses was that entertainment generally involved communicating the entire event (the full match). However, the distinction is much more difficult to make in relation to the various communication platforms on which sport is now accessed by the public.

It is a question of balancing the interests involved. On the one hand are the sports organisations, seeking to control access to their events in order to protect income streams, the funds from which are needed to develop and promote their sports. On the other hand are the news organisations seeking reasonable access to sports news content for a burgeoning range of media platforms. An appropriate balance is also needed between the public's right to access various sources of information using the new types of digital media and the need for sporting organisations to limit access to their events, so they are in a position to offer an attractive product to commercial interests.

The Australian government has so far declined to intervene by way of legislation. The advice from two recent reviews (ECA, IDP) is that at this stage it is preferable for the industry players to negotiate arrangements between themselves. However, one of the reviews (ECA) recommended that if agreement could not be reached, a mandatory industry code would be one way to achieve some resolution in the face of competing business interests. The government will be looking closely at the operation of the new voluntary code of practice for sports news reporting to see if further steps are necessary in this area.

This is an important area reflecting significant copyright and ethical issues emerging from a changing communications environment. The developments in Australia reflect what is happening in the wider international context. Precedents set in one country may influence the bargains being made in other jurisdictions, so there is considerable international interest in how Australia is working towards solutions in this area.

REFERENCES

Attorney-General's Department. (2005). *Review of fair use and other copyright exceptions*. Retrieved January 22, 2010, from http://www.ag.gov.au

Australian Communications and Media Authority. (2010). *Broadcasting codes index*. Retrieved January 25, 2010, from http://www.acma.gov.au

Australian Competition and Consumer Commission. (2005). *Guidelines for developing effective voluntary industry codes of conduct*. Retrieved January 25, 2010, from http://www.accc.gov.au

Blais, J. (1992). The protection of exclusive television rights to sporting events held in public venues: An overview of the law in Australia and Canada. *Melbourne University Law Review, 18*, 503–539.

Broadcasting Services Act1992 (Cwlth).

Code of Conduct for Copyright Collecting Societies. (2008). Retrieved January 26, 2010, from http://www.apra-amcos.com.au

Code of Practice for Sports News Reporting. *(Text, photography and data)*. (2010). Retrieved September 7, 2010 from http://www.minister.dbcde.gov.au

Competition and Consumer Act2010 (Cwlth) (formerly *Trade Practices Act 1974* (Cwlth)).

Copyright Act1968 (Cwlth).

Copyright Law Review Committee. (1994). *Report on journalists' copyright*. Retrieved.

Copyright Law Review Committee. (2002). *Copyright and contract*. Retrieved January 22, 2010, from http://www.ag.gov.au/clrc

Craufurd Smith, R., & Bottcher, B. (2002). Football and fundamental rights: Regulating access to major sporting events on television. *European Public Law, 8*(1), 107–133. doi:10.1023/A:1014594625408

De Garis v. Neville Jeffress Pidler Pty Ltd. (1990). FCA 218.

Department of Broadband, Communications and the Digital Economy. (2009). *Sport on television: A review of the anti-siphoning scheme in the contemporary digital environment*. Retrieved January 21, 2010, from http://www.dbcde.gov.au

Deutsch, A. (2000). Sports broadcasting and virtual advertising: Defining the limits of copyright law and the law of unfair competition. *Marquette Sports Law Review*, *11*(1), 41–86.

Getty Images, N. S. W. (2009). *Submission to the Senate Standing Committee on Environment, Communications and the Arts*. Retrieved May 14, 2009, from http://www.aph.gov.au/senate/committee/eca_ctte/sports_news/submissions.htm

Hutchison Telecoms. (2009). *Submission to the Senate Standing Committee on Environment, Communications and the Arts*. Retrieved May 14, 2009, from http://www.aph.gov.au/senate/committee/eca_ctte/sports_news/submissions.htm

Independent Sport Panel. (2009). *The future of sport in Australia*. Barton: Australian Government. Retrieved January 21, 2010, from http://www.sportpanel.org.au

January 22, 2010, from http://www.ag.gov.au/clrc

Mellis, M. (2008). Internet piracy of live sports telecasts. *Marquette Sports Law Review*, *18*(2), 259–284.

NetResult Ltd. (2008). *Background report on digital piracy of sporting events*. Retrieved.

Nine Network Australia Pty Ltd v. Australian Broadcasting Corp. (1999). FCA 1864.

Perez-Pena, R. (2009, April 7). A.P. seeks to rein in sites using its content. *The New York Times*. Retrieved April 9, 2009, from http://www.nytimes.com

Senate Standing Committee on Environment, Communications and the Arts. (2009). *The reporting of sports news and the emergence of digital media report*. Retrieved June 1, 2009, from http://www.aph.gov.au/senate/committee/eca_ctte/completed_inquiries/index.htm

September 1, 2009, from http://www.alliance-againstiptheft.uk

Sinclair, L. (2010, January 21). Google enters fight for sports broadcast rights. *The Australian*, (p. 5).

Sky Channel Pty Ltd v. Austar Entertainment Pty Ltd. (2005). NSWSC 815.

Sports and General Press Agency Ltd v 'Our Dogs' Publishing Co. Ltd. (1917). 2 KB 125.

TCN Channel Nine Pty Ltd v. Network Ten Pty Ltd. (2002). FCAFC 146.

Telstra Corporation Pty Ltd v. Premier Media Group Pty Ltd. (2007). FCA 568.

The Associated Press. (2009). *Submission to the Senate Standing Committee on Environment, Communications and the Arts*. Retrieved May 14, 2009, from http://www.aph.gov.au/senate/committee/eca_ctte/sports_news/submissions.htm

Thoroughvision Pty Ltd v. Sky Channel Pty Ltd. (2005). FCA 1527.

Victoria Park Racing and Recreation Grounds Company Ltd v. Taylor. (1937). 58 CLR 479.

West Australian Newspapers Ltd. (2009). *Submission to the Senate Standing Committee on Environment, Communications and the Arts*. Retrieved May 14, 2009, from http://www.aph.gov.au/senate/committee/eca_ctte/sports_news/submissions.htm

ADDITIONAL READING

Australian Broadcasting Corporation. ABC Radio National, The Sports Factor programme transcripts: Playing hard ball: New media and sport (May 11, 2007) and Privatising sport (August 10, 2007). Retrieved May 20, 2009, from http://www.abc.net.au/rn/sportsfactor.

Australian Communications & Media Authority website http://www.acma.gov.au.

Australian Subscription Television & Radio Association website http://www.astra.org.au.

Baulch, L., Green, M., & Wyburn, M. (Eds.). (1999). *The boundaries of copyright: Its proper limitations and exceptions*. Sydney: Australian Copyright Council.

Butler, D., & Rodrick, S. (2007). *Australian media law*. Sydney: LawbookCo.

De Zwart, M. (2003). Seriously entertaining: The Panel and the future of fair dealing. *Media and Arts Law Review, 8*(1), 1–18.

Fitzgerald, B., Fitzgerald, A., Middleton, G., Lim, Y., & Beale, T. (2007). *Internet and e-commerce law: Technology, law and policy* (pp. 153–288). Sydney: Thomson LawbookCo.

Free TV Australia website http://www.freetv.com.au.

Hartman, L. (2005). *Perspectives in business ethics* (3rd ed.). New York: McGraw-Hill Irwin.

Murphy, P., Laczniak, G., Bowie, N., & Klein, T. (2005). *Ethical marketing*. New Jersey: Pearson Prentice Hall.

Organisation for Economic Co-operation and Development. (2009). *Piracy of digital content*. Chapter 4, Case study: The sports rights owners sector, pp. 87-115.

Productivity Commission. (2000). *Broadcasting inquiry report*. Chapter 12, Television broadcasting of sport, pp. 423-445. Retrieved June 1, 2009, from http://www.pc.gov.au.

Retrieved January 19, 2010, from SourceOECD.

Ricketson, S., & Creswell, C. (2009). *The Law of intellectual property: Copyright, designs & confidential Information*. Sydney: Thomson LawbookCo.

Ricketson, S., Richardson, M., & Davison, M. (2009). *Intellectual property: Cases, materials and commentary* (4th ed., pp. 39–518). Sydney: LexisNexis Butterworths.

Rosen, J., & Nordell, P. (Eds.). (2001). *Copyright, related rights and media convergence in the digital context*. Stockholm: Swedish Copyright Society and Nordic Intellectual Property Review.

Turner, C. (2009). *Australian commercial law* (27th ed., pp. 698–773). Sydney: Thomson Lawbook Co.

KEY TERMS AND DEFINITIONS

Copyright: A set of exclusive statutory rights (for example, to reproduce, to communicate (make available online or electronically transmit) to the public) granted to the owner over particular categories of material (works: for example, literary work (book, computer program) and subject matter other than works: for example, film, sound recording, broadcast (television and radio)).

Copyright Infringement: When a party other than the owner of copyright, without the authority of the copyright owner, does any of the acts within the bundle of exclusive rights of the copyright owner, in relation to all or a substantial part of a copyright work or other subject matter.

Defence to Copyright Infringement: A set of exceptions that permit the use of copyright material without the permission of the copyright owner.

Fair dealing defences: defences that permit the use of copyright material for free where the use is fair and for one of the listed purposes (for example, news reporting, research or study, criticism or review, parody or satire).

Industry Code of Conduct: A code of conduct either agreed to voluntarily or a mandatory industry code imposed under the *Competition and Consumer Act 2010* (Cwlth) (formerly *Trade*

Practices Act 1974 (Cwlth)) or a code developed under the *Broadcasting Services Act 1992* (Cwlth).

News: Originally seen as limited to current events and not including entertainment but now expanding to include a wider range of information and it may include some aspects of entertainment.

News Agency: An agency which does not publish news itself but creates images and news reports that it then sells to (news and non-news) third parties.

Section 2
Ethical Concerns in the Handling and Delivery of Health and Safety Information

Chapter 5

The Protocols of Privileged Information Handling in an E–Health Context:
Australia

Juanita Fernando
Monash University, Australia

ABSTRACT

In this chapter, the author analyzes adherence to privileged health information handling protocols in the clinical context to inform work plans pioneering an ostensibly private and secure Australian national e-health scheme. The analysis leverages findings from new and emerging literature and data from a study involving twenty-three medical, nursing, and allied health clinicians working at public hospitals in Victoria, combined with data collected for a new case study from nine information technology (IT) support staff working at the same hospitals. In both case studies, data collection was based on the Questerview technique to examine the privacy of clinical e-health work for patient care. The research approach provided a rich source of qualitative data for analysis.

The evidence suggests a socio-material mismatch between privileged information handling protocols and clinical work in the natural hospital environment. The protocols foster a range of information privacy threats that may affect patient care outcomes. The risks incorporate data confidentiality, integrity, and availability. That is, health data is accessible only to those with the required level of authorization, it is accurate and complete, and all authorized end users can obtain information when and where required. Reflecting international findings, some Australian clinicians avoid or work around the protections provided by health privacy legal frameworks. Although fixes for several privacy threats are available, they do not appear to be in common use. Rather than analyze and rectify privacy threats embedded into the socio-material interface of patient care settings before pioneering e-health schemes, authorities propose to amend the Privacy Act and weaken identification rules to advance the national unified record. At the same time, unresolved work tension exists between clinicians and IT support staff. The mismatch trig-

DOI: 10.4018/978-1-60960-573-5.ch005

gered a series of responses that this chapter argues do not benefit either the clinician or the patient, and may hamper the introduction of a unified Australian e-health scheme more generally.

Health authorities need to review the privacy and security of real-life work contexts before pioneering new, privileged information handling protocols as a foundation of a new national e-health scheme.

INTRODUCTION

Reflecting global trends, Australia is increasingly adopting unified, national electronic health (e-health) frameworks to improve standards of patient care while containing service costs. The term "e-health" refers to the electronic management and exchange of patient health information using information and communication technology (ICT). The ICT includes databases, mobile phones, faxes, computerized devices and the Internet. Threats to health information stored on computer networks are complex and jeopardize the privacy of millions of patient-care records rather than, as reported prior to e-health, perhaps hundreds of paper records per incident (Zajac 2010). Evidence suggests privileged e-health information handling protocols are a broad and complex subject area, yet few studies analyze their impact in relation to complicated social and material, or socio-material, interactions in patient care settings (Orlikowski, 2007; Westbrook *et al.*, 2007). This chapter attempts to rectify the shortcoming, adding to knowledge about the protocols of privileged-information handling and informing national e-health framework strategies.

BACKGROUND

Information privacy and security (P&S), information technology (IT) and health care are complex domains that often use similar language in dissimilar ways. Thus we attempt to provide a shared understanding of the key terms used here. Privileged information handling protocols encompass a wide range of complicated issues and activities, from physical security to technical and administrative security. The convergence between physical security and technical or administrative security threats has contributed to an increasing number of serious incidents in recent years (Zajac, 2010). For the purposes of this chapter we define privileged information handling protocols as all measures that protect information privacy and security.

A false dichotomy often exists between privacy and security. Yet individuals cannot have one without the other. The term "security" refers to all implementations that protect information privacy. "Privacy" concerns control over access to information about One's self and associated data, including health information, as enshrined in legislative frameworks (Clarke, 2006). Complete information privacy cannot exist without security while there can be security without complete information privacy.

Clinical work can be subdivided into several tasks or streams. The streams incorporate medical tasks and administrative tasks. Some of the administrative tasks of care provision associated with third party requirements, such as health service organizations, insurance companies, professional associations or governments, are beyond the scope of this study. Medical tasks include clinical observations, assessments of health conditions (such as progress notes and diagnoses) and treatment, and services (such as medication, surgery, physical and psychological therapy). Legislation about medical tasks related to emergency health care are

Table 1. An overview of findings drawn from informatics studies about the application of HIT to HIS P&S from (Fernando & Dawson, 2009) p.819 (© IEEE 2009 Used with permission)

Affects	Security influence	Study findings
Data fragmentation	Control	Enhances data integrity & data availability
	Threat	Exacerbates data integrity & data availability shortcomings
Transcription	Control	Ends transcription, writing legible
	Threat	Entrenches transcription as clinicians collude to transcribe updates to an electronic health record (EHR)
Usability	Control	Reduces number & range of threats to private information
	Threat	Increases number and range of existing threats as well as some new ones
Productivity	Control	Can enhance efficiency (user skill, ends duplication of work)
	Threat	Hinders efficiency (productivity trade-offs)
Audit	Control	Auditable, tailored access to health records
	Threat	Non-auditable, clinician collusion over the highest level of access to health records
Cost	Control	IT devices reduce pressure on inadequate budgets due to increased efficiency
	Threat	IT devices magnify pressure on inadequate budgets due to ongoing maintenance and technology investment costs
Information security	Control	Robust e-health P&S implementations will control information threat & ensure that health records can be shared (data availability/integrity)
	Threat	Greatly increased magnitude of information threat on an e-health system (data confidentiality/availability/integrity)

different from those concerning non-emergency direct patient care and are beyond the scope of this study. Thus, unless otherwise specified in this chapter, the term "clinical work" describes all of the non-emergency medical tasks that apply to the way clinicians provide direct patient care.

Successful implementations hinge on citizen trust underpinned by national and international standards and robust e-health privacy legal frameworks (NEHTA, 2009). The frameworks ostensibly inform the design of e-health systems, so embedding robust security controls. Yet new and emerging evidence often supports the notion of a mismatch between complex privileged information handling protocols and work with patient-health information in the natural hospital environment (NHE). The NHE is characterized by unhelpful socio-material interactions that are intended to support clinical work (Fernando & Dawson, 2009; Robert, Greenhalgh, MacFarlane & Peacock, 2009) *Table 1: An overview of find-*

ings drawn from informatics studies about the application of HIT to health information P&S illustrates these contradictions. Concerns about privileged information handling protocols, the NHE and e-health systems have been published in the peer-reviewed literature from at least 1988 (Shortliffe, 1988; Hannan, 1999). Most of these concerns still remain to be addressed while new and emerging challenges have been added, suggesting clinician and citizen concern about a mismatch between P&S protocols and actual patient care have been overlooked as an important issue for several decades.

A growing number of researchers have begun to analyze these P&S concerns in an e-health context, especially as it pertains to unified national frameworks (Timmons, 2003; Pagliari, 2007; Williams, 2008; Schiff & Bates, 2010). The analyses focus on the inappropriate use of patient-specific information by health workers, who have access to those data as part of their regular work, emphasizing the mismatch between complex privileged information handling protocols and clinical work in the NHE. The mismatch fosters a range of data-CIA breaches that affect patient care. Data-CIA is a term used by IT security professionals. It refers to data confidentiality, integrity and availability; that is, data is accessible only to those with the required level of authorization, it is accurate and complete and all authorized end users can obtain information when and where required. As this chapter indicates, these mismatches trigger a series of responses that benefit neither clinician nor patient, let alone the implementation of national e-health frameworks.

Unintended Consequences

The socio-material mismatch between complex privileged information handling protocols and e-health tools in patient care settings is fostering worldwide research about the unintended consequences of e-health implementations (Han *et al.* 2005; Koppel, Wetterneck, Telles & Karsh, 2008; Greenhalgh *et al.* 2010; Zajac, 2010; Schiff & Bates, 2010). Theorists have begun to link e-health data-CIA shortcomings to a range of medical errors and adverse health outcomes (Han *et al.*, 2005; Williams, 2008; Fernando & Dawson, 2009). The evidence suggests current e-health system implementations can slow down the delivery of patient care and cause unintentional harm to many patients.

Research findings about the unintended and often adverse consequences of e-health, such as those reported by Han *et al.* (2005) analyzing the impact of the implementations on patients using time-dependent therapies, are persuasive. Data-CIA threats linked to e-health implementations may actually cause harm to some patients. A recent US survey claimed nearly nineteen per cent of 819 respondents had either uninstalled or were uninstalling e-health systems (MRI, 2007). Variable data accuracy and trouble accessing appropriate prescribing information are the key

problems many clinicians seem to associate with e-health systems (Koppel *et al.*, 2008; Schiff & Bates, 2010). Many clinicians are now devising workarounds to e-health systems to avoid the unintended patient care consequences linked to such implementations (Fernando & Dawson, 2009).

During December 2009 several medical organizations found e-health tools linked to a statewide trial of a new e-health system in NSW (Australia), known as Healthelink, so cumbersome that they reverted to paper records. The clinicians concerned were worried by the patient care shortcomings they experienced with the new e-health system (Staff Reporter, 2009). The media report fosters clinician scepticism about the utility of many current systems used in the NHE.

The DepressioNET service, an e-health online counselling service for patients and funded by the Australian government, allegedly published the logs from dozens of therapeutic sessions on the Internet in December 2009. The patient at the heart of the incident had searched for her name using a commercially available search engine. Internet search results returned transcripts of her online consultations with counsellors as well as information about other patients. Material published on the Internet included, but was not confined to, patients' first names, infidelities, sexuality, suicide attempts of self and children, fertility treatments, number of children, suburb and state (Scott, 2009). Information about the DepressioNET matter remains available on an international website, recoveryourlife.com ('Mystery of Life' & 'Jonboy', 2010). The alleged data breaches reported here, as well as many others, confirm clinician scepticism about the utility of e-health, while decreasing patient trust in the capacity of the systems to protect their P&S (Mansfield-Devine, 2006; Croll, 2009).

Multi-Country E-Health Overview

This chapter is informed by a multi-country e-health overview that places Australian implementations in an international context. The 'Global e-Health Atlas' evaluates international progress by country against a number of benchmarks including source systems, usage and access, and national integration and sharing (CSC, 2010). A recent multi-country comparison of e-health program analyzes privileged information handling protocols across several countries (Deutsch, Duftschmid & Dorda, 2010). Thus we sample the global e-health progress summaries, focusing on developed countries that include the United States of America (USA), the European Union (EU), the United Kingdom (UK) and Australia.

The USA

The ninth annual survey of national health information record implementations suggests interoperability barriers and clinician adherence to several clinical terminologies still hamper e-health benefits (MRI, 2007). Despite these challenges, a significant injection of government funds means lessons learned from this and other reviews may provide the foundation for future national e-health implementations (Kuperman, Blair, Franck, Devaraj & Low, 2010; Zajac, 2010). Government authorities in the USA are currently focused on developing the standards necessary in order to lead the country towards devising 'meaningful use' rules that will be applied to privileged e-health information handling protocols and so advance e-health implementations (Kuperman *et al.*, 2010).

EU

The dearth of suitably qualified clinicians with regard to privileged information handling protocols in the EU has become increasingly apparent, despite some success in implementing e-health frameworks in several countries over the years. The EU has established a forum on the Internet to help health informaticians and clinicians (some of whom are informaticians too), network, share information and browse case studies to offer

insight into real-life implementations. The 'Governance' and 'Policy and Communicating Security and ICT' communication groups on the site are particularly useful to those seeking information about actual rather than theoretical work with privileged information handling protocols across the health sector (EU, 2010).

The UK

In 2009, a review of organizational factors influencing technology adoption and assimilation in the NHS analyzed 99 empirical studies to further an academic understanding of the organizational processes and systems that inhibit or support the adoption of technological innovation in the National Health System (NHS) (Robert *et al.*, 2009). The UK work also reviewed cultural and organizational factors in the NHE to see whether and how they might differ from other organizations. The researchers wanted to understand the process of interaction between innovation and the complex organizational setting in which it is to be used. Their findings indicated that health services should assess the relevant social and material aspects of their context and the specific nature of the technological innovation under construction prior to implementation of such. The authors concluded the review by emphasizing the importance of multi-level research. These findings are supported by the findings of a recent evaluation of the Summary Care Record (SCR) and HealthSpace (an Internet-accessible personal organizer for UK patients) programmes for e-health, which was conducted in 2010 by researchers from University College London (Greenhalgh *et al*. 2010) It seems the clinical team is one of the most important organizational levels at which work is negotiated and information is communicated. The authors conclude that there is an unmet demand for rigorous, longitudinal and qualitative studies to improve explanatory models with regards to the adoption, implementation and assimilation of e-health innovations in the NHE (Robert *et al.* 2009).

Australia

An Australian study, contracted by health authorities and looking at a similar subject in the domestic context, was published in November 2009, the same year as the UK review. It was designed to provide a security and risk assessment of the unique health identifier (UHI). The UHI provides a numerical bridge to enable a national e-health framework (NEHTA, 2009). The UHI consists of a birth to grave identifying number that is allocated to each resident to provide a bridge or key for the services sharing their health information. Government authorities suggest the system will ensure the right information about the right patient is available to clinicians at the right time, so minimizing adverse health error due to misinformation (NEHTA, 2009).

Study findings from government-contracted risk assessment showed that clinicians tended to share user credentials in an emergency or trauma context to provide patient care (NEHTA, 2009). This is borne out by other research findings suggesting routine sharing of user credentials and security breaches occur in the NHE (Timmons, 2003; Williams, 2008; Greenhalgh *et al.* 2010). The National E-Health Transition Authority (NEHTA) plans to mitigate the threat by circulating a process and procedure manual to guide Australian clinicians about privileged information handling protocols in care settings (NEHTA, 2009).

RESEARCH DESIGN

The research design for this chapter mixes findings from new and emerging literature with case study data. Both case study participant groups were drawn from a purposive sample of clinicians and IT staff at three public hospitals in Victoria (Australia). Participants were recruited from tertiary hospitals in rural, urban and suburban locations. After human ethics clearance, managers passed on recruitment material for the study during regular meetings with groups of staff. Nine medical, eight nursing, nine allied health clinicians and, later, nine IT support staff volunteered to participate in the studies.

The case studies relied on the 'questerview' technique, which asks standardized questions during qualitative data collection (Fernando & Dawson, 2009). Participant interviews were tape recorded for later qualitative analysis. Audio recordings and transcripts were added into an nVivo project data base storing survey data that was entered shortly after each interview. nVivo is computer software designed to facilitate qualitative software analysis (QSR, 2003). nVivo linked the research data in order to prepare it for thematic data analysis.

Study Limitations

Study limitations are outlined here to define the variables considered beyond the scope of this study. First, case study participants are drawn from three Victorian sites, so simplifying data collection for the researcher. Only legislative frameworks relating to direct patient care were considered for this study. We exclude pharmaceutical technological innovation at the hospitals. Other limitations included an exclusive focus on non-emergency patient care tasks post admission and pre-discharge from public hospital wards. Finally, the range of cases was limited by the number of participants who volunteered to participate in the study. We assume these participants were more interested in the protocols of privileged patient information handling for clinical work than their counterparts, although the study was not intended to provide quantitative or statistical data. Nonetheless, if confirmatory, practice-based evidence were found in other work, additional case studies would strengthen the evidence presented here.

RIGHTS AND RESPONSIBILITIES

Rights and responsibilities are at the heart of all privacy legislation, but these are not always well understood. The legislation itself can be confusing, especially in countries like Australia or the USA, where a plethora of competing legislative frameworks combine to bewilder clinicians in patient care settings (Fernando *et al*., 2004). For instance, Australian government attempts to regulate health information privacy contradict state legislative frameworks. Controversial plans to introduce health identifier (HI) enabling legislation, weakening current regulatory protection of health care information, were enabled by Parliament in mid-2010. The weakened legislation is designed to support e-health innovation contradicting both state and national legislative frameworks. Clinicians will depend on this confusing health privacy legal framework for patient care until the information handling protocols are harmonized (NEHTA, 2009). Confusion about the application of e-health legal frameworks is likely to be an ongoing concern across the domain for some time.

Clinicians provide patient care in a complex, overlapping and uncertain legal context. Their confusion regarding privacy systems is magnified when one considers that both public sector and private sector health practice services in Australia are offered through public hospitals. The privacy rules are applied differently for services provided under the public sector and those in the private domain. For example, medical services in the private sector come under the auspices of the extended Privacy Act (2001), whereas in the public sector the relevant state or territory laws apply (Fernando, 2004). Deciding what is "right" is complex at the "doing end" of patient care (Fitzpatrick, 2000 p.2).

Bundled consent authorization is a foundation of privileged information handling protocols at the hospitals studied. "Bundled consent" refers to a protocol whereby health practices bundle together patient consent to a wide range of uses

and disclosures of privileged information into a single authority (Legg & Lovelock, 2007). The authorizations do not breach legal health privacy frameworks and it seems logical to assume these were introduced in clinical environments to ease the practice burden posed by the confusing legal frameworks. However, as a recent survey by the Health Informatics Society of Australia (HISA) indicates, the authorizations mean clinicians and their patients may not understand the specific health information handling practices agreed to as part of the terms and conditions of receiving medical services (Legg & Lovelock, 2007). The sites from which participants were recruited did not seem to offer alternative consent protocols to patients. Whether a fact or not, bundled consent authorizations were apparently a condition of receiving health care at the hospitals where this study was conducted.

Practice Conformance

Participant feedback about the need for practice conformance concerning about health policy laws emerged strongly from the clinician case study. Many clinicians indicated the regulatory environment for work with privileged information was interpreted differently by peers at each health service. Information exchanges were hampered by the independent interpretations.

Discussions evidently occurred on a patient-by-patient basis to make clinical practices conform to the contradictory regulatory environment. Even so, it seems some clinicians steadfastly refused to apply the national Act as drafted. This may be due to an overzealous application of the information handling protocols relating to shared patient information (Wimberley, Walden, Wiggins, Miller & Stacy, 2005). Nonetheless, negotiating practice conformance issue sometimes meant health professionals at one organization refused to allow others access to a range of health information permitted by all legal frameworks (Fernando & Dawson, 2009).

One of the clinicians interviewed for the study about the way they work with privileged information handling protocols in patient care environments was a doctor wanting to secure the data yet feeling utterly confused about how to do so. He said: "... it's a hassle ... it would be nice if there was a standard thing and everything was right across the board and [there was] a Gantt chart you followed". The clinicians' frustrations and confusion about health privacy laws emerged throughout the interviews. The evidence suggests that until privileged information handling protocols, including bundled consent rules, are harmonized, clinicians want and need to be trained as to the application of complex and confusing privacy rules when providing care, possibly in the same way as one does when obtaining a medical, driving or other license.

THE NATURAL HOSPITAL ENVIRONMENT (NHE)

Organizational factors have been shown to influence e-health assimilation into the clinical context (Robert *et al.*; 2009). Patient care tension resulting from clinician perceptions of the confusion they associate with punitive health privacy legal frameworks in care settings is often embedded into the socio-material interface they experience in the NHE.

The NHE refers to the socio-materiality of public hospital care settings. The interface is characterized by:

1. poor or non-existent training
2. shared workspaces and IT devices
3. aural privacy shortcomings
4. a highly interruptive clinical context
5. limited budget
6. pervasive use of old and slow computers and networks and
7. outdated hospital infrastructure (Fernando & Dawson, 2009).

Emerging studies indicate similar socio-material shortcomings occur in private practice (Timpka, Nordqvist & Lindqvist, 2009; Vogelsmeier, Halbesleben & Scott-Cawiezell, 2008, Williams, 2008). The socio-material interface of both office and ward work contradict clinician attempts to provide patient care according to confusing privileged information handling protocols. Accordingly, feedback about each element of the NHE is examined below.

Training

Clinician feedback suggests workplace training sessions about contextual privileged information handling protocols were of poor quality at the hospitals. Although some benchmarks exist, the training specification vacuum means health practices rely on recommendations from a myriad of sources to meet their training needs (Fernando & Dawson, 2008). The clinicians indicated that each hospital authority independently decided on workplace P&S training specifications to comply with privileged information handling protocols. The training sessions were neither ongoing nor related to practice concerns. One clinician, a nurse, asked "What do ... [the protocols] ... mean today when I'm ringing a client?" A Social Worker, summing up the views of many participants, described the sessions as "irrelevant". At the same time, doctors in private practice at the hospitals were not eligible to receive the training, further complicating an already vexed process. Clinician training is evidently an intricate logistical matter as well as a patient care concern.

Several of the clinicians reported that training information, when provided, was often presented in a written format. It was commonly embedded into contracts of employment, or they received booklets or protocol updates stapled to pay slips; the latter is presumably based on the belief that clinicians might read the material when not at work. The clinicians believed the format was unsatisfactory.

The e-health training strategies were not helpful at work should a clinician require assistance to remember how to handle the security of private information because trainers were generally unavailable or difficult to contact. One clinician explained she often felt alone when making information handling decisions. An allied health worker, she continued on to say "I have no information about how to protect patient security …" The privileged information handling training sessions also took the clinicians away from patient care work, fostering discomfort with the entire training process. Finally, some clinicians were not trained at all in how to manage privileged information handling protocols.

Participant feedback implies the organizational change needed to support e-health should be tailored to the actual information handling needs of clinicians working in the NHE rather than the dissemination of written guidelines or manuals. NEHTA proposals to circulate a process and procedure manual to clinicians as an effective risk-mitigation strategy (see the section 'Australia' above) may prove inadequate. The strategy seems unlikely to engender patient or clinician trust in a national e-health system.

Shared Workspaces & IT Devices

The subject of shared clinical workspace permeated questerview feedback, although it was sometimes incidental to specific subjects. In this study, the term "shared clinical workspace" incorporates locations open to a number of people, such as on the ward, in shared office space or at the patient bedside, unless otherwise specified. One participant, an allied health worker, commented that due to a poor planning process, clinicians trying to protect patient privacy generally held whispered consultations in passageways outside wards. Others worked in office space located in the corridors, where all passers by could see or hear patient information without effort.

Most participants indicated that "lots of patient care information" was stored on their open desk in shared workspace. The clinicians also worried about public access to bedside information on the ward. A nurse queried "… you should be able to [read your private health information], but whether your visitors should be able to [sic]?" It seems shared workspace meant that many clinicians could not control access to private patient information in the NHE at all.

Shared IT Devices

Timmons (2003) studied UK nurses who did not have access to a sufficient number of shared computers on the ward. He concluded this often resulted in patient care information not always being updated into e-health systems (Timmons, 2003). Questerview evidence indicates the computers provided to clinicians in the Australian NHE were also shared.

Most of the clinicians queued for access to an inadequate number of computers on a ward. The shortage resulted in collusion over user credentials to avoid the time cost they associated with the machines. Queues for access to the shared computers irritated clinicians and delayed patient care tasks. Irritation with the queues was aggravated by the time spent logging on and off between the various applications to paint a complete diagnostic picture of the patient. One doctor explained that current e-health systems meant "… you've got to be jumping between systems or screens and closing on and off and that kind of thing."

By contrast, an injection of government funds to two hospitals piloting e-health trials meant there were "many computers" for medical clinicians on the ward. The evidence from these participants indicates Doctors' queues were alleviated by expanding the number of computers allocated to end-user environments, although authorities had denied similar availability to nursing and allied health clinicians. The finding suggests technology reinvestment in the number of computers on wards may address the clinicians' perceptions of queues in the NHE. This is especially so if the importance of information from all disciplines is acknowledged by increased computer access time throughout clinical professions.

Shared Handover Sheets

Fitzpatrick (2000) argues paper records, such as shared handover sheets, sustain communication between clinicians to support patient care practice. The subject of "handover sheets" as they were called by study participants permeated every part of clinician feedback during interview. It seems the sheets were constructed from paper print-outs of medical records cobbled together from fragmented e-health systems to provide complete patient information upon which to base care. Clinicians regularly borrowed user credentials to log into e-health systems at the highest level of authorization to complete the handover sheets. Handover sheets provided an ostensibly functional way for these participants to work with privileged patient care information.

Handover sheets were based on transcribed patient care notes, which the literature describes as a potential cause of data fragmentation and medical error (NEHTA, 2009). Participants called the sheets "an important medical tool". The sheets were printed and circulated to all clinicians on a shift to provide a mobile paper-based record. One nurse-manager explained she printed "60 plus" of the sheets to share with other clinicians for every shift on the ward. Updated information on the records were integrated and later transcribed back into e-health applications after a shift. The clinicians believed the handover sheets saved them "inordinate amounts of time" to spend on patient care work.

Health authorities claim the introduction of e-health will address transcription and other privileged information handling concerns in the clinical context (NEHTA, 2010). Yet the evidence presented here suggests this is not case. Moves to pioneer e-health implementations are unlikely to be the panacea for the data fragmentation shortcomings discussed in this section.

Aural Privacy Shortcomings

The need for aural privacy is a legal requirement of work with privileged information. Concerns about the affect of aural privacy on patient care have emerged in the peer-reviewed literature (Sellers, Grams & Horty, 1977; Ancona, Coscia, Rubattino & Megliola, 2003; Karro, Dent & Farish, 2005). Patient stress reactions apparently escalate when presented with private information in public environments (Little & Briggs, 2009). Participant feedback suggests the same may be true for clinicians when collecting diagnostic evidence from patients.

The privacy shortcomings evidently mean some patients withhold relevant diagnostic information, while many of the clinicians interviewed for this work reported they didn't always ask questions during consultation in care settings. The oversight is notable because it signifies unreliable or incomplete patient e-health records, exacerbating problems of data fragmentation. One clinician interviewed for this work explained that teams of clinicians share her office and she can understand what is occurring in their office space while going about her ordinary business. Others reported they routinely heard and understood the telephone conversations of colleagues in shared offices despite their lack of involvement in the patient's ongoing care.

One nurse explained that despite drawing the bedside curtain, she knew the person in the next door bed was "listening to every word" of consultations on the ward. Another participant, a manager, facetiously summed up the views of colleagues when she suggested the only way clinicians could ensure aural privacy in the NHE was to "use sign language". In short, the clinicians believed aural privacy influenced patient consultations and hampered the collection and storage of complete e-health information and so medical treatment, potentially effecting health outcomes.

The clinicians' experiences suggest that irrespective of how many robust P&S measures are put in place at a technical level, people may always be able to overhear what others say. Patients and clinicians are perturbed by the threat, which influences the quality of diagnostic information made available to clinicians. Controls such as installing soundproof drapes for bedside curtains are available to ameliorate the concerns (Sellers *et al.*, 2005). We suggest that although healthcare may never be conducted in a soundproof vacuum in shared workspaces, pragmatic measures exist to protect the P&S of privileged information exchange, maximizing aural privacy controls. The installation of these controls may help to reassure clinicians concerned by aural privacy threats.

Old Computers and Networks

UK research suggests old computers and networks foster collusion in clinical settings (Timmons, 2003).. The time-cost associated with fragmented system logons were a foundation for shared user information between clinicians and sometimes extended to other health professionals. As with the findings of the UK review discussed earlier (see section 'The UK'), the socio-material interface influences clinician acceptance of new technologies in practice settings (Robert *et al.*, 2009).

Participants from the clinician case study believed slow and inefficient computers shaped privileged information handling protocols in care settings. The systems influenced clinical work, causing delays that impeded care and hampered clinical productivity. One clinician argued that slow system speed, due to the mishmash of fragmented applications stored on e-health systems, may ultimately jeopardize attempts to insure hospitals against the risk of information breaches. The clinicians believed old computers and networks were unacceptably slow and inefficient for patient care tasks.

It seems shared computers were often outdated, sometimes fitted with monochrome displays. The computers were configured with various iterations of software that was frequently decades old. These computers were slow to use and were affected by the number of end users logged in at a given time. Network speeds slowed noticeably when many clinicians were using e-health, as borne out by one doctor's comment; he described the systems as "sluggish". The clinicians commonly spoke about the "large times issue" needing to be resolved before using e-health implementations in their "busy workplace[s]".

Interoperability shortcomings exacerbated the productivity cost of establishing access to patient information, with one nurse mentioning individuals "who were literally red with rage" about trying to work with the systems. It seems many e-health applications were frequently so old that they were unable to communicate with others, even when located on the same computer. Ongoing system demands, such as those linked with screensavers requiring a password to dismiss, increased the period before a time-poor clinician could return to diagnostic work with patient information. One allied health worker explained that every time a screensaver initiated, she has "to wait for [the logon prompt] … to click up, I have to wait for it to go through a little exit thing and whatever, so it can take couple of minutes before I can even get access to anything". A few medical clinicians suggested the systems shortcomings in the NHE meant that some patient e-health records were "not updated at all", affecting the reliability of information stored there. Participants believed that e-health systems cost "inordinate" amounts of patient care time in clinical settings. Therefore user credentials at the hospital sites were frequently shared between all the clinicians on a ward.

An Interruptive Work Environment

Research finding show clinical work is highly interruptive (Fitzpatrick, 2000; Westbrook *et al.*, 2007; Schiff & Bates, 2010). An observational study by Westbrook, Ampt, Kearney & Rob (2008) found that, on average, clinicians are interrupted every twenty one minutes in care settings. Password-based system logon prompts and cumbersome information systems contribute to the time cost of many interruptions to patient care tasks (NEHTA, 2009). Many clinical participants described a "trade-off between what would be great security and what becomes inconvenient" in care settings. Thus, when e-health privileged information handling protocols interfere with end-user tasks and medical communication, the former may be avoided to ensure productivity (Post & Kagan, 2007).

Some participants complained that, while thinking a diagnosis through, P&S system demands, such as password-based screensaver prompts, often interrupted their thought processes. Others spoke of wireless networks that shut down when a screen saver triggered. One clinician complained, "the wireless system shuts down and it [the computer] can't find the [database] cell again until you log it back in again. … It just ruins the wireless [network] because it actually shuts down the wireless as well. Your password doesn't work. The wireless isn't even working until you've put the password in and … it just doesn't work so you actually have to close down the computer and reload it all back up again [sic]". These participants consequently "disabled" security tool impediments to workflow.

Participants believed machine rules on e-health systems did not correspond to everyday practice behavior. The feedback suggests privileged information handling protocols were often weighed against the impact they had on clinical workflow. Therefore, some clinicians avoided e-health P&S protocols entirely, as a pragmatic response to the highly interruptive nature of work in the NHE.

Limited Budgets

According to Boston Consulting, over the last twenty years or so, other information intensive sectors, such as finance and insurance, generally outlay five to ten percent of total budget on IT, while healthcare has spent between one and three percent (BCG, 2004). IT investment has exacerbated financial pressure on the inadequate health budgets. During 2003, Australia invested only two percent of health funding on IT while the US spent around five percent on health care related IT initiatives (Fernando & Savelyich *et al.* 2004). A renewed emphasis on e-health funding concerns has occurred recently as national systems have become more important to authorities (Moore, 2010).

In an effort to overcome financial concerns, the Australian government plans to increase e-health budgets over several years. The government is primarily concerned to cut costs due to an ageing population, increased chronic health concerns and the projected cost of providing healthcare to patients over the next few decades. Commentators do not contest the point; rather they are concerned the budget increases will not be adequate to support a useful and effective unified national e-health initiative. Despite increased e-health budgets overall, Australian investment in the system is significantly smaller than that of many other nations (Moore, 2010).

The clinicians interviewed for this work were pragmatic when discussing budgets for patient care work and private patient information. One clinician's view was typical of participant feedback about the budget shortcomings. She said "Well where you've got shared wards and also clinicians are in shared offices as well, [privileged information handling protocols] are not possible [to achieve]." IT investments and associated change management requirements magnify demands on inadequate hospital budgets for implementing contextual privilege information handling process. The budget shortcomings, which seem unlikely to be addressed in the near future, probably underpin the poor quality of IT devices described by study participants, presenting a major challenge for clinicians working in the NHE to improve patient care outcomes.

Hospital Infrastructure

The feedback from participants interviewed for the clinician case study indicates hospital infrastructure developments have been limited by budgetary constraints for several years. For this chapter, *infrastructure* refers to the physical layout of resources provided to clinicians by the hospitals for patient care. Research evidence has demonstrated the mismatch between hospital infrastructure and privileged information handling protocols in the NHE for some years (Post & Kagan, 2007; Koppel *et al.*, 2008; Robert *et al.*, 2009)

The clinicians from the case study spoke about shared office workspace in hospital corridors, with one participant's office located on the path to emergency care. Diagnostic consultations also occurred in crowded ward areas and the lack of aural privacy hampered privileged information handling protocols and so the quality of patient care information collected. During questerview, participants from two hospitals presently being refurbished described the requests they had made to senior management about the need for private, walled resources for work with privileged health information. Most participants apparently self-censored in an effort to manage the private information threats they perceived at the hospitals. One clinician, an allied health worker, said "I'm conscious of what I say ... and who's listening". It seems privileged information handling protocols were "untenable" to achieve at the hospitals, due to the unhelpful layout of clinical infrastructure.

Summary

The unhelpful layout of the NHE is borne out by the research evidence provided by the clinicians.

There was no provision for aural privacy in clinical workspaces, system demands embedded in information security tools hampered workflow, applications could not communicate even when on the same computer and an insufficient number of poor quality IT resources meant the latter were apportioned between all personnel, often requiring queued access to obtain fragmented health information. The feedback supports the notion that e-health systems are not necessarily always reliable for care purposes. Clinicians simply could not control privileged information handling protocols or data reliability when relying on shared and outmoded infrastructure for patient care in the NHE.

PKI AND NASH

By the time this chapter is published, Australian health authorities will have begun implementing a new program of security credentials. Known as the National Authentication Service for Health (NASH), the credential will be assigned to registered healthcare provider individuals and organizations (NEHTA, 2010). However public debate about adequate funding, governance and managerial mechanisms by successive governments may mean a unified national Australian e-health system, and so NASH authentication, may never actually occur. Instead, regional and local initiatives would supersede the national system (Hodgkinson, 2010).

NASH is based on public key infrastructure (PKI); it consists of a smart card that stores an UHI and digital certificates (NEHTA, 2009). PKI is a technology designed to secure private communication on the Internet. PKI frameworks incorporate digital signatures and digital certificates, which are protected by passwords or keys, to decipher encrypted data. The protocol relies on evidence of identity, generally a face-to-face check, conducted by the issuing authority (HESA, 2006). When used as designed, PKI is a robust information security tool. Using smartcard technology, clinicians will apparently insert their PKI-based, NASH-enabled smart card into a reader for access to the authorized level of an e-health system, so bypassing the need for system passwords. Anecdotally, we understand the cards will also open electronic doors and store logon combinations that are tailored to an individual's level of authorization. For clinicians, the combination of services will add value to other identification or access services that might be stored on the card.

Publicly available information outlining the similarities and differences between the NASH system and PKI are difficult to locate. It is also unclear as to whether NASH identities will be issued to teams of clinicians or individuals at the grass roots level of patient care. Health authorities have indicated that authorized end users will be issued with a NASH certificate in person, by phone, fax or mail or by using a PKI certificate, over a period of several years (NEHTA, 2009). A dearth of publicly available information about the mechanisms designed to support NASH identification processes means we are uncertain whether a face-to-face identity check, as currently required for PKI frameworks, is required for a certificate to be issued to clinicians. The incremental confirmation of identification (ID) without a face-to-face check over several years means clinicians and their patients will remain uncertain as to the reliability of the NASH system to protect privileged information handling protocols for some time.

During interviews with clinicians about privileged information handling protocols, it seems that many were familiar with the concept of PKI. However the clinicians were uneasy about the time needed to learn how to use the tool and lacked confidence in the way PKI was configured in patient care settings. They were dubious about the effectiveness of their respective IT departments and PKI implementations because the system needed to work every time without fail to be effective. The clinicians also indicated PKI passwords were routinely shared between clinical

teams that included casuals, contract and temporary personnel as well as part time and permanent staff. One clinician, summing up the views of many said "You can get an individual key and I've got my own individual key, but you can also have a group key …and so …about three or two people can use that." She concluded "…individual keys …have problems in if that individual is away or sick then nobody can access it [PKI]". Finally, it seems group PKI accounts and collusion over PKI passwords ensured that departments could function when there was a large staff turnover or when particular individuals were ill or absent from the hospitals.

The clinicians' experiences are borne out by end-user threat and risk assessment recently conducted by Australian health authorities (see section "Australia") and supported by research findings (Timmons, 2003; Pagliari, 2007; Williams, 2008; Greenhalgh *et al.* 2010). We question whether clinicians might not share the smartcards in the same way as they currently share passwords, if NASH systems are used in health. It is also conceivable that a smart card may be damaged, misplaced or lost. Logically the NASH system may be no more secure than any other technology at the point of patient care. Hence, NASH may not provide an effective protocol for confirming security credentials when clinicians use e-health data in the NHE.

Biometrics

Health authorities sometimes look to biometric technologies as a way to secure privileged information (DHS, 2006). "Table 2 Biometrics overview" is taken from Scheuermann, Schwiderski-Grosche & Struif (2000) and summarizes key features of some of the more popular tools. The table shows that even costly biometric systems can be difficult to use and require ongoing investment in maintenance costs. The tools are fairly simple and cheap to get around too. For example, the television program "Mythbusters" (2007) demonstrates how to

Table 2. Biometrics overview from Scheuermann et al. (2000) p.34

Biometric	Cost	Usability	Maintenance
Face	Medium	Difficult	Medium
	High		
Iris	High	Easy	Medium
Signature dynamics	Medium	Easy	Medium
Keystrokes	Low	Medium	Low
Facial thermograph	Medium	Difficult	Medium

beat quite sophisticated fingerprint security (Gams & Tušar, 2007). Biometric devices, while useful, do not necessarily secure private information.

None of the participants from the clinician study were aware of actual biometric implementations that had been used in patient care settings, although several knew of future plans to do so. The clinician saw "no real need" for this security control in patient care settings. One clinician summed up the view of most participants. He said, "In the end the [health] system works on trust whatever bits and pieces you've got in the place." The feedback supports the literature, suggesting that should clinicians establish an effective way to avoid biometric implementations or other P&S tools to support a more efficient work flow, they will do so.

Review of the literature and of clinician feedback suggests that combined, NASH embedded PKI certificates and biometric security controls may improve clinical workflow and so enhance actual privileged information handling practices in the NHE. Biometric authentication devices installed on e-health systems for each end user may counter moves to share smart cards or collude over access to e-health systems. The devices can also signal to clinicians working with privileged information that collusion over access to the information is not an acceptable patient care practice. Further research about combining smartcards storing NASH certificates with a biometric control, installed on e-health systems would provide valuable insight into this P&S

option, and contribute to analyses of privileged information handling protocols.

IT SUPPORT

Nine IT support staff from a second case study, drawn from the same hospital sites as the clinicians, volunteered to participate in a study looking at their perceptions of work in the NHE. The interdisciplinary nature of e-health has already been noted by some health services researchers (Timmons, 2003; Pagliari, 2007; Schiff & Bates, 2010). Despite the findings reported by Pagliari (2007) about a lack of understanding, mutual awareness and respect for each others' methods, "epistemologies, and contextual drivers", work "recognizing and harnessing potential synergies" between the cohorts is difficult to locate. The common pattern of working in discipline-based silos has supported the development of an IT environment that tends to run in parallel with the clinical user-level. Review of the literature supports the evidence from clinicians who participated in the first case study about IT support.

Many of the clinicians' beliefs about e-health in the NHE were borne out by the response, or lack of it, of an IT team to a survey devised and conducted by a social worker and his colleagues at the rural hospital site. The researchers were not able to obtain or analyze a copy of the survey during data collection, so it is not illustrated in this chapter. It seems survey findings expressed clinician dissatisfaction with the usability of e-health devices at the user level, and were evidently the substance of a complaint to IT staff, asking for further training. The clinician concerned explained that after IT had received survey findings, "nothing happened". Several other clinicians believed IT departments "really don't meet the times [sic]". In short, most of the twenty six clinicians from the first case study believed IT departments could not or would not adequately support privileged information handling protocols in the NHE.

By contrast, IT staff from the second case study consistently referred to shortages of technical resources and skilled staff throughout the interview. They frequently spoke of the small size of IT teams that were, by necessity, multiskilled. One IT participant said, "We are so small …I think everyone bogs in these days … you have to, haven't got much choice". Her views were echoed by another staff member. He said, "I haven't got teams of specialist people, they're all multiskilled and, as an example, one of my colleagues did an upgrade yesterday … half past five last night we're ringing him up to find out certain things because the documentation was incomplete". Regardless the teams were expected to support hundreds, if not thousands, of e-health deployments at the tertiary hospitals twenty-four hours per day, seven days per week, every day of the year.

The IT staff had observed shared computers on which many clinicians used stick-it notes to store passwords locally. They were also concerned by clinician responses to locked down USB ports and CD and DVD readers and writers at the hospitals. One staff member said "every Tom, Dick and Harry uses their USB to take [data] home". The same participant continued on to remark that at the hospital where he worked "Flash memories come in and people can just walk in and out with the bloody stuff [sic]". The context of the comment implies the "people" referred to were clinicians and the "stuff" was private e-health data.

Ensuring an e-health clinical setting complied with legal privileged information handling pro-

tocols was evidently hard work. One IT support professional bitterly commented "we will tell the business manager the password and they will give it to … [others]". Another participant said "… we've got to … get security into … [end users] … so it's included as part and parcel of the [clinicians'] procedures". The evidence bolsters earlier clinician feedback with regard to sharing security credentials. The IT participants' frustration with the habits of some end users was palpable.

The IT staff participants explained that their e-health responsibilities were, as with the clinicians, also interruptive at the hospitals. One said "What I am doing is not complete by itself, for many things I go back to [my manager]." Any change to a clinical e-health configuration was always authorized by relevant change managers throughout the hospitals. Staff shortages (as noted), as well as the reported segregation of many duties, ensured IT participants tended to be disconnected from each other and from the user-level environment.

IT staff described their experience of hospital processes auditing the P&S of NHE settings. Most participants believed they were more accountable to the external auditors and so the protection of physical network gateways to meet legal and funding obligations, than the P&S of clinical work in user-level environments. One IT participant said "we have policies here … we have the auditor general's office come in … Our review has found that the process in place at [the site] are adequate in all areas examined". Auditors did not review actual IT staff performance in clinical settings. Another IT support participant, when referring to the P&S audits, said they "lay a solid foundation for information security and practices … the audits are not instructional and do not affect the rules which must be adhered to by the persons responsible for carrying on security processes. IT support staff seemed to believe external auditors and hospital executives were primarily concerned to enforce legislative policy frameworks at the organizational level rather than the NHE.

The clinicians need for support with privileged information handling protocols and e-health were only a small part of IT staff responsibilities more generally. Logically, then, contradictions between the clinical work goals of improved patient care outcomes and those of IT staff at the hospitals to pass external audits may have colored the opinions of the groups of participants from both case studies about each other.

Evidence from both the first and second studies suggests unresolved tensions exist between clinician and IT support staff in the NHE. This situation evidently manifests as an e-health system that seems disconnected from patient care work. Actual compliance with privileged information handling protocols in the NHE was not the highest work priority of either the IT staff or the clinicians interviewed for this research Yet the potential for the integration of both approaches to e-health may prove beneficial to upholding private and secure patient information handling protocols in care settings. An exploration of the socio-material interaction between these discipline-based silos is the subject of our current research.

FUTURE RESEARCH DIRECTIONS

Several future research directions are outlined below.

First, case studies to analyze actually, rather than potentially, useful and interoperable e-health systems are required. Clinical work is interruptive and focused on improved patient care outcomes rather than the study of various e-health controls in the NHE. Studies that reflect and encompass clinician needs are required to provide exemplars to governments and other authorities across the health sector.

Research looking at ways to devise a workplace training matrix that specifies mechanisms, content and structure by technology, context and discipline would benefit global e-health efforts. One might examine champions in particular clinical fields.

This work would probably be best broken down into several research studies.

Further work is needed to build clinician and patient faith, and so reliance on, e-health services to improve global use of the systems. Such work might focus on professional groups or specific communities or patient groups. Logically, it seems reasonable to assume effective research efforts in this domain would ultimately relieve budget costs for health service provision over several years.

A study of various combinations of biometric device installed on e-health systems in concert with PKI implementations and perhaps other authentication measures is also required. The work would ensure clinicians obtain access on the basis of authorization rather than collusion over logon details, ensuring only qualified personnel are able to update an electronic health record. Some of the unintended consequences linked to e-health implementations might be avoided when privileged information handling protocols do not intrude on clinician patient care work.

Finally, the common pattern of working in discipline-based IT and clinician silos partly contributes to unintended patient care consequences in e-health settings. Our ongoing research in this domain needs to be supplemented by other efforts to enable an international and more detailed understanding of the phenomena in order to realize the synergies in this work. National policy strategies need to focus on and fund research developing usable privileged information handling protocols for clinicians working in patient care settings prior to pioneering national e-health frameworks.

CONCLUSION

This chapter shows that data supporting the importance of developing privileged information handling protocols for e-health to reduce adverse health errors and manage care efficiently and effectively, while improving the quality of patient outcomes, are clear. Clinician concerns about privileged information handling protocols and e-health have been published in peer-reviewed publications for several decades. Yet these as well as other concerns discussed in this chapter need to be resolved.

The socio-material mismatch between health authorities' responsibility to protect patients' rights to the P&S of health information and privileged information handling protocols in the NHE are significant. Rights and responsibilities are at the heart of e-health and privileged information handling protocols. Yet, Australian health privacy legal frameworks are complex and in a state of flux. Clinicians are not well trained to interpret these to protect P&S in care environments.

The NHE also obstructs the capacity of clinicians to control information handling protocols in patient care settings. The obstruction results in the persistence of paper records inefficient work practices, partially used health systems and shared user details, and entrenches clinician scepticism. The time-poor clinicians' experience of authenticated access to e-health systems is likely to compromise NASH and PKI security protocols.

Biometric platforms, although not inherently robust, might complement Australian NASH and other PKI-based authentication efforts and reduce the probability of collusion between clinicians. However, siloed work contexts for clinicians and IT support staff hinder integration of the platforms into the proposed Australian smart card systems. The siloed work experience is likely to confirm the tension that currently exists between IT staff and clinicians. Their conflicting work goals may contribute to some of the unintended patient care consequences linked to e-health applications.

In summary, many time-poor clinicians cannot understand how e-health systems are efficient, let alone relevant, to improved patient care outcomes. Legal health privacy frameworks, which may possibly be weakened in the future, are complex, and confuse clinicians working in care settings. P&S tools on e-health implementations constantly threaten clinician control of access to patient care

information. Participant feedback from both case studies, and supported by the literature, suggests e-health systems often present an obstacle that clinicians try to avoid or overcome in practice settings. Budget limitations, fragmented e-health systems, threats of punitive measures linked to security audits by governments, disciplinary silos and computer system demands combine to contribute to clinician e-health avoidance techniques. These techniques can be linked to adverse patient health outcomes. The utility of P&S implementations are seriously hampered by socio-material shortcoming in the NHE. Ongoing research work to understand and so address these concerns is urgently required.

REFERENCES

Ancona, M., Coscia, C., Rubattino, M., & Megliola, M. (2003). *Horizontal versus vertical development of the HCI in the Wardinhand project.* Genova, Italy: University of Genova.

Boston Consulting Group (BCG). (2004). *National health information management and information and communications technology strategy: National Health Information Group (NHIG) and Australian Health Information Council.* Retrieved 26 February, 2010, from http://www.moreassoc.com.au/downloads/bcg.pdf

Clarke, R. (2006). NSW health e-link: NSW trials of electronic health record. *Health E Link NSW.* Retrieved 8 May, 2010, from http://www.privacy.org.au/Campaigns/E_Health_Record/HealthElink.html

Computer Sciences Corporation (CSC). (2010). *CSC global e-health atlas.* Retrieved 12 February, 2010, from http://www.csc.com/au/ds/33253/33346-global_e_health_atlas

Croll, P. (2009). *Health privacy breaches and news.* Retrieved May 18, 2010, from http://healthprivacy.com.au/index_files/Breaches.htm

Department of Human Services (DHS). (2006). *Consumer and privacy taskforce discussion paper no. 1: The Australian government health and services access card*. Retrieved 17 June, 2006, from http://www.humanservices.gov.au/access/consumer_privacy_taskforce.htm

Deutsch, E., Duftschmid, G., & Dorda, W. (2010). Critical areas of national electronic health record programs-is our focus correct? *International Journal of Medical Informatics, 79*(3), 211–222. doi:10.1016/j.ijmedinf.2009.12.002

European Union (EU). (2010). *E-practice, EU*. Retrieved 23 February, 2010, from http://www.epractice.eu/

Fernando, B., Savelyich, B. S. P., Avery, A. J., Sheikh, A., Bainbridge, M., Horsfield, P., & Teasdale, S. (2004). Prescribing safety features of general practice computer systems: Evaluation using simulated test cases. *British Medical Journal, 328*(7449), 1171–1172. doi:10.1136/bmj.328.7449.1171

Fernando, J. (2004). Factors that have contributed to a lack of integration in health information system security. *The Journal on Information Technology in Healthcare, 2*(5), 313–328.

Fernando, J., & Dawson, L. (2008). Clinician assessments of workplace security training—an informatics perspective. *Electronic Journal of Health Informatics, 3*(1), e7.

Fernando, J., & Dawson, L. (2009). The health information system security threat lifecycle: An informatics theory. *International Journal of Medical Informatics, 78*(12), 815–826. doi:10.1016/j.ijmedinf.2009.08.006

Fitzpatrick, G. (2000). *Understanding the paper health record in practice: Implications for EHRs*. Paper presented at the Health Informatics Conference 2000: Integrating Information for Health Care, 3–6 Sept, Adelaide.

Gams, M., & Tušar, T. (2007). Intelligent high-security access control. *Informatica, 31*, 469–477.

Greenhalgh, T., Strammer, K., Bratan, K., Byrne, E., Russell, J., Hinder, S., & Potts, H. (2010). *The devil's in the detail. Final report of the independent evaluation of the Summary Care Record and HealthSpace programmes*. London: University College London.

Han, Y. Y., Carcillo, J. A., Venkataraman, S. T., Clark, R. S. B., Watson, R. S., Nguyen, T. C., & Orr, R. (2005). Unexpected increased mortality after implementation of a commercially sold computerized physician order entry system. *Pediatrics, 116*(6), 1506–1512. doi:10.1542/peds.2005-1287

Hannan, T. J. (1999). The Regenstrief medical record system. *International Journal of Medical Informatics, 54*(3), 225–253. doi:10.1016/S1386-5056(99)00009-X

Health eSignature Authority (HESA). (2006). *Health e-signature authority*. Retrieved 25 July, 2006, from www.hesa.com.au

Hodgkinson, S. (2010, 13 January 2010). National e-health strategy progress in Australia. *2010 Trends to Watch: Healthcare Technology*. Retrieved 3 February, 2010, from http://www.ovum.com

Karro, J., Dent, A. W., & Farish, S. (2005). Patient perceptions of privacy infringements in an emergency department. *Emergency Medicine Australasia, 17*(2), 117–123. doi:10.1111/j.1742-6723.2005.00702.x

Koppel, R., Wetterneck, T., Telles, J. L., & Karsh, B.-T. (2008). Workarounds to barcode medication administration systems: Their occurrences, causes, and threats to patient safety. *Journal of the American Medical Informatics Association*, M2616.

Kuperman, G. J., Blair, J. S., Franck, R. A., Devaraj, S., & Low, A. F. H. (2010). Developing data content specifications for the nationwide health information network trial implementations. *Journal of the American Medical Informatics Association, 17*(1), 6–12. doi:10.1197/jamia.M3282

Legg, M., & Lovelock, B. (2007). *HISA submission to the Boston Consulting Group NEHTA review*. Health Informatics Society, Australia Ltd.

Little, L., & Briggs, P. (2009). Private whispers/public eyes: Is receiving highly personal information in a public place stressful? *Interacting with Computers, 21*(4), 316–312. doi:10.1016/j.intcom.2009.06.002

Mansfield-Devine, S. (Ed.). (2006). News: Privacy group keeps tab on security breach victims. *Computer Fraud & Security*, (2): 2.

Medical Records Institute (MRI). (2007). *Ninth annual survey of electronic medical record trends and usage*. Retrieved 1 November, 2007, from http://www.medrecinst.com/07survey_press.html

Moore, D. (2010). *Australian health information technology: Rudd's options on healthcare costs are alarmist and misleading*. Retrieved 20 February, 2010, from http://www.aushealthit.blogspot.com/

Mystery of Life & Jonboy. (2010, 13 March 2010). *Thread: Depression chats leaked on web*. Retrieved 11 May, 2010, from http://www.recoveryourlife.com/forum/showthread.php?t=121759&highlight=DepressioNet

Mythbusters. (2007). *Mythbusters beat fingerprint security system*. Retrieved 11 May, 2010, from http://www.youtube.com/watch?v=LA4Xx5Noxyo

National, E. -Health Transition Authority (NEHTA). (2009). *HI service and security access framework version 1.0*. Sydney, Australia: NEHTA. Retrieved 13 November, 2009, from http://www.nehta.gov.au/component/docman/doc_download/877-security-and-access-framework

National, E. -Health Transition Authority (NEHTA). (2010). *Patient privacy to improve under new system*. Retrieved 23 January, 2010, from http://www.nehta.gov.au/media-centre/nehta-news/585-patient-privacy

Orlikowski, W. J. (2007). Sociomaterial practices: Exploring technology at work. *Organization Studies, 28*(9), 1435–1448. doi:10.1177/0170840607081138

Pagliari, C. (2007). Design and evaluation in e-health: Challenges and implications for an interdisciplinary field. *Journal of Medical Internet Research, 9*(2), e15. doi:10.2196/jmir.9.2.e15

Post, G. V., & Kagan, A. (2007). Evaluating information security tradeoffs: Restricting access can interfere with user tasks. *Computers & Security, 26*(3), 229–237. doi:10.1016/j.cose.2006.10.004

QSR International Pty Ltd. (2003, 2006). *QSR International*. Retrieved 17 October, 2006, from http://www.qsrinternational.com/

Robert, G., Greenhalgh, T., MacFarlane, F., & Peacock, R. (2009). *Organisational factors influencing technology adoption and assimilation in the NHS: A systematic literature review—June 2009*. National Health Service NIHR Service Delivery & Organisation (SDO) programme.

Scheuermann, D., Schwiderski-Grosche, S., & Struif, B. (2000). *Usability of biometrics in relation to electronic signatures*. (EU Case study 502533/8 Ver 1.0), September 12. Retrieved January 26, 2010, from http://www.cse.lehigh.edu/prr/Biometrics/Archive/Papers/eubiosig.pdf

Schiff, G. D., & Bates, D. W. (2010). Can electronic clinical documentation help prevent diagnostic errors? *The New England Journal of Medicine, 362*(12), 1066–1069. doi:10.1056/NEJMp0911734

Scott, S. (2009, 10 December 2009). *Depression chats leaked on the web*. Retrieved 8 May, 2010, from http://www.abc.net.au/news/stories/2009/12/09/2766589.htm

Sellers, D., Grams, R., & Horty, T. (1977). Documentation of hospital communication noise levels. *Journal of Medical Systems, 1*(1), 87–97. doi:10.1007/BF02222880

Shortliffe, E. H. (1998). *Semi-plenary: The evolution of health-care records in the era of the Internet*. Paper presented at the MedInfo Conference, Seoul, Korea.

Staff Reporter. (2009, 22 December). Fear for patients amid e-record troubles. *The Australian Financial Review (AFR)*. Retrieved 26 February, 2010, from http://www.afr.com/

Timmons, S. (2003). Nurses resisting information technology. *Nursing Inquiry, 10*(4), 257–269. doi:10.1046/j.1440-1800.2003.00177.x

Timpka, T., Nordqvist, C., & Lindqvist, K. (2009). Infrastructural requirements for local implementation of safety policies: The discordance between top-down and bottom-up systems of action. *BMC Health Services Research, 9*(1), 45. doi:10.1186/1472-6963-9-45

Vogelsmeier, A. A., Halbesleben, J. R. B., & Scott-Cawiezell, J. R. (2008). Technology implementation and workarounds in the nursing home. *Journal of the American Medical Informatics Association, 15*(1), 114–119. doi:10.1197/jamia.M2378

Westbrook, J. I., Ampt, A., Kearney, L., & Rob, M. I. (2008). All in a day's work: An observational study to quantify how and with whom doctors on hospital wards spend their time. *Electronic Medical Journal of Australia, 188*(9), 506–508.

Westbrook, J. I., Braithwaite, J., Georgiou, A., Ampt, A., Creswick, N., & Coiera, E. (2007). Multimethod evaluation of information and communication technologies in health in the context of wicked problems and sociotechnical theory. *Journal of the American Medical Informatics Association, 14*(6), 746–755. doi:10.1197/jamia.M2462

Williams, P. A. H. (2008). When trust defies common security sense. *Health Informatics Journal, 14*(3), 211–221. doi:10.1177/1081180X08092831

Wimberley, P., & Walden, D., Wiggins, Miller, R., & Stacy, A. (2005). HIPAA and nursing education: How to teach in a paranoid health care environment. *The Journal of Nursing Education, 44*(11), 489–492.

Zajac, J. D. (2010). Medical identity fraud in the United States: Could it happen here? *The Medical Journal of Australia, 192*(3), 19.

ADDITIONAL READING

Aarts, J., & Gorman, P. (2007). IT in Health Care: Sociotechnical Approaches 'To err is system'. *International Journal of Medical Informatics, 76*(Supplement 1), S1–S3. doi:10.1016/S1386-5056(07)00078-0

Amatayakul, M. K. (2009). *Electronic Health Records; A practical guide for professionals and organizations*. American Health Information Management Association (AHiMA), Chicago.

Australian Privacy Foundation (APF). (2010). *Selected APF papers sorted by policy topic; Health care*. Retrieved February 26, 2010 from http://www.privacy.org.au/Papers/indexPolicies.html#Health

Beale, T. (2008). *openEHR: an open health computing platform for Europe?* Presented at the BCS/EFMI Special Topic Conference, London, Sep 2008. Retrieved February 21 2010 from http://www.openehr.org/sharedresources/getting_started/government_orgs.html

Brogan, M. W., Lin, C. P., Pai, R., & Kalet, I. J. (2007). Implementing a mandatory password change policy at an academic medical institution. *AMIA Annual Symposium Proceedings,* 884. Washington, USA.

Byrne, J. M., Elliott, S., & Firek, A. (2009). Initial experience with patient-clinician secure messaging at a VA medical center. *Journal of the American Medical Informatics Association, 16*(2), 267–270. doi:10.1197/jamia.M2835

Coiera, E. (2003). *Guide to Health Informatics* (2nd ed.). NY: Oxford University Press.

Dawson, L., Ling, S., Indrawan, M., Weeding, S., & Fernando, J. (2008). Towards a framework for mobile information environments: a hospital-based example, paper presented at the *1st Mobile Collaborative Hospital-based Healthcare Workshop, in conjunction with the 10th @WAS International Conference on Information Integration and Web-based Applications & Services (iiWAS2008),* Lintz, Austria.

Dix, A. (2010). Human–computer interaction: A stable discipline, a nascent science, and the growth of the long tail. *Interacting with Computers, 22*(1), 13–27. doi:10.1016/j.intcom.2009.11.007

Englebardt, S. P., & Nelson, R. (2001). *Health care informatics: An interdisciplinary approach.* USA: Elsevier Science.

Fernando, J. (2009). The elephant in the room: Health information system security and the user-level environment. Paper presented at the *4th International Conference for Internet Technology and Secured Transactions '09,* London. Retrieved May 11 2010 from http://ieeexplore.ieee.org/xpl/mostRecentIssue.jsp?punumber=5393958

Greenhalgh, T., Swinglehurst, D., Myall, M., & Russell, J. (2010, December 29). Ethnographic study of ICT-supported collaborative work routines in general practice. *BMC Health Services Research, 10,* 348. doi:10.1186/1472-6963-10-348

Health Information Management Systems Society (HIMSS). (2010). *Value of electronic health records.* Retrieved February 26 2010 from http://www.himss.org/content/files/vantagepoint/v antagepoint_201002.asp

Karmel, R., Anderson, P., Gibson, D., Peut, A., Duckett, S., & Wells, Y. (2010). Empirical aspects of record linkage across multiple data sets using statistical linkage keys: the experience of the PIAC cohort study. *BMC Health Services Research, 41*(10), 10–14.

Keuhn, B. M. (2009). IT vulnerabilities highlighted by errors, malfunctions at Veterans' Medical Centers. *Journal of the American Medical Informatics Association, 301*(9), 540–553.

Kjeldskov, J., Skov, M. B., & Stage, J. (2010). A longitudinal study of usability in health care: Does time heal? *International Journal of Medical Informatics, 79*(6), e135–e43. doi:10.1016/j.ijmedinf.2008.07.008

Kohn, L. T., Corrigan, J. M., & Donaldson, M. S. (Eds.). (2000). '*To err is human*' IOM report. Committee on Quality of Health Care in America. Retrieved 26 February 2010 from http://www.nap.edu/openbook.php?isbn=0309068371

Koppel, R., & Kreda, D. (2009). Healthcare information technology vendors' 'Hold Harmless' clause: Implications for patients and clinicians. *Journal of the American Medical Informatics Association, 301*(12), 64–71.

Kuperman, G. J., Blair, J. S., Franck, R. A., Devaraj, S., & Low, A. F. H. (2010). Developing data content specifications for the Nationwide Health Information Network Trial Implementations. *Journal of the American Medical Informatics Association, 17*(1), 6–12. doi:10.1197/jamia.M3282

Leape, L. L., & Berwick, D. M. (2005). Five years after to err is human: What have we learned? *Journal of the American Medical Informatics Association, 293*(19), 461–465.

O'Connor, M., Erwin, T., & Dawson, L. (2009). A means to an end—A web-based client management system in palliative care. *Health Informatics Journal, 15*(1), 41–54. doi:10.1177/1460458208099867

Orr, M. (2005). The Challenges of privacy and security and the implementation of health knowledge management systems in Bali, R. K. (Ed.) *Clinical Knowledge Management: Opportunities and Challenges*. Idea Group Publishing, National Technical University of Athens.

Quigley, M. (Ed.). (2007). *Encyclopedia of Information Ethics and Security*. PA, USA.

Sellier, E., Colombet, I., Sabatier, B., Breton, G., Nies, J., & Zapletal, E. (2009). Effect of alerts for drug dosage adjustment in inpatients with renal insufficiency. *Journal of the American Medical Informatics Association, 16*(2), 203–210. doi:10.1197/jamia.M2805

Shachak, A., & Jadad, A. R. (2010). Electronic health records in the age of social networks and global telecommunications. *Journal of the American Medical Association, 303*(5), 452–453. doi:10.1001/jama.2010.63

Sittig, D. F., & Classen, D. C. (2010). Safe electronic health record use requires a comprehensive monitoring and evaluation framework. *Journal of the American Medical Association, 303*(5), 450–451. doi:10.1001/jama.2010.61

van der Linden, H., Kalra, D., Hasman, A., & Talmon, J. (2008). Inter-organizational future proof EHR systems A review of the security and privacy related issues. *International Journal of Medical Informatics, 3*(78), 141–160.

KEY TERMS AND DEFINITIONS

Bundled Consent: A protocol whereby health practices bundle together patient consent to a wide range of uses and disclosures of privileged information into a single authority.

Direct Patient Care: Patient care tasks including clinical observations, assessments of health conditions (such as progress notes and diagnoses) and treatment services (such as medication, surgery, physical and psychological therapy).

E-Health: Encompasses 'NASH' (National Authentication Service for Health) and consists of a smart card that stores an unique health identifier and digital certificates (NEHTA, 2009).

Public Key Infrastructure (PKI): A framework incorporating digital signatures and digital certificates to secure private communication over the Internet.

Privacy: Control over oneself and associated information according to legal guidelines.

Security: Refers to all administrative, physical and technical safeguards that protect information security.

Smartcard: Are tokens embedded with microprocessors to process data and authenticate end users.

Standards: Are the documented example of an agreed specification against which a series of benchmarks or best practices for a process or technology can be evaluated; often authorized by standards organizations.

The Natural Hospital Environment (NHE): Characterized by unhelpful and often outdated infrastructure resources that are intended to support clinicians with patient care work.

Unique Health Identifier (UHI): A birth to grave, Australian, identifying number that is allocated to each citizen to provide a bridge or key for the services sharing their health information.

Chapter 6
The Changing World of ICT and Health:
Crossing the Digital Divide

Prajesh Chhanabhai
University of Otago, New Zealand

Alec Holt
University of Otago, New Zealand

ABSTRACT

Information and Communication Technology (ICT) has undergone rapid change in the last decade and it is now readily accessible within many communities. This change has resulted in a revolution in the healthcare sector as technology has steadily empowered the health consumer. However, the problem of the digital divide remains and may be widening with the growth of technology. This chapter will examine how developing countries have overcome this problem by using varying communication techniques to share health information. The chapter also suggests how mobile phones can provide a more accessible conduit for sharing health information in developing countries as opposed to the Internet alone. These changes need to be embraced in order to provide a framework that will allow ICT to narrow, rather than widen the gap between the information poor and the information rich.

INTRODUCTION

The Digital Divide is a common term that has been utilised as frequently as exponential growth of technology has taken place. This term has numerous definitions, depending on the area it is focused in as well as the role that technology plays in that area. In this chapter, the definition given by Chircu and Mahajan (2009) will be used as it provides a holistic definition. They have defined the Digital Divide as "*the gap among individuals, households, businesses, and geographic areas in accessing and using information and communication technologies (ICTs) such as telephones,*

DOI: 10.4018/978-1-60960-573-5.ch006

personal computers (PCs), mainframes, and the Internet". The concept of the Digital Divide refers to any gap created by technology irrespective of socio economic status; however it is more commonly associated when addressing the difference between the developing and the developed world, where the Divide is more apparent and tangible. As the fields of technology and medicine converge, the impact of the Digital Divide has further implications in areas and communities that are under developed. The purpose of this chapter is to highlight this impact.

This chapter has three main foci:

1. *The empowerment of the health consumer.* As technologies have developed, the role of the patient has changed. Patients have become more informed and thus have access or the ability to access health information that was previously not available. The effects of communication technologies on public health, the patient-professional relationship, and society is an area of research which will be addressed in the chapter.

2. *The use of converging communication.* We examine how communication mediums have converged through the need to share health information. We also focus on how the lack of technology in some areas has resulted in the convergence of traditional methods of communication. Convergent communications through technology will also be addressed with a focus on the importance of the quality of information that can be transmitted by the various technologies and the level of understanding that patients/consumers will get from them.

3. *Access and the use of health information in the developing world.* There are a number of issues associated with developing countries that are not experienced in the developed world. Due to their lack of finance, civil strife and various other socio-economic problems

developing countries have a host of different situations that further enlarge the Digital Divide, especially in healthcare. In this chapter a developing country is defined as any country that that has a gross national income (GNI) per capita of US$10 000 or less (Mahajan & Banga, 2006).

By addressing these three areas, this chapter will focus on topical issues that are surrounding healthcare, the emphasis being that there is a technological change that is taking place which will affect healthcare. This, in turn, will introduce concerns surrounding security and ethical implications. The chapter will show that the mere existence of the technology does not mean that it is getting to the people that may require its full benefits, to utilise it in a manner that befits a community as opposed to oneself, especially in developing countries. Gibbons (2005) reports that the primary reasons why some groups have less access to information technology and resources are related to geography, literacy, disability, local infrastructure requirements, and cultural differences, some of which are not easily overcome simply by increasing personal computer ownership. Even if equity in personal computer and Internet access were achieved, this may still not achieve the goal that is require by the health sector. Providing health information is like marketing, it is all about ensuring that the correct communication channels are used to reach out to the right people on a large scale (Gibbons, 2005).

According to Kreps (2005) many of the people who are at most risk from serious health conditions come from underserved populations: populations that are generally made up of individuals who are of low socioeconomic status, possess a low level of health literacy and are members of marginalised ethnic and minority groups. These underserved and vulnerable populations often have limited access to relevant health information, especially information that is otherwise easily available over the Internet (Tang & Lansky, 2005). This is one of the symptoms of the Digital Divide. Many of the characteristics that identify those on the "have not" side of the Digital Divide also apply to those who suffer from the negative effects of health disparities. While information and knowledge are not guarantors of good health care decisions and adherence to recommended health behaviour, their ease of availability has shown to contribute to them (Tang & Lansky, 2005, Harris et al., 2004). This has been recognised by the White House, who in their *Healthy People 2010* report indicated that health communication through the use of computer technologies is a means of bridging the digital health divide (Department of Health and Human Services, 2000).

It is thus imperative when examining technology based health communication to understand who and what the communication is designed for. The goals of health promotion and disease prevention communication efforts are to help health consumers and information seekers gain knowledge about health issues and improve health. The goals of communication of health care delivery are to treat illness, maintain or improve health among patients and increase cost and delivery efficiencies (Balka *et al.*, 2010). Health communication efforts are designed to improve lifestyle behaviours, reduce risk factors for disease, and increase compliance with a medication or treatment plan, better self manage a condition, provide social support or provide help with decision making procedures (Crean, 2010). Within developing countries, the Digital Divide is not restricted only to the access to technology, but factors such as complementary resources and social inclusion need to be addressed. The introduction of technology in these communities may be seen as enabling elements, however they may do more harm than good if they are introduced without fully understanding the existing relationships and social norms in the community (Askonas & Steward, 2000).

THE PATIENT AS A CONSUMER

The theme "convergence of communications" is one that has become prevalent as technologies have evolved in ways that allow a single device to have a number of communication functions. This technological shift has not only had an impact on how businesses market themselves and run their organisations, but it has also seen the empowerment of the consumer, as they are now able to communicate and access information from the convenience of a single device. Increasingly, consumers are seen as a separate entity, rather, they have become an integral part of the production, marketing and decision making process. The consumer is now becoming an empowered individual through the use of and access to convergent technologies. This has led to a shift in the healthcare sector as patients are now being treated as consumers, and through the aid of technology, they are becoming better informed about their health care choices.

Within health care, communication technologies can be used by the healthcare provider to empower and educate patients/consumers while building a new relationship with their caregiver. These technologies have the ability to change the traditional doctor-patient relationship into a partnership. By having a more proactive role in their own health care, the patient/consumer will begin to understand their treatment plans and their health condition. This is already happening for patients with diseases like diabetes, as they have to self administer their insulin doses. By utilising the proper communication technologies, this empowerment will not have to be only for those who have various disease conditions, or those who can afford it, but rather for all health consumers.

The emergence of communication technologies and the incentives in the health sector to include consumers in their operations are some of the factors increasing the importance of the consumer in the healthcare setting (Friedman, 2001). The increasing availability of interactive information has enabled many services to be made available online. Health information is now only a button click away, with many Internet users visiting websites that contain health information and treatment options. The growth of discussion boards, bulletin boards, social network sites and micro blogging tools has allowed individuals to share experiences of specific diseases and treatments. This has introduced another dimension in to the healthcare industry where consumers are more knowledgeable and understanding of the terminology and procedures that are used in the health sector.

According to Eysenbach (2000), initially the technology had focused on development and growth through the eyes of the medical professional. This has changed and has seen the birth of consumer health informatics. Consumer health informatics is defined by Eysenbach (2000) as "*the branch of medical informatics that analyses consumers' needs for information; studies and implements methods of making information accessible to consumers; and models and integrates consumers' preferences into medical information systems.*"(p1713). As this definition indicates, the focus here is on the patient as a consumer and the technology being customised to empower the patient. Jones (2008a) provides a succinct summary on the ways technology has been developed and used specifically for patients to feel empowered in their health treatment plan.

One must remember though, that simply providing technology does not mean that a patient will automatically be empowered. Also, the provision of technology needs to occur in a manner that is accessible to a large population. As mentioned earlier, the case for the Digital Divide is that it is the "have nots" that require the information. There is a need for education in order to allow the technology to reach its full potential (Bertot, 2003). Educating users and their community about the positive uses of technology will allow users to feel more empowered. The case of the "hole in the wall" experiment as described by Warschauer,

(2002) is a good example of how just providing technology is inadequate. In this experiment, the Government of New Delhi wanted to provide computer access to the street children. They placed a five-station computer kiosk in one of the poorest slums and observed their behaviour. The positive findings indicated that these kiosks were popular with the children, and they learnt basic computer skills within 24 hours. However, the reality of the situation was that more than half the time the Internet that these kiosks were connected to did not work and content was delivered in English rather than the local language, thus it was used more as a portal to play computer games. Parents of the children felt that the introduction of these kiosks meant that their children were not focusing on their school work but rather playing games thus there was a decline in their academic outcomes. Families also felt that this decline in academic outcomes negatively affected the families' perceived social status. (Warschauer, 2002) This experiment has shown that empowering a consumer does not just mean giving them technology and letting them use it. There is a clear need for educating, and building the system to suit the community. In a healthcare setting, education needs to incorporate educating the user about the technology, about various simple healthcare concepts, and also about the power that the technology provides them, in terms of access to knowledge.

EMPOWERING THROUGH CONVERGING COMMUNICATIONS

Access to information in any sector is a key element, not only for decision making, but also for transferring knowledge from the "knowledge rich" population to the "knowledge poor" (Jones 2008b). Information transfer is essential in the healthcare scenario. This section introduces the concept of converging communications and the power that this approach has in narrowing the existing knowledge gap that exists in the developing country setting.

Health professionals, irrespective of the state of the country, depend on their ability to communicate effectively with colleagues and the health consumer in the performance of their healthcare duties. The communication can involve a simple enquiry into how the health consumer is feeling, to the explanation a pharmacist gives to a health consumer on the effects of a certain drug they may be taking (Stewart, 1995). In each case, the health professional depends on their ability to communicate effectively in order to get the correct information to the patient. In many cases however, the information that is required by the health consumer is needed well before they meet the healthcare professional. It is the old adage of "prevention is better than cure" and in the context of the health sector; this prevention message has to be easily understood by the health consumer (Jones, 2008a).

Communication technologies within the health context play an important role, especially as information flow between healthcare givers and from the health care provider to the health consumer is crucial. With the advent of various technologies however, there is a growth in the use of communication technology in consumer empowerment (Kriz, 2008). This empowerment is either self sought or empowerment that is enabled by the health system. This is the empowerment that is missing in a developing country setting, as the power of communication technologies is in the speed and updatedness of the information that can be accessed (Schilderman, 2002).

THE EVOLUTION OF COMMUNICATION MEDIUMS

From starting off as a static, one way dissemination tool, the Internet has transformed dramatically, especially with the advent of Web 2.0 which has also resulted in the growth of Health 2.0. There is no simple definition for Web 2.0. Broadly put, it is a paradigm shift in the way the Internet is used. Web 2.0 involves a more open approach to the Internet, in particular user-generated content, such as blogs, podcasts, social media, review sites, Wikipedia, and so on (O'Reilly, 2005). Web 2.0 has engineered the use of terminology such as "prosumer" to describe the fact that the traditional Web 1.0 "consumers" of information are now Web 2.0 producers of information (Doherty, 2008). Other common Web 2.0 terms include "architecture of participation" and "people-centric Web", indicating the involvement of users in the production of web content and the collaborative nature of the Web 2.0 environment (O'Reilly, 2005). Finally, the term "collaborationware" has been applied to the range of Web 2.0 technologies to express their potential for enabling people to work together online (Doherty, 2008). The question though is can this new paradigm shift be incorporated into the health setting and more specifically, into a developing country setting?

Health 2.0 has been defined in a number of different ways and there is as yet, no authoritative definition of the term. However, the various definitions together with usage on the web itself point to three distinct understandings of the term. Health 2.0 can be understood as the use of Web 2.0 technologies within healthcare to affect healthcare for the better, particularly in terms of increased consumer participation in health provision (Eysenbach, 2008). Health 2.0 can also refer to the transformation of the traditional Web 1.0 sites to include Web 2.0 tools and the provision of up-to-date personalised health care information for health consumers (Bos *et al.*, 2008). Finally, Health 2.0 can refer to a fundamental change in the way in which healthcare is delivered and conveyed (Hawn, 2009).

The next step is to see what Health2.0 means for communication technologies. The utopia of a convergent communication tools are Internet enabled phones, such as the Apple iPhone (Grossman, 2007). By placing the iPhone into the hands of the health consumer, the possibilities seem endless. Being a mobile device, it means that a user is not limited by geographic location, a problem that is faced by rural communities in developing countries. Thus in theory, the user in any setting is able to make contact with a healthcare provider, be it via the phone capabilities or through its Wi-Fi capabilities. The iPhone is the perfect platform where communication technologies are converging onto one medium. However, as it is an expensive investment, it is not a viable solution for access to health information in a developing country. The essence of the iPhone is that it is a mobile device and many mobile devices now even some of the cheaper range models, do have a number of different media types associated with them. The advent of the Google Android phone is an example of how this concept of a "one stop device" indicates the impact that the iPhone has had on increasing the capabilities of mobile devices.

The other emerging technology/forum for converging media in a communicative manner is the use of social networks. Networks such as Facebook, MySpace and Bebo are growing in popularity as well as the applications that are being attached to them. Therefore it is quite feasible that the information on the Internet will slowly start being filtered and customised for each user via such social networks. According to Surowiecki (2005, p 4) *"groups are remarkably intelligent and are often smarter than the smartest person in them"*. Groups don't have to be led by the smartest person to be smart. When placed in a healthcare scenario, social networks have the following impact. When patients are managing the same condition, their own observations are shared. This collective wisdom can yield clinical insights that are more informative than any one patient or healthcare professional will provide (Sarasohn, 2008). Social networks also have favourable outcomes for healthcare providers in that they can exchange case notes with providers globally and thus gain insights that would not be available locally. In a health setting, group opinion

has a greater impact than individual perspectives. It also allows individuals to start taking ownership of their own health as they are confident that there are social support networks easily available for them to gauge their condition (Sarasohn, 2008). Twitter, for example, is a free micro-blogging service that allows its users to send updates which are text-based posts of up to 140 characters in length. The impact of this easy to use interface within the health sector may have many positive impacts. One such impact would be the ease of informing a multiple number of users on viral outbreaks such as SARS or Bird Flu, in a simple and effective manner. This is already being researched in the HealthMap project.(Culotta, 2010).

INTERNET PENETRATION VS. MOBILE PENETRATION

With Internet penetration increasing in most regions, the impact of social networks and their form of convergent communications will be a growing trend within healthcare. This is an important paradigm shift that is being observed in the developed world but the same cannot be said for the developing world. Internet usage statistics show that despite the growth of the Internet, there is still a large gap between the developed world and the developing world. The overall percentage of the access to the Internet in Africa is 6.7% of the population. This indicates that the Internet is still limited to exclusive groups within the wider population thus excluding the critical mass (ISU, 2010).

The Internet is dependent on infrastructure. Developing countries and a number of developed countries still have dial up copper cables as the mainstay of their Internet. This requires putting up and maintaining the infrastructure (Edejer, 2008). Also, the Internet is not affordable for a large proportion of the rural and under developed populations especially within developing countries (Edejer, 2008). The low Internet penetration rate suggests that it does not in fact make it a feasible solution to bridging the data gap and whilst mobile phone penetration rates have tripled for developing countries, there is still a gap between access for those in urban and rural areas, although this gap is not as large as the Internet divide (Fong, 2009, James, 2009).

Over the last few years, mobile telephony has become the principal gateway to ICT access and use. In the developing world, many countries have skipped fixed-line infrastructure and leapfrogged directly into mobile technology. At the beginning of the twenty-first century, the average number of mobile phones per 100 inhabitants in Asia, Africa and Latin America and the Caribbean has risen by 400% in five years (UNCTAD, 2007). While developing countries are still lagging behind high-income countries in overall ICT usage and application, the marked increase in mobile phone penetration rates in developing countries especially should be recognised as a potential "digital bridge" for the Digital Divide. According to the *Information Economy Report 2007-2008* (McQueen et al., 2007) the number of mobile phone subscribers in the developing world has tripled in the last five years. The growth has been phenomenal and now these subscribers make up 58% of all mobile phone users worldwide. Despite this high growth, there is still a gap that exists between subscriber numbers and penetration rate. This can once again be put down to the urban and rural setting that plays a big role in different lifestyle approaches.

However, by comparing Internet penetration figures with mobile phone penetration figures, it can be seen that, especially in the developing world, the penetration rate of mobile phones is significantly higher than the Internet penetration rate (McQueen et al., 2007). With the increasing mobile coverage and the expansion to rural areas - something that the Internet has still not achieved - mobile technology is a more viable solution for making health prevention and medical care more effective for the world's poorest people. Rashid

and Elder (2009) found that mobiles offer the poor a relatively affordable and accessible option, compared to other ICTs. Also, mobile phones help to strengthen social ties among the poor and provide them with an opportunity to communicate in the case of emergencies (Atun & Sittampalan, 2006). Chircu and Mahajan (2009) conducted a review in which they conclude that there is little evidence of a Digital Divide in terms of mobile technology service breadth. Although this study was restricted to Brazil, Russia, China and India, (identified as the largest developing countries), a comparison to other developed countries found that these countries equalled or sometimes surpassed the developed countries' mobile technology breadth overall and in most categories of mobile services available worldwide. These findings indicate the strength and the power of the mobile phone, thus indicating that the Divide can be narrowed if the correct tool is used.

Mobile phones have now transcended the notion that they are meant exclusively for the wealthy and, according to Katz and Sugiyama (2006), they are now an icon that symbolises a conduit of trusted communication. As mobile phones not only provide the technology to deliver content, they allow this delivery to occur over greater ranges and quicker times than many other devices (Richardson & Lenarcic, 2008). Mobile phones increase the ability to contact individuals who are busy, remote or on the move. In healthcare, mobile phones offer opportunities for efficient and effective service delivery. The benefits that are offered by mobile technologies are not limited to rural areas. Privacy and confidentiality, especially in healthcare, is important. Mobile phones are more often than not personal rather than shared devices, thus it is easier for people to access and address personal information on their devices. Their use by teenagers to obtain healthcare information via phone calls has been documented as successful as they are aware that no one can over hear their conversation as they can go into secluded areas to talk

In addition to the advantages of mobile phones that have been described by Adler (2009) and Richardson and Lenarcic (2008), one of their most powerful capabilities is their ability to send and receive SMS (text) messages. Texting has many advantages over other modes of communication. As mobile phones are not restrained by cables or data points, it means their texting ability is not restrained to fixed locations. It is fast: transmitted messages are received almost immediately. It is convenient: messages can be stored in the phone until the recipient is ready to read them, or will be received as soon as the phone is turned on, thus making the message a very personal means of communication in a health sense. The cost of sending messages is also relatively low (approximately 20 New Zealand cents). Messages can be sent from mobile phones, computers and some fixed-line telephones. Messages can be sent to multiple recipients simultaneously. A report by CTIA (2009) estimated that over 1 trillion text messages were sent and received globally in 2008, with an average of 3.5 billion text messages being sent and received daily. The usage statistics and the pervasive nature of texting make it a very strong contender to be used in health applications

The text message itself is a simple form of data transfer usually communicated person to person but which can also be sent from a computer to person and vice versa. The Internet and email have some of the same characteristics but, in the context of healthcare management, the fact that the device is held by, and is personal to, the user (patient) is the point of difference (Oshun-loye, 2009). Mobility has the further potential to increase efficiency by the ability to reach the patient directly. Apart from its widespread usage, the SMS application also has many further characteristics that make it appropriate for use in a healthcare context. The 'one-to-many' feature of SMS systems means that messages can be sent to many recipients simultaneously and potentially in several different languages. These messages can also be pre-written, minimising time and effort in

data entry and communication for providers, but it also allows manual or custom messaging. Many studies have been carried out that show the use of SMS messages in various healthcare application. A study by Mahmud et al (2010) addressed the impact of SMS interventions in a rural setting and found that they provide a cost-effective solution to communication barriers in the setting of rural hospitals in the developing world.

Despite the disruptive nature of the Internet, the lack of Internet penetration into developing countries has resulted in the Digital Divide increasing. The implications of this affect the health sector, as both health care providers and health consumers are not able to access information that is readily available to their counterparts in the developed world. However, the exponential growth of mobile phones and mobile technology has seen the narrowing of this Divide as these devices are more accessible in the developing nations. The power of the mobile phone is thus in the hands of both the health care provider and the health care consumer. The mobile phone can act not only as a communication device between the two parties but also as a means of getting information "pushed" to them from various health agencies, which in turn leads to an empowered health consumer.

ACCESS TO HEALTH INFORMATION: DEVELOPING COUNTRY PERSPECTIVE

According to Whitehead (2007, pg 473) *"there is a growing acknowledgement that many countries face serious social inequalities in health"*. This Divide is more visible in developing countries. In such countries, the information poor are those that need the information the most (Prata, 2009). However, before the divide can be fully understood one has to understand the concept of equity in healthcare. Equity is an ethical concept that means different things to different people. It equates to social justice. Equity implies that in the allocation of resources, one should look at the need for the resources rather than the privilege of the people/ areas receiving these resources (Whitehead, 2007). Thus equity in health can be understood to mean striving to reduce avoidable disparities in physical and psychological wellbeing, as well as in the determinants of that wellbeing. This can be systemically observed between groups of people with different levels of underlying social status such as wealth, power and prestige. In virtually every society in the world, social privilege varies among groups of people that are categorised not only by economic resources, but also by gender, geographic location, ethnic and religious differences and by age (Whitehead, 2007). These inequalities become very pronounced when shifted into the health setting.

In developing countries, inequality is not just based on the grass root level, but by merely being a developing country it is already on the back foot. Lack of infrastructure makes even the most simplest of tasks a monumental effort. However, such countries develop systems to adapt to their situation (Morel *et al.*, 2005). The only area where adaptation is still an area of concern is in the area of quality health information. If the information is not portrayed in a correct manner, it may lead to negative consequences or lack of uptake. The important point about health information is to make it work as a trigger for behavioural change that will support healthy lifestyles.

Access to quality health information is essential, especially in the development of health education, health promotion and in any community is probably regarded as a critical determinant of health. It contributes to enhanced patient care, the development of health policies, management of healthcare systems and the understanding of health conditions by the health consumer. In developing countries, the impact of the "know do" gap is prominent (Braveman & Tarimo, 2002). The "know do" gap is the gap that is created from knowledge/awareness to action/behaviour

change (WHO, 2005). The growth of the Internet and especially Web 2.0 technologies, means this has become the universal media for publication, preservation, indexing, dissemination and access to up-to-date scientific, technical and factual information. It has become a universal library capable of extending equitable access to quality health information (Braveman & Tarimo, 2002).

Thus the Internet is ideally seen as the bridge between inequality of information sharing. However, this is not always the case. Despite its growth and the availability of health and scientific information, there are still numerous barriers that pose a challenge to allow for universal access and thus a promise of an equitable health society. According to Pandita and Singh (2008) barriers include, but are not solely limited to:

1. **Connectivity:** how to expand and maximise the availability and use of different and new media to communicate health information, knowledge and evidence to the general public. In particular, how to ensure that the information flow and knowledge is ubiquitous to the health consumer.
2. **Information technology literacy:** how to facilitate the use of technologies to access quality health information through various technological mediums.
3. **Cultural:** how to make information that is culturally acceptable and relevant within different settings and domains while keeping the end user in mind.
4. **Economic:** how to make quality health information open and accessible to all communities.

These are the barriers that affect the health consumer directly. Other barriers are: critical appraisal, copyright, local, national and regional visibility and accessibility and lack of government funding and support. With the existence of these barriers, developing countries have already had to adapt to using various traditional communication methodologies to transfer health information. In developing countries, a large proportion of the population, including health professionals, has no or only poor access to the Internet. Even printed material, such as up-to-date books, current journals and newspapers are scarce. In this situation, professionals rely on the knowledge they obtained during their training to care for patients, prevent disease and educate patients (Mouhouelo, 2006).

According to Kickbusch (2001), eighty percent of the world's population live in oral and visual cultures: cultures that learn through listening and watching, not through reading or writing. It can be argued that the Internet is heading in this direction as visual cues and multimedia are becoming more of a norm on health information websites. Crossman (1999) predicts that developed societies are embracing the visual and oral cultures via the Internet as well and that reading and writing have been, historically, an interim phenomenon.

With this in mind, many developing countries have utilised traditional media to communicate health information. The World Health Organisation (WHO) has identified the following traditional media communication sources (WHO, 2009):

1. **Using Soap Operas:** Cambodia launched a soap opera with an AIDS theme. This is Cambodia's way of shifting their focus to families as the sex trade is a very prominent industry in this country. They hope to educate families on the dangerous of promiscuous activity as well as the impact of AIDs on peoples' lives while also normalising it to show that a person with AIDs still needs to be taken care of and given attention.

2. **Using Bicycles:** In China, most of the television, radio and newspapers are controlled by the government thus it is very hard to promote health information in an acceptable manner. As Beijing has one of the highest bicycle populations in the world, the health boards have used this to their advantage to pass on health information. They do this by dressing up a large group of riders in identical clothing which has a specific health message and having them to ride together in a single file thus attracting attention (Blair et al., 2003).

3. **Sports Stars against smoking:** In Fiji, sport is a common denominator for all people and the passion for sport has become a great conduit for health information promotion. The National Centre for Health Promotion has used sports stars in an anti-smoking campaign. Their campaign slogan: "Winners don't smoke. Be smart, don't start", has used the country's netball secondary school teams as well as their relay teams as role models. The impact has been paramount with the campaign posters being visible at schools, community centres and even on phone cards.

4. **Using Puppets:** In Laos, there are 46 different ethnic groups and five spoken languages with a very low literacy rate, thus choosing the correct channel of communications is very difficult. UNICEF has gone back to a traditional medium to promote health education: community theatre. Puppet shows and theatre are strong parts of the Lao culture. Plays and puppet shows have been customised to carry health messages and have reported a high impact.

5. **Diverse channels for diverse communities:** Malaysia is made up of a diverse range of ethnicities. Like most developing countries, mainstream media is not always available in rural settings, thus their campaign is focused on using a combination of mediums to pass on the health messages. Mass media advertisements have included newspapers, television, radio, billboards and posters. However, these do not always have an effect, as it is very easy to drive past a billboard without reading it. Thus the different strategies include putting slogans on the back seats of buses as they remain at the eye level of the reader for a longer period. Printing health messages onto mugs, placemats and handbooks are some of

the other techniques used. Within the rural setting as well, workshops are run at the local communal markets on the importance of hygiene.

6. **Telephones:** In Mongolia, 85% of health promotion materials are in a printed format but these are not always effective. A very commonly used health promotion tool is the use of hotlines. In fact, a major source of information for young people who refuse to discuss safe sex with their parents is provided via such hotlines. In 2002, this particular health information hotline received 101 080 phone calls.

7. **Acting:** Papua New Guinea is the country that is most affected by the AIDS pandemic in the Pacific region, with over 45000 people being HIV positive (UNAIDS, 2009). Mass media has not worked due to the taboo that is associated with talking about sex and sexually transmitted infections. As the literacy rate is barely above 50%, print media has no impact on educating a vast majority of the people. The health ministry has gone back to storytelling as a means of promoting HIV/AIDS education. Unlike in Laos, the story telling here is focused totally on getting the message about AIDS. It is not a complicated story line and it falls in line with the traditional Wantok system of beliefs in Papua New Guinea.

8. **Using the village elders:** This is a technique that has been used widely in Africa and also Samoa. It involves educating and informing the village elders and chiefs on the importance of preventing disease through some intervention. Examples include condom use in Africa and the importance of good hygiene in Samoa. By getting the chief statesmen to accept and acknowledge these inventions, the uptake from the rural surroundings is much higher (Allen and Heald, 2004).

9. **Pictures:** Using pictures as an effective communication tool has been a major breakthrough in the barriers of understanding. Mapara (2006) utilised this effectively in Zambia as a methods of educating communities about HIV/AIDS. The impact was immediate as individuals could relate to the items in the pictures. No words were used: the pictures themselves told the story.

As it can be seen from these few but different examples, the importance of health education and promotion in developing countries has led to the development of innovative methods of communicating health information. Information is power and informing the lay person about the importance of good health practices will be beneficial to individuals and community groups. The impact of technology in developing countries is slowly becoming a reality, however the focus is still low. As was mentioned earlier, in these countries, the information poor will be the last to receive direct interaction with technologies, thus it is important to merge traditional methods with modern techniques and tools (Whitehead, 2007).

By merging the power of traditional methods with technology, communities will be empowered thus allowing for access and dissemination of health information, informed decision making, promoting healthy behaviours in the community, increased self-care, managing the demand for health services and lowering direct medical costs. Information is crucial, but not sufficient by itself to address many of the major challenges faced by disenfranchised and marginalised populations. Components of health empowerment, such as access to information and knowledge, informed consent, and negotiating skills and most importantly, health literacy, must constitute part of the overall empowerment effort. Far from being able to weigh the risks of various alternatives, people frequently have no choices. As options and complexities grow in developed countries, the health gap becomes ever more obvious on a global scale. Just as a broader, more modern concept of health includes physical, mental and social well-being, a broader understanding of health empowerment includes a range of skills to obtain technology, navigate the technology to turn information into knowledge and applying the knowledge. Health empowerment depends not only on technology but also on the ability to use the technology to access information that can be turned into knowledge in order for marginalised communities to function in a rapidly changing society

FUTURE RESEARCH DIRECTIONS

This chapter has highlighted the possibilities offered by technology to healthcare. It has also highlighted the "elephant in the room": with the increase of technology the traditional concept of the Digital Divide is also affecting the health sector. Disadvantaged populations are not experiencing the full advantages offered by technology to healthcare. There are many factors that need to be considered and these should not be focused solely on the monetary aspect. Future research in this area of bridging the Digital Divide in healthcare needs to focus on empowering these communities and using technology not as a disruptive commodity, but rather as a tool that works with the value system and social structure of these communities. By allowing communities to integrate traditional methods of communication and technology driven methods it should lead to better health outcomes. Thus research needs to be conducted to identify how communities can be empowered without further creating a divide within the community and how this will best serve the health interest - not only of the community but also each of the empowered individuals in that community.

Future research will also need to be conducted as to how governments can use existing technologies to implement policies that do not require large output on creating infrastructure that may become obsolete through the lack of use due to the lack of economic sustainability. Studies may have to be conducted via projects that are already opera-

tional in various developing world populations as opposed to setting up randomised control trials to observe the effectiveness of empowering the health consumer through convergent technologies. Tackling the problem of the Digital Divide in healthcare needs to address the two effects of the Digital Divide: access to the technology and the inequality that exists in the ability to use the technology among those who do have access.

Research will also need to be conducted on how the changing face of healthcare through the introduction of technology will initiate problems of security of electronic health communication and storage. Ethical dilemmas that are inherent in healthcare settings would also have to be researched as the marriage between technology and healthcare will introduce a new and varying set of ethical issues. Future research in these areas will only succeed in a better understanding of the full potential of technology in healthcare within a secure environment

CONCLUSION

The Digital Divide is becoming more apparent as the number of people using technology as a medium for obtaining health information grows. As stated before, it is those that are in dire need of the information that lack the resources to obtain this information. This chapter has highlighted this divide and has introduced the concept of health consumer empowerment. Empowering health consumers in disadvantaged communities will not only aid the individual; the positive effects will flow onto the rest of the community. The idea of converging communication technologies was also addressed, both in terms of the accepted view of combining various technologies in a convergent manner to provide a communication medium and through examples of how some traditional methods are being used in convergence with other communication mediums in an attempt to educate communities about various health conditions. The aim of this chapter was not only to introduce these ideas and concepts and demonstrate how they are being tackled in various areas, but also to highlight that the marriage of technology and health requires a shift in thinking when addressing underserved populations. The chapter also indicated that in this changing world, the age old problems of security and ethical issues will need to be addressed in innovative and new ways.

REFERENCES

Adler, R. (2009). The landscape of texting 4 health. In Fogg, B. J., & Adler, R. (Eds.), *Texting 4 health: A simple, powerful way to improve lives* (pp. 9–19). Stanford University Press.

Allen, T., & Heald, S. (2004). HIV/AIDS policy in Africa: What has worked in Uganda and what has failed in Botswana? *Journal of International Development*, *16*(8), 1141–1154. doi:10.1002/jid.1168

Anderson, D. G., & Stenzel, C. (2001). Internet patient care applications in ambulatory care. *The Journal of Ambulatory Care Management*, *24*, 1–38.

Askonas, P., & Steward, A. (2000). *Social inclusion: Possibilities and tensions*. London, UK: Macmillan.

Atun, R. A., & Sittampalam, S. R. (2006). *A review of the characteristics and benefits of SMS in delivering healthcare. The role of mobile phones in increasing accessibility and efficiency in healthcare*. Vodafone Policy Paper Series Number 4 2006, (pp. 18-28).

Balka, E., Green, E., & Heinswood, F. (Eds.). (2010). *Gender, health and Information Technology in context (health, technology and society)*. Basingstoke, UK: Palgrave Macmllan Ltd.

Bertot, J. C. (2001). The multiple dimensions of the digital divide: More than the technology haves and have nots. *Government Information Quarterly*, *20*(2), 185–191. doi:10.1016/S0740-624X(03)00036-4

Blair, M., Armstrong, R., & Murphy, M. (2003). *The 360 degree brand in Asia: Creating more effective marketing communications*. Asia John Wiley and Sons.

Bos, L., Marsh, A., Carroll, D., Gupta, S., & Rees, M. (2008). Patient 2.0 empowerment. In H. R. Arabnia, & A. Marsh (Eds.), *Proceedings of the 2008 International Conference on Semantic Web and Web Services*, (pp. 164-167).

Braveman, P., & Tarimo, E. (2002). Social inequalities in health within countries: Not only an issue for affluent nations. *Social Science & Medicine*, *54*(11), 1621–1635. doi:10.1016/S0277-9536(01)00331-8

Chhanabhai, P. N., & Holt, A. (2007). Consumers are ready to accept the transition to on-line and electronic records if they can be assured of the security measures. *Medscape General Medicine*, *9*(1), 8. Retrieved from http://medgenmed.medscape.com/viewarticle/549468

Chircu, A. M., & Mahajan, V. (2009). Revisiting the digital divide: An analysis of mobile technology depth and service breadth in BRIC countries. *Journal of Product Innovation Management*, *26*(4), 455–466. doi:10.1111/j.1540-5885.2009.00671.x

Crean, K. W. (2010). Accelerating innovation in information and communication technology for health. *Health Affairs*, *29*(20), 278–283. doi:10.1377/hlthaff.2009.0795

Crossman, W. (1999). The coming of age of talking computers. *The Futurist*, *33*, 42–48.

CTIA- The Wireless Association. (2009). *CTIA survey* (Spring 2009). Retrieved February 3, 2010, from http://ctia.orAg

Culotta, A. (2010). *Toward detecting influenza epidemics by analyzing Twitter messages.* 1st Workshop on Social Media Analytics July 2010. Washington DC. Retrieved June 1, 2010, from http://www.selu.edu/Academics/Faculty/aculotta/pubs/culotta10towards.pdf

Department of Health and Human Services. (2000). Healthy people 2010. Retrieved 6th May, 2006, from http://www.cdc.gov/nchs/about/other-act/hpdata2010/abouthp.htm

Dhillon, A. S., Albersheim, S. G., Alsaad, S., Pargass, N. S., & Zupancic, J. A. F. (2003). Internet use and perceptions of information reliability by parents in a Neonatal Intensive Care Unit. *Journal of Perinatology, 23,* 420–424. doi:10.1038/sj.jp.7210945

Dijkstra, A., De Vries, H., & Roijackers, J. (1998). Computerized tailored feedback to change cognitive determinants of smoking: A Dutch field experiment. *Health Education Research, 13,* 197–206. doi:10.1093/her/13.2.197

Doherthy, I. (2008). Web 2.0: A movement within the health community. *Health Care and Informatics Review Online.* Retrieved December 2, 2009, from http://www.hinz.org.nz/journal/2008/06/-Web-2-0---A-Movement-Within-The-Health-Community/991

Edejer, T. T.-T. (2000). Disseminating health information in developing countries: The role of the Internet. *British Medical Journal, 321,* 797–800. doi:10.1136/bmj.321.7264.797

Eng, T. R. (2001). The e-health landscape: A terrain map of emerging information and communication technologies in health and health care. *The Informatics Review.* Retrieved 5 May, 2006, from http://www.informatics-review.com/thoughts/rwjf.html

Eysenbach, G. (2000). Recent advances: Consumer health informatics. *British Medical Journal, 320,* 1713–1716. doi:10.1136/bmj.320.7251.1713

Eysenbach, G. (2008). Medicine 2.0. Social networking, collaboration, participation, apomediation, and openness. *Journal of Medical Internet Research, 10*(e22)..doi:10.2196/jmir.1030

Fong, M. (2009). Digital divide between urban and rural regions in China. *The Electronic Journal of Information Systems in Developing Countries, 36*(6), 1–12.

Friedman, M. (2001). How to cure health care. *The Public Interest, 142*(Winter), 3–30.

Friedman, R. H., Kazis, L. E., Jette, A., Smith, M. B., Stollerman, J., Torgerson, J., & Carey, K. (1996). A telecommunications system for monitoring and counseling patients with hypertension. Impact on medication adherence and blood pressure control. *American Journal of Hypertension, 9,* 285–292. doi:10.1016/0895-7061(95)00353-3

Grossman, L. (2007, Oct 30). Invention of the year: The iPhone. Retrieved December 23, 2009, from http://www.time.com/time/specials/2007/article/0,28804,1677329_1678542_1677891,00.html

Harris, L., Dresser, C., & Kreps, G. L. (2004). E-health as dialogue: Communication and quality of cancer care. *Dialogue Systems for Health Communication.* Retrieved 6th May, 2006, from http://www.ccs.neu.edu/home/bickmore/dshc/kreps.pdf

Hawn, C. (2009). Take two aspirin and Tweet me in the morning: How Twitter, Facebook, and other social media are reshaping healthcare. *Health Affairs, 2,* 361–369. doi:10.1377/hlthaff.28.2.361

Internet Usage Statistics. (2010). Retrieved February 1, 2010, from http://www.internetworldstats.com/stats.htm

James, J. (2009). From the relative to the absolute digital divide in developing countries. *Technological Forecasting and Social Change, 76*(8), 1124–1129. doi:10.1016/j.techfore.2009.01.004

Jones, B. F. (2008). *The knowledge trap: Human capital and development reconsidered.* (NBER Working Paper No. 14138).

Jones, R. (2008). Developments in consumer health informatics in the next decade. *Health Libraries Review, 17*(1), 26–31. doi:10.1046/j.1365-2532.2000.00257.x

Katz, J. E., & Sugiyama, S. (2006). Mobile phones as fashion statements: Evidence from student surveys in the US and Japan. *New Media & Society, 8*(2), 321–337. doi:10.1177/1461444806061950

Kickbusch, I. S. (2001). Health literacy: Addressing the health and education divide. *Health Promotion International, 16*(3), 289–297. doi:10.1093/heapro/16.3.289

Kreps, G. L. (2005). Disseminating relevant health information to underserved audiences: Implications of the digital divide pilot projects. *Journal of the Medical Library Association, 93*, 68–73.

Kriz, C. J. (2008). *The patient will see you now: How advances in science, medicine, and technology will lead to a personalized health care system.* New York, NY: Rowman & Littlefield Publishers Ltd.

Lansdale, M. W., & Ormrod, T. C. (1994). *Understanding interfaces: A handbook of human-computer dialogue.* London, UK: Academic Press.

Mahajan, V., & Banga, K. (2006). *The 86% solution: How to succeed in the biggest market opportunity of the next 50 years.* Upper Saddle River, NJ: Wharton School of Publishing.

Mahmud, N., Rodriguez, J., & Nesbit, J. (2010). A text message-based intervention to bridge the healthcare communication gap in the rural developing world. *Technology and Health Care, 18*(2), 137–144.

Mapara, E. M. (2006). *Pictures as a health promotion strategy in addressing HIV/AIDS in the developed countries.* Retrieved 30 December, 2009, from http://www.ahpn.org/downloads/publications/Pictures_as_a_Health_Promotion_Strategy_Adobe.pdf

Massachusetts Institute of Technology. (2000). *Hippocratic oath* (Hippocrates, 400 BC). Retrieved 10 March, 2005, from http://classics.mit.edu/Hippocrates/hippooath.html

McQueen, D., Newman, M., Patterson, G., Roberts, M., & Nick, L. (2007). *Mobile industry outlook 2007.* United Kingdom: Informa Media and Telecom.

Morel, C., Broun, D., Dangi, A., Elias, C., Gardener, C., & Gupta, R. K. (2005). Health innovation in developing countries to address diseases of the poor. *Innovation Strategy Today, 1*, 1–15.

Mouhouelo, P., Okessi, A., & Kabore, M. P. (2006). Where there is no Internet: Delivering health information via the Blue Trunk Libraries. *Public Library of Science Medicine, 3*(3), e77.

O'Reilly, T. (2005). What Is Web 2.0? Design patterns and business models for the next generation of software. Retrieved December 1, 2009, from http://oreilly.com/web2/archive/what-is-web-20.html

Oshunloye, A. O. (2009). ICT in marketing. Unpublished Masters Thesis, Blekinge Institute of Technology.

Pandita, N., & Singh, S. (2008). Barriers to equitable access to quality health information with emphasis on developing countries. *Proceedings of the Making the eHealth Connection: Global Partnerships, Local Solutions conference*, Bellagio, Italy.

Prata, N. (2009). Making family planning accessible in resource-poor settings. *Philosophical Transactions of The Royal Society B, 364*(1532), 3093–3099. doi:10.1098/rstb.2009.0172

Rashid, A., & Elder, L. (2009). Mobile phones and development: An analysis of IDRC-supported projects. *The Electronic Journal on Information Systems in Developing Countries, 36*(2), 1–16.

Richardson, J., & Lenarcic, J. (2008). Text messaging as a catalyst for mobile student administration: The trigger experience. *International Journal of Emerging Technologies and Society, 6*(2), 140–155.

Sarasohn-Kahn, J. (2008). *The wisdom of patients: Healthcare meets online social media*. Oakland, CA: California Healthcare Foundation.

Schilderman, T. (2002). Strengthening the knowledge and information systems of the urban poor. DFID/ITDG. Retrieved on October 13, 1999, from www.id21.org/society/s4bts1g1.html

Stewart, M. (1995). Effective physician-patient communication and health outcomes: A review. *Canadian Medical Association Journal, 152*(9), 1423–1433.

Suggs, S. L. (2006). A 10-year retrospective of research in new technologies for health communication. *Journal of Health Communication, 11*, 61–77. doi:10.1080/10810730500461083

Surowiecki, J. (2005). *The wisdom of crowds: Why the many are smarter than the few and how collective wisdom shapes business, economies, societies and nations*. New York, NY: Random House Inc.

Tang, P. C., & Lansky, D. (2005). The missing link: Bridging the patient-provider health information gap. *Health Tracking, 24*, 1290–1295.

UNAIDS. (2009). *Papua New Guinea: Country progress report*. Retrieved July 12, 2009, from http://data.unaids.org/pub/Report/2008/papua_new_guinea_2008_country_progress_report_en.pdf

UNCTAD. (2007). *Information economy report 2007-2008 science and technology for development: The new paradigm of ICT*. Geneva, Switzerland: United Nations Publication.

Warschauer, M. (2002). Reconceptualizing the digital divide. *First Monday, 7*(7).

Whitehead, M. (2007). A typology of actions to tackle social inequalities in health. *Journal of Epidemiology and Community Health, 61*, 473–478. doi:10.1136/jech.2005.037242

World Health Organisation. (2005). *The know do gap*. Geneva: Proceedings from Gap Knowledge Translation in Global Health.

World Health Organisation. (2009) *Choosing the channels of communication*. Retrieved July 1, 2009, from http://www.wpro.who.int/internet/resources.ashx/TFI/choosing+the+channels+of+communication.pdf

ADDITIONAL READING

Adams, S., & Bal, R. (2009). Practicing Reliability: Reconstructing Traditional Boundaries in the Gray Areas of Health Information Review on the Web. *Science, Technology & Human Values, 34*, 34–54. doi:10.1177/0162243907311267

Bartley, M. (2004). *Health inequality: an introduction to theories, concepts and methods*. Cambridge: Polity Press.

Bates, D. W. (2002). The quality case for information technology in healthcare. *BMC Medical Informatics and Decision Making, 2*, 7. Available from http://www.biomedcentral.com/content/pdf/1472-6947-2-7.pdf. doi:10.1186/1472-6947-2-7

Chhanabhai, P. Holt. (2009). "One mobile per child: a tractable global health intervention." *Journal of Health Informatics in Developing Countries*, **3**(2). Available from http://www.jhidc.org/index.php/jhidc/article/view/37/69

Committee on Quality of Health Care in America and Institute of Medicine. (2001). *Crossing the Quality Chasm: A New Health System for the 21st Century*. Washington, DC: National Academic Press.

Cotten, S. R., & Gupta, S. S. (2004). Characteristics of Online and Offline Health Information Seekers and Factors that Discriminate between Them. *Social Science & Medicine*, *9*(59), 1795–1806. doi:10.1016/j.socscimed.2004.02.020

Dewan, S., & Rigginas, F. J. (2005). The Digital Divide: current and future research directions. *Journal of the Association for Information Systems*, *6*(12), 298–33.

DiMaggio, P., & Hargittai, E. (2001). "From the 'Digital Divide' to 'digital inequality': Studying Internet use as penetration increases," *Princeton University Center for Arts and Cultural Policy Studies, Working Paper Series number 15*.

Edwards, A., & Elwyn, G. (2001). Developing professional ability to involve patients in their care: pull or push? *Quality & Safety in Health Care*, *10*, 129–13. doi:10.1136/qhc.0100129

Gerber, T., Olazabal, V., Brown, K., & Pablos-Mendez, A. (2010). An agenda for action on global e-health. *Health Affairs*, *29*(2), 235–238. doi:10.1377/hlthaff.2009.0934

Hargittai, E. (2004). Internet Access and Use in Context. *New Media & Society*, *6*(1), 137–143. doi:10.1177/1461444804042310

Heese, B. W. (2010) *Technology-mediated social participation in health and healthcare*. Available from http://www.tmsp.umd.edu/position%20papers/technology%20mediated%20social%20participaiton%20in%20health,%20Hesse%20(2010).pdf

Herzlinger, R. E. (2004). *Consumer-Driven health care*. United States of America: Jossey Bass.

Kling, R. (1998). Technological and social access to computing, information, and communication technologies. Available from http://rkcsi.indiana.edu/archive/kling/pubs/NGI.htm

Marmot, M. (2005). Social determinants of health inequalities. *Lancet*, *365*(9464), 1099–1104.

McCray, A. T. (2004). Promoting Health Literacy. *Journal of the American Medical Informatics Association*, *12*, 152–163. doi:10.1197/jamia.M1687

Mossberger, K., Tolbert, C. J., & Stansbury, M. (2003). *Virtual Inequality: Beyond the Digital Divide*. Washington, DC: Georgetown University Press.

Norris, P. (2003). *Digital Divide, civic engagement, information poverty, and the Internet worldwide*. Cambridge: Cambridge University Press.

Pauwels, C., & Kalimo, H. (2009). The convergent media and communications environment. In Pauwels, C., Kalimo, H., Donders, K., & Van Rompuy, B. (Eds.), *Rethinking European media and communications policy* (pp. 11–42). Brussels: Brussels University Press.

Rice, R. E., & Katz, J. E. (2003). Comparing Internet and Mobile Phone Usage: Digital Divides of Usage, Adoption, and Dropouts. *Telecommunications Policy*, *8/9*(27), 597–623. doi:10.1016/S0308-5961(03)00068-5

Rogers, E. M. (1995). *Diffusion of Innovations*. New York, NY: Free Press.

Rose, G. (2001). Sick individuals and sick populations. *Bulletin of the World Health Organization, 79*(10). Available from http://www.scielosp.org/scielo.php?script=sci_arttext&pid=S0042-96862001001000015&lng=en&nrm=iso.

Servon, L. J. (2002). *Bridging the Digital Divide: technology, community and policy.* Oxford: Blackwell Publishing. doi:10.1002/9780470773529

Tustin, N. (2010). The Role of Patient Satisfaction in Online Health Information Seeking. *Journal of Health Communication, 15*(1), 3–17. doi:10.1080/10810730903465491

Warschauer, M. (2004). *Technology and social inclusion: rethinking the Digital Divide.* United States of America: MIT Press.

Waverman, P. (2007) Mobiles, the Digital Divide, and Google Available from http://video.google.com/videoplay?docid=4640463281465283349#

Woottton, R., Patil, N. G., Scott, R. E., & Ho, K. (Eds.). (2009). *Telehealth in the developing world.* United Kingdom: Royal Society of Medicine Press Ltd.

Zhang, M., & Wolff, R. S. (2004). Crossing the Digital Divide: Cost-Effective Broadband Wireless Access for Rural and Remote Areas. *IEEE Communications Magazine, 2*(42), 99–105. doi:10.1109/MCOM.2003.1267107

Zoller, H. And Dutta, M.J. (2008). *Emerging Perspectives in Health Communication: Meaning, Culture, and Power.* United Kingdom, Routledge.

KEY TERMS AND DEFINITIONS

Converging Communications: The unification of communication mediums from many different types to a single type. This includes the joining of traditional communication models and modes and evolving models and modes of communication

Digital Divide: The gap that has been created by the growth in the use of technology. It includes access to the technology, ability to use the technology, potential gains and losses that are directly and indirectly linked to the advent of the technology.

Digital Health: The use of any form of digital device to aid, enable and monitor healthcare.

Health Consumer: Traditionally known as a "patient", this term reflects the choice that an individual now has when it comes to healthcare. The choice is not limited to choice of physician but includes the ability to use the wisdom of the crowd (crowd source) in self-care.

M-Health: The use of mobile phones to communicate and access information that pertains to health. It is also the use of mobile phones to aid in healthcare delivery, education, promotion and recovery.

Technology Mediated Social Networks: The use of technology, such as the Internet, mobile phones, radio devices to form a community of peers that engage in information exchange. The peers are not limited to being experts in any given area rather they use their own experiences as an information source.

Underserved Communities: Communities that suffer from the lack of infrastructure, access to information and access to education that is otherwise regarded as norm for a community to have. This is not restricted to developing countries but is applicable to any country.

Chapter 7
The Socio–Ethical Considerations Surrounding Government Mandated Location–Based Services during Emergencies:
An Australian Case Study

Anas Aloudat
University of Wollongong, Australia

Katina Michael
University of Wollongong, Australia

ABSTRACT

The adoption of mobile technologies for emergency management has the capacity to save lives. In Australia in February 2009, the Victorian bushfires claimed 173 lives, the worst peace-time disaster in the nation's history. The Australian government responded swiftly to the tragedy by going to tender for mobile applications that could be used during emergencies, such as mobile alerts and location services. These applications have the ability to deliver personalized information direct to the citizen during crises, complementing traditional broadcasting mediums like television and radio. Indeed governments have a responsibility to their citizens to safeguard them against both natural and human-made hazards, and today, national security has grown to encapsulate such societal and economic securitization. However, some citizens and lobby groups have emphasized that such breakthrough technologies need to be deployed with caution as they are fraught with ethical considerations, including the potential for breaches in privacy, security, and trust.

DOI: 10.4018/978-1-60960-573-5.ch007

INTRODUCTION

The aim of this chapter is to present a case study on how modern technologies, namely mobile applications, are changing the landscape of emergency management in Australia. The chapter begins by providing a general overview of emergency management and location-based services and then specifically places the reader in an Australian context by describing recent trends in emergency response, especially post the Victorian Bushfires of February 2009. The introduction of new warning and alerting methods and techniques will be a critical element in securing the nation against diverse natural hazards such as bushfires and floods. In today's modern age of technological innovation, it is difficult to comprehend how 173 persons perished and 414 persons were injured during the Black Saturday crisis, partly as a result of accessibility to timely and relevant information on how to respond to the emergency.

The recently deployed national emergency warning system (NEWS), as well as future "location-enabled" components, will be discussed before socio-ethical considerations are explored. It is anticipated that NEWS will force amendments to the *Telecommunications Act 1997*; an issue that was first tabled by the Australian Federal Government. With the pending introduction of such advanced technologies, it was also deemed that the regulations governing the use of the Integrated Public Number Database (IPND) also be reviewed. The IPND grants some government agencies access to Australia-wide consumer telecommunications details during emergencies and is maintained by one commercial mobile operator but may need to be accessed by more than one commercial entity during an emergency.

There are thus a number of socio-ethical considerations which need to be taken into account when reviewing both regulation and legislation in this domain. Despite the potential for breaches in privacy, mobile technologies and specifically location-based services offer a state-of-the art solution to the age old problem of personalized information dissemination based on context. Where a new technology can act as a life-sustaining tool, privacy issues are generally considered less important and wholly overshadowed by issues related to trust. Very few people would opt not to disclose their real-time physical location in the name of privacy, if it meant that they could survive a natural disaster. What is of greater concern to the success of an emergency service offering however, is that users can trust the technology, can trust the supplier of the service, and can trust that the accuracy, reliability and timeliness of the communicated message during a crisis. The findings of the study demonstrate that location-based services are a plausible solution to emergency management problems in Australia and that the benefits to citizens of using such innovations during natural disasters are clear. This does not mean however that government mandated services to citizens are not without their specific risks.

EMERGENCY MANAGEMENT IN AUSTRALIA

Defining Natural and Human-Made Hazards

Managing emergencies with regard to their socially-constructed context is one of the reasons that has led Australia to adopt the all-hazards approach in responding to risks associated with physical phenomena (Templeman & Bergin, 2008). A hazard is any source of potential harm or a situation with a potential to cause loss (Emergency Management Australia, 2004b). Emergency Management Australia (EMA) defines many types of hazards, which are broadly classified. Most of the known hazards are considered natural because they have their origins in the surrounding natural environment. Examples include bushfires, floods, cyclones, tsunamis, landslides, windstorms and earthquakes. Several other hazards are identified

Table 1. Hazard types

Hazard Classification	Types
Natural hazard	Bushfires, Cyclones, Earthquakes, Floods, Hurricanes, Land gales, Landslides, Mudslides, Storm surges, Tidal waves, Torrential rain, Tsunamis
Technological hazards	Blackouts or main power failures, Explosions, Mining or industry incidents, Pollution, Smog, Transportation incidents, Urban structure fires
Chemical, biological and radiological hazards	Chemical emissions, Epidemics / Pandemics, Exotic animal diseases, Insect or vermin plagues, Toxic spills
Social in origin hazards	Civil unrests, Hijackings, Riots, Sabotage, Shooting Massacres, Sieges, Terrorism

as technological, which are the result of failures in human-made systems and services, or are the outcome of human actions. For example, these include urban structure fires, explosions, and transportation incidents. Some hazards are classified as chemical, biological or radiological due to their specific origin. Some examples of these are toxic material releases, human epidemics and pandemics, exotic animal diseases, and insect and vermin plagues. Remaining hazards can be classified as social in origin, which include civil unrests and acts of violence such as riots, sieges, shooting massacres, hijackings, sabotage and terrorism (Emergency Management Australia, 2008). Table 1 summarizes the different types of hazards.

Throughout history, communities have battled hazards and responded to emergencies with the commensurate technology available to them. Organized attempts to counter emergencies, however, did not occur until much later in modern times (Haddow, Bullock, & Coppola, 2006). These attempts have evolved from simple precautions and scattered actions into systematized and sophisticated policies, programs and applications that include preparedness, response, mitigation, recovery and protection strategies (Canton, 2007). Modern emergency management (EM) could be defined as the discipline dealing with risk and risk avoidance and primarily concerned with developing and improving arrangements and programs that contribute to the goal of a safer, more sustainable community (Haddow, Bullock, & Coppola, 2006).

Emergencies in Australia

The Commonwealth of Australia covers a land mass of approximately 7,692 million square kilometers with a population of about 22 million. Around 85 percent of the population live in cities within 50 kilometers of the coast, where much of the country's commercial and industrial activity takes place (Australia.gov.au Website, 2010). Australia is divided into six States and two Territories. Each State or Territory has its own government, legislature and constitution. The legislature of Australia comprises a bicameral federal parliament, with a Prime Minister and Cabinet (PM&C).

As a physically large country with a diverse climate and geographic landscape, Australia experiences many types of hazards on a regular basis (Boughton, 1998). In addition, communities across Australia continue to settle into hazard-prone areas, particularly in coastal and river valley regions, exposing themselves to risks from a variety of sources including cyclones, floods and bushfires (The Victorian Bushfires Royal Commission, 2009). Even in regional areas, and as a result of inadequate risk assessments and mitigation actions, transport infrastructure, such as road and rail links, are usually flooded annually, which cause disruption to the carriage of commodities for communities and business, and the supply of materials for industry (The Australian Government: Department of Transport and Regional Services, 2004).

Reliable information on the frequency of emergencies and disasters in Australia extends only from 1967; nonetheless, the number of events has shown an upward trend in frequency over the last 20 years (The Victorian Bushfires Royal Commission, 2009). The same trend is noted worldwide both in the developed and developing countries, caused by several factors including an increase in human activities in hazard-prone areas, military conflicts and climate change (Coyle & Meier, 2009; United Nations News Centre, 2010). Despite that the frequency of emergencies and the numbers of people who live or work in risk-prone areas have increased in Australia, deaths per 100,000 population have continued to fall due to better emergency management policies, arrangements and applications (The Australian Government: Department of Transport and Regional Services, 2004).

Emergency Management Arrangements in Australia

Under Australia's constitutional arrangements, the country takes a Federal approach to emergency management in which the local, state and territory governments have responsibility within their own jurisdiction and have the laws, funding mechanisms and organizational arrangements in place to deal with emergencies. Each sphere of government has a different set of roles and responsibilities for emergency planning, preparedness and mitigation in relation to land, property and the environment, assets and infrastructures, agencies and programmes (Emergency Management Australia, 2009a).

Given that individual States and Territories are highly autonomous, the approach to emergency planning and alerting in Australia is not standardized (The Australian Government: Department of Transport and Regional Services, 2004). Nonetheless, there are similarities in approach that have emerged between states. For example, should a state of emergency be declared, a state-level emergency/disaster response and coordination committee/executive acts as the interface responsible for coordinating the state resources, seeking Commonwealth support if needed, and providing up-to-date reports to the media (Victorian State Parliamentary Offices, 2003). When activated, the committee is mainly responsible for:

1. Information collection, analysis and dissemination of intelligence to emergency response agencies;
2. Coordination of the provision of resources required by divisional emergency response coordinators;
3. Allocation of resources on a priority basis;
4. Requesting Commonwealth physical resources;
5. Briefing the Coordinator in Chief; and
6. Dissemination of information to the media and general public (The Victorian Bushfires Royal Commission, 2009).

The level of emergency response coordination depends on the scope of the emergency. In the first instance, the response to an emergency takes place at the municipal level. If the emergency calls for resources beyond those available at the municipal level, the emergency response coordination is stepped up to the divisional level. An emergency that extends beyond the division will be progressed to the State level (The Victorian Bushfires Royal Commission, 2009).

Although the prime responsibility for the protection of life, property and the environment rests with the states and territories, the Commonwealth Government is strongly committed to supporting local and state governments in developing their capacity for dealing with emergencies and disasters, providing physical assistance and mobilizing resources to States or Territories when they cannot reasonably cope during large-scale events (Emergency Management Australia, 2009a). On the national level, the basis for managing major emergencies and combating disasters is a partnership between the Federal, State and Territory, Local Governments, the community, and the private sector. Accordingly, this national framework for emergency management requires a high level of collaboration and coordination across all spheres of government, and with other non-government stakeholders as well (Emergency Management Australia, 2009a).

Emergency Management Committees and Organizations in Australia

Emergency and disaster management committees and organizations exist at National and State/Territory levels in Australia with specific responsibilities for local governments within their jurisdiction. The main emergency management bodies in Australia include:

1. **The Commonwealth Counter Disaster Task Force:** A senior interdepartmental committee, chaired by the Department of the Prime Minister and Cabinet. It is the peak Commonwealth body with emergency management responsibilities composed of representatives of Commonwealth Government departments and agencies with a significant role to play in the provision of disaster relief or rehabilitation assistance. On the advice of the Director General of the Emergency Management Australia (EMA) agency, the Chair may activate the committee during the response and recovery phase of a disaster in support of EMA's activities (Emergency Management Australia, 2004a).

2. **The Australian Emergency Management Committee:** Australia's principal consultative emergency management forum. It is chaired by the Director General of EMA, and comprises chairpersons and executive officers of State and Territory emergency management committees. The Committee meets bi-annually to provide advice and direction on the coordination and advance-

ment of Commonwealth and State interests related to emergency management issues. As required, it establishes working parties to examine particular issues (Emergency Management Australia, 2004a).

3. **The State and Territory Emergency/ Disaster Management Organizations:** Each State and Territory has established a committee of senior members of appropriate departments and agencies to consider emergency management matters. The names and functions of these organizations differ from State to State, but they are responsible for ensuring that proper plans and arrangements are made at State or Territory and local government level, to alert the public to and deal with emergencies and disasters (Emergency Management Australia, 1996).

4. **Emergency Management Australia (EMA):** The Federal agency through which the Attorney-General exercises the responsibility of providing national leadership in the development of emergency management measures to reduce the impact of emergencies on the Australian community (Emergency Management Australia, 2004b). EMA is mainly responsible for shaping and advancing emergency management strategies and policies throughout Australia, advocating emergency management education, and assisting state and territory local emergency management agencies. EMA also plays a key role in coordinating interstate and international assistance at times of major emergencies and disasters (Emergency Management Australia, 2004b). EMA has an established collaborative relationship with other Commonwealth agencies such as the Department of Finance and Administration, Geoscience Australia and the Bureau of Meteorology. In doing so, EMA seeks to encourage an all hazards, all agencies approach to the prevention or mitigation of emergencies, preparedness for their impact,

response to that impact and recovery from the consequences (Emergency Management Australia, 2009b).

5. **Other committees and organizations exist at the State level in Australia.** The names and functions of these organizations and committees differ from State to State but there are similar patterns that have been developed between them in regard to their roles and functions that include the identification of various threats and hazards, the coordination of volunteers and community resources during significant emergency events, hazard management guidelines, declaration of state of emergency, emergency management training and education, and the arranging of warnings in emergencies to the public (The Australian Government: Department of Transport and Regional Services, 2004).

An All-Hazards Approach to National security in Australia

The Changing Face of Emergency Management

Until recently emergencies were quantified in terms of the loss of life, extent of damage, or based on an event's physical attributes (Emergency Management Australia, 2004b). Emergencies have been traditionally associated to the notion of a "disaster" when the number of casualties and the allocated resources to a given event have been high (Canton, 2007). More contemporary viewpoints, especially from the social sciences have begun to question the validity of traditional classification schemes that have long defined emergencies and disasters or distinguished them according to their origin or scale. Social studies started to perceive these events as social constructions, defined by the nature and the volume of their impact on social systems (Perry, 2007; Quarantelli, 1986; Rosenthal, 1998).

The focus in understanding emergencies has now shifted toward the actual situation created by such phenomena, rather than simply considering the physical attributes that caused them (Emergency Management Australia, 2004b). This shift has come as a result of a growing realization that although there are many different types of emergency events, whether natural- or human-caused, they all have comparable capacity to bring social, economic, environmental and political consequences on the communities they impact (Buzan, Wver, & Wilde, 1998; Rosenthal, 1998). Thus an emergency impacts the organization of human communities and can be thought of only within a larger framework involving the society as a whole (Gilbert, 1998). It is what has caused a redefinition of national security to incorporate large-scale emergencies, and not just things to do with the military. How a government responds to a large scale emergency today has as much to do with national security as traditional security-centric actions like border control. Yet while the government aims to protect the well-being of its citizenry through blanket coverage technologies such as location-based services, they still need to maintain an individual-level of consent. For example, the government's adoption of sophisticated unmanned aerial vehicles (UAVs) to keep out illegal immigrants is very different to the government communicating with citizens via their personal mobile phones, especially when an entity's real-time location can be determined.

The Comprehensive and Integrated Approaches

Australia has adopted both a comprehensive and integrated all-hazards approach to the development of its arrangements and programs. The approach can be summarized as follows.

Under the comprehensive approach there is a general acknowledgment that a potential threat could originate from various types of hazards which have a comparable capacity to impact severely on communities and infrastructure. The all hazards approach to emergency management involves a recognition that most emergency event types cause similar problems and that many of the measures required to deal with them are generic (The Victorian Bushfires Royal Commission, 2009). Australia's comprehensive approach to emergency management identifies four strategies that contribute to the reduction or elimination of hazards, and an increase in community and environmental resilience. EMA (2004b) defines these strategies as follows:

1. **Prevention/mitigation**: Seek to eliminate or reduce the impact of hazards and/or to increase the resilience of the community subject to the impact of those hazards.
2. **Preparedness:** Concerned with establishing arrangements and plans and with providing education and information so as to prepare the community to deal with emergencies and disasters as they may arise.
3. **Response:** Covers the methods that are used to properly activate the preparedness arrangements and plans so as to deal with emergencies and disasters if and when they occur.
4. **Recovery:** Defines the set of arrangements practiced to assist a community affected by an emergency or disaster in reconstruction of the physical infrastructure and restoration of emotional, social, economic and physical well-being.

These emergency management strategies, although tightly related, could be developed independently of each other (Haddow, Bullock, & Coppola, 2006). Nonetheless, under the comprehensive approach to emergency management there is an emphasis that all of the activities, under these strategies, should effectively function as one seamless emergency management framework

(Emergency Management Australia, 2004b; Haddow, Bullock, & Coppola, 2006).

The integrated approach emphasizes the need to coordinate different emergency management programs and strategies with the support of other government agencies, and with the community and the private sector (Emergency Management Australia, 2004b). For the comprehensive approach to emergency management to be workable there should be effective arrangements for the coordination of the activities of governments and of the large number of organizations that need to be involved in emergency management activities. These arrangements need to be set within a legislative and public policy framework (Emergency Management Australia, 2004b). It therefore follows that technological solutions deployed to protect citizens also need to be set within a legislative and public policy framework. The problem however with "emergencies", whether they are natural or human-made is that they strike with little warning, if any, and therefore the deployment of specific technologies during a given emergency (e.g. with the requirement for access of citizenry personal data) undergoes limited discussion.

THE EMERGENCE OF LOCATION-BASED SERVICES SOLUTIONS

What are Location-Based Services?

Location-based services (LBS) are also known as location-dependent services, location-related services, location-enabled services, location-sensitive services and location services. See for example the definitions given by Hjelm (2002), Jensen (2002), Holma et al. (2004), Lopez (2004), Spiekermann (2004), Bernardos et al. (2007) and Uhlirz (2007). Küpper (2005) has previously noted this and argued that one possible reason for terms being used interchangeably is that the character and appearance of LBS have been specified and implemented by different communities and industries, especially in the telecommunications sector and the ubiquitous computing area for a variety of applications. In the context of LBS, *location* always refers to a spatial geographical location that is associated with a physical point or region relative to the surface of the Earth (Dawson, Winterbottom, & Thomson, 2007). Accordingly, LBS are classified as a subset of a larger set called context-aware services, which are electronic services that automatically adapt their behavior (e.g. filtering or presenting information) to one or more parameters (time, location, identity or activity) so as to reflect the context (personal, technical, spatial, social, or physical) of a target (person, animal or object) (Küpper, 2005).

LBS as a concept denotes applications that utilize the available geographic location information of a target device, being fixed, handheld, wearable or implantable, in order to add value to the provided service (Perusco & Michael, 2007; The 3rd Generation Partnership Project, 2009). Astroth (2003) defines a LBS as "any application that offers information, communication, or a transaction that satisfies the specific needs of a user in a particular place." Harvey (2008) simply defined LBS as "technologies that add geographical functions to other technologies." Gruber and Winter (2002) argued that a LBS is "any value-added service that takes into account a mobile agent's actual location." Shiode et al. (2002) delineate LBS as "services that provide geographically-orientated data and information services to users across mobile telecommunication networks."

Samsioe and Samsioe (2002) assert however that an electronic service that has location capabilities, should be able to fulfill the following three separate activities to be accurately defined as a LBS:

1.   Estimate the location of the device;

2.   Produce a service based on the estimated location; and

3.   Deliver the location-enhanced service to that device.

Based on Samsioe and Samsioe (2002), this strict definition excludes several services that employ location technologies in mobile telecommunications networks such as the cell broadcasting service, since these services cannot change their content when the physical location of a mobile handset changes. However, in the emergency management context, it should be understood that any service that provides information pertinent to the current location of the active mobile handset at a specific period of time can be viewed as a location-based service, regardless of the underlying delivery technology used to convey its information. Although this interpretation may extend to other types of services as well, it is nonetheless, an understanding that harmonizes several different forms of LBS such as those depicted by Holma et al. (2004), Grothe et al. (2005), Guan et al. (2007), Oh and Haas (2007), Stojanović et al. (2007) and Aitenbichler (2008).

The text-based message is the most realized form of LBS, but there are several other possible forms where the service could be received as a bitmap image, voice message, multimedia message (with rich content such as animated image formats), interactive maps or video. However, the final form of the delivered LBS depends on several factors that include existing and dedicated network resources, underlying technologies and protocols, market trends and handset capabilities/ limitations (Spiekermann, 2004).

Operational and Non-Operational Stakeholders

Effective deployment of location-based services requires the coordinated effort of multiple stakeholders in the services value chain, each of which provide specific components of the total solution (Astroth, 2003). A stakeholder represents an autonomous entity like a person, a company or an organization, each maintaining or performing one or several roles that characterize either the interests or functions it fulfils from a technical perspective, or the impact it exercises on LBS from an economic or regulatory position (Küpper, 2005).

Roles of LBS stakeholders can be classified as operational and non-operational. The operational roles define the players that cooperate during the operation of the service, which requires each stakeholder to maintain technical infrastructure, ranging from users' mobile handsets to service providers' farm servers to carrier's telecommunications networks, so as to facilitate the request and the provision of sub-services during LBS execution (Küpper, 2005). During an LBS operation, the interaction between these actors takes place through reference points that are defined by a set of protocols and connectivity services offered by various networks, and often determined by Service Level Agreements (SLAs). SLAs are agreed upon and adopted between the participating parties, prior to the provisioning of the services, for fixing quality of service and accounting conditions (Küpper, 2005). With so many stakeholders involved in a single LBS offering, upkeeping locational privacy is not easy. This is where industry level guidelines, contractual agreements between stakeholders, or even company level codes of conduct can play a pivotal role in protecting citizen rights.

A non-operational stakeholder is the one that does not directly engage in the technical operation of LBS but has an indirect impact on the services, either by dictating economic or regulatory circumstances of LBS operation or through the influence it exercises on the adoption of technical service standards (Küpper, 2005). An example from the Australian context could be Australian Communications and Media Authority (ACMA) which exercises a direct influence in regulating (by law) the utilization of location data to protect the privacy of individuals and for other purposes

such as lawful interception (The Australian Communications and Media Authority, 2004).

Location-Based Emergency Services in Mobile Networks

Emergency services represent one of the most obvious application areas where the deployment of location technology makes sense (Küpper, 2005). Still, location-based emergency services are in their infancy in several countries around the world including Australia (Küpper, 2005). One reason for this, beyond the socio-ethical issues are technical problems, including location determination mechanisms and accuracy standards, and also issues related to identifying different requirements for emergency systems which have yet to be fully resolved (The European Telecommunications Standards Institute, 2010; Togt, Beinat, Zlatanova, & Scholten, 2005)

In general, there are two types of location-based emergency service applications in mobile telecommunications networks (The European Telecommunications Standards Institute, 2006a). The first is initiated by a person in the form of a phone call or a distress Short Message Service (SMS) in a life-threatening or time-critical situation. The second type is initiated usually by the government in collaboration with telecommunications carriers, in which safety alerts and early warning messages are disseminated (pushed) to all active mobile handsets located in designated threatened area(s) before, during or after a large-scale event. The fundamental idea behind the first type of location-based emergency service application is for of an emergency service organization (ESO) (i.e. police force, fire brigade or ambulance service) to reach the caller (or the message sender) with some precision, based on the location information provided by the caller's mobile service provider. In many cases the person will be unable to communicate his or her current location or simply does not know it, so the ESO relies on handset data (Küpper, 2005). The prem-

137

ise behind the second type of emergency service application is to utilize the mobile handset as an additional information channel that is capable of reaching people wherever they are but within the threatened area.

EMERGENCY WARNING AND ALERTING METHODS IN AUSTRALIA

Traditional Warning and Alert Systems

Under emergency management arrangements in Australia, one of the main responsibilities of the government is to communicate and disseminate warnings and safety information to the general public in case of a large-scale emergency (The Australian Government: Department of Transport and Regional Services, 2004). In principle, any means of ensuring that a warning is quickly disseminated to those actually or potentially affected should be used. However, conventional broadcasting systems consisting primarily of local community radio stations and television networks are still the main channels that are currently used for disseminating alerts and warnings to the Australian public (Betts, 2003).

Australians also rely on several other sources of information, including relevant government websites and hotlines, to stay updated with the latest news about events as they unfold. In addition, traditional warning methods are used across the country including banners, door-to-door knocking and signage. Australia also still relies on what are known as triggers, such as the standard emergency warning signal (SEWS) and associated sirens, which are merely techniques prompting the audience to listen carefully for a warning and/ or to search for more information (The Victorian Bushfires Royal Commission, 2009).

Modern Warning and Alert Systems: The Short Message Service and Beyond

Other means and methods such as emails, landline and mobile phone calls, and short message service (SMS) have also been considered or used. For example, Telstra (the incumbent telecommunications operator) partnered with the state of Victoria in 2005, to trial the Community Information Warning System (CIWS) that was able to simultaneously telephone every household in a designated area. More than 660 calls were made, on an opt-in basis, to the residents of one specific area who had volunteered to participate in the trial (The Minister for Police and Emergency Services, 2005).

In 2007, SMS and email alerts were considered by the Victorian State Government for the purpose of geographically targeting people in specified areas with information about terror attacks or natural disasters (Dunn & Collier, 2007). In the same year, the New South Wales Premier proposed a warning system for metropolitan Sydney whereby residents could opt-in to real time Government SMS and email air pollution health alerts. The proposal came in response to key recommendations from a Parliamentary air quality inquiry in 2006, which warned that 1600 people were dying every year from air pollution related illness in New South Wales. This project was under the Department of Environment authority (Benson, 2007). The New South Wales Government also proposed an electronic warning system that, in principle, should have allowed ESOs, such as Police, Fire and Ambulance services, to send SMS alerts to all mobile handsets in terrorism or emergency target zones across the State. The design concept identified the system's need to be operable across all telecommunications carrier networks operating in Australia, and was to provide evacuation information, safety advice and alternate routes to avoid the emergency area (The Australian, 2007).

A similar system is now active in Sydney, New South Wales. The SydneyAlert system is a free, opt-in service that is meant to alert the general public in the event of an emergency in the Sydney and North Sydney Central Business Districts (CBDs). The system provides building managers, emergency wardens and security staff with safety information and instructions to help them manage and assist occupants, staff and others in their buildings during a serious incident. The system uses existing commercial communications networks to disseminate warnings, specifically SMS and e-mail. The State Emergency Operations Centre Controller, a senior NSW Police Officer, is the authority that determines if the system should be activated. This officer also determines who on the subscription list is contacted and what message is sent. The message is sent to the contact details supplied by those who have subscribed to SydneyAlert. The message is simple, giving clear guidance on what needs to be done. Example messages include: "Evacuate to a safety site", "Stay indoors and close windows", or "all clear message and situation is back to normal" (New South Wales Government, 2007).

Despite the SMS technology being available before the Victorian Bushfires, it was not until after the fires in 2009 that it was used to alert Victorians about severe weather conditions and other threatening bushfires (Dobbin, 2009; Ife, 2009). With fire risk and high wind predicted across the state, Telstra, Optus and 3 Hutchison- the three main mobile service providers in Australia- sent SMSs on the third of March 2009, on behalf of the Victorian Government and Victorian Police to more than 3 million mobile subscribers, advising recipients to listen to the Australian Broadcasting Corporation (ABC) radio for emergency updates (Dobbin, 2009; Ife, 2009). The messages were sent using commercial services (i.e. as part of a community service obligation), and not part of any State or National emergency warning system (ABC News, 2009). Some citizens reported receiving the SMS late, while others reported being

frightened or made nervous by the message content which was later considered to be over-the-top. In this particular trial, citizens were not warned about the impending message which meant that when they received it, hundreds of anxious citizens called triple zero concerned about the pending adverse weather conditions. While this is a typical response to interpreting instant messages during emergencies by a small portion of the population, more research needs to be done into effective and clear communications via mobile phones (Michael et al, 2006).

Queensland, in particular, faces the risks of cyclones, bushfires, storm surges and floods on an annual basis. In 2009, the Council of Townsville City started to provide an early warning service to its residents on an opt-in basis. The Early Warning Network (EWN) sends alerts 30 minutes ahead of severe weather conditions via a variety of electronic channels including email, SMS and landline phone call (Chudleigh, 2009). The cost of each message sent is borne by the Council. This system is believed to be the "the world's only location based early warning system for severe weather events" with the ability to pinpoint the area that information is needed "with accuracy to within 10m" according to EWN managing director Mr. Kerry Plowright (The Australian Early Warning Network, 2009).

The National Emergency Warning System of Australia

Not until recently was the standardization of a national emergency planning and alerting approach to public warning across Australia considered for actual implementation. A national emergency warning system has been the subject of discussion between the Commonwealth, States and Territories since 2004. In 2005, there was a prevailing view of the need to introduce a warning system on a national level but it was not subject to agreement by all States and Territories (The Victorian Bushfires Royal Commission, 2009). However, by July 2008, the Council of Australian Governments (COAG) finally reached an agreement to establish a national telephone-based emergency warning system in Australia (The Australian Government: Attorney General's Department, 2009). But according to the Prime Minister of Australia, privacy and data security restrictions in the *Telecommunications Act 1997* combined with interstate disagreements over funding schemes, delayed the system's introduction till after the Victorian bushfires in February 2009 (Bita & Sainsbury, 2009).

New innovations are often subject to a multitude of social-ethical issues such as privacy and security concerns in their incubation period. In this instance, the changes needed to the Telecommunications Act were not made in a timely fashion thus stifling the roll out of the telephone based warning system. This is an example of where the law lags behind new technologies or services. Despite that this system was to merely send a message to a telephone, the appropriate legislative process had not taken place. Laws or amendments to current laws do not usually happen overnight. However, following the worst bushfire season in Australia's history in 2009, the Federal Australian Government, COAG and the State and Territory Governments identified the compelling need for the immediate deployment of the national warning system which would enable them to deliver warnings to landline and mobile telephones based on the billing address of the subscriber (The Australian Government: Department of Broadband Communications and the Digital Economy, 2009). It should be stressed here that after the Victorian Bushfires, it only took several days for Honorable Senator John Faulkner, a Cabinet Secretary and Special Minister of the State, to sign the Emergency Bushfires Declaration No.1 on behalf of the Victorian Government. The declaration was made under Section 80J of the *Privacy Act 1988*. Section 80J is primarily concerned with the declaration of an emergency or an event of national significance and only the

Prime Minister of Australia or the Minister of relevance may make such a declaration.

The National Emergency Warning System (NEWS) was operational in October 2009 in all States and Territories except Western Australia (WA) which delivered its emergency warning messages through the use of its own WA State Alert system (The Victorian Department of Treasury and Finance, 2009). Under the COAG agreement, States and Territories retained autonomy of the warning systems they choose to implement (The Australian Government: Attorney General's Department, 2009). NEWS is meant to supplement, and not to replace, the range of traditional measures currently used to warn the public of emergencies, including television and radio, public address systems, door knocking, sirens, signage and the internet (Gibbons, 2009).

Granting NEWS Stakeholders Access to the Integrated Public Number Database

The second stage of NEWS is presently under deliberation, in particular the ability for Australian telecommunications carriers to meet the long term requirements of a national emergency alerting and warning system utilizing location-based technologies to identify active mobile handsets of all carriers within a defined emergency area (The Victorian Department of Treasury and Finance, 2009). For the first stage of NEWS to operate, access to the IPND was required in order to obtain the number and address upon which the warning is disseminated (The Australian Government: Department of Broadband Communications and the Digital Economy, 2009). IPND is an industry-wide, commonwealth-owned database that contains all the residential and business telephone numbers, both listed and unlisted, and other subscriber information such as name, address, and the type of service delivered by each number (i.e. landline, fax, mobile, pager, etc.) (The Australian Communications and Media

Authority, 2009). IPND was established and is maintained by Telstra, as a condition of its carrier license. All telecommunications carriers and service providers are required to provide Telstra with subscriber information in order to populate and maintain the database (The Australian Government: Department of Broadband Communications and the Digital Economy, 2009). Maintaining accurate IPND data is extremely important to ESOs as these organizations rely on the IPND to respond to emergency calls from the public in a timely manner (The Australian Communications and Media Authority, 2009).

In accordance with the States and Territories agreement to establish NEWS, the Federal Government immediately commenced drafting legislation to authorize access to the IPND. This was not without some controversy, despite the obvious benefits of the new warning system, even the potential to save lives. Given the sensitive nature of the information contained in the IPND, the *Telecommunications Act 1997*, Sections 276 and 277, restricts access and prohibits disclosure or use of information from the database save for a few exceptions. These exceptions are explicitly specified in the legislation which allow for the release of personal information for a number of reasons including emergency calls, law enforcement and national security purposes (The Australian Communications and Media Authority, 2009).

In 2009, the Federal Government introduced into Parliament *the Telecommunications Amendment Integrated Public Number Database 2009 Bill* that proposed amendments to the *Telecommunications Act 1997* in order to enable access to the IPND for NEWS purposes, in connection with the provision of telephony-based emergency warnings and for the supply of location-based emergency services (The Australian Government: Department of Broadband Communications and the Digital Economy, 2009).

In light of the Victorian Bushfires, the government sought advice from the Solicitor-General on an interim measure to allow immediate access to

the IPND by any State or Territory that wished to implement a more limited system, as soon as possible. This interim access was not a substitute for the amendments to the Telecommunications Act contained in the Bill and the planned future access arrangements for the IPND (Gibbons, 2009), but some citizens and civil liberties groups did voice concern over the potential for breaches in information privacy. The amendments to the Telecommunications Act contain a number of privacy protection provisions, which are intended to ensure that subscriber data obtained from the IPND is not used or disclosed for any other purpose than to provide telephone-based emergency warnings. Specifically, emergency agencies will only be permitted to access the data in the event of an actual emergency, in the event of a likely emergency or for testing purposes (i.e. to test whether in the event of an emergency the alert would have reached the people that it needed to) (Gibbons, 2009).

The amendments provide the Attorney-General, as the Minister with portfolio responsibility for emergency management issues, with powers to specify, by legislative instrument, who can use IPND information in the event of an emergency or disaster (The Australian Government: Attorney General's Department, 2009). The amendments also contain accountability measures including a reporting requirement for any government agency that activates a telephony-based emergency warning using IPND data. The agency will be required to report each usage of IPND information to the Attorney-General and to the ACMA, as soon as practicable after each incident occurs (The Australian Government: Department of Broadband Communications and the Digital Economy, 2009). Agencies will be required to report on the nature and location of the emergency or disaster, the number of telephone numbers disclosed, the number of persons to whom the numbers were disclosed and why. Agencies will also be required to report annually to ACMA and to the Office of the Privacy Commissioner (OPC) on each disclosure (The Australian Government: Department of Broadband Communications and the Digital Economy, 2009).

With regard to the location-based emergency services phase of NEWS, the bill clarifies the Telecommunications Act by explicitly allowing carriers and service providers supplying LBS to access listed public number information in the IPND, since the current Telecommunications Act does not contain express authority for use of information in the IPND for the purpose of providing LBS on a large scale (Gibbons, 2009). The Bill seeks to explicitly permit access to IPND data for the purpose of providing location-based emergency services and only limited to that information necessary to provide such services. The amendments also extend the existing secondary usage provisions of the Telecommunications Act to prohibit the use or disclosure of IPND data obtained for the purpose of providing the services, except for the purposes permitted under the Act. The prohibition against secondary usage applies to either the carrier or service provider, which initially requested the data and to any other party who may receive the information (The Australian Government: Department of Broadband Communications and the Digital Economy, 2009)

Location-Based Emergency Services in Australia

Unlike in the United States, technical feasibility in the context of location accuracy standards for emergency purposes does not yet exist in Australia. In addition, the commitments for telecommunications carriers are less restrictive since Australian regulators, primarily the ACMA, do not enforce accuracy levels on carriers (The Australian Communications and Media Authority, 2004). At present, a call from a mobile handset to an emergency call service is accompanied by very broad mobile location information (MoLI) relating to what is known as a standardized mobile service area (SMSA). These SMSAs can range in size from 2,000 to 500,000 square kilometers, according to the cell's size from where the emergency call is originated, and are thus too broad to assist ESOs to find someone in an emergency. Rather, the SMSAs are used by the emergency call person to identify the requested ESO answering point that is closest to his or her location, a process known as jurisdiction determination (The Australian Communications and Media Authority, 2004). Many aspects of these services are regulated and monitored by ACMA under the primary legislation, namely the *Telecommunications (Consumer Protection and Service Standards) Act 1999* and *Telecommunications Act 1997*, and through two subordinate legislative instruments: (i) *Telecommunications (Emergency Call Service) Determination 2002*; and (ii) *Telecommunications (Emergency Call Persons) Determination 1999* (The Australian Communications and Media Authority, 2004).

High accuracy location techniques to provide accurate MoLI in emergency situations are yet to be implemented in Australia but one future aim is to reach accuracy levels within 50 to 500 meters (The Australian Communications and Media Authority, 2004). Currently, location methods that can identify the mobile base station being used to carry an emergency handset call, thus providing MoLI generally within 500 meters to 30 kilometers of accuracy, are available and ready to be used in Australia but prior to 2009 were not extensively deployed by the country's telecommunications carriers (The Australian Communications and Media Authority, 2004). However, this is expected to change as the feasibility of high accuracy location methods are currently under investigation after the Federal Australian Government, Council of Australian Governments (COAG) and the States and Territories identified the compelling need for this technology in Australia, following the tragic 2009 bushfires (The Victorian Bushfires Royal Commission, 2009).

Accordingly, in regard to the second type of location-based emergency service application, which is initiated by government agencies to people in the event of an emergency, the Victorian Government released a tender in August 2009 on behalf of COAG. The tender sought responses for the purpose of determining the capacity and capability of the Australian telecommunications carriers in meeting the long term future requirements for a national emergency alerting and warning system utilizing location-based technologies to identify the active mobile handsets of all carriers, within a defined emergency area (The Victorian Department of Treasury and Finance, 2009). The tender document envisaged the underlying technology to be capable of the following:

1. The technology will have the ability to receive notifications about any new mobile device entering a previously specified emergency area to alert the user that, for example, an emergency services vehicle has arrived at a location, or a civilian has entered the area and may be unaware of the emergency.
2. The technology will include the ability to receive notifications for any mobile device exiting the defined emergency area. This could facilitate the creation of an evacuation list of people who are still remaining in the emergency area.
3. The technology will be able to locate specific mobile devices in both 2G and 3G networks, and overlay their position onto a map.
4. The technology will have the ability to provide sufficient privacy and authentication checking mechanisms to ensure mobile location security (The Victorian Department of Treasury and Finance, 2009)

SOCIO-ETHICAL CONSIDERATIONS

The location-based emergency warning system should allow the government to determine the almost exact geographic coordinates of all active mobile handsets in a defined emergency area(s) or locate mobile handsets in real time within specific threatened zone(s), and then to disseminate, and be able to re-disseminate when necessary, a warning message to these mobile handsets. Determining and/or locating the mobile handset whereabouts does not necessarily require an explicit consent from its user as pertinent government departments and law enforcement agencies have the power, under the *Privacy Act 1988*, to temporarily waive the person's right to privacy in emergencies based on the assumption that the consent is already implied in such situations.

It is quite true that emergencies do represent unique contexts where privacy is most likely to be one of our least concerns. In theory, the location/determination processes cannot trigger concerns being employed specifically for emergency management, but the perception of the uninterrupted availability of these technologies in the hands of governments during normal daily life situations has the potential to raise concerns about the possibility of utilizing them for other purposes, specially under a one-year long emergency declaration. In addition, the implications of waiving away the consent, even temporarily, has the power to impact adversely on the individual's trust in the government and its mandated LBS solutions. These concerns have the potential to add impetus to the ongoing debate of how much individuals are truly willing to relinquish their right to privacy in exchange for a sense of continuous security. This is especially now true in the current political climate of the so-called "war on terror" where governments have started to bestow additional powers on themselves to monitor, track and gather personal information in a way that never could have been previously justified (Perusco & Michael, 2007). In the name of national security, such measures have become justified albeit in exceptional situations. Despite being beyond the established rule of law these exceptions are now considered an absolute necessity to maintain the security of society and its interdependent critical infrastructures (Cavelty, 2007).

When location-based services are employed by governments the individual may never know the true extent of the location/determination on his or her handset's whereabouts or the breadth of location information being collected. Location information is a particularly sensitive kind of personal information that can have intrusive consequences on individual lives if misused (The Australian Communications and Media Authority, 2004). This kind of information can be collected, stored, aggregated and when correlated with other personal information a broad view of behavioral patterns or detailed portraits of individual habits can be created (Clarke & Wigan, 2008; Parenti, 2003). One need only ponder on what personal data is available on social networking sites. Nicola Green posited that location-based technologies might be used one day to hold individuals institutionally accountable for their day-to-day activities (2001). In his work about location-based profiling, Ronald Leenes provides two cases of where location data was used in criminal investigations (2008). Indeed, this profiling of individuals is what makes people uneasy about LBS being in the hands of governments, because of concerns about privacy in general as well as fears of being incorrectly profiled (Holtzman, 2006). Consider the sensitivity of location information pertaining to minors or the elderly who are vulnerable in different ways, or those persons suffering from mental illness.

In this age of "permanent emergency" (Parenti, 2003), perhaps now more than ever, LBS do emerge as promising technologies that can add significant value to the all-hazards approach governments are advocating in national security. Nonetheless, a transparent society where privacy is completely abolished by governments in the name of security is neither feasible nor acceptable. This is because of the inherent value of privacy for both the individual and society (Schneier, 2008). Privacy is indispensable in a community that recognizes social freedom as good and where many people dislike exposure of

their private actions, not because they have acted irregularly but because their psychological nature requires privacy (Ben-Ze'ev, 2003). Accordingly, governments have to incur an ethical obligation of defining clear limits on privacy intrusions if these intrusions are to be framed in the name of security. Harkin (2003) raised this issue when he stated that "unless there are clear limits on how government can employ the information that it gleans from our mobile communications – and in the current climate of international terrorism, few governments are keen to impose limits on their own meddling – there may well be a backlash that will impede the development of the technology itself".

Requirements for Location-Based Emergency Systems: Equity and Access

Location-based emergency systems are part of all-hazard alert and warning systems that include other emergency notification mechanisms (The Federal Communications Commission, 2005). Several national authorities, international standards organizations, and a number of specialist researchers have undertaken extensive studies to identify and document different requirements for different public emergency warning systems that should in principle allow support for all current and future emergency event types. In these studies, many aspects were given attention, including legislative, regulatory, administrative, operational, technical, organizational and ethical requirements. Some of these contributions have been by Mileti and Sorensen (1990), the Cellular Emergency Alert Systems Association (2002), ETSI (2003; The European Telecommunications Standards Institute, 2006a, 2006b, 2010), Tsalgatidou et al. (2003), FCC (2005), McGinley et al. (2006), the International Telecommunications Union (2007), The 3rd Generation Partnership Project (2008; The 3rd Generation Partnership Project, 2009), Fernandes (2008), The Victorian Bushfires Royal Commission (2009), The Victorian Department of

Treasury and Finance (2009), and Jagtman (2009), Sanders (2009), and Setten and Sanders (2009) under the European Commission's CHORIST Project (2009).

In general, defining requirements serves several objectives such as establishing a standardized way of developing and implementing a system, prioritizing the system's future functionality while providing guidance on the system's expected performance levels, preventing duplicative reporting for the system's stakeholders (The United States Department of Homeland Security, 2008), and ensuring that people who want access to LBS services during emergencies can have them in addition to other mechanisms they have traditionally enjoyed. With regard to location-based emergency systems, no explicit requirements, specifically legal and administrative requirements, currently exist anywhere in the world (Togt, Beinat, Zlatanova, & Scholten, 2005). Nonetheless, based on the concepts and principles outlined in the above-mentioned works, the following specific requirements have been drawn from the literature for location-based emergency warning and alerting systems. These requirements include, but are not limited to:

1. Ability to be integrated or used along with other alerting and warning systems.
2. Be fully accessible to the right authorities.
3. Be only accessible by the right authorities.
4. Be flexible to allow support for all current and future types or categories of emergency events and not to be designed to support specific type(s) of emergencies or events requiring notification.
5. Ability to operate independently of a specific telecommunications carrier network.
6. The underlying technology should be supported by all telecommunications carriers in the country.
7. Be able to accommodate newer technologies to enable futuristic enhanced transfer modes (e.g. messages with large data content such

as video within the warning notification in order to send, for example, a map of safe area or emergency facilities).
8. Have the ability to provide sufficient privacy and authentication checking mechanisms to ensure mobile location security.
9. Support both pre-planned and dynamic notification events.
10. Reach an unrestricted number of people, ranging from hundreds in rural areas to millions in urban and metropolitan cities.
11. Deliver messages simultaneously to a large number of recipients.
12. Deliver the message in near real-time or within a planned specified time.
13. Reach the appropriate recipients, as efficiently as possible, through the ability of the underlying technology to segment the message recipients by geographic locations.
14. Allow the opportunity to send different messages to different groups of people (e.g. recommend different safety areas for different groups or messages can be targeted at people in the immediate vicinity of an emergency to do one thing, and people traveling to an affected area to do another).
15. Reach all kinds of existing mobile handsets including legacy devices that are largely still in use.
16. Support delivery of messages to those with special needs and unique devices, such as handsets for hearing and vision impaired persons.
17. Reach the residents of remote areas, and people roaming from other mobile telecommunications networks, including visitors from other countries.
18. Support the transmission in languages in addition to English to the extent where it is practical and feasible.
19. Be able to deliver the message under network-congested conditions.
20. Have a message redelivery mechanism when the initial message delivery fails.

21. Have a message reiteration mechanism for as long as the message is valid.

In addition to the base requirements for the location-based emergency system, the requirements for the service/message itself should consider, but are not limited to, the following:

1. Message creation is driven by the country's specific characteristics and its own list of emergencies.
2. Message template is consistent across different warning sources from different emergency authorities.
3. Message is based on standardized digital format for expressing and disseminating a consistent warning message simultaneously over different informative and media channels.
4. Specifically recognizable as being an emergency message that cannot be mistaken for an ordinary message.
5. Credible, secure and authentic.
6. Location-specific, to minimize social anxiety.
7. Relevant, to ensure that recipients realize that the warning relates to their personal situation.
8. Timely, to prevent wrong actions and to provide those at risk with enough time to take protective action.
9. Accurate, to indicate the degree severity, or the predicted severity, of the event.
10. Complete, to offer sufficient details about the situation.
11. Concise, to avoid lengthy messages.
12. Provide adequate instructions to recipients regarding what should and should not be done to protect them.
13. Fully clear and comprehensible to all people including young and senior recipients.
14. Positive, rather than negative to advocate people on what to do.

One of the greatest threats to such service implementation comes from the potential for instant message hoaxes during times of crisis (i.e., disinformation) from unscrupulous citizens to other unsuspecting citizens, as was reported in the fight against SARs (Severe Acute Respiratory Syndrome) in Hong Kong in 2003 (Jardin, 2003). These are not only disruptive to emergency services but can also be life-threatening to individuals who are misinformed. There is unfortunately little authorities can do to guard against such communications.

CONCLUSION

Large scale emergencies, that have the potential to disrupt the orderly manner of civil society, are now considered a type of national security challenge. While there is a growing trend by governments to deploy more socially constructed security measures to counter the threatening consequences of extreme events, the public reception has not always been favorable. In Australia, some citizens and lobby groups see the introduction of laws mandating access to certain types of personal information to aid in the gradual relinquishing of individual privacy rights. Beyond unauthorized access and disclosure of citizen personal details is the public perception that authorities will be able to perform continuous tracking after legitimately deploying a one year long emergency declaration. With a limited effort from the government to raise public awareness about the deployed system, most of the concerns, although they may merely be misconceptions, have the power to impact negatively on the practiced emergency response measures while devaluing the purpose of the alert and warning system in the eyes of the public. The time to intervene is now as governments, like Australia, move to introduce basic systems moving to more sophisticated and fully-fledged location based services into the future. It is important for governments, telecommunications carriers and relevant stakeholders to discuss the possible socio-ethical implications of advanced technologies like location based services before they are rolled out in a ubiquitous manner. In trying to respond to the challenge of national security, governments will ironically need to invest even more money into such areas as database security to ensure that private citizen details are not disclosed to unauthorized parties.

REFERENCES

Aitenbichler, E. (2008). A focus on location context. In Mühlhäuser, M., & Gurevych, I. (Eds.), *Handbook of research on ubiquitous computing technology for real time enterprises* (pp. 257–281). Hershey, PA: IGI Global. doi:10.4018/9781599048321.ch012

Astroth, J. (2003). Location-based services: Criteria for adoption and solution deployment. In Mennecke, B. E., & Strader, T. J. (Eds.), *Mobile commerce: Technology, theory, and applications* (pp. 229–236). Hershey, PA: Idea Group Publishing. doi:10.4018/9781591400448.ch015

Australia.gov.au Website. (2010). *The Australian continent*. Retrieved 10 March, 2010, from http://australia.gov.au/about-australia/our-country/the-australian-continent

Ben-Ze'ev, A. (2003). Privacy, emotional closeness, and openness in cyberspace. *Computers in Human Behavior*, *19*(4), 451–467. doi:10.1016/S0747-5632(02)00078-X

Benson, S. (2007). *SMS smog alerts for Sydney*.

Bernardos, A. M., Casar, J. R., & Tarrio, P. (2007). *Building a framework to characterize location-based services*.

Betts, R. (2003). The missing links in community warning systems: Findings from two Victorian community warning system projects. *The Australian Journal of Emergency Management*, *18*(3), 35–45.

Bita, N., & Sainsbury, M. (2009). *Bungling silenced Victoria bushfires warning*. The Australian.

Boughton, G. (1998). The community: Central to emergency risk management. *Australian Journal of Emergency Management*, 2-5.

Buzan, B., Wver, O., & Wilde, J. D. (1998). *Security: A new framework for analysis* (1st ed.). London, UK: Lynne Rienner Publishers.

Canton, L. G. (2007). *Emergency management: Concepts and strategies for effective programs* (1st ed.). Hoboken, NJ: John Wiley & Sons, Inc.

Cavelty, M. D. (2007). Cyber-terror–looming threat or phantom menace? The framing of the US cyber-threat debate. *Journal of Information Technology & Politics*, *4*(1). doi:10.1300/J516v04n01_03

Chudleigh, J. (2009, November 10). Earlier alert system for severe weather. *The Courier-Mail*.

Clarke, R., & Wigan, M. (2008). You are where you have been. In Michael, K., & Michael, M. G. (Eds.), *Australia and the new technologies: Evidence based policy in public administration* (pp. 100–114). Canberra, Australia: University of Wollongong.

Coyle, D., & Meier, P. (2009). *New technologies in emergencies and conflicts: The role of information and social networks*.

Dawson, M., Winterbottom, J., & Thomson, M. (2007). *IP location* (1st ed.). New York, NY: McGraw-Hill.

Dobbin, M. (2009, March 3). Victorians receive fire text warning. *The Age*.

Dunn, M., & Collier, K. (2007, February 27). Plan to use SMS for SOS. Retrieved 6 June 2007, Factiva

Emergency Management Australia. (1996). *Australian counter disaster handbook* (5th ed., *Vol. 2*). Canberra, Australia: Emergency Management Australia.

Emergency Management Australia. (2004a). *Disaster recovery: Safer sustainable communities*. Retrieved 27 November, 2007, from http://www.ema.gov.au/www/emaweb/rwpattach.nsf/VAP/(3273BD3F76A7A5DEDAE36942A54D7D90)~Manual10-Recovery.pdf/$file/Manual10-Recovery.pdf

Emergency Management Australia. (2004b). *Emergency management in Australia: Concepts and principles*. Retrieved 27 November, 2007, from http://www.ema.gov.au/www/emaweb/rwpattach.nsf/VAP/(3273BD3F76A7A5DEDAE36942A54D7D90)~Manual01-Emergency-ManagementinAustralia-ConceptsandPrinciples.pdf/$file/Manual01-EmergencyManagementin-Australia-ConceptsandPrinciples.pdf

Emergency Management Australia. (2008). Disasters database. Retrieved 04 January, 2008, from http://www.ema.gov.au/www/emaweb/emaweb.nsf/Page/Resources_DisastersDatabase_DisastersDatabase

Emergency Management Australia. (2009a). *Australian emergency management arrangements*. Retrieved 27 November, 2009, from http://www.ema.gov.au/www/emaweb/rwpattach.nsf/VAP/(3A6790B96C927794AF1031D9395C5C20)~Australian+Emergency+Management+Arrangements.pdf/$file/Australian+Emergency+Management+Arrangements.pdf

Emergency Management Australia. (2009b). Emergency management. Retrieved 08 December, 2008, from http://www.ema.gov.au/www/emaweb/emaweb.nsf/Page/Emergency_Management

Fernandes, J. P. (2008). Emergency warnings with short message service. In Coskun, H. G., Cigizoglu, H. K., & Maktav, M. D. (Eds.), *Integration of information for environmental security* (pp. 205–210). Dordrecht, The Netherlands: Springer. doi:10.1007/978-1-4020-6575-0_14

Gibbons, S. (2009). *Telecommunications amendment (Integrated Public Number Database) bill 2009: Second reading*. Retrieved 6 August, 2009, from http://parlinfo.aph.gov.au/parlInfo/genpdf/chamber/hansardr/2009-02-26/0032/hansard_frag.pdf;fileType=application%2Fpdf

Gilbert, C. (1998). Studying disaster: Changes in the main conceptual tools. In Quarantelli, E. L. (Ed.), *What is a disaster? A dozen perspectives on the question* (pp. 3–12). New York, NY: Routledge.

Green, N. (2001). Who's watching whom? Monitoring and accountability in mobile relations. In Brown, B., Green, N., & Harper, R. (Eds.), *Wireless world: Social and interactional aspects of the mobile age* (pp. 32–45). New York, NY: Springer-Verlag.

Grothe, M. J. M., Landa, H. C., & Steenbruggen, J. G. M. (2005). The value of Gi4DM for transport & water management. In P. v. Oosterom, S. Zlatanova & E. M. Fendel (Eds.), *Geo-information for disaster management* (pp. 129-154). Delft, The Netherlands: Springer.

Gruber, B., & Winter, S. (2002). *Location based services using a database federation*. Paper presented at the 5th AGILE Conference on Geographic Information Science, Palma, Spain.

Guan, J., Zhou, S., Zhou, J., & Zhu, F. (2007). Providing location-based services under Web services framework. In Taniar, D. (Ed.), *Encyclopedia of mobile computing and commerce* (pp. 789–795). London, UK: Information Science Reference. doi:10.4018/9781599040028.ch134

Haddow, G. D., Bullock, J. A., & Coppola, D. P. (2006). *Introduction to emergency management* (2nd ed.). Burlington, MA: Elsevier Butterworth–Heinemann.

Harkin, J. (2003). *Mobilisation: The growing public interest in mobile technology* (1st ed.). London, UK: Demos.

Harvey, F. (2008). *A primer of GIS: Fundamental geographic and cartographic* (1st ed.). New York, NY: The Guilford Press.

Hjelm, J. (2002). *Creating location services for the wireless Web* (1st ed.). New York, NY: John Wiley & Sons, Inc.

Holma, H., Kristensson, M., Salonen, J., & Toskala, A. (2004). UMTS services and applications. In Holma, H., & Toskala, A. (Eds.), *WCDMA for UMTS: Radio access for third generation mobile communications* (3rd ed., pp. 11–46). West Sussex, UK: John Wiley & Sons Ltd. doi:10.1002/0470870982.ch2

Holtzman, D. H. (2006). *Privacy lost: How technology is endangering your privacy* (1st ed.). San Francisco, CA: Jossey-Bass.

Ife, H. (2009, March 02). Texts alert Victorians of fire danger. *Herald Sun*.

Jagtman, E. (2009). *Reaching citizens with CHORIST: Everything but technology*. Retrieved 18 October, 2009, from http://www.chorist.eu/index.php?page=1&sel=1

Jardin, X. (2003). Text messaging feeds SARS rumors. *Wired*. Retrieved 17 October, 2009, from http://www.wired.com/medtech/health/news/2003/04/58506

Jensen, C. S. (2002,). *Research challenges in location-enabled m-services*. Paper presented at the Third IEEE International Conference on Mobile Data Management, 08-11 January, Singapore.

Küpper, A. (2005). *Location-based services: Fundamentals and operation* (1st ed.). Chichester/ West Sussex, UK: John Wiley & Sons Ltd. doi:10.1002/0470092335

Leenes, R. (2008). Reply: Mind my step? In Hildebrandt, M., & Gutwirth, S. (Eds.), *Profiling the European citizen: Cross-disciplinary perspectives* (pp. 160–168). Dordrecht, The Netherlands: Springer.

Lopez, X. R. (2004). Location-based services. In Karimi, H. A., & Hammand, A. (Eds.), *Telegeoinformatics: Location-based computing and services* (pp. 144–159). New York, NY: CRC Press LLC.

McGinley, M., Turk, A., & Bennett, D. (2006). *Design criteria for public emergency warning systems*. Paper presented at The 3rd International Conference on Information Systems for Crisis Response and Management (ISCRAM), Newark, New Jersey.

Michael, K., Stroh, B., Berry, O., Muhlhauber, A., & Nicholls, T. (2006). The avian flu tracker-a location service proof of concept. *Recent Advances in Security Technology: Proceedings of the 2006 RNSA Security Technology Conference, Australian Homeland Security Research Centre*, Canberra, 19-21 September, (pp. 244-258).

Mileti, D. S., & Sorensen, J. H. (1990). *Communication of emergency public warnings: A social science perspective and state-of-the-art assessment*. Retrieved 08 August, 2007, from http://emc.ornl.gov/EMCWeb/EMC/PDF/CommunicationFinal.pdf

New South Wales Government. (2007). About sydneyALERT. Retrieved 17 April, 2008, from http://www.sydneyalert.nsw.gov.au/content.php/36.html

ABC News. (2009, Mar 4). *Bushfire SMS to assist in warning system development*. The Australian Broadcasting Corporation.

Oh, J., & Haas, Z. J. (2007). A scheme for location-based Internet broadcasting and its applications. *IEEE Communications Magazine, 45*(11), 136–141. doi:10.1109/MCOM.2007.4378333

Parenti, C. (2003). *The soft cage: Surveillance in America from slavery to the war on terror* (1st ed.). New York, NY: Basic Books.

Perry, R. W. (2007). What is a disaster? In H. a. Rodr'ıguez, E. L. Quarantelli & R. Dynes (Eds.), *Handbook of disaster research* (pp. 1-16). Springer Science+Business Media, LLC.

Perusco, L., & Michael, K. (2007). Control, trust, privacy, and security: Evaluating location-based services. *IEEE Technology and Society Magazine, 26,* 4–16. doi:10.1109/MTAS.2007.335564

Quarantelli, E. L. (1986). What should we study? Questions and suggestions for researchers about the concept of disasters. *International Journal of Mass Emergencies and Disasters, 5*(1), 7–32.

Rosenthal, U. (1998). Future disasters, future definitions. In Quarantelli, E. L. (Ed.), *What is a disaster? A dozen perspectives on the question* (pp. 147–160). New York, NY: Routledge.

Samsioe, J., & Samsioe, A. (2002). Introduction to location based services: Markets and technologies. In Reichwald, R. (Ed.), *Mobile Kommunikation: Wertschöpfung, Technologien, neue Dienste* (pp. 417–438). Wiesbaden, Germany: Gabler.

Sanders, P. (2009). *The CB way forward.* Retrieved 18 October, 2009, from http://www.chorist.eu/index.php?page=1&sel=1

Schneier, B. (2008). *The myth of the transparent society.* Wired Magazine.

Setten, W. v., & Sanders, P. (2009). *Citizen alert with cell broadcasting: The technology, the standards and the way forward.* Retrieved 18 October, 2009, from http://www.chorist.eu/index.php?page=1&sel=1

Shiode, N., Li, C., Batty, M., Longley, P., & Maguire, D. (2002). *The impact and penetration of location-based services* (pp. 1–16). London, UK: Centre for Advanced Spatial Analysis, University College London.

Spiekermann, S. (2004). General aspects of location-based services. In Schiller, J., & Voisard, A. (Eds.), *Location-based services* (pp. 9–26). San Francisco, CA: Elsevier. doi:10.1016/B978-155860929-7/50002-9

Stojanović, D., Djordjevic-Kajan, S., Papadopoulos, A. N., & Nanopoulos, A. (2007). Monitoring and tracking moving objects in mobile environments. In Taniar, D. (Ed.), *Encyclopedia of mobile computing and commerce* (pp. 660–665). London, UK: Information Science Reference. doi:10.4018/9781599040028.ch110

Templeman, D., & Bergin, A. (2008). *Taking a punch: Building a more resilient Australia.* Retrieved 02 February, 2009, from http://www.aspi.org.au/publications/publication_details.aspx?ContentID=165

The 3rd Generation Partnership Project. (2008). *Technical specification group services and system aspects: Study for requirements for a public warning system (PWS) service (Release 8).* Retrieved 13 April, 2009, from http://www.3gpp.org/ftp/tsg_sa/WG1_Serv/TSGS1_37_Orlando/Docs/S1-070824.doc

The 3rd Generation Partnership Project. (2009). *Technical specification group services and system aspects: Functional stage 2 description of location services (LCS) (Release 9).* Retrieved 16 January, 2010, from http://www.3gpp.org/ftp/Specs/archive/23_series/23.271/

The Australian. (2007, February, 26). *Premier promises mobile phone terrorism alert.* Factiva.

The Australian Communications and Media Authority. (2004). *Location location location: The future use of location information to enhance the handling of emergency mobile phone calls.* Retrieved 21 October, 2007, from http://acma.gov.au/webwr/consumer_info/location.pdf

The Australian Communications and Media Authority. (2009). *Australia's emergency call service in a changing environment*. Retrieved 25 September, 2009, from http://www.acma.gov.au/webwr/_assets/main/lib311250/future_of_emergency_call_svces.pdf

The Australian Early Warning Network. (2009). Townsville city council signs up to the early warning network. Retrieved 7 December, 2009, from http://www.ewn.com.au/media/townsville_city_council.aspx

The Australian Government: Attorney General's Department. (2009). *Rudd government implements COAG agreement on telephone-based emergency warning systems (Joint Media Release)*. Retrieved 02 August, 2009, from http://www.ag.gov.au/www/ministers/mcclelland.nsf/Page/MediaReleases_2009_FirstQuarter_23February2009RuddGovernmentImplementsCOAGAgreementonTelephone-BasedEmergencyWarningSystems

The Australian Government: Department of Broadband Communications and the Digital Economy. (2009). *Telecommunications amendment (integrated public number database) bill 2009: Explanatory memorandum*. Retrieved 6 August, 2009, from http://parlinfo.aph.gov.au/parlInfo/download/legislation/ems/r4062_ems_d2937505-3da94059b9cbe382e891dd23/upload_word/TelAm(IPND)_EM.doc;fileType=application%2Fmsword

The Australian Government: Department of Transport and Regional Services. (2004). *Natural disasters in Australia: Reforming mitigation, relief and recovery arrangements*. Retrieved 18 February, 2009, from http://www.ema.gov.au/www/emaweb/rwpattach.nsf/VAP/(99292794923AE8E7CBABC6FB71541EE1)~Natural+Disasters+in+Australia+-+Review.pdf/$file/Natural+Disasters+in+Australia+-+Review.pdf

The Cellular Emergency Alert Systems Association. (2002). *Handset requirements specification: Reaching millions in a matter of seconds*. Retrieved 02 April, 2007, from http://www.ceasa-int.org/library/Handset_Requirements_Specification.pdf

The European Commission. (2009). *The CHORIST project: Integrating communications for enhanced environmental risk management and citizens safety*. Retrieved 07 November, 2009, from http://www.chorist.eu/index.php?page=1&sel=1

The European Telecommunications Standards Institute. (2003). *Requirements for communication of ctizens with authorities/organizations in case of distress (emergency call handling)*. Retrieved 10 May, 2007, from http://etsi.org/WebSite/homepage.aspx

The European Telecommunications Standards Institute. (2006a). *Analysis of the short message service and cell broadcast service for emergency messaging applications: Emergency messaging, SMS and CBS*. Retrieved 10 May, 2007, from http://etsi.org/WebSite/homepage.aspx

The European Telecommunications Standards Institute. (2006b). *Emergency communications (EMTEL): Requirements for communications from authorities/organizations to individuals, groups or the general public during emergencies*. Retrieved 10 May, 2007, from http://etsi.org/WebSite/homepage.aspx

The European Telecommunications Standards Institute. (2010). *Study for requirements for a public warning system (PWS) service*. Retrieved 10 Feb, 2010, from http://webstats.3gpp.org/ftp/Specs/html-info/22968.htm

The Federal Communications Commission. (2005). *Review of the emergency alert system*. Retrieved 13 April, 2008, from http://www.fcc.gov/eb/Orders/2005/FCC-05-191A1.html

The International Telecommunications Union. (2007). *Compendium of ITU'S work on emergency telecommunications.* Geneva, Switzerland: The United Nations Agency for Information and Communication Technologies.

The Minister for Police and Emergency Services. (2005). *First calls made as part of early warning trial.* Retrieved 04 June, 2007, from http://www.legislation.vic.gov.au/domino/Web_Notes/newmedia.nsf/35504bc71d3adebcca256cfc0082c2b8/4ae0fe91bdeb3e8aca25704d000729b0!OpenDocument

The United States Department of Homeland Security. (2008). *National emergency communications plan.* Retrieved 06 October, 2009, from http://www.dhs.gov/xlibrary/assets/national_emergency_communications_plan.pdf

The Victorian Bushfires Royal Commission. (2009). *Victorian bushfires royal commission interim report.*

The Victorian Department of Treasury and Finance. (2009). *Request for information (RFI) for: Location based identification of active mobile handsets for emergency notification purposes.* (RFI Number: SS-06-2009). Retrieved 19 November, 2009, from https://www.tenders.vic.gov.au/tenders/tender/display/tender-details.do?id=87&action=display-tender-details&returnUrl=%2Ftender%2Fsearch%2Ftender-search.do%3Faction%3Dadvanced-tender-search-closed-tender

Togt, R., Beinat, E., Zlatanova, S., & Scholten, H. (2005). Location interoperability services for medical emergency operations during disasters. In P. v. Oosterom, S. Zlatanova & E. M. Fendel (Eds.), *Geo-information for disaster management* (pp. 1127-1141). Berlin/ Heidelberg, Germany: Springer

Tsalgatidou, A., Veijalainen, J., Markkula, J., Katasonov, A., & Hadjiefthymiades, S. (2003). *Mobile e-commerce and location-based services: Technology and requirements.* Paper presented at the The 9th Scandinavian Research Conference on Geographical Information Sciences, Espoo, Finland.

Uhlirz, M. (2007). A market and user view on LBS. In Gartner, G., Cartwright, W., & Peterson, M. P. (Eds.), *Location based services and telecartography* (pp. 47–58). Berlin/ Heidelberg, Germany: Springer. doi:10.1007/978-3-540-36728-4_4

United Nations News Centre. (2010). *Earthquakes the deadliest of all disasters during past decade.* Retrieved 29 January, 2010, from http://www.un.org/apps/news/printnews.asp?nid=33613

Victorian State Parliamentary Offices. (2003). *Watching brief on the war on terrorism: Submission by the state Of Victoria to the joint standing committee on foreign Affairs, defence and trade hearing on Australia's counter terrorism capabilities.* Retrieved 18 January, 2009, from http://www.aph.gov.au/House/committee/jfadt/terrorism/subs/sub13.pdf

ADDITIONAL READING

Aloudat, A., Michael, K., & Jun, Y. (2007). Location-Based Services in Emergency Management- from Government to Citizens: Global Case Studies. In Mendis, P., Lai, J., Dawson, E., & Abbass, H. (Eds.), *Recent Advances in Security Technology* (pp. 190–201). Melbourne: Australian Homeland Security Research Centre.

Brin, D. (1998). *The Transparent Society: Will Technology Force Us to Choose between Privacy and Freedom?* (1st ed.). Boulder, Colorado: Perseus Press.

Cantwell, B. (2002). *Why Technical Breakthroughs Fail: A History of Public Concern with Emerging Technologies*. Working Paper, Auto-ID Center, Massachusetts Institute of Technology, Cambridge, Massachusetts. Retrieved 17 August 2009.

Carter, L., & Bélanger, F. (2005). The utilization of e-government services: citizen trust, innovation and acceptance factors. *Information Systems Journal, 15*(1), 5–25. doi:10.1111/j.1365-2575.2005.00183.x

Code of Practice of Passive Location Services in the UK. (2006). Industry Code of Practice For the use of mobile phone technology to provide passive location services in the UK. Retrieved 23 August 2007, from http://www.mobilebroadbandgroup.com/documents/UKCoP_location_servs_210706v_pub_clean.pdf

Gow, G. A. (2005). Pinpointing Consent: Location Privacy and Mobile Phones. In Nyíri, K. (Ed.), *A sense of place: The global and the local in mobile communication* (pp. 139–150). Vienna: Passagen Verlag.

Holtzman, D. H. (2006). *Privacy Lost: How Technology Is Endangering Your Privacy* (1st ed.). San Francisco, California: Jossey-Bass.

Kiefer, J. J., Mancini, J. A., Morrow, B. H., Gladwin, H., & Stewart, T. A. (2008). *Providing Access to Resilience-Enhancing Technologies for Disadvantaged Communities and Vulnerable Populations*. Retrieved from www.orau.org/university-partnerships/files/The-PARET-Report.pdf.

Kim, D. J., Braynov, S. B., Rao, H. R., & Song, Y. I. (2001, 2-5 August). *A B-to-C Trust Model for Online Exchange*. Paper presented at the Seventh Americas Conference on Information Systems, Boston, Massachusetts.

Kini, A., & Choobineh, J. (1998). *Trust in Electronic Commerce: Definition and Theoretical Considerations*. Paper presented at the Thirty-First Annual Hawaii International Conference on System Sciences.

Krishnamurthy, N. (2002). *Using SMS to deliver location-based services*. Paper presented at the 2002 IEEE International Conference on Personal Wireless Communications.

Marx, G. T. (1999). What's in a Name? Some Reflections on the Sociology of Anonymity. [Article]. *The Information Society, 15*(2), 99–112. doi:10.1080/019722499128565

McAdams, J. (2006). SMS does SOS: Short Message Service Earns Valued Role as a Link of Last Resort for Crisis Communications. Retrieved 02 February 2007, from http://fcw.com/articles/2006/04/03/sms-does-sos.aspx?sc_lang=en

McKnight, D. H., & Chervany, N. L. (2001). What Trust Means in E-Commerce Customer Relationships: An Interdisciplinary Conceptual Typology. *International Journal of Electronic Commerce, 6*(2), 35–59.

Perusco, L., Michael, K., & Michael, M. G. (2006, 11-13 Oct.). *Location-Based Services and the Privacy-Security Dichotomy*. Paper presented at the Third International Conference on Mobile Computing and Ubiquitous Networking, London.

Pura, M. (2005). Linking perceived value and loyalty in location-based mobile services. *Managing Service Quality, 15*(6), 509–538. doi:10.1108/09604520510634005

Schneier, B. (2008). The Myth of the 'Transparent Society'. *Wired Magazine*. Retrieved from http://www.wired.com/politics/security/commentary/securitymatters/2008/03/securitymatters_0306

Tan, Y.-H., & Thoen, W. (2001). Toward a Generic Model of Trust for Electronic Commerce. *International Journal of Electronic Commerce, 5*(2), 61–74.

The Australian Communications and Media Authority. (2004). *Location Location Location: The Future Use of Location Information to Enhance the Handling of Emergency Mobile Phone Calls*. Retrieved from http://acma.gov.au/webwr/consumer_info/location.pdf.

The Australian Government: Attorney General's Department. (2008). Privacy Act 1988: Act No.119 of 1988 as amended. Retrieved 02 August 2008, from http://www.comlaw.gov.au/ComLaw/Legislation/ActCompilation1.nsf/0/63C00ADD09B982ECCA257490002B9D57/$file/Privacy1988_WD02HYP.pdf

Weiss, D., Kramer, I., Treu, G., & Kupper, A. (2006). *Zone Services - An Approach for Location-Based Data Collection*. Paper presented at the The 8th IEEE International Conference on E-Commerce Technology, The 3rd IEEE International Conference on Enterprise Computing, E-Commerce, and E-Services.

KEY TERMS AND DEFINITIONS

Emergency Management: Typically has four stages including prevention/mitigation, preparedness, response and recovery. Emergency management is integral to a nation's national security from the perspective of societal securitization.

Hazards: These can be natural or technological. Natural hazards are those that have their origin in the natural environment such as bushfires. Technological hazards are a result of failures in human-made systems, such as oil spills. Hazards can also be categorized as chemical, biological or radiological.

Integrated Public Number Database (IPND): An industry-wide, commonwealth-owned database that contains all the residential and business telephone numbers (listed and unlisted) of Australia. The IPND also stores subscriber information such as name, address, and the type of service delivered by each number (e.g. landline or mobile).

Information Privacy: The interest an individual has in controlling the handling of data about themselves.

Information Risk: Personal data being accessed or modified by unauthorized persons.

Location-Based Services: Services that use the location of the target for adding value to the service, where the target is the "entity" to be located. Typical LBS consumer applications include roadside assistance and who is nearest, and typical LBS business applications include fleet management and field service personnel management.

Mandate: A command or an authorization given by a political electorate to its representative often supported by laws and regulations.

Mobile Alerts: A message disseminated during an emergency to mobile devices, typically sent from an authorized government agency.

Security: Freedom from risk or danger; safety. Freedom from doubt, anxiety, or fear.

Short Message Service: SMS is a well-known and accepted asynchronous protocol of communication. It is capable of transmitting a limited size of binary or text messages to one or more recipients. SMS offers virtual guarantee for message delivery to its destination.

Section 3
Ethics and Security in Organisations

Chapter 8
Monitoring Employee Actions in the Workplace:
Good Business Practice or Unethical Behaviour?

Cliona McParland
Dublin City University, Ireland

Regina Connolly
Dublin City University, Ireland

ABSTRACT

While the use of Internet based technologies empower organisations immensely, the recent surge of pervasive technologies into the workplace environment has created situations whereby employees are becoming increasingly aware of the ways in which management can employ these technologies to monitor their email and computer interactions. Although it is apparent that in some cases management may have legitimate reasons to monitor employees' actions it is becoming increasingly evident that emerging issues and subsequent privacy concerns resulting from the use of these technologies have the potential to negatively impact organisational productivity and employee morale. This chapter outlines some of the major issues relating to workplace surveillance, identifying the emerging issues and subsequent privacy concerns from the employee's perspective, as well as the motivation behind managements' decision to employ monitoring technologies in the workplace.

INTRODUCTION

While the exponential growth of Internet-based technologies has empowered organisations immensely, the recent surge of pervasive technologies into the workplace environment has generated privacy concerns amongst employees. The pervasive computing environment is characterised by the seamless integration of technologies into society, and it is this transparent nature which has fuelled much of these privacy concerns. For example, employees are becoming increasingly aware of the ways in which management can employ such technologies to monitor their email and computer interactions in the workplace. Profit driven organisations however, aim to manage their

DOI: 10.4018/978-1-60960-573-5.ch008

business in an efficient and productive manner. As such, it is perhaps unrealistic to expect that such organisations would not avail themselves with the obvious empowering benefits that these communication monitoring technologies afford them. Furthermore, it can be argued that they may in fact have legitimate reasons to monitor employee actions in the first place.

Many questions surround the issue of workplace surveillance, in particular, relating to the ethical nature of managements ability to monitor employees computer interactions. The aim of this chapter therefore, is to outline some of the major issues relating to workplace surveillance, identifying the emerging issues and subsequent privacy concerns from the employee's perspective, as well as the motivation behind managements' decision to employ monitoring technologies in the workplace. As such, this chapter explores the ethical impact of monitoring in the computer-mediated work environment, addressing whether management's ability to monitor employee actions in the workplace represents good business practice or constitutes an invasion of privacy.

BACKGROUND

It is a common belief that one of the greatest threats to personal privacy lies in the monitoring and surveillance capabilities of modern technology. Privacy is a complex construct that remains beset by conceptual and operational confusion. It is an ambiguous concept that for many is difficult to either define or understand. For example, for every definition of privacy sourced from the literature, a counterexample can be easily produced (Introna, 1996). Understandably therefore, privacy is often defined and measured in terms of a specific study, event or situation and as a result, the conceptual confusion that surrounds the construct as well as the ways in which best to manage it remains a hot discussion topic. In order to gain a full understanding of the privacy construct, it is

reasonable to suggest that one considers it from a multiplicity of viewpoints and as such, privacy is often examined as a psychological state, a form of power, an inherent right or an aspect of freedom (Parker, 1974; Acquisti, 2002; Rust *et al.,* 2002)

One aspect of privacy which for many is central to our understanding of the construct is the issue of control, specifically the individual's need to have control over their personal information. Control has been defined as *"the power of directing command, the power of restraining"* (Oxford, 1996: 291) and is consistently proposed in the literature as a key factor in relation to understanding individual privacy concerns. Personal control is important as it relates to the interest of individuals to control or significantly influence the handling of personal data (Clarke, 1988). Practitioner reports confirm the importance that individuals attribute to being able to control their personal information, particularly in relation to the use of Internet-based systems. For example, a 1999 Louis Harris poll indicated that 70% of online users felt uncomfortable disclosing personal information while a 2003 Harris poll of 1010 adults also found that 69% of those surveyed described their ability to control the collection of personal information as being 'exceptionally important'. Statistics like these indicate the increasing concern of individuals regarding the violation of their privacy and their desire to be able to control their personal information.

Interestingly, while individuals' sensitivity to control of private information is an issue of increasing concern, the truth regarding the extent of control over that personal information is often misunderstood, particularly amongst the Internet-using public. This is confirmed by a 2005 study by the Annenberg Public Policy Centre which discovered that 47% of the 1500 adults surveyed falsely believed they were able to control personal information distributed about them online simply because they had the right to view data collated by the on-line vendor, while a further 50% falsely believed they could control the depth of information contained on them by having the ability to edit information as and when they saw fit (Turow *et al.*, 2005). The value of such practitioner reports lies in the acknowledgement that individuals yearn to become empowered decision makers relating to the level of control they maintain over their sensitive information, thus providing a basis for future research from a rigour and relevance perspective.

This issue of control and privacy may not always be as clear cut as it at first seems, however. In fact, it can be argued that not every loss or gain of control necessarily constitutes a loss or gain of privacy (Parker, 1974). For example, a user of an Internet-based technology who voluntarily provides personal information in the course of their interaction may not necessarily view this as a loss of control and consequently a loss of privacy. Even if the knowledge that each of their computer-based interactions leaves behind a detailed trail of information regarding who they are, their behaviour and habits and other potentially sensitive information about themselves – it may not necessarily constitute a lack of control or loss of privacy in their eyes. Once again, it becomes apparent that the definition and scope of privacy is dependent upon the situation or event in question as well as the attitudes and perceptions of those involved.

There is a general consensus that the advent of the information age has made the art of communication significantly easier. However, as previously noted, the influx and increased adoption of technology has also made it significantly easier for third parties to intercept and collate communications by others (Ghosh, 1998). In fact, the adoption of the Internet for both business and recreational purposes simply fuels the privacy debate as the potential for individuals to gain unauthorised access to electronic networks poses a significant threat (Laudon and Laudon, 2002). The increasing pervasiveness of technologies into our working lives has opened up a spectrum of unregulated behaviour whereby previously accepted distinctions regarding cor-

rect and immoral behaviour are no longer always clear (Turban, 2006). Researchers such as Safire (2002) note how extreme pervasive surveillance tends to result in a 'creepy feeling' among those being monitored despite the fact that they may have done nothing wrong to merit such scrutiny. In some cases, individuals may be conscious that they are being monitored, they are just not sure of the extent and detail of that monitoring. Neither are they aware of how that collated information is being used by the monitoring body. As such, it is clear that there are two distinct issues relating to surveillance – one relating to the actual act of monitoring or surveillance itself, the second relating to how the collated information can be used.

While it is clear that the exponential growth of Internet-based technologies has changed the scope and indeed the capabilities of such practices, it is important to note that many of these monitoring techniques have a long established presence in the offline world also. One of the earliest known examples relates to an observation unit known as the Panopticon, which was designed to house prison inmates in the 18th century. The unit was designed to allow an observer to observe undetected so that prison inmates were seamlessly individualised, were made constantly visible, were always seen but could never see themselves (Foucault, 1977). In this way they were a constant source of information but subsequently unable to communicate in the existing relationship. The basic principles of this observation system played on the fundamental vulnerability of human nature, turning visibility into a trap and ensuring that a covert presence held the power.

Examples of modern day computer-mediated surveillance techniques rely heavily on these basic principles. Clarke (1988) coined the term dataveillance to describe the systematic monitoring of the actions or communications of individuals. Modern technologies provide the opportunity for constant observation and continuous data collection ensuring that surveillance is employed through an individual, not over them. In fact, the monitoring of employees' computer-related interactions has previously been described as an 'electronic whip' used unfairly by management (Tavani, 2004). In this way, employees are now facing an electronic form of panopticism whereby they can be observed by an electronic supervisor who never leaves the office (Wen *et al.,* 2007).

SURVEILLANCE

Surveillance: An Employee Perspective

The rapid growth of the Internet has been matched by an explosion in the use of email and Internet for business use in the workplace environment. In fact, email is very much a fundamental part of the communication structure of many organisations today. While the speed and productivity benefits of email are immense from an organisational perspective, the placing of stringent controls by management on the use of email systems may also jeopardise an employee's privacy. For example, a recent study carried out by AMA (2005) found that as many as 55% of US firms not only retain but review an employee's email messages, a figure which has risen 8% since 2001. Managements' ability to monitor employee actions also stretches to use of the Internet within the workplace. AMA (2005) further revealed that 76% of organisations monitor an employee's Internet usage, 65% of which are blocking access to particular websites, highlighting Web surfing as a primary concern for many organisations. It is now estimated that as many as 80% of organisations monitor employee activities in the workplace – a figure which has doubled since 1997 (AMA, 2001; D'Urso, 2006).

Despite the fact that management are entitled to monitor employee behaviour primarily for 'business-related reasons', a recent study carried out by McParland and Connolly (2009) found that only 45% of employees surveyed knew their actions could be monitored by management while in the workplace. From this, only 22% believed that their actions were monitored on a regular – such as daily or weekly – basis. Interestingly however, a significant number of respondents indicated a strong degree of privacy concerns in relation to managements' ability to monitor their email interactions in the workplace, despite the fact that many were unsure of whether or not such activities actually occurred. For example, 35% were concerned that employers could log into and record their personal emails, 42% were concerned that they could access their emails without their knowledge and 45% were concerned with how management would or could use information obtained from their personal emails. Employees indicated a stronger level of concern regarding the monitoring of personal emails they receive (32%) as opposed to those they send themselves from their work email account (12%), confirming the notion that control is an important aspect in relation to privacy issues.

The concept and art of surveillance is based on the notion that one is 'under watch' or being observed in some way. However based on the fundamental principles of the 'Hawthorne Effect', it is reasonable to assume that if one is aware they are under observation they may alter their actions accordingly. For example, McParland and Connolly (2009) found that 84% of employees surveyed were careful about the type of information they would send in an email while in the workplace with only 32% sending a personal email if they thought their employer could not see them. Furthermore, 57% sent emails from their own personal (yahoo, gmail) account in order to prevent management from tracking their behaviour with only 54% of the overall sample accepting managements' right to monitor staff email interactions in the workplace.

While it is apparent that employees often alter or modify their behaviour in response to management monitoring activities, it is important to note that the use of such techniques may result in other more worrying outcomes. For example, many workers experience high degrees of stress because their activities and interactions can be monitored by employers (Tavani, 2004). Once again, based on the fundamental principles of panopticism, the question can be raised as to whether it is the presence of the 'invisible supervisor' that generates or in part fuels this distress. Ironically however, it is the computer-based information worker whose work is dependent upon the use of computer systems that is often the one most subjected to this form of monitoring. In a study carried out by McParland and Connolly (2009), it was found that many individuals felt extremely uncomfortable being under watch by management, expressing explicit concerns, questioning how the information collated is used and in some instances, even translating it into a failing performance or lack of ability on their behalf. This obvious negative impact that such surveillance techniques have on employee morale is a serious issue and one which must be addressed. In fact, the use of electronic surveillance in the workplace has been compared to that of a work environment tantamount to an 'electronic sweatshop' in some instances (Tavani, 2004).

Workplace surveillance clearly raises many ethical and social issues. However, in order to adequately address many of these issues, we must first consider the motivations behind management's decision to employ monitoring technologies in the first place.

Surveillance: Managements' Motivation

While many reports emphasise the risks faced by the employee, it is reasonable to assume that in some instances, management may have legitimate reasons to monitor their employees' actions. For example, profit driven organisations aim to manage their business in an efficient and productive manner and as such it may be unreasonable to expect that such companies would not avail themselves of methods or employ technologies to ensure that their employees are completing the

job they are being paid to do. Furthermore and perhaps more notably, organisations continually face the risk of adverse publicity resulting from offensive or explicit material circulating within the company and as such, many employ monitoring technologies to protect themselves from costly litigation claims (Laudon & Laudon, 2001). The Internet has increased the possible threat of hostile work environment claims by providing access to inappropriate jokes or images that can be transmitted internally or externally at the click of a button (Lane, 2003). In fact, a study carried out in 2000 concluded that 70% of the traffic on pornographic websites occurs during office hours, with ComScore networks reporting 37% of such visits actually taking place in the office environment (Alder *et al.*, 2006).

Moreover, the risks to organisations stretch also to the abuse of the email system, with virtually all the respondents in an AMA (2003) survey reporting some sort of disruption resulting from employees' email use. For example, 33% of the respondents experienced a computer virus, 34% reporting business interruptions and 38% of whom had a computer system disabled for some time as the result of a bogus email. In a similar vein, Jackson *et al.*, (2001) conducted a study to investigate the cost management endure as a result of such email interruption. The study indicated that it took the average employee between 1 and 44 seconds to respond to a new email when the icon or pop up box appeared on their screen. 70% of these mails were reacted to within 6 seconds of them appearing and a further 15% were reacted to within a 2 minute time period. Overall, the study found that it took on average, 64 seconds for an employee to return to a productive state of work for every one new email sent. Other practitioner reports also identify the potential cost of email usage with as many as 76% reporting a loss of business time due to email problems, 24% of which estimating a significant two day loss of company time (AMA, 2003). These statistics are not so surprising given the amount of time the average employee spends online. The survey further reported that the average employee spends 25% of his or her working day solely on their emails, with a further 90% admitting to sending and receiving personal mails during company time.

Whilst the need to improve productivity is a common rationale for employee monitoring, other motivations such as minimising theft and preventing workplace litigation can be considered equally justifiable in the eyes of management seeking to protect the interests of the organisation. The former motivation is particularly understandable as research shows that employees stole over 15 billion dollars in inventory from their employers in the year 2001 alone (Lane, 2003). In addition, the seamless integration of technology into the workplace has increased the threat of internal attacks with Lane (2003) noting the ease at which sensitive corporate data and trade secrets can be downloaded, transmitted, copied or posted onto a Web page by an aggrieved employee. Internal attacks typically target specific exploitable information, causing significant amounts of damage to an organisation (IBM, 2006). Management need to ensure that their employees use their working time productively and are therefore benefiting the organisation as a whole (Nord *et al.,* 2006). It is apparent however, that tensions will remain constant between both parties unless some form of harmony or balance between the interests of both the employer and employee is achieved.

In order to balance this conflict of interests however, it is vital that clearly defined rules and disciplinary offences are implemented into the workplace (Craver, 2006). The need for structure becomes all the more apparent when one considers the differing views and tolerance levels certain managers may hold (Selmi, 2006). For example, if an employee is hired to work, then technically they should refrain from sending personal emails or shopping online during working hours. However, as a general rule, most management will overlook these misdemeanours as good practice or in order to boost worker morale. The situation becomes

more serious however when the abuse of Internet privileges threatens to affect the company itself, be it through loss of profits or adverse publicity for the company. Furthermore, the problem increases as boundaries in the modern workplace begin to blur and confusion between formal and informal working conditions arise (Evans, 2007). For example by allowing an employee to take a company laptop into the privacy of their own home, management could be sending out a message that the computer can be used for personal use which may lead to the employee storing personal data on management's property. Legally, the employer would have claims over all of the data stored on the computer and could use it to discipline or even terminate an employee. In fact, it is this apparent lack of natural limit in regard to what is acceptable or indeed unacceptable relating to workplace privacy which makes the task of defining appropriate principles all the more difficult to comprehend (Godfrey, 2001).

An Ethical Paradox: Organisational Justice, Trust and Risk in Workplace Surveillance

The recent surge in the use of communication monitoring technologies within the computer-mediated work environment has further brought the issues of justice and fairness centre stage in the literature. In fact, justice and fairness are often cited as key drivers in managing the ethical and privacy concerns of employees who are subjected to monitoring practices within the computer-mediated work environment (Stanton, 2000a and 2000b; Zweig & Webster, 2002). Organisational justice is an overarching term used to describe individuals' perceptions of what is fair and just within the workplace. For researchers such as Stanton (2000b) justice theories thus provide researchers with a solid framework to help predict the perceived fairness of specific organisational procedures, outcomes and actions.

Justice perceptions for the main are separated into three specific forms, notably *(1) procedural justice, (2) distributive justice* and *(3) interactional justice.* The first of these antecedents, procedural justice centres around an individuals' perception that the organisational decision-making process will produce fair and just outcomes (Barrett-Howard and Tyler, 1986; Stanton, 2000b & Hauenstein *et al.,* 2001). In this way, procedural justice acts as a critical factor for understanding the relations between the supervisors' social power and the employees' subsequent reactions to it whereby they perceive positive outcomes in a more favourable light (Mossholder *et al.,* 1998). Distributive justice refers to the distribution of outcomes, measuring the extent to which employees feel recognised and therefore appropriately rewarded for their efforts within the workplace (Stanton, 2000b; Cohen-Charash and Spector, 2001 and Hauenstein *et al.,* 2001). In this way management are required to treat employees who are similar in respect to a certain outcome in the same manner, as opposed to basing decisions on arbitrary characteristics (Daft, 2000). According to Cohen-Charash & Spector (2001) if a distributive injustice is perceived, it will affect an employee's emotions, cognitions and their overall behaviour. The final facet of organisational justice, interactional justice stems from the interpersonal communications of the workplace, examining the quality of the interpersonal treatment employees experience at the hands of the company power- holders (Bies & Moag, 1986; Cohen-Charash & Spector, 2001). More specifically, it examines the extent to which employees' believe they have been treated with dignity, sincerity and respect during the distribution of outcomes as well as the process undertaken to achieve them by company decision-makers (Stanton, 2000b; Helne, 2005). Consequently, if an employee perceives interpersonal injustice they are more likely to act negatively towards their direct supervisor as opposed to the organisation or the injustice in question (Cohen-Charash & Spector, 2001).

Organisational justice theories have been linked to research on performance monitoring – specifically electronic performance monitoring [EPM] in the literature (Stanton & Barnes-Farrell, 1991; Stanton, 2000a; Stanton, 2000b). EPM differs from traditional (non-electronic) forms of monitoring in that it can be carried out on a continuous, large scale basis recording multiple dimensions of a single workers performance (Stanton, 2000a). The ubiquitous nature of these monitoring technologies contributes to the employees' ethical concerns relating to loss of personal privacy in the workplace.

Trust and risk perceptions also play an important role in the issue of workplace surveillance. For example, studies on trust – in particular relating to trust in leaders - are becoming increasingly prominent in the literature. Mayer *et al.,* (1995) for example, developed a model which suggested that integrity, benevolence and ability were major factors which had the potential to affect an individual's perception of trustworthiness in a leader. Similarly, a study carried out by Robinson and Rousseau (1994) found that as many as 55% of respondents reported a reduced level of trust in an employer as a result of management violating a psychological contract with them. The seamless integration of communication-monitoring technologies into the workplace can influence an employee's perception of the risks they face working in the computer-mediated environment. Therefore, it is conceivable that an employees' attitude towards the technology will act as an important determinant in the implementation process of communication-monitoring technologies into the workplace.

Furthermore, it is apparent that risk perceptions can affect how an individual makes specific decisions, subsequently influencing their behaviour. In fact, studies show that when an employee is aware they are under surveillance, they modify their behaviour accordingly. For example, a recent study carried out by SHRM in 2005 found that as many as 75% of employees display a certain degree of caution in relation to what they write in emails due to possible monitoring by the organisation. Similarly, the study showed that 47% are equally cautious in relation to telephone conversations while in the workplace environment. Studies show however, that the degree of risk perceived by an individual can be reduced if trust exists in a particular situation (So & Sculli, 2002). In this way, the significance of trust within studies on risk perception cannot be understated. In fact, an individuals' need to trust often relates directly to the risks involved in a given situation and consequently, the pervasive nature of communication-monitoring practices within the computer-mediated organisation hold risks that are unique to that context (Mayer *et al.*, 1995). In order for trust to be engendered however, employees must feel confident that the boundaries between what is acceptable and unacceptable in relation to information monitoring are clearly and openly stated. Those companies that are successful at building that trust and managing the uncertainty associated with communication monitoring practices will benefit from increased employee confidence.

It is becoming increasingly apparent that there is a significant disparity between management and employee perspectives on the issue of workplace surveillance. The uncertainty and lack of control related to the use of these communication monitoring technologies in the workplace reflects the significant asymmetry that exists in terms of what they mean to management versus the employee. While it is apparent that technology has created better, faster and cheaper ways for individuals to satisfy their own needs, the capability to leverage this technology is far higher for companies than for the employee. Because unequal forces, leading to asymmetric information availability, tilt the playing field significantly in favour of industry, such technologies do not create market benefit to all parties in an equitable manner (Prakhaber, 2000). As such, one of the major tasks facing the computer-mediated organisation is that of identi-

fying the factors to improve employees' attitudes and behavioural reactions towards surveillance in the workplace. There is a distinct need for the implementation of clear measures that govern the effective and fair use of communication technologies in the workplace, allowing management to monitor their staff in a reasonable and rational manner. Management should consider the ethical and social impacts that surveillance techniques may have within the workplace and employ specific policies which may both minimise the negative implications associated with the use of such technology as well as helping to improve employee receptiveness overall.

A Code of Ethics for Workplace Surveillance

Organisations looking for ways in which to balance this conflict of interest between management and employees are focusing towards the use of workplace policies, many of which are framed on established or predefined codes of ethics. For example, Marx and Sherizen (1991) argue that employees should be made aware in advance of any monitoring practices conducted in the workplace before they actually occur. In this way, the individual can electively decide whether or not he or she wishes to work for that particular organisation. Furthermore the authors suggest that the employee should have the right to both view information collated on them and challenge inaccurate information before it can be used against them. This idea of 'transparency' in relation to surveillance methods is commonly supported by privacy advocates however it can be argued that it goes against fundamental principles of the act of surveillance. Similarly, we can once again note the impact of the 'Hawthorne Effect' in that individuals will alter their behaviour if they believe they are being observed in some way. In this way management need to have clearly defined sanctions in place within the organisation informing employees of the depth and detail of monitoring practices in the company whilst deterring them from abusing workplace systems.

Other ethical strategies focus solely on how management use the information collated on employees in the workplace. Again, we can note that the scope of surveillance is generally divided into two main components - one relating to the actual act of monitoring or surveillance itself, the second relating to how the collated information can be used. In some cases, it is reasonable to assume that employees may not fear the act of surveillance but more so how the information could be used and whether or not employers will make subsequent judgements about them (Introna, 2001). For example, McParland and Connolly (2009) found that 33% of employees they surveyed were concerned that their employers would react negatively to their use of personal email in the workplace, however, 24% still thought it was reasonable to use work email to chat freely with their friends and colleagues. Once again, the lines regarding what are acceptable or indeed unacceptable forms of behaviour begin to blur.

In order to alleviate much of this confusion, other researchers such as Turban *et al.,* (2010) apply the basic ethical principles to information collected in an online environment. It is apparent however, that these basic ethical principles can also be applied to the use of communication-monitoring technologies in the workplace environment, thus providing a solid framework to guide management in their efforts to monitor employees in a fair and effective manner. The basic principles include the following:

1. **Notice or awareness**: employees should be made aware of the extent and detail of monitoring techniques, prior to the collection or use of personal information.
2. **Choice or consent**: employees should be made aware of how the collated information can be used and consent must be granted by the employee by signing a workplace policy

or notification which outlines the companies monitoring practices.
3. **Access or participation**: Employees should be able to access certain information on them and challenge the validity of the data.
4. **Integration or security**: Employees should be assured that their personal information is kept secure within the organisation and can not be used in a way which was not intended.
5. **Enforcement or redress**: Employees must be made aware of organisational sanctions set in place such that a misuse of workplace systems will be detected and punished by management. Otherwise, there is no deterrent or indeed, enforceability to protect privacy.

Effective workplace policies need to protect the interests of all parties involved. A code needs to be developed that protects the interests of both the employee and the employer. Little progress can be made in this area however, unless the current privacy legislation is addressed.

Legal Protections: The Role of Privacy Legislation

Privacy legislation differs considerably between Europe and the United States. While both Europe and the United States define privacy in a similar way, it is the fundamental objective of their information privacy laws that signifies the major difference between the two. For example, in Europe, privacy protection is considerably stronger than in the United States as it focuses on controlling and regulating managements' collection and use of employee data. While the European Directive is based on the Fair Information Doctrine of the United States, it extends the level of control an individual can exercise over their own personal information (Laudon & Traver, 2010). In this way, European law lends itself more to the protection of data – and therefore the individual – compared to the United States which focuses more on the use and collection of data. Any country that is a member state of the European Union [EU] must comply with the legislation that is passed by any one of its major institutions as well as any national laws or regulations set in place. Furthermore, under the Directive 95/46/EC and Article 29 WP55, all monitoring in the organisation must pass a number of specified criteria before being implemented into the workplace.

Under current EU legislation, the employer must prove that electronic observation is a necessary course of action for a specific purpose before engaging in it. In this way, management are encouraged to consider traditional and less intrusive measures of observation before resorting to electronic means (Directive 95/46/EC). For the purpose of Internet or indeed email surveillance, it is likely that some form of electronic monitoring would be enlisted, however, in such instances, the employer by law, can keep the data in question no longer than necessary for the specific monitoring action. In a similar vein, the second principle of finality denotes that any data collected must be used for an explicit purpose and therefore cannot be processed or used for any other purpose than initially intended (Directive 95/46/EC).

Under EU law, management must also be clear and open regarding the surveillance practices of the organisation and are therefore obliged to provide employees with information regarding organisational monitoring policies. In this way, employees are advised of improper procedures and disciplinary offences that justify the scope of invasive monitoring techniques (Directive 95/46/EC). Furthermore, details of the surveillance measures undertaken are also provided so as the employee will know who is monitoring them, how they are being monitored, as well as when these actions are taking place. This principle of transparency also provides individuals with access rights to personal data processed or collated by management, allowing them to request its rectification or deletion where appropriate (Directive 95/46/EC).

The fourth criterion, legitimacy, is similar to that of necessity in so far as data can only be obtained for a justifiable purpose and must not contravene an employee's fundamental or inherent right to privacy. Under this element of the legislation however, data of a very sensitive nature can be deemed too personal to collect and collection therefore must be specifically authorised by a national law in extreme circumstances (Directive 95/46/EC). Organisations must also comply with the notion of proportionality, using the most non-intrusive or least excessive action in order to obtain the desired information. For example, the monitoring of emails should, if possible, focus on the general information such as the time and transmission as opposed to the content, if the situation permits. If, however, viewing of the email content is deemed necessary, then the law presides that the privacy of those outside of the organisation should also be taken into account and that reasonable efforts be made to inform the outside world of any monitoring practices (Directive 95/46/EC).

Any data that is collated on an employee must only be retained for as long as is necessary under this European law and data that is no longer needed should then be deleted. Management should specify a particular retention period based on their business needs so that employees are constantly aware of the ongoing process (Directive 95/46/EC). Furthermore, provisions should be set in place to ensure that any data that is held by the employer will remain secure and safe from any form of intrusion or disturbance. The employer is also required to protect the technological medium from the threat of viruses as a further means of protecting the personal data (Directive 95/46/EC).

It is apparent that the central concept of the European Directive relates to the processing and flow of information (Elgesem, 1999). As a result, researchers such as Evans (2007) note how the existence of these European laws that favour the employee are consequently putting considerable pressure on the United States to adopt similar laws. In fact, it has been previously suggested that the various proposals and directives – or at least the relevant aspects of them - should be combined into one robust comprehensive model (Tavani, 2004). While such a model combining the interests of both the organisation and the employee would appear to be a sensible solution, for Wang, Lee and Wang (1998) it poses 'one of the most challenging public policy issues of the information age'.

FUTURE RESEARCH DIRECTIONS

The themes identified in this chapter have implications for future academic work in the area of workplace surveillance. Although there is increasing evidence that workplace surveillance is on the rise, the factors influencing management to electively employ monitoring technologies remains ambiguous. Furthermore, the lines regarding what are correct and moral forms of behaviour continually blur thus limiting our overall understanding of the main issues involved as well as the ways in which to target them. In fact, the use of Internet-based technologies in the workplace presents businesses and employees with opportunities to engage in behaviours for which comprehensive understandings or rules have not yet been established.

As such, it is imperative that future research aims to alleviate this confusion by addressing these issues from both a rigorous and relevant perspective. In order to examine and understand the factors that inhibit and amplify workplace surveillance issues, future researchers must begin by exploring these issues directly with those that face them. There is significant scope for a large scale detailed study to be conducted that addresses some, if not all of these issues from both an employee and employer perspective. A study conducted in such a manner could not only identify the frequent concerns that exist in response to workplace surveillance techniques but could further explore what technologies IS departments employ to monitor activities and

perhaps, more importantly, why. Only then can we try to establish some form of balance or harmony between both parties in the computer-mediated workplace environment.

Further research into the main issues of workplace surveillance will be of great significance and interest to practitioners also. Employees are the lifeblood of any organisation and only by understanding the behavioural outcomes of such individuals can we begin to understand the factors that predict the perceptions, attitudes and beliefs that are generated through the implementation of communication monitoring techniques in the workplace. Consequently future research into some of these major issues will have significant and important consequences for the businesses that employ these growing and developing technologies.

CONCLUSION

The primary objective of this chapter was to address the issue of electronic monitoring in the computer-mediated work environment. This chapter explored the ethical impact of monitoring in the computer-mediated work environment, addressing whether management's ability to monitor employee actions in the workplace represents good business practice or constitutes an invasion of privacy. While it is apparent that management may have legitimate reasons to monitor employees' actions in the workplace, the privacy rights of the employee cannot be ignored. In this way, it is paramount that some form of harmony or balance between the interests of the employer and the employee is achieved.

In general however, studies on workplace surveillance issues are limited in the literature. While surveillance issues have long been of concern for many, the increased ability of management to use technology to gather, store and analyse sensitive information on employees on a continuously updated basis has increased the acuteness of such concerns. It is apparent that European laws favour the rights of the employee, however, within the literature, no hierarchy of privacy or ethical concerns on the part of employers and employees has yet been identified. Moreover, as far as it is possible to ascertain, the factors influencing employers and IS managers in their decisions to electively employ surveillance technologies have not been explored. As a result, our understanding of these issues, and the ways in which employee privacy concerns could be diminished - thus positively impacting productivity and morale - remains a matter of speculation and a fruitful avenue for researchers to explore.

REFERENCES

Acquisti, A. (2002). *Protecting privacy with economic: Economic incentives for preventive technologies in ubiquitous computing environment.* Workshop on Socially-informed Design of Privacy-enhancing Solutions in Ubiquitous Computing: Ubicomp 2002.

Alder, G. S., Noel, T. W., & Ambrose, M. L. (2006). Clarifying the effects of Internet monitoring on job attitudes: The mediating role of employee trust. *Information & Management*, *43*(7), 894–903. doi:10.1016/j.im.2006.08.008

Barrett-Howard, E., & Tyler, T. R. (1986). Procedural justice as a criterion in allocation decisions. *Journal of Personality and Social Psychology*, *50*(2), 296–304. doi:10.1037/0022-3514.50.2.296

Bies, R. J., & Moag, J. F. (1986). Interactional justice: Communication criteria of fairness. In Lewicki, R. J., Sheppard, B. H., & Bazerman, M. H. (Eds.), *Research on negotiations in organisations* (1st ed., pp. 43–55). Greenwich, CT: JAI Press.

Clarke, R. A. (1988). Information Technology and dataveillance. *Communications of the ACM*, *31*(5), 498–512. doi:10.1145/42411.42413

Cohen-Charash, Y., & Spector, P. E. (2001). The role of justice in organizations: A meta-analysis. *Organizational Behavior and Human Decision Processes*, *86*(2), 278–321. doi:10.1006/obhd.2001.2958

Craver, C. B. (2006). Privacy issues affecting employers, employees and labour organizations. *Louisiana Law Review*, *66*, 1057–1078.

D'Urso, S. C. (2006). Who's watching us at work? Toward a structural-perceptual model of electronic monitoring and surveillance in organisations. *Communication Theory*, *16*, 281–303. doi:10.1111/j.1468-2885.2006.00271.x

Daft, R. L. (2000). *Management* (5th ed.). Fort Worth, TX: The Dryden Press, Harcourt College Publishers.

Directive 95/46/EC (2002). *Article 29 WP55 2002*. Retrieved from http://ec.europa.eu/justice_home/fsj/privacy/docs/wpdocs/2002/wpss_en.pdf

Elgesem, D. (1999). The structure of rights in directive 95/46/EC on the protection of individuals with regard to the processing of personal data and the free movement of such data. *Ethics and Information Technology*, *1*(4), 283–293. doi:10.1023/A:1010076422893

Evans, L. (2007). Monitoring technology in the American workplace: Would adopting English privacy standards better balance employee privacy and productivity? *California Law Review*, *95*, 1115–1149.

Foucault, M. (1977). *Discipline and punish: The birth of the prison.* Great Britain: Penguin Books.

Ghosh, A. P. (1998). *E-commerce security–weak links, best defences.* N.J.: John Wiley and Sons, Inc.

Godfrey, B. (2001). Electronic work monitoring: An ethical model. *Australian Computer Society*, 18-21.

Harris Poll. (2003). *Harris interactive*. Retrieved from http://www.harrisinteractive.com/ harris_poll/ index.asp? PID=365

Hauenstein, N. M. A., McGonigle, T., & Flinder, S. W. (2001). A meta-analysis of the relationship between procedural justice and distributive justice: Implications for justice research. *Employee Responsibilities and Rights Journal, 13*(1), 39–56. doi:10.1023/A:1014482124497

Helne, C. A. (2005). Predicting workplace deviance from the interaction between organizational justice and personality. *Journal of Managerial Issues, 11*(2), 247–263.

IBM. (2006). Stopping insider attacks: How organizations can protect their sensitive information. Retrieved from http://www-935.ibm.com/ services/ us/imc/ pdf/ gsw00316-usen-0 0-insider-threats-w p.pdf

Introna, L. D. (1996). Privacy and the computer: Why we need privacy in the information society. *Ethicomp e-Journal, 1*.

Introna, L. D. (2001). Workplace surveillance, privacy and distributive justice. In Spinello, R. A., & Tavani, H. T. (Eds.), *Readings in cyberethics* (pp. 519–532). Sudbury, MA: Jones and Barlett Publishers.

Jackson, T., Dawson, R., & Wilson, D. (2001). *The cost of email interruption*. Loughborough University Institutional Repository: Item 2134/495. Retrieved from http://km.lboro.ac.uk/ iii/ pdf/ JOSIT% 2020 01.pdf

Lane, F. S. (2003). *The naked employee: How technology is compromising workplace privacy*. New York, NY: AMACOM, American Management Association.

Laudon, K. C., & Laudon, J. P. (2001). *Essentials of management Information Systems: Organisation and technology in the networked enterprise* (4th ed.). Prentice Hall.

Laudon, K. C., & Laudon, J. P. (2002). *Management Information Systems: Managing the digital firm* (7th ed.). New Jersey: Prentice Hall International.

Laudon, K. C., & Traver, C. G. (2010). *E-commerce 2010–business, technology, society* (6th ed.). Boston, MA: Pearson.

Louis Harris Poll. (1999). Louis Harris and associates. Retrieved from http://www.natlconsumersleague.org/ FNLSUM1.PDF

Marx, G., & Sherizen, S. (1991). Monitoring on the job: How to protect privacy as well as property. In Forester, T. (Ed.), *Computers in the human context: Information Technology, productivity, and people* (pp. 397–406). Cambridge, MA: MIT Press.

Mayer, R. C., Davis, J. D., & Schoorman, F. D. (1995). An integrative model of organisational trust. *Academy of Management Review, 20*(3), 709–734. doi:10.2307/258792

McParland, C., & Connolly, R. (2009). *The role of dataveillance in the organsiation: Some emerging trends*. Irish Academy of Management Conference, Galway, 2009.

Mossholder, K. W., Bennett, N., Kemery, E. R., & Wesolowski, M. A. (1998). Relationships between bases of power and work reactions: The mediational role of procedural justice. *Journal of Management, 24*(4), 533–552. doi:10.1016/ S0149-2063(99)80072-5

Nord, G. D., McCubbins, T. F., & Horn Nord, J. (2006). Email monitoring in the workplace: Privacy, legislation, and surveillance software. *Communications of the ACM, 49*(8), 73–77.

Parker, R. B. (1974). A definition of privacy. *Rutgers Law Review, 27*(1), 275.

Prakhaber, P. R. (2000). Who owns the online consumer? *Journal of Consumer Marketing, 17*(2), 158–171. doi:10.1108/07363760010317213

Robinson, S. L., & Rousseau, D. M. (1994). Violating the psychological contract: Not the exception but the norm. *Journal of Organizational Behavior*, *15*(3), 245–259. doi:10.1002/job.4030150306

Rust, R. T., Kannan, P. K., & Peng, N. (2002). The customer economics of Internet privacy. *Journal of the Academy of Marketing Science*, *30*(4), 455–464. doi:10.1177/009207002236917

Safire, W. (2002). The great unwatched. *New York Times*. Retrieved from http://query.nytimes.com/ gst/ fullpage.html ?res=9A03 E7DB1E3FF93B A25751C0A964 9C8B63

Selmi, M. (2006). Privacy for the working class: Public work and private lives. *Louisiana Law Review*, *66*, 1035–1056.

SHRM. (2005). *Workplace privacy–poll findings*. A Study by the Society for Human Resource Management and CareerJournal.com.

So, M. W. C., & Sculli, D. (2002). The role of trust, quality, value and risk in conducting e-business. *Industrial Management & Data Systems*, *102*(9), 503–512. doi:10.1108/02635570210450181

Stanton, J. M. (2000a). Reactions to employee performance monitoring: Framework, review, and research directions. *Human Performance*, *13*(1), 85–113. doi:10.1207/S15327043HUP1301_4

Stanton, J. M. (2000b). Traditional and electronic monitoring from an organizational justice perspective. *Journal of Business and Psychology*, *15*(1), 129–147. doi:10.1023/A:1007775020214

Stanton, J. M., & Barnes-Farrell, J. L. (1996). Effects of electronic performance-monitoring on personal control, satisfaction and performance. *The Journal of Applied Psychology*, *81*, 738–745. doi:10.1037/0021-9010.81.6.738

Survey, A. M. A. (2001). Workplace monitoring and surveillance. Retrieved from http://www. amanet.org/ research /pdfs/ ems_short20 01.pdf

Survey, A. M. A. (2003). Email rules, policies and practices survey. Retrieved from http://www. amanet.org/ research/ pdfs/ email_policies_practices.pdf

Survey, A. M. A. (2005). Electronic monitoring and surveillance survey. Retrieved from http://www. amanet.org/ research/ pdfs/ ems_summary0 5.pdf

Tavani, H. T. (2004). *Ethics and technology: Ethical issues in an age of information and communication technology. Wiley* (International Edition). John Wiley and Sons.

Turban, E., King, D., Lee, J., Liang, T. P., & Turban, D. (2010). *Electronic commerce 2010: A managerial perspective* (6th ed.). Boston, MA: Pearson.

Turban, E., Leidner, D., McClean, E., & Wetherbe, J. (2006). *Information Technology for management–transforming organisations in the digital economy* (5th ed.). USA: John Wiley & Sons Inc.

Turow, J., Feldman, L., & Metlzer, K. (2005). *Open to exploitation: American shoppers online and offline*. A Report from the Annenberg Public Policy Centre of the University of Pennsylvania.

Wang, H., Lee, M. K. O., & Wang, C. (1998). Consumer privacy concerns about Internet marketing. *Communications of the ACM*, *41*(3), 63–70. doi:10.1145/272287.272299

Wen, H. J., Schwieger, D., & Gershuny, P. (2007). Internet usage monitoring in the workplace: Its legal challenges and implementation strategies. *Information Systems Management*, *24*, 185–196. doi:10.1080/10580530701221072

Zweig, D., & Webster, J. (2002). Where is the line between benign and invasive? An examination of psychological barriers to the acceptance of awareness monitoring system. *Journal of Organizational Behavior*, *23*(5), 605–633. doi:10.1002/job.157

ADDITIONAL READING

Adams, A. (1999). Users' Perception of Privacy in Multimedia Communication, IN: *Proceedings of CHI'99*. Pittsburg P.A.

Adams, A., & Sasse, M. A. (2001). Privacy in Multimedia Communications: Protecting Users Not Just Data, IN: *Proceedings of IMH HCPOI*, Lille pp49-64.

Agranoff, M. H. (1993). Controlling the Threat to Personal Privacy. *Journal of Information Systems Management, 8*(3), 48–52.

Ajzen, I. (1988). *Attitudes, Personality, and Behaviour*. Milton Keynes: Open University Press.

Beal, G. M., & Bohlean, J. M. (1957). The Diffusion Process, IN: *Special Report No.18 Iowa State University of Science and Technology,* Reprinted Nov 1981.

Beldiman, D. (2002). An Information Society Approach to Privacy Legislation: How to Enhance Privacy while Maximizing Information Value. *Review of Intellectual Property Law, 2*(1), 71–94.

Boatright, R. J. (2004). *Ethics and the Conduct of Business*. London: Pearson Education.

Culnan, M. J. (2000). Protecting Privacy Online: Is Self-Regulation Working? *Journal of Public Policy & Marketing, 19*(Spring), 20–26. doi:10.1509/jppm.19.1.20.16944

Davis, F.D. (1989). Perceived Usefulness, Perceived Ease of Use, and User Acceptance of Information Technology, *MIS Quarterly*, Sept.

Davis, F. D. (1993). User Acceptance of Information Technology: System Charactoristics, User Perceptions and Behavioural Impacts. *International Journal of Man-Machine Studies, 38*, 475–478. doi:10.1006/imms.1993.1022

Davis, F. D. (1996). A Critical Assessment of Potential Measurement Biases n the Technology Acceptance Model: Three Experiments. *International Journal of Human-Computer Studies, 45*, 19–45. doi:10.1006/ijhc.1996.0040

Davis, F. D., Bagozzi, R. P., & Warshaw, P. R. (1989). User Acceptance of Computer Technology: A Comparison of Two Theorectical Models. *Management Science, 35*(8), 982–1003. doi:10.1287/mnsc.35.8.982

De Boni, M., & Prigmore, M. (2002). Cultural Aspects of Internet Privacy, IN: *Proceedings of the 7th Annual UK Academy for Information Systems Conference* (UKAIS'02), Leeds.

Dryer, D. C., Eisbach, C., & Ark, W. S. (1999). At What Cost Pervasive? A Social Computing View of Mobile Computing Systems. *IBM Systems Journal, 38*(4), 652–676. doi:10.1147/sj.384.0652

Elgesem, D. (1999). *Privacy, Respect for Persons, and Risk. Philosophical Perspectives on Computer Mediated Communication, edited by C.* Ess, New York: State University of New York Press.

Galanxhi-Janaqi, H., & Fui-Hoon Nah, F. (2004). U-commerce: Emerging Trends and Research Issues. *Industrial Management & Data Systems, 104*(9), 744–755. doi:10.1108/02635570410567739

Galanxhi-Janaqi, H., & Fui-Hoon Nah, F. (2006). Privacy Issues in the Era of Ubiquitous Commerce. *Electronic Markets, 16*(3), 222–232. doi:10.1080/10196780600841894

Gefen, D. (2000). E-Commerce: The Role of Familiarity and Trust. *Omega: The International Journal of Management Science, 28*(6), 725–737. doi:10.1016/S0305-0483(00)00021-9

Langheinrich (2001). Privacy by Design – Principles of Privacy – Aware Ubiquitous Systems, IN: *Proceedings of the 3rd International Conference on Ubiquitous Computing*, Atlanta, Georgia. Springer-Verlag LCNS 2201, pp273-291.

Lederer, S. (2003). Designing Disclosure: Interactive Personal Privacy at the Dawn of Ubiquitous Computing, *M.S Report,* Computer Science Division University of California at Berkley December 2003.

Lederer, S., Dey, A. K., & Mankoff, J. (2002a). A Conceptual Model and Metaphor of Everyday Privacy in Ubiquitous Computing, Intel *Research Technical Report*, Berkeley.

Lederer, S., Dey, A. K., & Mankoff, J. (2002b). Everyday Privacy in Ubiquitous Computing Environments, IN: *Ubicomp Workshop on Socially-Informed Design of Privacy-Enhancing Solutions in Ubiquitous Computing*

Miller, A. R. (1971). *The Assault on Privacy*. University of Michigan Press.

Singh, S., Puradkar, S., & Lee, Y. (2005). *Ubiquitous Computing: Connecting Pervasive Computing through Semantic Web*. Springer-Verlag.

Smith, A. D. (2005). Exploring Radio Frequency Identification Technology and its Impact on Business Systems. *Information Management & Computer Security*, *13*(1), 16–28. doi:10.1108/09685220510582647

Stone, E. F., Gardner, D. G., Gueutal, H. G., & McClure, S. (1983). A Field Experiment Comparing Information-Privacy Values, Beliefs, and Attitudes Across Several Types of Organizations. *The Journal of Applied Psychology*, *68*(3), 459–468. doi:10.1037/0021-9010.68.3.459

Tavani, H. T. (1999). Internet Privacy: Some Distinctions between Internet Specific and Internet-Enhanced Privacy Concerns. *The ETHICOMP E-Journal*, *1*, 1999.

Tavani, H.T (2001). Privacy Protection, Control of Information and Privacy Enhancing Technologies, *Computers and Society,* March.

KEY TERMS AND DEFINITIONS

Dataveillance: The monitoring or surveillance of data

Workplace Surveillance: Monitoring individuals' actions in the workplace.

Computer-Mediated Surveillance: Monitoring individuals' computer interactions.

Pervasive Computing Environment: An environment which is characterised by the seamless integration of technologies into society.

Electronic Panopticism: A form of electronic surveillance whereby you are unsure of when exactly your actions are being monitored.

Chapter 9

Policy and Issues in Deploying Automated Plagiarism Detection Systems in Academic Communities:
A Case Study of VeriGuide

Chi Hong Cheong
The Chinese University of Hong Kong, Hong Kong

Tak Pang Lau
The Chinese University of Hong Kong, Hong Kong

Irwin King
The Chinese University of Hong Kong, Hong Kong

ABSTRACT

Plagiarism is becoming prevalent through the use of the Internet. Educational institutions are seeking technology to combat plagiarism. This chapter describes policy and issues encountered by an educational institution that deploys an automated plagiarism detection system. Background information of plagiarism and the benefits of using automated plagiarism detection systems are presented as motivation. A detailed account on the benefits of using automated plagiarism detection system in the academic setting is given. Associated policy issues (administrative issues, submission policy issues, disciplinary issues, copyright issues, security and privacy issues, and ethical issues) and resources needed to deploy such a system are discussed in details. VeriGuide, an automated plagiarism detection system designed and implemented at the Chinese University of Hong Kong, is presented as a case study on how the technology can be used to alleviate workload for the teachers and also provide a fair academic environment for the students. It is hoped that the case study would be helpful for those who are interested in using such a system to promote academic quality and integrity.

DOI: 10.4018/978-1-60960-573-5.ch009

INTRODUCTION

Plagiarism refers to the dishonest act of taking credit for someone else's intellectual properties. It can appear in many forms, such as copying text, programming codes, images, and music (BBC news, 2010; Mcdonell, T. B., 2008; Tahaghoghi, S., 2008). In the case of academic writing, plagiarizing is copying or borrowing ideas without properly citing the source. It is sometimes possible that a person may not realize that he or she is plagiarizing when he or she does. Nevertheless, ignorance is never an excuse for plagiarism (Goodwin, D. K., 2002; Plotz, D., 2002). There are five types of plagiarism, namely copy and paste plagiarism, word switch plagiarism, style plagiarism, metaphor plagiarism, and idea plagiarism (Barnbaum, C., n.d.; Liles, J. A., & Rozalski, M. E., 2004). Copy and paste plagiarism involves cutting and pasting text from the Internet or electronic sources. Word switch plagiarism is similar to copy and paste plagiarism with the exception of changing a few words to evade detection. Style plagiarism copies the text by paraphrasing it. Metaphor plagiarism means copying the metaphors from the source article. Idea plagiarism is the failure to distinguish between public domain information and creative ideas in the source article. All five categories of academic plagiarism involve taking credit for ideas that belongs to somebody else by failing to give proper citations to the original authors.

Academic plagiarism is a growing problem all over the world. The vast amount of readily available resources in the Internet has made plagiarism easier. Even though the severity of the problem can be mitigated by moral education, it is foreseeable that the problem is here to stay. In the United States, a survey by Rutgers University (Beam, A., 2003) based on 18,000 college students, 2,600 faculty members, and 650 teaching assistants from 23 campuses suggests that 10% of students surveyed used the Internet to plagiarize in 2000; but the figure grew to 38% in 2003. Furthermore, almost 50% of students surveyed

did not consider Internet plagiarism as cheating. In 2008, the student newspaper Varsity reported that: "49 per cent of Cambridge students have committed some form of plagiaristic act whilst at the University" (Stothard, M., 2008). Moreover, plagiarism is not exclusive to students. There are reported cases of faculty members copying from conference and journal papers (Kock, N., 1999; Smallwood, S., 2004; BBC news, 2008). The seriousness of the problem is augmented by students' lack of a proper concept of plagiarism. Some students think that plagiarism is either not wrong or wrong only if they are caught. This phenomenon was reported by BBC News (2006a). The open secret was publicly confirmed when some students admitted that they had searched the Internet for model essays or copied their friends' work (BBC news, 2006b).

The consequences of plagiarism are summarized as follows from different viewpoints (Dey, S. K., & Sobhan, M. A., 2006; Harris, R. A., 2001; Howard, R. M., 1999):

Student. Widespread plagiarism deteriorates the learning attitudes of students and results in an unfair learning environment and scoring. The motivation to do the hard work of learning new knowledge will be weakened if students have the option to choose the easy way out by cheating. An environment that tolerates plagiarism is unfair to those students who are honest. Sooner or later, even the honest students will start plagiarizing in order to compete. The vicious circle continues.

Teacher. In order to stop plagiarism, teachers have to spend extra time and energy to verify submitted work (Bjaaland, P. C., & Lederman, A., 1973). For example, they would invent countermeasures, such as requiring students to link the assignments with activities in the classroom (Satterwhite. R., & Gerein,. M., 2001) or using obscured topics in student assignments. The problem worsens when the class size is large and when students are experienced in counter-detection methods such as extensive paraphrasing and copying from multiple references. When too much resource is tied up in the detection process, the quality of teaching will likely suffer.

Institution. The prospect of unfair scoring, the prevalence of unmotivated students and deteriorating teaching quality will eventually be reflected in the institution's reputation. On the fundamental level, the school will have failed its mission to produce well-trained graduates and to promote academic excellence.

Society. A society invests in education to instill beneficial qualities, such as creativity, originality, productivity, and morality, in the next generation. Plagiarism is counter-productive toward this end.

Plagiarism has serious negative impacts on all aspects of the educational enterprise. Therefore it must be stopped. Some ways to discourage plagiarism are to publish a clear school policy regarding plagiarism, educate students on plagiarism and proper citations, promote ethical academic behaviors, design assignments and assessments in such a way that students have difficulties in committing plagiarism, and teach students how to summarize ideas or words from their properly cited materials (Carroll, J., 2001; Cogdell, B., & Aidulis, D., 2007; Porter, J.E., 2005). Nevertheless, these measures cannot completely prevent students from committing plagiarism. Hence, an efficient way to detect plagiarism is still needed, such as deploying an automated plagiarism detection system.

An automated plagiarism detection system computerizes the plagiarism detection process that is difficult and time consuming to perform manually. Its main function is to search for plagiarized sentences in students' submissions automatically. The system provides other functions such as the search of reference materials from the Internet. In general, an automated plagiarism detection system promotes and upholds academic integrity. More precisely, such a system offers the following advantages:

Objectivity. The computerized system offers an objective measurement of plagiarized work. Decision as to whether the work is plagiarized is based on statistical analysis in a systematic manner without bias.

Automation. The automated system relieves teachers from the otherwise tedious, repetitive, and error-prone tasks of plagiarism checking when done by hand. By reducing the labor-intensive work, the teacher has more time for other teaching-related activities.

Scalability. As the information on the Internet continues to increase at a rapid rate, the system is able to keep up with the breadth and depth of the data used in plagiarism detection making the system robust over time.

Flexibility. The system provides adjustable parameters to meet the teacher's specific needs such as scope matching and leniency level. (These terms will be explained later.)

In summary, an automated plagiarism detection system is a step toward a better learning environment. It has the potential of encouraging students to be more self-disciplined in doing creative and original work and teachers to be more productive. The end result is hopefully better academic performance and higher moral standard in an institution as a whole.

The deployment of an automated plagiarism detection system typically involves three types of stakeholders. They are policy maker, executor, and supporter.

Policy Maker. A policy maker (such as the senate committee of the education institution) sets the policy for the automated plagiarism detection system (such as who should submit the assignments to the system and whether the submission is mandatory). In addition, the policy maker has to define the protocol when a case of suspected plagiarism is identified and the appropriate punishment when the case is verified. The policy maker may have to discuss with all the relevant constituents (e.g., students, teachers, and the disciplinary committee) during the course of deciding the policy. Furthermore, the policy maker has to be aware of issues related to copyright, privacy, and security and to delegate responsibilities to the appropriate constituents. Once the policy is set and the system is deployed, the policy maker has to evaluate the effectiveness of the system, collect feedback from the constituents, and be ready to make changes if necessary.

Executor. After the policy is made and the procedures are defined, certain constituents have to enforce the policy and implement the procedures. For example, teachers may have to either submit students' assignments to the automated plagiarism detection system or teach the students to submit their assignments to the system themselves. The disciplinary committee has to follow the procedures set by the policy maker to handle plagiarism cases and to decide on the appropriate punishment within the guidelines set by the policy.

Supporter. The smooth operation of the automated plagiarism detection system depends on a support team providing technical, legal, and logistic supports. The IT department needs to collect data from the constituents and to create accounts for students, teachers, and courses. Once the system is deployed, the IT department has to maintain the system and to protect it from hackers. Workshops need to be organized to teach teachers and students how to use the system. The library and the licensing office have to deal with the copyright and legal issues of the digital resources used by the system. They need to obtain permission from the owners to use these resources in the system and reports generated by the system.

Plagiarism is a serious problem worldwide. It affects everyone involved, such as students, teachers, administrators, and the society at large. In order to combat plagiarism, the appropriate infrastructure and technologies are needed. The goal of the rest of this chapter is to explain in details the aforementioned issues related to the deployment of an automatic plagiarism detection system in an educational institution. For each issue, solutions and their pros and cons are discussed. Resources needed for the system are clearly stated so that an educational institution can assess its readiness to deploy the system. Finally, a case study of Veri-

Guide (an automated plagiarism detection system deployed at the Chinese University of Hong Kong since 2005) is used as a reference to provide further insights on how to deploy plagiarism software in an academic institution.

POLICY AND ISSUES

In this section, common issues encountered by an educational institution on the deployment of an automatic plagiarism detection system (administration, submission policy, disciplinary actions, copyright, security, privacy, and ethics) are explained. It is hoped that general readers who are interested in the automatic plagiarism detection system can find all of the relevant information in this brief discussion.

Administrative Issues

There are two basic modes of submission: the student-oriented vs. the teacher-oriented. The student-oriented version refers to the case in which students submit their assignments to the system directly. Alternatively the teacher-oriented version allows the teachers to collect students' assignments first and then submit them to the system. No matter which version is used, the reports generated by the system are always sent to the teachers and it is the duty of the teachers to send reports of suspicious cases to the disciplinary committee. An example of the flow of the assignments and the routing of reports in the student-oriented and teacher-oriented versions are summarized in Figure 1.

In the student-oriented version, students know that their assignments will be checked by the system and are more likely to refrain from plagiarizing. The workload of teachers is reduced by virtue of letting the students submit their assignments to the system themselves. As long as reports are not distributed to students so that none of them can use the feedback in the reports to figure out ways to break the system, it does not count as a

Figure 1. The flow of assignments and reports for the student-oriented and the teacher-oriented versions

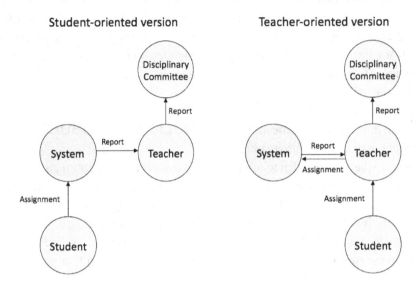

disadvantage of the student-oriented version. However, the cost of maintenance is higher because additional accounts have to be created for students and the system has to handle more users. The teacher-oriented version gives teachers a tighter control over the submission process. The price of more control is that the workload of teachers is increased since they have to submit the assignments for the students. The pros and cons of the two versions are summarized in Table 1.

The student-oriented version is more suitable for educational institutions with a large number of students because of the volume of submissions to the system. In the Chinese University of Hong Kong, the plagiarism detection system received over 42,000 student submissions in term 1 of 2009. Some courses can have more than 100

students. Teachers' workload can be decreased if the student-oriented version is deployed. On the other hand, the teacher-oriented version is more suitable for elementary schools because it is difficult to teach young students to submit assignments to the system. At the end, the choice between student-oriented versus teacher-oriented version is dependent on the importance assigned to the pros and cons in a particular situation.

Submission Policy Issues

Assignment submission to the system can be either mandatory or optional. Mandatory submission policy mandates that assignments for all courses and all students must be submitted to the system for detecting plagiarism. This way, more students and teachers use the system (higher adoption rate)

Table 1. The pros and cons of the student-oriented version and the teacher-oriented version

	Student-oriented version	Teacher-oriented version
Pros	• Students are less likely to plagiarize when they know that they are being checked • The workload of the teachers is reduced	• Teachers have more control over the submission process
Cons	• Higher cost of support	• The workload of teachers is increased

Table 2. The pros and cons of the mandatory submission policy and the optional submission policy

	Mandatory submission policy	Optional submission policy
Pros	• Higher adoption rate • Higher usage volume	• Less resistance from students • Less resource is needed
Cons	• More resistance from students • More resource is needed	• Lower adoption rate • Lower usage volume

and thus the impact of the system to the educational institution is greater. When more submissions are stored in the system (higher usage volume), the system is more effective in detecting plagiarism that involves assignments submitted by other students over a period of many years. In the case of optional submission policy, only selected assignments are submitted to the system. In this scenario, students are likely to be less resistant against the deployment of the system. In addition, the system supports fewer users and submissions so that less resource is needed. The pros and cons of the two submission policies are summarized in Table 2.

Since most of the plagiarism detection systems do not handle non-text such as drawings, images, equations, programming codes, and multimedia materials, the mandatory submission policy requires some fine-tuning. An example is to create two sub-categories: the full mandatory submission policy and the partial mandatory submission policy. The full mandatory submission policy checks all types of assignments from all students for all courses, regardless of whether the system is capable of detecting plagiarism for all types of assignments. This policy is suitable for the educational institution that uses the plagiarism detection system for the purpose of collecting assignments. Under the partial mandatory submission policy, only the types of assignments that the system supports are submitted. This policy is suitable for the educational institution that uses the system specifically for detecting plagiarism. Teachers have other means to collect assignments.

When the student-oriented version is used to detect plagiarism but not to collect assignments,

additional measures must be installed to prevent students from submitting two versions of assignments—doctored assignments submitted to the system to avoid detection of plagiarism and regular assignments submitted to teachers for grading. In other words, there must be ways to ensure that assignments received by the teachers are the same as those submitted to the system. A possible solution is to ask the student to sign an agreement to declare that the submitted assignment is original and is the same as the one submitted to the teacher for grading. The agreement may also include other statements such as granting the copyright of the assignments to the system for later reference. More details of the copyright issue will be discussed later.

It is possible for a university to have different submission policies for undergraduate and graduate students. Although plagiarism is unacceptable for both undergraduates and graduates, plagiarism in graduate theses is much more serious. Hence, even if a university decides to adopt the optional submission policy, it may still want to consider a mandatory submission policy for theses.

Disciplinary Issues

The education institution needs to establish a final authority on judging plagiarism cases. The function of an automatic plagiarism detection system is merely to identify contents that are similar to other sources. Teachers have to identify suspicious plagiarism cases based on such information and then pass these cases to the disciplinary committee for handling and making final decisions. There are "four fairly well-defined phases" for civil procedure in United States (Inc. Merriam-Webster, 1996)—(1) pleadings, (2) discovery, (3) trial and judgment, and (4) conclusion of litigation. Similar phases can be adopted for the disciplinary committee to handle a plagiarism case.

Pleadings. The disciplinary committee has to define parameters of the plagiarism case. Some possible parameters are:

1. Which student is involved?
2. Which assignment is involved?
3. Does the student copy others' work or allow others to copy his or her work?
4. If the student copies others' work, what is the source?

This information should be included in the report generated by the system.

Discovery. The disciplinary committee collects evidence of plagiarism and investigates the report generated by the system in the next phase. Some of the questions that the disciplinary committee wants to answer are:

1. Has the student committed plagiarism before?
2. How many students are involved in the plagiarism case?
3. If the case involves a student copying another student's work, can the source be identified?

The above questions are explained as follows. For the first question, if the student has committed plagiarism before, a more severe punishment should be enforced if he or she commits plagiarism again. The second and the third questions should be answered if there are a number of suspicious cases involving submissions that are similar to each other. The disciplinary committee has to figure out how many students are involved and whose work is copied by other students. Some educational institutions have a policy that the student who let another student copy his or her work receives a lighter punishment than the student who copies. Hence, information of the source is needed for administering punishment in this case. The disciplinary committee needs to collect the aforesaid information before the trial and judgment phase.

Trial and Judgment. The disciplinary committee should not base the final verdict merely on the report generated by the system and the evidence collected in the discovery phase. The suspected students should be given the chance to defend themselves before the disciplinary committee. The students are presumed innocent until proven guilty during the trial. The disciplinary committee has the responsibility to ensure a fair trial. At the end of the trial, the following questions ought to be answered:

1. Has the student committed plagiarism?
2. If so, what is the punishment?

If guilt is proven, the disciplinary committee has to decide on the punishment. Wendy Sutherland-Smith (2010) reported several penalties enforced in some universities: (1) Reprimand the student, (2) fine the student, (3) fail the student for the plagiarized assignment, (4) fail the student for the entire course, (4) suspend scholarship granted to the student, (5) suspend the student from study for a fixed period of time, (6) expel the student from the school, and (7) rescind or downgrade the degree granted to the student. Many factors are considered in the decision of an appropriate punishment. Repeated offenders often receive more severe punishment. The punishment is usually heavier if the extent of the plagiarized work is larger. However it is also possible that a fixed punishment is administered regardless of the extent of the plagiarized work. The disciplinary committee decides whether a student who let another student copy his or her works receives the same level of punishment as the student who copies. Universities need to decide if the same level of punishment applies to both undergraduate and graduate students who are caught plagiarizing. As a general rule, punishment ought to be consistent. For example, star students and athletes should not be given a lighter sentence or no punishment even though they might be very valuable in terms of bringing fame to the institution.

Conclusion of Litigation. The trial phase ends as soon as the disciplinary committee pronounces a verdict and hands down a judgment. However some questions still need to be answered:

1. Is it possible for the student to appeal the judgment and punishment?
2. Who is responsible for handling the appeal case?
3. What is the consequence if the student fails or refuses to accept the punishment?

In general, the student should be allowed to appeal if he or she disagrees with the judgment and/or punishment. If possible, the senate committee should handle the appeal cases. Students have to be informed of the appeal procedure and the consequences of failing to accept the punishment.

To avoid the prospect of counter-litigation, students have to be informed of the definition of plagiarism. Obviously, copying source materials without proper acknowledgement is regarded as plagiarism. However there are also some less obvious cases that would require clarification. An example is when a student submits an assignment from another course as the assignment of a course even though he or she has not copied source materials illegally in the process. In addition, the students are to be informed of the procedures that the disciplinary committee will follow if a plagiarism case is found and the possible punishment if guilt is proven. The educational institution can clarify these issues to the students by setting up a website or by distributing booklets to them. This information will reduce the student's anxiety about being falsely accused of plagiarism due to imperfections in the automatic plagiarism detection system. It will also let the students know that

plagiarism is not tolerable and that the school is serious about fighting it.

Copyright Issues

There are several copyright issues that the education institution will have to encounter when the plagiarism detection system is deployed. The issues can be divided into two categories: student submissions and source materials.

Student Submissions. Some copyright issues related to assignments submitted by students are:

1. Does the student own the copyright of the submission after he or she has submitted the assignment to the system?
2. Does the system have the right to use students' past assignments for detecting plagiarism?

One option commonly implemented is to let the student own the copyright of the submission after he or she has submitted the assignment to the system. The system is only entitled to use the submission to detect plagiarism under the principles of fair use. Nevertheless the system may archive and use student's assignments for detecting plagiarism of other students' assignments later. This approach is "explicitly recognized by the United States District Court for the Eastern District of Virginia and the United States Court of Appeals for the Fourth Circuit in A.V. et al. v. iParadigms, LLC, 562 F.3d 630 (4th Cir. 2009)" (Answers to Common Legal Questions About Turnitin, 2009). It is recommended that these issues are included in the agreement that the student has to accept when he or she submits the assignment.

Source Materials. Information of source materials is included in the reports to indicate which part of the assignment is plagiarized—e.g., materials from digital libraries and online resources. However, some copyright issues about the source materials need to be considered:

1. Can the content of the source materials be directly shown on the report or shown only indirectly via a hyperlink?
2. Can the sources of the source materials be shown on the report?

The questions can only be answered with the help of source provider, such as the owner of the database or the digital library.

In summary, the educational institute has to consider the copyright issues regarding student assignments and source materials. The former has to be handled by the agreement that the student signs when the student submits the assignment and the latter has to be discussed with the provider of the source materials.

Security and Privacy Issues

The system has to provide security measures to ensure that there is no leakage of sensitive information, such as student ID and reports of plagiarism. In general, the system has to provide the following two functions:

Authentication. The system has to verify the identities of users.

Authorization. The system allows users to access only those resources for which they are given the right of access. For instance, students can only access their own submitted assignments but teachers can access all assignments and reports for their courses.

One way to implement authentication and authorization is to create accounts for different users such that different accounts have different privileges to access resource in the system. In the case of the automatic plagiarism detection system, student accounts should have the lowest privilege that only allow students to submit assignments and view submissions. Teacher accounts should have the rights to manage submitted assignments of their courses and access the reports generated by the system. Some educational institutions may want to create accounts with higher privileges for

the disciplinary committee, the department, the faculty, or the head of the school, so that they can follow up on plagiarism cases and monitor system usage and statistics. Administrative accounts normally have the highest privilege to ensure the availability of services and maintain the system.

The system should be protected against unauthorized persons and hackers by putting the system behind a firewall that allows limited access to the outside world. Moreover, the system administrator should be vigilant in monitoring abnormal network traffic that may be related to hacking activities and formulate plans if such activities are detected.

Besides the aforesaid security measures, the system should not ask for more than the absolutely necessary personal information at the very start to lower the security risk further. In regard to the personal information submitted to the system, two main privacy issues need to be considered:

1. Which types of personal information are considered private so that it is off limit to data acquisition of the system?
2. In case the system maintains an assignment archive for future reference, which types of contents should not be archived?

Some assignments may contain private contents, such as personal journal, diary, and medical records. There should be an exclusion list to show which types of contents are considered private and should not be submitted to the system. Personal data that may identify the owner of the assignment, such as student's names and student ID, should be removed before the assignment is archived.

Ethical Issues

In this subsection, ethical questions of whether an automatic plagiarism detection system should be deployed as well as the ethical issues after such a system is deployed are considered.

Ethics tries to answer the question of what is right and wrong or what is good and evil. Nowadays, more and more software engineers are beginning to consider ethical issues during the system design and development process. In general, the issues at stake are users' privacy, copyright, and impact to the society. Miller and Selgelid (2007) observed that science and technology can be used for both good and evil. The two-pronged nature of technology is what they call the "dual-use dilemma." In essence, dual-use dilemma simply refers to the dilemma in which something can be used for both good and evil. Technology itself is ethically neutral. It is up to the persons who control the technology in how technology is used. Take nuclear weapons for example: the good of the weapon is that it can be used to deter large scale war among superpowers by the virtue of the threat of mutual destruction. The evil is that terrorists and rogue states can actually use nuclear weapons to destroy the lives of innocent people or as a means of nuclear blackmail. The concept of dual-use dilemma can be extended to software engineering in the sense that computer technology can be used in both good and bad ways (Rashid, A., Weckert, J., & Lucas, R., 2009). Unfortunately, some systems have inherent ethical issues that cannot be resolved easily. For example, Google Maps provides 3D street images, which allow users to have a better view of an area. However people who live in the area may feel that their privacy is violated. In extreme cases, terrorists and robbers may exploit this technology to find new targets (Rashid, A., Weckert, J., & Lucas, R., 2009).

The dual-use dilemma also applies to automatic plagiarism detection systems. On one hand, this technology helps the teachers to catch cheaters more efficiently. On the other hand, it also creates a new environment for a cat-and-mouse game for those ill-motivated students who focus on out-smarting the system instead of learning the old-fashioned value of honest hard work. In addition, if the system cannot detect all the plagiarism cases (Royce, J., 2003), deploying such a system

may give a false sense of confidence (Martin, B., 2004). Satterwhite and Gerein (2001) suggested that the deployment of automatic detection system can erode the trust between professors and students. Despite the dual-use nature of technology, it does not mean that automatic plagiarism detection system should not be deployed. When confronted by the ethical dilemmas of deploying a new technology, Miller and Selgelid (2007) are always in favor of work-around to avoid the ethical problems of the technology. Given the usefulness of an automatic plagiarism detection system in terms of promoting academic honesty and integrity, it is expected that this technology will rate high in ethical weight. Assuming the unlikely event of the contrary, a better solution is to actively seek alternative means to bypass any ethical dilemma instead of rejecting the deployment of the automatic plagiarism detection system.

Wendy Sutherland-Smith (2010) suggested that education is key to combating plagiarism in an educational institution. In addition to the deployment of the automatic plagiarism detection system, an educational institution should educate students about the unethical nature of plagiarism and the importance of honesty and academic integrity. Students have to understand what plagiarism is and how to avoid it. They have to be reminded that they cannot get an education by plagiarizing (Cogdell, B., & Aidulis, D., 2007). The above suggestions are consistent with the results of the experiments conducted by Dee and Jacob (2010) in that the number of plagiarism cases is significantly reduced if web-based tutorials on plagiarism and its avoidance are provided for the students. The automatic plagiarism detection system may cure the symptoms but not the ill. School policy and deployment of technology to fight plagiarism is only a part of education. Moral education must be done in the old-fashioned way.

Once the automatic plagiarism detection system is deployed, there are still additional ethical issues that need to be considered.

Policy Adjustment. The policy makers of the school have to ensure that the adopted policy is effective, appropriate, and fair. They have to (1) review the existing policy, (2) listen to the feedback from students and teachers, and (3) make changes to the existing policy if necessary. As an example, imagine the scenario in which the optional submission policy is used and teachers complain that the system is not very helpful in detecting plagiarism due to low system utility. The policy maker may consider switching the optional submission policy to the mandatory submission policy in order to improve the effectiveness of the system.

Human Intervention and Fairness. To be fair to students, human judgment has to be involved in deciding whether a student has committed plagiarism. Since there is no perfect system/algorithm to detect plagiarism, the system should not be the one that makes the final decision. Teachers have to investigate the cases reported by the system to verify suspicious plagiarism cases. Suspicious cases identified by teachers are then reported to the disciplinary committee. The disciplinary committee further investigates the case and meets the involved students before deciding whether the students have committed plagiarism. The student should be given a fair trial, presumed innocent until proven guilty, and have the right to appeal the decision handed down by the disciplinary committee.

Avoidance of the Misuse of System Data. The school has to regulate and monitor how the system data are used. The data stored in and generated by the system, such as the students' assignments and the reports generated by the system, cannot be disclosed to others and used by anyone to generate profits or other kinds of benefits. Inevitably, system technicians and administrators have higher privileges than teachers and students in the system. System staff members have to follow regulations on the proper use of data. In addition, only a limited number of privileged staff members, such as the highest administrator, have full access of the system.

Fair Use. Although certain types of data usage are prohibited, some other types of usage are considered fair use and thus are allowed. Some examples of fair use are the checking of future assignments submitted by other students, research, and statistical calculations.

Staff Training. Proper staff training is necessary to prevent the misuse of the system, and to increase the effectiveness and fairness of using the system to combat plagiarism. System technicians and administrators should follow regulations to avoid the misuse of system data. Workshops should be made available to teachers and disciplinary committee members to teach them how to read the reports generated by the system and handle suspicious plagiarism cases properly.

Right to Know. Students have the right to know the school definition of plagiarism, the course of action that the disciplinary committee will take when a plagiarism case is found, and the punishment when the student is found guilty. In addition, students should be notified of other fair usages of their assignment submissions besides detecting plagiarism.

Security and Privacy. The information stored in the system is considered private; the system has the obligation to protect the data from being leaked to unauthorized persons. Hence, the security and privacy of the system fall under the category of ethical issues. Some security and privacy protocols are mandatory, such as authentication, authorization, and the exclusion list of personal information, as discussed in the previous section. In the following, we will discuss some other security and privacy issues that are not mandatory, but are still worth mentioning. They are separation of duties and single sign-on.

Separation of Duties. Separation of duties refers to the division of privileges into several parts owned by different staff members to complete a task (Botha, R.A., Eloff, J.H.P., 2001). The advantage of this policy is setting in place accountability to deter fraud. If a staff member were to cheat, such as modifying the report of a student, he has to obtain privilege from other staff member(s). This way, cheating is made more difficult and hopefully discouraged. However, separation of duties is labor intensive and may not feasible for a small administrative/support team.

Single Sign-On. Single sign-on allows a user to obtain access to all related but independent systems by logging in only once. If the automatic plagiarism detection system is integrated with existing systems of the school, such as the assignment collection system, the school should consider whether single sign-on is a good idea. Some of the advantages suggested by Chris Dunne (2003) are the simplification of user accounts administration, time reduction for multiple user logins, and saving the hassle of remembering different usernames and passwords. On the other hand, the disadvantages are increased cost to the system, a single point of attack for hackers, and the increased vulnerability of the system if the username and password are compromised (Chris Dunne, 2003).

Pre-Requisites to Deploy an Automated Plagiarism Detection System

An educational institution has to meet certain pre-requisites before it is ready to deploy an automated plagiarism detection system. First, the school has to have existing ethical guidelines to educate students about plagiarism. The guideline should include an official definition of plagiarism and some practical ways to avoid plagiarism. As mentioned earlier, the automated plagiarism detection system should not be the only means to fight plagiarism. The promotion of creativity, originality, and also integrity should be carried out concurrently to fight plagiarism. Secondly, the school has to have a disciplinary committee to handle plagiarism cases. Technology only helps

teachers to identify suspicious cases but cannot make the final decision on whether the student has committed plagiarism. Once a plagiarism case is found, the disciplinary committee has to define the parameters of the suspicious case, collect evidence, give a fair trial to the student involved, make the judgment, and decide the punishment if the suspicious case is proven. Thirdly, the education institution has to have an IT department to maintain and monitor the system, and to support teachers and students to use the system. The system should have implemented authentication and authorization functions to deal with security and privacy issues. For example, teachers and students need accounts to login to the system to check reports (for teachers only) and submit assignments. Hence, the IT department has to create accounts and then distribute them to these users. In addition, the IT department is also responsible for protecting the system from unauthorized persons and hackers and monitoring for abnormal network traffic that may be related to hacking activities.

CASE STUDY: VERIGUIDE IN CUHK

VeriGuide is an automated plagiarism detection system that has been deployed at the Chinese University of Hong Kong (CUHK) since 2005 to ensure that the assignments submitted by students are original works. In the academic year 2008-2009, VeriGuide received over 80,000 submissions serving over 15,000 students and 1,000 teachers in about 3,000 classes offered by 8 faculties. The benefits of deploying VeriGuide in CUHK are (1) the provision of fair assessments for our students, (2) the promotion of deep learning of the subjects, (3) the accountability for our students to cite the sources properly, and (4) the enhancement of the prestige of the degrees offered by CUHK (Honesty in academic works: A guide for students and teachers, 2008). The reasons of deploying VeriGuide but not other similar systems are (1) its bilingual feature (Chinese and English) and (2) convenience for our teachers. VeriGuide is developed by CUHK and the designers have firsthand knowledge of how to make the system fit the needs of the teachers. For instance, VeriGuide can directly obtain information of students, teachers, and courses from the CUHK Registry system (Honesty in academic works: A guide for students and teachers, 2008).

Overview of VeriGuide

VeriGuide is a web-based system with course assignment management functions in parallel with plagiarism detection. Figure 2 shows the first page of VeriGuide (2010). VeriGuide can be used in a wide range of disciplines and courses whose assignments are in the form of textual essay-type writings. Courses at any levels that accept articles, essays, term papers, reports, and theses from students can use this system.

VeriGuide is composed of several modules as illustrated in Figure 3. They include the front-end module, the parameter module, the core engine, and the report generator, which are briefly explained as follows.

Front-End Module. Users interact with VeriGuide through the front-end module, which provides course management functions so that teachers can create records for their courses, assignments associated with each course, lists of students enrolled, and archive assignment submissions. The front-end module also interacts with the parameter modules to invoke the core engine.

Parameter Module. The parameter module specifies the batch of documents to undergo the detection process and the control parameters governing the detection behavior. After obtaining all the necessary information from teachers through the front-end module, the parameter module registers a new detection job in the submission queue. The submission queue keeps the submitted assignments and the control parameters until the core engine is ready to process the submitted jobs.

Core Engine. The core engine is responsible for checking the submitted assignments against different sources, such as identifying plagiarism amongst essays in the same submission batch, checking if the assignment is plagiarized from the work of other students from other courses or from previous years, as well as from other sources such as journal articles or materials from the Internet.

Figure 2. The first page of VeriGuide

Figure 3. Architecture of VeriGuide

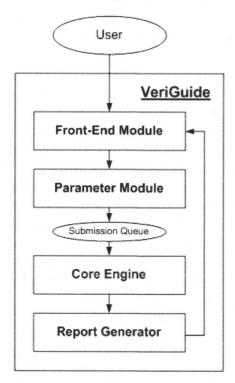

Report Generator. The report generator summaries and converts the plagiarism identification results obtained by the core engine into HTML format so that teachers can review the result online using Web browsers. Once the report is ready, VeriGuide sends an e-mail to notify the user of its availability.

Features of VeriGuide

The main function of VeriGuide is to help teachers search for sentences in students' submissions that are similar to other sources. To facilitate the main function, VeriGuide has to increase accuracy in detecting plagiarized sentences and reduce time and effort needed by teachers to complete plagiarism detection tasks. To increase accuracy, VeriGuide provides several features to broaden the search area and accommodate various situations. By minimizing time and effort, VeriGuide is made to be convenient to users. The features of VeriGuide and their functions are summarized in Table 3.

In order to broaden the search area, VeriGuide includes the following features:

Automatic Search for Reference Materials. VeriGuide automatically extracts keywords in the document and searches for reference materials using those keywords. The search will cover both copyrighted and freely available materials. The system searches in the digital library of a number of collaborating publishers to look for scholarly articles that may have been used as plagiarism sources. Teachers can also provide keywords or phrases related to that assignment to fine-tune the search. The automatic search for reference materials help the system to detect plagiarized sentences that copy from the Internet and other materials.

Table 3. The features of VeriGuide and their functions

Main Function of VeriGuide	Ways to Facilitate the Main Function	Feature Categories	Features of VeriGuide
Helping teachers to search for sentences in students' submissions that are similar to other sources	Increased accuracy in detecting plagiarized sentences	Broadening the search area	Automatic search for reference materials
			Assignment archive
		Accommodating various situations	Chinese plagiarism detection
			Leniency control
	Reduced time and effort needed by teachers to complete plagiarism detection tasks	Making the system more convenient for users	Detection report with side-by-side comparison and filters
			Assignment management with embedded plagiarism detection function

Assignment Archive. All assignments submitted to the system are archived. This does not only provide data for future research but also serves as a database for future plagiarism detection as students sometimes copy assignments from previous years. Teachers can adjust the matching scope in VeriGuide to select the range of years and courses in archived materials to be used to check current submissions.

To accommodate various situations, VeriGuide includes the following features:

Chinese Plagiarism Detection. VeriGuide is the first automatic Chinese and English plagiarism detection system. It accepts both Chinese and English documents as input. A dedicated Chinese plagiarism detection method is used to satisfy the needs of detecting plagiarism in assignments in Chinese.

Leniency Control. Leniency reflects the standard of what plagiarism is. The judgment of whether a piece of writing is plagiarized or not can be somewhat subjective. Different people may have different standards for defining the threshold of plagiarism. In addition, the level of leniency varies in different subject areas. Hence, VeriGuide allows the teacher to define this threshold. The leniency parameters select the minimum length of sentences to be checked and the degree of tolerance for paraphrasing. The parameters tune the balance between high sensitivity and high rate of false positives. Teachers can control the leniency by setting the matching method and the associated parameters: "Quick match" performs a coarse check on the assignment, while "detailed match" performs a more detailed check to detect higher degree of paraphrasing. Leniency control can help the system to check students' assignments in the ways that fit the circumstances.

To make the system more convenient for users, VeriGuide includes the following features:

Detection Report with Side-by-Side Comparison and Filters. An originality report will be generated when plagiarism detection finishes. In addition to printing out typical information (such

as the likelihood that the document is plagiarized and the text being plagiarized), VeriGuide also provides a side-by-side comparison such that one side shows the student's assignment and another side shows the document that contains similar sentences. This feature facilitates a visual inspection of the plagiarized text and allows teachers to use their personal judgment to detect plagiarism. In addition, VeriGuide provides various filters in the report to help teachers screen out potential common sentences and assignments from the same group, where such cases should not be treated as plagiarism (more details of the filters will be discussed later). These features help the teachers to read the report in a more convenient way.

Assignment Management with Embedded Plagiarism Detection Function. VeriGuide also supports some assignment management features. It has an assignment management interface so that every plagiarism detection task is labeled with the course code and assignment number instead of an arbitrary file name. This helps teachers to organize the assignments and peruse the detection results more easily. In terms of assignment collection, the submission interface allows the assignments to be submitted either by the teachers as a batch or individually by the students via a Web interface. With respect to teacher submission, teachers need to compress the assignments into a ZIP file before submitting it to the interface. With respect to student submission, students need to provide their personal information for authentication when they submit the assignments. In terms of plagiarism detection, the system accepts text documents with various popular file formats, such as Adobe PDF, Microsoft Word, and HTML. In this way, VeriGuide can help teachers to manage the assignments in certain extends.

Stakeholders of VeriGuide

VeriGuide is developed and administrated by the VeriGuide team, which also provides real time supports to VeriGuide's users, such as staff from

CUHK or other educational institutions. The VeriGuide team is a part of the Department of Computer Science and Engineering in CUHK, which provides computing resources and infrastructure such as computer network and firewall.

VeriGuide has many stakeholders in CUHK. The Pro Vice Chancellor, the Senate Committee, and the Academic and Quality Section are the policymakers. Teachers receive the originality reports generated by VeriGuide. They report plagiarism cases to the Disciplinary Committee. The Disciplinary Committee investigates the suspected cases, meets with the students involved, and decides the penalties. The Senate Committee handles appeal cases and the cases that are exceptionally serious. The Information Technology Services Centre (ITSC) authenticates users for VeriGuide. When a user tries to login to VeriGuide, the login name and password are redirected to ITSC. After the authentication is checked, the control will be passed back to VeriGuide. CUHK Library discusses the copyright issues with the resource owners whenever resources are used by VeriGuide to detect plagiarism. The Registration and Examinations Section provides information on courses and students to VeriGuide. The Centre for Learning Enhancement And Research (CLEAR)

organizes workshops to teach CUHK users to use VeriGuide. The Technology Licensing Office deals with the legal issues, such as registering the logo and the patent for VeriGuide, and preparing agreements and contracts with constituents outside CUHK. The stakeholders of VeriGuide are shown in Figure 4.

Policy and Issues in Deploying VeriGuide in CUHK

This subsection presents the policy and issues in deploying VeriGuide in CUHK. The plagiarism policy of CUHK described in this subsection can be used as sample policy for policy makers in other institutions.

Administrative Issues. CUHK adopts the student-oriented version in order to lighten teachers' workload in using VeriGuide to fight plagiarism. VeriGuide is intentionally made simple to use for teachers so that each teacher only needs to ask each student in the course to upload a soft copy of the completed assignment to VeriGuide at a specified URL. The student logins to the VeriGuide system using his or her regular university account information. After the student has submitted the assignment, the student will be issued a receipt

Figure 4. Stakeholders of VeriGuide

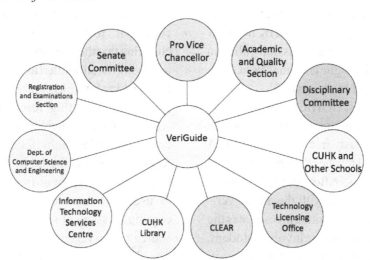

that contains a statement confessing honesty. The student has to sign the statement, attach it to the hard copy of the assignment, and then submit the certified assignment to the teacher. At the same time, the system detects plagiarism by comparing student submissions against each other and other documents in the databases and digital libraries. Finally, an originality report per assignment will be sent to the teacher via e-mail. Teachers do not submit assignments to VeriGuide. When students submit their assignments, they are asked to input the assignment numbers and deadlines to Veri-Guide. This information is used by VeriGuide to determine the time to invoke the plagiarism detection process, the teacher of the course, and the email address of the teacher for sending the originality reports. Hence, teachers' workload in using VeriGuide to detect plagiarism is minimized.

Submission Policy Issues. In the beginning, CUHK adopted the optional submission policy so that not all assignments were submitted to Veri-Guide. It was found that the system usage was not high. In order to emphasize that CUHK places a very high priority on academic honesty, starting from the academic year 2008-2009, the mandatory submission policy is adopted so that all student assignments that are principally text-based have to be submitted via VeriGuide. However, several types of assignments are excluded—e.g. calculations in science, brief laboratory reports, drawings in fine arts and architecture, and programming code. More precisely speaking, CUHK has now adopted a partial mandatory submission policy in that only the types of assignments that VeriGuide supports are submitted to the system.

Disciplinary Issues. CUHK has released the disciplinary guidelines for handling the suspected plagiarism cases (Honesty in academic works: A guide for students and teachers, 2008), which are summarized as follows. After teachers identify suspected plagiarism cases with the aid of Veri-Guide, the disciplinary committee investigates the reported case and meets with the involved student. If guilt is proven, the disciplinary committee will

decide on the penalty and notify the student of its decision. According to the penalty guideline, the penalty for a student who commits plagiarism is one demerit (or two demerits if the student has committed plagiarism before) and a zero mark for the assignment. If the case is serious (e.g. the extent of the plagiarized materials is large), the disciplinary committee has the right to give a zero mark for the entire course. If the student allows others to copy his or her assignment but he or she has not plagiarized, the disciplinary committee has the option of giving out only demerit(s) but not a zero mark. The Senate Committee also participates in disciplinary issues. It handles appeal cases of students who are not satisfied with the decisions handed down by the disciplinary committee. It also has the right to give out a heavier penalty, such as suspension or termination of the student from the University, for exceptionally serious plagiarism cases or a less severe penalty for extenuating circumstances. The above disciplinary guidelines are listed in a website to let students know that CUHK is serious in fighting plagiarism.

Copyright Issues. We are aware of the copyright issues for deploying VeriGuide and varies measures are needed to handle such issues. When a student submits his or her assignment to VeriGuide, he or she has to sign the agreement indicating that he or she owns the copyright of his or her submission but grants "a worldwide irrevocable non-exclusive perpetual license in respect of the copyright" to the University and VeriGuide for checking that the submitted assignment is original, archiving the submitted assignment anonymously for checking future assignments submitted by other students, conducting research, and calculating statistics. On the other hand, since VeriGuide also compares student submissions with other digital resources such as digital libraries, the university has to obtain approval from resource providers to use their resources. The approval includes copyright issues of showing the content and the source of the resources in the originality report. The above measures indicate that VeriGuide does not infringe the copyright of students' assignments and other digital resources.

Security and Privacy Issues. For security reasons, each user of VeriGuide needs to authenticate himself or herself in order to use the system. Each student, teacher, and staff in CUHK has a login name and a password for the Campus-wide E-mail System (CWEM) administrated by the Information Technology Services Centre (ITSC). ITSC makes it possible for students and the teachers in CUHK to use their CWEM login names and passwords to login to VeriGuide. Most importantly, VeriGuide does not store CWEM login names and passwords for security reasons. Whenever a user tries to login to VeriGuide, the login name and password will be encrypted and redirected to ITSC for authentication. ITSC will send VeriGuide the authentication result to indicate whether the login process is successful. In addition, the servers for VeriGuide are put behind a firewall to protect them from hackers and unauthorized access. On the other hand, for privacy reasons, teachers may withhold the submission of those assignments that contain private contents (such as personal journal, diary, and medical records) to VeriGuide even though CUHK has a mandatory submission policy. As an extra protection, VeriGuide removes information from the submitted assignments that identifies the owners of the assignments (such as students' names and student's IDs) before they are archived for future reference. In summary, VeriGuide is protected by various security measures and no unnecessary private information is stored in VeriGuide.

Ethical Issues. As mentioned in the previous section, certain ethical issues may arise when VeriGuide is deployed. For instance, some students may spend more time trying to figure out ways to beat the system than simply doing the work itself. In order to combat plagiarism from its root, CUHK not only deploys VeriGuide, but also tries to educate students about plagiarism by setting up a website and distributing booklets to encourage honesty in academic work. The

website (Honesty in academic works: A guide for students and teachers, 2008) defines plagiarism and details the proper use of source materials and online resources. It also includes regulations on academic honesty and disciplinary procedures for handling plagiarism cases. Students should get an unmistaken impression that plagiarism is a serious offence and that CUHK places a very high priority on academic honesty. The Pro Vice Chancellor, the Senate Committee, and the Academic and Quality Section review the existing policy and listen to the feedback from students and teachers from time to time. Changes to the existing policy are made whenever necessary. For example, the submission policy was switched from optional to mandatory in the academic year 2008-2009 after receiving the feedback that system usage was not high. To be fair to students, VeriGuide does not make the final decision in judging plagiarism. Instead, VeriGuide sends the report to the teachers to identify suspicious plagiarism cases. Teachers are taught how to use VeriGuide and handle suspicious plagiarism cases through workshops and regulations. Beside plagiarism detection, the VeriGuide system uses the submitted assignments and generated reports only for the purpose of checking future assignments submitted by other students, conducting research, and calculating statistics. Such usages are fair uses. Students are informed of such usages when they submit the assignment to the system. Members of the VeriGuide team are required to follow regulations written by the Department of Computer Science and Engineering in CUHK. They cannot use VeriGuide to obtain personal gains. These measures indicate that CUHK is concerned about the ethical aspects of deploying VeriGuide and has developed some expertise in dealing with these issues.

Discussion of Technical Issues of VeriGuide

Technical issues of developing and deploying VeriGuide are discussed as follows.

Scalability. Besides CUHK, more and more educational institutions in Hong Kong are using VeriGuide to detect plagiarism and collect student assignments. Scalability is an important issue in the system design phase of the development cycle of VeriGuide. The system has to be divided into modules having different functions—e.g. the front-end module for user interactions, the core engine for detecting plagiarism, and the report generator. The scalability problem can be solved easily by upgrading the hardware for the particular module that lacks enough resources due to high usage volume.

False Positives and False Negatives. There is no perfect algorithm for detecting plagiarism such that the system may occasionally produce false positives (reporting non-plagiarized cases to be plagiarized cases) and false negatives (reporting plagiarized cases to be non-plagiarized cases) results. However, it is still possible to tune the parameters of the system to shift the balance between false positives and false negatives based on the teacher's need. For example, if the minimum number of keywords of a sentence for checking plagiarism is set to be higher, the confidence for each case (quality) increases but the number of identified cases (quantity) decreases. In other words, the number of false negatives increases but the number of false positives decreases. On the other hand, we can incorporate a filter to screen common sentences that should not be regarded as plagiarized sentences even though they appear frequently elsewhere, such as the questions of the assignment, definitions of terms, proverbs, and famous quotes. Such a filter reduces the number of false positives and hence helps teachers to identify real plagiarism cases.

Filters for Group or Same Submissions. If the assignment is group-based, it is possible for the system to receive duplicate submissions from different students in the same group even though students have already been told that only one student in each group has to submit the assignment to the system. As a result, the system will wrongfully report this case as plagiarism. To prevent this scenario, a filter is developed to help teachers to identify duplicate submissions in the event of a group-based assignment. On the other hand, a re-submission of the same assignment that is rightfully similar to a previous submission should not be reported as plagiarism. An example of this scenario is that a student may be required by the teacher to re-submit a project after modifying an earlier submission. Another example is that the student accidentally inputs a wrong assignment number to the system the first time and resubmits the assignment again with the correct assignment number the second time. Filters for these various scenarios are developed to help teachers to identify group or same submissions that should not be identified as plagiarism cases.

Chinese Issues. VeriGuide supports plagiarism detection in Chinese and there are several technical issues in handling Chinese. One issue is related to the Chinese encoding scheme. It is trivial to tell if a text is written in English or Chinese because English text is encoded in ASCII characters. However, there are various encoding standards for the computer representation of Chinese text (Lunde, K., 1999). With these different encoding standards, an encoding detector is implemented in VeriGuide to determine the correct one and converts text in different encodings into a unique encoding, UTF8 in our case, to facilitate subsequent identification. Another issue concerning Chinese is on the identification of "words". English is delimited explicitly by non-alphabetic elements such as space and punctuation. Chinese, on the other hand, does not separate words with spaces so that the segmentation of Chinese text into words is non-trivial. To solve this problem, a technique called "LMR-RC tagging", which is an improved version of "LMR tagging" (Xue, N., & Shen, L., 2003), is implemented in VeriGuide (Lau, T. P., & King, I., 2005; Lau, T. P., 2006). The VeriGuide team has to solve the aforesaid technical issues in order for VeriGuide to detect plagiarism in Chinese.

FUTURE RESEARCH DIRECTIONS

There are two aspects in future research directions, namely policy and system, which are discussed as follows.

Policy. Experience sharing between new and existing policy/issues is helpful for those who are interested in using such a system to promote academic quality and integrity. On one hand, it is possible that new policy and issues may arise when the system is deployed in different schools and under different situations besides those discussed in this chapter. On the other hand, the policy makers of the school currently deploying an automatic plagiarism detection system have to review the adopted policy from time to time to ensure that the existing policy are effective and appropriate. Such experiences are valuable to the policy makers of other schools that have or will have an automatic plagiarism detection system deployed.

System. Existing automatic plagiarism detection systems can be improved in two ways: accuracy and user-friendliness. With regard to accuracy, since there is no perfect algorithm for detecting plagiarism, there is always room for improvement to reduce false positives and false negatives. As per user-friendliness, some users of the system may not be familiar with computers and new technologies. Hence, system developers should listen to the feedback of the users to improve the interface and the workflow of the system so that the system is easier to use.

CONCLUSION

In light of the prevalence of plagiarism, an automatic plagiarism detection system is needed to promote and uphold academic integrity and honesty. However, even if an educational institution has the technological savvy to maintain an automatic plagiarism detection system, it still needs to consider many policy issues. This chap-

ter offers a guideline by discussing the pros and cons of different policies. A school can choose a suitable policy to meet its needs. Deploying an automatic system reduces the workload of the teachers. However, it also introduces a new impact to students and teachers in the school. First, this technology affects how students submit their assignments and how teachers handle assignments (administrative and submission policy issues). Secondly, the number of plagiarism cases that can be identified is expected to increase dramatically. In order to ensure the consistency for handling such cases, the school has to decide on the proper procedures whenever a plagiarism case is identified and the possible penalties when guilt is proven (disciplinary issues). Thirdly, the system not only compares an assignment with other assignments, it may also compare it against copyrighted digital resources. Copyright and legal issues have to be discussed with the owners of digital resources outside the school (copyright issues). Fourthly, the system may store sensitive information of students. Security measures have to be implemented to protect the information stored in the system from leakage (security and privacy issues). Finally, this technology is expected to raise ethical issues and encounter resistance from students. The educational institution should not rely on the system alone to fight plagiarism but should also educate students about the ill of plagiarism, the proper use of source material, and how to avoid plagiarizing unintentionally (ethical issues). VeriGuide, an automated plagiarism detection system deployed at the Chinese University of Hong Kong since 2005, is used as an example in this chapter. Preference in policymaking and the relationship between VeriGuide and its stakeholders are explained. It is hoped that this case study is helpful for those who are interested in using an automated plagiarism detection system to promote academic integrity and honesty and provide a fair academic environment.

REFERENCES

Barnbaum, C. (n.d.). Plagiarism: A student's guide to recognizing it and avoiding it. Retrieved February, 2010, from http://www.valdosta.edu /~cbarnbau/ personal/ teaching_MISC/ plagiarism.htm

BBC news. (2006). *Net students think copying OK.* Retrieved February, 2010, from http://news.bbc.co.uk/2/hi/ uk_news/ education/ 5093286.stm

BBC news. (2008). *Media doctor admits to plagiarism.* Retrieved February, 2010, from http://news.bbc.co.uk /2/hi/ 7452877.stm

BBC news. (2010). *Men At Work lose plagiarism case in Australia.* Retrieved February, 2010, from http://news.bbc.co.uk/ 2/hi/entertainment /8497433.stm

Beam, A. (2003). Survey shows plagiarism is up. *Daily Gamecock.* Retrieve February, 2010, from http://www.dailygamecock.com/ 2.3455/ survey-shows- plagiarism-is- up-1.381072

Bjaaland, P. C., & Lederman, A. (1973). The detection of plagiarism. *The Educational Forum, 37,* 201–206. doi:10.1080/00131727309339183

Botha, R. A., & Eloff, J. H. P. (2001). Separation of duties for access control enforcement in workflow environments. *IBM Systems Journal, 40,* 666–682. doi:10.1147/sj.403.0666

Carroll, J. (2001). *What kinds of solutions can we find for plagiarism?* Retrieved May, 2010, from www.gla.ac.uk/ media/ media_13513_en.pdf

Cogdell, B., & Aidulis, D. (2007). Dealing with plagiarism as an ethical issue. In Roberts, T. S. (Ed.), *Student plagiarism in an online world: Problems and solutions* (pp. 38–59). Hershey, PA: Idea Group Inc.doi:10.4018/9781599048017.ch004

Dee, T. S., & Jacob, B. A. (2010). *Rational ignorance in education: A field experiment in student plagiarism.* (National Bureau of Economic Research Working Paper no. 15672).

Dey, S. K., & Sobhan, M. A. (2006). *Impact of unethical practices of plagiarism on learning, teaching and research in higher education: Some combating strategies.* In 7th International Conference on Information Technology Based Higher Education and Training, 2006, (pp. 388–393).

Dunne, C. (2003). *Build and implement a single sign-on solution.* Retrieved May 2010, from http:// www.ibm.com/ developerworks/ web/library/ wa-singlesign/

Goodwin, D. K. (2002). How I caused that story. *Time.* Retrieved February, 2010, from http://www.time.com/ time/nation/ article/ 0,8599,197614,00.html

Harris, R. A. (2001). *The plagiarism handbook.* Pyrczak Publishing.

Honesty in academic works: A guide for students and teachers. (2008). Retrieved February, 2010, from http://www.cuhk.edu.hk/ policy/ academichonesty/ index.htm

Howard, R. M. (1999). *Standing in the shadow of giants: Plagiarists, authors, collaborators.* Alex Publishing Corporation.

Kock, N. (1999). A case of academic plagiarism. *Communications of the ACM, 42,* 96–104. doi:10.1145/306549.306594

Lau, T. P. (2006). *Chinese readability analysis and its applications on the Internet.* Unpublished Master's thesis, The Chinese University of Hong Kong.

Lau, T. P., & King, I. (2005). Two-phase LMR-RC tagging for Chinese word segmentation. In *Proceedings of the 4th SIGHAN Workshop on Chinese Language Processing,* (pp. 183–186).

Liles, J. A., & Rozalski, M. E. (2004). It's a matter of style: A style manual workshops for preventing plagiarism. *College & Undergraduate Libraries, 11*(2), 91–101. doi:10.1300/J106v11n02_08

Lunde, K. (1999). *CJKV information processing.* O'Reilly and Associates.

Martin, B. (2004). Plagiarism: Policy against cheating or policy for learning. *Nexus, 16*(2), 15–16.

Mcdonell, T. B. (2008). *Plagiarism in writing and in art.* Retrieved February, 2010, from http:// tommypaints.blogspot.com/2008/11/plagiarism-in-writing-and-in-art.html

Merriam-Webster Inc. (1996). *Merriam-Webster's dictionary of law.* Merriam-Webster.

Miller, S., & Selgelid, M. J. (2007). Ethical and philosophical consideration of the dual-use dilemma in the biological sciences. [Springer Netherlands.]. *Science and Engineering Ethics,* 523–580. doi:10.1007/s11948-007-9043-4

Plotz, D. (2002). The plagiarist: Why Stephen Ambrose is a vampire. *Slate.* Retrieved February, 2010, from http://slate.msn.com/?id=2060618

Porter, J. E. (2005). *Discourage plagiarism by promoting academic honesty: A proactive approach for teachers.* Retrieved May, 2010, from http://kairos.wide.msu.edu/ porter/ teach_plagiarism.pdf

Rashid, A., Weckert, J., & Lucas, R. (2009). Software engineering ethics in a digital world. *IEEE Computer, 42*(6), 34–41.

Royce, J. (2003). Trust or trussed? Has turnitin. com got it all wrapped up? *Teacher Librarian, 30*(4), 26–30.

Satterwhite, R., & Gerein, M. (2001). *Downloading detectives: Searching for online plagiarism.* Retrieved February, 2010, from http://www. coloradocollege.edu/ Library/Course/ downloading_detectives_paper.htm

Smallwood, S. (2004). Arts professor at new school U. resigns after admitting plagiarism. *The Chronicle of Higher Education.* Retrieved February, 2010, from http://www.skidmore.edu/ ~rscarce/ Writing_Tips/ Art_Professor's_Plagiarism.html

Stothard, M. (2008). 1 in 2 admits to plagiarism. *Varsity.* Retrieved February, 2010, from http:// www.varsity.co.uk/news/1058

Sutherland-Smith, W. (2010). Retribution, deterrence and reform: The dilemmas of plagiarism management in universities. *Journal of Higher Education Policy and Management, 32*(1), 5–16. doi:10.1080/13600800903440519

Tahaghoghi, S. (2008). *Avoiding plagiarism–program code.* RMT University. Retrieved February, 2010, from http://mams.rmit.edu.au/ 14rfpbr1vh3t.pdf

Turnitin. (2009). *Answers to common legal questions about Turnitin.* Retrieved February, 2010, from http://www.turnitin.com/ resources/documentation /turnitin/sales/ Turnitin_FAQ_Legal. pdf

VeriGuide. (2010). *Homepage information.* Retrieved May, 2010, from http://www.veriguide.org

Xue, N., & Shen, L. (2003). Chinese word segmentation as lmr tagging. In *Proceedings of Second SIGHAN Workshop on Chinese Language Processing,* (pp. 176–179).

ADDITIONAL READING

Ashworth, P., Bannister, P., & Thorne, P. (1997). Guilty in whose eyes? University students' perceptions of cheating and plagiarism in academic work and assessment. *Studies in Higher Education, 22*(2), 187–203. doi:10.1080/0307507971 2331381034

Ashworth, P., Freewood, M., & Macdonald, R. (2003). The student lifeworld and the meanings of plagiarism. *Journal of Phenomenological Psychology, 34*(2), 257–278. doi:10.1163/156916203322847164

Barrett, R., & Malcolm, J. (2006). Embedding plagiarism education in the assessment process. *International Journal for Educational Integrity, 2*(1), 38–45.

Carroll, J. (2002). *A handbook for deterring plagiarism in higher education.* Oxford: Oxford Centre for Staff and Learning Development.

Carroll, J. (2003). *Deterring student plagiarism: Where best to start. Improving student learning theory and practice—10 years on* (pp. 365–373). Oxford: Oxford Centre for Staff and Learning Development.

Carroll, J. (2003). Six things I did not know four years ago about dealing with plagiarism. In: H. Marsden & M. Hicks (Eds.), *Educational integrity: plagiarism and other perplexities, Proceedings of the Inaugural Educational Integrity Conference* (pp. 12-18), University of South Australia, Adelaide.

Chanock, K. (2003). Before we hang that highwayman: the LAS advisers' perspective on plagiarism. In: H. Marsden & M. Hicks (Eds.), *Educational integrity: plagiarism and other perplexities, Proceedings of the Inaugural Educational Integrity Conference* (pp. 19-25), University of South Australia, Adelaide.

Clarke, R. (2006). Plagiarism by academics: More complex than it seems. *Journal of the Association for Information Systems, 7*(2), 91–121.

Clerehan, R., & Johnson, A. (2003). Ending the war on plagiarism: appropriation context. In: H. Marsden & M. Hicks (Eds.), *Educational integrity: plagiarism and other perplexities, Proceedings of the Inaugural Educational Integrity Conference* (pp. 88-96), University of South Australia, Adelaide.

Davis, S. (2000). Teaching practices that encourage or eliminate student plagiarism. In Lathrop, A., & Foss, K. (Eds.), *Student cheating and plagiarism in the Internet era—a wake-up call* (pp. 182–187). Englewood, CO: Libraries Unlimited.

Evans, R. (2006). Evaluating an electronic plagiarism detection service. *Active Learning in Higher Education, 7*(10), 87–99. doi:10.1177/1469787406061150

Freewood, M., Macdonald, R., & Ashworth, P. D. (2003). *Why simply policing plagiarism is not enough. Improving student learning theory and practice—10 years on* (pp. 374–383). Oxford: Oxford Centre for Staff and Learning Development.

Hamilton, D., Hinton, L., & Hawkins, K. (2003). Educational integrity, plagiarism and other perplexities. In: H. Marsden & M. Hicks (Eds.), *Educational integrity: plagiarism and other perplexities, Proceedings of the Inaugural Educational Integrity Conference* (pp. 54–59), University of South Australia, Adelaide.

Introna, L., Hayes, N., Blair, L., & Wood, E. (2003). *Cultural attitudes Towards Plagiarism: Developing a Better Understanding of the Needs of Students from Diverse Cultural Backgrounds Relating to Issues of Plagiarism.* Lancaster, UK: Lancaster University.

Kock, N., & Davison, R. (2003). Dealing with plagiarism in the IS research community: A look at factors that drive plagiarism and ways to address them. *Management Information Systems Quarterly, 27*(4), 511–532.

Larkham, P. J., & Manns, S. (2002). Plagiarism and its treatment in higher education. *Journal of Further and Higher Education, 26*(4), 341–349. doi:10.1080/0309877022000021748

Leask, B. (2006). Plagiarism, cultural diversity and metaphor – implications for academicdevelopment. *Assessment & Evaluation in Higher Education, 31*(2), 183–199. doi:10.1080/02602930500262486

Mason, M. (2001). The ethics of integrity: Educational values beyond postmodern ethics. *Journal of Philosophy of Education, 35*(1), 47–69. doi:10.1111/1467-9752.00209

McCabe, D. (2003). Promoting academic integrity: a US/Canadian perspective. In: H. Marsden & M. Hicks (Eds.), *Educational integrity: plagiarism and other perplexities, Proceedings of the Inaugural Educational Integrity Conference* (pp. 3-11), University of South Australia, Adelaide.

Park, C. (2003). In other (people's) words: plagiarism by university students—literature and lessons. *Assessment & Evaluation in Higher Education, 28*(5), 471–488. doi:10.1080/02602930301677

Samuelson, P. (1994). Self-plagiarism or fair use? *Communications of the ACM, 37*(August), 21–25. doi:10.1145/179606.179731

Sutherland-Smith, W. (2008). *Plagiarism, the Internet and academic writing: Improving academic integrity*. London: Routledge.

Thompson, L. C., & Williams, P. G. (2000). But I changed three words! Plagiarism in the ESL Classroom. In Lathrop, A., & Foss, K. (Eds.), *Student cheating and plagiarism in the Internet era— a wake-up call*. Englewood, CO: Libraries Unlimited.

Tierney, A. M., Brown, A., & Neil, D. (2006). Tackling plagiarism in the Level One Biology class—A work in progress. *Practice and Evidence of Scholarship of Teaching and Learning in Higher Education, 1*(1), 13–21.

Walker, J. (1998). Student plagiarism in universities: what are we doing about it? *Higher Education Research & Development, 17*(1), 89–106. doi:10.1080/0729436980170105

Zobel, J., & Hamilton, M. (2002). Managing student plagiarism in large academic departments. *Australian Universities Review, 45*(2), 23–30.

KEY TERMS AND DEFINITIONS

Plagiarism: The dishonest act of taking credit for someone else's intellectual properties.

Automatic Plagiarism Detection System: The computerized system that helps teachers to search for sentences in students' submissions that are similar to other sources.

Academic Quality: The standard that describes the learning environment provided for students.

Academic integrity: Honesty and high moral standard in academic.

Policy (in deploying an automatic detection system): The decisions and plans that are concerned with the deployment of an automatic plagiarism detection system.

Stakeholders (of an automatic plagiarism detection system): The group of people who help to deploy an automatic plagiarism detection system.

VeriGuide: The web-based automated plagiarism detection system that has been deployed at the Chinese University of Hong Kong (CUHK) since 2005. (URL: http://www.veriguide.org)

Chapter 10
Security Technologies and Policies in Organisations

Nickolas J. G. Falkner
The University of Adelaide, Australia

ABSTRACT

The ability to perform actions that were previously impossible or unfeasible has been one of the most challenging aspects that has accompanied the introduction of electronic systems for data management. This, in turn, has required a rethinking of a number of behaviours that had apparently been driven by a strong ethical code but now appear to have been more strongly controlled by the impossibility of the action. This chapter proposes a hybrid ethical approach to address the complex issues surrounding modern computer systems, having first identified the reasons why a simplistic approach is insufficient.

INTRODUCTION

When invasion of privacy required a search of numerous buildings and searching through boxes, the action was restricted to those who had strong motivation – the 'average' employee had neither the will nor the access required to carry out the act. With the ability to search, link and change data at the press of a switch, an ethical vacuum has become apparent in that the perceived impact of a highly invasive or destructive act is not recognised by those carrying out the action and, when confronted, there is not sufficient ethical context for the perpetrator to judge the gravity of the situation. In addition, the existence of the notion of 'Hackers' Ethics' provides a basis for immoral and unethical actions from a business perspective. While a person may react to being caught, it does not necessarily follow that they will integrate this into their worldview to imply that the action itself was wrong.

In this chapter, I will provide a set of case studies and general rules that can be applied to provide an ethical basis for the development and implementation of security policies. In the second half of the chapter, I will address the teleological, deontological and virtue-oriented aspects of the

DOI: 10.4018/978-1-60960-573-5.ch010

ethics surrounding organisational ICT security policy to provide a more theoretical basis for an ethical organisation.

INFORMATION FOR MANAGERS

Your business is not secure in the absence of a formal policy on the responsible, secure and ethical use of technology. An individual's capacity for rationalisation, the possibility of unethical or ethically-ignorant employees, and the capabilities of modern technology combine to make it possible for an organisation's security to be compromised quickly, easily and with devastating effect (Harris & Ogbonna, 2010).

As we will discuss, existing professional codes of ethics may be useful, but there must be a well-established code of ethics that binds the organisation as a whole. These codes of ethics must be flexible, extensible and practical. Because of this, we are going to take the most suitable aspects from all of the frameworks, and propose a system that can be adapted to any business.

The core points of this chapter, for management, are:

1. Be ethically consistent. Apply one rule across your company, your employees and your clients.
2. Use as much security technology as you need to protect your systems and to carry out work efficiently.
3. Consider the impact on your staff of encouraging (or forcing) them to act unethically, even implicitly.
4. Clearly identify what the core ethical rules are for your business in plain language.
5. Provide clear guidance as to which professional ethics bodies you believe are the closest fit for your organisation.
6. Provide clear and explanatory duty statements to all of your staff.

7. Do not presume 'common sense' or a shared notion of reasonable behaviour. Your corporate culture cannot be based on "Well, you should have known that", it should be clearly written down and available.
8. A perfect security policy is only as good as the staff and equipment that implement it.

BACKGROUND

As more technology enters the workplace, we have seen the development of new professions and trades, or trade specialisations, to support office staff and business activities. Electricians are now often licensed as network cabling experts, systems administrators maintain software, hardware and networking systems, and business information specialists spend a great deal of time analysing and optimising the business processes for their clients. Information, and access to it, is a valuable commodity.

Information and Communication Technology (ICT)-rich businesses may be generally characterised as businesses that have a high proportion of their staff using a computer on a daily basis and depend upon the availability of the data stored in the firm's computer systems. There is also active use of the Internet.

ICT-rich businesses require at least two different staff roles: those staff whose core activities relate to the delivery of the company's products and those staff whose core activities provide the ICT support required to allow this to occur. Depending on the size, nature and maturity of the business, this second staff role may be provided by a third party, through a dedicated person or team of people, or through placing additional support roles onto another staff member.

Professional staff may already have a professional code of ethics that they can draw upon. The educational background required to perform competently, the level of accreditation required for employment in a number of sectors, and the impact of incompetence provide a strong argument that ICT staff should act as professionals, even in the absence of licensing or binding professional bodies. They should also adhere to the ethical standards and codes of practice provided by international and national bodies, such as the ACM, IEEE and Australian Computer Society (ACM, 1992; IEEE, 2006; ACS, 2005). It should be noted that certain industry certifications, such as Cisco Certification for a range of network specialities, provides a *de facto* professional framework, as the certifications expire after 2 or 3 years (Cisco, 2010). Professional staff also have to learn and conform to the code of conduct and ethics of their employer.

A significant number of businesses employ external ICT support staff. Depending on the terms of their employment, such staff may be required to observe the codes of practice of two organisations, potentially have multiple supervising staff and may not necessarily spend all of their time on the one business site. Third-party staff must adhere to at least two corporate codes of ethics: those of their primary employer and those of the organisation to which they are attached. This immediately introduces at least one level of conflict, unless both organisations have achieved a very high level of agreement.

We need ethical consistency across all of our staff and this has to be driven from the top.

CASE STUDY 0

A new employee at Badger and Rat (Aquatic), a dual partner organisation, is told to install software onto a set of computers by one of the partners. She is handed an obviously copied DVD containing office productivity software, database software and photo manipulation software. The serial numbers for all of these pieces of software are the same for all of the machines. She asks the partner, somewhat naively, if there are some other disks she can use, as she is worried about copy-right issues. The partner waves off her concerns, citing the unreasonable price of the software as a justification.

Still concerned, the employee goes to the other partner, who takes the disks from her and tells her not to worry about it. Some time later, the employee goes to use one of the new machines and discovers the copied software installed.

What are the security considerations implicit in this case study and what are the responsibilities of the actors?

The major security concern here is that the business is now open to legitimate legal action launched by a body such as the Business Software Alliance (BSA), a group of leading software makers working to stop copyright infringement. Successful litigation has a financial cost and a potential loss of reputation for the company involved. If the organisation has a restricted cash flow, a sufficiently large fine could result in the business being wound up.

The secondary consideration is that pirated, or illegally unlocked, software may contain security back doors or other malware, installed deliberately or accidentally during the copying process.

The ethical argument regarding pirated software is often framed in a 'Robin Hood' apparatus. The software creator is charging an unjustifiably high fee for their services and the partners are avoiding paying an unjust fee. This is a very shallow and immediately dismissible framework, within an ethical framework, as no counter argument of greater good is being made here and a law is being broken with no consideration to its wider application. Partner One is claiming that the fee is too high but is offering no offset benefit to justify theft. Partner Two is, apparently, deceiving the employee and then allowing the unethical behaviour to take place. The new employee is arguably complicit in this misuse if she remains with the company and takes no action about it. The first and second partners are actively involved in unethical behaviour.

The partners are responsible for the success of the company, as a duty to each other, and this activity is not in the long-term interests of the company. The employee is responsible for the ethical discharge of their own job and, unless they actively signed a contract agreeing to pirate software, may be required to resign, remove the software, or approach the BSA, as dictated by their moral compass. The employee may also have no faith in the management structure and the ethical structure of the company is also highly questionable. What else is being dealt with in this manner?

Case study 0 shows a company with an explicit disregard for the correct ethical behaviour, but what happens when we have a company with, apparently, implicit disregard?

CASE STUDY 1

The University of Example provides computing resources to staff and students and, to prevent unauthorised usage, maintains a strong password system. For many years, a warning is shown to all users, when they log in, to inform users of their rights and the penalties that apply if the resources are misused.

Recently, a student has been discovered running an illicit warez server, serving illegally copied material, on a University machine. The student is brought before a disciplinary hearing and argues that they were unaware of these limitations on usage. On further questioning, it transpires that the 'warning message' is only seen when students log in using a particular mechanism. New computers purchased in the current year no longer show this warning because they do not connect to the servers in the same way.

Fortunately for the University, a site-wide policy has also been created that binds all students to authorised use of the University's facilities, superseding the warning message. All students agree to this policy as a condition of enrolment.

The student still argues that they were unaware that they were doing anything wrong, as they were not informed at time of login. The disciplinary board finds them guilty of misconduct and the student's account privileges are suspended for two weeks and all illegal material is purged from the server.

Who is responsible for the student's actions? What is the security impact?

Despite the student's assertions, all information required has been provided to him, even if he has chosen not to read it. However, it is becoming increasingly apparent that certain groups, including young people, are neither reading end-user licence agreements nor service agreements (Bryce & Klang, 2009). The "click to accept" is seen as the price to pay to use the service, without integrating the contract that is being explicitly established by the acceptance.

Because of the way that the warning has been presented, not once at the start of a semester but at every log in, can the University be seen to be undermining its own case? The frequency of this warning appears to signal that the warning is still active. What happens if it disappears?

The security impact of the lack of warning is straightforward. Can one expect better behaviour from a prisoner in the Panopticon when they are unaware that they are in the Panopticon (Bentham, 1995)? The security impact of the warez site is subtler. Not only does it provide a gathering place within the University's walls, but it also leaves the University open to legal action from copyright groups. The University must take action to shut down the service, be seen to be active in their opposition to such activity and to take steps to prevent this from happening again.

The management focus here is of clearly stating what is expected of your employees and ensuring that this message is available to everyone.

Before further discussing the ethical implications of actions taken within a business, and the motivation and rationale of actors, we need to consider the most likely security threats that will be encountered by these businesses.

COMMON SECURITY ISSUES

The first security issue is controlling access to resources and the second is maintaining the availability of resources (Garfinkel, 2003).

The simplest way to address access control is to limit access completely and maintain isolated systems, with strong authentication procedures. Unfortunately, this isolation deprives the business of the benefits of linking systems together to share data, distribute workload and provide intra-office communication. Removing legitimate connections also may encourage illicit connection formation, which we will discuss shortly. Access control corresponds to the locked door that prevents burglars from entering a house, while allowing the owner the ability to enter, leave and share their entry privileges with trusted associates. As we will see, not everyone who is trusted with a key can be considered truly trustworthy (Kurose & Ross, 2010; Nemeth, 2008b).

Access control is not restricted to protecting resources from external agencies. A very high percentage of security threats arise from within businesses and access control is as important for the employees of a company as it is for the malign entities beyond their borders. Similarly, it is much easier for an internal agent to restrict or deny access to resources.

In the majority of cases, preventing these potential threats from becoming an actual threat to the business is possible if the security staff are doing their job correctly. Even if a single event does occur, timely detection will greatly reduce the severity of the incident and prevent re-occurrence. Security and systems staff must be alert to all of these threats and should respond to them in a timely fashion and take all instances seriously. However, this responsibility is often difficult to implement if it is not clear what constitutes one of these actions,

due to a policy vacuum, or if executive staff in the business are the culprits. An important part of this responsibility is an obligation to be aware of the problems that can occur, actively attempt to detect them and regularly update both the list of potential security problems, the detection methods and the prevention mechanisms that are deployed. This will be addressed further in the section "The Duties of Security Staff" (Nemeth, 2008a).

It is important to note that the role of the staff is essential to system reliability and security, to the extent that inaction can have as great an impact on users as malign action. The significant threats are far more likely to occur and to have an impact when insufficient maintenance has been carried out on the system. The task of upgrading and updating computer systems is referred to as 'patching', and is vital as modern operating systems may have exploitable problems from the day of release. But what of those who would actually attack the system, even when it is well maintained?

THE HACKER 'ETHIC'

Many organisations divide their security concerns into two partitions: those who are outside and who cannot be trusted; and those who are inside and can be trusted.

To discuss the outsiders, we will begin by addressing the 'core values' of hackers as initially outlined (Levy, 1984), which first introduced the values of the MIT hacker community. Although the contemporary use of the term hacker implies a person who performs acts that are of a criminal or questionably legal nature, the original use of the term was to describe projects that achieved constructive and enjoyable outcomes. Thus, when the first MIT students started trying to achieve more with the computers that they had access to, they were hacking – achieving a constructive goal that gave them a great deal of pleasure.

While there is no formal codex of hacker behaviour, the implicit ethics of the MIT hackers were well established. In this section, we will discuss the core hacker ethics: unlimited access, free information, decentralisation, meritocratic advancement, seek beauty and computers can enrich your life.

- **Unlimited access**, or the Hands-On imperative, proposes that improvement can only come when all previous ideas and systems are available for examination. Otherwise, hackers risk re-inventing the wheel, rather than taking ideas to the next level. The notion of 'access' is not just restricted to inspection, but extends to disassembly and potential improvement of an existing system
- **Free information** is the principle that all information about the systems should also be available to everyone.
- **Decentralisation** reduces the possibility of a single entity, such as a bureaucracy, government or corporation from controlling access to systems or data. This provides a borderless environment to encourage the flow of ideas.
- **Meritocratic advancement** builds a community of hackers that ignores qualifications, race, creed, age or gender in favour of a measure of worth based on hacking skills. The goal is to produce an equal opportunity environment.
- Hackers may **seek beauty** in many ways, including the careful construction of a program to look beautiful as well as to produce beautiful things and the use of innovative techniques to achieve artistic results.

The increasing availability of computers and ease of joining the network has increased the community of potential hackers. The exploitation and false adoption of the original 'hacker ethic' increased in the 1990s, to justify actions that were criminal or, at best, self-centred. The original statements were now employed in a manner that rationalised selfish, and sometimes destructive, actions by placing adherence to a hacker ethic 'rule' as being more important than individual rights to privacy. Often, this misuse was combined with a questionable application of Marxist theory to justify unauthorised access to resources (Heller, 1998). Recall Case Study 0 and the use of a 'Robin Hood' argument to steal software. Similar arguments take place all of the time to justify any number of criminal computer-related activities.

As the Internet has grown, a number of practices have become standards, or *de facto* standards, to deal with the continued operation and use of a globally-linked, multi-computer network (Kurose & Ross, 2010). A number of these practices are at odds with the idealism of the original hacker ethic. Unlimited access and free information are not available to the majority of users. Users may access their own materials and those to which they have been granted access. In many cases, the rights granted to users do not allow unlimited access for changing and replacing existing systems with 'improved' systems. In order to pay for the systems and networks, a great number of resources are centralised and this has had significant impact on issues such as information access, censorship and the legal umbrella under which actions take place. Uncertified skills are not widely regarded, unless concrete evidence can be provided.

In the face of a growing hacker community, who are faced with an increasingly restrictive and hacker-hostile environment, the role of the corresponding staff that protects systems from immoral activity is essential. The next section outlines the duties of these staff.

The most important aspect of these rules, with regard to policy formation, is that we cannot depend upon social mores to prevent hackers from exploiting the system as the 'traditional' social systems are at odds with the social standards of the hacker community. Our policies cannot depend upon an individual's sense of what is right as rationalisation and lack of thought may still lead to immoral actions being taken.

THE DUTIES OF SECURITY STAFF

The duties of the security staff in an organisation can be viewed from two perspectives: that of the company who has employed them within a well defined job specification, and that of those who use the services of these staff. The company, explicitly or not, employs security staff to reduce risk, manage threats and maximise resource availability. However, the users of the systems have an expectation that any security measures taken will not unduly affect their ability to use the systems. The systems that are being administered will often dictate how the security can be applied, and how the actions of the staff and users will be perceived.

The security models that are available can also have an impact on the efficacy of the staff, as modern operating system can have a complex, fine-grained security model or can have a system where the user has a very small number of privileges, or all of them! A fine-grained system, or capability model, may allow an administrator to have total control over one aspect of the system, without the risk of having more power than is required. The 'all-or-nothing' alternative provides all power to the administrator who has been allowed to increase, or escalate, their level of privilege. This has an effect on the ease with which hackers can achieve new privileges in the system. In a capability model, they have to achieve all of the capabilities required individually. In an 'all-or-nothing' model, a hacker can achieve total power in a single act of escalation.

Even the most secure mechanism can still be bypassed by hackers because, if anyone can gain access, all the hacker has to do is to find who has the access and convince that person to pass on the access code or mechanism. Obtaining access in this way, social engineering, is one of the significant causes of security problems. It is often tempting for management to deal with this problem by requiring many levels of security, hardware artefacts and incredibly frequent password changes. This inconveniences users and, unfortunately, the response of users to inconvenience is often to devise a mechanism to circumvent the measure.

CASE STUDY 2

International Widget has a new security manager who institutes a monthly password change cycle and the use of RSA SecurID hardware tokens as part of a two-factor authentication system. To drive the importance home, the loss of the SecurID token is a sacking offence. (Bank cards are also two-factor mechanisms as you must have both the card and the PIN to gain access.) Three months into this new cycle, a random sweep determines that a number of staff have started writing the passwords down and placing them into insecure locations, such as a sticky note placed on a monitor or in a drawer, with very little attempt to conceal the password. Worse, several of the field staff have started leaving their tokens in their desks as well, as they have been concerned about losing them while out on client sites. This also means that these staff cannot legitimately remotely access their machines while on the road. The final problem uncovered is that the field staff have installed a remote dial-in point that they can connect to while outside that allows them access to their systems. To get around the lack of token, the dial-in point is pre-authenticated, with the credentials expiring in 12 hours.

There is nothing intrinsically wrong with the approach proposed above from a security perspective. However, it is obvious that there is a great deal of staff resistance. From a management perspective, whoever installed an incredibly large hole in the corporate security systems will, at least, have a great deal of explaining to do. (A pre-authenticated gateway allows anyone who knows how to access the dial-in point to use the privileges of the pre-authenticated user.)

What is less than ideal in Case Study 2 is that it took several months to uncover what was going on. The partitioning of insider versus outsider often leads to the incorrect assumption that security mechanisms only need to observe the gateways and attempts to come in. Realistically, all resource usage should be tracked and periodically audited to ensure that no-one, inside or outside, is misusing the resources. The requirement for everyone to act ethically requires that everyone be prepared to be placed within a panopticon, at least as far as their corporate resource usage is concerned.

The following questions need to be asked:

1. What level of security do I actually need? Staff in high-security jobs can generally meet the security requirements required for the job. Staff in a clerical firm on monthly rolling passwords will wonder why they are doing it.
2. Have I provided enough training for the new system? Any good security system will need some time to bed in and user confidence will assist in uptake. Again, stressing the importance of the new model and combining that with a clear statement on why this is being done is essential.
3. Have you considered your staff as well as your business? Do you have mobile staff that may be connecting over low-bandwidth mobile connections, using a range of devices that may not be able to run all of your security mechanisms? Then consider placing a part of your systems into a more accessible area. Some parts of the system may need to be heavily protected, but maybe not as many as you think.
4. Am I at risk of encouraging my staff to take an unethical path to circumvent my security mechanisms? If the daily demands of a job require a level of response and agility that cannot be met and still conform to the secu-

rity mechanisms, you are asking your staff to choose between doing their job well or doing their job ethically.

If we are going to observe everyone, then management must also institute recording and logging mechanisms that cannot be circumvented or easily altered by a small group of people. This adds a fifth requirement.

5. Clearly identify security mechanisms that could be considered intrusive. The use of plain language is essential here - do not use examples or euphemism.

As always, your staff need to know that there is a guard and that they are being watched as it will alter their behaviour, at least in the short term (Wang and Hong, 2010). If a staff member does something, accidentally or deliberately, and no action is taken, then there may as well be no monitoring. We also address a sensitive issue in terms of staff system usage: the illusion of privacy.

Users make, often incorrect, assumptions regarding the privacy and ownership of the data that is stored on systems. Institutional ownership of equipment, services and facilities is generally perceived to be the provision of resources to undertake the core business of the institution. Users, however, often have an implicit assumption of privacy and ownership of materials that they have generated in the system. This is reflected in the number of users who use their work e-mail address for private activity, or the storage of materials (often of a humorous or trivial nature) on work servers. Privacy, however, is surprisingly hard to maintain in any system that doesn't employ a very fine-grained access control mechanism. In 'all-or-nothing' systems, the system becomes completely visible to any user who escalates their privilege, becoming the *superuser*. The security staff now face another set of issues concerning how they monitor and inspect the systems under their control in order to determine if unethical

Table 1. Applications of the threats

Threat	Pre-Computer Application	Computer Application
Denial of Service Attack	Burning a library	Shutting down web server
Access Subversion	Reading bank ledgers	Reading e-mail
Network Sniffing	Steaming open mail	Wireless snooping
Resource Misuse	Stealing materials	Running a warez site

behaviour is taking place, or the system is at risk. The moment that their investigations take them into user data, such as e-mails or files on disk, they have violated the user's expectations of privacy. Investigation as an action is easy to carry out but harder to justify, and much harder to provide a moral framework for, if the investigation is to have an ethical basis (Harris, Pritchard and Rabins, 2010).

Security staff are the direct opponents of hackers, as they wish to control access, limit information flow, and enforce the authority of the owning body. This now gives the system administrators three conflicting groups with whom they have to deal: management, users and hackers. In the absence of a well-established set of guidelines, as part of a larger ethical framework, security staff will be required to try to resolve the conflicts using their own judgement, or based on what they have done previously. Both of these risk applying solutions inconsistently or, worse, having issues ignored because they are too hard to deal with.

THE POWER TO MOVE MOUNTAINS

Why has this now become such an issue? The threats discussed previously are not unique to the computing environment, nor is the role of servant with many masters an unprecedented one. Table 1 contains some of the possible applications of the threats, for both the pre-computer and computer age.

The most significant difference between the pre- and post-computer threat realisations is the physical presence required to carry out the action. More specifically, each action requires one person to be actively involved. The computer applications can all be very effectively automated and, because of that, can be carried out in parallel and in high volumes.

This is the power to move mountains: we can now carry out actions in a time frame that was previously unrealised, as actions did not scale beyond "one person-one task". It can be argued that one person could move a mountain singled-handed, providing that that person was sufficiently long-lived and the mountain was sufficiently small. As an example, consider the pyramids of the Egyptians: impossible to build unless one had access to sufficient slaves. However, with the scaling offered by computerisation and networking, one person can enlist a large number of resources to provide the necessary 'hands' to move the mountain.

Consider the increased capabilities now extended to staff through the use of computing infrastructure that either has a primitive security and control mechanism, or a non-existent security and control mechanism. This includes systems where the 'convenience versus security' argument has resulted in an otherwise secure system being bypassed or disabled in some way. Now the data of the system is widely available and, at the same time, contains the resources to allow the inspection of its own data. This ease of access is unprecedented in the physical sphere due to the nature of real objects. Even if a big pile of paper is unsecured, it is harder to search than its electronic analogue and any searching has to be carried out at the location of the paper. The storage of real objects can be quite difficult, as British Airways discovered after the failure of the baggage handling system in their new Terminal 5. The entire luggage backlog was moved to Italy, which was a far more efficient location from which to sort and dispatch the luggage effectively (Balakrishnan, 2008). Conversely, the electronic equivalent of this, an e-mail backlog due to the failure of mail delivery, is much easier to resolve. E-mail will accumulate for as long as disk space is available and, once service resumes, can be redirected, redispatched or shared with other machines to clear the backlog. Even if the e-mail is, effectively, 'sent to Italy' it will not be in a way that is overly visible to the users.

THE THEFT OF THE INTANGIBLE

The Motion Picture Association of America (MPAA) produced advertisements in 2004 to address the downloading of films in electronic format, with a number of statements along the lines of "You wouldn't steal a (object)", thereby identifying film downloading as stealing (IPOS, 2004). However, the theft of the intangible lacks the traditional outcome of theft, which is the deprivation of one party of the object that is stolen by the other party. Theft is defined as the illegal taking of one person's property without that person's express consent. In this case, however, nothing has been taken; instead we have taken advantage of a new data model to produce a new copy of the original object. The act is the unauthorised taking of the data, but the intention must be dishonesty, or the deliberate intent to retain the data permanently.

It is important to realise that deprivation may still have occurred, as the copying of the original may have deprived the owner of either remuneration, due recognition or their rights of ownership. Recent changes to Australian Copyright Law, dealing with "space shifting" and designed to al-

low for MP3 players to be legitimately used, have made it legal to transfer data from one format to another, such as ripping a CD to place MP3 files on an iPod, while still making it illegal to then share that data with a third party (ACC, 2006).

The theft of intangible objects through copying is a major issue in any system, as the ease with which copying can be achieved and post-hoc rationalisation on the part of the user often leads to a very high volume of copying of this type. Within the University example, the theft of intangibles also extends to plagiarism and the copying of assignment components in order to receive benefit for work performed by other beings, without due attribution.

Modern distribution technologies, such as BitTorrent or, in its previous form, Napster, allow the sharing of these copied data forms with many other users (Quinn, 2006). At the point that a copying user places the copy onto a distribution point, we have both the act and the intent, as the user has lost the ability to remove the data at the point at which the first download completes – their theft is now unarguably permanent. This has been reflected in recent legal cases undertaken on behalf of the Record Industry Association of America (RIAA).

CASE STUDY 3

A supermarket company has a shopper rewards program that allows customers to accumulate points that can be redeemed for holidays or vouchers. The card IDs are associated with a customer's purchases on any day that they use the card. The company then uses the store location and the customer's specified postcode to determine the best and worst days to sell certain products, on a geographical basis. This approach is considered preferable to just indexing store location as the customer's postcode also shows those customers who are willing to travel to a specific location for a product, special or because this store forms part of their commute (Jilcott et al, 2009).

A new sales manager takes over the company and identifies that a certain brand of cheese never sells well on Tuesday and proposes that anyone who buys that cheese on Tuesday should receive a special offer taking 10% off the price. After discussion, and much data analysis, it is revealed that a certain geographical group are the major contributors to the deficit. Instead of a general, and profit-reducing, special offer, an alternative suggestion is put forward where all of the customers who fall into this group and are on the loyalty program are sent a voucher in the mail to use in conjunction with their card.

The plan is followed and, while a large number of shoppers use the vouchers, a number of shoppers register complaints that their data has been misused. The supermarket group has strict privacy constraints on the release of data to third-parties and have kept all processing house. The supermarket does have a clause in their card usage agreement that specifies that they may use the card data for limited and in-house promotional activities, which they argue is relevant in this case.

To whom does this new, inferred, data belong? The clients are the owners of their geographical data but have chosen to make this available to the supermarket. The supermarket is the owner of their supply chain data but has chosen to make their analyses available to the customers, in a limited fashion, for the customer's benefit. This view of the data that shows the marriage of the two ownerships is a 21st Century intangible product. If it were stolen, or copied, then both the privacy of the original client and the business interests of the company are compromised.

Ethically speaking, neither party has done anything wrong but the perception of wrongdoing is very powerful and, as previously mentioned, users may not read end-user licence agreements. This is, however, an illustration of using technology unnecessarily. Instead of providing such a targeted approach, the supermarket chain could have provided a discount to particular store locations on the Tuesday. The majority of users in that

region will shop at a given store habitually - what is needed is a motivator to change the timing of their actual habits.

An ideal employee, or employer, will be predictable in many important ways, not the least of which is their ability to carry out ethical actions as required in the pursuit of their objectives. Up until now, we have provided a more applied framework and examples to direct how we can assess the ethical nature of action. The following sections provide a more theoretical framework for those managers seeking to understand where the ethical bases for the previous arguments have come from.

PRODUCING A CONSISTENT ETHICAL FRAMEWORK

The original hackers had always, at least implicitly, discounted the role of ownership and rejected the notion of privacy. Thus, their right to intellectual freedom was seen to transcend property and privacy rights in other individuals. Their justification was based on their perception of the *right to improve*, which was construed as a global benefit. However, as this consequence is both subjective in interpretation and requires perfect behaviour on the part of the hacker, it is questionable whether it is actually a benefit. From an ethical perspective, this privileged position fails to satisfy the Kantian Categorical Imperative, as we cannot apply the principle universally – not everyone should attempt to modify systems merely because they *believe* that they can improve it (Kant, 1989). The utilitarian interpretation also finds this approach to be immoral, as the application of this as a rule is not guaranteed to increase overall benefit. There is also no social contract here as we have two distinct groups, the privileged and the non-privileged, and one group is applying changes of no demonstrated benefit and unknown costs to another group who is incapable of reciprocating these changes. Ultimately, the only possible justification for the core of the hacker ethic is an act-based utilitarian view if, for an individual act, the demonstrated benefit is sufficiently large to justify ignoring privacy and ownership. It is always essential, therefore, to consider the consequences of a hacker's action, in order to determine if the action is moral or immoral. There is also an aspect of *moral luck* to be considered, where an action that is intended to be immoral accidentally provides a moral consequence, and vice versa. An example of this is the situation where someone breaks into a computer system to steal data and uncovers embezzlement, which they then share with the company. If the value of the stolen data is less than the value to the company of exposing the embezzlement, we have a net benefit and a utilitarian moral action. However, any deontological system will reject this as the rules "Don't steal" or "Don't break in" are being broken here, despite the positive outcome.

A Deontological Basis for a Consistent Ethical Framework

Deontological ethics focus on adherence to rules, and on duty and obligation, rather than on the consequences of the act (Ross, 2003). To eliminate the role of moral luck in this discussion, we consider the effect of moral absolutism, where an immoral act cannot be redeemed by accidentally having moral consequences (Kant, 1989).

A rule-based approach is highly inflexible, especially when the consequences cannot be taken into account (Kamm, 1996). A significant problem can arise when duty statements and personal moral codes are interpreted as an exclusive list of reasonable actions. For example, the maxim "protect the system from misuse" is a valid duty statement but depends on a usable definition of 'misuse'. How do we define misuse: as a list of unacceptable activities or as the inverse of a list of acceptable activities? The first approach will exclude known unacceptable activities but will allow unknown or novel activities until they are reclassified (Kamm, 2007). The second ap-

proach completely prevents novel unacceptable behaviours from being allowed but slows down the introduction and adoption of new, acceptable behaviours. We now have a choice between better support of our users and allowing them to pursue new approaches, or better protection of the system and the potential limiting of user activity in a counter-productive way.

This is further compounded by a staff member's personal moral code providing an additional layer of interpretation of the acts listed on either the 'acceptable' list or 'unacceptable' list. A great deal of training, mentoring and feedback will be required to ensure that the staff member's interpretation is going to meet the expectations of management. This presupposes that the rules that have been put in place have been formed with careful thought and are not inherently contradictory. For example, "protect the system from misuse" and "maximise ease of access" are contradictory rules in this sphere. Maximising the ease of access would require a number of security measures to be toned down or switched off, which immediately leaves the system open to misuse. The first act of any employee who is required to enforce a rule-based approach should be to check the rules for inconsistency.

Another issue with a purely deontological approach in the area of ICT is that an incorrect application reasoning by analogy can lead to the formation of rules that are potentially immoral in their application. Once the rule is in place, the consequences of the rule will not be relevant, and can cause major problems. Regarding the corporate file servers as if they were a direct analogue to the ledger storeroom in a pre-computing business could lead to the maxim "Any investigations of security incidents may take place over the corporate file servers." The problem is that, with a low granularity security model, the ease with which all data can be searched is far greater than the ease with which one can pick up every ledger in the storeroom. This rule can very easily be implemented in a way that reduces the legitimate privacy rights of every user on the server, and also leads to consequences where the rule is used as a post-hoc rationalisation for immoral actions taken by malign actors on the security staff.

A Teleological Basis for a Consistent Ethical Framework

This section focuses on the consequences of the actions taken by staff and the importance of understanding the impact of actions (Bentham, 1996; Mill, 1993). The major problems with a framework consequentially are that, firstly, consequences may not be the result of deliberate acts or match the intention behind the act, and, secondly, that a poor understanding of the possible consequences of an act can lead to immoral actions. There is a surprisingly poor knowledge of computer systems found in many organisations, often where staff are asked to perform system duties part-time, and this often leads to poor decision-making as the impact of the actions cannot be correctly assessed.

Moral luck becomes a more significant issue here, as an action that should result in an immoral consequence may result in a moral consequence, accidentally. It is also difficult to quantify the exact nature of the benefits that we wish to maximise for the business, its users and customers, as each group has a different perspective on the most beneficial aspects (Moore, 2004).

Let us assume that we can specify some essential consequences, and that we can maximise the benefit to all participants. How do we implement this in an environment where increasing protection of the system has a direct impact on the usability of the system for any users? Any member of staff will have to consider the effects of their protective actions on the perceived benefit of the user. If they wish to improve the user experience, will this decrease the benefit allotted to the system?

This difficult balancing act, which must be carried out for every decision in the system, is further compounded by a lack of knowledge of what the true consequences are, and immoral

acts with moral consequences. As an example of the consequences of lack of knowledge, consider the University of Exemplar and an application for transmitting examination results to students. Students can register to receive live updates as their examination results are posted, via e-mail. The system programmer who develops the system makes two mistakes due to inexperience: the first is that they allow the user to specify their University user ID on the electronic request form, and the second is that the user is allowed to change their e-mail address in case they wish to send it to a second account while they are on holiday. The legitimate benefit to students is that they can now be advised of their examination results, wherever they are. This has come at a substantial cost to the system security and individual privacy, as anyone who can view the form can now request the examination results of an arbitrary student, and have it sent to an arbitrary e-mail address. Now malign agents can inspect the examination results of any student. This is an example of the lack of knowledge of the consequences of the actions taken in programming.

Taking a Utilitarian perspective, benefit and 'happiness' can be difficult to quantify in business terms, which are, ultimately, the focus of an ICT business. It could be argued that the overall benefit in the scenario above is a net positive if the students legitimately using the system are happier, very few students have their information stolen but a large number of malign actors derive great benefit from the theft. There is a similar situation with the theft of intellectual property from a company. If the stolen information is then transferred to a company who uses it to produce a better product, at a lower price, that is then used by far more people, has there been an increase or decrease in benefit? The originating company would argue a net loss but, depending on the number of users who increase their benefit, it could be argued that this is a net positive.

To summarise, utilitarianism by itself is insufficient for two reasons: the assessment of benefit may differ, and incompetence in the assessment of consequences will undermine this approach.

Virtue as a Basis for a Consistent Ethical Framework

A virtue-based approach (Devettere, 2002) is one of the most challenging to posit in an ICT framework as the nature of virtue and vice is highly subjective and, in a pragmatic sense, many businesses require ICT actions that would be better supported by vices, while actively suppressing virtues. A virtuous being will embody a set of desirable characteristics, which makes them both moral and virtuous. This immediately raises the question of what is a virtue, in the context of ICT and systems management? From most perspectives, it is possible to produce a short list of virtues that most participants will agree upon. These virtues include honesty, integrity, trustworthiness, knowledge, and fairness. An employer may wish to add commitment, diligence and obedience to this list, where an employee may wish to add self-confidence and independence to the list.

An employer's desire for an employee to be virtuously obedient may lead to immoral actions on the part of the employee as, if they strictly adhere to obedience, they may be required to act in a way that ignores a novel situation, not covered by the guidelines to which they are adhering. This then compromises other virtues and results in a negative result for all participants, except possibility for the malign actors. Also, when two virtues are in conflict, which should be obeyed? Should an employee be honest with all parties, including those malign actors that he or she is currently investigating? Or should the employee be diligent in their duties and trustworthy, from the corporate perspective, by limiting the flow of information that could compromise an individual investigation?

The perspective that we take, and the contextual framework in which we operate, are important in establishing a virtue-based approach but we still find situations where virtues are in conflict between participants or for an individual. Even with the notion of a virtuous 'good citizen', who adheres to all their virtues absolutely, we have no guarantee that this will result in an ethical result. This is also a highly flexible definition as one person's 'good citizen' may behave in a way that is culturally unacceptable and, hence, immoral in a different perspective.

Let us reduce this to the logical minimum: can we guarantee that all of our employees are virtuous and in agreement with us? No. Then this is not enough.

A Hybrid Approach for a Consistent Ethical Framework

This section separates the distinct components of security policies into groups where a specific ethical approach may be employed. We provide examples of a policy and policy component structure that allows each section to be treated consistently. Our goal is utilitarian, ultimately, based on our desire to maximise the benefits to the users of the business and the staff to whom the policies apply. However, because of the diverse nature of underlying tasks that must be considered for a consistent policy, we have no choice except to provide a fusion of duty, goals and virtues. This hybrid approach maximises the overall benefit and allow all participants to retain flexibility and the ability to act morally with a high expectation of their actions being seen as moral.

Our ultimate requirement is to provide a framework that is sufficiently constrained to restrict the loose interpretation, or deliberate corruption, of a personal moral code, while still allowing sufficient flexibility to allow moral acts to occur that have not been previously considered. We start with our expectations of staff, and the employer, in an ICT rich environment.

There is little controversy regarding the pursuit of virtue but, as discussed, it is the definition of the virtues that raises problems, as does the perspective employed. If there are statements regarding the consequences, and rules to govern the application, then we can more easily provide a set of virtues and limit their misuse.

The key virtues for an ethical employee are, as previously mentioned, trustworthiness, integrity, honesty, fairness and knowledge. We must be able to trust the employee, expect them to act in a consistent manner, deal with us honestly, be fair and reasonable in their application of the duties and to have the knowledge required to undertake their duties correctly. The first two virtues are vital if we are to apply consequential or deontological rules or act descriptions to bind the employee to our code of ethics. The remaining virtues are merely those that we would expect from a good employee – that they do their job well and represent all their actions honestly. The reader will note that none of these virtues have a direct bearing on how the employee will determine how to allocate benefit, how to choose between two possible consequences, or to resolve a conflict in rules.

We must now consider the role of benefit and this is a far more difficult matter to decide. While it would be trivial for a company to claim that "in a dilemma, choose the outcome that maximises benefit for the company", this is far more likely to lead to immoral behaviour than not. While a company may be considered, legally, a person, and has an impact on many lives, there are a number of situations where maximising profit or minimising loss can lead to severe consequences on a large number of beings. Part of the model that we adopt employs the rule utilitarian approach to develop a set of rules that will minimise loss of benefit to customer, user and company (Garner, 1967). By focusing on the minimisation of loss of benefit, a negative utilitarianism approach, we are always forced to consider the impact of our actions in terms of how badly it will affect others, rather than how well it will affect us. A starting point for such a rule is "Always act in a way that minimises the loss of benefit for customer, user and company." This may also consist of many,

smaller, rules such as "The user has a right to information and a right to be heard", where it is understood that this is a statement of a user's rights in discussions and treatment, minimising their loss of benefit in a legitimate conflict with the company.

Finally, and in parallel with virtuous employees and a rule utilitarian approach, we must provide sufficient ethical guidance to maintain a morality that meets the social contract of the culture in which we are living. Many of these rules will naturally stem from the rule utilitarian approach that has been developed, but some will be purely deontological. For example, we earlier proposed a utilitarian approach that justified the theft of software, if the receiver provided a derived product that benefited the most people. A virtuous employee could still, within the virtue of fairness, remove material from a hoarding employer and share it with another, to increase benefit and fairly distribute materials of benefit. If there was no other rule to bind them from this course, then the other virtues could be bypassed (more commonly, rationalised). A duty-based framework provides the missing elements to restrict activities to the ethical framework. A rule such as "Do not redistribute material that you do not have a legal reason to distribute" prevents code theft and bit-torrent distribution of music or software. It does not, however, prevent an employee from acting on the virtues of integrity and fairness, and in conjunction with the rule that minimises loss of benefit, to become a whistleblower and distribute company documents revealing illegal activity to authorised persons. Whether the employee is still acting morally if they distribute the material to the media is more debatable, although the eventual outcome will most likely be the same and is acceptable if the authorities in question are also acting in a malign manner. It does not, however, provide a moral argument for an employee to justify selling whistleblower information.

CONCLUSION

We began this chapter by providing an introduction to the issues and types of business that we encounter in ICT and also introduced the hacker ethic – the set of values that guide those people who threaten the ethical companies that we wish to form. Revisiting those ethics, the subjective nature of the leading points is too great to be able to depend on a sufficiently virtuous being, with the correct interpretation, to render all acts derived from these ethics as moral. We must reject the hacker ethic as a complete statement, and understand it as a rationalisation of behaviour that ultimately derived from the privileged position of an academic elite. However, there are degrees to which we can adopt some of the aspects of the hacker ethic, providing that we do not depend on interpretation or intellectual arrogance to assign benefit values.

There is no argument that computers can and are changing the world. This is one of the driving forces for producing a strong ethical code in ICT businesses. We have codified this as the rule utilitarian principle in our hybrid framework. Seeking beauty, or the minimisation of ugliness, is also represented in this consequential principle. What is lacking from the hacker ethic is any form of constraint and, ultimately, it can be reduced to "Do what you want as long as you think it's a good idea", which is an egotistical ethic at best. By providing and codifying virtue and non-consequential rules in a hybrid ethical framework, we can still enjoy some of the high ideals of the hacker ethic, such as freedom of information and access, without contravening individual rights and still provide a fair and consistent ethical framework.

User and staff education and awareness raising are essential tools to develop and maintain the ethical framework for an organisation. All actors in the environment should be encouraged to develop their virtues. The nature and interpretation of all of the virtues, consequences and rules that are part of the company framework must be consistent and formed in a way that genuinely encourages ethical behaviour. Parts of the system that are unethical will ultimately lead to immoral behaviour and, most likely, real-world repercussions in the form of company failure, financial distress, public censure or criminal prosecution. The ethical framework in an ICT company must also reflect the nature of the company and be designed to deal with the new data forms that are now in use, with all of the new threats that exist.

Unless an ICT company is willing to develop a strong and consistent ethical framework, which is actively in use, they have chosen to act in an immoral manner, in the same way as someone who parks their car on a road without setting park brake. While they have not actively set an immoral act in motion, their negligence to do so, given the obvious nature of the act, can lead to a great loss of benefit, does not follow established rules and is not an example of a virtue. It is, by all interpretations, immoral.

REFERENCES

ACC. (2006). *2006 copyright amendments*. Redfern, Australia: Australian Copyright Council.

ACM. (1992). *ACM code of ethics and professional conduct*. Retrieved from http://www.acm.org/ about/ code-of-ethics

ACS. (2005). *ACS code of ethics*. Retrieved from http://www.acs.org.au/ attachments/ Code of Ethics.pdf

Balakrishnan, A. (2008). *BA sending luggage surplus to Italian warehouse*. Retrieved from http://www.guardian.co.uk/ travel/2008/apr /02/ heathrowterminal 5.transport

Bentham, J. (1996). *An introduction to the principles of morals and legislation*. USA: Oxford University Press.

Bryce, J., & Klang, M. (2009). Young people, disclosure of personal information and online privacy: Control, choice and consequences. [Elsevier.]. *Information Security Technical Report, 14*(3), 160–166. doi:10.1016/j.istr.2009.10.007

Cisco. (2010). *Certifications overview*. Retrieved from http://www.cisco.com/ web/learning/ le3/ learning certification overview.html

Devettere, R. J. (2002). *Introduction to virtue ethics: Insights of the ancient Greeks*. Washington, DC: Georgetown University Press.

Duska, R. F. (2007). *Contemporary reflections on business ethics*. The Netherlands: Springer.

Garfinkel, S., Spafford, G., & Schwartz, A. (2003). *Practical UNIX and Internet security* (3rd ed.). O'Reilly Media.

Garner, R. T., & Rosen, B. (1967). *Moral philosophy: A systematic introduction to normative ethics and meta-ethics*. New York, NY: Macmillan.

Harris, C. E. Jr, Pritchard, M. S., & Rabins, M. J. (2005). *Engineering ethics: Concepts & cases* (3rd ed.). Thomson Wadsworth.

Harris, L. C., & Ogbonna, E. (2010). Antecedents and consequences of management-espoused organizational cultural control. *Journal of Business Research*. doi:.doi:10.1016/j.jbusres.2010.03.002

Heller, M. A. (1998). The tragedy of the anticommons: Property in the transition from Marx to markets. *Harvard Law Review, 111*(3), 621–688. doi:10.2307/1342203

IEEE. (2006). *IEEE code of ethics*. Retrieved from http://www.ieee.org /portal/pages /iportals/ aboutus /ethics /code.html

IPOS. (2004). *Launch of anti-piracy movie trailer*. Retrieved from http://www.ipos.gov.sg/ topNav/ news /pre/ 2004/Launch +of+anti+piracy +movie+ trailer.htm

Jilcott, S. B., Laraia, B. A., Evenson, K. R., & Ammerman, A. S. (2009). Perceptions of the community food environment and related influences on food choice among midlife women residing in rural and urban areas: A qualitative analysis. [Routledge.]. *Women & Health, 49*(2-3), 164–180. doi:10.1080/03630240902915085

Johnson, D. G. (2001). *Computer ethics* (3rd ed.). Upper Saddle River, NJ: Prentice Hall. Kamm, F. M. (1996). *Morality, mortality vol. II: Rights, duties, and status*. New York, NY: Oxford University Press.

Kamm, F. M. (2007). *Intricate ethics: Rights, responsibilities, and permissible harm*. New York, NY: Oxford University Press.

Kant, I. (1989). What is enlightenment? In *Foundations of the metaphysics of morals* (2nd ed.). Rochester, NY: Prentice Hall.

Kurose, J. F., & Ross, K. W. (2010). *Computer networking: A top-down approach* (5th ed.). Addison Wesley.

Levy, S. (1984). *Hackers: Heroes of the computer revolution*. Garden City, NY: Anchor Press/ Doubleday.

Mill, J. S. (1993). *On liberty and utilitarianism*. New York, NY: Bantam Books.

Moore, G. E. (2004). *Principia ethica*. Mineola, NY: Dover Publications.

Nemeth, E., Snyder, G., Hein, T., & Whaley, B. (2008a). Policy and politics. In *Unix and Linux system administration handbook* (4th ed.). Upper Saddle River, NJ: Prentice Hall.

Nemeth, E., Snyder, G., Hein, T., & Whaley, B. (2008b). Security. In *Unix and Linux system administration handbook* (4th ed.). Upper Saddle River, NJ: Prentice Hall.

Quinn, M. J. (2006). *Ethics for the information age* (2nd ed.). Addison Wesley.

Ross, W. D. (2003). *The right and the good* (Stratton-Lake, P., Ed.). New York, NY: Oxford University Press.

Wang, S. S., & Hong, J. (2010). Discourse behind the forbidden realm: Internet surveillance and its implications on China's blogosphere. [Elsevier.]. *Telematics and Informatics, 27*(1), 67–78. doi:10.1016/j.tele.2009.03.004

ADDITIONAL READING

Bentham, J. (1995). *The Panopticon Writings.* Verso. (Original work published 1787)

Hannah, S. A. & Harris, M. H. (1996, Winter) *Information Technology and the Future of Work.* Progressive Librarian, 10/11.

Lyon, D. (2006). The search for surveillance theories. In Lyon, D. (Ed.), *Theorizing Surveillance: The Panopticon And Beyond.* UK: Willan Publishing.

Stoll, C. (2000). *The Cuckoo's Egg. New York, NY: Pocket Books. Kidder, T. (2000). The Soul of a New Machine.* New York, NY: Back Bay Books.

KEY TERMS AND DEFINITIONS

Hacker (Original): Someone who achieves a constructive goal that provided joy during attainment and at completion.

Hacker (Current): Someone who conducts illegal activities concerning computers to circumvent established security procedures.

MP3: A compressed music file, using the MPEG 4-Layer 3 encoding.

Space Shifting: The act of moving electronic data, such as music or video, from one storage format to another, such as from CD to MP3 on computer.

User: A person who uses computer systems, without having administrative privileges or the knowledge to make major modifications to the system.

Chapter 11
Critical Infrastructure Protection:
An Ethical Choice

Graeme Pye
Deakin University, Australia

Matthew Warren
Deakin University, Australia

William Hutchinson
Edith Cowan University, Australia

ABSTRACT

The protection of Australian critical infrastructures and the choices made in terms of priorities and cost all impact upon the planning, precautions, and security aspects of protecting these important systems. Often, the choices made will have an ethical imperative that is difficult to assess at the time the decision is taken, and it is only after an incident that the truth of the choices made become fully evident. This is the focus of this discussion that highlights the issues of earlier resource funding choices made and how an ethical choice had to be made, with regard to protecting the security of a water supply infrastructure, or that of a community under the threat of bushfire as outlined in the case study.

INTRODUCTION

The provision and delivery of many of the services that modern society enjoys are the result of ubiquitous critical infrastructure systems that permeate many sectors of the Australian community. Moreover, the integration of technological enhancements and networking interconnections

between critical infrastructure systems has heightened system availability and resilience, including the efficient delivery of services to consumers throughout Australia. However, the reliance on these services and their supporting systems is ever more critical: as the removal, temporary loss, degradation or destruction of a single or multiple systems would have a detrimental impact across many sectors of Australian society. With this increasing system integration and societal

DOI: 10.4018/978-1-60960-573-5.ch011

dependence on critical infrastructure systems, their security, availability and protection becomes increasingly significant.

The broader Australian community has an expectation that services such as power and water will be available when desired and that it will be provided as expected in a safe manner. These services and others are provided by various infrastructure systems dedicated to producing and or providing these services seamlessly to all consumers within our modern society. Therefore, by community expectation and necessity, the protection of these critical infrastructure systems is an imperative to governments, infrastructure owners and consumers.

Australia's modern industrialised society, like those of other western nations, is increasingly reliant on the crucial services delivered by various physical and virtual infrastructure systems to maintain the comfortable standard of living and convenience that the population largely enjoy. Furthermore, the diffusion of information and communication technologies and their incorporation into these crucial systems enables greater system interconnections, which form relationally cooperative networks that facilitate communication, automation and control of infrastructure services supply. Thereby, the maintenance of high-levels of system availability, responsiveness and resilience in terms of their ongoing service supply is required, as is largely the expectation of the community and individual consumers.

The nature of these critical infrastructure systems and their systematic interconnection display attributes of highly structured, complex interconnected networks that characterise the issues of dependency and interdependency relationships, which by necessity exist between infrastructures to facilitate the supply of services. This is particularly prevalent when considering the energy sector, where for instance the continuity of the supply of electricity is crucial to many other sectors of Australia's critical infrastructure for their ongoing provision of services to the community at large (Scott 2005).

In the Australian context some common examples of critical infrastructure systems and services to the community, rely on electricity; water; gas and fuel; health services; telecommunication; and banking and financial services to name a few (AGD 2008). Furthermore, other services that are regarded as critical infrastructures in other national contexts may include: air transportation; ground transportation (interstate trucking, railroads, highways, bridges); telephone; cellular telephone; internet; sewers; food distribution and social events (shopping, sports, entertainment) (Smith 2002). However, critical infrastructures are vulnerable and can be damaged, destroyed or disrupted by breakdowns, negligence, natural disasters, accidents, cyber incidents, illegal criminal activity and malicious damage. So it is for these and other reasons that drives the need to protect the continuity of supply against such hazards and threats. It is the aim of government policy and that of infrastructure owners and operators, to ensure continued supply through identifying and implementing improved security, protective safeguards and analysis in response to the identified threats, vulnerabilities and weaknesses posed (Scott 2005, Bentley 2006).

The impact of disrupting one or more of these services that critical infrastructures supply and the potential inconvenience to the wider community is an ongoing concern to national decision makers. This is due largely in part to the physical magnitude of many of these infrastructures and the complexity of their interconnections and relationships with other systems. Furthermore, system availability coupled with system security analysis of the infrastructure operation and environment may provide sufficient insights into the potential vulnerabilities of these assets. Although this represents a significant challenge, critical infrastructure industry owners and operators including the various levels of government must remain cognisant of the potential consequences of system compromise. This requires critical infrastructure stakeholders to seek ways in which to address, analyse, cope, plan and comprehend the complexities of the twenty first century security of critical infrastructures (Smith, 2002).

Therefore, protecting critical infrastructure systems from damage and maintaining system functionality, resilience and delivery of the services to the community, requires ethical choices to be made by governments, owners and emergency services, particularly during times of natural disaster. This research investigates the ethical choices that arise with regard to managing threats to critical infrastructure systems during times of disaster, which may impinge upon the availability and quality of the resources that critical infrastructure systems supply to the community.

At the outset, a background discussion will provide an understanding of what critical infrastructures are in the Australian context and describe some past events that exemplify the criticality of these systems to the community. The issue of critical infrastructure system protection is broadly explained, before outlining the ethical issues surrounding the critical infrastructure system case study presented. Finally, a discussion of the ethical choices made in response to the evolving situation within the context of the case study is undertaken and outcomes are discussed, before presenting conclusions and identifying future research opportunities.

BACKGROUND

In terms of defining critical infrastructure, the specific Australian determination is as follows (TISN 2004b, p.3): "Critical infrastructure is defined as those physical facilities, supply chains, information technologies and communication networks which, if destroyed, degraded or rendered unavailable for an extended period, would significantly impact on the social or economic well-being of the nation, or affect Australia's ability to conduct national defence and ensure national security."

The diffusion of critical infrastructures permeates across many sectors of the Australian community and economy including banking and finance, transport and distribution, energy, utilities, health, food supply, communications and even key government services and national icons. Some elements are not strictly physical infrastructure and may be 'virtual' in terms of internet-based electronic supply chains for example, or other networks that support the delivery of all important products, information or services (TISN, 2003, 2004b). Generally, these modern critical infrastructure systems exist securely and seamlessly within our environment and provide many of the services and resources that Australians utilise on an everyday basis; be it at home, work or leisure.

Ethical Decision Making

In society, whether in a business context or in a day to day situation, the majority of decisions that are made are based upon an ethical viewpoint. The ethical reasoning could be due to a number of factors including political views, upbringing and personal values have long been associated with individual decision behaviour. There has been extensive research into the ethical decision making in a business context (Hunt & Vitell (1986), Singhapakdi and Vitell (1991); Mayo and Marks (1990), Hunt and Vasquez-Parraga (1993), Herndon (1996) and Harrington (1997)).

The role played by personal values in decision making within an organization is less clear (Fritzhe 1995). Prior research into individuals ethical decision making (Wagner & Sanders 2001) had determined that individual characteristics, such as religion and the issue under consideration are expected to affect the ethical evaluation that an individual goes through based on their underlying ethical philosophies and cognition (level of moral development). The evaluation stage of ethical decision making involves an individual evaluating or determining the rightness or wrongness of aspects of a particular issue. The individual considers aspects or alternatives of the issue such as whether he deems them to be just or unjust, acceptable to himself or to others, conforming to society and government expectations. Ethical evaluations result in a judgment regarding the ethical issue and also impact the intended actions of the individual. An ethical judgment is the determination of an action as being ethical or not ethical. An individual's intention is the probability that they will engage in an action presented to them as an outcome to an ethical situation.

Wagner and Sanders (2001) proposed a theoretical model (as shown by Figure 1) which illustrated the stages that an individual passes through in determining a course of action when confronted with an ethical issue. An individual is considered to be an active agent within the context of their social, economic and organizational environments.

In a security context, ethical decision making may not always apply. In a security or emergency situation, the magnitude of consequences is the main issue that has to be considered. Jones (1991) identified six major factors that should be considered when the magnitude of consequences are reviewed. The major factors are:

Magnitude of Consequences

The magnitude of consequences of the moral issue is defined as the sum of the harms (or benefits) done to victims (or beneficiaries) of the moral act in question. For example, an act that causes 1,000 people to suffer a particular injury is of greater magnitude of consequence than an act that causes 10 people to suffer the same injury.

Social Consensus

The social consensus of the moral issue is defined as the degree of social agreement that a proposed act is evil (or good). For example, the evil involved in discriminating against minority job candidates has greater social consensus than the evil involved in refusing to act affirmatively on behalf of minority job candidates.

Probability of Effect

The probability of effect of the moral act in question is a joint function of the probability that the act in question will actually take place and the act in question will actually cause the harm (benefit) predicted. For example, producing a vehicle that would be dangerous to occupants during routine driving has greater probability of harm than producing a vehicle that endangers occupants only during rear-end collisions.

Figure 1. Decision making in an ethical context

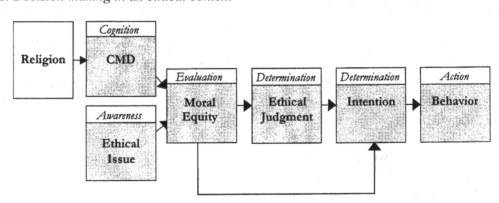

Temporal Immediacy

The temporal immediacy of the moral issue is the length of time between the present and the onset of consequences of the moral act in question (shorter length of time implies greater immediacy). For example, releasing a drug that will cause 1 percent of the people who take it to have acute nervous reactions soon after they take it has greater temporal immediacy than releasing a drug that will cause 1 percent of those who take it to develop nervous disorders after 20 years.

Proximity

The proximity of the moral issue is the feeling of nearness (social, cultural, psychological, or physical) that the moral agent has for victims (beneficiaries) of the evil (beneficial) act in question. For example, layoffs in a person's work unit have greater moral proximity (physical and psychological) than do layoffs in a remote plant.

Concentration of Effect

The concentration of effect of the moral act is an inverse function of the number of people affected by an act of given magnitude. For example, a change in a warranty policy denying coverage to 10 people with claims of $10,000 has a more concentrated effect than a change denying coverage to 10,000 people with claims of $10.00.

Security and the Environment

Likewise environmental change and its effect can have an impact on human security in a number of ways. If considered from an anthropogenic perspective, it can cause conflict and it can degrade the resources available to human societies (for example, by decreasing biodiversity, by clearing such items as mangrove swamps and forests, by decreasing cropland). Furthermore, such impacts upon the environment can disrupt the very economic base of societies. So to summarise the impact of the natural environment on security, it can be stated that:

- Future changes could provide a source of conflict over natural resources and services by their decrease/depletion and unequal distribution (Klare, 2001, Renner, 2002), e.g. conflict over water, failure of water supplies for major cities;
- Environmental change can affect human security by producing situations that adversely affect human health and well-being for example, drought, food shortages, bio-security threats, chemical contamination and availability of usable land. Also it can directly affect society's infrastructure, for example, climate change can cause an increase in bushfires which in themselves can threaten water supplies (by contamination) and power supply (by destruction of power lines and generation facilities);
- Human military and industrial activity can seriously affect environmental health and therefore human security.

However, this is taking a very human-centred approach where the object to be 'secured' is the human and associated systems. A more eco-centric viewpoint would be concerned with the security of regional or global eco-systems. Even the concept of sustainability – both 'weak' and 'strong' which determine whether natural and human capital are considered complements rather than substitutes are considered from a human perspective. In a sense, it is difficult not to do this. However, it is possible to attempt to draw the boundary around a security problem to actively include them on an equal footing with infrastructure systems.

Modern Critical Infrastructure Systems

Modern infrastructure systems are the product of a steady development, improvement and expansion throughout the twentieth century into the present day. Furthermore, the incorporation of new technologies continues to improve the functionality and reliability of these systems and the essential services they deliver to the greater community. Modern infrastructures deliver a variety of services to the modern industrialised societies that have permeated into both the public and private lives of its citizens. This pervasive phenomenon has increasingly become the focus of concern from a national security perspective, particularly with regard to protecting critical infrastructure systems and maintaining system availability.

The conceptual notion of a national critical infrastructure was ushered into the public arena in the mid 1990s when the United States began to acknowledge that a set of infrastructure facilities and services were critical to the ongoing well-being of the nation and its citizens. Initially the US critical infrastructure systems and organisations identified were those providing electricity, water, fuel supply, communications, transport, the finance sector, government and public services. Although infrastructure system failures do happen and multiple failures are possible, the belief was that as long as they were not significant or long term in duration, there would be no threat to the governance of the nation or the wellbeing of the population. It remains evident that infrastructure facilities and services are critical to government and the people and require protection at times of civil unrest, and wars where it is essential to protect food, water and energy supplies (Jones, 2007a).

Furthermore, during the twentieth century the advances in technology and its incorporation, particularly the internet, has led to the realisation that physical protection is simply not enough. This connectivity introduces another avenue to perpetrate an act involving an infrastructure system without being physically present to commit the act. Many of these changes in the security attitude and protection of critical infrastructures are the result of various incidents that have occurred since the 9/11 attacks of 2001 in the US. This has resulted in the adoption of tighter security attitudes being adopted by other nations (Jones, 2007a).

Additionally, it is the benefits of the technological capabilities incorporated into today's infrastructure systems that are a measure of a nation's economic prosperity and development. The outcome is high quality and reliable infrastructure services that contribute to higher living standards for the community generally. Additionally, these infrastructure systems play an important part in attracting private sector investment that in turn contribute to ongoing national economic growth and increasing prosperity (COAG, 2007).

Modern infrastructures are prevalent across numerous sectors of today's community such as energy, utilities, transport, communications, health, food supply, finance, manufacturing, mining, government services and national icons (NCTC, 2004). Although not a fully inclusive list, it is through these underpinning infrastructure distribution networks that essential products and services reach the community and other jurisdictions as required. For the most part, the infrastructures identified here are relevant to most industrialised nations, with a few variations to those listed attributing to specific needs or a particular approach taken by a particular nation towards infrastructures that underpin the standard of living (Marasea & Warren, 2004).

Furthermore, it is the convenience and availability of the infrastructure services, together with community expectations, that potentially leads to adverse social issues when these systems fail, falter or experience a reduced level of service supply or availability to the community. Depending upon magnitude and which infrastructures or multiple infrastructures are affected, will invariably determine the community reaction and influence the likely response contingencies evoked at governmental, business, personal and wider economical levels (Pye & Warren, 2008; 2009).

Exemplifying the Criticality of Infrastructures

Modern industrialised societies are increasingly reliant on key infrastructures and their support systems to reliably produce and deliver their services. Electricity supply and distribution, water supply, fuel supplies and distribution, telecommunication services, transportation and distribution systems and emergency response services to list some of these infrastructures systems, are critical to a modern industrial society. Furthermore, consider adding to these the stock exchange, banking and financial systems, health services and food supply systems. It soon becomes apparent that the potential impact upon the community is significant if such critical infrastructure systems were to fail (Slay & Koronios, 2006).

The loss of these systems even for a short time can result in significant, severe disruptions to the activities of business and the greater community at large, as evidenced by the Victorian gas crisis in 1999. In this instance, the state of Victoria, Australia was without gas supplies for a number of weeks with the associated costs to business and government estimated in the billions of dollars; not discounting the major inconvenience presented to householders with no gas for cooking and heating purposes (ANAO, 2000).

Two other relevant examples of critical infrastructure system failure were the separate 1998 power outages following generator and grid infrastructure failures in Brisbane, Australia and Auckland, New Zealand. In both cases, sections of the cities were without reliable power supplies and government and business alike had to operate in this environment for an extended period (ANAO, 2000). The recent gas plant explosion at the Apache Energy's facility on Varanus Island off Karratha in the Pilbara region of Western Australia (WA) on 3rd of June 2008 exemplifies another critical

infrastructure system failure. The explosion and fire affected gas export pipelines that carry the gas supply south to the domestic market and cut supply by one-third indefinitely, with estimates of at least two months before even partial gas production could resume (Williams, 2008; Le May, 2008). As Apache Energy was the second biggest supplier of gas, the WA state government had no option but to ration gas supplies to the industrial, manufacturing and mining sectors forcing sharp cutbacks in production for at least two months due to their dependency on a consistent supply of gas (Chambers, 2008; Gosch, 2008).

Furthermore, from an information and communications technology (ICT) perspective, a recent Australian federal government review of its use of ICT found that power agencies had raised concerns regarding the electricity supply to federal government data centres in the Australian Capital Territory (ACT). The critical issue was that the ACT's single electricity distribution grid is currently fed by two supply feeds from the larger New South Wales (NSW) electricity supply grid, with one feed supplying 85 percent of the ACT's electricity requirements and the smaller 15 percent feed only supplying the immediate localised suburban area of Fyshwick. What this electricity supply reliance imbalance indicates, was that the smaller electricity power feed was insufficient to support government agency needs and that government agency data centres situated in Canberra remain vulnerable, due to their ongoing dependence on the larger, single ACT electricity supply feed (Gershon, 2008).

Additionally, during the summers of 2007, 2008 and 2009 Victoria's electricity generation, distribution and transmission system has been unable to cope with demand due to a combination of extreme hot weather and bushfire events (Dowling, 2009). During the 2009 heatwave, electricity demand out stripped supply capability resulting in rolling 'blackouts' across the state affecting more than one hundred thousand homes, businesses and industries (Dobbin & Dowling, 2009;

Moran, 2009). This illustrates the consequences of a dependency relationship, as exhibited by the electrified suburban train system. The contracted service provider was forced to cancel nearly 40 percent of its services on the worst day leaving many passengers stranded, because of intermittent power supplies and issues regarding the buckling railway tracks' inability to cope with the extreme heat, even when power was available (Economou, 2009; Houston & Reilly, 2009; Lucas, 2009a; Lucas, 2009b).

In essence, what these examples illustrate is the importance and criticality of maintaining service supply security of critical infrastructure systems. This is a consequence of the pervasiveness of the services these systems provide and the sophistication of information technology (IT) functioning within these systems, coupled with physical service supply and community expectations. This reliance upon critical infrastructure systems has permeated into nearly every corner of Australian daily life, with the community now largely dependent upon the many infrastructure systems and services they deliver for their day-to-day activities, which the community largely takes for granted, and feel secure in the expectation that critical infrastructure system services remain available when needed and on demand.

It is at this point, when the greater community cannot do without the services these systems provide, that they become critical infrastructures because of the crucial services they deliver to the ongoing wealth and well-being of society in general. Therefore, the logical extension of this assumption is that service assurance and integrity of the system progressively attains a condition that is fundamentally essential to most modern, secure, industrialised and stable societies. Additionally, it is from the national security perspective that governments begin to realise the potential threat of interrupting, denigrating performance or the destruction of a nation's critical infrastructure systems and the potential flow-on effects of such scenarios. Therefore, in order to effectively plan

for and protect critical infrastructure systems, it is imperative that a comprehensive understanding of the system structure, operational intricacies, security characteristics and vulnerabilities is attained, which is central to developing a considered assessment of the soundness of these physically large and geographically distributed systems (TISN, 2006).

As identified, critical infrastructure systems provide essential services and capabilities to modern industrialised societies that have become an intrinsic concern in terms of national security and the potential security vulnerabilities of their technological interconnection, networking and increasingly the reliance on the availability of services that critical infrastructure systems deliver to the community. Therefore, the protection of critical infrastructure systems continues to be the subject of security scrutiny as national governments recognise the importance of maintaining secure system availability as an imperative to the national interest.

Critical Infrastructure Protection

The implementation of protective measures aimed at securing critical infrastructure systems requires a considered approach, as there are many variables involved in establishing and maintaining a balance between security and functionality of service delivery and system availability. A key part of the greater national infrastructure security picture is the continued availability of critical infrastructure systems that provide and deliver services to the community that, largely, have become increasingly reliant.

The underlying premise is that through their pervasiveness nature, these systems and services have become crucial to an improved standard of living for the community generally. Therefore, it is the convenience and availability of these critical infrastructure system services, together with the community's expectations, which leads to potential social issues when the security of these systems is threatened, fails or experiences a reduced level of service and availability. Depending upon the amount of time, how and which critical infrastructure system or multiple systems thereof are affected, will invariably determine community reaction, incident management and contingency responses that will in turn influence the likely response and recovery actions instigated at governmental, business, personal and wider economic levels.

The perception is that critical infrastructure systems and the services they deliver remain largely in the background, seamlessly providing the services that support the standard of living enjoyed by most highly industrialised societies, with their contribution largely going unnoticed until an incident occurs.

Protecting Critical Infrastructures: Why?

The primary area that continues to emerge as the central theme to critical infrastructures is security and the protection of critical infrastructure systems from damage, attack or disaster. This requires continued vigilance and a focus on sustaining and ameliorating the resilience of critical infrastructure systems and their ability to maintain service integrity, recover and remain available in the face of adverse conditions and events.

Modern societies and governments continue to invest in infrastructure systems to meet current demand and future needs and furthermore, these infrastructure systems have continued to evolve through the integration of new technologies. This has changed infrastructure systems from simple, localised, single focus systems to more distributed, complex and integrated ones to increase efficiency of operation, improve service availability and reliability and offer greater consumer choice and safety generally. The alternative of diminishing infrastructure systems moves the society it supports toward less comfort and safety, from plenty to scarcity, from richness to want. Societies and

governments recognise their essential dependence on these systems and adopt policies and processes to distribute infrastructure and services widely and to protect them from physical damage and misuse (Lukasik *et al.*, 1998).

The physical security threats to critical infrastructure system assets are many and varied and can manifest themselves as fires, floods, natural disasters, accidents, sabotage, human error, lightning strikes, earthquakes and climate change, to name some of the more recognisable physical threat possibilities. The likelihood and frequency of such physical events occurring depends on location and geographical environmental characteristics.

However, critical infrastructure systems remain exposed to a myriad of operational and environmental threats, each with a unique ability to disrupt operations. For example, road networks are vulnerable to flooding, landslides, traffic congestion and major accidents. Telecommunication networks are vulnerable to denial of service attacks, computer viruses, targeted infrastructure attacks and congestion. In fact, all critical network infrastructures, to some degree, are vulnerable to either technological or natural hazards and it for these and other reasons that protection of critical infrastructure systems remains an important necessity (Murray & Grubesic, 2007) One such example in the Australian context is the threat of bushfires to the availability of critical infrastructures services in the form of Melbourne's metropolitan water supply.

Protecting Water Infrastructure and Catchments

As an example of the need to protect critical infrastructures, maintaining a safe, secure and reliable water supply to any population centre, especially a large city such as Melbourne, is an imperative across all levels of government. In this instance approximately 80 percent of Melbourne's drinking water is collected and stored in catchments located in the Yarra Ranges east of Melbourne (Melbourne Water, 2009a).

The catchment areas consist of some 157,000 hectares of protected native forests that naturally filter the rainwater as it flows into the catchment reservoirs via creeks and rivers. These areas have been closed to the public for over 100 years to protect the quality of the water and to protect against unauthorised public entry, erosion and bushfires. These actions reduce the risks of disease or contamination of the drinking water supply system and the likelihood of bushfires occurring within the catchment bushland areas (Melbourne Water, 2009a).

The bushfire threat is of particular concern to the quality and security of the drinking water supply. It is the resultant the loss of vegetation that negates the natural filtering effect and fails to slow the flow of water, thereby enabling contaminated water to flow into the reservoir. Another long term effect is that the loss of mature forest trees results in forest regeneration activity where the immature saplings can use up to 50percent more water than mature trees (Melbourne Water, 2009a).

The following case study outlines just such a scenario as part of the ethical discussion undertaken here with regard to protecting critical infrastructure systems.

THE CRITICAL INFRASTRUCTURE PROTECTION CASE STUDY

The following Case Study: Victorian bushfires and its environmental security impact, discusses the impact of a natural threat impact a critical infrastructure (Hutchinson & Warren 2009).

The 7th of February, 2009 was a day of unprecedented tragedy in the state of Victoria, Australia. One hundred and seventy-three people died in one of the worst bushfires in Australian history. About 430,000 hectares of land were burnt, as well as 2000 properties and 61 businesses (Teague *et al.*, 2009). One of the issues that has not been dis-

cussed about the tragic event has been the security implications and in particular the environmental security repercussions.

Victoria is one of the smaller states in mainland Australia with a population of 5.17 million (Australian Bureau of Statistics, 2008), and its capital city Melbourne has a population of 3.19 million (Australian Bureau of Statistics, 2009). This highlights that in the state of Victoria, the majority of the population lives within a single city. This has implications for a number of key services that relate to Melbourne, one of the most important issues being the provision of water.

The majority of Melbourne's water comes from within 160,000 hectares of uninhabited forested catchments north east of Melbourne, Victoria (Melbourne Water, 2009a). The impact of the Victorian bushfire was that around 30 percent of Melbourne's catchments were damaged by fire. This was mostly centred on the O'Shannassy and Maroondah catchments (Melbourne Water, 2009b). A detailed analysis of the damage is shown in Table 1.

During the actual bushfire, a number of key actions were taken and issues raised, regarding water supplies, these included (Roberts, 2009):

- The transfer of ten billion litres of water in pipes from the Upper Yarra dam to smaller dams, this was to safeguard the existing water supply;
- Identifying the major concern that the ash residue left from the bushfire would be transported by subsequent rain water 'run-off' into reservoirs and would contaminate Melbourne's water supplies. If reservoirs were contaminated, it would be contaminated for three months and impact 24 percent of Melbourne's drinking water.

Fortunately, the impact of damages caused by bushfire upon catchments areas was not as great as first feared and was limited as follows to (Melbourne Water, 2009c):

Table 1. Catchment impact table (Melbourne Water, 2009b)

Catchment	Fire affected	Area burnt estimate	Share of total reservoir inflow
Reservoirs with catch-ment			
Thomson	No	None	36%
Upper Yarra	Yes	About 2% burnt	19%
Maroondah	Yes	About 75% burnt	12%
O'Shannassy	Yes	About 93% burnt	12%
Yan Yean	No	None	2% (not in supply)
Tarago	Yes	About 50% burnt	Nil (not used for Melbourne's water supply)

• Damage to water supply infrastructure was limited to minor things such as weir gates;

• The Maroondah aqueduct system escaped major damage but had been experiencing blockages in places by fallen trees and landslides;

• Some movement of soil following the rains since the fires, particularly in the Wallaby Creek area. This is usual with high intensity fires;

• Wallaby Creek sustained considerable damage in burned area and infrastructure;

• A number of buildings have been lost, including the historic Wallaby Creek Quarters complex.

The Victorian bushfires had the potential to damage the water supply of a major global city. Thankfully, the impact was not as severe as first thought. From a critical infrastructure protection perspective it raises an interesting question about how you can protect against such an occurrence. The issue is that you can only build reservoirs in areas of high rainfall, alternative solutions such as building pipelines to transfer water across the state can be very expensive, and they would not be immune to fire damage and could cause an unacceptable environmental impact. Perhaps the announcement of the building of a new desalination plant in the State of Victoria, that will provide 150 billion litres of water a year, could be a the solution from a security perspective (Brumby 2009).

Ethical Analysis of Case Study

As discussed previously, when looking at a security or emergency related situation, it is the magnitude of consequences that have to be assessed when making decisions. As an example, the Victorian bushfires and its environmental security impact will be studied using the Jones (1991) consequence model. The major factors are:

Magnitude of Consequences

The magnitude of the Victorian bushfires was considerable. The outcome of the fire was 430,000 hectares of land were burnt, as well as 2000 properties and 61 businesses. Melbourne's water supply was at risk and one hundred and seventy-three people died.

Social Consensus

The social consensus was that the fire had to be stopped at all costs.

Probability of Effect

The impact of the effect of the fire was that it was far greater than anything experienced before.

Temporal Immediacy

Due to the fact the fire spread very quickly, decisions had to be made regarding the protection of people, property and critical infrastructure.

Proximity

The fire had the potential to spread directly into Melbourne, a city of over three million people.

Concentration of Effect

The fire had the potential to impact the majority of the population in the state of Victoria.

Post Script

The Australia's Commonwealth Scientific and Industrial Research Organisation (CSIRO) undertake a major review on the impact of climate change and infrastructure on behalf of the Victorian State Government.

The CSIRO Report (CSIRO, 2006) predicts that enhanced conditions for major bushfires events in the catchments of dams and reservoirs will generate immediate impacts on water quality and availability as well as medium-term reduction in water yield. Costly short-term water quality solutions will be needed should this occur in major catchments

The main areas of concern are with regard to the Bushfire and Water (CSIRO, 2006):

- An increase in bushfire within the main water catchment for cities and towns causing an immediate loss of water supply from ash, debris, sediments and fire fighting chemicals affecting the water quality of the dams and reservoirs. The Canberra Fires in 2004 are an example of this impact;
- A financial cost impact resulting from a bushfire through key water harvesting catchments could also be the technology

expenditure to utilise the water affected in the short term through, for example installation of cleaning or membrane filtration technology to treat water to meet quality standards. Such technology is not currently installed for any of the major Melbourne catchments;
- Financial impact to water dependent industries and water supply agencies;
- Significant community hardship and outrage;
- Expensive transport of water and extraction from other water constrained areas;
- Several years of reduced water yield from catchments due to increased water use during tree regrowth.

The CSIRO Report rates the chance of catastrophic bushfire in the state of the Victoria as being (CSIRO, 2006):

- **2050:** Prediction of a Moderate–High risk level of a catastrophic bushfire occurring in Victoria;
- **2070:** Prediction of a High–Extreme risk level of a catastrophic bushfire occurring in Victoria;

It may be postulated that the catastrophic bushfire event of 2009 may have occurred forty years to early in terms of the CSIRO Report, however this event my serve to exemplify and draw attention to the potential impact of future bushfires in Victoria.

OUTLINING THE ETHICAL DILEMMA

The ethical dilemma is the allocation of bushfire fighting resources in relation to the protection of the water supply infrastructure catchment areas and managing the water supply under threat

Critical Infrastructure Protection and the Victorian Bushfires

The infrastructure is the contamination of the public water supply through the damage caused to parts of the water supply storage and catchment areas including the water grid infrastructure.

The Ethical Perspectives

The Ethical issues relate to a number of different situations:

- **Consumers:** should the people of Melbourne expect that their water supply should be secured?
- **Melbourne Water:** is the role of Melbourne Water just to provide water to its customers or to provide a secure service that is available under any situation?
- **Fire Fighters:** should fire fighting resources be moved from protecting centres of population (protecting people and homes) to critical infrastructure protection (protecting the water supply of Melbourne)?

As well as the ethical issues, there are also a number of environmental issues that cause an impact upon this decision making:

- The impact of a lack of resources due to state governmental budget cuts for the funding for full time and casual fire fighters (financial issue);
- The impact of a lack of planned burning to reduce fuel loads and the impact this would have upon localised eco-systems (ecological/social issue);
- Possible link to global weather change (global issue).

All these ethical issues and perspectives each individually raise relevant issues for priority resource management, protection including aspects

of government budgetary consideration and financial investment in infrastructure security. In reality choices are made in an attempt to strike a balance between perceived risk to consumers, protecting and securing the resource and the likelihood of an adverse water infrastructure incident impinging upon consumer well-being, including the cost.

SOLUTIONS AND RECOMMENDATIONS

As this ethical dilemma highlights, the choices are never clear cut or straightforward, but with the benefit of hindsight and a lessons learned approach, this can aid in evaluating, planning and targeting strategic investment in the future. It must be acknowledged that those making decisions at the time of any incident do so with the best intentions acting on the information at hand. In this situation the choice was to concentrate on the protection of critical water infrastructures and the threat to public health through contamination of the water supply or to the fighting fight the bushfires threatening individual people and their homes.

FUTURE RESEARCH DIRECTIONS

The Critical Infrastructure Protection Case study helps to identify and analyse the impact that critical infrastructures protection and weather change can have upon a society. The aim is of the future research is to develop security models that will help to protected against the future security issues that related to critical infrastructure protection and in particular the impact that weather changes could have upon those key critical infrastructures.

CONCLUSION

Security implications are inherent in all but the very minor environmentally related decisions made. Decision makers should be aware of the stance and assumptions they are making with regard to these issues and be aware of the implications of the stand point taken. Those who wish to promote sustainable use of natural resources should also embrace the notion of security as it is a pragmatic way to encourage politicians and the public to consider other options rather than the biased traditional economic and political approaches taken to come to a decision. The problem of water security in Australia will become an even greater issue and the ethical considerations will also become a greater problem.

REFERENCES

AGD. (2008). *Critical infrastructure protection.* Australian Government Attorney-General's Department. Retrieved April 2008, from http://www. ag.gov.au/ www/agd /agd.nsf/Page/ Nationalsecurity_Critical Infrastructure Protection

ANAO. (2000). *Business continuity management.* Australian National Audit Office (ANAO), Canberra, ACT, best practice guide.

Australian Bureau of Statistics. (2008). *Report 1301-yearbook Australia, 2008.* Canberra, Australia.

Australian Bureau of Statistics. (2009). *Report 3218-regional population growth, Australia, 2007-08.* Canberra, Australia.

Bentley, A. (2006). Infrastructure: Critical mass. *CSIRO Solve, 7.*

Brumby, J. (2009). *Australia's biggest desalination plant to secure water and jobs.* Victorian State Government, 30th July.

Chambers, M. (2008, June 5). Gas crisis threat over Apache pipeline fire. *The Australian,* (pp. 22).

CISRO (Commonwealth Scientific and Industrial Research Organisation). (2006). *Infrastructure and climate change risk assessment for Victoria.*

COAG. (2007). *Victoria's infrastructure: Status and prospects. Council of Australian Governments.* COAG.

Dobbin, M., & Dowling, J. (2009, January 29). Blackouts hit thousands. *Age, 7.*

Dowling, J. (2009, January 27). Power supplies secure as heatwave sweeps state-scorching week. *Age, 2.*

Economou, N. (2009, January 18). Besieged Kosky may get ticket to ride a little longer. *Age, 21.*

Fritzhe, D. (1995). Personal values: Potential keys to ethical decision making. [Kluwer Academic Publishers, The Netherlands.]. *Journal of Business Ethics, 14,* 909–922. doi:10.1007/BF00882069

Harrington, S. J. (1997). A test of a person–issue contingent model of ethical decision making in organizations. [Kluwer Academic Publishers, The Netherlands.]. *Journal of Business Ethics, 16,* 363–375. doi:10.1023/A:1017900615637

Herndon, N. C. Jr. (1996). A new context for ethics education objectives in a college of business: Ethical decision-making models. *Journal of Business Ethics, 15,* 501–510. doi:10.1007/BF00381926

Houston, C., & Reilly, T. (2009). Heat leaves $100m black hole. *Age, 1.*

Hunt, S. D., & Vasquez-Parraga, A. V. (1993). Organizational consequences, marketing ethics, and salesforce supervision. *Journal of Marketing Research, 30*(February), 78–90. Gershon, P. (2008). *Review of the Australian government's use of Information and Communication Technology.* Attorney General's Department, Barton, ACT, Government Review Report. Gosch, E. (2008, June 5). Gas cuts after blast spark supply fears. *The Australian,* (pp. 7).

Hunt, S. D., & Vitell, S. (1986). A general theory of marketing ethics. *Journal of Macromarketing, (Spring)*, 5–16.

Hutchinson, W., & Warren, M. (2009). Security as an element in environmental assessment and decision making. *Proceedings of The 2009 Conference of the Australia and New Zealand Society for Ecological Economics (ANZSEE): Green Mileage in the Global Meltdown: An Ecological Economics Way Forward*, Darwin, Australia, 27th-30th October 2009.

Jones, A. (2007a). *Critical infrastructure protection-developments since the inception of the concept*. In 6th European Conference on Information Warfare and Security, ACI (Academic Conferences International), Shrivenham, UK, (pp. 131-138).

Jones, T. (1991). Ethical decision making by individuals in organizations: An issue-contingent model. *Academy of Management Review, 16*(2), 366–395. doi:10.2307/258867

Klare, M. T. (2001). *Resources wars: The new landscape of global conflict*. New York, NY: Metropolitan Books.

Le May, R. (2008, June 7). Two months to sort gas plant. The Advertiser, (pp. 87).

Lucas, C. (2009a, January 29). Train blame heats up as patrons wilt. *Age*, 1.

Lucas, C. (2009b, January 29). Tracks buckle and so does rail system. *Age*, 1.

Lukasik, S. J., Greenberg, L. T., & Goodman, S. E. (1998). Protecting an invaluable and ever-widening infrastructure. *Communications of the ACM, 41*(6), 11–16. doi:10.1145/276609.276610

Marasea, P., & Warren, M. (2004). *Critical infrastructure protection: Comparison of countries*. In 3rd European Conference on Information Warfare and Security, Academic Conferences International (ACI), University of London, (pp. 249-260).

Mayo, M. A., & Marks, L. J. (1990). An empirical investigation of a general theory of marketing ethics. *Journal of the Academy of Marketing Science, 18*(2), 163–171. doi:10.1007/BF02726432

Melbourne Water. (2009a). *Bushfires in catchments*. Retrieved on September 21, 1999, from http://www.melbournewater.com.au/ content/ water_storages /bushfires_in_catchments /bushfires_in_catchments.asp

Melbourne Water. (2009b). Catchment impact table. Retrieved September 21, 2009, from http://www.melbournewater.com.au/ content/ water_storages/ bushfires_in_catchments/ february_2009 _-_catchment _impact_table.asp

Melbourne Water. (2009c). *Bushfire recovery community update*.

Moran, A. (2009, February 2). Ease the squeeze on power utilities. *Age*, 9.

Murray, A. T., & Grubesic, T. H. (2007). Overview of reliability and vulnerability in critical infrastructure . In *Critical infrastructure* (pp. 1–8). Berlin/ Heidelberg, Germany: Springer. doi:10.1007/978-3-540-68056-7_1

NCTC. (2004). *Critical infrastructure protection in Australia. National counter-terrorism committee*. TISN.

Pye, G., & Warren, M. J. (2008). *Considerations for modelling critical infrastructure systems*. In 7th European Conference on Information Warfare and Security, Academic Conferences International (ACI), Plymouth, UK, (pp. 185-196).

Pye, G., & Warren, M. J. (2009). An emergent security risk: Critical infrastructures and information warfare. *Journal of Information Warfare, 8*(3), 14–26.

Renner, M. (2002). *The anatomy of resource wars. (World Watch Paper 162)*. USA: Worldwatch Institute.

Roberts, G. (2009, February, 17). Vic bushfires may affect water supplies. *The Age Newspaper.*

Scott G. (2005). Protecting the nation. *AUSGEO News, 79.*

Singhapakdi, A., & Vitell, S. (1991). Research note: Selected factors influencing marketers' deontological norms. *Journal of the Academy of Marketing Science, 19*(1), 37–42. doi:10.1007/BF02723422

Slay, J., & Koronios, A. (2006). *Information Technology security & risk management.* John Wiley Sons Australia Ltd, Milton Qld.

Smith, R. (2002). *Complexities of simulating domestic infrastructure protection.* Titan Systems Corporation, Orlando, FA, USA.

Teague, B., McLeaod, R., & Pascoe, S. (2009). *2009 Victorian bushfire royal commission interim report.* Victorian State Government.

TISN. (2003). *Fact sheet: What is critical infrastructure? Trusted Information Sharing Network.* Canberra: TISN.

TISN. (2004b). *Critical infrastructure protection national strategy.* Trusted Information Sharing Network (TISN). Retrieved from http://www.tisn.gov.au/agd /WWW/rwpattach.nsf /VAP/ (930C12A91 01F61D4349 3D44C70E84EAA) ~National+CIP+ Strategy+2.1+ final.PDF/$file/ National +CIP +Strategy+ 2.1+final.PDF

TISN. (2006). *Critical infrastructure protection: Whose responsibility is it?* Trusted Information Sharing Network (TISN). Retrieved from http://www.tisn.gov.au/

Wagner, S., & Sanders, G. (2001). Considerations in ethical decision making. [Kluwer Academic Publishers, The Netherlands.]. *Journal of Business Ethics, 29,* 161–167. doi:10.1023/A:1006415514200

Williams, F. (2008, June 5). Blast disrupts gas supply to miners. Herald Sun, (p. 78).

ADDITIONAL READING

Barnett, J. (2001). *The Meaning of Environmental Security: Ecological Politic and Policy in the New Security Era.* London: Zed Books.

Barnett, J. (2007). Environmental Security . In *Contemporary Security Studies, A. Collins* [ed.]. (pp. 183–203). Oxford: Oxford University Press.

Bertrell, R. (2000). *Planet Earth – the Latest Weapon of War: A Critical Study into the Military and the Environment.* London: Women's Press Ltd.

Dalby, S. (2002). *Environmental Security.* Minneapolis: University of Minnesota Press Malden.

Dalby, S. (2009). *Security and Environmental Change.* Malden, MA: Polity Press.

Dyer, G. (2008). *Climate Wars.* Melbourne: Scribe.

Hough, P. (2004). *Understanding Global Security.* London: Routledge.

Klare, M. T. (2001). *Resources Wars: The New Landscape of Global Conflict.* New York: Metropolitan Books.

Masher, D. E., Lachman, B. E., Greenberg, M. D., Nichols, T., Rosen, B., & Willis, H. H. (2008). *Green Warriors: Army Environmental Considerations for Contingency Operation form Planning through Post-Conflict.* Santa Monica, CA: RAND.

O'Riordan, T. (1989). *The challenge for environmentalism in: New Models in Geography - volume one, R. Peet, N. Thrift* [Eds.]. London: Unwin Hyman.

Schubert, R., Schellnhuber, H. J., Buchmann, N., Epiney, A., Grießhammer, R., & Kulessa, M. (2008). *Climate Change as a Security Risk.* London: Earthscan.

Teague, B., McLeaod, R., & Pascoe, S. (2009). *2009 - Victorian Bushfire Royal Commission Interim Report*. Victorian State Government.

KEY TERMS AND DEFINITIONS

Critical Infrastructure: The physical facilities, supply chains, information technologies and communication networks which, if destroyed, degraded or rendered unavailable for an extended period, would significantly impact on the social or economic well-being of the nation, or affect Australia's ability to conduct national defence and ensure national security.

Risk: The possibility of suffering harm or loss; danger.

Security: Something that gives or assures safety, as: (1) Measures adopted by a government to prevent espionage, sabotage, or attack; (2) Measures adopted, as by a business or homeowner, to prevent a crime.

Threat: An indication of impending danger or harm.

Chapter 12
Effective Infrastructure Protection through Virtualization

Dennis C. Guster
St. Cloud State University, USA

Olivia F. Lee
St. Cloud State University, USA

ABSTRACT

In this current digital era, organizations are increasingly aware of the need to protect their computer infrastructure to maintain continuity of operations. This process involves a number of different concerns including: managing natural disasters, equipment failure, security breaches, poor data management, inadequate design, and complex/impractical design. The purpose of this chapter is to delineate how virtualization of hosts can be used to address the concerns above resulting in improved computer infrastructure that can easily be restored following a natural disaster and which features fault tolerant hosts/components, isolates applications security attacks, is simpler in design, and is easier to manage.

INTRODUCTION

Numerous types of disasters, both natural and manmade, can be catastrophic to businesses. Without a well thought out disaster recover (DR) plan, such events can seriously disrupt routine business operations. Often times, it is difficult to comprehend the devastation of an unknown future event, let alone create a comprehensive approach to meet and survive it. The most critical challenges are related to understanding the scope and complexity of DR requirements and the risk of inadequate deployment of recovery efforts. This lack of understanding is especially applicable to small or medium size businesses (Hill, 2008) due to the limited IT resources they have available. Larger firms are able to apply economy of scale to develop an information technology (IT) depart-

DOI: 10.4018/978-1-60960-573-5.ch012

ment that equips them with the basic infrastructure to support the addition of DR mechanisms. Small and medium sized businesses, on the other hand, often do not have adequate infrastructure and since they operate on smaller profit margins, devising and supporting a DR plan can be a huge burden. Recently, Search Security.com reported that disaster recovery often accounts for as much as 25% of the IT budget. Hence, sound disaster recovery planning is a very important undertaking not only due to what might be lost, but also from a budget perspective. Hence, devising a strong DR infrastructure is further justified by the "information intensity" structure of many companies in the 21st Century.

Specifically, for many companies in the 21st century, information resources are their livelihood. The loss or unexpected long term disruption of information or data could have a detrimental effect on business operations. Phillippi (2008) reports that 92% of small businesses that experience significant data loss due to a major disaster go out of business within five years. Indeed, due to the high level of internet connectivity required by most operation functions today, the risks are high and warrant a well thought-out plan with appropriate risk assessment (e.g., Hiles, 1992; Jones & Keyes, 2001; Stephens, 2003). Although security risks of the internet increase the need for an effective disaster recovery mechanism, the internet connectivity is nevertheless advantageous as it can be effectively used in the data replication process. An efficient and cost-effective disaster recovery strategy is to utilize the geographic distribution of the critical components model (Adam, 2002). The connectivity can be inexpensively provided by the internet provided secure transmission methods, such as virtual private networks or VPNs (a way of isolating and double encrypting data sent across the internet), are used, and using the internet can minimize the huge cost of leasing dedicated lines (such as T1 a non-switched digital phone line). The data replicas should be at least 150 miles from the data center headquarters (Phillippi, 2008).

Information resource or data recovery can take many forms. In the past, pools of computers, on which a few members worked together and shared resources, could be used to house backup systems. While this approach still has some merits and fits reasonably within a service oriented architecture approach (SOA), for small businesses with remote sites and existing corporate partners, there are major trust issues to resolve in regard to the partners that make up the pool. An alternative is the use of virtualization which can potentially minimize costs and server density (Safigan, 2008). Organizations can logically partition one high-end computer and place each of its production servers on it in separate zones, thereby reducing management overhead. Another concept to consider is automation as it may significantly reduce the recovery time during an unexpected disaster. Whatever the chosen method, it is important to consider the expensive and on-going personnel costs which could be significantly higher than the additional hardware required.

Another data recovery aspect organizations must consider is the effect of distributed processing in disaster recovery. The advent of distributed processing and cluster computing vastly altered the manner in which data is stored and how access is granted to resources in an enterprise computing environment. No longer are projects simply done on a stand-alone computer. In fact, any given project may share and retrieve resources from several computers. While such processes often improve performance and lead to some degree of fault tolerance, organizations are required to have a resource profile on each required host. As a result, data spread out among hosts, in separate login accounts, can rapidly become an end-user's nightmare. However, by using a global file (such as NFS) and authentication system (such as LDAP) that allows single sign-in capability, as well as a file system that is attached to that sign-in no matter which host is being accessed, the above problems can be rectified.

Global systems often reside on one large enterprise level server. Notwithstanding the aforementioned ease of end-user management and system or network administrative advantages, global systems place a vast majority of the installation resources in "one basket." Such an approach, if properly replicated, not only can enable network administrators to retain the ease of management, but also provide better performance and reliability through the use of replicas. If there are multiple replicas and they are geographically spread out, they can provide the core infrastructure for a disaster recovery plan. In other words, multiple data centers can act as disaster-recovery sites. Recognizing that developing a recovery plan is imperative in distributed business networks, this chapter presents a disaster recovery plan based on computer virtualization that is designed to maintain performance and security while at the same time reducing cost. Specifically, eight topics related to virtualization will be discussed in the Topics in Virtualization section:

1. Managing Infrastructure Complexity
2. The Virtualization Model
3. Understanding Fault Tolerance
4. Virtualization and Security Issues
5. Green Virtualization
6. Cost Effectiveness Via a Virtualized Disaster Recovery Plan
7. WAN Connectivity and Optimization
8. Secured Infrastructure Practices and Policy

BACKGROUND

DR Considerations

Information resource management is a key success and survival factor in today's heavily connected business landscape. An interruption of normal business operations' information can occur as a result of many unforeseen events. Record and information management (RIM) professionals have long argued the importance of developing appropriate administrative programs to protect vital information during disasters (e.g., Dearstyne, 2006; Jones & Keyes, 2001; Wellheiser & Scott, 2002). Any interruption must be prevented or detected early; damage assessment and recovery must be promptly carried out. For smaller organizations, the ability to successfully respond to disasters can not be viewed as an optional management initiative but is an essential component of survival (Stephen, 2003). Indeed, top executives generally agreed that developing disaster recovery infrastructure is paramount to business survival.

(Pervan, 1998). Although advocates of disaster planning agree that preparedness makes all the difference, disaster preparedness *per se* is not limited to planning. Rather, it involves assessing and reducing risks, identifying critical business functions, re-evaluating back-up needs, testing the feasibility of recovery plans, and developing relationships with business partners who can be counted on during emergencies (Dearstyne, 2006). A successful disaster recovery plan is a continuous loop of planning, implementing, reevaluating and refining to optimize the plan through each cycle. Such a process results in a structured protocol that covers possible scenarios along with a carefully thought-out recovery plan designed to address disasters and mitigate risk in a methodical and organized manner (Tura et al. 2004).

Paramount in disaster infrastructure design is recovery time. Recovery time is addressed by Guo (2006) who determined that there was a level of tolerance in regard to recovery time. Guo's study pointed out that recovery time in today's complex world of internetworking is somewhat unpredictable due to the concept of primary/secondary paths and the effects of variable workload on any given network segment.

Obviously the supporting infrastructure needs to be designed to minimize this time interval at a cost the company can justify.

The future of disaster recovery will certainly involve increasing virtualization. Safigan (2008) discusses virtualization as an important option because of its speed. Balaouras (2007) compiled results of an online survey concerning disaster recovery and its costs depending on business size. His work is a useful report which includes statistics on how much organizations are spending on disaster preparedness, their disaster testing methodologies, current recovery objectives, and company confidence in the recovery practices they employ. His results verified that there is a relationship between firm size and what expenses can be justified.

Traditional backup plans simply provide a copy of the data. In the event of a disaster, this backup can be used to restore the system, on new hardware, to its original state when the backup was made. The problem with this approach is that the media is set to a daily backup. As a result, a failure of 12 hours into the next cycle would result in 12 hours of data loss because it was assumed that the 12 hours would be backed up on a redundant array of inexpensive disks (RAID) within the host. Natural disasters, such as earthquakes or floods, could cause severe damage to the host and RAID causing both of them to become completely unusable. In these instances, off-site storage of backups cannot be overlooked. Therefore, a good disaster recovery plan should go beyond off-site storage to restoring a system to its prior state which leads to the concept of host replication. By storing the entire system on one enterprise level host (with or without virtualization of multiple hosts) where global authentication and global file systems are used, it is possible, through the use of WAN's, to have many "baskets" geographically scattered either locally or globally. In the event of a disaster at headquarters, it is possible to switch operations to a replica located well away from the site of the disaster. To accomplish this goal, there are plans of varying degrees of sophistication. For example, using a transparent high performance plan based on commercial software is a costly solution. For small and medium size businesses, it is more

sensible to sacrifice a little to performance and vendor support for a cost effective solution.

Virtualization Models

The concept of a virtualized operating system is not new in PC (personal computer) architecture; in fact it goes back at least 20 years (Borden, Hennessy & Rymarczyk, 1989). However, widespread usage of this concept has only occurred in the last five years or so. This willingness to embrace the concept can probably be traced to a commonly available design that made the transition from best effort provisioning to stable platforms but did not compromise secure operations and was still able to provide adequate performance and functionality (Barham, et al., 2003). In other words, the technology of today provides the necessary performance, isolation, ease of use and reliability to make virtualization both practical and effective.

In effect, virtualization allows any given computer to be "multiplexed" or shared among multiple applications. The traditional one computer one application model typically results in much idle time per computer and a much more complex environment to manage. There are several structural models that can be employed when adopting virtualization within a data center (Rosenblum, 2009). One of the most common is server consolidation. This model simply transfers the functionality of a single computer to a logical zone on a host computer. For example, a business might be running three applications such as accounts receivable, accounts payable and general ledger with each housed on a separate physical computer. Server consolidation would allow each application to be housed in a single host computer with each application being logically separated into virtual zones. This solution would still provide the desired isolation for security reason, but would result in less CPU idle time and be easier to manage.

A more sophisticated model that builds on the server consolidation idea is the addition of distributed resource management. In this model, the number of virtual hosts per physical host could be varied so that the environment can adapt dynamically to workload. This model tends to optimize computing power better than the basic server consolidation model in which the virtual zones are defined statically. This model then can be said to employ on demand computing (Nellitheertha, 2006) which, in effect, is the reallocation of unused resources to other applications.

The most sophisticated structural model employs the dynamic logic not just to a few physical virtual hosts but to all hosts in the data center resulting in a data center wide virtualization layer which means that all the hardware then can be treated as a hardware pool of resources. This creates a highly flexible environment that can be easily adapted to any usage profile resulting in a highly optimized solution. Once again, this would be a variant of on demand computing but more efficient than the previous model because the resource pool is much larger.

To this point, the models have all focused on optimizing processing resources. However, the same basic logic can be applied to storage as well (Nellitheertha, 2006). The primary idea behind this model is to link together a number of heterogeneous storage devices of varying size and model so that they appear as a single virtual resource (Massiglia and Bunn, 2003). Once again this model is highly flexible and allows for better access times, high availability, high data capacity, and reduces the operation cost per megabyte of storage.

Green Computing and Virtualization

Another important reason to increase use of OS virtualization deals with the concept of sustainability and "green" IT solutions. Data centers experienced rapid growth over the past 10 years to accommodate distributed systems that now have world-wide reach due to the Internet and the access it provides to support a global economy.

Prior research on virtual operating systems contribution to a data center's infrastructure has shown that it is certainly possible to reduce the number of physical computers required to perform the same functions. This new architecture draws less power, generates less heat, and takes up less physical space (Armitage and Harrop, 2005). Further, because fewer computers are required in the data center, additional advantages are also gained in regard to less physical maintenance and simplicity of design (Lowell, Saito, & Samberg, 2004). Further, the advantages include the need for fewer employees and given the highest cost within the IT budget is typically personnel, this would be a most welcome reduction.

Besides the readily apparent advantages such as sustainability that green computing through virtualization provides, other advantages may result that are related to fault tolerance and performance. In the physical model, if a host failed only the application actually running on that host would fail. In the virtual model, if the physical host fails all the virtual zones and their respective applications fail as well. So, one could view the virtual model structure as putting all of your "eggs" (running applications) in one basket. This is a troubling scenario, so for this model to be effective, multiple baskets are needed (Guster, McCann, Krzenski & Lee 2008).

Replication and Fault Tolerance in Virtualized Models

It would be a good idea to make sure the main production virtualized host would be backed up at least twice. More specifically, two exact copies (or as close as the updating delay would permit) should be kept, one on site and one off-site, providing two degrees of fault tolerance. In the event the main site failed then the first replica would become the new production site. In addition to offering fault tolerance capability the replicas can also be used to improve performance by being configured for load balancing. More specifically not all of the data inquiries would be sent to the main production server; rather, they would be equally distributed among the main production host and the available replicas. Some research has shown that the load balancing technique can in fact help improve performance (Lin et al., 2007). This load balancing technique can extend performance which is important given that the virtualized model in its basic form reduces an application's access to computer resources.

While "greening" the data center, reducing complexity, and enhancing fault tolerance provide strong support for the concept of host virtualization, it is still important to address the security concept of isolating applications. Many worry that the logical isolation it provides is adequate when compared with the physical isolation model. However, given the dire security consequences of being connected to the Internet perhaps it is virtualization's flexible high profile isolation services that are its best attributes. The work of Laureano, Maziero, and Jamhour (2007) provides a good example. They describe the importance of intrusion detection applications to help safeguard against outside attacks and point out the application's vulnerability to external tampering or disabling when run in a straight unvirualized physical host. As one might expect, intrusion detection is the cornerstone of any security strategy and should be protected to the utmost. Further, they were able to use virtualization to successfully isolate the intrusion detection application in their data center, thereby making it invisible and inaccessible to intruders.

Based on the review above, clearly numerous advantages can be gained from integrating virtualization into the computing infrastructure. The main focus of this chapter will be to delineate specifics within the eight topics presented in the Introduction section above.

TOPICS IN VIRTUALIZATION

Managing Infrastructure Complexity

As a basis for understanding infrastructure complexity, we will use the scale-free degree distribution formula.

Complexity does not necessarily translate into sounder infrastructure. In fact, complexity can lead to infrastructure that is both challenging to use and expensive to manage. One factor in assessing complexity is the number of physical hosts housed in the computer system infrastructure. Many autonomous systems have experienced rapid uncontrolled growth in the number of physical hosts often utilized under the guise of application separation or improved performance. Each added host and its network connection (s) add to infrastructure complexity. A curve linear relationship occurs when one realizes that each host must communicate with every other host in an autonomous system. To provide an understanding of this situation, a series of infrastructure examples will be analyzed using the scale-free distribution formulae to assess the number of failure points (i.e., a host or a host connection). Further, several examples will be presented that will delineate how virtualized hosts can reduce complexity while maintaining acceptable security and performance.

Currently, there are three commonly available data backup site categories: cold, warm or hot sites. Through virtualization we will also introduce the modified hot site. A cold site is typically the most inexpensive back-up option to operate and involves minimal set up costs. A cold site has no functioning backup copies of the data at the primary data center, and often no additional hardware is required if the tape backup systems are already available. The recovery methodology is essentially restoration from tape to hardware at a remote site with daily updates.

A warm site is an alternate location where data could be retrieved after disruption. It is equipped with hardware similar to the primary site but does

Figure 1. Recovery expenses vs. recovery time

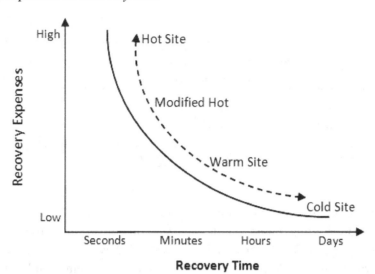

not store exact copies of the data. Often the updates take place hourly. A warm site is moderately expensive to operate and the cost largely depends on the desired speed of recovery.

A hot site is the most expensive DR option with full technological capacity that enables a seemingly fool-proof recovery process. Due to its sophisticated information technology (IT) infrastructure, hot sites allow real time synchronization between the primary and alternate back-up site, allowing a complete mirroring of the original data using wide area network links (in our case two independent leased links) and advanced software. Following a disruption to the primary location, the data processing can be quickly relocated to the hot site with minimal loss to routine operations.

A modified hot site is a recovery option that provides partial benefits of a hot site with a lower DR investment. We propose this option based on our success in leveraging the benefits of host virtualization via creating multiple logical computers (partitioning the resources of one physical computer into six virtualized resource sets) in one single physical computer. Because all production hosts are virtualized into one physical host, this option generates a smaller complexity index and, as a result, has fewer failure points.

Figure 1 is a graphical representation of the various available options in regard to recovery expenses (investment) versus recovery time. Infrastructure complexity and investment cost are the two major considerations in choosing an appropriate DR model. For small and medium-sized businesses, the availability of technologies and size of the DR budget dictate reasonable recovery spending. However, even with resource limitations, well thought out models can still yield effective benefits. Therefore, decisions related to allocating these resources are important in ensuring organizational sustainability. Bryson et al. 2002, advocates using mathematical modeling in analyzing and designing DR models. Past research indicated that the more physical components (hosts) in the DR infrastructure, the greater the probability of a hardware failure. Certainly, additional hardware can provide additional fault tolerance, but it will also increase the DR expenses, particularly from a personnel perspective.

To illustrate the concepts of complexity within this chapter, we employ the scale-free degree distribution theory to determine network growth by applying the formula $N*(N-1)/2$ to assess the complexity of the communication path within each DR model (Baccaletti, 2006). Our

Table 1. Disaster recovery models for a six-host model

Model	Synchronize Time	Recovery Time	Back-up Site Characteristics	No. of Computers	Model Complexity	Tolerance Support
Cold	Days	>24 Hours	Off site backups	12	18	Limited
Warm	Hours	1-24 hours	Limited physical mirroring	18	40	Moderate
Modified Hot	Minutes	1 hour	Virtual mirror image	6	10	High
Hot	Seconds	Minutes	Physical mirror image	30	251	Very high
Note: There is no remote backup site in the cold model. Hence, the total no. of hosts = 2 computers per instance.						

assumption rests on the premise that a complex model will result in more possible failure points and be more difficult to support from a personnel perspective. The formula allows us to discover the complexity of communication paths and possible failure points based on the total number of computers in production and the configuration of the replication process. In a simple client/server model that typically consists of a client computer, a server computer, and a network (LAN) connecting them, the complexity index would be one and result in three total model failure points. In this example, a network complexity of one reflects a very simple model. The number of individual possible failure points is three, which is arrived at by adding the number of computers (N) to the network complexity (C). Because this backup scenario is applied to only one host (one instance), the model's total number of failure points is still three.

For the rest of the computations presented in this section of the chapter, we based our assumptions on a six-host production model because such a quantity is regarded as a representative model for many small and medium sized businesses. Furthermore, that is the number of production hosts in our computing domain and we had experience working with that number. However, any number of hosts (computers) might occur. It is common for organizations to have separate hosts for various applications such as accounting and inventory to manage security and performance indicators.

Further, additional hosts are often required to support networking activities such as world wide web (WWW), domain name service (DNS) and remote file systems. Table 1 presents a summary of the characteristics of each of the basic models in which a six physical host production domain was replicated. The modified hot model based on virtualization significantly reduced the number of physical computers required and offered performance that was superior to every model except the hot model which is significantly more complex and vastly more expensive. For a detailed explanation of these models and calculations used to derive the model complexities (Lee, Guster, Schmidt & McCann 2009).

Virtualization Model

This topic will describe how to use virtualized hosts to build an entire production network in a single box.

The number of physical hosts required to support the networking and application functions of an autonomous system can often be housed in a single "virtualized" physical box. This method reduces complexity and results in a network that is easier to manage. To illustrate this concept, an example from the authors' autonomous system in which nine physical production hosts were reduced to nine virtual zones in a single physical computer will be described in detail.

Table 2. Virtual host partitions (zones)

Partition No.	Description
Host	Time Server, Virtual Machine host (Running LINUX)
1	Main client access server, secure access server (Firewall will forward all port22 traffic to this partition)
2	Secondary client access server, backup secure access server (Firewall will forward alternate port to this partition, port22)
3	Global authentication server (OpenLDAP/Kerberos5-MIT)
4	Network address resolution server (DNS/DHCP/LDAP)
5	E-Mail server (LINUX Mail Server installed)
6	Web server (Apache Tomcat)
7	Global file system server for home folders (NFS Mounted)
8	Financial applications server (accounting, sales, payroll and etc.)
9	Production server to support application services (inventory, product development, advertising and etc.)

The computing domain used in this case study is designed to mirror the functionality of a manufacturing company that sells its own products and maintains its own IT infrastructure. In an environment such as this, numerous physical production hosts serve a variety of needs. If the traditional physical model is followed, each service or application would be housed in separate physical computers to provide isolation for security purposes. The assumption in the design delineated here is that in all cases performance in the separate physical host model was acceptable from a performance perspective and that unused CPU cycles were observed for all hosts. Therefore, one could expect that the core production hosts could be effectively converted to a virtualized host design. The security related assumption then is that the virtual partitions would provide the required isolation needed for security purposes while the performance requirements would still be reasonable. In other words, since all the original physical hosts were using only a fraction of their available computing resources they should function at an acceptable level in a shared virtual host (Lee, Guster, Schmidt & McCann, 2009). In this case study, nine physical hosts are restructured into virtual zones in a single physical host. In theory, this should mean that each is limited to about 1/9 of the available computing resources. However, the LINUX operating system can be configured to utilize dynamic resource allocation, meaning that the total available resources can be viewed as a pool and any unused resources can be allocated to any virtual partition. The dynamic allocation methodology works well as long as there are several fairly idle virtual machines. If an intense workload is distributed across all nine virtual partitions, performance would fall very rapidly and a priority scheme would be needed to control resource allocation. The purpose of each of the nine original physical hosts providing IT infrastructure for a typical medium size business that engages in Ecommerce is described below in Table 2. Each partition corresponds to a separate physical host.

The first row in the table describes the characteristics of the physical host for the nine partitions (zones) to follow. This host contains the network time server (using network time protocol, NTP) that is used to synchronize all hosts (both virtual and physical) within the domain. It is critical for client/server and database applications that all hosts in the domain be synchronized for data integrity and security purposes. This physical host is configured with the Linux operating system.

Partition number 1 contains the main client access server used to allow people within the company and customers to access IT resources in a secure manner. Because this domain is connected to the internet to support E-commerce activity and financially related applications are run in the domain, it is crucial to monitor client traffic. Therefore, both incoming and outgoing traffic to this partition are tightly filtered at the firewall level and terminal access is only available through secure shell (ssh) which uses a sophisticated encryption stream.

Partition 2 provides a secondary version of virtual zone 1 (described above). This zone provides a backup to partition 1 so that clients have an alternate way to connect to the domain in the event partition 1 becomes corrupted. Because the domain uses a global authentication system (active directory), single sign-on can be provided to users so that they are granted access to both partitions one and two, with the same login information.

The global authentication described above is hosted in virtual partition number 3. This global authentication is provided by lightweight directory access protocol which IT managers often select due to its robustness and scalability (Guster, Hall, Herath, Jansen & Mikluch, 2008). In an effort to provide heightened security to this critical component in the IT security structure, Kerberos (developed by MIT) is used which increases the robustness of the encryption and uses a mechanism so that the password does not have to be sent remotely across the network by the client.

Partition 4 provides the network address resolution services. Specifically, domain name service (DNS) and the dynamic host configuration protocol (DHCP) are hosted in this zone. These services allow resolution of network layers and client work stations to be allocated to a temporary network (IP) address. Domain service would be provided to all domains in the company's enterprise because a given company might support more than one domain name (such as chevy.com and chevrolet.com).

Email services are provided in virtual zone 5. This virtual partition hosts a mail system which provides standard mail services and a browser based email interface that is linked to a standard apache tomcat web server (hosted in partition 6). Both secure and unsecured mail services are supported. Standard web services are supported in partition 6 and, as mentioned earlier, apache tomcat is the web server software of choice. This web service also hosts domain related home pages, web interfaces for company employees, and E-commerce activities.

The global file system is hosted in partition 7 and uses the network file system protocol. This file system can be described as the central depository of company data and allows all user/company data to be stored in a central location for ease of access and management. Further, this global orientation allows a user's home directory (or directory maps) to follow that user no matter which host (virtual or physical) he/she is logged into. The user always has the same default directory no matter which host (virtual or otherwise) he/she is referencing. The concept of centralizing all data at a single location provides management advantages; however, it involves risk in that all the "eggs" (data) are in one basket (location). Therefore, it is critical to have the data reside at multiple locations to provide the multiple "basket" logic. Virtualization makes it easy to accomplish this since the functionality of the entire domain can be hosted in a single physical computer. Placing several computers, all configured with the same file synchronization logic, at various locations world-wide can provide excellent fault tolerance and backup.

Virtual partition 8 is designed to support financial related applications. The software required to run all financial operations is hosted in this zone. This includes applications such as payroll, accounting and sales. Direct access to this zone would not be allowed, so a user would have to authenticate through partition 1 (or 2) and access the application via SSH or some form of tunneled web browser.

The last partition contains the virtual zone that contains the product related application server. This partition would support applications such as inventory, product development and advertising. Once again because security is paramount, direct access to this zone would not be allowed. A user would have to authenticate through partition 1 or 2 and access the application via SSH or some form of tunneled web browser.

Understanding Fault Tolerance

In this section we will describe how to use multiple "virtualized" boxes to provide fault tolerance, load balancing and archiving.

If the functionality of nine computers is placed into one and it fails, the results could be catastrophic; it is synonymous with placing all of your "eggs" (hosts) in one basket. For this strategy to be effective the autonomous system must have multiple baskets (i.e., replicas of the virtualized host). To illustrate how multiple replicas can provide effective fault tolerance, load balancing and data archiving an example will be described from the authors' autonomous system that features three replicas and two archival hosts.

Virtualization makes it easy to provide fault tolerance by simplification of IT infrastructure and easy deployment of replicas housed in a single physical computer. In Topic 2 above, we explained that a whole production domain consisting of nine hosts could be virtualized into one physical computer. So, to replicate that whole domain, only one physical computer virtualized into the nine zones would be required. Figure 2 below illustrates how this scenario might be used to provide three levels of replication while only using four computers.

This figure indicates that the first level replica will be housed in the same equipment room as the production virtualized host and, in addition to providing fault tolerance, could be used for load balancing. The design features two other replicas one in a different building, but in the same town and one in a different town at least 300 miles away. Therefore, different levels of disasters are considered, from a building specific disaster such as a localized flood to a disaster that might affect the whole town such as a tornado, in which case operations could be switched to the town 300 miles away.

Further, the same virtualized replicas that provide a multi-level fault tolerance plan can also be used to improve system performance. Inquiry

Figure 2. Fault tolerance through virtualized replicas

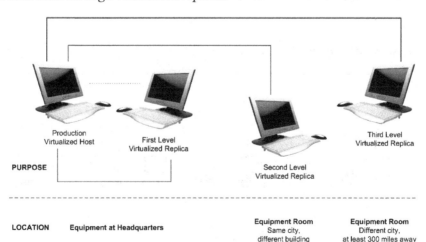

workload can be distributed among the various replicas by using a "load balancing" technique. This technique means that any given replica in the enterprise will be less busy which translates to less service time (wait time) for any given transaction. Distributing the replicas at key geographic locations within a company's global market can also enhance performance by reducing the distance any client needs to travel across the network (internet). For example, a company based in New York may do business in Paris. In a centralized model, a customer in Belgium would need to connect to the main server in New York. With the decentralized virtual model that same customer could connect to the replica server in Paris, thereby reducing network travel and response time delay.

Virtualization and Security Issues

This section will describe how virtualization can be used to isolate applications for security reasons.

One of the primary reasons that multiple hosts are housed in different autonomous systems is the need to isolate applications for the sake of security. The logic behind this concept is that if any one host is compromised only the application running on that host will be effected. However, it is also possible to achieve the same isolation via software rather than physical borders and that is what host virtualization does. Thus, in a virtualized host, if one virtual zone is compromised all other zones

are not affected. More specifically, virtualization, as its name implies, is used in virtual memory and virtual machines. A proven technology, it allows speedy transformation of information among connected networks of computers. Virtualization is the core principle in overlays, allowing a computer to carry out the tasks of multiple computers by sharing resources of a single computer within the network and across multiple environments. In essence, virtualization allows several services that are housed on separate physical hosts to be concentrated, and logically, be partitioned into individual zones on a single computer, and still provide necessary isolation required for security purposes (Peterson, Shenker & Yurner, 2005).

In the example delineated earlier in Topic 2, nine physical computers were reduced to nine zones in a single physical computer to provide application isolation. Each zone is completely protected from traffic entering another zone within that physical computer. In fact even the network interface is multiplexed, and each logic interface is linked only to the appropriate zone in the virtual hosts. Figure 3 illustrates this concept using the previous nine zone model. Once again, each zone is independent and isolated and has its own unique network node address even though only one network interface card is installed. This configuration does however require each zone be placed on the same network, which in this case

Figure 3. Security isolation in a virtual host model

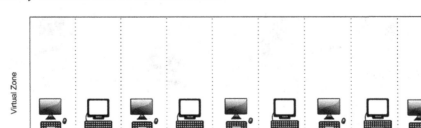

would be the internet protocol network style dotted decimal address is 192.1.1.0.

Green Virtualization

In this section, we will describe how virtualization can be used to promote green computing.

Many feel the energy cost to run computer systems is getting out of hand; some estimates suggest it is as high as 2% of all U.S. energy usage. Virtualization of hosts can reduce the number of physical hosts required to do the same information processing job. By reducing the number of computers, the 110 volt and the cooling power are reduced, resulting in a "greener" foot print for the IT infrastructure. To illustrate this concept, the example from the authors' autonomous system described earlier in which nine computers were virtualized into one will serve as a case study to illustrate how virtualization can result in a $900 a year savings in power consumption.

In the computing domain serving this case study, numerous physical production hosts serve a variety of needs. They were originally placed in separate physical computers to provide isolation for security purposes. In all cases, performance in the separate physical host model was generally excellent and unused CPU cycles were observed in all cases. Therefore, these core production hosts offered an excellent test case for virtualized hosts. The assumption was the virtual partitions would provide the isolation needed for security purposes, and the performance requirements for any one host could be met in a shared resource environment. Specifically, since all hosts were using only a fraction of their available computing resources on their physical host, they would function at an acceptable level in a shared virtual host (Lee, Guster, Schmidt, McCann, 2009). As stated earlier in the chapter, our case study nine physical hosts are restructured as virtual machines in a single physical host. In theory, that would

mean that they would each be limited to 1/9 of the available computing resources. However, in the operating system utilized, the resource allocation is dynamic, meaning that the resources are viewed as a pool and any unused resources can be allocated to any virtual machine. This methodology works well as long as there are several fairly idle virtual machines. In the unlikely scenario of intense workload across all nine virtual machines performance would decay exponentially and a priority scheme would need to be used to control the resource allocation. As you will recall the purpose of each of the nine original physical hosts described in partition numbers 1-9 is in Table 2 (Virtual Hosts Zones) was also provided earlier in this chapter.

To ascertain the effectiveness of the virtual model, a nine day period was selected and power consumption data (using a standard meter) was collected for both the old physical configuration and the new virtual configuration. The result of this comparison is depicted in Table 3 (a). As expected, the virtual model improved upon the physical model. In fact, the cost per KWH for the virtual model was only about 20% of the physical model. This translated into a yearly cost difference (assuming a price of $.07 per KWH) of almost $600.

Table 3 (b) provides information about the cooling requirements for each architecture. The methodology applied is adapted from Larabie (2003). Again, as expected, the virtual model consumed significantly fewer resources than did the physical model. Further, it appears that the ratio of consumption was, as expected, similar. The cooling cost difference was about $300 higher for the physical model and that coupled with the approximate $600 figure on power consumption, reveals that the physical model would cost almost $900 more a year to run than the virtual model.

Table 3. (a). Power consumption physical vs. virtual architecture. (b) Cooling consumption physical vs. virtual architecture

a. Power consumption physical vs. virtual architecture				
Architecture	**Cumulative KWH**	**Average KWH**	**Cost per KWH ($)**	**Yearly Cost ($)**
Physical	266.24	1.232592593	8.63	755.83
Virtual	55.25	0.255787037	1.79	156.85
			Yearly difference	598.98

b. Cooling consumption physical vs. virtual architecture				
Architecture	**Cumulative KWH**	**BTU per hour**	**Cost to Cool per BTU ($)**	**Yearly Cost ($)**
Physical	266.24	642703.36	4.37	382.51
Virtual	55.25	133373.5	0.91	79.38
			Yearly difference	303.14

Cost Effectiveness via a Virtualized Disaster Recovery Plan

A description of how virtualized hosts can serve as the cornerstone of a disaster recovery plan from a cost effectiveness perspective will be presented in this section. Too often, companies tend to skimp on the plan because if they selected a hot model (a complete replication of their entire IT infrastructure) it in effect doubles their infrastructure budget. Virtualization of hosts can provide much of the functionality of a hot model at a fraction of the cost. Once again this will be illustrated using the nine zone virtualized model presented in Table 2, and the characteristics of virtualized models such as cost, reliability, recovery time, complexity and ease of management will be compared to the three common disaster recovery models.

Overview of Replica Strategies

To gain some understanding of the complexity, it may be useful to examine a common fault tolerance concept, the RAID (redundant array of inexpensive disks) logic. In the modified hot site option, the array concept can be expanded to the host level, and the RAIH (redundant array of inexpensive hosts (computers)) concept might be more appropriate because we are mirroring hosts instead of just disks. In a six-host model, all six computers of the production site are equipped with computing power for an instructional domain. These six hosts perform the following functions: host DNS (domain name service), maintain a global file system, enable website service, allow email communication, serve as a firewall, and provide instructional support. The capability of RAIH allows the data to support all functions to be replicated across all hosts, and, therefore, the data is available for any given function when needed to support its primary purpose. In a six-host model, each local disk will have to be logically divided into six separate partitions. Although this model offers excellent fault tolerance, it is inherently complex, and sophisticated personnel are required for system support. In a LAN environment, the additional complexity and inter-processor communication might be practical because there is adequate bandwidth to support them. However, in a WAN environment, the additional communication overhead may negate the model due to the network's inability to complete the needed updates timely and cost effectively due to the slower speeds and the additional number of bytes that a RAIH would generate.

Software Costs

In regard to software, the costs vary based on the complexity of the model and whether shareware or commercial software is used. For the cold site, a commercial tape backup package with nine licenses was selected. In the case of the warm model, a commercial backup/replica package with nine licenses was chosen. Since the modified warm model was devised from scratch using the Unix operating system the openness allowed the use of shareware software at no cost. The complexity and high reliability needs of the hot model necessitated an enterprise level backup replica package with unlimited server licenses.

Hardware Costs

As would be expected, the variance in complexity led to variation in the hardware needs. In all cases we are assuming the production side hardware was in place, as well as the networking infrastructure minus the WAN bandwidth costs. For the cold model, nine low end PCs with tape drives at $1,000 each (this allows for simultaneous backup of all six hosts) were required. In the warm model, nine mid range server level hosts (at $1,000 each) were needed. For the modified hot virtualization model, the hardware needs were reduced to three mid range server level hosts at $1,000 each. Lastly, as expected, the hot model required the most hardware, 18 high range enterprise server level hosts at $10,000 each.

Bandwidth Costs

In regard to band width, the tape back up equipment would reside on site so there are no WAN bandwidth requirements for the cold site. A traditional warm site would rely on leased lines for the sake of security. In this case, a leased line (point to point) at 300 miles at 16mbs was selected to meet the bandwidth requirements. The modified hot site developed to save money risks using the internet to provide connectivity (a VPN is used to enhance security) and an internet cable connection at 12mbs has been selected based on the data observed in Guster, Safonov, Hall and Sundheim (2003). To provide the massive bandwidth and reliability required by the hot site, dual 40 Mbs leased lines at 300 miles were the configuration chosen.

Personnel Cost

Lastly, the personnel costs also varied greatly from model to model. In the cold model, the primary operational costs were tape backup operations and the personnel cost is estimated at 10 hours a week at the rate of $20 an hour. In the warm model, we estimated that 10 hours a week, at $50 an hour, for system/network engineering personnel would be required. The lower complexity of the modified hot model reduces the personnel needs down to five hours a week (due to reduced hardware) at $50 an hour for system/network engineering personnel. The hot site had the greatest personnel needs estimated at 20 hours a week (due to added hardware) at $50 an hour for system/network engineering personnel. This criteria need to be carefully assessed because personnel is probably the most important component in the DR strategy. (Krojnewski & Nager, 2006). Table 4 provides a summary of estimated costs incurred for each of the four models that might be used to provide DR for the nine host model described in Table 2.

Table 4. Disaster recovery investment and annual maintenance costs (S) based on nine instances

Recovery Sites	Software: Server Site	Hardware: Remote Site	Bandwidth Cost (WAN)	Personnel Cost	Total Cost
Cold	3,225	9,000	0	10,400	22,625
Warm	6,650	9,000	6,384	26,000	48,034
Modified Hot	0	3,000	1,596	13,000	17,596
Hot	66,500	180,000	120,000	52,000	418,500

WAN Connectivity and Optimization

In this section we will describe how virtualized hosts can be integrated into an archiving methodology that relies on WAN connectivity.

One of the concerns with any disaster recovery plan is to have the data spread out over an acceptable geographic distance in the event the whole region might be affected. A basic rule of thumb is that data should be spread out at least 300 miles. However, designing an archival network with replication at remote sites requires a cost effective and secure means of data transfer. Leasing private lines to support connectivity can be costly and WANs in general have significantly less bandwidth than LANs. Therefore, often the only affordable alternative is to use the internet to transfer the archival information from the main host to the archival replica. Data collected on the authors' autonomous system will be used to illus-trate how security can be employed to protect the archival data and how an Internet WAN link can be optimized to support this data intensive transfer. To ascertain if the encryption overhead on this link would not jeopardize performance, a series of experiments were undertaken. Figure 4 depicts the difference in inter-arrival times between the encrypted and non-encrypted traffic. It is clear that the unencrypted traffic arrives much more quickly and would result in a quicker completion of the replica update process.

Then the encrypted backup software was run several times with the fairly intense backup scenario, first without and then with the two types of encryption (tunneled and secure shell, SSH). Since one of the replicas was connected remotely via a WAN, different line speeds were tested to ascertain available bandwidths' influence on performance.

Figure 4. Packet inter-arrival times encrypted vs. unencrypted sessions (Wan 1.5 MBS)

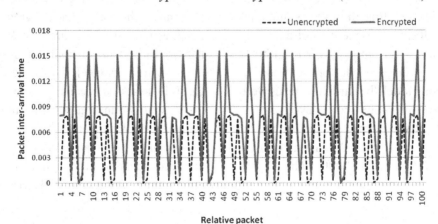

The findings of this experiment provided some interesting results, particularly for the WAN links. On the LAN link, it was clear that the overhead generated by the encryption process contributed to longer transmission times, but only about 10% longer. With the WAN links, line speed makes a major difference in regard to efficiency and if backup scenarios of this magnitude are expected, investing in additional line speed becomes important. In our example, at 1.5Mbs it takes approximately 500 minutes to complete the intense back up scenario tested (about 50 GB), while at 6Mbs it only takes about 100 minutes. It is also worthwhile to note that the influence of encryption overhead is lessened at slower speeds. Indeed, it takes longer for non-encrypted data than with encrypted data. One plausible explanation is the large dependence on buffering the data. Since the data can leave the PC easily at 100Mbs, there is little bandwidth restriction when entering the LAN. In the case of the WANs, the data sits in a buffer for long time periods and as long as the application can keep the buffer full, there is less time loss in actual network transmission. Further, the CPU usage levels provide a similar pattern for the un-encrypted traffic. It took 225 seconds (unencrypted) on the LAN level versus 250 seconds for the encrypted tunneled traffic. In summary, these results show it is possible to conduct the replica backup/update securely across an internet link if adequate bandwidth is provided (about 10 Mbs in our example).

Secured Infrastructure Practices and Policy Considerations

In this section we will provide some sample policy statements related to the integration of virtualized hosts in an IT infrastructure. Any change in infrastructure needs a framework to follow. Security concerns such as partition design, archival updating across the internet, and firewall settings involving inter-host communications which would not be a concern under the old physical model will be discussed. A series of policy statements derived from the authors' virtualized network will be presented below and discussed.

The first policy area to be discussed will involve disaster recovery. Instead of two computers with the same physical image, all logical zones on a virtualized host must be backed up in their entirety to a separate physical machine from that of the virtualization server machine. In other words, it does not make sense to backup to a second logical zone in the same virtual machine. Further, because in a sense you are putting all of "eggs" (data) in one basket there is a need for multiple baskets. Therefore, with virtualization a policy in regard to replication might be: there must be a minimum of the production system, and three duplicate replica backups of that production virtualized host. One backup must be onsite of with the production system, and the second must be housed in a separate building located at least 500 meters from the production system and the third must be housed at least 300 miles away.

A second area of virtualization policy might be related to general operations which might warrant a policy as follows. Because the virtual zones are logical and truly transparent all logical zone installations must be documented in the organization network diagram schematics and on all system hosts files. No logical zone may be created or used for any purpose for which the chief information officer has not authorized in writing.

The last area of discussion will be related to system maintenance. Because the hard drive(s) on a virtual host are supporting data from multiple applications performance and management are paramount. So a policy related to disk defragmentation might look as follows: virtualization servers housing logical zones must have the hard disks defragmented at least once per month. Further, the logical implementations themselves must have their disk partitions defragmented at least once every three months.

SOLUTIONS AND RECOMMENDATIONS

Disaster tolerance, as previously stated, is the ability to maintain ongoing productive operations even in the face of a catastrophe. This is an important consideration since high availability is achieved by providing redundant components; if one fails, another part is still available to do the job. To provide a better understanding of the key issues involved in selecting a recovery site, we undertook complexity analysis of the various model's communication paths and possible failure points. In reality, the most challenging goals surrounding DR planning are related to deciding on the appropriate number of hosts, degree of fault tolerance desired, appropriate granularity and attainment of all of those goals within the available budget. Our analysis indicated that there were some real benefits in adapting the virtual model. Of course, the key advantage for the proposed modified hot site is cost effectiveness. By deploying virtualization to reduce the number of physical hosts and using shareware software, firms can develop a structured and actionable DR plan that has many of the basic benefits of a hot site model. The application of virtualization is a formal approach to DR planning which enables effective DR solutions that are less complex, more cost effective, and close to the performance level of the hot model. We suspect that the proposed virtual option is an optimal solution for small and medium sized businesses due to its capabilities to enable firms to simplistically map out the dependencies between critical business processes, people, IT assets, and other resources. It can also perform simultaneous functions such as hosting DNS, maintaining a global file system, enabling website service, allowing email communication, serving as a firewall, and providing application support, all in a single physical host, while still maintaining the separation of those services for performance and security purposes.

In addition to the numerous benefits of virtual computing that were described in this chapter (such as application isolation, load balancing, simplicity of design, reduced personnel requirements) it is the "green" benefits that a timely focus to this paper. In that regard, Tables 2 and 3 provide interesting data that supports the "green" benefits of virtual computing. We took nine physical computers and virtualized them into nine different zones in a single virtual host computer (see Table 2). While the data does not indicate that it reduced power consumption by a ratio of nine times less, the savings are still significant. The observed ratio was more in the range of a reduction of five times. This can be explained by the fact that the virtual host was newer, more powerful, and had a larger power supply than the majority of the original physical hosts. Further, because it was housing nine applications, the new virtual host tended to be loaded at a higher level which led to more power consumption. Cost savings on power were about $600 a year and on cooling about $300 a year. This yields an annual combined savings of about $900 a year. If a data center was larger and was a candidate for virtualization and the saving ratio observed is transferrable then reduction of cooling and power costs by a factor of five would be a most welcome development. Further, if that reduction is realized, the added benefit of reducing the physical space to store the equipment could be attained as well. In summary, virtualization offers many benefits and may be applied to classes of problems in which isolation is the primary rationale for running an application in a separate physical computer. It is not designed for situations in which increasing performance is the primary motivation for multiple physical computers (such as a cluster). The data herein certainly indicate that there are sustainability benefits to be gained from virtualization of physical hosts.

Further, the data collected show some interesting results in regard to model sophistication and cost. Often the basic perception of outsourcing is that it is superior to devising an in-house model. In our case, had we not devised a hybrid virtualized model that built upon our existing in-house technical expertise and the adaptation of virtualization/internet access, our solution would have probably been the out-sourced model. While the cold model was relatively inexpensive, it simply was not sophisticated enough. The warm model probably would have been adequate with some tuning on the granularity level, but it was too expensive, while the hot model was a luxury way beyond our budget. It was also interesting that the virtualized model and the outsourcing price tag in our case were very similar. While the design and preparation time for devising and implementing the virtualized model were substantial, we suspect that it was not significantly greater than what would be required to define and convey our backup needs and strategies to an outsourcing company. As one would suspect, effective communication with the outsourcing company is crucial.

Our success in part was related to our staff's sound foundation in technical areas such as virtualization and network encryption techniques. We were able to use existing personnel to accomplish our goal and justify some of the costs by piggy-backing the concept of performance improvement through load balancing via replication within the project. Companies without in house expert perhaps should carefully consider the advantages of outsourcing due to the high cost of personnel. While we did not greatly consider the ethics of trusting an outsourcing company with our sensitive data, we suspect it could be an important issue for some companies (especially if they do not already have internal IT personnel resources).

Last, the preliminary results obtained herein are encouraging. First, the hardware and infrastructure required for this plan are inexpensive and would fit into any small business' budget. Second, we were able to inexpensively use shareware software to provide the functionality, ease of use, and performance necessary to create and update the required replicas. Third, the internet WAN connection was viable because the overhead generated by the encryption process was minimal, and it can be effectively employed to protect the transmission of the backup data.

FUTURE RESEARCH DIRECTIONS

Additional research is needed that would replicate the model design effectiveness. Of particular interest would be how well virtualization would scale in larger computing domains. Also, the question of how to best provide inter-connectivity among replicas connected by a WAN needs additional examination, but with backup scenarios that require a much larger volume of data.

Also, the current research did not address in detail the effect that line speed would have upon this process. Because these experiments were conducted on a LAN with line speeds of 100 Mbs, the success obtained herein might not transfer to a WAN situation in which the line speed would probably not exceed 10Mbs at best.

One positive finding from the experiment is related to the majority of the extra overhead related to CPU time. It is easy and relatively inexpensive to obtain and deploy additional CPU resources. From a management perspective, dealing with CPU bottlenecks is much easier than network bottlenecks, especially in regard to high priced WANs. The fact that the total number of bytes increased by only 2% on the encrypted data stream suggests that the network overhead might scale at an acceptable rate as workload intensity increases.

Lastly, the question of how effective virtualization is in fostering personnel savings; personnel should receive further review, again with larger computing domains. This is an especially important question because personnel are the largest portion of the IT budget.

CONCLUSION

The importance of a disaster recovery strategy cannot be underestimated. If a recovery strategy is well thought-out, effectively managed, and cost effective, it is easier to deploy within organizations (Toigo, 1996; 2002). This chapter presented recovery plans for small and medium sized businesses and determined that there were many advantages to adopting a virtualized model.

In conclusion, it appears that the physical traditional models while providing a sound foundation do not provide the flexibility needed in today's internet oriented virtualized world. In fact, the recent work of Ardagna, Tanelli, Lovera and Zhang (2010) confirms the ability of virtualized servers to provide excellent performance in supporting web delivered applications. Based on our observations, for in-house solutions to be competitive with outsourcing, hybrid models that incorporate parts of the traditional models and expand on recent technology such as virtualization offer the best and most flexible solution in regard to balancing cost versus reliability/low granularity which brings up the question of transferability of the models presented herein to other sites. While there is not direct transferability of the models to other data centers, the basic ideas certainly are. For example, our virtualization model as depicted in Table 2 featured nine virtual zones. The same basic server consolidation model could be accomplished using a different number of zones and of course the number of zones required would be a function of the applications needed. Of course, on demand virtual solutions add a degree of complexity, but result in even more flexibility and efficiency. The authors are just beginning to adapt to on demand models. First, by replicating the existing server consolidation models so that if a primary virtualized host fails a second replica of that host automatically takes over. Second, experimentation with "cloud" computing software is being undertaken which in effect takes the resources of the entire autonomous system and allocates them dynamically. As described previously, cloud computing is the operational deployment of the data center wide on demand computing model where its complexity requires a well thought out transition strategy. Based on the authors' experience, it makes sense to begin with simple server consolidation (perhaps on a department level), then migrate to some form of on demand computing with that basic consolidation and then, after gaining significant experience, carefully begin the transition to a data center wide plan (perhaps using existing "cloud" computing software).

REFERENCES

Adams, K. (2002). Geographically distributed system for catastrophic recovery. *Proceedings of 16th USENIX Conference on System Administration,* (pp. 47-64).

Ardagna, D., Tanelli, M., Lovera, M., & Zhang, L. (2010). Black-box performance models for virtualized web service applications. *Proceeding of the First Joint WOSP/SIPEW International Conference on Performance Engineering,* (pp. 153-164).

Armitage, G., & Harrop, W. (2005). Teaching IP networking fundamentals in resource constrained educational environments. *Australasian Journal of Educational Technology, 21*(2), 263–283.

Baccaletti, S., Latora, V., Morento, Y., Chavez, M., & Hwang, D. U. (2006). Complex networks: structure and dynamics. *Physics Reports, 424,* 175–308. doi:10.1016/j.physrep.2005.10.009

Balaouras, S. (2007). The state of DR preparedness. *Forester/Disaster Recovery Journal.* Retrieved July 7, 2010, from http://www.drj.com/ index.php? option=com_conten t&task=view&id= 794&Itemid =159& ed= 10

Barham, P., Dragovic, B., Fraser, K., Hand, S., Harris, T., & Ho, A. ... Warfield, A. (2003). Xen and the art of virtualization. In *Proceedings of the 19th Symposium on Operating Systems Principles*, (pp. 164–177). Bolton Landing, NY, USA, October 2003.

Borden, T. L., Hennessy, J. P., & Rymarczyk, J. W. (1989). Multiple operating systems on one processor complex. *IBM Systems Journal, 28*(1), 104–123. doi:10.1147/sj.281.0104

De Tura, N., Reilly, S. M., Narasimhan, S., & Yin, Z. J. (2004). Disaster recovery preparedness through continuous process optimization. *Bell Labs Technical Journal, 9*(2), 147–162. doi:10.1002/bltj.20031

Dearstyne, B. W. (2006). Taking charge: Disaster fallout reinforces RIM's importance. *The Information Management Journal, July/August*, 37-43.

Guo, L. (2006). Recovery time guaranteed heuristic routing for improving computation complexity in survivable WDM networks. *Computer Communications, 30*, 1331–1336. doi:10.1016/j.comcom.2006.12.014

Guster, D. C. Hall, C., Herath, S., Jansen, B., & Mikluch, L. (2008). A comparison of popular global authentication systems. *Proceeding of the Third International Conference on Information Warfare and Security* (ICIW), Omaha, NE.

Guster, D. C., McCann, B. P., Kizenski, K., & Lee, O. F. (2008). Cost effective, safe and simple method to provide disaster recovery for small and medium sized businesses. *Review of Business Research, 8*(4), 63–71.

Guster, D. C., Safonov, P., Hall, C., & Sundheim, R. (2003). Using simulation to predict performance characteristics of mirrored WWW hosts. *Issues in Information Systems, 4*(2), 479–485.

Hiles, A. (1992). Surviving a computer disaster. *Engineering Management Journal, 2*(6), 271–274. doi:10.1049/em:19920071

Hiles, A. (2007). *The definitive handbook of business continuity management.* John Wiley and Sons.

Jones, V. A., & Keyes, K. (2001). *Emergency management for records and information management programs.* Lenexa, KS: Conservation Information Network, ARMA International.

Krojnewski, R., & Nager, B. (2006). Disaster recovery: It's not just an IT problem. *Forrester Report*, November 13, 2006.

Laureano, M., Maziero, C., & Jamhour, E. (2007). Protecting host-based intrusion detectors through virtual machines, computer networks. *The International Journal of Computer and Telecommunications Networking, 51*(5), 1275–1283.

Lee, O. F., Guster, D. C., Schmidt, M. B., & McCann, B. (2009). Applying the scale-free degree distribution algorithm to assess communication complexity and failure points in disaster recovery model. *Journal of Information Technology Management, 20*(2), 35–45.

Lin, Q., Neo, H., Zhang, L., Huang, G., & Gay, R. (2007). Grid-based large-scale web3D collaborative virtual environment. *Proceeding of the 12th International Conference on 3D Web Technology*, (pp. 123-132).

Massiglia, P., & Bunn, F. (2003). *Virtual storage redefined: Technologies and applications for storage virtualization.* Veritas Publishing.

Nellitheertha, H. (2006). *Virtualization technologies.* Infosys White Paper.

Pervan, G. (1998). How chief executive officers in large organizations view the management of their information systems. *Journal of Information Technology, 13*(2), 95–109. doi:10.1080/026839698344882

Phillippi, M. (2008). An effective SME disaster recovery strategy for branch offices. *Computer Technology Review*. Retrieved February 15, 2010, from http://www.thefreelibrary.com/ An+effective+ SME+disaster +recovery +strategy+ for+branch +offices.-a0168 214596

Rosenblum, M. (2009). *The impact of virtualization on modern computing environments*. Virginia Technological University Distinguished Lecture Series. Retrieved from http://www.cs.vt.edu/ Distinguished Lectures/ Mendel Rosenblum

Safigan, C. (2008). Disaster recovery for the masses–the role of OS-level server virtualization in disaster recovery. *Computer Technology Review*. Retrieved July 7, 2010, from http://www.wwpi. com/index.php ?option=com_ content&task=vie w&id=1151&Item id= 64

Stephens, D. (2003). Protecting records in the face of chaos, calamity, and cataclysm. *The Information Management Journal, January/February*, 33-40.

Toigo, J. W. (1996). *Disaster recovery planning: For computers and communication resources*. John Wiley & Sons, Inc.

Toigo, J. W. (2002). *Disaster recovery planning: Preparing for the unthinkable* (3rd ed.). Prentice Hall.

Wellheiser, J., & Scott, J. (2002). *An ounce of prevention: Integrated disaster planning for archives, libraries, and record centers*, 2nd ed. Scarecrow Press. The Canadian Archives Foundation. Lenexa, KS: ARMA International.

ADDITIONAL READING

Balaouras, S., & Schreck, G. (2008). Maximizing data center investments for disaster recovery and business resiliency. *Forrester Report*, October 5, 2008.

Boyd, T., & Dasgupta, P. (2002). Process migration: A generalized approach using a virtual operating system, proceedings of the 22nd International Conference on Distributed Computing Systems, 385.

Davison, C. (2007). Ethics of business continuity and disaster recovery technologies: A conceptual orientation. *International Journal of Computers, Systems and Signals, 8*(1), 54–63.

Grier, D.A. (2009). Virtual walls, *Computers*, 8-10.

Henrickson, K. (2006). Health plan decision support: Used and useful, *Forrester Research*, March 21, 2006.

Hill, J. (2008) Business continuity: Implementing disaster recovery strategies and technologies, *Aberdeen Benchmark Report*, March, 2008.

Lee, O. F., Guster, D. C., & Schmidt, M. B. (2009). Wan line speed and its implications for the support of globally remote replicas in a disaster recovery model. *Business Research Yearbook, 16*(1), 349–354.

Lowell, D., Saito, Y., & Samberg, E. (2004). De-virtualizable virtual machines enabling general, single node, online maintenance, Proceedings of the 11th International Conference on Architectural Support for Programming Languages and Operating Systems, 211-223.

Meier, J. D., Carlos, F., Prashant, B., Scott, B., & Dennis, R. (2007). Quantifying end-user response time goals, Microsoft pattern & practices developer center. Available at: http://msdn.microsoft. com/en-us/library/bb924365.aspx. Last accessed on: July 31, 2010.

Peterson, L., Shenker, S., & Turner, J. (2005). Overcoming the internet impasse through virtualization. *Computer, 38*(4), 34–41. doi:10.1109/ MC.2005.136

Smith, J., & Nair, R. (2005). The architecture of virtual machines. *Computer*, *38*(5), 32–38. doi:10.1109/MC.2005.173

Xu, J., Zhao, M., Fortes, J., Carpenter, R., & Yousif, M. (2008). Autonomic resource management in virtualized data centers using fuzzy logic-based approaches. *Cluster Computing*, *11*(3), 213–227. doi:10.1007/s10586-008-0060-0

KEY TERMS AND DEFINITIONS

Autonomous Systems: A collection of internet protocol routing logic that control one or more network operations which presents a globally defined routing policy to the internet.

Backup Site: A location where a firm can relocate following a disaster.

Cold Site: The most inexpensive backup site that neither includes hardware infrastructure nor backed up copies of data and information from the original location of a firm. Following a disaster, a cold site requires additional time to resume operations.

Disaster Recovery: A process and protocol for the preparation of recovery or continuation of technology infrastructure critical to a firm.

Fault Tolerance: Also referred to as graceful degradation. It is a system in place to resume normal operation in the event of any unforeseen failure.

Green Virtualization: An environmentally friendly logically segmented computing system.

Hot Site: The most expensive backup site for a firm with fully computerized systems and near-complete duplicates of the original data. Following a disaster, a hot site enables efficient recovery to resume normal operations.

LAN: A local area network or a computer network system that covers a physical location.

NFS: Network File System

RAID: redundant array of inexpensive disks

Virtualized Host: A method for hosting multiple logical computers contained in one physical computer.

VPN: Virtual private networks

WAN: A wide area network that covers a broad area such as an area across metropolitan, regional or national boundaries.

Warm Site: A moderately expensive backup site between a cold and hot site. Hardware infrastructure is established with ready connectivity. Following a disaster, a warm site can require up to several days to resume normal operations

Chapter 13
Firewall Rulebase Management:
Tools and Techniques

Michael J. Chapple
University of Notre Dame, USA

Aaron Striegel
University of Notre Dame, USA

Charles R. Crowell
University of Notre Dame, USA

ABSTRACT

The network firewall serves as one of the foundational network components for modern day computer security. A key challenge with respect to firewalls is the on-going maintenance of the rules of the various firewall devices, namely how does one keep the firewall at maximum security effectiveness in the face of changing security threats and enterprise application needs? To that end, this chapter focuses on contributions in two key areas with respect to the practice of firewall rulebase management. First, the chapter presents a general model for the auditing and analysis of installed firewalls that ensures compliance with security policy requirements and technical specifications. Second, the chapter provides insight for the proactive identification of rules that possess a high likelihood of becoming orphaned in the future based upon their similarity to previously orphaned firewall rules.

INTRODUCTION

The introduction of the modern computer network has revolutionized how computing is used in the workplace. Whether it is through simple sharing files via common storage locations or accessing a wealth of information through both external Internet sources and internal intranet sources, the

modern network has become a necessity for nearly all companies to deploy. Technology and application growth seem to continue unbounded raising the question of what the next technology will be after smart phones, Twitter, or social networking. Unfortunately, the very act of communication that opens up such a wealth of information serves as a double-edged sword, both allowing helpful, requested information to flow but also offering

DOI: 10.4018/978-1-60960-573-5.ch013

a new opportunity for malicious individuals to attack the digital enterprise environment.

In the enterprise security environment, the *firewall* serves as the front-line security device effectively delineating the perimeter between various zones of security control within the network of an organization. These *zones of control* can range from guarding sensitive data repositories such as a large database of personnel information to separating individual departments from one another to simply protecting the internal network from outside attacks originating in the Internet. Moreover, firewalls have become nearly ubiquitous with deployment levels approaching nearly 97% within modern enterprises (Richardson, 2007).

While other security tools such as virus scanners also enjoy similar deployment rates, the firewall is the de facto tool for enforcing network security. Analogous to the gate officer of old, firewalls operate as the network "traffic cop," determining which connections can start and stop and to whom communications can go or from whom they can be received. Due to the current and growing significance of firewalls in computer security for the enterprise, this chapter has the following goals.

- **Overview of firewalls and networking**: We begin with a brief overview of computer networks and describe the core approaches on how firewalls and the network interact. Particularly, we focus on the rules or logic of the firewall, i.e. how does the device decide what traffic may pass and how do the rules governing that activity emerge from company policy and / or history?

- **Discussion of rulebase management:** We continue with a discussion of the current state of affairs with respect to firewall rulebase management. Given that the enterprise and its applications are ever changing, what is the current state of the industry and most organizations with respect to

keeping their firewall rule sets in peak running condition. What are the most common approaches to this task?

- **An important but neglected aspect of rulebase management:** We conclude the chapter with a case study regarding the notion of orphaned rules. We discuss why orphaned rules offer an excellent case study regarding the importance of proper organizational security leadership and we describe specific tools we have created to address this matter.

Overview of Firewalls and Networking

The foundation of the modern computer network rests on multiple layers of technology described by what is called the "Open System Interconnection" (OSI) model. This model involves several key layers including the *physical layer* (how devices are connected and communicate at the lowest level), the *network layer* (how to find a particular device), the *transport layer* (how data is split up for sending), and the *application layer* (the actual executable programs used). At the lowest physical layer, devices are typically connected to the network via wires through Ethernet (IEEE 802.3) or wirelessly through WiFi (IEEE 802.11). Switches connect computers in the wired case while access points (APs) implement wireless connectivity in the wireless case.

Conversely, the highest application layer represents the applications that are using the network. Common applications would include web browsers (Firefox, Internet Explorer, Safari), e-mail clients (Outlook, Thunderbird), and various communication-centric applications (Skype, Instant Messenger, etc.). Similarly, file sharing such as a roaming profile or network drive could also be viewed through the lens of the application layer. Communications across the network take place between a pair of applications in that a client such as an e-mail client talks to an e-mail server to fetch / send e-mails.

The applications use the intermediate network and transport layers to identify where to find the various applications that will be communicating with one another across the network. The network layer provides an identifier for a particular machine, akin to the street address of a house or apartment building. A machine receives its network address from devices on the network (during startup) and uses that identifier as the "return address" for all communications. For the majority of computers on the Internet today, the dominant network protocol (i.e., addressing scheme) is IP particularly IPv4 also known as Internet Protocol version 4. An address under IPv4 consists of a 32-bit binary number frequently expressed using a more human-readable dot notation containing four numbers, each ranging from 0 to 255. Thus, a machine on the network (e.g., *MyWebServer*) on boot would receive its address for instance as 192.168.25.74, meaning that its IP address is that particular dotted number. Thus, any machine wishing to talk to *MyWebServer* would send communication packets to 192.168.25.74. The Domain Name Service allows the network to translate well-known names (ex. www.amazon.com) to their respective IP addresses.

Network addresses are assigned in a manner analogous to the way in which telephone area codes are assigned with geographically proximal devices receiving similar addresses. Each computer on the network is part of a *subnet* or common portion of the IP address where similar subnets often share similar functionality. Thus, analogous to how all telephones phones with the same area code and prefix number (e.g., 555-666-) would likely be in the same city, machines in the 192.168.25 subset would also be in a similar geographic area. The inclusion of a slash and number after the address (192.168.25 / 24) is used to refer to the binary bit length of the common address, which tells an application or network device how to treat that particular address. Based on the fact that each

grouping of numbers in the dot notation takes up eight of the 32 binary bits, the number following the slash denotes the length of the common address signifying which part of the full dotted address can be ignored. For example, a subnet identifier of 192.168 / 16 means that anything sharing the first 16 bits (i.e., 192.168) is part of that subnet or block while 192.168.85 / 24 means that anything sharing the first 24 bits (i.e., 192.168.85) is part of that subnet. As will be shown later, subnets will be used to simplify the firewall rules in a logical manner, since it is easier to state that all machines in a subnet follow a particular rule rather than it is to make individual rules for each different machine (i.e., each unique 32-bit IP address).

While network addresses and subnets work to allow data to be routed (sent) between different machines, how does a machine know which application to send the data to once it arrives via the wire or via wireless? The transport layer works in tandem with the network layer to allow a machine to route information to multiple applications running on that same machine by virtue of assigning each application one or more *ports*. While the network address can be thought of as the street address, the port number can be thought of as the correct apartment number. The port number allows traffic destined for different applications to get to their proper destinations. Moreover, common server applications tend to always be assigned the same port. For instance, web servers might always "listen" at port 80 while secure mail servers might always "listen" on port 993. Alternatively, other client applications may get assigned a port number randomly by the operating system. One might think of server applications (e.g., web/email) as being similar to one's home or business address (i.e., the port doesn't change often and always needs to be valid) in contrast to other client applications that don't need stability/permanency and thus are assigned the next available open room at a hotel (i.e., the specific port doesn't matter, as long as it's open, because it will be valid only for a limited time).

Taken together, the address and port of the network work with the transport layers to insure that a stream of data (i.e., *network flow*) moves back and forth between intended applications on the network. Each network flow is then identified by four components, the two network addresses (sending address, receiving address) and two ports (sending port, receiving port). This address group (also known as a "*tuple*") is contained in every data transmission between the two applications. From the perspective of security and in particular the firewall, it is this tuple of information that is most relevant to effectively controlling the network. With servers frequently using similar ports, one can then begin to create rules or filters that either allow or deny communications to between services or locations. The rule base or rule set that emerges contains a series of tuples that are compared against incoming and outgoing information "packets" (discreet pieces of the communication stream) sent between the applications. This rule base effectively controls which applications in the organization are allowed to communicate with which other applications inside or outside the organization. The resulting "firewall" becomes the foundational embodiment of the organization's overarching security policy realized at the lowest level such that, for example, company employees may not be allowed to browse to certain websites

that are deemed "undesirable." Firewall rulebases must be created and maintained by specific company employees (i.e., firewall administrators) with designated authority.

Firewall Deployment Example

Figure 1 shows a common firewall topology at the perimeter of an organization representing a typical network deployment. In this example, known as a *triple-homed firewall deployment* topology, the firewall device has three network interface zones corresponding to a protected internal network (intranet), a demilitarized zone (DMZ or screened subnet), and the greater Internet. The zones in this particular example are denoted by subnets whereby all machines with the 192.168.1 prefix are part of the DMZ, all machines with the 192.168.2 prefix are part of the intranet, and the rest are considered part of the Internet. The *intranet* contains those internal systems not designed to be accessible from the Internet. Intranets normally contain both internal servers and user productivity workstations, although the intranet may be further subdivided into separate security zones in some deployments. Conversely, the DMZ contains systems designed to be accessed from both the intranet and the Internet. In this example, the DMZ contains a web server (192.168.1.1) that offers services to

Figure 1. Sample firewalled network

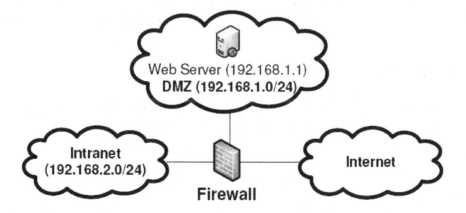

both intranet and Internet users. The purpose of the DMZ is to provide an isolation domain as systems exposed to the Internet are presumed to be at a significantly higher risk of compromise than those in the intranet. The DMZ serves as an additional layer of protection, limiting the ability a user who successfully compromises a DMZ system to compromise sensitive intranet systems.

As noted earlier, the heart of any firewall is the administrator-developed rulebase that maps the company level security policy to the underlying security mechanism of the firewall. With a typical default rule to deny unless explicitly noted, the rules of the firewall form the list of allowed traffic that can pass through the protected perimeter. In short, if one does not know or approve of the general class of communications in advance, it should not be allowed otherwise. In their most basic form, firewall rules contain four elements:

- **Action:** the action that should be taken when the rule is triggered (normally either allow or deny)
- **Source IP:** the IP address range of source systems affected by the rule listed either by individual addresses or subnets
- **Destination IP:** the IP address range of destination systems affected by the rule listed either by individual addresses or subnets
- **Destination Port:** the destination port corresponding to the type of service offered by the server

While a typical firewall offers significantly more complicated rule elements, this simplified version of the firewall rule model is sufficiently complete for the discussion in this chapter[1]. The complete syntax of firewall rules varies from platform to platform and typically includes additional elements that facilitate customization of rules. For example, some platforms allow the restriction of access to particular times of day or the requirement of individual user authentication.

Table 1 shows a sample firewall rulebase based on the following simplified security policy:

- External and internal parties can communicate with the web server either via normal communication or via secure communication.
- All e-mails from inside the company network must go through the company mail server to ensure proper compliance with regulatory agencies.
- Any computer internally can communicate with any external computer.
- No external computer can initiate a communication with an internal computer.

The first two rules enable access to the web server located in the DMZ on ports 80 (HTTP) and 443 (HTTPS – Secure HTTP). The "any" source address permits access from both the intranet and the Internet. The third rule blocks access from the internal network to external mail servers on port 25 (SMTP) to force all outbound mail to the company mail server while the fourth rule permits

Table 1. Sample firewall rules

Rule Number	Action	Source IP	Destination IP	Destination Port
1	Allow	Any	192.168.1.1	80
2	Allow	Any	192.168.1.1	443
3	Deny	192.168.2.0/24	any	25
4	Allow	192.168.2.0/24	any	any
5	Deny	any	any	any

all other outbound access. Finally, the last rule, known as the "cleanup rule" or the default deny all rule, blocks any other access, implementing the fundamental *principle of least privilege*: denying any access which is not explicitly authorized.

Although firewall rules are reasonably straight-forward in this simple case, enterprise rules often encompass hundreds if not thousands of individual rules. Hence, firewall rulebases frequently contain errors resulting from many distinct causes, including misspecification of business requirements, improper implementation of rules, changing technical environments and typographical error. This chapter proposes the following taxonomy of erroneous rules to provide a consistent framework for discussion:

- **Promiscuous rules** allow more access than necessary to meet the stated business requirements. Examples of promiscuous rules include allowing access to a system from all IP addresses when access is only necessary from a single subnet and allowing access to a system on multiple ports when only a subset of those ports is required.

- **Redundant rules** result when one rule duplicates all or a portion of the access permitted or denied by an existing rule. An example of a redundant rule is one that allows a single IP address to access a server on a particular port when an existing rule already allows all IP addresses to access that port. Similarly, an administrator creates a redundant rule when creating a rule that allows access to a port on that system when another rule allows that access due to the port's membership in a service group.

- **Shadowed rules** result when the incorrect ordering of rules in a firewall rulebase completely prevents the execution of one or more firewall rules. Examples of shadowed rules include placing a rule that denies access to a particular website below

a rule that allows access to all websites and placing a rule that allows access to a server on a single port from a single IP address below a rule that blocks all access to the server from all IP addresses. Referring back to the example rulebase in Table 1.1, if the administrator accidentally inverted rules three and four, rule four would shadow rule three, rendering it useless.

- **Orphaned rules** exist in the firewall rulebase but are never exercised by traffic passing through the firewall. Examples of orphaned rules include a rule designed to allow access to a database server that incorrectly specifies a non-existent destination IP address and a rule designed to allow access to a web server that no longer hosts a website.

- **Rule specification errors** include errors made in the conversion process between business requirements and the firewall rule definition. Some examples of rule specification errors include specifying the incorrect port for a service (e.g. creating a rule for port 88 when the business requirement was for web service on port 80), specifying rules that do not meet business requirements based upon a misunderstanding of business requirements, and failing to specify a rule necessary to meet business requirements.

- **Data entry errors** include errors made when converting a technical rule definition into the firewall policy format and entering that rule into the firewall rulebase. Some examples of data entry errors include mistyping a port number (e.g. creating a rule for port 52 when the technical specification indicated port 25), mistyping a source or destination address (e.g. creating a rule for 129.47.0.0/24 instead of 129.74.0.0/24), and failing to input a rule included in the technical specification.

It is significant to note that errors may commonly fall into more than one classification in this taxonomy. For example, consider a rule that is designed to allow traffic to a server from systems in the 192.168.1.0/24 subnet. If the firewall administrator implementing this rule commits a data entry error and mistypes the subnet using a /16 subnet mask, this data entry error also results in a promiscuous rule error, as systems outside of the intended range will be able to access the host. On the other hand, if the administrator mistypes the IP address of the server, instead entering a non-existent IP address, this data entry error will also produce an orphaned rule, as no traffic will ever exercise a rule to a nonexistent host.

Other Firewall Topologies

Other firewall topologies in addition to the above-described triple-homed firewall include the *bastion host* and the *dual firewall* topology. In the bastion host topology the firewall is placed between the Internet and the protected network. It filters all traffic entering or leaving the network. The bastion host topology is well suited for relatively simple networks (e.g. those that don't offer any public Internet services.) The key factor to keep in mind about this firewall arrangement is that it offers only a single boundary. Once someone manages to penetrate that boundary, they've gained unrestricted access (at least from a perimeter protection perspective) to the protected network. This may be acceptable for organizations merely using the firewall to protect a corporate network that is used mainly for surfing the Internet, but is probably not sufficient for those hosting a Web site or e-mail server.

The most secure (and most expensive) option is to implement the dual firewall topology, which involves a screened subnet (i.e., DMZ) and uses two firewalls. In this case, the DMZ is placed between the two firewalls. The use of two firewalls still allows the organization to offer services to Internet users through the use of a DMZ, but

provides an added layer of protection. It's very common for security architects to implement this scheme using firewall technology from two different vendors. This provides an added level of security in the event a malicious individual discovers a software-specific exploitable vulnerability in one of the firewall systems.

Firewall Enforcement Methodologies

Firewalls also can be classified depending on how/where they enforce security protocols. Three main categories here include *packet filtering* firewalls, *stateful inspection* firewalls, and *application proxy* firewalls. Packet filtering firewalls screen traffic by examining data from packet headers. Usually, the rules are concerned with source, destination and port addresses. Using this type of static filtering, a firewall is unable to provide user authentication or to tell whether a packet originated from inside or outside of a private network, which means these firewalls can be easily fooled with spoofed packets. Static packet filtering firewalls operate at the Network layer of the OSI Model and are often also called screening routers.

Stateful inspection firewalls examine "connection state," which means they evaluate current network traffic in the context of preceding traffic. By examining source and destination addresses, application usage, source of origin and relationship between current packets and previous packets of the same session, stateful inspection firewalls are able to control a broader range of access for authorized users and activities and are able more actively to watch for unauthorized access attempts. These firewalls operate at the Network and Transport layers of the OSI Model.

Application proxy firewalls do not allow packets to cross directly between network segments. Instead, they first evaluate each packet using stateful inspection techniques and then create a copy of the packet that is readdressed using network address translation (NAT) functionality so that the packets can be forwarded to a private network address located behind the firewall. This allows a greater degree of isolation between the public network and the protected network. Application proxy firewalls also offer the significant benefit of allowing the firewall to inspect packets all the way down to the OSI Model's Application layer. The firewall can perform a detailed analysis of the packet and then make allow/deny decisions based upon additional factors. For example, an application proxy firewall might be configured to allow requests to receive information (e.g., HTTP GET requests) but deny requests to send/submit inform (e.g., HTTP POST requests). Even more granularly, the firewall might allow POST requests only to certain URLs or from certain source IP ranges. Application proxy firewalls also can look for violations of protocol standards that may be indicative of an attack attempt.

These technologies vary in both financial and computational cost, with packet filtering firewalls falling on the lower end of both spectrums, application proxy firewalls falling on the higher end and stateful inspection appearing in the middle range. For this reason, it's important to carefully select firewalls that provide adequate protection to meet an organization's security requirements but without incurring excessive costs or management overhead.

Chapter Contribution

Later in this chapter, we will focus on orphaned rules because they have a high likelihood of occurrence (as we have noted elsewhere, see Chapple, D'Arcy, &, Striegel, 2009) and because the existence of such rules introduces risk into the enterprise. We will contend that it is much more likely an orphaned rule will introduce risk into a firewall architecture than a redundant rule, due to the nature of the misconfiguration. An orphaned rule allows access through the firewall for an unused or nonexistent service. If such a rule becomes inadvertently active as a result of a common organizational practice like recycling

IP addresses, there is a chance that the rule could then allow unintended access to the network. As redundant rules by their nature duplicate functionality implemented by other rules, they do not allow additional access to a protected network and only introduce unnecessary complexity.

This chapter will make two main contributions to the practice of firewall rulebase management. First, it will present a general model for the auditing and analysis of installed firewalls that will ensure compliance with security policy requirements and technical specifications. Second, it will provide a technique for the proactive identification of rules that possess a high likelihood of becoming orphaned in the future based upon their similarity to previously orphaned firewall rules. While these specific contributions could be viewed as narrow in focus, the fact is that both of these topics have not received yet received sufficient attention within the literature in our opinion.

BACKGROUND

Despite significant research on policy validation, there exists little research on the adoption of practical firewall management techniques within an organization or on the current state of firewall management across an enterprise. Indeed, a review of common security and firewall training materials reveals significant attention to the design of firewall topologies and the implementation of rulebases, but little or no discussion of proper firewall management practices. Accordingly, in earlier work (Chapple, D'Arcy, &, Striegel, 2009), we developed a survey instrument that combined open- and closed-ended questions designed to probe the actual behaviors of firewall administrators in each of the identified best practice areas. It also included questions designed to assess the state of their firewall rulebases based upon the number of rules in place and the frequency of change. Finally, it asked several questions designed to elicit administrator opinions about the state of their rulebases. Based upon the results of this study, we were able to draw three main conclusions:

- Firewall rulebase complexity greatly exceeded that discovered in prior research and administrators felt this complexity was a major contributing factor to rulebase configuration errors.
- Evidence indicated that administrators made errors on a routine basis and most considered it likely that their rulebases contained undetected errors that exposed their organization to risk.
- In general, firewall administrators did not follow recognized best practices for firewall administration on a regular basis.

Little scholarly research exists on the identification and management of the firewall rulebase lifecycle. The most relevant work is that of Schuba and Spafford (1997), which focuses on a reference model for the development of a firewall platform, rather than the management of an existing firewall rulebase.

A number of current research efforts address the conversion of high-level security policies into firewall rulesets. In Bartal, Mayer, Nissim, and Wool (2004), a high-level language is used to automate the mapping of policy into firewall rules. Verbowski (2006) extends this work to the configuration and management of distributed firewalls. FANG (Mayer, Wool, & Ziskind, 2000) is a query-based firewall configuration analysis engine designed to answer basic policy implementation questions, such as 'Is service X allowed from host A to host B?'. FANG was later extended to the more general Firewall Analyzer by Mayer, Wool, & Ziskind (2005).

Tools are also available to perform offline analysis of a firewall rulebase. Eronen and Zitting (2001) built an expert system to analyze firewall rules for misconfigurations, based upon the expert knowledge contained in the system's knowledge base. Al-Shaer and Hamed (2004) described a Firewall Policy Advisor that is capable of analyzing a rulebase for inherent anomalies including shadowing, correlation, generalization, redundancy and irrelevance.

More recently, the commercially available AlgoSec Firewall Analyzer offers administrators a toolkit for rule workflow management and the proactive identification of redundant rules (AlgoSec, Inc., 2009)

Hamed and Al-Shaer (2006) make the case for ordering firewall rulebases in a manner that optimizes performance, known as the optimal rule ordering (ORO) problem and provide evidence that such optimization has a significant impact on the performance of firewall devices. They also demonstrate that the ORO problem is NP-complete via reduction to the single machine job scheduling problem with precedence constraints (Lawler, 1978)

The only known effort to analyze firewall audit logs for anomalous activity is described in Gaspary, Melchiors, Locatelli, and Dillenburg (2004) and uses case-based reasoning to identify potentially malicious activity within firewall logs.

FIREWALL RULEBASE MANAGEMENT

Our earlier work (see Chapple, D'Arcy, &, Striegel, 2009) revealed a clear gap between the current and desired state of firewall management practices in the modern enterprise.

For example, 89% of administrators surveyed did not use an automated process to detect orphaned firewall rules. Only 2% used a fully automated process while the remainder required at least some degree of manual tabulation. Detecting and removing orphaned rules is a trivial way to manage rulebase complexity, yet the vast majority of enterprises do not practice this simple technique. Additionally, only a small majority (58%) of administrators used a formal

Figure 2. Firewall rulebase lifecycle model

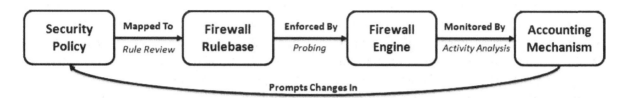

change control process to govern modifications to firewall policies.

We believe this gap is in large part due to a lack of available tools to automate the firewall rulebase management process. Therefore, in this section, we outline and explore frameworks for firewall rulebase auditing and present a set of tools designed to assist in the reactive and proactive identification of orphaned firewall rules.

Auditing Framework

Auditing system controls can ensure ongoing correctness and compliance with policy, regulations, and best-practice. ISO 17799 states "Information systems should be regularly checked for compliance with security implementation standards" (ISO/TEC, 2005). While a large number of procedures and guidelines exist for the auditing of workstations, servers, networking devices and other computing systems, no framework currently exists for the complete auditing of firewall rulebases. This section presents a general model of the firewall rulebase lifecycle, and describes three auditing techniques that may be used to verify the correct implementation of a rulebase.

Firewall Rulebase Lifecycle Model

This model considers the firewall lifecycle as a four-stage process beginning when a change in business requirements motivates a modification of an organization's security policy and continuing through the creation and enforcement of corresponding firewall rules, which are subsequently

monitored by accounting procedures that may, in turn, prompt additional changes in business requirements. A graphic interpretation of this process appears in Figure 2.

In the first stage of the process, the organization's management analyzes the business requirements of the enterprise and uses this analysis to formulate the basis for the organization's security policy, standards and guidelines. In many organizations, this results in a formal, written statement regarding the acceptable level of risk to the enterprise and an enumeration of permissible and/or impermissible activities. Less mature organizations may not opt for formal documentation of these principles but instead may rely upon an institutional knowledge of acceptable and unacceptable practice. The former approach lends itself to a traceable (and, therefore, auditable) path from the statement of business requirements to the eventual implementation and execution of controls, while the latter approach is likely to be deemed unacceptable by auditors.

Upon the completion and promulgation of the organization's security policy, firewall administrators must translate the written language of the security policy into firewall rules that provide the technical specifications instructing the firewall to either allow or deny specific types of traffic depending upon its nature. For example, a security policy might state the following requirement:

"It is the policy of XYZ Corporation that all accesses to customer data taking place over a public network connection must use strong encryption."

The security analyst reading this requirement must first determine the appropriate implementation of this requirement within the technical context of the enterprise. For example, if an organization uses a web-based customer relationship management (CRM) system, the analyst might derive the following technical specification of that requirement:

- Users on the internal network (192.168.2.0/24) may access the server using an unencrypted HTTP connection on port 80, as the policy does not require encryption for non-public network connections.
- Users who have connected to the organization's Virtual Private Network (VPN) (192.168.3.0/24) may access the server using an unencrypted HTTP connection on port 80, as the VPN already provides suitable encryption.
- Users from any location may access the server using an encrypted HTTPS connection on port 443, as the HTTPS connection provides encryption meeting the organization's security policy.

This technical specification is purely an intermediate requirement, as it then must be expressed in proper firewall rule syntax. An example of this translation appears in Table 2, assuming that the CRM web server resides in a DMZ in the context of the network specified in Figure 1 with the address 192.168.1.2.

Upon completion of rule specification, the administrator uploads the newly created rules to the firewall and depends upon the device to correctly interpret the rules and apply them to inbound traffic. Best practice dictates that the enterprise then perform accounting activities to monitor security decisions made by the firewall and ensure that traffic is appropriately allowed or blocked by the device, although this final step is rarely performed in practice due to the resource intensive nature of the task.

Rule Review

Rule review is an auditing technique that verifies the first step of the firewall rulebase lifecycle process: mapping the organization's written business requirements to a technical specification of firewall rules. Due to the tedious, technical nature of this work, errors regularly occur in this stage of the process as the result of typographical errors, misinterpretations and inattention to configuration details.

In the rule review, a subject matter expert performs a comparison between the extant firewall rulebase and those actions that should follow directly from the spirit of the network security policy. This may be facilitated by an organizational policy requiring administrators to annotate any new entries into the rulebase with notes in the associated comments fields regarding the policy basis of the rule, preferably referencing a specific statement or section of the organization's security policy.

Table 2. CRM firewall rulebase

Rule Number	Action	Source IP	Destination IP	Destination Port
1	Allow	192.168.2.0/24	192.168.1.2	80
2	Allow	192.168.3.0/24	192.168.1.2	80
3	Allow	Any	192.168.1.2	443
4	Deny	Any	Any	Any

Earlier work attempted to automate the rule review process through the design of languages that facilitate the mapping of policy statements to firewall rules (Bartal et al., 2004). However, these efforts have not been widely (if at all) adopted by the security community due to their burdensome nature. The manual "desk check" rule review process remains the most common and effective technique for the verification of policy implementation correctness.

In addition to verifying the correct implementation of the firewall policy, rule review techniques may be used to perform static analysis on the firewall rulebase to identify several of the common configuration errors described above, including redundant rules. The Firewall Policy Advisor developed by Al-Shaer and Hamed (2004) represents earlier work in this area. Our approach, described in the next section, differs in that it performs dynamic analysis, taking actual usage patterns into account, specifically with respect to considering the case of orphaned rules.

Penetration Testing

Penetration testing provides verification of the correct function of the second transition in the firewall rulebase lifecycle: enforcement of the firewall rulebase by the firewall engine. Normally, enterprises make use of commercial firewall products and do not have access to the product's source code. This renders impossible the verification of the firewall's correct implementation via code review. Therefore, administrators seeking to verify the correct functioning of the firewall have no option other than to gather empirical evidence to verify that the firewall is correctly enforcing the rulebase's access control entries.

The most direct way to gather this evidence is through the generation of customized packets that exercise each of the firewall's rules. Due to the prohibitively large number of potential rules, administrators must develop test scenarios that properly exercise the likely success and failure conditions rather than to attempt an exhaustive search. Some guiding principles for this type of verification include:

- Perform verification of all TCP and UDP ports for external addresses given privileged access through the firewall. For example, if a rule allows LDAP traffic from a specific host, best practice dictates performing an exhaustive test to confirm that address is not provided excessive access.
- Perform bounds testing on subnets allowed access through the firewall. This test confirms that the firewall correctly identifies the starting and ending addresses for subnets used in access control entries.
- Perform exhaustive testing of all TCP and UDP ports for a small sample of addresses not provided privileged access through the firewall. These addresses may be randomly selected or chosen by administrators based upon local conditions. This test confirms the level of access provided to arbitrary public hosts.

Auditors should always consult administrators with domain knowledge of the local firewall rulebase and computing environment when designing these tests to ensure that any special conditions are captured in the test scenarios.

Conducting these tests manually would be quite tedious and time-consuming. Fortunately, a large body of prior work exists on this topic and there are several tools available that can generate artificial traffic designed to perform the desired test scenarios. Examples include Nmap (Lyon, 1997), Hping (Sanfilippo, 2006), Nemesis (Nathan, 2003), and Packet (Bounds, 2007).

Activity Analysis

The final auditing tool, *activity analysis*, allows the auditor to take advantage of the monitoring function of firewalls to detect errors in the firewall rulebase configuration and confirm that the firewall both meets the specific requirements of the network security policy and serves the organization's business requirements. In particular, by reviewing firewall logs the administrator or auditor should be able to establish statistics about firewall traffic and identify rulebase configuration errors that are not detectable with traditional static analysis techniques.

For example, orphaned rule identification, a focus of the next section, is not possible without performing dynamic analysis that incorporates information about rule utilization found in firewall log data. Other anomalies found in these logs that may reveal configuration errors include:

- Denied traffic that may indicate the absence of a required rule. Analysts should pay particular attention to denied traffic originating from a known host, as this may indicate a trusted host attempting to access a legitimate service that the firewall is unintentionally blocking.
- Invalid IP addresses appearing in the logs that may indicate an improperly configured host on the network. For example, the presence of a public Internet address on a private subnet may indicate a host with a network configuration error. Similarly, the presence of a host with an address invalid on the subject subnet that would be valid on another subnet may indicate a switching layer configuration error (VLAN, etc.).
- Security alerts and invalid attempts to establish administrative connections to the firewall itself that may indicate an attack in progress and should be the subject of particular scrutiny.
- Counts of rule utilization on particular paths that may be analyzed and trended over time to identify security and network issues.

Activity analysis plays an extremely important role in the ongoing management and monitoring of firewalls, as it incorporates actual usage information that is essential to identifying a number of configuration errors that simply cannot be detected with offline static analysis techniques.

CASE STUDY: ORPHANED RULE IDENTIFICATION AND PREVENTION

Orphaned firewall rules are at best undesirable and, in the worst case, pose a significant risk to enterprise security for several reasons:

- Orphaned firewall rules may unintentionally allow unintended access to the internal network if the original business requirement for the rule no longer exists but the service remains to meet other needs.
- Orphaned rules unnecessarily increase the complexity of the firewall rulebase, increasing the possibility of error in the future and simultaneously increasing the burden of performing firewall rule reviews during the audit process.
- Orphaned rules place added processing burden on the firewall which must futilely compare each incoming connection against the orphaned ACLs in the rulebase. This increases ongoing enterprise maintenance costs by demanding critical hardware resources for an insignificant purpose.

To that end, we propose a two-component set of tools to (a) identify extant orphaned firewall rules in a production firewall based upon dynamic rulebase analysis, and (b) proactively alert administrators when they attempt to create a rule that has a high likelihood of becoming orphaned in the future. The first element of this set is the *Firewall Audit Support Tool (FAST)*. FAST processes firewall logs in near real-time and tracks the utilization of specific firewall rules over time, alerting administrators when specific rule use falls below a threshold signaling orphan status. The second element of the set is the *Firewall ACL Creation Tool (FACT)* which uses the results of enterprise-specific decision tree analysis to model orphaned rule characteristics and apply that model to future rules as a predictor of the rule's future orphan status.

Together, the tools of the FAST/FACT set provide firewall administrators with a previously unavailable deep look into the orphaned rules in their production environments. After development of these tools, we deployed them in the production environment of a local organization to which we had access. The first deployment yielded immediate benefit, resulting in a greater than 50% reduction in the overall size of the rulebase and allowing the postponement of a previously planned infrastructure upgrade necessitated by enormity of the firewall rulebase.

Orphaned Rule Identification

To identify orphaned rules in a rulebase we used the straightforward approach described by the algorithm shown in Figure 3. This approach required that administrators create a database table containing basic information about each rule in the rulebase and update that table subsequent to any rulebase modification. We developed an automated script based on this algorithm that functioned on Sidewinder G2 firewalls but that may be adapted for any arbitrary platform allowing plaintext rulebase export.

In short, the algorithm takes two inputs for consideration, the log of connection entries as gained by a product such as Cisco NetFlows (providing an identical view of what the firewall would see with respect to the connection tuple) and the table of the firewall rules including all historical changes applied to the rulebase. Using a hash function, the algorithm then explores each rule and updates the last time that the rule was "hit" or used by a connection as well as various other appropriate statistical properties. Based on the aforementioned results, the statistics with respect to rule usage can then be used to identify the orphaned rules, (i.e. rules that have not seen recent activity).

Orphaned Rule Threshold

A system designed to identify orphaned rules must be based upon a precise definition of what it means to be orphaned. In contrast to the subjective definition presented earlier in this chapter, an orphaned rule detection system seeking to make a

Figure 3. Algorithm for orphaned rule identification

Input: Log of connection entries (L)
Input: Database table of firewall rules (R)
Output: Database table of firewall rules (R) with updated timestamps
$h \leftarrow \oslash$
foreach *log entry l* **do**
    if $l_{rulename}$ *does not exist in h* **then**
        $h\{l_{rulename}\} \leftarrow l_{timestamp}$
    end
end
foreach *hash entry h{i}* **do**
    lookup record h{i} in R update timestamp on record to value of h{i}
end

Boolean judgment must have precise criteria that specify when a rule is indeed orphaned.

Figure 4 shows the results of a threshold analysis of orphaned rules based upon the rulebase we employed in our research. The graph shows the number of rules in the rulebase identified as orphaned at each possible threshold value, where the threshold value is the number of time periods elapsed since the rule was last activated. For example, if the threshold value were set to 25, any rules that had not appeared in the previous 25 time periods would be flagged as orphaned.

This straightforward technique is non-optimal because experience tells us that not all firewall rules are triggered at even intervals. It is quite common to have rules triggered in every time period (e.g. rules that allow access to an organization's main web server) as well as those triggered infrequently (e.g. those that allow access to a system accessed only at certain times of the year).

In a similar vein, it is important to note that an incorrect diagnosis of a rule as being orphaned could have significant repercussions. While there exists incentive for the administrator to create new rules for connectivity (new business service and its accompanying productivity), the converse is not always readily apparent despite the lingering

security issues. In the absence of users being made to periodically justify the existence of a rule (e.g., a soft state approach similar to renewing a license or certification), an administrator must be reasonably certain that said rule is inactive. Whereas the security threat to the organization is a more uncertain future risk, the incorrect removal of an active but perceived to be orphaned rule certainly might have concrete and immediate career repercussions for the administrator.

Therefore, in developing FAST, we adopted a methodology in which rule-specific thresholds were created based on analyzing past patterns of use for each rule, looking at the number of days that typically passed between executions of the rule. If the current gap was more than three standard deviations larger than the mean gap, FAST identified the rule as potentially orphaned. This approach allowed FAST to accommodate rules that typically were used on an infrequent basis without triggering excessive false positive alerts.

Firewall Audit Support Tool

FAST's orphaned rule detection algorithm processed in memory all connection entries recorded in a firewall's log for a particular interval (e.g.

Figure 4. Orphan threshold analysis

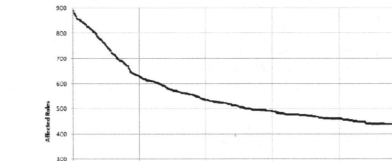

one day). Upon completion of this processing, the algorithm updated the timestamp stored in each rule's database entry to correspond to the timestamp of the log file being processed.

FAST automatically triggered orphaned rule detection processing on a nightly basis, although this time period was configurable. During the nightly processing, FAST identified those rules that appeared to be orphaned based upon their presence in one of two categories:

- **Rules that had never been used:** These rules were prioritized by the number of days elapsed since the time they were first created, in descending order. These rules were likely either misspecified or misinterpreted upon creation or requested in anticipation of a business requirement that had never materialized.
- **Rules that had not been used in abnormally long periods of time, prioritized by the number of days since last use in descending order:** FAST detected these

rules based upon the thresholding technique described in the previous section.

FAST then e-mailed a report of the rulebase status to the firewall administrators. A brief excerpt from a FAST report appears in Figure 5.

FAST Results

The FAST system was deployed in a production environment that had an original rulebase consisting of 806 rules. Prior to deploying the tools, interviews with administrators revealed that they were aware the rulebase contained orphaned rules but they did not know which rules were orphaned. Moreover, administrators greatly underestimated the pervasive nature of the orphaned rules, estimating that approximately 25-30% of the rulebase might consist of orphaned rules.

Expert analysis identified that approximately 50% of the rules contained in the rulebase were indeed orphaned and, with the assistance of FAST, administrators were able to reduce the size of the

Figure 5. FAST Output

Orphaned Rule Analysis

The rulebase contains 806 proxy rules. Of these, 53% appear to be orphaned

The following 116 rules appear to have never been used:

vpn-sa-untrust-wwwproxy-pvcspprd created 975 days ago

vpn-sa-untrust-pvcsin-pvcspprd created 857 days ago

untrust-untrust-ssh-oracledb1 created 182 days ago

DMZ-Admindmz-httpsportalprod2-webfms created 107 days ago

...

The following 304 rules appear to have been orphaned:

vpn-sa-admindmz-pvcs-pvcspprd01 last used 723 days ago

untrust-untrust-wts-dpac-wts-devl last used 626 days ago

admin-dmz-untrust-9100-hp-printer-wcp35 last used 267 days ago

dmz-coresvcs-mssql-oit-cfmx-prod3-sqlprod-p5 last used 94 days ago

...

rulebase significantly and postpone a planned in-frastructure upgrade project that would have been necessitated by the excessive size of the rulebase.

Decision Tree Analysis of Orphaned Rules

The FAST system played an important role in the management of firewall rulebases, allowing administrators to detect the presence of orphaned rules in their systems, but it was strictly an *ex post facto* system. Desiring insight into the causal factors behind orphaned rules, a decision tree analysis of those rules was performed using the J48 decision tree algorithm in the Weka data mining package (University of Waikato, 2005). This algorithm can be used to predict a binary outcome (e.g., whether a rule is ORPHAN or ACTIVE) based on a set of attributes characterizing that rule such as what source it considers (e.g., DMZ, internal private network, Internet), what destination it considers, what port service it pertains to (e.g., 80-HTTP), etc. This type of analysis was the preferred technique in this instance due to the intuitive nature of its output as well as the desire to share the resulting models with practicing firewall administrators. The analysis requires a "training set" of rules for which the attributes and outcomes already are known. In this case, the training set consisted of the same 806 rules used in the prior section's FAST analysis, thereby also allowing for cross-validation of the previous results.

The resultant decision tree appears in Figure 6. While a detailed explanation of this tree is beyond the scope of the present discussion, the tree reveals which specific combinations of rule attributes were associated with correct or incorrect classification of those rules as ACTIVE or ORPHAN. The parentheses to the far right of each row indicate the respective number of instances observed in the rulebase with that particular combination of attributes, together with the classification errors for that set. Overall, this tree had a true positive

classification rate of 70.3% with a 76.4% true positive rate for the orphaned rule class.

A receiver operating characteristic (ROC) curve also may be used to visualize the predictive power (i.e., ability to correctively classify rule as ACTIVE vs. ORPHAN) of the decision tree classification performance. An ROC curve plots the true positive classification rate against the false positive rate. In such a curve, a 45-degree diagonal line through the origin would represent random classification performance such as might result from flipping a coin. Points above that line toward the upper left would represent good (i.e., better than random) classification performance.

Figure 6. J48 Decision Tree

```
sourcetype = none
|   destburb = none: ACTIVE (8.0/3.0)
|   destburb = Untrusted: ACTIVE (48.0/10.0)
|   destburb = NNAT-DMZ: ACTIVE (9.0/4.0)
|   destburb = Mon-Tw: ACTIVE (9.0)
|   destburb = Core-Svcs: ACTIVE (8.0/1.0)
|   destburb = Admin-DMZ: ORPHAN (12.0/5.0)
|   destburb = DMZ: ORPHAN (7.0/2.0)
|   destburb = vpn-sa: ORPHAN (3.0)
|   destburb = Firewall: ORPHAN (1.0)
|   destburb = Heartbeat: ORPHAN (2.0)
sourcetype = netgroup
|   numtargets <= 28
|   |   sourceburb = Untrusted
|   |   |   numtargets <= 12: ACTIVE (62.0/22.0)
|   |   |   numtargets > 12: ORPHAN (12.0/2.0)
|   |   sourceburb = DMZ: ORPHAN (47.0/16.0)
|   |   sourceburb = Core-Svcs
|   |   |   numtargets <= 13: ORPHAN (12.0/2.0)
|   |   |   numtargets > 13: ACTIVE (15.0/4.0)
|   |   sourceburb = NNAT-DMZ: ORPHAN (10.0/3.0)
|   |   sourceburb = Admin-DMZ
|   |   |   numtargets <= 1: ACTIVE (32.0/11.0)
|   |   |   numtargets > 1: ORPHAN (29.0/12.0)
|   |   sourceburb = Mon-Tw: ACTIVE (12.0/3.0)
|   numtargets > 28: ACTIVE (33.0)
sourcetype = subnet
|   destburb = Untrusted
|   |   sourceburb = none: ORPHAN (1.0)
|   |   sourceburb = Untrusted: ACTIVE (87.0/40.0)
|   |   sourceburb = Admin-DMZ: ORPHAN (2.0)
|   |   sourceburb = vpn-sa: ACTIVE (8.0/4.0)
|   destburb = NNAT-DMZ: ACTIVE (1.0)
|   destburb = Core-Svcs: ORPHAN (7.0/1.0)
|   destburb = Admin-DMZ: ACTIVE (19.0/9.0)
|   destburb = DMZ: ORPHAN (15.0/4.0)
|   destburb = DMZ2: ACTIVE (1.0)
sourcetype = ipaddr: ORPHAN (281.0/93.0)
sourcetype = netmap: ORPHAN (13.0/5.0)
```

The ROC curve associated with the decision tree analysis is shown in Figure 7. This curve shows an area of 73.9% under the curve, which demonstrates a high predictive value for this tool. In effect, this area represents the likelihood that when a pair of examples (one true positive and one false positive) is selected randomly, the classification would assign a higher score to the true positive than to the false positive example. The next section on FACT creates an embodiment of the decision tree realized through a GUI interface.

Interviews with firewall administrators then sought insight into the features selected by the decision tree analysis. In this way we were able to confirm that the features selected by the algorithm were intuitively correct, as they corresponded to several technical and personnel factors used in firewall rule creation. The presence of these factors resulted in an enterprise-specific decision tree model. This model, shown in Figure 6, obviously was specific to the technical and personal characteristics of the environment and administrators studied in this research. However, it is highly likely that the technique proposed here can be successfully generalized to, and implemented in, other organizations.

Firewall ACL Creation Tool

FACT used the results of decision tree analysis in a prophylactic fashion: informing administrators before they created a rule that appears likely to become orphaned. FACT is a web-based system that used the interface shown in Figure 8 to allow administrators to specify a rule. The drop-down boxes that allowed selection of the source and destination attributes drew input directly from the firewall information database. This eliminated the possibility of typographical errors by restricting feature values to those extant in the firewall database.

Once an administrator entered the rule specification, FACT performed two types of analyses to inform the administrator's decision to deploy the rule onto the production firewall:

1. Rules were checked against the organization's business requirements. For example, security policy might dictate that no rule allow direct traffic between the Internet and any internal zone other than the DMZ. FACT enforced these requirements, informing administrators when they created a rule that

Figure 7. Receiver operating characteristic (ROC) curve

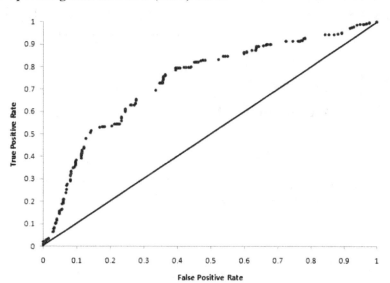

Figure 8. FACT rule specification

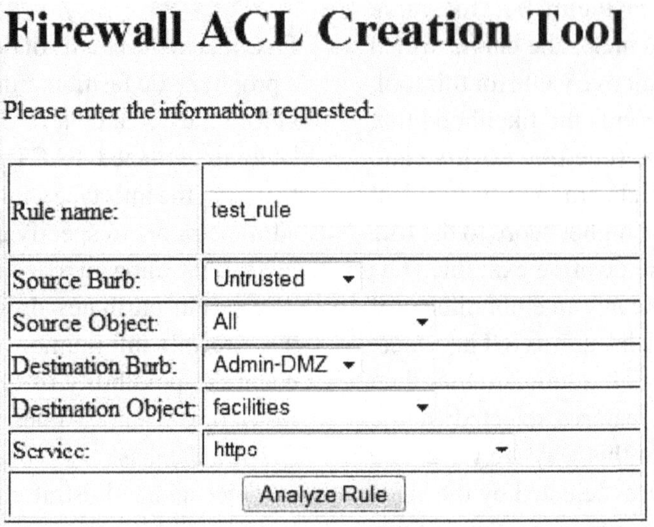

Firewall ACL Creation Tool

Please enter the information requested:

Rule name:	test_rule
Source Burb:	Untrusted ▼
Source Object:	All ▼
Destination Burb:	Admin-DMZ ▼
Destination Object:	facilities ▼
Service:	https ▼
	Analyze Rule

failed to comply with one or more business requirements and, optionally, not allowing the creation of such a rule.

2. Rules were processed through the decision tree model generated in the previous section to determine a likelihood of future orphan status. If the model predicted that a rule might become orphaned, FACT provided the administrator with information on the number of instances that informed the model at that particular leaf node and recommended a careful analysis prior to deployment.

An example of FACT output appears in Figure 9.

Finally, FACT limited the likelihood of transcription errors by providing administrators with a textbox containing a cut-and-paste version of a firewall ACL implementing the specified requirements in a manner suitable for use on a Sidewinder G2 firewall. The FACT source code can be easily altered to accommodate the rulebase format of any other firewall that allows text-based rule entry.

The deployment of FACT in a production environment was simulated by gathering data

Figure 9. FACT output

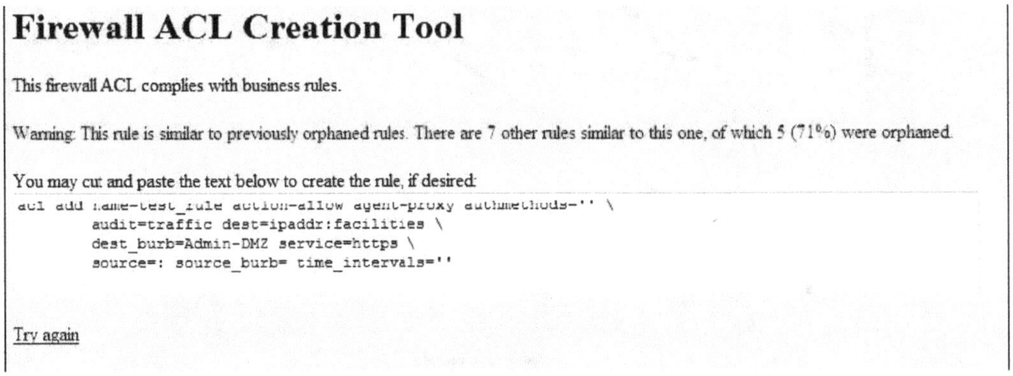

Firewall ACL Creation Tool

This firewall ACL complies with business rules.

Warning: This rule is similar to previously orphaned rules. There are 7 other rules similar to this one, of which 5 (71%) were orphaned.

You may cut and paste the text below to create the rule, if desired:

```
acl add name=test_rule action=allow agent=proxy authmethods='' \
        audit=traffic dest=ipaddr:facilities \
        dest_burb=Admin-DMZ service=https \
        source=: source_burb= time_intervals=''
```

Try again

on the next 50 rules created on the same firewall studied in the previous section. FACT identified 14 of those rules as being potentially orphaned rules and a manual follow-up analysis of those rules indicated that at least 10 contained errors in their specifications that likely would have resulted in those rules becoming orphaned in the future. While 14 out of 50 was a significantly lower rate of orphaning than initially was found in the rulebase for this enterprise (50%), this reduction may be attributed to the attention called to orphaned rules due to publicity created within the organization after the training period (but prior to the evaluation period) as a result of the study reported by Chapple et al. (2009).

FUTURE RESEARCH DIRECTIONS

This work provides the first careful analysis of the orphaned firewall rule problem and offers two tools for the proactive and reactive identification and elimination of these rules from firewall rulebases. There are many possibilities for future research based on this work. First, these techniques may prove useful in the proactive ordering of firewall rulebases, stemming from prior reactive work in this area by Al-Shaer and Hamed (2004). It may also be possible to extend the techniques used in FAST to identify promiscuous firewall rules that do not ever become orphaned but allow a much larger scope of traffic than necessary to meet business requirements. Other future research might involve the extension of static firewall analysis techniques to generate a template for penetration testing suitable for use in industry-standard probing tools, such as a Nessus Attack Scripting Language (NASL) template for use with the Nessus scanner. The security community would also benefit from the development of a "watchdog"' system for firewall rules that monitors suspect rules (i.e., those tagged by the decision tree model) for a period of time to identify whether they do indeed become orphaned and, optionally, then au-

tomatically disabling and/or removing them from the rulebase after a specified period of inactivity. Specific future research questions include:

- Can the techniques used to proactively identify potential orphaned rules be extended to the rulebase ordering problem?
- How can the FAST/FACT suite be extended to address the problem of promiscuous firewall rules? Could one derive how rules could be slightly decreased (promiscuous) or increased (orphaned) in scope to arrive at the correct rule?
- Would the generation of penetration testing templates based upon FAST/FACT results offer performance and/or security benefits over traditional penetration testing techniques?
- How can a "watchdog"' system be implemented that monitors suspect rules over time to provide administrators with additional information on the likelihood that a rule is orphaned?
- What trends and patterns of activity may be detected through the extension of the firewall management survey to a longitudinal deployment? To what extent are current problems slowing organizational reactions/solutions to those problems?
- How could one better align incentives for the enterprise to encourage security and balance the potential productivity losses from aggressive rule management versus the uncertain risk associated with stagnant rulebases?

CONCLUSION

The orphaned rule analysis techniques proposed in this work are of immediate value to enterprises of all sizes seeking to control the efficiency and effectiveness of their firewall rulebases. The elimination of orphaned rules and the prevention of new orphaned rule creation promises to limit unnecessary rulebase complexity, reduce the risk to enterprise security and make effective use of firewall administrator time.

The general framework described in this chapter including the notion of a firewall rule life cycle may be used as a basis for the management activities of system administrators, security analysts, and auditors. The use of this framework and the associated tools provides administrators with a practical, effective means to combat the types of pervasive errors uncovered in earlier work.

REFERENCES

Al-Shaer, E. S., & Hamed, H. H. (2004). Modeling and management of firewall policies. *IEEE Transactions on Network and Service Management, 1*(1), 2–10. doi:10.1109/TNSM.2004.4623689

AlgoSec, Inc. (2009). *FireFlow intelligent workflow for network security*. Retrieved on May 25, 2009, from http://www.algosec.com/en/products/fireflow key features.php

Bartal, Y., Mayer, A., Nissim, K., & Wool, A. (2004). Firmato: A novel firewall management toolkit. *ACM Transactions on Computer Systems, 22*(4), 381–420. doi:10.1145/1035582.1035583

Bounds, D. (2007). *Packet - network injection and capture*. Retrieved on September 18, 2007, from http://www.intrusense.com/software/packit/

Chapple, M. J., D'Arcy, J. M., & Striegel, A. (2009). An analysis of firewall rulebase (mis) management practices. *Journal of the Information Systems Security Association, 7*, 12–18.

Eronen, P., & Zitting, J. (2001). An expert system for analyzing firewall rules. In *Proceedings of the 6th Nordic Workshop on Secure IT Systems*, (pp. 100-107). Copenhagen, Denmark: Technical University of Denmark.

Gaspary, L. P., Melchiors, C., Locatelli, F. E., & Dillenburg, F. (2004). Identification of intrustion scenarios through classification, characterization and analysis of firewall events. In *LCN '04: Proceedings of the 29th Annual IEEE International Conference on Local Computer Networks* (pp. 327–334). Washington, DC: IEEE Computer Society.

Hamed, H., & Al-Shaer, E. (2006). On autonomic optimization of firewall policy organization. *Journal of High Speed Networks, 15*, 209–227.

ISO/IEC. (2005). *Information Technology - security techniques - code of practice for information security management*. Geneva, Switzerland: ISO/IEC.

Lawler, E. (1978). Sequencing jobs to minimize total weighted completion time subject to precedence constraints. *Annals of Discrete Mathematics, 2*, 75–90. doi:10.1016/S0167-5060(08)70323-6

Lyon, G. (1997). The art of port scanning. *Phrack Magazine, 7*(51). Retrieved on February 2, 2010, from http://www.phrack.com/issues.html?issue=51&id=11

Mayer, A., Wool, A., & Ziskind, E. (2000). Fang: A firewall analysis engine. In *SP '00: Proceedings of the 2000 IEEE Symposium on Security and Privacy* (p. 177). Washington, DC: IEEE Computer Society.

Mayer, A., Wool, A., & Ziskind, E. (2005). Offline firewall analysis. *International Journal of Information Security, 3*, 125–144.

Nathan, J. (2003). *Nemesis*. Retrieved on September 18, 2007, from http://nemesis.sourceforge.net/

Richardson, R. (2007). *12th annual computer crime and security survey*. Retrieved on September 18, 2007, from http://www.gocsi.com/forms/csi survey.jhtml

Sanfilippo, S. (2006). *Hping*. Retrived on September 18, 2007, from http://www.hping.org/

Schuba, C. L., & Spafford, E. H. (1997). A reference model for firewall technology. In *Proceedings of the Thirteenth Annual Computer Security Applications Conference*, (pp 133–145). San Diego, CA: IEEE.

University of Waikato. (2005). *Waikato environment for data analysis* v3.5.3. Retrieved on October 8, 2006, from http://www.cs.waikato.ac.nz /ml/ weka/

Verbowski, C. (2006). System administration: Drowning in management complexity. In *LISA 2006: Proceedings of the 20th Large Installation System Administration Conference*. Washington, DC: USENIX. Retrieved on February 2, 2010, from http://www.usenix.org/media/events/lisa06/tech/mp3/ verbowski_mgt_complexity.mp3

ADDITIONAL READING

Anderson, J. P. (1980). *Computer security threat monitoring and surveillance. Technical report.* National Institute of Standards and Technology.

Bandel, D. A. (2001). Taming the wild netfilter. *Linux Journal, 89*, 2.

Barford, P., Kline, J., Plonka, D., & Ron, A. (2002). A signal analysis of network trafficanomalies. In *IMW '02: Proceedings of the 2nd ACM SIGCOMM Workshop on Internet Measurment*, (pp. 71–82), New York, NY: ACM Press.

Bartal, Y., Mayer, A., Nissim, K., & Wool, A. (2004). Firmato: A novel firewall management toolkit. *ACM Transactions on Computer Systems, 22*(4), 381–420. doi:10.1145/1035582.1035583

Bellovin, S. M. (1999). Distributed firewalls. Retrieved on February 2, 2010 from http://www1.cs.columbia.edu /~smb/ papers/ distfw.pdf.

Bishop, M. A. (2003). *The Art and Science of Computer Security.* Boston, MA: Addison-Wesley.

Brackney, R. C., & Anderson, R. H. (2004). Understanding the insider threat. In *Proceedings of a March 2004 Workshop*, (pp. 1–137), Santa Monica, CA: RAND National Security Research Division.

Cabrera, J. B. D., Ravichandran, B., & Mehra, R. K. (2000). Statistical traffic modeling for network intrusion detection. In *Proceedings of the 8th International Symposium on Modeling, Analysis and Simulation of Computer and Telecommunication Systems*, (pp. 466–473), Washington, DC: IEEE Computer Society.

Chapple, M. J., Chawla, N., & Striegel, A. (2007). Authentication anomaly detection: A case study on a virtual private network. In *Proceedings of the ACM Workshop on Mining Network Data (MINENET 2007)*, (pp. 494-501). San Diego, CA: ACM Press.

Chapple, M. J., Wright, T. E., & Winding, R. M. (2006). Flow anomaly detection in firewalled networks. In *WENS 2006: Proceedings of the 2006 Workshop on Enterprise Network Security*, (pp. 120-132), Baltimore, MD: IEEE Computer Society.

Cheswick, W. R., Bellovin, S. M., & Rubin, A. D. (2003). *Firewalls and Internet Security, Repelling the Wily Hacker.* Boston, MA: Pearson Education.

Epstein, J., Thomas, L., & Monteith, E. (2000). Using operating system wrappers to increase the resiliency of commercial firewalls. In *ACSAC '00: Proceedings of the 16th Annual Computer Security Applications Conference*, (p. 236), Washington, DC: IEEE Computer Society.

Gaspary, L., Melchiors, C., Locatelli, F., & Dillenburg, F. (2004). Identification of intrusion scenarios through classification, characterization and analysis of firewall events. In *Proceedings of the IEEE Conference on Local Computer Networks*, (pp 327-344). Tampa, FL: IEEE Computer Society.

Hamed, H., & Al-Shaer, E. (2006). On autonomic optimization of firewall policy organization. *Journal of High Speed Networks, 15*, 209–227.

Hartmeier, D. (2002). Design and performance of the openbsd stateful packet filter (pf). In *Proceedings of the FREENIX Track: 2002 USENIX Annual Technical Conference*, (pp. 171–180), Berkeley, CA: USENIX Association.

Ioannidis, S., Keromytis, A. D., Bellovin, S. M., & Smith, J. M. (2000). Implementing a distributed firewall. In *CCS '00: Proceedings of the 7th ACM Conference on Computer and Communications Security*, (pp. 190–199), New York, NY: ACM Press.

Kim, M.-S., Kang, H.-J., Hong, S.-C., Chung, S.-H., & Hong, J. W. (2004). A flow-based method for abnormal network traffic detection. In *Proceedings of the IEEE/IFIP Network Operations and Management Symposium*, (pp. 599–612), Seoul, Korea: IEEE Computer Society.

Microsoft. (2004). *Understanding Windows Firewall*. Retrieved on May 21, 2007 from http://www.microsoft.com/.

Noonan, W. J., & Dubrawsky, I. (2006). *Firewall Fundamentals*. Indianapolis, IN: Cisco Press.

Secure Passage. (2009). *What Happens When Firewall Policies Become Too Complex?* Overland Park, KS: Secure Passage.

Tsudik, G., & Summers, R. (1990). AudES: An expert system for security auditing. In *Proceedings of the AAAI Conference on Innovative Application in Artificial Intelligence*, (pp 89-93), Washington, DC: AAAI.

Witten, H., & Frank, E. (2005). *Data Mining: Practical Machine Learning Tools and Techniques. Morgan Kaufmann Series in Data Management Systems* (2nd ed.). New York: Morgan Kaufmann.

Wool, A. (2004). A quantitative study of firewall configuration errors. *IEEE Computer*, *37*(6), 62–67.

KEY TERMS AND DEFINITIONS

Firewall: A network device that enforces network security policies, determining what packets may enter and/or leave the network.

Firewall Rule: A specific firewall policy statement that specifies the action that the firewall should take when it encounters traffic matching the source and destination addresses and port contained within the rule.

Firewall Rulebase: The collection of all rules enforced by a specific firewall.

Orphaned Rule: A firewall rule that exists in the firewall rulebase but is never exercised by traffic passing through the firewall.

Promiscuous Rule: A firewall rule that allows more access than necessary to meet the stated business requirements.

Redundant Rule: A firewall rule that results when one rule duplicates all or a portion of the access permitted or denied by an existing rule.

Shadowed Rule: A firewall rule that results when the incorrect ordering of rules in a firewall rulebase completely prevents the execution of one or more firewall rules.

ENDNOTE

[1] Rules incorporating source port would fall into that category.

Chapter 14

Integration of COBIT, Balanced Scorecard and SSE–CMM as an Organizational & Strategic Information Security Management (ISM) Framework

James E. Goldman
Purdue University, USA

Suchit Ahuja
Purdue University, USA

ABSTRACT

The purpose of this chapter is to present an integrated framework that addresses the need for organizational information security requirements as well as alignment between business, IT and information security strategies. This is achieved via the integrated use of control objectives for Information Technology (COBIT) and balanced scorecard (BSC) frameworks, in conjunction with Systems Security Engineering Capability Maturity Model (SSE-CMM) as a tool for performance measurement and evaluation, in order to ensure the adoption of a continuous improvement approach for successful sustainability. This integrated framework has been presented at the IEEE Symposium on Security & Privacy (2009) and the International Conference on Business/IT Alignment (2009). The goal is to investigate the strengths, implementation techniques, and potential benefits of such an integrated approach. The integrated use of COBIT, BSC, and SSE-CMM can provide a more comprehensive mechanism for strategic information security management–one that is fully aligned with business, IT, and information security strategies.

INTRODUCTION

Threats security of information assets and privacy of individuals have been growing at a tremendous rate. It is reported that more than 250 million records containing sensitive personal information were involved in security breaches in the U.S. since January 2005 (Privacy Rights Clearinghouse, 2009). In order to proactively deal with such growing threats to security and privacy of information-based assets, organizations are increasingly adopting information security man-

DOI: 10.4018/978-1-60960-573-5.ch014

agement systems (ISMS). Although organizations use several established international standards and frameworks like ISO27001, ISO 27799, ISO 27002, NIST, FIPS, ANSI, etc. for information security controls and management, the primary driving factor for such implementations are regulatory compliance requirements (Turner, Oltsik & McKnight, 2008). In order to be compliant with requirements of applicable industry regulations like Health Insurance Portability and Accountability Act (HIPAA), Sarbanes-Oxley (SOX), Gramm Leach Bliley Act (GLBA), Children's Online Privacy Protection Act (COPPA), Family Educational Rights and Privacy Act (FERPA), etc., organizations adopt ISMS and frameworks. The IT organization also adopts best practices and supporting tools like IT Infrastructure Library (ITIL), Control Objectives for Information Technology (COBIT), Capability Maturity Model Integration (CMMI), Six Sigma, etc. for IT service, support, quality management and information security management.

A standalone framework mostly addresses only a single functional area within the organization. Therefore, organizations often use a combination of frameworks to address the challenges of business, IT and operational information security. Nevertheless, integration of these frameworks and tools is not easy for organizations, as successful implementation is dependent on factors ranging from organizational culture to training of employees (Elci, Ors & Preneel, 2008). In the same way, organizations can gain additional value and benefits by using a combination of standards and best practices for strategic ISM. This view is also supported by studies that demonstrate a combination of standards such as ISO 17799 and SSE-CMM for metrics based security assessment (Goldman & Christie, 2004) and other studies that illustrate the mapping of processes for effective integration of COBIT and SEI-CMM (IT Governance Institute, 2007a). Several other studies also show that using a combination of standards and

best practices can lead to effective management and alignment of IT with business.

Taking into account the above discussion, the goal of this chapter is to present an integrated framework that addresses the need for organizational information security requirements as well as alignment between business, IT and information security strategies. This is achieved via the integrated use of Control Objectives for Information Technology (COBIT) and Balanced Scorecard (BSC) frameworks, in conjunction with Systems Security Engineering Capability Maturity Model (SSE-CMM) as a tool for performance measurement and evaluation, in order to ensure the adoption of a continuous improvement approach for successful sustainability. The purpose is to investigate the strengths, implementation techniques, and potential benefits of such an integrated approach, while simultaneously aligning business, IT and information security strategies.

PROBLEM & SIGNIFICANCE

Lack of a Comprehensive Approach to Information Security

Organizations are increasingly using ISM frameworks in order to mitigate risks and reduce threats to business assets (mainly information assets). A purely technical approach to implementation of information security controls proves insufficient in addressing the strategic objectives of the organization. According to the results of a Global Information Security Survey (Ernst & Young, 2008), the primary drivers for investment and implementation of such ISM frameworks are regulatory compliance requirements, loss of revenue, loss of stakeholder confidence, loss to brand and reputation, etc. Thus, investments made by the organization (for technology alone) often provide low or inadequate returns, resulting in revenue losses and higher operational expenditures. It also establishes the fact that there is a gap between the information security controls and the overall business and IT strategy of the organization. Hence, a more comprehensive approach to ISM is being recommended by several IT security and governance organizations.

Since the implementation of ISM frameworks is more reactive than proactive, the tendency is to focus on implementation of technical controls to prevent security and privacy breaches. As a result, the strategic significance of the ISM framework is either never realized fully or the true potential to transform the business by using the ISM framework strategically, is ignored. This leads to the deployment of ISM processes and procedures that are not aligned with the business objectives of the organization. E&Y's survey results show that only 18% of the organizations surveyed had information security strategy as an integrated part of their overall business strategy (Ernst & Young, 2008). The results of this survey clearly imply that alignment between business, IT and information security strategies is still not being taken into consideration while deploying ISM processes.

Lack of Alignment in IT-Business-Information Security Strategies

A well-aligned approach will not only help mitigate risks and apply technical controls, but also potentially provide benefits to the business. Interestingly, a small number of organizations have started realizing the value of investing in well-aligned business, IT and information security strategies, thereby boosting investment in governance, risk and compliance management. According to AMR Research (2008), governance, risk management, and compliance (GRC) spending exceeded $32B for 2008, up 7.4% from 2007, as companies shift towards identifying, assessing, and managing risk across numerous business and IT areas. According to a survey conducted by Society for Information Management (2008), a lack of alignment of business, IT, and information security translates into lower revenues for companies. The fact stated

above is further validated by an IT Governance Global Status Report (IT Governance Institute, 2008) indicating that between 2005 and 2008 the number of organizations reporting disconnect between IT strategy and business strategy increased by almost 30%.

Another important reason for the low success rate of ISM programs across various organizations is the lack of corporate governance and ownership of information security issues. Information security management must be considered as part of the business and it is imperative to assign responsibility for managing information security to board level, as business information is a valuable and critical corporate asset. In order to mitigate risks caused by inadequate corporate governance with respect to information security management, a holistic and comprehensive framework for information security management must be developed such that it not only addresses technical aspects of security but also takes into account business alignment, IT governance, and measurement and evaluation (Von Solms, 2001).

THE NEED FOR A STRATEGIC ISM FRAMEWORK

Considering the above discussion, any strategic ISM framework must address not only information security processes and controls, but also the alignment of such processes and controls with an organization's overall business and IT strategies. Furthermore, it is imperative to take into consideration the aspects of governance, risk and compliance to build a truly comprehensive framework.

Components of the Proposed Framework

The main components of such an organizational ISM framework consist of:

1. *Information Security Process Management and Control System.* COBIT is an international open standard that defines requirements for the control and security of sensitive data and provides a reference framework (IT Governance Institute, 2007b). COBIT consists of process domains and detailed process controls that can be applied to the ISM functions within an organization. COBIT positions itself as 'the tool for information technology governance' and it is therefore not exclusive to information security (Von Solms, 2005). It also embeds Information Security governance within a wider Information Technology governance framework, which is beneficial because it provides an integrated platform (architecture/ structure) for wider Information Technology governance. Thus, COBIT can be used to satisfy the requirement of a management and control system for ISM. According to PriceWaterhouseCoopers (2006), between 2003 and 2006, the awareness of COBIT has tripled amongst the general IT population, while awareness in the general population of the existence of COBIT has increased by 50 percent.

2. *Business/IT/Information Security Alignment Mechanism.* The existence of a management and control framework for ISM does not necessarily guarantee that the ISM practices are aligned with business and IT strategy. Hence, a mechanism that aligns business, IT and information security strategies is extremely crucial for the successful implementation of a comprehensive ISM framework. An ISM framework that provides robust security and controls but does not fit the organizational objectives would fail to achieve its full purpose and may prove to be detrimental to business functions. In order to prevent this, it is important to use an alignment mechanism. The balanced scorecard (BSC) is a strategic planning and management system that is used

extensively in business and industry, government, and nonprofit organizations worldwide to align business activities to the vision and strategy of the organization, improve internal and external communications, and monitor organization performance against strategic goals (Balanced Scorecard Institute [BSCI], 2009). The usefulness of the BSC has made it arguably the most successful and widely accepted mechanism that organizations adopt in order to achieve strategic alignment. The total usage of BSC has doubled between 1993 and 2006 with about 57% of global companies working with the BSC in one or more functions (Rigby, 2009). The use of a cascading BSC approach can lead to the effective communication of the key drivers of success to every business unit and employee within an organization, while also providing an opportunity for contribution to the overall success of an organization (Niven, 2006). Therefore, it is imperative to use a BSC approach in conjunction with COBIT, in order to align information security processes and controls with the broader business strategy while simultaneously ensuring the development of a strategic ISM framework.

3. *Measurement and Performance Evaluation Mechanism.* The implementation of a strategic framework for ISM would be incomplete if its success cannot be quantitatively measured. In order to achieve this, a standardized performance management and evaluation mechanism is required. COBIT provides a stand-alone maturity model for each of its domains, but it cannot be used as a comprehensive measurement tool (Simonsson, Johnson, & Wijkström, 2007). The SSE-CMM model describes the essential characteristics of an organization's security engineering process that must exist to ensure good security engineering (SSE-CMM. org, 2009). SSE-CMM is an internationally recognized and widely accepted model for

measurement and evaluation of the maturity of security processes and controls across the organization. The use of SSE-CMM can help the organization develop a continuous improvement approach to ISM and achieve higher levels of competence and capability as related to ISM processes and procedures. Table 1 provides a description of SSE-CMM levels.

The integration of COBIT, Balanced Scorecard and SSE-CMM, can potentially lead to the development of a strategically aligned ISM framework. In order to fulfill the requirements for such a comprehensive framework, organizations are increasingly using an integrated approach of more than one tool or mechanism. The IT Governance Global Status Report (IT Governance Institute, 2008) shows a large number of organizations use an internally developed framework to address their ISM requirements. Such internally developed frameworks usually consist of more than one recognized tool or mechanism.

BACKGROUND & EXISTING RESEARCH

Purpose of COBIT: IT Governance or Security Controls?

COBIT is a flexible framework that runs across several domains within an organization. The purpose of implementing COBIT framework can be interpreted in several different ways due to its broad scale and flexibility. Hence, there have been differing opinions about the derived benefits of a COBIT implementation, ranging from improved IT governance to efficient IT support. The exact purpose of COBIT can vary depending on organizational requirements and the derived benefits depend on the quality of deployment of processes.

By definition, COBIT is an IT governance framework and supporting toolset that allows

managers to bridge the gap between control requirements, technical issues and business risks (IT Governance Institute, 2007b). According to the IT Governance Institute (2007a), COBIT enables clear policy development and good practice for IT control throughout organizations. COBIT emphasizes regulatory compliance, helps organizations in increasing the value attained from IT, and enables business/IT alignment (Ridley, Young, & Carroll, 2004; Larsen, Pedersen, & Andersen, 2006; Debraceny, 2006). However, this perspective does not provide details about how COBIT can support a business-IT-security alignment strategy or how IT security controls can be implemented.

Interestingly, the definition of IT Governance itself is not very strict and is open to interpretation by the organization. IT Governance is defined by Massachusetts Institute of Technology's (MIT) Sloan School of Management - Center for Information Systems Research (CISR) as the decision

Table 1. SSE-CMM levels

Maturity Level	LEVEL	Description
Level 1	1.1	Base Practices are Performed
Level 2	2.1	Planning Performance
	2.2	Disciplined Performance
	2.3	Verifying Performance
	2.4	Tracking Performance
Level 3	3.1	Defining a Standard Process
	3.2	Perform the Defined Process
	3.3	Coordinate the Process
Level 4	4.1	Establishing Measurable Quality Goals
	4.2	Objectively Managing Performance
Level 5	5.1	Improving Organizational Capability
	5.2	Improving Process Effectiveness

making rights and the framework of responsibilities to promote desirable behavior in the use of IT (Weill & Ross, 2004). Thus by default, due to its popularity as a governance tool, COBIT is often categorized as a tool that can only be used for management purposes. This categorization of COBIT focuses only on management aspects (like decision-making) and ignores the process-level controls that the COBIT framework is built on. Nevertheless, COBIT was developed to "bridge the gap" between currently existing business-control models and IT-control models (Curtis & Wu, 2000). Contrarily, this purpose has mostly been overshadowed by the more popular opinion that COBIT is purely a management tool used to ensure effective IT finance and governance by senior management (IT Governance Institute, 2007).

Implementing COBIT domains and the sub-processes within each domain is difficult due to the lack of defined "ownership" of the organizational processes. This is a problem of mapping corporate governance to IT governance and even if COBIT does not prescribe "process ownership", such a problem may point to lack of alignment between organizational and governance objectives (Remenyi, 2005). Additionally, COBIT lacks the tactical direction that some organizations need in strategic ISM areas (Schlarman, 2007). There are instances of using COBIT as an alignment tool but the alignment starts only at the prescribed COBIT process levels instead of using an alignment methodology that has been cascaded from the organizational-level mission to the information security controls (Haes & Grembergen, 2005). Hence, the obtained solution remains incomplete in terms of business-IT-security alignment.

Strengths of COBIT

COBIT originated from an attempt to improve auditing and this makes it a perfect frame of reference for the internal control of IT, guaranteeing performance measurement, value creation and risk management (Rouyet-Ruiz, 2008). As an advantage, these fields are inherently defined in process orientation and in the structured metrics system that measures those processes. COBIT has become a de-facto standard especially in financial organizations (Robinson, 2005) thereby making it universally applicable. It is a comprehensive, independent, evolving, large body of knowledge and educational support. It has a common language and maturity model (when used in combination with CMM) for IT process improvement (Lainhart 2000; ITGI 2007). There are many examples of using COBIT in conjunction with SEI-CMM in order to measure the maturity of processes within an organization (ITGI, 2007; Mallette, 2005). It is detailed in its description of process-level controls. COBIT has important business value, including increased compliance, corporate risk reduction, good accountability, and proves to be a useful tool to establish a baseline for process maturity (Haes & Grembergen, 2005).

Weaknesses of COBIT (from an ISM Perspective)

Although IT governance is considered to be an enabler for business/IT alignment, COBIT lacks in the establishment of responsibilities and a methodological alignment with business strategy – especially when COBIT processes are used for enabling information security strategy management (Rouyet-Ruiz, 2008; Ernest 2007). This is by far the most significant gap that needs to be plugged by using another framework; otherwise the purpose of using COBIT would be defeated if the recommended controls and processes are not aligned with the business strategy. The following weaknesses are further observed by Simonsson, Johnson & Wijkström (2007):

- *COBIT contains all the processes, activities, documents, etc. needed to represent all IT Governance concerns. Nonetheless, some incongruence exists within COBIT like control objectives not being effectively* mapped to process areas and not aligned with business requirements.

- *COBIT provides a vast amount of metrics that can be used to assess the maturity of IT governance. Each COBIT domain specifies its own maturity measurement model, based on process areas within that domain. These maturity levels are not arranged in a way such that the aggregation from separate domain-level metrics can be aggregated into a comprehensive maturity level for the organization or business unit.*
- *COBIT does not aid efficient data collection and it does not provide guidelines or options for partial implementation. Analysis and data collection are not clearly separated and must both be carried out by experienced analysts.*
- *The analysis of a COBIT implementation is difficult to achieve and cannot be automated. The result of a COBIT supported IT governance maturity assessment might vary from one time to another depending on several factors like the time when an analysis was conducted, the person who conducts the analysis, the processes that are being analyzed, etc.*
- *COBIT uses a maturity model that is mainly a stand-alone analysis tool that provides only a very shallow analysis. Due to this constraint, it takes an experienced analyst to conduct a credible maturity assessment of an IT organization by the use of COBIT.*

COBIT is not fully prescriptive in its methodology in order to match the control objectives with specific technology-level controls (Ritchie, 2004). It is a very broad framework for implementation of organizational processes. The CPA Journal (Curtis & Wu, 2000) states that as COBIT controls are exercised at the domain and process level, it is often difficult to adapt to specific areas within an organization and is therefore resisted in terms of implementation. The downside of us-

ing COBIT for Information Security governance is that it is not always very detailed in terms of 'how' controls can be implemented (Von Solms, 2005; Lainhart, 2000).

Purpose of Balanced Scorecard (BSC)

Balanced Scorecard (Kaplan & Norton, 1996) by definition is a performance management system that enables businesses, business units and functional business areas to drive strategies based on goal definitions, measurement and follow-up (Grembergen & Haes, 2005). The balanced scorecard usually consists of four specific domains:

- The business contribution perspective capturing the business value created from various investments (in the context of this research, security investments will also be considered)
- The user perspective representing the user evaluation
- The operational excellence perspective evaluating the IT processes employed to develop and deliver applications
- The future perspective representing the human and technology resources needed by information security to deliver its services over time

The perspectives within BSC can be tweaked to fit the information security strategy, thereby making it a useful and flexible tool. In order to achieve business-IT-information security alignment (Microsoft, 2007), it is important to use the cascading BSC approach. According to the Balanced Scorecard Institute (2009), "cascading a balanced scorecard means to translate the corporate-wide scorecard (referred to as Tier 1) down to first business units, support units or departments (Tier 2) and then teams or individuals (Tier 3). The result should be to focus across all levels of the organization that is consistent. The organization alignment should be clearly visible through strategy, using the strategy map, performance measures and targets, and initiatives. Scorecards are used to improve accountability through objective and performance measure ownership, and desired employee behaviors are incentivized with recognition and rewards."

In recent times, BSC has gone through an evolution and there has been extensive research to fine-tune the original BSC approach and implement it (Cobbold and Lawrie, 2002). This process can help achieve a better fit for the organization and provide a customized scorecard that can produce improved results. The cascading balanced scorecard approach (between business and IT) can be successfully used as a strategic management tool (Kaplan, 1996; Kaplan, 2005; Martinsons, 1999).

Weaknesses of Balanced Scorecard (from an ISM Perspective)

The BSC approach to effective strategic management is often seen as subjective and difficult to implement. The use of BSC can cause disagreement and tension between top and middle management regarding the appropriateness of specific aspects of the BSC as a communication, control and evaluation mechanism (Malina & Selto, 2001). This is one of the most significant drawbacks of using BSC and in order to minimize risks that may arise, it is important to use a governance mechanism that sets the priority for evaluation parameters (as a guideline for executive management) within the context of the BSC approach. It can be hard to provide evidence of causal relations between effective management control, motivation, strategic alignment and beneficial effects of the BSC. Ineffective communication and management control cause poor motivation and conflict over the use of the BSC as an evaluation device (Ahn, 2001; Malina & Selto, 2001). There is disagreement about how the balanced scorecard can link strategy to operational metrics that managers can understand and influence (Nor-

reklit, 2000). Considering an ISM perspective in context of this research study, it is also difficult to establish traceability from the business-level down to the information security-level without using a governance framework to steer information criticality and set appropriate priority, which can in turn influence the information security strategy.

The above discussion indicates that BSC is a multi-purpose tool that can be used as a performance management system (Rohm & Halbach, 2005), IT governance mechanism (Grembergen, 2000) and as a strategic alignment framework (Kaplan & Norton, 1996). BSC is a powerful framework for aligning business/IT strategy, but when it is used as a standalone mechanism for comprehensive alignment of business/IT/security strategies, its weaknesses and gaps are exposed. These weaknesses range from management conflicts due to lack of an ideal set of parameters for information security (that the BSC must operate on) to the lack of a reporting mechanism for low-level information security metrics.

Similarly, COBIT is highly effective when used as a standalone mechanism for IT governance (in comparison to BSC), but is lacking when assessed from a business/IT alignment perspective. To that end, if COBIT is used for business/IT/information security alignment purposes, the gaps in business/IT alignment must be plugged before the security control objectives that are prescribed by COBIT process areas can be implemented.

Importance of Systems Security Engineering Capability Maturity Model (SSE-CMM) within the Proposed Framework

It is difficult to measure security controls and security processes, both qualitatively and quantitatively (Wang & Wulf, 1997; Chapin & Akridge, 2005; Ozkan, Hackney & Bilgen, 2007). It is extremely crucial to measure the performance of processes that are deployed for information security management, in conjunction with security controls, in order to derive accurate results. Traditionally risk assessment, risk mitigation, and residual risk were used as mechanisms to balance security risks and requirements, considering business needs, budget, and other resources (Chapin & Akridge, 2005). Further, with the advent of globalization, business structures have become more complex, with outsourcing and off-shoring now acting as business drivers, thereby increasing global threats to information and information systems. In order to counter such a vast range of potential vulnerabilities and the enormous scale of threats, a strategic approach to measurement of the maturity of security processes and controls is required (AMR Research, 2008). SSE-CMM provides a model that is useful in assessment of the level of security maturity in an organization's systems, regardless of the methodology used to implement the systems, thereby making it "methodology neutral" (Goldman & Christie, 2004).

The success of such a security measurement and performance evaluation approach is significantly dependent upon tracking and reporting of accurate security metrics. The key to the strategic use of security metrics is to obtain measurements that have the following ideal characteristics (Chapin & Akridge, 2005):

- They should measure organizationally meaningful things
- They should be reproducible
- They should be objective and unbiased
- Over time, they should be able to measure some type of progression towards a goal

The accurate use of information security "process and control metrics" can lead to better return on investment (for security investments), while moving the organization towards a continuous improvement approach – thereby ensuring the sustainability of the security management practices. To that end, there is requirement of an ISM process maturity framework, which is applicable across the organization and is deployed from a strategic perspective. This requirement can be fulfilled by the SSE-CMM maturity model as it facilitates synergy between system life cycle phases, increases efficiency, reduces wastage, and results in more secure solutions with greater assurance and lower costs (Goldman & Christie, 2004).

Various frameworks for measuring security maturity like NIST CSEAT IT Security Maturity Model, Citigroup's Information Security Evaluation Model (CITI-ISEM), CERT/CSO Security Capability Assessment, etc. are widely used in areas like software engineering and information technology (Ozkan, Hackney & Bilgen, 2007). Nonetheless, each framework has its own advantages and disadvantages, although adoption is dependent on a set of organizational requirements. The internal maturity model within COBIT is narrow in scope and covers only individual COBIT domains. There is no provision for aggregation of metrics across domains in order to implement a comprehensive, organization-wide maturity model (Simonsson, Johnson & Wijkström, 2007). In contrast, SSE-CMM is a widely accepted security 'process reference' model that is used across various business units within an organization due to its "methodology neutral" approach.

The objective of the SSE-CMM is to advance security engineering as a defined, mature, and measurable discipline by leveraging the following key factors (SSE-CMM.org, 2009):

- The organization must be able to justify focused investments in security engineering tools, training, process definition, management practices, and improvements.
- Capability-based assurance or trustworthiness based on confidence in the maturity of an organization's security practices and processes
- Selection of appropriately qualified providers of security processes through differentiating by capability levels and associated programmatic risks

SSE-CMM applies a comprehensive engineering-based approach to security measurement (SSE-CMM.org, 2009). This provides good justification, in part, for its use in a diverse process area /domain specific environment such as the one being proposed.

Balancing the Strengths and Weaknesses of the Components

The above discussions show the strengths of the cascading balanced scorecard approach, for alignment between business-IT-information security strategies. On the other hand, the potential weaknesses (when used in a standalone approach) range from lack of information governance to conflicts in prioritization of implementation of objectives. Similarly, the strengths of COBIT that are highlighted include enabling IT governance (including information assets), comprehensive approach to process controls, and an audit-based approach to information security. The weaknesses of COBIT (when used as a standalone approach) are that the processes within each of COBIT's process domains are not aligned with the overall business strategy and this may lead to ineffectiveness in the application of information security controls (Rouyet-Ruiz, 2008; Ernest, 2007). This may prove to be a detrimental factor while conducting information security audits, as the results potentially may not be useful to the business.

The challenge is to formulate an integrated framework for ISM, using both cascading BSC and COBIT, to enable a comprehensive approach that is aligned with the strategic business focus of the organization. The ISM framework itself would not be able to provide meaningful audit-based performance evaluation reports to the business, solely based on the COBIT control objectives that are applied to information security processes. Therefore, in order to provide meaningful ISM process maturity reports to the business and to build a framework that enables a continuous

improvement approach, the use of SSE-CMM as a measurement and performance evaluation tool is required.

FORMULATION OF THE INTEGRATED FRAMEWORK (METHODOLOGY)

The proposed comprehensive framework is a conceptual integration of cascading BSC, COBIT, and SSE-CMM for strategic ISM within an organization. It is imperative to study where the gaps may exist and where synergy can be obtained during the integration process. Hence, the methodology used consists of the following steps:

1. Gap analysis of COBIT and BSC frameworks
2. Mitigation of gaps based on previous research and added value from current efforts
3. The formulation of the integrated framework

Gap Analysis of COBIT and BSC Frameworks

BSC and COBIT frameworks are displayed separately in Figure 1 and Figure 2 respectively, following a top-down approach starting from business information and going down to 'information security management' processes and controls. Figure 1 and Figure 2 depict the following two scenarios:

Scenario 1: The Standalone Use of Balanced Scorecard (BSC) in Order to Achieve Alignment between Business Strategy, IT Strategy, and ISM Strategy

The mission and vision of the business are the driving factors behind the BSC approach. The purpose of existence of the organization is determined by its mission and the value of the services it aims to provide is detailed in the vision. A strategy document that is drafted and formulated by upper management ensures that the mission and vision are duly supported throughout the organization and sustained via organizational processes. This is a general strategy for the whole organization and may be fine-tuned by various business units and departments within the organization to fit their purpose. Department-level (e.g. IT) objectives can be formulated and every business unit can follow its own specific objectives in accordance with those listed in the broader organization-wide document. A cascading BSC approach may be used for aligning the business strategy to the IT strategy and for further alignment of IT strategy with information security strategy. The objectives of business BSC and IT BSC can be adopted in the information security BSC with appropriate

relevance. Information security BSC is closest to the operational level of the organization and metrics defined at the business-level can be applied via the information security BSC. Targets are benchmarks set by management (for each objective) and can be tweaked according to the business unit and organizational requirements. Initiatives are at the bottom of the BSC pyramid and represent "actions" that must be performed in order to achieve the strategy set by the upper layers.

Figure 1. BSC Gaps from an ISM perspective – standalone scenario – Scenario 1

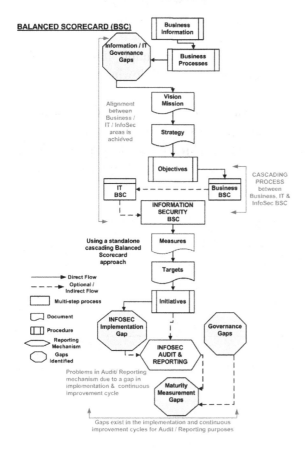

Figure 2. COBIT Gaps from an ISM perspective – standalone scenario – Scenario 2

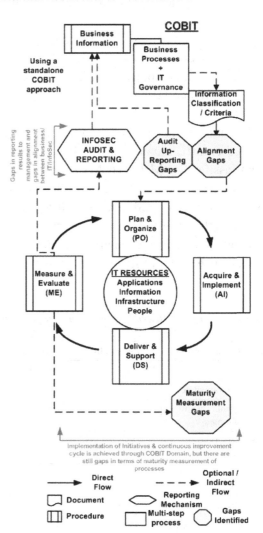

The following illustrations provide a detailed explanation of the gaps in a standalone BSC scenario:

1. **Information / IT Governance Gap**: This refers to the lack of a well-defined information classification mechanism within the organization. The lack of such a mechanism can lead to:
   - Risks in terms of information-asset ownership
   - Increased cost of information protection due to lack of a clear expenditure strategy on assets based on their value to the organization
   - Redundancy in information security processes
   - Complexities in mitigation of data loss
   - Non-compliance with regulatory requirements

For information security management purposes, the most commonly used tool is an Information Classification Matrix (ICM). A sample ICM is illustrated in Table 2. The criteria that are used for classification of information are listed across the top of the table and the various categories or domains of the information are listed in the first column on the left. The standard for classification

of information is to assign a rating of High (H), Medium (M), or Low (L) for each criterion within an information category. These should ideally be provided by an "information governance" committee or by using business drivers as a guideline. Once established, an ICM not only provides clear information classification but also can help with resolving any conflicts about information protection strategy, practices, and expenditures.

2. **Infosec Implementation Gap**: This gap results due to the termination of the balanced scorecard at the "initiatives" level. The implementation of processes and procedures that support or enable these initiatives are open to organizational interpretation. A sample illustration of Business-IT BSC (cascading) and their respective strategies is provided in Table 3 below. In order to maintain the length limitations of the chapter, only a single Strategy-Objective combination for each BSC is shown.

Table 3 provides a sample illustration of a Business BSC with the following features:

- **Business Strategy:** Strategic use of technology to achieve organizational goals
- **Business Objectives:** O1-Upgrade clinical technology, O2-Support core clinical func-

Table 2. Sample illustration of information classification matrix

Information Criteria	Confidentiality	Accuracy	Availability	Privacy	Compliance	Audit-ability
	H-M-L	H-M-L	H-M-L	H-M-L	H-M-L	H-M-L
Patient information	H	H	H	H	H	H
Intellectual Property (IP) information	H	H	M	H	H	H
Operational systems information	M	H	H	M	H	H
Research subject information	H	M	M	H	H	H
Business partnership information	H	H	M	M	H	M

tions, O3-Patient data management, O4-Universal accessibility

Table 4 provides a sample illustration of IT BSC with the following features:

- **IT Strategy:** Strategic use of technology to achieve organizational goals
- **IT Objectives:** O1-Leverage IT to improve clinical outcomes, O2-Develop clinical informatics practices, O3-Patient lifecycle automation, O4-Provide clinical and physician support

Interestingly, "Enterprise Single Sign-On" and "Remote Access" are generally part of core security function or security/service functions within an organization. Therefore, it is clear that the initiatives at the IT level only provide guidance in terms of implementation of technical controls and operational security initiatives still need to be addressed. While implementing such operational

and information security initiatives, it is imperative to consider changes in organizational factors such as policy, people, processes, procedures, and technology – as these tend to have a wider impact across the organization. In order to enable this, another level of cascading BSC must be added to the Business and IT (the solution will be called Infosec BSC).

Taking into account the other two gaps i.e. Governance gaps and Maturity Measurement gaps, it is important to mention that there is no inherent mechanism within the BSC framework that enables it to address these gaps independently. The questions to be asked within the context of the framework are the following:

i. Is the BSC framework alone enough to address all aspects of Governance? Even with the presence of a "Corporate/Business Governance Committee" and supporting processes, can IT and information security governance be guaranteed? For example:

Table 3. Sample illustration of business BSC

Initiative (I)	Measurement Details (M)	Target (T)	Initiatives (I)
S1-O1-M1-T1-I1 S1-O1-M2-T1-I1	% Automated clinical care tasks % Users of eHealth applications	70% 75%	Deployment of point-of-care devices Development of eHealth programs
S1-O2-M1-T1-I1 S1-O2-M2-T1-I1 S1-O2-M3-T1-I1	% increase in process automation % of technology enable requests % automated reporting / audit	50% 50% 75%	Implement process training programs and tools Deploy new Hospital Information System modules Deploy enterprise software for **audit and reporting**
S1-O3-M1-T1-I1 S1-O3-M2-T1-I1 S1-O3-M3-T1-I1	% data availability # of transaction errors % electronic data mgmt.	99.5% < 10/wk 60%	Upgrade network and system infrastructure Improve information / data services Conversion into e-records
S1-O4-M1-T1-I1 S1-O4-M2-T1-I1 S1-O4-M3-T1-I1	% systems using single sign-on % universal applications % online user base	80% 65% 85%	**Enterprise single sign-on solution** Deploy **remote-access solutions** and web services Promote online scheduling, EMR, knowledge base

Table 4. Sample illustration of IT BSC

Initiative	Measurement Details	Target	Initiatives
S1-O1-M1-T1-I1 S1-O1-M2-T1-I1	% Physician CPOE # Physician Portal Usage (Knowledge)	70% 75%	CPOE Module integration with Hospital Info. Sys. Enable & Integrate Physician Portal online

Who owns which data assets within the domains of the ICM? Is a clear mapping between business level strategy and information security strategy available?

ii. In order to ensure sustainability, how can the success of information security and security management processes be measured? Is there a process maturity scale provided by the BSC framework? For example: Can the performance of security processes within the organization be tracked, measured, verified and standardized or is the operation purely ad-hoc?

However, these questions must be addressed because of the need to provide a *comprehensive* framework for strategic information security management.

Summarizing the above points, the following gaps and weaknesses in the BSC approach are observed:

1. The initiatives can be either a set of controls (applications, systems, etc.) or a set of processes. However, BSC does not fulfill all requirements for implementation of the set of initiatives as the critical aspect of "how" the initiatives must be implemented is missing.

2. The conversion of the overall initiatives into information security initiatives that are well-aligned with the business are performed by using the BSC approach. Nevertheless, additional tools or frameworks are required in order to ensure that a process lifecycle is established for the management of initiatives (either individually or as a set).

3. BSC traceability terminates at the "Initiatives" level without indicating the processes that need to be implemented.

4. Ad-Hoc BSC implementation can cause disagreement and tension between top and middle management regarding the appropriateness of specific aspects of BSC, as

a communication, control and evaluation mechanism.

5. Audit and Information Security reporting gaps that can lead to lack of information flow between upper management and implementation teams.

Scenario 2: The Standalone Use of COBIT for ISM

COBIT has always been projected as an IT governance framework, although it prescribes more than 200 process controls. According to the IT Governance Institute (ITGI, 2007), COBIT enables clear policy development and good practice for IT control throughout organizations. COBIT emphasizes regulatory compliance, helps organizations to increase the value attained from IT and enables alignment. COBIT is a comprehensive model for enterprise control of the IT environment / IT Governance and is divided into four domains:

1. Planning and Organization (PO)
2. Acquisition and Implementation (AI)
3. Delivery and Support (DS)
4. Monitor and Evaluate (ME)

Each of the above four domains consists of several detailed processes that recommend control objectives in order to create a mapping among the various areas within an organization. The information being processed in the four domains can be classified into the following criteria in order to provide a map for rating information criticality:

1. Effectiveness (EFT)
2. Efficiency (EF)
3. Confidentiality (CF)
4. Integrity (I)
5. Availability (A)
6. Compliance (C)
7. Reliability (R)

The following illustrations provide a detailed explanation of the gaps in a standalone COBIT scenario:

1. **Alignment gap between business strategy and COBIT process areas**: It is important to remember the context within which this gap exists. There is a lack of direct relationship between COBIT processes that enable the implementation of initiatives for realizing business level goals with respect to information security. Table 5 provides an illustration of such a scenario. Although the definition of goals, objectives and metrics is clear at the business and IT levels of the BSC (using Operational Excellence perspective); and the applicable processes areas of COBIT are known (Rouyet-Ruiz, Spauwen, & Aguilar, 2010) there is still a gap in terms of conversion of the IT-level initiatives into initiatives and metrics that can be directly applied to the information security entity of the organization.

2. **A gap in aggregation and consolidation of metrics**: COBIT 4.1 provides a large number of processes that can be used to track metrics required by the business and IT units. However, there is no methodology defined for aggregation of such metrics that are derived from COBIT process domains, business requirements, IT organization, and IT security organization. As seen in Figure 3, the performance of business, IT, and information security goals can be tracked by establishing metrics like Key Performance Indicators (KPIs). Nevertheless, at the COBIT domains level, each domain has its own metric system (and a corresponding maturity model as shown in Figure 3). Additionally, business KPIs, IT KPIs, and Infosec KPIs can constitute a varied and broad set of metrics. In order to provide a

Table 5. Sample illustration of gaps between cascading BSC and COBIT process areas

Business Balanced Scorecard – Operational Excellence Perspective		
Business Goals	**Objectives**	**Metrics**
Lower process costs	Direct cost savings from all processes including business, IT and IT security.	Reduce operational budget by $2M
High productivity of operational processes	Operational processes for business, IT and security are highly efficient and no resource wastage occurs	Ensure 100% availability and reliability
IT Balanced Scorecard – Operational Excellence Perspective		
IT Goals	**Objectives**	**Metrics**
Ensure seamless integration of applications into business processes. Ensure proper use and performance of the applications and technology solutions.	Process compliance Efficient IT infrastructure Optimize utilization of IT resources	Percent of development efforts spent maintaining existing IT systems Number of errors causing loss of production Percent of platforms not in line with defined IT architecture standards Reduced cost to produce/maintain user documentation, operation procedures and training materials
Translational into Security BSC? → This is where a gap exists		
Security Goals	**Security Objectives**	**Security Metrics**
X	X	X
Applicable COBIT Process Areas that support the implementation • PO2 – Define Information Architecture • AI2 – Acquire and maintain application software • AI3 – Acquire and maintain technology infrastructure • AI4 – Enable operation and use • DS3 – Manage performance and capacity • DS8 – Manage service desk and incidents • DS9 – Manage configuration • ME1 – Manage and evaluate IT performance		

unified metric system across the organization such that the metrics provide meaningful data about the performance of organization-wide processes, it is indeed necessary to create a mapping between them or to integrate them as required to realize business goals.

3. **A gap in terms of providing an "organiza-tion-wide" maturity model**: In the COBIT 4.1 framework, every domain consists of its own maturity model and scale. Although the maturity scale is consistent across the domains, every domain can have a different level of maturity as shown in Figure 4. In addition, it is important to also consider maturity of processes for information security management, IT governance, IT/business alignment and risk & compliance management. As a result, it is difficult to derive an "organization-wide" maturity model by simply considering the maturity of COBIT processes.

4. **Audit and information security report-ing gaps**: As shown in Figure 5, organizations often use performance dashboards to track the performance of key applications, processes and technology infrastructure.

With respect to information security management, the result of an audit is usually a major driver for reporting and performance improvements. Consequently, key metrics defined for information security processes and systems are tracked, reported and updated. While reporting "information security performance" independently from IT performance or operational performance, an incomplete assessment might be projected to upper management. This can result in ineffective or inefficient strategy in terms of COBIT process implementation and improvement. Therefore, such a gap must be and mitigated by trying to create a more comprehensive audit and reporting mechanism that includes inputs from information security, IT, and internal audit business units within the organization.

Summarizing the above, the following gaps have been observed in the COBIT framework:

1. Lack of alignment of process areas with business strategy.

Figure 3. Sample illustration of gap in "aggregation" of metrics in business, IT and Infosec

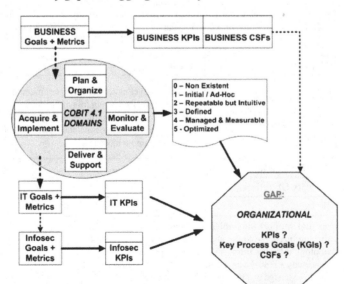

Figure 4. Sample illustration of gap in implementation of "organization-wide" maturity model

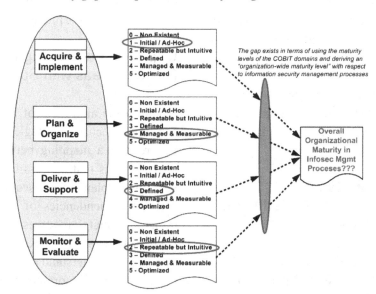

2. A maturity model that is mainly a standalone analysis tool that provides only a very shallow analysis of the situation.
3. COBIT provides a vast amount of metrics that can be used to assess the maturity of

IT governance. These are however not arranged in a way such that the aggregation from separate metrics into a comprehensive maturity level is supported.

Figure 5. Sample illustration of gap in Audit and Information Security reporting

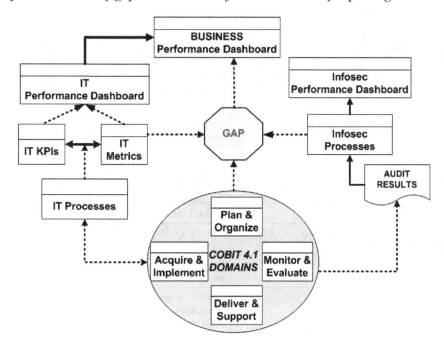

4. Audit and Information Security reporting gaps that can lead to lack of information flow between upper management and implementation teams.

Table 6 shown below is a summary of the identified gaps and lists some potential mitigation mechanisms that will be further elaborated in the next section.

Mitigation of Gaps Based on Previous Research and Added Value from Current Efforts

The mitigation of gaps that are derived from Figure 1 and Figure 2 (also listed in Table 6) can be conducted by either addressing each one separately

or by grouping them together (wherever synergies exist within the processes being considered):

Gap #1.1: Lack of Alignment of COBIT Process Areas with Business Strategy

A gap in the alignment of business, IT and information security strategies can be addressed by creating a mapping between those COBIT process areas that address the formulation of a strategic IT plan and a cascading BSC approach. The interdependencies of COBIT domains in terms of inputs-processes-outputs has already been established (ISACA, 2009a) and it is very important to understand that the processes within these domains support the rest of the framework, while maintaining the input-process-output paradigm. The aim is to demonstrate that a cascading

Table 6. Weaknesses in BSC & COBIT and potential mitigation solutions

#	Weaknesses / Risks / Gaps	Potential Mitigation Mechanism
1	**COBIT**	
1.1	Lack of alignment of COBIT process areas with business strategy	Use a cascading balanced scorecard approach to align business strategy with information security strategy that can be used as input to COBIT process areas
1.2	A vast amount of metrics that can be used to assess the maturity of IT governance processes. These are however not arranged in a way such that the aggregation from separate metrics into a comprehensive maturity level is supported	Use metrics from cascading BSC and Key Performance Indicators (KPI), Key Goal Indicators (KGI) and Critical Success Factors (CSF) to aggregate the metrics towards a comprehensive maturity level; using maturity levels prescribed by SSE-CMM as a guideline
1.3	A maturity model that is mainly a stand-alone analysis tool that provides only a very shallow analysis of the organizational situation	Use SSE-CMM mapping to COBIT areas. There are previous examples of SEI-CMM to COBIT mapping. Using a similar approach, a maturity model can be developed
1.4	Audit and Information Security reporting gaps	Using a cascading balanced scorecard approach would establish an information security reporting mechanism via KPIs, KGIs and CSFs while measuring maturity via SSE-CMM
2	**Balanced Scorecard**	
2.1	Can cause disagreement and tension between top and middle management regarding the appropriateness of specific aspects of the BSC as a communication, control and evaluation mechanism	The use of COBIT as a governance tool for business, IT and information security management strategies. The use of COBIT Information Classification / Criteria, with clear prioritization can mitigate risks arising from conflicts
2.2	Terminates at the "Initiatives" level without indicating what processes need to be implemented	Create a mapping between COBIT processes and BSC initiatives
2.3	Lack of traceability to information security level	Use of COBIT control processes over appropriate process areas that are related to information security management
2.4	Audit and Information Security reporting gaps	Using a cascading balanced scorecard approach would establish an information security reporting mechanism via KPIs, KGIs and CSFs while measuring maturity via SSE-CMM

BSC approach can enable implementation of the alignment processes. It is important to distinguish between the application of the COBIT and BSC frameworks, at the tactical and strategic organizational levels (Da Cruz & Labuschagne, 2006). BSC is generally used to determine the strategy of the organization in terms of its business, IT and ISM goals, while COBIT is used to implement the strategy tactically, using its "best practices" methodology. Therefore it is important to remember that the implementation of the alignment of business, IT and information security strategies, using these two frameworks (and their usage at respective levels in the organization) are not interchangeable – BSC is used at the strategic level while COBIT must be used at the tactical level as shown in Figure 6.

Initially, in order to ensure alignment of IT and Infosec BSC with COBIT processes and to establish traceability, a mapping must be created between organizational drivers (or goals) derived from business BSC, COBIT domain processes and objectives of IT/Infosec BSC. Table 7 provides a sample illustration of such a mapping.

Figure 6. Application of frameworks at different levels of the organization for security management

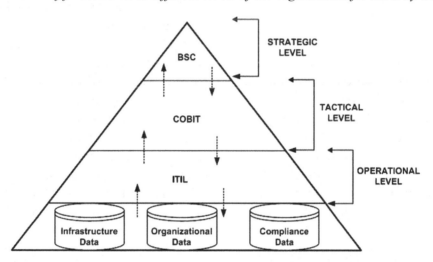

Table 7. Illustration of sample mapping between business goals, COBIT and IT/Infosec BSC

Organizational Drivers	IT + InfoSec BSC Mapping	COBIT Mapping {PO+AI+DS+ME}
1. Information System Activity Review	*Service Line Development* o CPOE Integration **(S1)** o EMR System	o Monitoring and Reporting o Problem Tracking and Audit Trail o Violations o Security Activity Reports
2. Security Awareness and Training	*Medical Education* o Online portal access (S2) o Educational Modules	o Security Reminders o Protection from Malicious Software o Log-in Monitoring o Password Management
3. Facility Access Controls	Operations (S3)	o Contingency Operations o Facility Security Plan o Access Control and Validation Procedures o Maintenance Records
4. Information Access Management	Technology components (S4)	o Identification, Authentication and Access Control o Security of Online Access to Data o User Account Management

In order to illustrate the points made above, consider the gaps shown via Table 3, Table 4 and Table 5. A balanced scorecard for information security can be used to mitigate the gaps. As a solution, Table 8 provides a sample illustration of Infosec BSC with the following features (only a single perspective of the BSC is shown due to length limitations):

- **Infosec Strategy:** Secure use of technology to ensure patient privacy
- **Infosec Objectives:** O1-Implement monitoring & reporting practices, O2-Enable problem tracking, O3-Track and measure violations

Thus, the installation of an IDS/IPS solution or expenses incurred via security training are traceable (up) to the business need of CPOE Integration and to the business driver of "Service Line Development", while at the same time mapping the involved processes to specific COBIT domains and process areas. To further expand in context of this framework, KPIs related to business, IT and information security processes and technologies can be extracted from the strategic BSC cascade.

B. Gap #1.2, 2.2: An Aggregation of Metrics is not Supported and Lack of Mapping between BSC and COBIT Processes

As shown by Grembergen & Haes (2005), these gaps can be mitigated using a mapping of the organizational Key Performance Indicators (KPIs) and Key Goal Indicators (KGIs) to the BSC initiatives and COBIT domain "Monitor & Evaluate". An example is shown in Figure 7. The approach can establish traceability between the metrics defined at the business level via the BSC approach and can tie them directly to organizational KPIs, KGIs as well as the metrics used in the COBIT processes. An important consideration at this stage is that COBIT is only a "best practices" or "control" framework for security processes. The concrete security metrics will come from the underlying physical security controls that must then be translated into meaningful organizational metrics in order to be useful to the business. This process can be facilitated via mitigation of gap #1.2 as well. In order to address gap #2.2, specific attention must be paid to COBIT domain "Measure & Evaluate" in order to implement the process correctly for

Table 8. Illustration of sample Infosec BSC

Objective	Objective Detail	Target ID	Measurement Details	Target
Strategy: **S1** Objective: O1 Secure CPOE Integration	Monitor & Report	S1-O1-M1-T1	% of security CPOE events generated per day vs. total CPOE events	< 10%
	Problem Tracking	S1-O2-M1-T1	% of reported security issues traced vs. unresolved	90%
	Violations	S1-O3-M1-T1	% of security violations detected per day	100%

Initiative	Measurement Details	Target	Initiatives
S1-O1-M1-T1-I1 *Objective: Secure CPOE Integration*	% of security CPOE events generated per day vs. total CPOE events	< 10%	Enhance CPOE security evaluation process Increasing physician awareness by providing additional training Increasing application awareness by providing additional training to configuration mgmt. teams
S1-O2-M1-T1-I1	% of reported security issues traced vs. unresolved	90%	Historical tracking tools, training for current staff, ticketing and reporting system
S1-O3-M1-T1-I1	% of security violations detected per day	100%	Installation of IDS / IPS

collection of the required security metrics that must be reported to management.

Gap #1.3, 1.4, 2.3, 2.4: Lack of a Comprehensive Maturity Model, Establishing Traceability in Information Security Processes and Bridging Audit Reporting Gaps

The combined use of methodology specified by Goldman and Christie (2004), Mallette (2005), IT Governance Institute (2007a), and IT Governance Institute (2008) can help mitigate these gaps. The basic idea is to create a mapping between COBIT domains and SSE-CMM process areas such that the organization can use this to streamline common functions and better understand the processes that need to be tracked and aligned in order to achieve an efficient ISM approach. Goldman & Christie

(2004) used SSE-CMM and ISO 17799 for metrics based evaluation, therefore the ten SSE-CMM Process Areas (PAs) can be re-used in this context, instead of considering the whole set (all PAs are displayed in Table 9). The other studies used SEI-CMM (which is primarily used to measure software development process maturity) to map to COBIT domains (Mallette, 2005). A potential solution would be to use this methodology and replace SEI-CMM PAs with SSE-CMM PAs.

Gap #2.1: Lack of a Clear Prioritization and Criticality of Information

The use of COBIT Information Criteria can result in effective classification of information, based on a clear set of criteria as defined by the organization, leading to lower risks and avoidance of conflicts between executive management (pertaining to

Figure 7. Information Security KPI & KGI mapping to business level

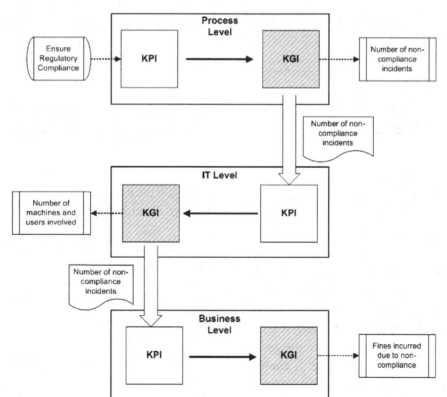

Table 9. SSE-CMM process areas

SSE-CMM (v. 3.0) Process Area	Description
PA 01	Administer Security Controls
PA 02	Assess Impact
PA 03	Assess Security Risk
PA 04	Assess Threat
PA 05	Assess Vulnerability
PA 06	Build Assurance Argument
PA 07	Coordinate Security
PA 08	Monitor Security Posture
PA 09	Provide Security Input
PA 10	Specify Security Needs
PA 11	Verify and Validate Security
PA 12	Ensure Quality
PA 13	Manage Configuration
PA 14	Manage Project Risk
PA 15	Monitor and Control Technical Effort
PA 16	Plan Technical Effort
PA 17	Define Organization's Systems Engineering Process
PA 18	Improve Organization's Systems Engineering Process
PA 19	Manage Product Line Evolution
PA 20	Manage Systems Engineering Support Environment
PA 21	Provide Ongoing Skills and Knowledge
PA 22	Coordinate with Suppliers

information criticality and prioritization). These criteria include Effectiveness (EFT), Efficiency (EF), Confidentiality (CF), Integrity (I), Availability (A), Compliance (C), and Reliability (R).

A comparison with other mechanisms for information governance and security, like the Information Criticality Matrix (ICM), which is part of the Infosec Assessment Methodology (IAM) developed by the National Security Agency (NSA), can provide some insight into the use of COBIT for information governance. It enables the prioritization of information (and informa-

tion assets) protection based on criteria set by the organization from a business perspective, and thus helps resolves any conflicts that may arise due to personal misinterpretation by executive management.

Formulation of the Proposed Integrated Framework

The true integration of COBIT, cascading BSC, and SSE-CMM can be shown with a comprehensive illustration of the mitigation of the gaps from the standalone frameworks. The gaps must not only be mitigated individually, but the mitigation must also help in enabling and facilitating integration of the three frameworks. Figure 8 below shows a high-level diagram of the integrated framework (i.e. COBIT, cascading BSC, and SSE-CMM) and in order to justify that the individual components of the comprehensive framework are functionally correct, further illustrations are provided in the next section. These illustrations would facilitate the implementation of the strategic ISM framework and ensure that the solution is universally understandable without being just restricted to technical staff or security experts.

JUSTIFICATION OF THE COMPONENTS (FINDINGS)

The following findings attempt to provide justification for the use of components and map them to the gaps identified and the mitigation mechanisms.

Information / IT Governance Gap (# 2.1)

The use of COBIT Information Criteria can result in effective classification of information, based on a clear set of criteria as defined by the organization, leading to lower risks and avoidance of conflicts between executive management (pertaining to information criticality and prioritization). These

Figure 8. The integrated framework showing the components and mitigation of gaps

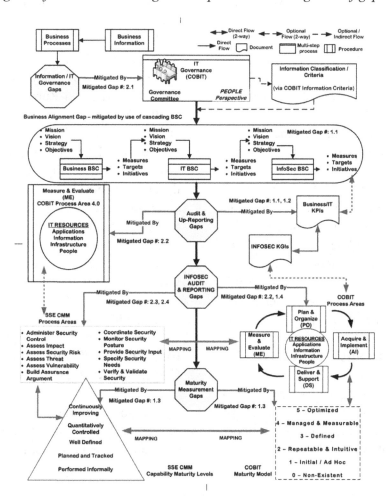

criteria include the following: Effectiveness (EFT), Efficiency (EF), Confidentiality (CF), Integrity (I), Availability (A), Compliance (C), and Reliability (R).

According to European University Information Systems (EUNIS), COBIT Information Criteria overlap largely with the audit criteria of Netherlands' Professional Association of Accountants NIVRA-53 (Mahnic & Zabkar, 2000), which provides standards for the auditor's statement relating to electronic data processing. Thus, using COBIT Information Criteria can help in the classification of information directly for audit purposes and establish ease of top-down traceability. The COBIT Information Criteria matrix is also similar

to the Information Criticality Matrix (ICM) that is part of the Infosec Assessment Methodology (IAM) developed by the National Security Agency (NSA). ICM enables the classification of information based on organizational requirements and is a widely accepted mechanism.

The ICM uses a standard C-I-A (Confidentiality-Integrity-Availability) model to classify information, while COBIT uses broader classification criteria, thereby providing flexibility to the organization, which can result in effective information governance. This concept can be mapped directly to the COBIT process area of "Plan & Organize", recommending that an organization must "Define the Information Architecture (PO2)" and consists of

- **PO2.1:** Enterprise Information Architecture Model
- **PO2.2:** Enterprise Data Dictionary and Data Syntax Rules
- **PO2.3:** Data Classification Scheme
- **PO2.4:** Integrity Management

To that end, using COBIT Information Criteria provides an appropriate platform for developing clear high-level priority for information protection as a guidance baseline for COBIT control processes. This enables alignment of business requirements directly with information security controls, while simplifying the implementation of information security tools and processes.

Business Alignment Gap (# 1.1)

The COBIT process area "Plan & Organize (PO1) requires the establishment of a strategic IT plan. Nevertheless, COBIT does not provide any tool or mechanism to enable the development or deploy-ment of a strategic IT plan. The use of a cascading BSC approach is required to address this gap (# 1.1) as shown in Figure 10 below. Such an approach for alignment of business and IT using COBIT as a tool and BSC as a platform has been recently established (Rouyet-Ruiz, Spauwen, & Aguila, 2010). The use of a cascading BSC establishes alignment between the business strategy (based on business processes and information), IT strategy and information security strategy, thereby enabling the extrapolation of a unified strategy across the organization from the executive management to the operational level. The cascading BSC approach usually consists of tiers, with each tier addressing the strategy, objectives, measurements, targets and initiatives at different business units within the organization (usually hierarchical – i.e. business, IT within business, and IT security within IT).

InfoSec Audit and Up-Reporting Gaps (# 1.2, 2.2)

In order to ensure traceability and conversion effectiveness between business and technical security goals and processes, SSE-CMM process areas

Figure 9. Information classification matrix & COBIT information criteria

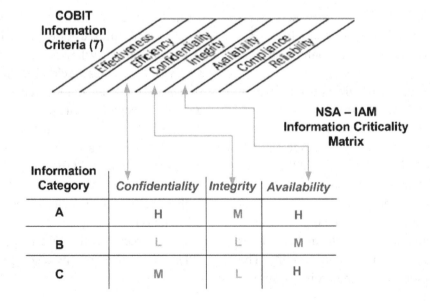

must be mapped to appropriate COBIT process controls. The resulting business metrics can be reported to upper management via the KPI/KGI cascade and the resulting information security metrics can be reported via the COBIT process area of "Measure and Evaluate (ME)". Figure 11 shows the metric reporting processes. The goal is to ensure continuous reporting of security metrics (to executive management) from both business and operational level security processes. In order to achieve this, it is important to establish traceability between the metrics that are established as part of the business, IT, and information security strategies. Metrics and targets established at the BSC level can be used a baseline for comparison. The Key Goal Indicators (KGIs) of the business and the initiatives from the cascading BSC must be synchronized. On the other hand, the process goals within COBIT must be clearly defined and mapped to the BSC initiatives. The KGIs and COBIT goals drive the Key Performance Indicators

(KPIs) of the information security BSC and the COBIT process area of "Measure & Evaluate" respectively. These in turn are used to measure the performance of the COBIT control processes that monitor the operational security controls. This type of a reporting mechanism supports the meaningful reporting of security audit data directly to the business level, thereby contributing towards enhancing the conversion effectiveness of operational security controls.

Following up on previous illustrations, an illustrative example for cascading KPIs is provided in Figure 12.

Maturity Measurement Gaps (# 1.3, 1.4, 2.3, 2.4)

The maturity levels defined in COBIT process areas are very generic. The definition and requirement to achieve a particular maturity level is dependent on organizational expectations and can

Figure 10. COBIT: Cascading BSC Mapping

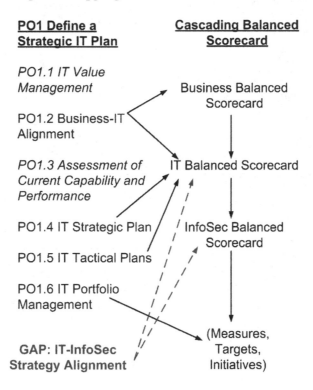

Figure 11. Cascading KPIs & KGIs for mitigation of Audit/Up-Reporting Gaps

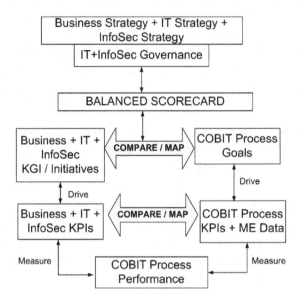

Figure 12. Sample illustration of cascading KPIs & KGIs

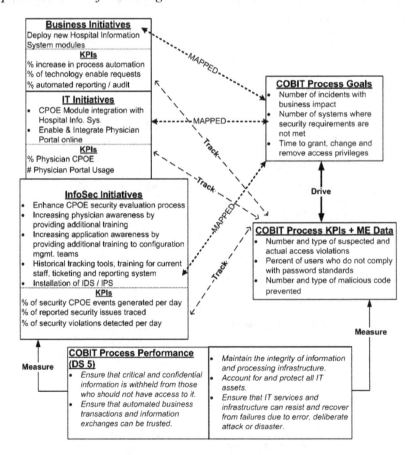

be easily misinterpreted. Therefore, a standardized mechanism to measure process-level maturity for information security is required. This can be achieved by using the maturity levels defined in SSE-CMM. With the purpose of achieving this, SSE-CMM maturity level definitions must be mapped to appropriate "COBIT process area" maturity levels, thereby providing a measureable and traceable mechanism to measure "information security process maturity". This will facilitate the establishment of a "continuous improvement" approach to information security. The fundamental idea is to create a mapping between COBIT domains and SSE-CMM process areas (PAs) such that the organization can use this to streamline the common functions and to align processes in order to achieve an efficient ISM approach. In this context, previous research has already established mapping between SEI-CMM (which is primarily used to measure software development "process maturity") and COBIT domains. A potential solution (for ISM purposes) is to use a similar methodology and replace SEI-CMM Process Areas with SSE-CMM Process Areas. A summary of the mapping structure is shown in Table 10. The SSE-CMM process areas (PA) and base practices (BP) are directly referenced from the SSE-CMM manual. The focus was on the "security" based COBIT domains and hence DS5-Ensure Systems Security was expanded, while only a high-level mapping of the other three domains is shown.

The points listed above justify the potential use of the mitigation mechanisms within the context of the integrated framework. The use of these components potentially ensures 'conversion effectiveness' between strategic business goals, adopted IT processes and the ISM initiatives in the organization.

RECOMMENDATIONS AND FUTURE RESEARCH

The proposed integrated framework consisting of COBIT, BSC and SSE-CMM for the purpose of strategic ISM is conceptual at this stage. Potential reasons for slow or resistant adoption of this framework consist of the following factors:

1. COBIT is a resource intensive framework that requires training and takes considerable time to implement and analyze. It would be difficult for an organization to integrate it within its existent ISM processes and align other frameworks solely to provide results for this research study. Hence, this study is not based on results from an implementation.
2. Although the ValIT (ISACA, 2009) framework is seen as more tightly integrated with COBIT, it was not considered for the purposes of this research due to its focus on information security from the perspective of investments, while the focus of this research is Business/IT/Information Security alignment. The extensive use of BSC in academic research and industry implementation provides quality literature and credibility. ValIT is a comparatively newer framework and does not possess a significantly large publication base.
3. Due to difficulty in standardization of KPIs and KGIs within an organizational unit and across different business units in the organization, collection of metrics is challenging.
4. Any new framework affects business processes and successful adoption is contingent on the support of executive management, user training and adoption, organizational culture and emphasis on a continuous improvement approach, business process maturity, etc.

Table 10. SSE-CMM and COBIT mapping

COBIT Processes	SSE-CMM Process Areas (PA) & Base Practices (BP) High Level Correlation	CMM Levels
Plan and Organize (PO)		
PO1 – PO 11	Managed by Business/IT Alignment	N/A
Acquire and Implement (AI)		
AI 1 – AI 6	Managed by organizational processes	N/A
Deliver and Support (DS)		
DS1 Define & Manage service levels	PA 01(BP: 1-4)	3 - 5
DS2 Manage third party services	PA 12 – PA 22	1 - 5
DS3 Manage performance & capacity	PA 12 – PA 22	1 - 5
DS4 Ensure continuous service	PA 12 – PA 22	3 - 5
DS5 Ensure systems security		
5.1 Mgmt. of IT Security	PA 01(1-4), PA 02(1-6), PA 03(1-6), PA 04(1-6), PA 05(1-5)	3 - 5
5.2 IT Security Plan	PA 06(1-5), PA 10(1-7)	1 - 3
5.3 Identity Mgmt.	PA 01 – PA 11	1 - 3
5.4 User Account Mgmt.	PA 01 – PA 11	1 - 3
5.5 Testing, surveillance, monitoring	PA 06(1-5), PA 08(1-7)	3 - 5
5.6 Security incident definition	PA 02 (1-6), PA 03(1-6)	3 - 5
5.7 Protection of security technology	PA 07(1-4), PA 08(1-7)	3 - 5
5.8 Cryptographic key mgmt.	PA 01 – PA 11	1 - 3
5.9 Prevention, detection & correction	PA 03(1-6), PA 07(1-4), PA 08(1-7)	3 - 5
5.10 Network Security	PA 01 – PA 11	1 - 3
DS6 Identify & allocate costs	PA 12 – PA 22	N/A
DS7 Educate & train users	PA 01(3), PA 09(5-6), PA 10(2)	3 - 5
DS8 Assist & advise customers	PA 10(1-7)	3 - 5
DS9 Manage configuration	PA 01(1-4), PA 07(1-4)	3 - 5
DS10 Manage incidents	PA 03(1-6), PA 07(1-4), PA 08(1-7)	3 - 5
DS11 Manage Data	PA 03(1-6), PA 07(1-4), PA 08(1-7)	3 - 5
DS12 Manage facilities	PA 12 – PA 22	N/A
DS13 Manage Operations	PA 12 – PA 22	N/A
Monitor and Evaluate (ME)		
ME1 Monitor & Evaluate IT performance	PA 11(1-5)	3 - 5
ME2 Assess internal control adequacy	PA 11(1-5), PA 8(1-7)	3 - 5
ME3 Ensure regulatory compliance	PA 10(2), PA 06(1-5), PA 11(1-5)	3 - 5
ME4 Provide IT Governance	PA 11(1-5), PA 03(1-6) + strategic alignment	4 - 5

Consequently, recommendations for future work related to this research include:

- Implementation of the proposed ISM framework within an organizational environment

- Reporting the performance of the information security processes prior to and post implementation

- Mapping of ValIT with this framework and mapping with ISO 38500 standard for IT Governance

- Assessing the ROI (return on investment) from the implementation of the framework
- Analyzing the effect of this framework on overall audit-based activities and reporting performance levels

Although it is important to provide a final justification in terms of cost and efficiency benefits to an organization, via adoption of this framework, it is also important to consider the complexities involved. Originally, COBIT itself is a vast framework and its adoption is dependent on organizational process maturity. Additionally, every organization uses different business drivers and goals for its IT and information security implementations. Thus, it is very difficult to provide one complete objective solution. The framework attempts to provide guidance in terms of achieving business value via use of information security management as a strategic asset, instead of the traditional perception of a supporting mechanism for IT.

CONCLUSION

In order to develop a comprehensive "strategic information security management" framework, it is critical to consider the alignment of the business, IT and information security strategies. It is also important to consider that the development of such a framework must take into account organizational entities such as applications, information, infrastructure and people. The success of the information security framework is dependent on the establishment of traceability between policy, process, people, procedures and technology.

The strategic ISM framework proposed in this study may find direct applicability in the governance, risk and compliance or GRC domain of business. COBIT is becoming a de facto standard control model and covers several organizational areas like responsibility, evaluation, acquisition, conformance, strategy, etc. These areas are directly related to ISO 38500, which is a standard model for IT Governance. Thus, the applicability of the strategic framework is broader than just security management.

The success of the strategic ISM framework is measured in terms of conversion effectiveness of the business goals into IT goals and IT goals into information security goals, thereby proving that the strategies are aligned and that the success of execution (of those strategies) is quantitatively measurable. The use of a gap analysis and gap mitigation methodology within the strategic ISM framework, along with input-process-output functionality, enables clear traceability and supports implementation. The traceability within this strategic, integrated framework is obtained by ensuring that the outputs (in terms of metrics, KPIs, targets, and initiatives) of one framework are aligned with the inputs (in terms of objectives, KGIs, mission, etc.) of the other framework, and vice-versa, thereby establishing a robust input-process-output methodology. Thus, this strategic ISM framework addresses the need for information security requirements as well as alignment between business, IT and information security strategies while providing objective metrics of security performance as well as value.

REFERENCES

Ahn, H. (2001). Applying the balanced scorecard concept: An experience report. *Long Range Planning*, *34*(4), 441–461. doi:10.1016/S0024-6301(01)00057-7

Balanced Scorecard Institute. (2009). *About-balanced scorecard.* Retrieved March 1, 2009, from http://www.balancedscorecard.org/BSCResources/ AbouttheBalancedScorecard/tabid/55/ Default.aspx

Chapin, D. A., & Akridge, S. (2005). How can security be measured? *Information Systems Control Journal, 2*(1). Retrieved from http://www.isaca.org/Content/ ContentGroups/Journal1/20058/ jpdf052-how-can-security.pdf

Cobbold, I. M., & Lawrie, G. J. G. (2002). *The development of balanced scorecard as a strategic management tool*. 2GC Active Management Ltd. Retrieved from http://humanresources.co.za/free/ Downloads/BSC.pdf

Curtis, M. B., & Wu, F. H. (2000). The components of a comprehensive framework of internal control. *The CPA Journal, 70*(3), 64–66.

Da Cruz, E., & Labuschagne, L. (2006). A new framework for bridging the gap between IT service management and IT governance from a security perspective. Retrieved from http://icsa.cs.up.ac.za/issa/2005/Proceedings/Full/072_Article.pdf

Debraceny, R. S. (2006). Re-engineering IT internal controls: Applying capability maturity models to the evaluation of IT controls. *Proceedings of the 39th Hawaii International Conference on System Sciences*. Kauai, Hawaii, USA.

Elci, A., Ors, S., & Preneel, B. (2008). Security of information and networks. *Proceedings of the first international conference on security of information and networks* (SIN 2007). Retrieved from http://books.google.com/books?id=z dsOFf9U8bkC&printsec=frontcover

Ernest, M. (2007). Adding value to the IT organization with the component business model. *IBM Systems Journal, 46*(3), 387–389. doi:10.1147/ sj.463.0387

Ernst & Young. (2008). *Global information security survey*. Retrieved from http://www.ey.com/ Global/assets.nsf/UK/ Global_Information_Security_Survey_2008/$file/ EY_Global_Information_Security_Survey_2008.pdf

Goldman, J. E., & Christie, V. R. (2004). Metrics based security assessment. In Quigley, M. (Ed.), *Information security and ethics: Social and organizational issues* (pp. 261–287). Hershey, PA: IRM Press.

Grembergen, W. (2000). The balanced scorecard and IT governance. *Information Systems Control Journal, 2*(1). Retrieved from http:// citeseerx.ist.psu.edu/viewdoc/download?doi =10.1.1.90.1125&rep=rep1&type=pdf

Grembergen, W., & Haes, S. (2005). COBIT's management guidelines revisited: The KGIs/KPIs cascade. Retrieved from http://www.itgi.org/ Template.cfm?Section=Home&CONTENTID =24398&TEMPLATE=/ContentManagement/ ContentDisplay.cfm#f3

Haes, S., & Grembergen, W. (2005). IT governance structures, processes and relational mechanisms: Achieving IT/business alignment in a major Belgian financial group. *Proceedings of the 38th Annual Hawaii International Conference on System Sciences* (HICSS'05) - Track 8. Big Island, Hawaii.

ISACA. (2009). *ValIT framework 2.0*. Retrieved from http://www.isaca.org/Template. cfm?Section=Val_IT4&Template=/ContentManagement/ContentDisplay.cfm&ContentID=39994

ISACA. (2009a). *Building the business case for COBIT and Val IT–executive briefing*. Retrieved from http://www.isaca.org/ContentManagement/ ContentDisplay.cfm?ContentID=53055

ISACA. (2009b). *COBIT focus*. vol 3, July 2009.

IT Governance Institute. (2007a). *COBIT 4.1 handbook*. Retrieved from http://www.itgi.org

IT Governance Institute. (2007b). *COBIT mapping: Mapping SEI's CMM for software with COBIT 4.0*. Retrieved from http://www. isaca.org/Template.cfm? Section=COBIT_ Mapping1&Template=/ContentManagement/ ContentDisplay.cfm&ContentID=27170

IT Governance Institute. (2007b). *Information security governance: Guidance for information security managers*. Retrieved from http://www.itgi.org

IT Governance Institute. (2008). *Aligning CO-BIT® 4.1, ITIL® V3 and ISO/IEC 27002 for business benefit*. Retrieved from http://www.isaca.org/Template.cfm?Section= COBIT_Mapping1&Template=/ContentManagement/ContentDisplay.cfm&ContentID=45932

Kaplan, R. S. (1996). Using the balanced scorecard as a strategic management system. *Harvard Business Review, 74*, 75–76.

Kaplan, R. S. (2005). The balanced scorecard: Measures that drive performance. *Harvard Business Review, 83*(7), 172–173.

Kaplan, R. S., & Norton, D. P. (1996). *Using the balanced scorecard as a strategic management system*. Harvard Business Review, January-February.

Lainhart, J. (2000). COBIT: A methodology for managing and controlling information and information technology risks and vulnerabilities. *Journal of Information Systems*. Retrieved from http://www.allbusiness.com/techn ology/computer-networking/715615-1.html

Larsen, H. M., Pedersen, K. M., & Viborg Andersen, V. K. (2006). IT governance-reviewing 17 IT governance tools and analysing the case of Novozymes A/S. *Proceedings of the 39th Hawaii International Conference on System Sciences*. Kauai, Hawaii, USA.

Mahnic, V., & Zabkar, N. (2000). The role of information system audits in the improvement of university information systems. *EUNIS 2000 Conference Proceedings*. Poznan, Poland.

Malina, A. M., & Selto, F. H. (2001). Communicating and controlling strategy: An empirical study of the effectiveness of the balanced scorecard approach. *Journal of Management Accounting Research*. doi: 10.2139/ssrn.278939

Mallette, D. (2005). *IT performance improvement with COBIT and SEI CMM*. Information Systems Audit and Control Association (ISACA). Retrieved from http://www.isaca.org/Template.cfm?Section=COBIT_Mapping1&Template=/ContentManagement/ContentDisplay.cfm&ContentID=25094

Martinsons, M. (1999). The balanced scorecard: A foundation for the strategic management of information systems. *Decision Support Systems, 25*(1), 71–74. doi:10.1016/S0167-9236(98)00086-4

Microsoft. (2007). *Balanced scorecard for information security introduction*. Microsoft TechNet – Security Tech Center. Retrieved April 5, 2009, from http://technet.microsoft.com/en-us/library/bb821240.aspx

Niven, R. P. (2006). *Balanced scorecard step-by-step: Maximizing performance and maintaining results*. Hoboken, NJ: Wiley.

Norreklit, H. (2000). The balance on the balanced scorecard a critical analysis of some of its assumptions. *Management Accounting Research, 11*(1), 65–88. doi:10.1006/mare.1999.0121

NSA. (2010). *Infosec assessment methodology and Infosec evaluation methodology* (NSA IAM/IEM). Retrieved from http://www.securityhorizon.com/resources.php

Ozkan, S., Hackney, R., & Bilgen, S. (2007). Process based information systems evaluation: Towards the attributes of PRISE. *Journal of Enterprise Information Management, 20*(6), 700–725. doi:10.1108/17410390710830736

PriceWaterhouseCoopers. (2006). *IT governance survey 2006*. Retrieved from http://www.pwc.com/Extweb/pwcpublications.nsf/docid/D3E2997D370F3C648025713300511A01

Privacy Rights Clearinghouse. (2009). *Data breaches*. Retrieved February 5, 2009, from http://www.privacyrights.org/ar/ChronDataBreaches.htm#2009

Remenyi, D. (2005). Centralization issues in IT governance: The role and responsibilities of the IT control officer from a European perspective. *Proceedings of the 12th European Conference on IT Evaluation*, (p. 96). Turku, Finland. Retrieved from http://books.google.com/books?id=2dTUA7-YHWQC&lpg= PR1 &ots=tj5CWKfpdw&dq=%22Proceedings%20 of%20the%2012th% 20European%20Conference%20on%20IT%20Evaluation%22&pg= PR1#v=onepage&q&f=false

Research, A. M. R. (2008). *The governance, risk management, and compliance spending report*. Retrieved from http://www.amrresearch.com/

Ridley, G., Young, J., & Carroll, P. (2004). COBIT and its utilization: A framework from the literature. *Proceedings of the 37th Hawaii International Conference on System Sciences*. Kauai, Hawaii, USA.

Rigby, D. (2009). *Management tools and trends 2007*. Bain & Company Publication. Retrieved March 5, 2009, from http://www.bain.com/management_tools/tools_balanced.asp?groupCode=2

Ritchie, W. (2007). Old school CIOs versus COBIT-avoiding COBIT is avoiding the emerging standards of IT accountability. *CIO Digest–Strategies and Analysis from Symantec*. Retrieved from http://www.symantec.com/ciodigest/articles/200704/old_school_cios_versus_cobit.html

Robinson, N. (2005). IT excellence starts with governance. *Journal of Investment Compliance*, *6*(3), 45–49. doi:10.1108/15285810510659310

Rohm, H., & Halbach, L. (2005). *Developing and using balanced scorecard performance systems*. Retrieved from http://www.google.com/url?sa=U&start=1 &q=http://www.performancesoft.com/pdfs/wp/

Rouyet-Ruiz, J. (2008). COBIT as a tool for IT governance: Between auditing and IT governance. *The European Journal for the Informatics Professional*, *9*(1). Retrieved from http://upgrade-cepis.net/issues/2008/1/upg9-1Rouyet.pdf.

Rouyet-Ruiz, J., Spauwen, W., & Aguilar, L. (2010). Using COBIT 4.1 to achieve business-IT alignment: A practical approach. *ISACA Journal Online*, *1*(1). Retrieved from http://www.isaca.org/Template.cfm? Section=Current_Issue&template=/TaggedPage /TaggedPageDisplay.cfm&TPLID=7&UserDefinedDate1=02/01/2010

Schlarman, S. (2007). Selecting an IT control framework. [Retrieved from ABI/INFORM Global database]. *EDPACS*, *35*(2), 11–17. doi:10.1080/07366980601148030

Simonsson, M., Johnson, P., & Wijkström, H. (2007). *Model-based IT governance maturity assessments with COBIT*. KTH Royal Institute of Technology - Publications and Reports of School of Electrical Engineering. Retrieved from http://www.ee.kth.se/php/modules /publications/reports/2007/IR-EE-ICS_2007_026.pdf

Society for Information Management. (2008). Retrieved February 5, 2009, from http://www.stevensnewsservice.com/pr/pr1206

SSE-CMM.org. (2009). *How secure is SSE-CMM?* Retrieved from http://www.secure-software-engineering.com/2008/02/19/how-secure-is-sse-cmm

Turner, M. J., Oltsik, J., & McKnight, J. (2008). *ISO, ITIL and COBIT triple play fosters optimal security management execution*. SC Magazine Awards 2009 - USA. Retrieved February 1, 2009 from http://www.scmagazin eus.com/ISO-ITIL-and-COBIT-triple-play-fosters-optimal-security-management -execution/article/108620/

Von Solms, B. (2005). Information security governance: COBIT or ISO 17799 or both? *Computers & Security*, *24*(2), 99–104. doi:10.1016/j.cose.2005.02.002

Wang, C., & Wulf, W. A. (1997). Towards a framework for security management. *NIST NISSC Conference Proceedings*. Retrieved from http://csrc.nist.gov/nissc/1997/proceedings/522.pdf

Weill, P., & Ross, J. W. (2004). *IT governance: How top performers manage IT decision rights for superior results*. Boston, MA: Harvard Business School Press.

ADDITIONAL READING

Harvard Business School Publishing. (1999). *Harvard Business Review on the business value of IT*. Boston, MA: Harvard Business School Publishing.

Kaplan, R. S., & Norton, D. P. (1996). *The Balanced Scorecard: Translating strategy into action*. Boston, MA: Harvard Business Press.

Krutz, R., & Russell, V. (2003). *The CISM Prep Guide: Mastering the five domains of Information Security Management*. Hoboken, NJ: Wiley.

LeVeque, V. (2006). *Information Security: A strategic approach*. Hoboken, NJ: Wiley-IEEE Computer Society Press.

Lucas, H. (1999). *Information technology and the productivity paradox: Assessing the value of investing in IT*. New York, NY: Oxford University Press.

Moeller, R. (2008). *Sarbanes-Oxley internal controls: Effective auditing with AS5, CobiT, and ITIL*. Hoboken, NJ: Wiley.

Sherwood, J., Clark, A., & Lynas, D. (2005). *Enterprise Security Architecture: A business driven approach*. San Francisco, CA: CMP Books. Available from http://www.sabsa.org

Tipton, H. F., & Krause, M. (2003). *Information security management handbook* (5th ed.). Boca Raton, FL: CRC Press.

Von Solms, S. H., & Von Solms, R. (2008). *Information security governance*. New York, NY: Springer Publication.

KEY TERMS AND DEFINITIONS

Information Security Management (ISM): refers to the management of information security controls, processes, policies, people, procedures, and systems as well as the evaluation of the performance of the implemented processes.

Strategic ISM: is the integration of the ISM as a core part of the business in order to leverage it for the creation of more business opportunities in addition to managing risks and mitigating threats.

COBIT: Control Objectives for Information and related Technology (COBIT – version 4.1) is a set of best practices for information technology (IT) management that provides managers, auditors, and IT users with a set of generally accepted measures, indicators, processes and best practices for use of IT and facilitates IT governance and control in a company.

Balanced Scorecard (BSC): is a strategic alignment system that is generally used for alignment of business and IT strategies within an organization.

Cascading BSC: The cascading approach to the use of BSC can be defined as the synchronization of strategies and objectives of various business units within an organization. The business units must follow their own BSC approach, in consideration of the wider, organizational BSC approach.

SSE-CMM: The Systems Security Engineering Capability Maturity Model (SSE-CMM) is a tool for engineering organizations to evaluate security-engineering practices and to define improvements to them (sse-cmm.org, 2009).

Compilation of References

ABC News. (2009, Mar 4). *Bushfire SMS to assist in warning system development.* The Australian Broadcasting Corporation.

Abdul-Rahman, A., & Hailes, S. (2000). Support trust in virtual communities. In *Proceedings of the 33rd Hawaii International on System Science, Maui, Hawaii, USA,* (pp. 1769-1777).

ACC. (2006). *2006 copyright amendments.* Redfern, Australia: Australian Copyright Council.

ACM. (1992). *ACM code of ethics and professional conduct.* Retrieved from http://www.acm.org/ about/ code-of-ethics

Acquisti, A. (2002). *Protecting privacy with economic: Economic incentives for preventive technologies in ubiquitous computing environment.* Workshop on Socially-informed Design of Privacy-enhancing Solutions in Ubiquitous Computing: Ubicomp 2002.

ACS. (2005). *ACS code of ethics.* Retrieved from http://www.acs.org.au/ attachments/ Code of Ethics.pdf

Adams, K. (2002). Geographically distributed system for catastrophic recovery. *Proceedings of 16th USENIX Conference on System Administration,* (pp. 47-64).

Adler, R. (2009). The landscape of texting 4 health. In Fogg, B. J., & Adler, R. (Eds.), *Texting 4 health: A simple, powerful way to improve lives* (pp. 9–19). Stanford University Press.

AGD. (2008). *Critical infrastructure protection.* Australian Government Attorney-General's Department. Retrieved April 2008, from http://www.ag.gov.au/ www/ agd /agd.nsf/Page/ Nationalsecurity_Critical Infrastructure Protection

Ahn, H. (2001). Applying the balanced scorecard concept: An experience report. *Long Range Planning, 34*(4), 441–461. doi:10.1016/S0024-6301(01)00057-7

Aitenbichler, E. (2008). A focus on location context. In Mühlhäuser, M., & Gurevych, I. (Eds.), *Handbook of research on ubiquitous computing technology for real time enterprises* (pp. 257–281). Hershey, PA: IGI Global. doi:10.4018/9781599048321.ch012

Alder, G. S., Noel, T. W., & Ambrose, M. L. (2006). Clarifying the effects of Internet monitoring on job attitudes: The mediating role of employee trust. *Information & Management, 43*(7), 894–903. doi:10.1016/j.im.2006.08.008

AlgoSec, Inc. (2009). *FireFlow intelligent workflow for network security.* Retrieved on May 25, 2009, from http://www.algosec.com /en/products /fireflow key features.php

Allen, T., & Heald, S. (2004). HIV/AIDS policy in Africa: What has worked in Uganda and what has failed in Botswana? *Journal of International Development, 16*(8), 1141–1154. doi:10.1002/jid.1168

Al-Shaer, E. S., & Hamed, H. H. (2004). Modeling and management of firewall policies. *IEEE Transactions on Network and Service Management, 1*(1), 2–10. doi:10.1109/TNSM.2004.4623689

ANAO. (2000). *Business continuity management.* Australian National Audit Office (ANAO), Canberra, ACT, best practice guide.

Ancona, M., Coscia, C., Rubattino, M., & Megliola, M. (2003). *Horizontal versus vertical development of the HCI in the Wardinhand project.* Genova, Italy: University of Genova.

310

Anderson, D. G., & Stenzel, C. (2001). Internet patient care applications in ambulatory care. *The Journal of Ambulatory Care Management, 24,* 1–38.

Ardagna, D., Tanelli, M., Lovera, M., & Zhang, L. (2010). Black-box performance models for virtualized web service applications. *Proceeding of the First Joint WOSP/SIPEW International Conference on Performance Engineering,* (pp. 153-164).

Armitage, G., & Harrop, W. (2005). Teaching IP networking fundamentals in resource constrained educational environments. *Australasian Journal of Educational Technology, 21*(2), 263–283.

Armstrong, A., & Hagel, J. (1996). The real value of online communities. *Harvard Business Review, 74*(3), 134–141.

Askonas, P., & Steward, A. (2000). *Social inclusion: Possibilities and tensions.* London, UK: Macmillan.

Astroth, J. (2003). Location-based services: Criteria for adoption and solution deployment. In Mennecke, B. E., & Strader, T. J. (Eds.), *Mobile commerce: Technology, theory, and applications* (pp. 229–236). Hershey, PA: Idea Group Publishing. doi:10.4018/9781591400448.ch015

Attorney-General's Department. (2005). *Review of fair use and other copyright exceptions.* Retrieved January 22, 2010, from http://www.ag.gov.au

Atun, R. A., & Sittampalam, S. R. (2006). *A review of the characteristics and benefits of SMS in delivering healthcare. The role of mobile phones in increasing accessibility and efficiency in healthcare.* Vodafone Policy Paper Series Number 4 2006, (pp. 18-28).

Australia.gov.au Website. (2010). *The Australian continent.* Retrieved 10 March, 2010, from http://australia.gov.au/about-australia/our-country/the-australian-continent

Australian Bureau of Statistics. (2008). *Report 1301-yearbook Australia, 2008.* Canberra, Australia.

Australian Bureau of Statistics. (2009). *Report 3218-regional population growth, Australia, 2007-08.* Canberra, Australia.

Australian Communications and Media Authority. (2010). *Broadcasting codes index.* Retrieved January 25, 2010, from http://www.acma.gov.au

Australian Competition and Consumer Commission. (2005). *Guidelines for developing effective voluntary industry codes of conduct.* Retrieved January 25, 2010, from http://www.accc.gov.au

Baccaletti, S., Latora, V., Morento, Y., Chavez, M., & Hwang, D. U. (2006). Complex networks: structure and dynamics. *Physics Reports, 424,* 175–308. doi:10.1016/j.physrep.2005.10.009

Baier, A. (1986). Trust and antitrust. *Ethics, 96,* 231–260. doi:10.1086/292745

Balakrishnan, A. (2008). *BA sending luggage surplus to Italian warehouse.* Retrieved from http://www.guardian.co.uk/travel/2008/apr/02/heathrowterminal5.transport

Balanced Scorecard Institute. (2009). *About-balanced scorecard.* Retrieved March 1, 2009, from http://www.balancedscorecard.org/BSCResources/AbouttheBalancedScorecard/tabid/55/Default.aspx

Balaouras, S. (2007). The state of DR preparedness. *Forester/Disaster Recovery Journal.* Retrieved July 7, 2010, from http://www.drj.com/index.php?option=com_content&task=view&id=794&Itemid=159&ed=10

Balka, E., Green, E., & Heinswood, F. (Eds.). (2010). *Gender, health and Information Technology in context (health, technology and society).* Basingstoke, UK: Palgrave Macmllan Ltd.

Barham, P., Dragovic, B., Fraser, K., Hand, S., Harris, T., & Ho, A. … Warfield, A. (2003). Xen and the art of virtualization. In *Proceedings of the 19th Symposium on Operating Systems Principles,* (pp. 164–177). Bolton Landing, NY, USA, October 2003.

Barnbaum, C. (n.d.). Plagiarism: A student's guide to recognizing it and avoiding it. Retrieved February, 2010, from http://www.valdosta.edu/~cbarnbau/personal/teaching_MISC/plagiarism.htm

Barnes, S. B. (2006). A privacy paradox: Social networking in the United States. *First Monday, 11*(9), 1–15.

Barrett-Howard, E., & Tyler, T. R. (1986). Procedural justice as a criterion in allocation decisions. *Journal of Personality and Social Psychology, 50*(2), 296–304. doi:10.1037/0022-3514.50.2.296

Bartal, Y., Mayer, A., Nissim, K., & Wool, A. (2004). Firmato: A novel firewall management toolkit. *ACM Transactions on Computer Systems*, *22*(4), 381–420. doi:10.1145/1035582.1035583

BBC news. (2006). *Net students think copying OK.* Retrieved February, 2010, from http://news.bbc.co.uk/ 2/hi/ uk_news/ education/ 5093286.stm

BBC news. (2008). *Media doctor admits to plagiarism.* Retrieved February, 2010, from http://news.bbc.co.uk /2/hi/ 7452877.stm

BBC news. (2010). *Men At Work lose plagiarism case in Australia.* Retrieved February, 2010, from http://news. bbc.co.uk/ 2/hi/entertainment /8497433.stm

BBC. (2009). *Facebook gives users more control of privacy.* Retrieved March 30th, 2010, from http://news.bbc. co.uk/2/hi/technology/8404284.stm

BBC. (2010). *The prisoners causing trouble on Facebook.* Retrieved March 30th, 2010, from http://news.bbc.co.uk/2/ hi/uk_news/8496658.stm

Beam, A. (2003). Survey shows plagiarism is up. *Daily Gamecock.* Retrieve February, 2010, from http://www. dailygamecock.com/ 2.3455/ survey-shows- plagiarism-is- up-1.381072

Benson, S. (2007). *SMS smog alerts for Sydney.*

Bentham, J. (1996). *An introduction to the principles of morals and legislation.* USA: Oxford University Press.

Bentley, A. (2006). Infrastructure: Critical mass. *CSIRO Solve, 7.*

Ben-Ze'ev, A. (2003). Privacy, emotional closeness, and openness in cyberspace. *Computers in Human Behavior*, *19*(4), 451–467. doi:10.1016/S0747-5632(02)00078-X

Bernardos, A. M., Casar, J. R., & Tarrio, P. (2007). *Building a framework to characterize location-based services.*

Bertot, J. C. (2001). The multiple dimensions of the digital divide: More than the technology haves and have nots. *Government Information Quarterly*, *20*(2), 185–191. doi:10.1016/S0740-624X(03)00036-4

Betts, R. (2003). The missing links in community warning systems: Findings from two Victorian community warning system projects. *The Australian Journal of Emergency Management*, *18*(3), 35–45.

Bhattacharyya, J. (2004). Theorizing community development. *Journal of the Community Development Society*, *34*(2), 5–34. doi:10.1080/15575330409490110

Bies, R. J., & Moag, J. F. (1986). Interactional justice: Communication criteria of fairness. In Lewicki, R. J., Sheppard, B. H., & Bazerman, M. H. (Eds.), *Research on negotiations in organisations* (1st ed., pp. 43–55). Greenwich, CT: JAI Press.

Bita, N., & Sainsbury, M. (2009). *Bungling silenced Victoria bushfires warning.* The Australian.

Bjaaland, P. C., & Lederman, A. (1973). The detection of plagiarism. *The Educational Forum*, *37*, 201–206. doi:10.1080/00131727309339183

Blair, M., Armstrong, R., & Murphy, M. (2003). *The 360 degree brand in Asia: Creating more effective marketing communications.* Asia John Wiley and Sons.

Blais, J. (1992). The protection of exclusive television rights to sporting events held in public venues: An overview of the law in Australia and Canada. *Melbourne University Law Review*, *18*, 503–539.

Borden, T. L., Hennessy, J. P., & Rymarczyk, J. W. (1989). Multiple operating systems on one processor complex. *IBM Systems Journal*, *28*(1), 104–123. doi:10.1147/sj.281.0104

Bos, L., Marsh, A., Carroll, D., Gupta, S., & Rees, M. (2008). Patient 2.0 empowerment. In H. R. Arabnia, & A. Marsh (Eds.), *Proceedings of the 2008 International Conference on Semantic Web and Web Services*, (pp. 164-167).

Boston Consulting Group (BCG). (2004). *National health information management and information and communications technology strategy: National Health Information Group (NHIG) and Australian Health Information Council.* Retrieved 26 February, 2010, from http://www. moreassoc.com.au/downloads/bcg.pdf

Botha, R. A., & Eloff, J. H. P. (2001). Separation of duties for access control enforcement in workflow environments. *IBM Systems Journal*, *40*, 666–682. doi:10.1147/sj.403.0666

Boughton, G. (1998). The community: Central to emergency risk management. *Australian Journal of Emergency Management*, 2-5.

Bounds, D. (2007). *Packet - network injection and capture*. Retrieved on September 18, 2007, from http://www.intrusense.com/ software /packit/

Boyd, D. (2008). Facebook's privacy trainwreck: Exposure, invasion, and social convergence. *Convergence*, *14*(1), 13–20.

Brandon, D. P., & Hollingshead, A. B. (2007). Characterizing online groups. In Joinson, A. N., McKenna, K. Y. A., Postmes, T., & Reips, U. D. (Eds.), *The Oxford handbook of Internet psychology* (pp. 105–119). Oxford, UK/ New York, NY: Oxford University Press.

Braveman, P., & Tarimo, E. (2002). Social inequalities in health within countries: Not only an issue for affluent nations. *Social Science & Medicine*, *54*(11), 1621–1635. doi:10.1016/S0277-9536(01)00331-8

Brenkert, G. (1998). Trust, business and business ethics: An introduction. *Business Ethics Quarterly*, *8*(2), 195–203.

Brown, J. (2000). Growing up digital: How the Web changes work, education, and the ways people learn. *CHANGE*.

Brumby, J. (2009). *Australia's biggest desalination plant to secure water and jobs*. Victorian State Government, 30th July.

Bryce, J., & Klang, M. (2009). Young people, disclosure of personal information and online privacy: Control, choice and consequences. [Elsevier.]. *Information Security Technical Report*, *14*(3), 160–166. doi:10.1016/j.istr.2009.10.007

Buchan, N. R., Croson, R., & Solnick, S. J. (2008). Trust and gender: An examination of behavior, biases, and beliefs in the investment game. *Journal of Economic Behavior & Organization*, *68*(3-4), 466–476. doi:10.1016/j.jebo.2007.10.006

Burauskas, G., & Aldama, J. I. (2008). *Trust in virtual community*. Unpublished master thesis, Lunds University, Lund, Sweden.

Buzan, B., Wver, O., & Wilde, J. D. (1998). *Security: A new framework for analysis* (1st ed.). London, UK: Lynne Rienner Publishers.

Canton, L. G. (2007). *Emergency management: Concepts and strategies for effective programs* (1st ed.). Hoboken, NJ: John Wiley & Sons, Inc.

Carroll, J. (2001). *What kinds of solutions can we find for plagiarism?* Retrieved May, 2010, from www.gla.ac.uk/media/ media_13513_en.pdf

Castelfranchi, C., & Tan, Y. H. (2001). *Trust and deception in virtual societies*. Dordrecht, The Netherlands: Kluwer Academic Publishers.

Cavelty, M. D. (2007). Cyber-terror–looming threat or phantom menace? The framing of the US cyber-threat debate. *Journal of Information Technology & Politics*, *4*(1). doi:10.1300/J516v04n01_03

Chambers, M. (2008, June 5). Gas crisis threat over Apache pipeline fire. *The Australian*, (pp. 22).

Chapin, D. A., & Akridge, S. (2005). How can security be measured? *Information Systems Control Journal*, *2*(1). Retrieved from http://www.isaca.org/Content/ Content-Groups/Journal1/20058/jpdf052-how-can-security.pdf

Chapple, M. J., D'Arcy, J. M., & Striegel, A. (2009). An analysis of firewall rulebase (mis)management practices. *Journal of the Information Systems Security Association*, *7*, 12–18.

Chen, S. C., & Dhillon, G. S. (2003). Interpreting dimensions of consumer in e-commerce. *Information Technology Management*, *4*(2-3), 303–318. doi:10.1023/A:1022962631249

Chhanabhai, P. N., & Holt, A. (2007). Consumers are ready to accept the transition to on-line and electronic records if they can be assured of the security measures. *Medscape General Medicine*, *9*(1), 8. Retrieved from http://medgenmed.medscape.com/viewarticle/549468

Chircu, A. M., & Mahajan, V. (2009). Revisiting the digital divide: An analysis of mobile technology depth and service breadth in BRIC countries. *Journal of Product Innovation Management*, *26*(4), 455–466. doi:10.1111/j.1540-5885.2009.00671.x

Chopra, K., & Wallace, W. A. (2003). Trust in electronic environments. In *Proceedings of the 36th Annual Hawaii international Conference on System Sciences (Hicss '03) - Track 9 - Volume 9* (January 06 - 09, 2003). HICSS. IEEE Computer Society, Washington, DC, 331.1.

Christenson, J., Fendley, K., & Robinson, J. (1994). Community development. In J. Christenson, & J. Robinson (Eds.). *Community development in perspective* (pp. 3-25). Ames, IO: Iowa State University.

Chudleigh, J. (2009, November 10). Earlier alert system for severe weather. *The Courier-Mail*.

Cisco. (2010). *Certifications overview*. Retrieved from http://www.cisco.com/ web/learning/ le3/ learning certification overview.html

CISRO (Commonwealth Scientific and Industrial Research Organisation). (2006). *Infrastructure and climate change risk assessment for Victoria*.

Clarke, R. A. (1988). Information Technology and dataveillance. *Communications of the ACM, 31*(5), 498–512. doi:10.1145/42411.42413

Clarke, R., & Wigan, M. (2008). You are where you have been. In Michael, K., & Michael, M. G. (Eds.), *Australia and the new technologies: Evidence based policy in public administration* (pp. 100–114). Canberra, Australia: University of Wollongong.

Clarke, R. (2006). NSW health e-link: NSW trials of electronic health record. *Health E Link NSW*. Retrieved 8 May, 2010, from http://www.privacy.org.au/Campaigns/E_Health_Record/HealthElink.html

Cluley, G. (2009). Denying staff access to SNSs will only drive them to find a way round the ban, social network: The business case. *IEEE Engineering and technology, 4*(10).

COAG. (2007). *Victoria's infrastructure: Status and prospects. Council of Australian Governments*. COAG.

Cobbold, I. M., & Lawrie, G. J. G. (2002). *The development of balanced scorecard as a strategic management tool*. 2GC Active Management Ltd. Retrieved from http://humanresources.co.za/free/Downloads/BSC.pdf

Code of Conduct for Copyright Collecting Societies. (2008). Retrieved January 26, 2010, from http://www.apra-amcos.com.au

Code of Practice for Sports News Reporting. *(Text, photography and data)*. (2010). Retrieved September 7, 2010 from http://www.minister.dbcde.gov.au

Cogdell, B., & Aidulis, D. (2007). Dealing with plagiarism as an ethical issue. In Roberts, T. S. (Ed.), *Student plagiarism in an online world: Problems and solutions* (pp. 38–59). Hershey, PA: Idea Group Inc. doi:10.4018/9781599048017.ch004

Cohen-Charash, Y., & Spector, P. E. (2001). The role of justice in organizations: A meta-analysis. *Organizational Behavior and Human Decision Processes, 86*(2), 278–321. doi:10.1006/obhd.2001.2958

Competition and Consumer Act 2010 (Cwlth) (formerly *Trade Practices Act 1974* (Cwlth)).

Computer Sciences Corporation (CSC). (2010). *CSC global e-health atlas*. Retrieved 12 February, 2010, from http://www.csc.com/au/ds/33253/33346-global_e_health_atlas

Connolly, R. (2008). Trust and the virtual environment: Research and methodological considerations. *International Journal of Networking and Virtual Organisation, 5*(3/4), 259–274. doi:10.1504/IJNVO.2008.018823

Connolly, R., & Bannister, F. (2007). Consumer trust in Internet shopping in Ireland: Towards the development of a more effective trust measurement instrument. *Journal of Information Technology, 22*(2), 102–118. doi:10.1057/palgrave.jit.2000071

Constant, D., Sproull, L., & Kiesler, S. (1996). The kindness of strangers: The usefulness of electronic weak ties for technical advice. *Organization Science, 7*(2), 119–135. doi:10.1287/orsc.7.2.119

Consumer Affairs. (2006). *Connecticut opens MySpace. com probe*. Retrieved July 12th, 2010, from http://www.consumeraffairs.com/news04/2006/02/myspace.html

Coppola, N., Hiltz, S. R., & Rotter, N. (2004). Building trust in virtual teams. *IEEE Transactions on Professional Communication, 47*(2), 95–104. doi:10.1109/TPC.2004.828203

Copyright Law Review Committee. (1994). *Report on journalists' copyright*. Retrieved.

Copyright Law Review Committee. (2002). *Copyright and contract*. Retrieved January 22, 2010, from http://www.ag.gov.au/clrc

Coyle, D., & Meier, P. (2009). *New technologies in emergencies and conflicts: The role of information and social networks.*

Craufurd Smith, R., & Bottcher, B. (2002). Football and fundamental rights: Regulating access to major sporting events on television. *European Public Law, 8*(1), 107–133. doi:10.1023/A:1014594625408

Craver, C. B. (2006). Privacy issues affecting employers, employees and labour organizations. *Louisiana Law Review, 66*, 1057–1078.

Crean, K. W. (2010). Accelerating innovation in information and communication technology for health. *Health Affairs, 29*(20), 278–283. doi:10.1377/hlthaff.2009.0795

Croll, P. (2009). *Health privacy breaches and news.* Retrieved May 18, 2010, from http://healthprivacy.com.au/index_files/Breaches.htm

Crossman, W. (1999). The coming of age of talking computers. *The Futurist, 33*, 42–48.

CTIA- The Wireless Association. (2009). *CTIA survey* (Spring 2009). Retrieved February 3, 2010, from http://ctia.orAg

Culotta, A. (2010). *Toward detecting influenza epidemics by analyzing Twitter messages.* 1st Workshop on Social Media Analytics July 2010. Washington DC. Retrieved June 1, 2010, from http://www.selu.edu/Academics/Faculty/aculotta/pubs/culotta10towards.pdf

Curtis, M. B., & Wu, F. H. (2000). The components of a comprehensive framework of internal control. *The CPA Journal, 70*(3), 64–66.

D'Urso, S. C. (2006). Who's watching us at work? Toward a structural-perceptual model of electronic monitoring and surveillance in organisations. *Communication Theory, 16*, 281–303. doi:10.1111/j.1468-2885.2006.00271.x

Da Cruz, E., & Labuschagne, L. (2006). A new framework for bridging the gap between IT service management and IT governance from a security perspective. Retrieved from http://icsa.cs.up.ac.za/issa/2005/Proceedings/Full/072_Article.pdf

Daft, R. L. (2000). *Management* (5th ed.). Fort Worth, TX: The Dryden Press, Harcourt College Publishers.

Davis, W. (2009). Facebook harassment suit could spur cyberbullying laws. *The Daily Online Examiner.* Retrieved November 25th, 2009, from http://www.mediapost.com/publications/index.cfm?fa=Articles.showArticle&art_aid=114854

Dawson, M., Winterbottom, J., & Thomson, M. (2007). *IP location* (1st ed.). New York, NY: McGraw-Hill.

De Garis v. Neville Jeffress Pidler Pty Ltd. (1990). FCA 218.

De Laat, P. B. (2005). Trusting virtual trust. *Ethics and Information Technology, 7*(3), 167–180. doi:10.1007/s10676-006-0002-6

De Souza, Z., & Dick, G. N. (2009). Disclosure of information by children in social networking–not just a case of you show me yours and I'll show you mine. *International Journal of Information Management, 29*, 255–261. doi:10.1016/j.ijinfomgt.2009.03.006

De Tura, N., Reilly, S. M., Narasimhan, S., & Yin, Z. J. (2004). Disaster recovery preparedness through continuous process optimization. *Bell Labs Technical Journal, 9*(2), 147–162. doi:10.1002/bltj.20031

Dearstyne, B. W. (2006). Taking charge: Disaster fallout reinforces RIM's importance. *The Information Management Journal, July/August*, 37-43.

Debraceny, R. S. (2006). Re-engineering IT internal controls: Applying capability maturity models to the evaluation of IT controls. *Proceedings of the 39th Hawaii International Conference on System Sciences.* Kauai, Hawaii, USA.

Dee, T. S., & Jacob, B. A. (2010). *Rational ignorance in education: A field experiment in student plagiarism.* (National Bureau of Economic Research Working Paper no. 15672).

DeGeorge, R. (2010). *Business ethics* (7th ed.). Upper Saddle River, NJ: Pearson Education Inc.

Dehnart, A. (1999). *Digital neighborhoods.* Retrieved January 12, 2010, from http://www.andydehnart.com/writing/articles/digital_neighborhoods/

Department of Broadband, Communications and the Digital Economy. (2009). *Sport on television: A review of the anti-siphoning scheme in the contemporary digital environment*. Retrieved January 21, 2010, from http://www.dbcde.gov.au

Department of Health and Human Services. (2000). Healthy people 2010. Retrieved 6th May, 2006, from http://www.cdc.gov/nchs/about/otheract/hpdata2010/abouthp.htm

Department of Human Services (DHS). (2006). *Consumer and privacy taskforce discussion paper no. 1: The Australian government health and services access card*. Retrieved 17 June, 2006, from http://www.humanservices.gov.au/access/consumer_privacy_taskforce.htm

DesJardins, J. (2009). *An introduction to business ethics* (3rd ed.). New York, NY: McGraw-Hill.

Deutsch, A. (2000). Sports broadcasting and virtual advertising: Defining the limits of copyright law and the law of unfair competition. *Marquette Sports Law Review*, *11*(1), 41–86.

Deutsch, E., Duftschmid, G., & Dorda, W. (2010). Critical areas of national electronic health record programs-is our focus correct? *International Journal of Medical Informatics*, *79*(3), 211–222. doi:10.1016/j.ijmedinf.2009.12.002

Devettere, R. J. (2002). *Introduction to virtue ethics: Insights of the ancient Greeks*. Washington, DC: Georgetown University Press.

Dey, S. K., & Sobhan, M. A. (2006). *Impact of unethical practices of plagiarism on learning, teaching and research in higher education: Some combating strategies*. In 7th International Conference on Information Technology Based Higher Education and Training, 2006, (pp. 388–393).

Dhillon, A. S., Albersheim, S. G., Alsaad, S., Pargass, N. S., & Zupancic, J. A. F. (2003). Internet use and perceptions of information reliability by parents in a Neonatal Intensive Care Unit. *Journal of Perinatology*, *23*, 420–424. doi:10.1038/sj.jp.7210945

Dibben, M. R., Morris, S. E., & Lean, M. E. J. (2000). Situational trust and co-operative partnerships between physicians and their patients: A theoretical explanation transferable from business practice. *QJM*, *93*(1), 55–61. doi:10.1093/qjmed/93.1.55

Dijkstra, A., De Vries, H., & Roijackers, J. (1998). Computerized tailored feedback to change cognitive determinants of smoking: A Dutch field experiment. *Health Education Research*, *13*, 197–206. doi:10.1093/her/13.2.197

DiMicco, J. M., & Millen, D. R. (2007). Identity management: Multiple presentations of self in Facebook. *Proceedings of the 2007 International ACM conference on Supporting group work, Florida, USA*.

DiMicco, J., Millen, D. R., Geyer, W., Dugan, C., Brownholtz, B., & Muller, M. (2008). Motivations for social networking at work. *Proceedings of the ACM Conference on Computer Supported Cooperative Work*. New York, NY: ACM.

Dimmel, B. (2008). *Identity theft worm hits Facebook*. Retrieved October 18th, 2009, from http://www.infopackets.com/news/security/2008/20081208_identity_theft_worm_hits_facebook.htm

Directive 95/46/EC (2002). *Article 29 WP55 2002*. Retrieved from http://ec.europa.eu/ justice_home /fsj/ privacy/ docs/ wpdocs/ 2002/ wpss_en.pdf

Dirks, K. T., & Ferrin, D. L. (2001). The role of trust in organizational settings. *Organization Science*, *12*(4), 450–467. doi:10.1287/orsc.12.4.450.10640

D'Monte, L. (2009). Swine flu's tweet tweet causes online flutter. *Business Standard*. Retrieved January 18th, 2010, from http://www.business-standard.com/india/news/swine-flu%5Cs-tweet-tweet-causes-online-flutter/356604/

Dobbin, M., & Dowling, J. (2009, January 29). Blackouts hit thousands. *Age*, 7.

Dobbin, M. (2009, March 3). Victorians receive fire text warning. *The Age*.

Doherthy, I. (2008). Web 2.0: A movement within the health community. *Health Care and Informatics Review Online*. Retrieved December 2, 2009, from http://www.hinz.org.nz/journal/2008/06/-Web-2-0---A-Movement-Within-The-Health-Community/991

Donath, J. (1998). Identity and deception in the virtual community. In Smith, M., & Kollock, P. (Eds.), *Communities in cyberspace* (pp. 29–59). London, UK: Rutledge.

Dowling, J. (2009, January 27). Power supplies secure as heatwave sweeps state-scorching week. *Age*, 2.

Dunn, J., & Schweitzer, M. (2005). Feeling and believing: The influence of emotion on trust. *Journal of Personality and Social Psychology*, 88, 736–748. doi:10.1037/0022-3514.88.5.736

Dunn, M., & Collier, K. (2007, February 27). Plan to use SMS for SOS. Retrieved 6 June 2007, Factiva

Dunne, C. (2003). *Build and implement a single sign-on solution*. Retrieved May 2010, from http://www.ibm.com/developerworks/ web/library/ wa-singlesign/

Duska, R. F. (2007). *Contemporary reflections on business ethics*. The Netherlands: Springer.

Dwyer, C., Hiltz, S., & Passerini, K. (2007). Trust and privacy concern within social networking sites: A comparison of Facebook and MySpace. *Proceedings of the Thirteenth Americas Conference on Information Systems*, Keystone, Colorado August 09 -12, 2007.

Economou, N. (2009, January 18). Besieged Kosky may get ticket to ride a little longer. *Age*, 21.

Edejer, T. T.-T. (2000). Disseminating health information in developing countries: The role of the Internet. *British Medical Journal*, *321*, 797–800. doi:10.1136/bmj.321.7264.797

Elci, A., Ors, S., & Preneel, B. (2008). Security of information and networks. *Proceedings of the first international conference on security of information and networks* (SIN 2007). Retrieved from http://books.google.com/books?id=z dsOFf9U8bkC&printsec=frontcover

Elgesem, D. (1999). The structure of rights in directive 95/46/EC on the protection of individuals with regard to the processing of personal data and the free movement of such data. *Ethics and Information Technology*, *1*(4), 283–293. doi:10.1023/A:1010076422893

Ellison, N., Steinfield, C., & Lampe, C. (2007). The benefits of Facebook friends: Exploring the relationship between college students' use of online social networks and social capital. *Journal of Computer-Mediated Communication, 12*(3). Retrieved July 30th, 2007, from http://jcmc.indiana.edu/vol12/issue4/ellison.html

Emergency Management Australia. (1996). *Australian counter disaster handbook* (5th ed., *Vol. 2*). Canberra, Australia: Emergency Management Australia.

Emergency Management Australia. (2004a). *Disaster recovery: Safer sustainable communities*. Retrieved 27 November, 2007, from http://www.ema.gov.au/www/emaweb/rwpattach.nsf/VAP/(3273BD3F76A7A5DEDAE36942A54D7D90)~Manual10-Recovery.pdf/$file/Manual10-Recovery.pdf

Emergency Management Australia. (2004b). *Emergency management in Australia: Concepts and principles*. Retrieved 27 November, 2007, from http://www.ema.gov.au/www/emaweb/rwpattach.nsf/VAP/(3273BD3F76A7A5DEDAE36942A54D7D90)~Manual01-EmergencyManagementinAustralia-ConceptsandPrinciples.pdf/$file/Manual01-EmergencyManagementinAustralia-ConceptsandPrinciples.pdf

Emergency Management Australia. (2008). Disasters database. Retrieved 04 January, 2008, from http://www.ema.gov.au/www/emaweb/emaweb.nsf/Page/Resources_DisastersDatabase_DisastersDatabase

Emergency Management Australia. (2009a). *Australian emergency management arrangements*. Retrieved 27 November, 2009, from http://www.ema.gov.au/www/emaweb/rwpattach.nsf/VAP/(3A6790B96C927794AF1031D9395C5C20)~Australian+Emergency+Management+Arrangements.pdf/$file/Australian+Emergency+Management+Arrangements.pdf

Emergency Management Australia. (2009b). Emergency management. Retrieved 08 December, 2008, from http://www.ema.gov.au/www/emaweb/emaweb.nsf/Page/Emergency_Management

Eng, T. R. (2001). The e-health landscape: A terrain map of emerging information and communication technologies in health and health care. *The Informatics Review*. Retrieved 5 May, 2006, from http://www.informatics-review.com/thoughts/rwjf.html

Ernest, M. (2007). Adding value to the IT organization with the component business model. *IBM Systems Journal*, *46*(3), 387–389. doi:10.1147/sj.463.0387

Ernst & Young. (2008). *Global information security survey*. Retrieved from http://www.ey.com/Global/assets.nsf/ UK/ Global_Information_Security_Survey_2008/$file/ EY_Global_Information_Security_Survey_2008.pdf

Eronen, P., & Zitting, J. (2001). An expert system for analyzing firewall rules. In *Proceedings of the 6th Nordic Workshop on Secure IT Systems*, (pp. 100-107). Copenhagen, Denmark: Technical University of Denmark.

European Union (EU). (2010). *E-practice, EU*. Retrieved 23 February, 2010, from http://www.epractice.eu/

Evans, L. (2007). Monitoring technology in the American workplace: Would adopting English privacy standards better balance employee privacy and productivity? *California Law Review*, *95*, 1115–1149.

Eysenbach, G. (2000). Recent advances: Consumer health informatics. *British Medical Journal*, *320*, 1713–1716. doi:10.1136/bmj.320.7251.1713

Eysenbach, G. (2008). Medicine 2.0. Social networking, collaboration, participation, apomediation, and openness. *Journal of Medical Internet Research*, *10*(e22).. doi:10.2196/jmir.1030

Facebook. (2009a). *Facebook facts*. Retrieved September 25th, 2009, from http://www.facebook.com/press/info. php?factsheet

Facebook. (2009b). *Facebook statistics*. Retrieved September 25th, 2009, from http://www.facebook.com/press/ info.php?statistics

Facebook. (2009c). *Facebook site governance: Facebook's privacy policy–full version*. Retrieved on November 7th, 2009, from http://www.facebook.com/note. php?note_id=%20322194465300

Facebook. (2010). *Facebook statistics*. Retrieved June 6th, 2010, from http://www.facebook.com/press/info. php?statistics

Fernandes, J. P. (2008). Emergency warnings with short message service. In Coskun, H. G., Cigizoglu, H. K., & Maktav, M. D. (Eds.), *Integration of information for environmental security* (pp. 205–210). Dordrecht, The Netherlands: Springer. doi:10.1007/978-1-4020-6575-0_14

Fernando, B., Savelyich, B. S. P., Avery, A. J., Sheikh, A., Bainbridge, M., Horsfield, P., & Teasdale, S. (2004). Prescribing safety features of general practice computer systems: Evaluation using simulated test cases. *British Medical Journal*, *328*(7449), 1171–1172. doi:10.1136/ bmj.328.7449.1171

Fernando, J. (2004). Factors that have contributed to a lack of integration in health information system security. *The Journal on Information Technology in Healthcare*, *2*(5), 313–328.

Fernando, J., & Dawson, L. (2008). Clinician assessments of workplace security training—an informatics perspective. *Electronic Journal of Health Informatics*, *3*(1), e7.

Fernando, J., & Dawson, L. (2009). The health information system security threat lifecycle: An informatics theory. *International Journal of Medical Informatics*, *78*(12), 815–826. doi:10.1016/j.ijmedinf.2009.08.006

Ferrell, O. C., Fraedrich, J., & Ferrell, L. (2008). *Business ethics: Ethical decision making and cases*. Boston, MA: Houghton Mifflin Company.

Festa, P. (2003). Investors snub Friendster in patent grab. *CNet News*. Retrieved July 7th, 2010, from http://news. com.com/2100-1032_3-5106136.html

Festinger, L., Pepitone, A., & Newcomb, T. (1952). Some consequences of deindividuation in a group. *Journal of Abnormal and Social Psychology*, *47*, 382–389. doi:10.1037/h0057906

Fitzpatrick, G. (2000). *Understanding the paper health record in practice: Implications for EHRs*. Paper presented at the Health Informatics Conference 2000: Integrating Information for Health Care, 3–6 Sept, Adelaide.

Fong, M. (2009). Digital divide between urban and rural regions in China. *The Electronic Journal of Information Systems in Developing Countries*, *36*(6), 1–12.

Foucault, M. (1977). *Discipline and punish: The birth of the prison*. Great Britain: Penguin Books.

Friedman, M. (2001). How to cure health care. *The Public Interest*, *142*(Winter), 3–30.

Friedman, R. H., Kazis, L. E., Jette, A., Smith, M. B., Stollerman, J., Torgerson, J., & Carey, K. (1996). A telecommunications system for monitoring and counseling patients with hypertension. Impact on medication adherence and blood pressure control. *American Journal of Hypertension, 9*, 285–292. doi:10.1016/0895-7061(95)00353-3

Fritzhe, D. (1995). Personal values: Potential keys to ethical decision making. [Kluwer Academic Publishers, The Netherlands.]. *Journal of Business Ethics, 14*, 909–922. doi:10.1007/BF00882069

Gambetta, D. (1988). Can we trust trust? In Gambetta, D. (Ed.), *Trust: Making and breaking cooperative relationships* (pp. 213–237). New York, NY: Basil Blackwell.

Gams, M., & Tušar, T. (2007). Intelligent high-security access control. *Informatica, 31*, 469–477.

Garfinkel, S., Spafford, G., & Schwartz, A. (2003). *Practical UNIX and Internet security* (3rd ed.). O'Reilly Media.

Garner, R. T., & Rosen, B. (1967). *Moral philosophy: A systematic introduction to normative ethics and metaethics*. New York, NY: Macmillan.

Gaspary, L. P., Melchiors, C., Locatelli, F. E., & Dillenburg, F. (2004). Identification of intrustion scenarios through classification, characterization and analysis of firewall events. In *LCN '04: Proceedings of the 29th Annual IEEE International Conference on Local Computer Networks* (pp. 327–334). Washington, DC: IEEE Computer Society.

Gefen, D. (2000). E-commerce: The role of familiarity and trust. *Omega: The International Journal of Management Science, 28*(6), 725–737. doi:10.1016/S0305-0483(00)00021-9

Gefen, D., Karahanna, E., & Straub, D. W. (2003). Trust and TAM in online shopping. *Management Information Systems Quarterly, 27*(1), 51–83.

Gefen, D., & Straub, D. W. (2004). Consumer trust in B2C e-commerce and the importance of social presence: Experiments in e-products and e-services. *Omega: The International Journal of Management Science, 32*(6), 407–424. doi:10.1016/j.omega.2004.01.006

Getty Images, N. S. W. (2009). *Submission to the Senate Standing Committee on Environment, Communications and the Arts*. Retrieved May 14, 2009, from http://www.aph.gov.au/senate/committee/eca_ctte/sports_news/submissions.htm

Ghillyer, A. (2008). *Business ethics: A real world approach*. New York, NY: McGraw-Hill Irwin.

Ghosh, A. P. (1998). *E-commerce security–weak links, best defences*. N.J.: John Wiley and Sons, Inc.

Gibbons, S. (2009). *Telecommunications amendment (Integrated Public Number Database) bill 2009: Second reading*. Retrieved 6 August, 2009, from http://parlinfo.aph.gov.au/parlInfo/genpdf/chamber/hansardr/2009-02-26/0032/hansard_frag.pdf;fileType=application%2Fpdf

Giffin, K. (1967). The contribution of studies of source credibility to a theory of interpersonal trust in the communication process. *Psychological Bulletin, 68*(2), 104–120. doi:10.1037/h0024833

Gilbert, C. (1998). Studying disaster: Changes in the main conceptual tools. In Quarantelli, E. L. (Ed.), *What is a disaster? A dozen perspectives on the question* (pp. 3–12). New York, NY: Routledge.

Godfrey, B. (2001). Electronic work monitoring: An ethical model. *Australian Computer Society*, 18-21.

Goldie, L. (2008). Facebook to discuss security with ICO after data leak. *New Media age*. Retrieved November 21st, 2009, from http://www.nma.co.uk/news/facebook-to-discuss-security-with-ico-after-private-data-leak/38591.article

Goldman, J. E., & Christie, V. R. (2004). Metrics based security assessment. In Quigley, M. (Ed.), *Information security and ethics: Social and organizational issues* (pp. 261–287). Hershey, PA: IRM Press.

Goodwin, D. K. (2002). How I caused that story. *Time*. Retrieved February, 2010, from http://www.time.com/time/nation/ article/ 0,8599,197614,00.html

Govier, T. (1997). *Social trust and human communities*. Montreal, Canada: McGill-Queen's University Press.

Grabner-Kräuter, S., Kaluscha, E. A., & Fladnitzer, M. (2006). Perspectives of online trust and similar constructs: A conceptual clarification. In *Proceedings of the 8th International Conference on Electronic Commerce: The New e-commerce: Innovations For Conquering Current Barriers, Obstacles and Limitations To Conducting Successful Business on the internet* (Fredericton, New Brunswick, Canada, August 13 - 16, 2006). (pp. 235-243). ICEC '06, Vol. 156. New York, NY: ACM. doi: 10.1145/1151454.1151496

Grandison, T., & Sloman, M. (2000). A survey of trust in Internet applications. In *IEEE Communications Surveys and Tutorials, 3*(4), 2-16.

Granovetter, M. S. (1985). Economic action and social structure: The problem of embeddedness. *American Journal of Sociology, 91*(3), 481–510. doi:10.1086/228311

Green, N. (2001). Who's watching whom? Monitoring and accountability in mobile relations. In Brown, B., Green, N., & Harper, R. (Eds.), *Wireless world: Social and interactional aspects of the mobile age* (pp. 32–45). New York, NY: Springer-Verlag.

Greenhalgh, T., Strammer, K., Bratan, K., Byrne, E., Russell, J., Hinder, S., & Potts, H. (2010). *The devil's in the detail. Final report of the independent evaluation of the Summary Care Record and HealthSpace programmes*. London: University College London.

Grembergen, W. (2000). The balanced scorecard and IT governance. *Information Systems Control Journal, 2*(1). Retrieved from http://citeseerx.ist.psu.edu/viewdoc/download?doi =10.1.1.90.1125&rep=rep1&type=pdf

Grembergen, W., & Haes, S. (2005). COBIT's management guidelines revisited: The KGIs/KPIs cascade. Retrieved from http://www.itgi.org/Template.cfm?Section=Home&CONTENTID=24398&TEMPLATE=/ContentManagement/ ContentDisplay.cfm#f3

Gross, R., & Acquisti, A. (2005). Information revelation and privacy in online social networks. *Proceedings of the ACM Workshop on Privacy in the Electronic Society* (pp. 71-80). New York, NY: ACM.

Grossman, L. (2007, Oct 30). Invention of the year: The iPhone. Retrieved December 23, 2009, from http://www.time.com/time/specials/2007/article/0,28804,1677329_1678542_1677891,00.html

Grothe, M. J. M., Landa, H. C., & Steenbruggen, J. G. M. (2005). The value of Gi4DM for transport & water management. In P. v. Oosterom, S. Zlatanova & E. M. Fendel (Eds.), *Geo-information for disaster management* (pp. 129-154). Delft, The Netherlands: Springer.

Gruber, B., & Winter, S. (2002). *Location based services using a database federation*. Paper presented at the 5th AGILE Conference on Geographic Information Science, Palma, Spain.

Guan, J., Zhou, S., Zhou, J., & Zhu, F. (2007). Providing location-based services under Web services framework. In Taniar, D. (Ed.), *Encyclopedia of mobile computing and commerce* (pp. 789–795). London, UK: Information Science Reference. doi:10.4018/9781599040028.ch134

Guo, L. (2006). Recovery time guaranteed heuristic routing for improving computation complexity in survivable WDM networks. *Computer Communications, 30*, 1331–1336. doi:10.1016/j.comcom.2006.12.014

Guster, D. C., McCann, B. P., Kizenski, K., & Lee, O. F. (2008). Cost effective, safe and simple method to provide disaster recovery for small and medium sized businesses. *Review of Business Research, 8*(4), 63–71.

Guster, D. C., Safonov, P., Hall, C., & Sundheim, R. (2003). Using simulation to predict performance characteristics of mirrored WWW hosts. *Issues in Information Systems, 4*(2), 479–485.

Guster, D. C. Hall, C., Herath, S., Jansen, B., & Mikluch, L. (2008). A comparison of popular global authentication systems. *Proceeding of the Third International Conference on Information Warfare and Security* (ICIW), Omaha, NE.

Haag, S., & Cummings, M. (2010). *Management Information Systems for the information age* (8th ed.). New York, NY: McGraw-Hill Irwin.

Haddow, G. D., Bullock, J. A., & Coppola, D. P. (2006). *Introduction to emergency management* (2nd ed.). Burlington, MA: Elsevier Butterworth–Heinemann.

Haes, S., & Grembergen, W. (2005). IT governance structures, processes and relational mechanisms: Achieving IT/business alignment in a major Belgian financial group. *Proceedings of the 38th Annual Hawaii International Conference on System Sciences* (HICSS'05) - Track 8. Big Island, Hawaii.

Hamed, H., & Al-Shaer, E. (2006). On autonomic optimization of firewall policy organization. *Journal of High Speed Networks, 15*, 209–227.

Han, Y. Y., Carcillo, J. A., Venkataraman, S. T., Clark, R. S. B., Watson, R. S., Nguyen, T. C., & Orr, R. (2005). Unexpected increased mortality after implementation of a commercially sold computerized physician order entry system. *Pediatrics, 116*(6), 1506–1512. doi:10.1542/peds.2005-1287

Hannan, T. J. (1999). The Regenstrief medical record system. *International Journal of Medical Informatics, 54*(3), 225–253. doi:10.1016/S1386-5056(99)00009-X

Hardin, R. (1992). The street-level epistemology of trust. *Analyse & Kritik, 14*, 152–176.

Harkin, J. (2003). *Mobilisation: The growing public interest in mobile technology* (1st ed.). London, UK: Demos.

Harrington, S. J. (1997). A test of a person–issue contingent model of ethical decision making in organizations. [Kluwer Academic Publishers, The Netherlands.]. *Journal of Business Ethics, 16*, 363–375. doi:10.1023/A:1017900615637

Harris, R. A. (2001). *The plagiarism handbook*. Pyrczak Publishing.

Harris, C. E. Jr, Pritchard, M. S., & Rabins, M. J. (2005). *Engineering ethics: Concepts & cases* (3rd ed.). Thomson Wadsworth.

Harris, L. C., & Ogbonna, E. (2010). Antecedents and consequences of management-espoused organizational cultural control. *Journal of Business Research*. doi:. doi:10.1016/j.jbusres.2010.03.002

Harris Poll. (2003). *Harris interactive*. Retrieved from http://www.harrisinteractive.com/ harris_poll/ index. asp? PID=365

Harris, L., Dresser, C., & Kreps, G. L. (2004). E-health as dialogue: Communication and quality of cancer care. *Dialogue Systems for Health Communication*. Retrieved 6th May, 2006, from http://www.ccs.neu.edu/home/bickmore/dshc/kreps.pdf

Hartman, L., & DesJardins, J. (2008). *Business ethics: Decision-making for personal integrity and social responsibility*. New York, NY: McGraw-Hill Irwin.

Harvey, F. (2008). *A primer of GIS: Fundamental geographic and cartographic* (1st ed.). New York, NY: The Guilford Press.

Hauenstein, N. M. A., McGonigle, T., & Flinder, S. W. (2001). A meta-analysis of the relationship between procedural justice and distributive justice: Implications for justice research. *Employee Responsibilities and Rights Journal, 13*(1), 39–56. doi:10.1023/A:1014482124497

Havenstein, H., Vijayan, J., & Perez, J. (2007, December, 10). Facebook fiasco may lead to closer look at online privacy issues. *Computerworld*.

Hawn, C. (2009). Take two aspirin and Tweet me in the morning: How Twitter, Facebook, and other social media are reshaping healthcare. *Health Affairs, 2*, 361–369. doi:10.1377/hlthaff.28.2.361

Hayden, A. (2009). *Facebook needs to improve privacy practices, investigation finds.* Office of the Privacy commissioner for Canada. Retrieved November 24th, 2009, from http://www.priv.gc.ca/media/nr-c/2009/nr-c_090716_e.cfm

Health eSignature Authority (HESA). (2006). *Health e-signature authority*. Retrieved 25 July, 2006, from www.hesa.com.au

Heller, M. A. (1998). The tragedy of the anticommons: Property in the transition from Marx to markets. *Harvard Law Review, 111*(3), 621–688. doi:10.2307/1342203

Helne, C. A. (2005). Predicting workplace deviance from the interaction between organizational justice and personality. *Journal of Managerial Issues, 11*(2), 247–263.

Herald Sun. (2010). Governments powerless to stop Facebook vandalism, says IT expert. Retrieved February 28th, 2010, from http://www.heraldsun.com.au/.../governments-powerless-to-stop-facebook-vandalism-says-it-expert/story-e6frf7jx-1225834291255

Herndon, N. C. Jr. (1996). A new context for ethics education objectives in a college of business: Ethical decision-making models. *Journal of Business Ethics, 15*, 501–510. doi:10.1007/BF00381926

Herring, S. C. (2002). Computer mediated communication on the Internet. *Annual Review of Information Science & Technology, 36*, 109–168. doi:10.1002/aris.1440360104

Hildebrand, J. (2009). *Facebook identity theft enough for jail*. Retrieved July 20th, 2010, from http://www.news.com.au/story/0,27574,25764253-421,00.html

Hiles, A. (1992). Surviving a computer disaster. *Engineering Management Journal, 2*(6), 271–274. doi:10.1049/em:19920071

Hiles, A. (2007). *The definitive handbook of business continuity management*. John Wiley and Sons.

Hilligoss, B., & Rieh, S. Y. (2008). Developing a unifying framework of credibility assessment: Construct, heuristics, and interaction in context. *Information Processing & Management, 44*(4), 1467–1484. doi:10.1016/j.ipm.2007.10.001

Hiltz, S. R., & Turoff, M. (1978). *The network nation: Human communication via computer*. Reading, MA: Addison-Wesley.

Hjelm, J. (2002). *Creating location services for the wireless Web* (1st ed.). New York, NY: John Wiley & Sons, Inc.

Hodgkinson, S. (2010, 13 January 2010). National e-health strategy progress in Australia. *2010 Trends to Watch: Healthcare Technology*. Retrieved 3 February, 2010, from http://www.ovum.com

Hoffman, R. R., Lee, J. D., Woods, D. D., Shadbolt, N., Miler, J., & Bradshaw, J. M. (2009). The dynamics of trust in cyberdomain. *IEEE Intelligent Systems, 24*(6), 5–11. doi:10.1109/MIS.2009.124

Hofstede, G. (1980). *Culture's consequences: International differences in work-related values*. Newbury Park, CA: Sage.

Holma, H., Kristensson, M., Salonen, J., & Toskala, A. (2004). UMTS services and applications. In Holma, H., & Toskala, A. (Eds.), *WCDMA for UMTS: Radio access for third generation mobile communications* (3rd ed., pp. 11–46). West Sussex, UK: John Wiley & Sons Ltd. doi:10.1002/0470870982.ch2

Holtzman, D. H. (2006). *Privacy lost: How technology is endangering your privacy* (1st ed.). San Francisco, CA: Jossey-Bass.

Honesty in academic works: A guide for students and teachers. (2008). Retrieved February, 2010, from http://www.cuhk.edu.hk/ policy/ academichonesty/ index.htm

Houston, C., & Reilly, T. (2009). Heat leaves $100m black hole. *Age*, 1.

Howard, R. M. (1999). *Standing in the shadow of giants: Plagiarists, authors, collaborators*. Alex Publishing Corporation.

Hsu, M. H., & Chiu, C. M. (2004). Internet self-efficacy and electronic service acceptance. *Decision Support Systems, 38*, 369–381. doi:10.1016/j.dss.2003.08.001

Hunt, S. D., & Morgan, R. M. (1994). Relationship marketing in the era of network competition. *Marketing Management, 3*(1), 18–28.

Hunt, S. D., & Vasquez-Parraga, A. V. (1993). Organizational consequences, marketing ethics, and salesforce supervision. *Journal of Marketing Research, 30*(February), 78–90. Gershon, P. (2008). *Review of the Australian government's use of Information and Communication Technology*. Attorney General's Department, Barton, ACT, Government Review Report. Gosch, E. (2008, June 5). Gas cuts after blast spark supply fears. *The Australian*, (pp. 7).

Hunt, S. D., & Vitell, S. (1986). A general theory of marketing ethics. *Journal of Macromarketing, (Spring)*, 5–16.

Hunter, B. (2002). Learning in the virtual community depends upon changes in local communities. In Renninger, K. A., & Shumar, W. (Eds.), *Building virtual communities: Learning and change in cyberspace* (pp. 96–126). Cambridge, UK: Cambridge University Press. doi:10.1017/CBO9780511606373.009

Hutchinson, W., & Warren, M. (2009). Security as an element in environmental assessment and decision making. *Proceedings of The 2009 Conference of the Australia and New Zealand Society for Ecological Economics (ANZSEE): Green Mileage in the Global Meltdown: An Ecological Economics Way Forward*, Darwin, Australia, 27th-30th October 2009.

Hutchison Telecoms. (2009). *Submission to the Senate Standing Committee on Environment, Communications and the Arts*. Retrieved May 14, 2009, from http://www.aph.gov.au/senate/committee/eca_ctte/sports_news/submissions.htm

IBM. (2006). Stopping insider attacks: How organizations can protect their sensitive information. Retrieved from http://www-935.ibm.com/ services/ us/imc/ pdf/ gsw00316-usen-0 0-insider-threats-w p.pdf

IEEE. (2006). *IEEE code of ethics*. Retrieved from http://www.ieee.org /portal/pages /iportals/ aboutus /ethics / code.html

Ife, H. (2009, March 02). Texts alert Victorians of fire danger. *Herald Sun*.

Independent Sport Panel. (2009). *The future of sport in Australia*. Barton: Australian Government. Retrieved January 21, 2010, from http://www.sportpanel.org.au

Internet Usage Statistics. (2010). Retrieved February 1, 2010, from http://www.internetworldstats.com/stats.htm

InternetWorld. (2009a). *Global internet statistics*. Retrieved September 25th, 2009, from http://www.internetworldstats.com/stats.htm

Introna, L. D. (2001). Workplace surveillance, privacy and distributive justice. In Spinello, R. A., & Tavani, H. T. (Eds.), *Readings in cyberethics* (pp. 519–532). Sudbury, MA: Jones and Barlett Publishers.

Introna, L. D. (1996). Privacy and the computer: Why we need privacy in the information society. *Ethicomp e-Journal, 1*.

IPOS. (2004). *Launch of anti-piracy movie trailer*. Retrieved from http://www.ipos.gov.sg/ topNav/news / pre/ 2004/Launch +of+anti+piracy +movie+ trailer.htm

ISACA. (2009). *ValIT framework 2.0*. Retrieved from http://www.isaca.org/Template.cfm?Section= Val_IT4&Template=/ContentManagement/ ContentDisplay.cfm&ContentID=39994

ISACA. (2009a). *Building the business case for COBIT and Val IT–executive briefing*. Retrieved from http://www.isaca.org/ContentManagement/ContentDisplay.cfm?ContentID=53055

ISACA. (2009b). *COBIT focus*. vol 3, July 2009.

ISO/IEC. (2005). *Information Technology - security techniques - code of practice for information security management*. Geneva, Switzerland: ISO/IEC.

IT Governance Institute. (2007a). *COBIT 4.1 handbook*. Retrieved from http://www.itgi.org

IT Governance Institute. (2007b). *COBIT mapping: Mapping SEI's CMM for software with COBIT 4.0*. Retrieved from http://www.isaca.org/Template.cfm? Section=COBIT_Mapping1&Template=/ContentManagement/ ContentDisplay.cfm&ContentID=27170

IT Governance Institute. (2007b). *Information security governance: Guidance for information security managers*. Retrieved from http://www.itgi.org

IT Governance Institute. (2008). *Aligning COBIT® 4.1, ITIL® V3 and ISO/IEC 27002 for business benefit*. Retrieved from http://www.isaca.org/Template. cfm?Section= COBIT_Mapping1&Template=/ContentManagement/ ContentDisplay.cfm&ContentID=45932

Jackson, T., Dawson, R., & Wilson, D. (2001). *The cost of email interruption*. Loughborough University Institutional Repository: Item 2134/495. Retrieved from http:// km.lboro.ac.uk/ iii/ pdf/ JOSIT% 2020 01.pdf

Jagtman, E. (2009). *Reaching citizens with CHORIST: Everything but technology*. Retrieved 18 October, 2009, from http://www.chorist.eu/index.php?page=1&sel=1

James, J. (2009). From the relative to the absolute digital divide in developing countries. *Technological Forecasting and Social Change, 76*(8), 1124–1129. doi:10.1016/j.techfore.2009.01.004

Jardin, X. (2003). Text messaging feeds SARS rumors. *Wired*. Retrieved 17 October, 2009, from http://www.wired.com/medtech/health/news/2003/04/58506

Jarvenpaa, S. L., Shaw, T. R., & Staples, D. S. (2004). Toward contextualized theories of trust: The role of trust in global virtual teams. *Information Systems Research, 15*(3), 250–267. doi:10.1287/isre.1040.0028

Jarvenpaa, S. L., Tractinsky, N., & Vitale, M. (2000). Consumer trust in an Internet store. *Information Technology Management, 1*(1-2), 45–71. doi:10.1023/A:1019104520776

Jarvenpaa, S. L., & Leidner, D. E. (1998). Communication and trust in global virtual teams. *Journal of Computer-Mediated Communication 3*(4). Retrieved on February 20, 2010, from http://jcmc.indiana.edu/vol3/issue4/jarvenpaa.html

Jensen, C. S. (2002,). *Research challenges in location-enabled m-services*. Paper presented at the Third IEEE International Conference on Mobile Data Management, 08-11 January, Singapore.

Jilcott, S. B., Laraia, B. A., Evenson, K. R., & Ammerman, A. S. (2009). Perceptions of the community food environment and related influences on food choice among midlife women residing in rural and urban areas: A qualitative analysis. [Routledge.]. *Women & Health, 49*(2-3), 164–180. doi:10.1080/03630240902915085

Johnson, D. G. (2001). *Computer ethics* (3rd ed.). Upper Saddle River, NJ: Prentice Hall. Kamm, F. M. (1996). *Morality, mortality vol. II: Rights, duties, and status*. New York, NY: Oxford University Press.

Jonas-Dwyer, D., & Pospisil, R. (2004). The millennial effect: Implications for academic development. *Proceedings of the HERDSA Conference* (pp. 194-207).

Jonassen, D. H., Peck, K. L., & Wilson, B. G. (1999). *Learning with technology: A constructivist perspective.* Upper Saddle River, NJ: Merrill.

Jones, R. (2008). Developments in consumer health informatics in the next decade. *Health Libraries Review, 17*(1), 26–31. doi:10.1046/j.1365-2532.2000.00257.x

Jones, T. (1991). Ethical decision making by individuals in organizations: An issue-contingent model. *Academy of Management Review, 16*(2), 366–395. doi:10.2307/258867

Jones, A. (2007a). *Critical infrastructure protection-developments since the inception of the concept.* In 6th European Conference on Information Warfare and Security, ACI (Academic Conferences International), Shrivenham, UK, (pp. 131-138).

Jones, B. F. (2008). *The knowledge trap: Human capital and development reconsidered.* (NBER Working Paper No. 14138).

Jones, S., Millermaier, S., Goya-Martinez, M., & Schuler, J. (2008). Whose space is MySpace? A content analysis of Myspace profiles. *First Monday, 13*(9). Retrieved September 25th, 2009, from http://www.uic.edu/htbin/cgiwrap/bin/ojs/index.php/fm/article/view/2202/2024

Jones, V. A., & Keyes, K. (2001). *Emergency management for records and information management programs.* Lenexa, KS: Conservation Information Network, ARMA International.

Jøsang, A. (1996). The right type of trust for distributed systems. New Security Paradigms Workshop, In *Proceedings of the 1996 Workshop on New Security Paradigms*, Lake Arrowhead, California, United States, (pp. 119-131).

Kahneman, D., & Tversky, A. (1979). Prospect theory: An analysis of decisions under risk. *Econometrica, 47*, 313–327. doi:10.2307/1914185

Kamm, F. M. (2007). *Intricate ethics: Rights, responsibilities, and permissible harm.* New York, NY: Oxford University Press.

Kanawattanachai, P., & Yoo, Y. (2007). The impact of knowledge coordination on virtual team performance over time. *Management Information Systems Quarterly, 31*(4), 783–808.

Kant, I. (1989). What is enlightenment? In *Foundations of the metaphysics of morals* (2nd ed.). Rochester, NY: Prentice Hall.

Kaplan, R. S. (1996). Using the balanced scorecard as a strategic management system. *Harvard Business Review, 74*, 75–76.

Kaplan, R. S. (2005). The balanced scorecard: Measures that drive performance. *Harvard Business Review, 83*(7), 172–173.

Karro, J., Dent, A. W., & Farish, S. (2005). Patient perceptions of privacy infringements in an emergency department. *Emergency Medicine Australasia, 17*(2), 117–123. doi:10.1111/j.1742-6723.2005.00702.x

Katz, J. E., & Sugiyama, S. (2006). Mobile phones as fashion statements: Evidence from student surveys in the US and Japan. *New Media & Society, 8*(2), 321–337. doi:10.1177/1461444806061950

Kelton, K., Fleischmann, K. R., & Wallace, W. A. (2008). Trust in digital information. *Journal of the American Society for Information Science and Technology, 59*(3), 363–374. doi:10.1002/asi.20722

Khodyakov, D. (2007). Trust as a process: A three-dimensional approach. *Sociology, 41*(1), 115–132.. doi:10.1177/0038038507072285

Kickbusch, I. S. (2001). Health literacy: Addressing the health and education divide. *Health Promotion International, 16*(3), 289–297. doi:10.1093/heapro/16.3.289

Kiesler, S. (1986). Thinking ahead: The hidden messages in computer networks. *Harvard Business Review*, (January-February): 46–60.

Kim, D. J. (2008). Self-perception-based versus transference-based trust determinants in computer-mediated transactions: A cross-cultural comparison study. *Journal of Management Information Systems, 24*(4), 13–45. doi:10.2753/MIS0742-1222240401

Kim, K.-H., & Yun, H. (2007). Cying for me, Cying for us: Relational dialectics in a Korean social network site. *Journal of Computer-Mediated Communication, 13*(1).

King, R. (2006). Social networks: Execs use them too. *Business Week*. Retrieved September 15th, 2009, from http://www.businessweek.com/technology/content/sep2006/tc20060911_414136.htm

Klare, M. T. (2001). *Resources wars: The new landscape of global conflict*. New York, NY: Metropolitan Books.

Klein, P. G. (2009). Risk, uncertainty, and economic organization. In J. G. Hülsmann, & S. Kinsella (Eds.), *Property, freedom, & society: Essays in honor of Hans-Hermann Hoppe* (pp. 325-338). Auburn, AL: Ludwig von Mises Institute. Retrieved on May 1st, 2010, from http://mises.org/daily/3779

Knight, F. H. (1921). *Risk, uncertainty, and profit*. New York, NY: Kelley and Millman, Inc.

Kock, N. (1999). A case of academic plagiarism. *Communications of the ACM, 42*, 96–104. doi:10.1145/306549.306594

Kollock, P. (1999). The production of trust in online markets. In Lawler, E. J., Macy, M., Thyne, S., & Walker, H. A. (Eds.), *Advanced in group process, 16* (pp. 99–123). Greenwich, CT: JAI Press.

Koppel, R., Wetterneck, T., Telles, J. L., & Karsh, B.-T. (2008). Workarounds to barcode medication administration systems: Their occurrences, causes, and threats to patient safety. *Journal of the American Medical Informatics Association*, M2616.

Kramer, R. M. (1999). Trust and distrust in organizations: Emerging perspectives, enduring questions. *Annual Review of Psychology, 50*, 569–598. doi:10.1146/annurev.psych.50.1.569

Kreps, G. L. (2005). Disseminating relevant health information to underserved audiences: Implications of the digital divide pilot projects. *Journal of the Medical Library Association, 93*, 68–73.

Krishnamurthy, B., & Wills, C. (2009). On the leakage of personally identifiable information via online social networks. *Proceedings of ACM Workshop on Online Social Networks*, Barcelona, Spain.

Kriz, C. J. (2008). *The patient will see you now: How advances in science, medicine, and technology will lead to a personalized health care system*. New York, NY: Rowman & Littlefield Publishers Ltd.

Krojnewski, R., & Nager, B. (2006). Disaster recovery: It's not just an IT problem. *Forrester Report*, November 13, 2006.

Kumar, R., Novak, J., & Tomkins, A. (2006). Structure and evolution of online social networks. *Proceedings of the ACM SIGKDD International Conference on Knowledge Discovery and Data Mining* (pp. 611-617). New York, NY: ACM.

Kuperman, G. J., Blair, J. S., Franck, R. A., Devaraj, S., & Low, A. F. H. (2010). Developing data content specifications for the nationwide health information network trial implementations. *Journal of the American Medical Informatics Association, 17*(1), 6–12. doi:10.1197/jamia.M3282

Küpper, A. (2005). *Location-based services: Fundamentals and operation* (1st ed.). Chichester/ West Sussex, UK: John Wiley & Sons Ltd.doi:10.1002/0470092335

Kurose, J. F., & Ross, K. W. (2010). *Computer networking: A top-down approach* (5th ed.). Addison Wesley.

Lainhart, J. (2000). COBIT: A methodology for managing and controlling information and information technology risks and vulnerabilities. *Journal of Information Systems*. Retrieved from http://www.allbusiness.com/technology/computer-networking/715615-1.html

Lane, F. S. (2003). *The naked employee: How technology is compromising workplace privacy*. New York, NY: AMACOM, American Management Association.

Lansdale, M. W., & Ormrod, T. C. (1994). *Understanding interfaces: A handbook of human-computer dialogue*. London, UK: Academic Press.

Larsen, H. M., Pedersen, K. M., & Viborg Andersen, V. K. (2006). IT governance-reviewing 17 IT governance tools and analysing the case of Novozymes A/S. *Proceedings of the 39th Hawaii International Conference on System Sciences*. Kauai, Hawaii, USA.

Lau, T. P. (2006). *Chinese readability analysis and its applications on the Internet*. Unpublished Master's thesis, The Chinese University of Hong Kong.

Lau, T. P., & King, I. (2005). Two-phase LMR-RC tagging for Chinese word segmentation. In *Proceedings of the 4th SIGHAN Workshop on Chinese Language Processing*, (pp. 183–186).

Laudon, K. C., & Laudon, J. P. (2001). *Essentials of management Information Systems: Organisation and technology in the networked enterprise* (4th ed.). Prentice Hall.

Laudon, K. C., & Laudon, J. P. (2002). *Management Information Systems: Managing the digital firm* (7th ed.). New Jersey: Prentice Hall International.

Laudon, K. C., & Traver, C. G. (2010). *E-commerce 2010–business, technology, society* (6th ed.). Boston, MA: Pearson.

Laureano, M., Maziero, C., & Jamhour, E. (2007). Protecting host-based intrusion detectors through virtual machines, computer networks. *The International Journal of Computer and Telecommunications Networking, 51*(5), 1275–1283.

Lawler, E. (1978). Sequencing jobs to minimize total weighted completion time subject to precedence constraints. *Annals of Discrete Mathematics, 2*, 75–90. doi:10.1016/S0167-5060(08)70323-6

Le May, R. (2008, June 7). Two months to sort gas plant. The Advertiser, (pp. 87).

Lea, M., & Spears, R. (1991). Computer-mediated communication, de-individuation and group decision-making. [Special Issue: Computer-supported cooperative work and groupware.]. *International Journal of Man-Machine Studies, 34*, 283–301. doi:10.1016/0020-7373(91)90045-9

Lee, O. F., Guster, D. C., Schmidt, M. B., & McCann, B. (2009). Applying the scale-free degree distribution algorithm to assess communication complexity and failure points in disaster recovery model. *Journal of Information Technology Management, 20*(2), 35–45.

Lee, C., & Warren, M. (2007). Security issues within virtual worlds such as Second Life. *Proceedings of the 5th Australian Information Security Management Conference*, Edith Cowan University, Western Australia.

Leenes, R. (2008). Reply: Mind my step? In Hildebrandt, M., & Gutwirth, S. (Eds.), *Profiling the European citizen: Cross-disciplinary perspectives* (pp. 160–168). Dordrecht, The Netherlands: Springer.

Legg, M., & Lovelock, B. (2007). *HISA submission to the Boston Consulting Group NEHTA review*. Health Informatics Society, Australia Ltd.

Leitch, S., & Warren, M. (2009). Security issues challenging Facebook. *Proceedings of the 8th Australian Information Security Management Conference*, Perth, Australia.

Lenhart, A. (2009a). *Adults and social network sites*. Pew Internet & American Life Project. Retrieved July 3rd, 2010, from http://www.pewinternet.org/~/media//Files/Reports/2009/PIP_Adult_social_networking_data_memo_FINAL.pdf

Lenhart, A. (2009b). *Social networks grow: Friending Mom and Dad*. Pew Internet & American Life Project. Retrieved July 10th, 2010, from http://pewresearch.org/pubs/1079/social-networks-grow

Lenhart, A., & Madden, M. (2007). *Social networking websites and teens: An overview*. Pew Internet & American Life Project. Retrieved January 19, 2010, from http://www.pewinternet.org/Reports/2007/Social-Networking-Websites-and-Teens.aspx

Letzing, J. (2010). AOL pulls plug on Bebo social networking effort. *The Wall Street Journal.* Retrieved July 6th, 2010, from http://www.marketwatch.com/story/aol-pulls-plug-on-bebo-social-networking-effort-2010-04-06

Levy, S. (1984). *Hackers: Heroes of the computer revolution*. Garden City, NY: Anchor Press/Doubleday.

Lewicki, R. J., McAllister, D. J., & Bies, R. J. (1998). Trust and distrust: New relationships and realities. *Academy of Management Review, 23*(3), 438–458. doi:10.2307/259288

Lewicki, R. J., & Wiethoff, C. (2000). Trust, trust development, and trust repair. In Deutsch, M., & Coleman, P. T. (Eds.), *The handbook of conflict resolution: Theory and practice* (pp. 86–107). San Francisco, CA: Jossey-Bass.

Lewicki, R. J., & Bunker, B. B. (1996). Developing and maintaining trust in work relationships. In Kramer, R. M., & Tyler, T. R. (Eds.), *Trust in organization: Frontiers of theory and research* (pp. 114–139). Thousand Oaks, CA: Sage.

Lewis, J. D. (1999). *Trusted partner: How companies build mutual trust and win together*. New York, NY: Simon & Schuter.

Lewis, J. D., & Weigert, A. J. (1985). Trust as a social reality. *Social Forces*, *63*(4), 967–985. doi:10.2307/2578601

Liao, Q., Luo, X., Gurung, A., & Li, L. (2009). Workplace management and employee misuse: Does punishment matter? *Journal of Computer Information Systems*, 49–59.

Liles, J. A., & Rozalski, M. E. (2004). It's a matter of style: A style manual workshops for preventing plagiarism. *College & Undergraduate Libraries*, *11*(2), 91–101. doi:10.1300/J106v11n02_08

Lin, Q., Neo, H., Zhang, L., Huang, G., & Gay, R. (2007). Grid-based large-scale web3D collaborative virtual environment. *Proceeding of the 12th International Conference on 3D Web Technology*, (pp. 123-132).

Lipnack, J., & Stamps, J. (1997). *Virtual teams*. New York, NY: John Wiley and Sons, Inc.

Little, L., & Briggs, P. (2009). Private whispers/public eyes: Is receiving highly personal information in a public place stressful? *Interacting with Computers*, *21*(4), 316–312. doi:10.1016/j.intcom.2009.06.002

Lopez, X. R. (2004). Location-based services. In Karimi, H. A., & Hammand, A. (Eds.), *Telegeoinformatics: Location-based computing and services* (pp. 144–159). New York, NY: CRC Press LLC.

Louis Harris Poll. (1999). Louis Harris and associates. Retrieved from http://www.natlconsumersleague.org/FNLSUM1.PDF

Lu, Y., Zhao, L., & Wang, B. (2009). (in press). From virtual community members to C2C e-commerce buyers: Trust in virtual communities and its effect on consumers' purchase intention. *Electronic Commerce Research and Applications*. doi:.doi:10.1016/j.elerap.2009.07.003

Lu, Y., Zhao, L., & Wang, B. (2008). Exploring factors affecting trust and purchase behavior in virtual communities. *IEEE Symposium on Advanced Management of Information for Globalized Enterprises, 2008. AMIGE, 2008*, (pp. 1-5).

Lucas, C. (2009a, January 29). Train blame heats up as patrons wilt. *Age*, 1.

Lucas, C. (2009b, January 29). Tracks buckle and so does rail system. *Age*, 1.

Luhmann, N. (1979). *Trust and power*. Toronto, Canada: John Wiley.

Luhmann, N. (1988). Familiarity, confidence, trust: Problems and alternatives. In Gamebetta, D. (Ed.), *Trust: Marking and breaking cooperative relations* (pp. 94–107). New York, NY: Basil Blackwell.

Lukasik, S. J., Greenberg, L. T., & Goodman, S. E. (1998). Protecting an invaluable and ever-widening infrastructure. *Communications of the ACM*, *41*(6), 11–16. doi:10.1145/276609.276610

Lunde, K. (1999). *CJKV information processing*. O'Reilly and Associates.

Lynch, C. (2001). When documents deceive: Trust and provenance as new factors for information retrieval in a tangled web. *Journal of the American Society for Information and Technology*, *52*(1), 12–17. doi:10.1002/1532-2890(2000)52:1<12::AID-ASI1062>3.0.CO;2-V

Lyon, G. (1997). The art of port scanning. *Phrack Magazine, 7*(51). Retrieved on February 2, 2010, from http://www.phrack.com/ issues.html? issue= 51&id=11

M86Security. (2009). *Social networking: The pros, the cons and the solution*. Retrieved November 20th, 2010, from http://www.m86security.com/documents/pdfs/white_papers/business/WP_SocialNetworking.pdf

Mahajan, V., & Banga, K. (2006). *The 86% solution: How to succeed in the biggest market opportunity of the next 50 years*. Upper Saddle River, NJ: Wharton School of Publishing.

Mahmud, N., Rodriguez, J., & Nesbit, J. (2010). A text message-based intervention to bridge the healthcare communication gap in the rural developing world. *Technology and Health Care*, *18*(2), 137–144.

Mahnic, V., & Zabkar, N. (2000). The role of information system audits in the improvement of university information systems. *EUNIS 2000 Conference Proceedings*. Poznan, Poland.

Malina, A. M., & Selto, F. H. (2001). Communicating and controlling strategy: An empirical study of the effectiveness of the balanced scorecard approach. *Journal of Management Accounting Research*. doi: 10.2139/ssrn.278939

Mallette, D. (2005). *IT performance improvement with COBIT and SEI CMM*. Information Systems Audit and Control Association (ISACA). Retrieved from http://www.isaca.org/Template.cfm?Section =COBIT_ Mapping1&Template=/ContentManagement/ Content-Display.cfm&ContentID=25094

Mansfield-Devine, S. (Ed.). (2006). News: Privacy group keeps tab on security breach victims. *Computer Fraud & Security*, (2): 2.

Mapara, E. M. (2006). *Pictures as a health promotion strategy in addressing HIV/AIDS in the developed countries*. Retrieved 30 December, 2009, from http://www.ahpn.org/ downloads/publications/Pictures_as_a_Health_Promotion_Strategy_Adobe.pdf

Maran, C. M. (2009). Parallel life on social network: A study. *The IUP Journal of Management Research*, *8*(12), 7–30.

Marasea, P., & Warren, M. (2004). *Critical infrastructure protection: Comparison of countries*. In 3rd European Conference on Information Warfare and Security, Academic Conferences International (ACI), University of London, (pp. 249-260).

Martin, B. (2004). Plagiarism: Policy against cheating or policy for learning. *Nexus*, *16*(2), 15–16.

Martinsons, M. (1999). The balanced scorecard: A foundation for the strategic management of information systems. *Decision Support Systems*, *25*(1), 71–74. doi:10.1016/S0167-9236(98)00086-4

Marx, G., & Sherizen, S. (1991). Monitoring on the job: How to protect privacy as well as property. In Forester, T. (Ed.), *Computers in the human context: Information Technology, productivity, and people* (pp. 397–406). Cambridge, MA: MIT Press.

Massachusetts Institute of Technology. (2000). *Hippocratic oath* (Hippocrates, 400 BC). Retrieved 10 March, 2005, from http://classics.mit.edu/Hippocrates/hippooath.html

Massiglia, P., & Bunn, F. (2003). *Virtual storage redefined: Technologies and applications for storage virtualization*. Veritas Publishing.

Mayer, R. C., Davis, J. H., & Schoorman, F. D. (1995). An integrative model of organization trust. *Academy of Management Review*, *20*(3), 709–734. doi:10.2307/258792

Mayer, A., Wool, A., & Ziskind, E. (2005). Offline firewall analysis. *International Journal of Information Security*, *3*, 125–144.

Mayer, A., Wool, A., & Ziskind, E. (2000). Fang: A firewall analysis engine. In *SP '00: Proceedings of the 2000 IEEE Symposium on Security and Privacy* (p. 177). Washington, DC: IEEE Computer Society.

Mayo, M. A., & Marks, L. J. (1990). An empirical investigation of a general theory of marketing ethics. *Journal of the Academy of Marketing Science*, *18*(2), 163–171. doi:10.1007/BF02726432

McAlister, D. J. (1995). Affect- and cognition-based trust as foundations for interpersonal cooperation in organizations. *Academy of Management Review*, *38*(1), 24–59. doi:10.2307/256727

McCarthy, C. (2008). You, there. Step back from the webcam. *Cnet News*, Retrieved November 20th, 2010, from http://news.cnet.com/8301-13577_3-9853908-36.html

Mcdonell, T. B. (2008). *Plagiarism in writing and in art*. Retrieved February, 2010, from http://tommypaints.blogspot.com/ 2008/ 11/ plagiarism-in-writing-and-in-art.html

McGinley, M., Turk, A., & Bennett, D. (2006). *Design criteria for public emergency warning systems*. Paper presented at The 3rd International Conference on Information Systems for Crisis Response and Management (ISCRAM), Newark, New Jersey.

McKnight, D. H., & Chervany, N. L. (2002). What trust means in e-commerce customer relationships: An interdisciplinary conceptual typology. *International Journal of Electronic Commerce*, *6*(2), 35–59.

McKnight, D. H., Cummings, L. L., & Chervany, N. L. (1998). Initial trust formation in new organizational relationships. *Academy of Management Review*, *23*(3), 473–490. doi:10.2307/259290

McKnight, D. H., & Chervany, N. L. (1996). *The meanings of trust* (Technical Report 94004). Carlson School of Management, University of Minnesota, retrieved on February 1st, 2010, from http://misrc.umn.edu/wpaper/WorkingPapers/9604.pdf

McKnight, D. H., & Chervany, N. L. (2001). Conceptualizing trust: A typology and e-commerce customer relationships model. *Hawaii International Conference on System Sciences*, 7, Los Alamitos, CA, USA: IEEE Computer Society. (pp. 7022-7031).

McKnight, D. H., & Chervany, N. L. (2006). Distrust and trust in B2C e-commerce: Do they differ? In *Proceedings of the Eighth International Conference on Electronic Commerce* (pp. 482-491). Fredericton, New Brunswick: Association for Computing Machinery.

McParland, C., & Connolly, R. (2009). *The role of dataveillance in the organsiation: Some emerging trends.* Irish Academy of Management Conference, Galway, 2009.

McQueen, D., Newman, M., Patterson, G., Roberts, M., & Nick, L. (2007). *Mobile industry outlook 2007*. United Kingdom: Informa Media and Telecom.

Medical Records Institute (MRI). (2007). *Ninth annual survey of electronic medical record trends and usage*. Retrieved 1 November, 2007, from http://www.medrecinst.com/07survey_press.html

Melbourne Water. (2009a). *Bushfires in catchments*. Retrieved on September 21, 1999, from http://www.melbournewater.com.au/ content/ water_storages /bushfires_in_catchments /bushfires_in_catchments.asp

Melbourne Water. (2009b). Catchment impact table. Retrieved September 21, 2009, from http://www.melbournewater.com.au/ content/water_storages/ bushfires_in_catchments/ february_2009 _-_catchment _impact_table.asp

Melbourne Water. (2009c). *Bushfire recovery community update*.

Mellis, M. (2008). Internet piracy of live sports telecasts. *Marquette Sports Law Review*, *18*(2), 259–284.

Merriam-Webster Inc. (1996). *Merriam-Webster's dictionary of law*. Merriam-Webster.

Michael, K., Stroh, B., Berry, O., Muhlhauber, A., & Nicholls, T. (2006). The avian flu tracker-a location service proof of concept. *Recent Advances in Security Technology: Proceedings of the 2006 RNSA Security Technology Conference, Australian Homeland Security Research Centre*, Canberra, 19-21 September, (pp. 244-258).

Microsoft. (2007). *Balanced scorecard for information security introduction*. Microsoft TechNet – Security Tech Center. Retrieved April 5, 2009, from http://technet.microsoft.com/en-us/library/bb821240.aspx

Mileti, D. S., & Sorensen, J. H. (1990). *Communication of emergency public warnings: A social science perspective and state-of-the-art assessment*. Retrieved 08 August, 2007, from http://emc.ornl.gov/EMCWeb/EMC/PDF/CommunicationFinal.pdf

Mill, J. S. (1993). *On liberty and utilitarianism*. New York, NY: Bantam Books.

Miller, S., & Selgelid, M. J. (2007). Ethical and philosophical consideration of the dual-use dilemma in the biological sciences. [Springer Netherlands.]. *Science and Engineering Ethics*, 523–580. doi:10.1007/s11948-007-9043-4

Mishna, F., Saini, M., & Solomon, S. (2009). Ongoing and online: Children and youth's perceptions of cyber bullying. *Children and Youth Services Review*, *31*, 1222–1228. doi:10.1016/j.childyouth.2009.05.004

Mitchell, A., & Zigurs, I. (2009). Trust in virtual teams: Solved or still a mystery? *The Data Base for Advances in Information Systems*, *40*(3), 61–83.

Moore, G. E. (2004). *Principia ethica*. Mineola, NY: Dover Publications.

Moore, D. (2010). *Australian health information technology: Rudd's options on healthcare costs are alarmist and misleading*. Retrieved 20 February, 2010, from http://www.aushealthit.blogspot.com/

Moran, A. (2009, February 2). Ease the squeeze on power utilities. *Age*, 9.

Morel, C., Broun, D., Dangi, A., Elias, C., Gardener, C., & Gupta, R. K. (2005). Health innovation in developing countries to address diseases of the poor. *Innovation Strategy Today*, *1*, 1–15.

Morrison, E. W., & Robinson, S. L. (1997). When employees feel betrayed: A model of how psychological contract violation develops. *Academy of Management Review*, *22*, 226–256. doi:10.2307/259230

Morse. (2009). *Press Release: Twitter and social networks cost UK businesses*. Retrieved January 10th, 2010, from http://www.morse.com/press_20.htm

Mossholder, K. W., Bennett, N., Kemery, E. R., & Wesolowski, M. A. (1998). Relationships between bases of power and work reactions: The mediational role of procedural justice. *Journal of Management, 24*(4), 533–552. doi:10.1016/S0149-2063(99)80072-5

Mouhouelo, P., Okessi, A., & Kabore, M. P. (2006). Where there is no Internet: Delivering health information via the Blue Trunk Libraries. *Public Library of Science Medicine, 3*(3), e77.

Mowshowitz, A. (1997). Virtual organization-introduction to the special section. *Communications of the ACM, 40*(9), 30–37. doi:10.1145/260750.260759

Murnighan, J. K., Malhotra, D., & Weber, J. M. (2004). Paradoxes of trust: Empirical and theoretical departures from a traditional model. In Kramer, R. M., & Cook, K. S. (Eds.), *Trust and distrust in organizations: Emerging perspectives, enduring questions* (pp. 293–326). New York, NY: Russell Sage Foundation.

Murray, A. T., & Grubesic, T. H. (2007). Overview of reliability and vulnerability in critical infrastructure. In *Critical infrastructure* (pp. 1–8). Berlin/ Heidelberg, Germany: Springer. doi:10.1007/978-3-540-68056-7_1

Myskja, B. K. (2008). The categorical imperative and the ethics of trust. *Ethics and Information Technology, 10*, 213–220. doi:10.1007/s10676-008-9173-7

Mystery of Life & Jonboy. (2010, 13 March 2010). *Thread: Depression chats leaked on web*. Retrieved 11 May, 2010, from http://www.recoveryourlife.com/forum/showthread.php?t=121759&highlight=DepressioNet

Mythbusters. (2007). *Mythbusters beat fingerprint security system*. Retrieved 11 May, 2010, from http://www.youtube.com/watch?v=LA4Xx5Noxyo

Nancy, F. (2009). *The e-policy handbook: Rules and best practices to safely manage your company's e-mail, blogs, social networking, and other electronic communication tools*. USA: American Management Association.

Nass, C., & Brave, S. (2005). *Wired for speech*. Cambridge, MA: MIT Press.

Nathan, J. (2003). *Nemesis*. Retrieved on September 18, 2007, from http://nemesis.sourceforge.net/

National, E. -Health Transition Authority (NEHTA). (2009). *HI service and security access framework version 1.0*. Sydney, Australia: NEHTA. Retrieved 13 November, 2009, from http://www.nehta.gov.au/component/docman/doc_download/877-security-and-access-framework

National, E. -Health Transition Authority (NEHTA). (2010). *Patient privacy to improve under new system*. Retrieved 23 January, 2010, from http://www.nehta.gov.au/media-centre/nehta-news/585-patient-privacy

NCTC. (2004). *Critical infrastructure protection in Australia. National counter-terrorism committee*. TISN.

Nellitheertha, H. (2006). *Virtualization technologies*. Infosys White Paper.

Nemeth, E., Snyder, G., Hein, T., & Whaley, B. (2008a). Policy and politics. In *Unix and Linux system administration handbook* (4th ed.). Upper Saddle River, NJ: Prentice Hall.

Nemeth, E., Snyder, G., Hein, T., & Whaley, B. (2008b). Security. In *Unix and Linux system administration handbook* (4th ed.). Upper Saddle River, NJ: Prentice Hall.

NetResult Ltd. (2008). *Background report on digital piracy of sporting events*. Retrieved.

New South Wales Government. (2007). About sydneyALERT. Retrieved 17 April, 2008, from http://www.sydneyalert.nsw.gov.au/content.php/36.html

New York Times. (2008). How to use social networking sites for marketing and PR. Retrieved November 22nd, 2009, from http://www.nytimes.com/allbusiness/AB11702023_primary.html

Nine Network Australia Pty Ltd v. Australian Broadcasting Corp. (1999). FCA 1864.

Niven, R. P. (2006). *Balanced scorecard step-by-step: Maximizing performance and maintaining results*. Hoboken, NJ: Wiley.

Nooteboom, B. (2002). *Trust: Forms, foundations, functions, failures and figures*. Cheltenham, UK/ Northampton, MA: Edward Elgar.

Nord, G. D., McCubbins, T. F., & Horn Nord, J. (2006). Email monitoring in the workplace: Privacy, legislation, and surveillance software. *Communications of the ACM, 49*(8), 73–77.

Norreklit, H. (2000). The balance on the balanced score-card a critical analysis of some of its assumptions. *Management Accounting Research*, *11*(1), 65–88. doi:10.1006/mare.1999.0121

NSA. (2010). *Infosec assessment methodology and Infosec evaluation methodology* (NSA IAM/IEM). Retrieved from http://www.securityhorizon.com/resources.php

O'Reilly, T. (2005). What Is Web 2.0? Design patterns and business models for the next generation of software. Retrieved December 1, 2009, from http://oreilly.com/web2/archive/what-is-web-20.html

O'Reilly, T., & Battelle, J. (2009). Web squared: Web 2.0 five years on. *Proceedings of Web 2.0 Summit*, San Francisco, USA.

Ofuonye, E., Beatty, P., Reay, I., Dick, S., & Miller, J. (2008). How do we build trust into e-commerce websites? *IEEE Software*, *25*(5), 7–9. doi:10.1109/MS.2008.136

Oh, J., & Haas, Z. J. (2007). A scheme for location-based Internet broadcasting and its applications. *IEEE Communications Magazine*, *45*(11), 136–141. doi:10.1109/MCOM.2007.4378333

Orlikowski, W. J. (2007). Sociomaterial practices: Exploring technology at work. *Organization Studies*, *28*(9), 1435–1448. doi:10.1177/0170840607081138

Oshunloye, A. O. (2009). ICT in marketing. Unpublished Masters Thesis, Blekinge Institute of Technology.

Ostrow, A. (2009). *Obama assassination poll on Facebook was created by a minor*. Retrieved October 1st, 2009, from http://mashable.com/2009/10/01/kill-obama-poll/

Ostwald, M. J. (1997). Virtual urban futures. In Holmes, D. (Ed.), *Virtual politics: Identity & community in cyberspace* (pp. 125–144). London, UK: Sage.

Owston, R. (1998). *Making the link: Teacher professional development on the Internet*. Portsmouth, NH: Heinemann.

Ozkan, S., Hackney, R., & Bilgen, S. (2007). Process based information systems evaluation: Towards the attributes of PRISE. *Journal of Enterprise Information Management*, *20*(6), 700–725. doi:10.1108/17410390710830736

Pagliari, C. (2007). Design and evaluation in e-health: Challenges and implications for an interdisciplinary field. *Journal of Medical Internet Research*, *9*(2), e15. doi:10.2196/jmir.9.2.e15

Pandita, N., & Singh, S. (2008). Barriers to equitable access to quality health information with emphasis on developing countries. *Proceedings of the Making the eHealth Connection: Global Partnerships, Local Solutions conference*, Bellagio, Italy.

Parenti, C. (2003). *The soft cage: Surveillance in America from slavery to the war on terror* (1st ed.). New York, NY: Basic Books.

Parker, R. B. (1974). A definition of privacy. *Rutgers Law Review*, *27*(1), 275.

Pavlou, P. A. (2003). Consumer acceptance of electronic commerce: Integrating trust and risk with the technology acceptance model. *International Journal of Electronic Commerce*, *7*(3), 69–103.

Perez-Pena, R. (2009, April 7). A.P. seeks to rein in sites using its content. *The New York Times*. Retrieved April 9, 2009, from http://www.nytimes.com

Perry, R. W. (2007). What is a disaster? In H. a. Rodr'ıguez, E. L. Quarantelli & R. Dynes (Eds.), *Handbook of disaster research* (pp. 1-16). Springer Science+Business Media, LLC.

Perusco, L., & Michael, K. (2007). Control, trust, privacy, and security: Evaluating location-based services. *IEEE Technology and Society Magazine*, *26*, 4–16. doi:10.1109/MTAS.2007.335564

Pervan, G. (1998). How chief executive officers in large organizations view the management of their information systems. *Journal of Information Technology*, *13*(2), 95–109. doi:10.1080/026839698344882

Pew Internet. (2008). *Dataset: Cloud computing, politics and adult social networking*. Pew Internet & American Life Project. Retrieved July 1st, 2010, from http://www.pewinternet.org/Shared-Content/Data-Sets/2008/May-2008--Cloud-computing-politics-and-adult-social-networking.aspx

Phillippi, M. (2008). An effective SME disaster recovery strategy for branch offices. *Computer Technology Review*. Retrieved February 15, 2010, from http://www.thefreelibrary.com /An+effective+ SME+disaster +recovery +strategy+ for+branch +offices.-a0168 214596

Plotz, D. (2002). The plagiarist: Why Stephen Ambrose is a vampire. *Slate*. Retrieved February, 2010, from http://slate.msn.com/?id=2060618

Porter, C. E. (2004). A typology of virtual communities: A multi-disciplinary foundation for future research. *Journal of Computer-Mediated Communication, 10*(1). Retrieved October 26, 2009, from http://jcmc.indiana.edu/vol10/issue1/porter.html

Porter, J. E. (2005). *Discourage plagiarism by promoting academic honesty: A proactive approach for teachers*. Retrieved May, 2010, from http://kairos.wide.msu.edu/porter/ teach_plagiarism.pdf

Post, G. V., & Kagan, A. (2007). Evaluating information security tradeoffs: Restricting access can interfere with user tasks. *Computers & Security, 26*(3), 229–237. doi:10.1016/j.cose.2006.10.004

Prakhaber, P. R. (2000). Who owns the online consumer? *Journal of Consumer Marketing, 17*(2), 158–171. doi:10.1108/07363760010317213

Prata, N. (2009). Making family planning accessible in resource-poor settings. *Philosophical Transactions of The Royal Society B, 364*(1532), 3093–3099. doi:10.1098/rstb.2009.0172

PriceWaterhouseCoopers. (2006). *IT governance survey 2006*. Retrieved from http://www.pwc.com/Extweb/pwcpublications.nsf/docid/ D3E2997D370F-3C648025713300511A01

Privacy Rights Clearinghouse. (2009). *Data breaches*. Retrieved February 5, 2009, from http://www.privacyrights.org/ar/ChronDataBreaches.htm#2009

Putnam, R. (1993). *Making democracy work: Civic tradition in modern Italy*. Princeton, NJ: Princeton University Press.

Putnam, R. (2000). *Bowling alone: The collapse and revival of American community*. New York, NY: Simon and Schuster.

Pye, G., & Warren, M. J. (2009). An emergent security risk: Critical infrastructures and information warfare. *Journal of Information Warfare, 8*(3), 14–26.

Pye, G., & Warren, M. J. (2008). *Considerations for modelling critical infrastructure systems*. In 7th European Conference on Information Warfare and Security, Academic Conferences International (ACI), Plymouth, UK, (pp. 185-196).

QSR International Pty Ltd. (2003, 2006). *QSR International*. Retrieved 17 October, 2006, from http://www.qsrinternational.com/

Quarantelli, E. L. (1986). What should we study? Questions and suggestions for researchers about the concept of disasters. *International Journal of Mass Emergencies and Disasters, 5*(1), 7–32.

Quinn, M. J. (2006). *Ethics for the information age* (2nd ed.). Addison Wesley.

Raacke, J., & Bonds-Raacke, J. (2008). MySpace and Facebook: Applying the uses and gratifications theory to exploring friend-networking sites. *Cyberpsychology & Behavior, 11*(2), 169–174. doi:10.1089/cpb.2007.0056

Radin, P. (2006). To me, it's my life: Medical communication, trust, and activism in cyberspace. *Social Science & Medicine, 62*, 591–601. doi:10.1016/j.socscimed.2005.06.022

Rashid, A., & Elder, L. (2009). Mobile phones and development: An analysis of IDRC-supported projects. *The Electronic Journal on Information Systems in Developing Countries, 36*(2), 1–16.

Rashid, A., Weckert, J., & Lucas, R. (2009). Software engineering ethics in a digital world. *IEEE Computer, 42*(6), 34–41.

Rawlins, B. (2009). Irrational trust. Retrieved on May 1st, 2010, from http://www.instituteforpr.org/essential_knowledge/detail/irrational_trust_rawlins/

Remenyi, D. (2005). Centralization issues in IT governance: The role and responsibilities of the IT control officer from a European perspective. *Proceedings of the 12th European Conference on IT Evaluation*, (p. 96). Turku, Finland. Retrieved from http://books.google.com/books?id=2dTUA7-YHWQC&lpg= PR1&ots=tj 5CWKfpdw&dq=%22Proceedings%20of%20the%20 12th% 20European%20Conference%20on%20IT%20 Evaluation%22&pg= PR1#v=onepage&q&f=false

Renner, M. (2002). *The anatomy of resource wars. (World Watch Paper 162)*. USA: Worldwatch Institute.

Research, A. M. R. (2008). *The governance, risk management, and compliance spending report*. Retrieved from http://www.amrresearch.com/

Reynolds, G. W. (2010). *Ethics in Information Technology* (3rd ed.). Boston, MA: Course Technology.

Rheingold, H. (1993). *The virtual community: Homesteading on the electronic frontier*. Reading, MA: Addison-Wesley.

Richardson, J., & Lenarcic, J. (2008). Text messaging as a catalyst for mobile student administration: The trigger experience. *International Journal of Emerging Technologies and Society*, *6*(2), 140–155.

Richardson, R. (2007). *12th annual computer crime and security survey*. Retrieved on September 18, 2007, from http://www.gocsi.com/ forms /csi survey.jhtml

Ridings, C. M., Gefen, D., & Arinze, B. (2002). Some antecedents and effects of trust in virtual communities. *The Journal of Strategic Information Systems*, *11*, 271–295. doi:10.1016/S0963-8687(02)00021-5

Ridings, C. M., & Gefen, D. (2004). Virtual community attraction: Why people hang out online. *Journal of Computer-Mediated Communication*, *10*(1). Retrieved on January 12, 2010 from http://jcmc.indiana.edu/vol10/ issue1/ridings_gefen.html

Ridley, G., Young, J., & Carroll, P. (2004). COBIT and its utilization: A framework from the literature. *Proceedings of the 37th Hawaii International Conference on System Sciences*. Kauai, Hawaii, USA.

Rieh, S. Y., & Danielson, D. R. (2007). Credibility: A multidisciplinary framework. *Annual Review of Information Science & Technology*, *41*, 307–364. doi:10.1002/ aris.2007.1440410114

Rigby, D. (2009). *Management tools and trends 2007*. Bain & Company Publication. Retrieved March 5, 2009, from http://www.bain.com/management_tools/tools_balanced.asp?groupCode=2

Ritchie, W. (2007). Old school CIOs versus COBIT-avoiding COBIT is avoiding the emerging standards of IT accountability. *CIO Digest–Strategies and Analysis from Symantec*. Retrieved from http://www.symantec. com/ciodigest/articles/ 200704/old_school_cios_versus_cobit.html

Robert, G., Greenhalgh, T., MacFarlane, F., & Peacock, R. (2009). *Organisational factors influencing technology adoption and assimilation in the NHS: A systematic literature review—June 2009*. National Health Service NIHR Service Delivery & Organisation (SDO) programme.

Roberts, G. (2009, February, 17). Vic bushfires may affect water supplies. *The Age Newspaper*.

Robinson, S. L., & Rousseau, D. M. (1994). Violating the psychological contract: Not the exception but the norm. *Journal of Organizational Behavior*, *15*(3), 245–259. doi:10.1002/job.4030150306

Robinson, N. (2005). IT excellence starts with governance. *Journal of Investment Compliance*, *6*(3), 45–49. doi:10.1108/15285810510659310

Rohm, H., & Halbach, L. (2005). *Developing and using balanced scorecard performance systems*. Retrieved from http://www.google.com/url?sa=U&start=1 &q=http:// www.performancesoft.com/pdfs/wp/

Rosenblum, M. (2009). *The impact of virtualization on modern computing environments*. Virginia Technological University Distinguished Lecture Series. Retrieved from http://www.cs.vt.edu/ Distinguished Lectures/ Mendel Rosenblum

Rosenthal, U. (1998). Future disasters, future definitions. In Quarantelli, E. L. (Ed.), *What is a disaster? A dozen perspectives on the question* (pp. 147–160). New York, NY: Routledge.

Ross, W. D. (2003). *The right and the good* (Stratton-Lake, P., Ed.). New York, NY: Oxford University Press.

Rousseau, D., Sitkin, S., Burt, R., & Camerer, C. (1998). Not so different after all: A cross-discipline view of trust. *Academy of Management Review*, 23(3), 393–404.

Rouyet-Ruiz, J. (2008). COBIT as a tool for IT governance: Between auditing and IT governance. *The European Journal for the Informatics Professional*, 9(1). Retrieved from http://upgrade-cepis.net/issues/2008/1/upg9-1Rouyet.pdf.

Rouyet-Ruiz, J., Spauwen, W., & Aguilar, L. (2010). Using COBIT 4.1 to achieve business-IT alignment: A practical approach. *ISACA JournalOnline, 1*(1). Retrieved from http://www.isaca.org/Template.cfm? Section=Current_Issue&template=/TaggedPage /TaggedPageDisplay.cfm &TPLID=7&UserDefinedDate1=02/01/2010

Royce, J. (2003). Trust or trussed? Has turnitin.com got it all wrapped up? *Teacher Librarian, 30*(4), 26–30.

Rust, R. T., Kannan, P. K., & Peng, N. (2002). The customer economics of Internet privacy. *Journal of the Academy of Marketing Science, 30*(4), 455–464. doi:10.1177/009207002236917

Safigan, C. (2008). Disaster recovery for the masses–the role of OS-level server virtualization in disaster recovery. *Computer Technology Review*. Retrieved July 7, 2010, from http://www.wwpi.com/index.php ?option=com_content&task=vie w&id=1151&Item id= 64

Safire, W. (2002). The great unwatched. *New York Times*. Retrieved from http://query.nytimes.com/ gst/ fullpage. html ?res=9A03 E7DB1E3FF93B A25751C0A964 9C8B63

Samsioe, J., & Samsioe, A. (2002). Introduction to location based services: Markets and technologies. In Reichwald, R. (Ed.), *Mobile Kommunikation: Wertschöpfung, Technologien, neue Dienste* (pp. 417–438). Wiesbaden, Germany: Gabler.

Sanders, P. (2009). *The CB way forward*. Retrieved 18 October, 2009, from http://www.chorist.eu/index.php?page=1&sel=1

Sanfilippo, S. (2006). *Hping*. Retrived on September 18, 2007, from http://www.hping.org/

Sarasohn-Kahn, J. (2008). *The wisdom of patients: Healthcare meets online social media*. Oakland, CA: California Healthcare Foundation.

Sarker, S., Valacich, J. S., & Sarker, S. (2003). Virtual team trust: Instrument development and validation. *Information Resources Management Journal, 16*(2), 35–55. doi:10.4018/irmj.2003040103

Satterwhite, R., & Gerein, M. (2001). *Downloading detectives: Searching for online plagiarism*. Retrieved February, 2010, from http://www.coloradocollege.edu/Library/Course/ downloading_detectives_paper.htm

Scheuermann, D., Schwiderski-Grosche, S., & Struif, B. (2000). *Usability of biometrics in relation to electronic signatures*. (EU Case study 502533/8 Ver 1.0), September 12. Retrieved January 26, 2010, from http://www.cse. lehigh.edu/prr/Biometrics/Archive/Papers/eubiosig.pdf

Schiff, G. D., & Bates, D. W. (2010). Can electronic clinical documentation help prevent diagnostic errors? *The New England Journal of Medicine, 362*(12), 1066–1069. doi:10.1056/NEJMp0911734

Schilderman, T. (2002). Strengthening the knowledge and information systems of the urban poor. DFID/ITDG. Retrieved on October 13, 1999, from www.id21.org/society/s4bts1g1.html

Schlarman, S. (2007). Selecting an IT control framework. [Retrieved from ABI/INFORM Global database]. *EDPACS, 35*(2), 11–17. doi:10.1080/07366980601148030

Schneier, B. (2008). *The myth of the transparent society*. Wired Magazine.

Schonfeld, E. (2010). Facebook closing in on 500 million visitors a month (ComScore). *TechCrunch*. Retrieved June 18th, 2010, from http://techcrunch.com/2010/04/21/facebook-500-million-visitors-comscore

Schoorman, F. D., Mayer, R. C., & Davis, J. H. (2007). An integrative model of organizational trust: Past, present and future. *Academy of Management Review, 32*, 344–354.

Schuba, C. L., & Spafford, E. H. (1997). A reference model for firewall technology. In *Proceedings of the Thirteenth Annual Computer Security Applications Conference*, (pp 133–145). San Diego, CA: IEEE.

Scott G. (2005). Protecting the nation. *AUSGEO News, 79*.

Scott, S. (2009, 10 December 2009). *Depression chats leaked on the web*. Retrieved 8 May, 2010, from http://www.abc.net.au/news/stories/2009/12/09/2766589.htm

Sellers, D., Grams, R., & Horty, T. (1977). Documentation of hospital communication noise levels. *Journal of Medical Systems*, *1*(1), 87–97. doi:10.1007/BF02222880

Selmi, M. (2006). Privacy for the working class: Public work and private lives. *Louisiana Law Review*, *66*, 1035–1056.

Senate Standing Committee on Environment, Communications and the Arts. (2009). *The reporting of sports news and the emergence of digital media report*. Retrieved June 1, 2009, from http://www.aph.gov.au/senate/committee/eca_ctte/completed_inquiries/index.htm

Serino, C., Furner, C. P., & Smatt, C. M. (2005). Making it personal: How personalization affects trust over time. *Proceedings of the Hawaii International Conference on System Sciences (ICIS)*, Waikoloa, HI.

Serrano, N., & Torres, J. (2010). *IEEE Software, May/June*. USA: IEEE Computer Society.

Setten, W. v., & Sanders, P. (2009). *Citizen alert with cell broadcasting: The technology, the standards and the way forward*. Retrieved 18 October, 2009, from http://www.chorist.eu/index.php?page=1&sel=1

Shankar, V., Urban, G. L., & Sultan, F. (2002). Online trust: A stakeholder perspective, concepts, implications, and future directions. *The Journal of Strategic Information Systems*, *11*(3-4), 325–344. doi:10.1016/S0963-8687(02)00022-7

Shapiro, S. P. (1987). The social control of impersonal trust. *American Journal of Sociology*, *93*(3), 623–658. doi:10.1086/228791

Sheppard, B. H., & Sherman, D. M. (1998). The grammars of trust: A model and general implications. *Academy of Management Review*, *23*(3), 422–437. doi:10.2307/259287

Shin, D. (2010). The effects of trust, security and privacy in social networking: A security-based approach to understand the pattern of adoption. *Interacting with Computers*, *3*(5).

Shiode, N., Li, C., Batty, M., Longley, P., & Maguire, D. (2002). *The impact and penetration of location-based services* (pp. 1–16). London, UK: Centre for Advanced Spatial Analysis, University College London.

Short, J., Williams, E., & Christie, B. (1976). *The social psychology of telecommunications*. New York, NY: John Wiley.

Shortliffe, E. H. (1998). *Semi-plenary: The evolution of health-care records in the era of the Internet*. Paper presented at the MedInfo Conference, Seoul, Korea.

SHRM. (2005). *Workplace privacy–poll findings*. A Study by the Society for Human Resource Management and CareerJournal.com.

Shuen, A. (2008). *Web 2.0: A strategy guide*. O'Reilly Media, Inc.

Siegrist, M., Cvetkovich, G. T., & Gutscher, H. (2001). Shared values, social trust, and the perception of geographic cancer clusters. *Risk Analysis*, *21*(6), 1047–1054. doi:10.1111/0272-4332.216173

Simonsson, M., Johnson, P., & Wijkström, H. (2007). *Model-based IT governance maturity assessments with COBIT*. KTH Royal Institute of Technology - Publications and Reports of School of Electrical Engineering. Retrieved from http://www.ee.kth.se/php/modules /publications/reports/2007/IR-EE-ICS_2007_026.pdf

Sinclair, L. (2010, January 21). Google enters fight for sports broadcast rights. *The Australian*, (p. 5).

Singhapakdi, A., & Vitell, S. (1991). Research note: Selected factors influencing marketers' deontological norms. *Journal of the Academy of Marketing Science*, *19*(1), 37–42. doi:10.1007/BF02723422

Sky Channel Pty Ltd v. Austar Entertainment Pty Ltd. (2005). NSWSC 815.

Slay, J., & Koronios, A. (2006). *Information Technology security & risk management*. John Wiley Sons Australia Ltd, Milton Qld.

Smallwood, S. (2004). Arts professor at new school U. resigns after admitting plagiarism. *The Chronicle of Higher Education*. Retrieved February, 2010, from http://www.skidmore.edu/~rscarce/Writing_Tips/Art_Professor's_Plagiarism.html

Smith, J. (2009). *Fastest growing demographic on Facebook: Women over 55*. Retrieved February 12th, 2010, from http://www.insidefacebook.com/2009/02/02/fastest-growing-demographic-on-facebook-women-over-55/

Smith, R. (2002). *Complexities of simulating domestic infrastructure protection*. Titan Systems Corporation, Orlando, FA, USA.

So, M. W. C., & Sculli, D. (2002). The role of trust, quality, value and risk in conducting e-business. *Industrial Management & Data Systems*, *102*(9), 503–512. doi:10.1108/02635570210450181

Socialman. (2009). Allowing staff to use Orkut? Better take care. *Social Unwire India*. Retrieved November 20th, 2009, from http://www.social.unwireindia.com/2009/07/allowing-staff-to-use-orkut-better-take-cover

Society for Information Management. (2008). Retrieved February 5, 2009, from http://www.stevensnewsservice.com/pr/pr1206

Song, J., & Kim, Y. J. (2006). Social influence process in the acceptance of a virtual community service. *Information Systems Frontiers*, *8*(3), 241–252. doi:10.1007/s10796-006-8782-0

Sophos. (2007). *Press release: Facebook members bare all on networks*. Retrieved November 20th, 2009, from http://www.sophos.com/pressoffice/news/articles/2007/10/facebook-network.html

Spears, R., Lea, M., Corneliessen, R. A., Postemes, T., & Ter Harr, W. (2002). Computer-mediated communication as a channel for social resistance: The strategic side of SIDE. *Small Group Research*, *33*(5), 555–574. doi:10.1177/104649602237170

Spears, R., & Lea, M. (1992). Social influence and the influence of the social in computer mediated communication. In Lea, M. (Ed.), *Contexts of computer-mediated communication* (pp. 30–65). Hemel Hempstead, UK: Harvester Wheatsheaf.

Spiekermann, S. (2004). General aspects of location-based services. In Schiller, J., & Voisard, A. (Eds.), *Location-based services* (pp. 9–26). San Francisco, CA: Elsevier. doi:10.1016/B978-155860929-7/50002-9

Sports and General Press Agency Ltd v 'Our Dogs' Publishing Co. Ltd. (1917). 2 KB 125.

Sproull, L., & Kiesler, S. (1991). Computers, networks and work. *Scientific American*, (September): 84–91.

Sproull, L., & Faraj, S. (1997). Atheism, sex and databases: The net as a social technology. In Kiesler, S. (Ed.), *Culture of the Internet* (pp. 35–51). Mahwah, NJ: Lawrence Erlbaum Associates.

SSE-CMM.org. (2009). *How secure is SSE-CMM?* Retrieved from http://www.secure-software-engineering.com/2008/02/19/how-secure-is-sse-cmm

Stabb, S., Bhargava, B., Lilien, L., Rosenthal, A., Winslett, M., & Sloman, M. (2004). The pudding of trust. *IEEE Intelligent Systems*, *19*(5), 74–88. doi:10.1109/MIS.2004.52

Staff Reporter. (2009, 22 December). Fear for patients amid e-record troubles. *The Australian Financial Review (AFR)*. Retrieved 26 February, 2010, from http://www.afr.com/

Stafford, T. F., Stafford, M. R., & Schkade, L. L. (2004). Determining uses and gratifications for the internet. *Decision Sciences*, *35*, 259–288. doi:10.1111/j.00117315.2004.02524.x

Stanton, J. M. (2000a). Reactions to employee performance monitoring: Framework, review, and research directions. *Human Performance*, *13*(1), 85–113. doi:10.1207/S15327043HUP1301_4

Stanton, J. M. (2000b). Traditional and electronic monitoring from an organizational justice perspective. *Journal of Business and Psychology*, *15*(1), 129–147. doi:10.1023/A:1007775020214

Stanton, J. M., & Barnes-Farrell, J. L. (1996). Effects of electronic performance-monitoring on personal control, satisfaction and performance. *The Journal of Applied Psychology*, *81*, 738–745. doi:10.1037/0021-9010.81.6.738

Stepanikova, I., Mollborn, S., Cook, K. S., Thom, D. H., & Kramer, R. M. (2006). Patients' race, ethnicity, language, and trust in a physician. *Journal of Health and Social Behavior*, *47*(4), 390–405. doi:10.1177/002214650604700406

Stephens, D. (2003). Protecting records in the face of chaos, calamity, and cataclysm. *The Information Management Journal, January/February*, 33-40.

Stewart, M. (1995). Effective physician-patient communication and health outcomes: A review. *Canadian Medical Association Journal*, *152*(9), 1423–1433.

Stojanović, D., Djordjevic-Kajan, S., Papadopoulos, A. N., & Nanopoulos, A. (2007). Monitoring and tracking moving objects in mobile environments. In Taniar, D. (Ed.), *Encyclopedia of mobile computing and commerce* (pp. 660–665). London, UK: Information Science Reference. doi:10.4018/9781599040028.ch110

Story, L. (2007, December 6). Apologetic, Facebook changes ad program. *New York Times.* USA.

Stothard, M. (2008). 1 in 2 admits to plagiarism. *Varsity.* Retrieved February, 2010, from http://www.varsity.co.uk/news/1058

Strater, K., & Richter, H. (2007). Examining privacy and disclosure in a social networking community. *ACM International Conference Proceeding Series, 229.* Pittsburgh, USA.

Suggs, S. L. (2006). A 10-year retrospective of research in new technologies for health communication. *Journal of Health Communication, 11,* 61–77. doi:10.1080/10810730500461083

Sunden, J. (2003). *Material virtualities.* New York, NY: Peter Lang.

Surowiecki, J. (2005). *The wisdom of crowds: Why the many are smarter than the few and how collective wisdom shapes business, economies, societies and nations.* New York, NY: Random House Inc.

Survey, A. M. A. (2001). Workplace monitoring and surveillance. Retrieved from http://www.amanet.org/research /pdfs/ ems_short20 01.pdf

Survey, A. M. A. (2003). Email rules, policies and practices survey. Retrieved from http://www.amanet.org/ research/ pdfs/ email_policies_practices.pdf

Survey, A. M. A. (2005). Electronic monitoring and surveillance survey. Retrieved from http://www.amanet.org/ research/ pdfs/ ems_summary0 5.pdf

Sutherland-Smith, W. (2010). Retribution, deterrence and reform: The dilemmas of plagiarism management in universities. *Journal of Higher Education Policy and Management, 32*(1), 5–16. doi:10.1080/13600800903440519

Swinth, K. R., & Blascovich, J. (2002). Perceiving and responding to others: Human-human and human-computer social interaction in collaborative virtual environments. *Proceedings of the 5th Annual International workshop on PRESENCE.* Porto, Portugal.

Tahaghoghi, S. (2008). *Avoiding plagiarism–program code.* RMT University. Retrieved February, 2010, from http://mams.rmit.edu.au/ 14rfpbr1vh3t.pdf

Tajfel, H., & Turner, J. C. (1986). *The social identity of intergroup relations.* Chicago, IL: Nelson-Hall.

Tang, P. C., & Lansky, D. (2005). The missing link: Bridging the patient-provider health information gap. *Health Tracking, 24,* 1290–1295.

Tavani, H. T. (2004). *Ethics and technology: Ethical issues in an age of information and communication technology. Wiley* (International Edition). John Wiley and Sons.

TCN Channel Nine Pty Ltd v. Network Ten Pty Ltd. (2002). FCAFC 146.

Teague, B., McLeaod, R., & Pascoe, S. (2009). *2009 Victorian bushfire royal commission interim report.* Victorian State Government.

Telstra (2009). *Social media policy–Telstra's 3R's of social media engagement.* Telstra, Australia. Retrieved November 20th, 2009, from http://www.telstra.com.au/abouttelstra/media/docs/social-media-company-policy_final_150409.pdf

Telstra Corporation Pty Ltd v. Premier Media Group Pty Ltd. (2007). FCA 568.

Templeman, D., & Bergin, A. (2008). *Taking a punch: Building a more resilient Australia.* Retrieved 02 February, 2009, from http://www.aspi.org.au/publications/publication_details.aspx?ContentID=165

The 3rd Generation Partnership Project. (2008). *Technical specification group services and system aspects: Study for requirements for a public warning system (PWS) service (Release 8).* Retrieved 13 April, 2009, from http://www.3gpp.org/ftp/tsg_sa/WG1_Serv/TSGS1_37_Orlando/Docs/S1-070824.doc

The 3rd Generation Partnership Project. (2009). *Technical specification group services and system aspects: Functional stage 2 description of location services (LCS) (Release 9)*. Retrieved 16 January, 2010, from http://www.3gpp.org/ftp/Specs/archive/23_series/23.271/

The Associated Press. (2009). *Submission to the Senate Standing Committee on Environment, Communications and the Arts*. Retrieved May 14, 2009, from http://www.aph.gov.au/senate/committee/eca_ctte/sports_news/submissions.htm

The Australian Communications and Media Authority. (2004). *Location location location: The future use of location information to enhance the handling of emergency mobile phone calls*. Retrieved 21 October, 2007, from http://acma.gov.au/webwr/consumer_info/location.pdf

The Australian Communications and Media Authority. (2009). *Australia's emergency call service in a changing environment*. Retrieved 25 September, 2009, from http://www.acma.gov.au/webwr/_assets/main/lib311250/future_of_emergency_call_svces.pdf

The Australian Early Warning Network. (2009). Townsville city council signs up to the early warning network. Retrieved 7 December, 2009, from http://www.ewn.com.au/media/townsville_city_council.aspx

The Australian Government: Attorney General's Department. (2009). *Rudd government implements COAG agreement on telephone-based emergency warning systems (Joint Media Release)*. Retrieved 02 August, 2009, from http://www.ag.gov.au/www/ministers/mcclelland.nsf/Page/MediaReleases_2009_FirstQuarter_23February20-09RuddGovernmentImplementsCOAGAgreementonTelephone-BasedEmergencyWarningSystems

The Australian Government: Department of Broadband Communications and the Digital Economy. (2009). *Telecommunications amendment (integrated public number database) bill 2009: Explanatory memorandum*. Retrieved 6 August, 2009, from http://parlinfo.aph.gov.au/parlInfo/download/legislation/ems/r4062_ems_d2937505-3da94059b9cbe382e891dd23/upload_word/TelAm(IPND)_EM.doc;fileType=application%2Fmsword

The Australian Government: Department of Transport and Regional Services. (2004). *Natural disasters in Australia: Reforming mitigation, relief and recovery arrangements*. Retrieved 18 February, 2009, from http://www.ema.gov.au/www/emaweb/rwpattach.nsf/VAP/(99292794923AE8E7CBABC6FB71541EE1)~Natural+Disasters+in+Australia+-+Review.pdf/$file/Natural+Disasters+in+Australia+-+Review.pdf

The Australian. (2007, February, 26). *Premier promises mobile phone terrorism alert*. Factiva.

The Australian. (2010a). *Bligh hits out at sick net sites*. Retrieved February 28th, 2010, from http://www.theaustralian.com.au/politics/state-politics/bligh-hits-out-at-sick-net-sites/story-e6frgczx-1225834063831

The Australian. (2010b). *Facebook vandal complaints futile*. Retrieved from http://www.theaustralian.com.au/australian-it/facebook-vandal-complaints-futile/story-e6frgakx-1225834303404, Accessed 28th February, 2010

The Australian. (2010c). *Online ombudsman for Facebook woes*. Retrieved February 20th, 2010, from http://www.theaustralian.com.au/australian-it/online-ombudsman-for-facebook-woes/story-e6frgakx-1225834756343

The Cellular Emergency Alert Systems Association. (2002). *Handset requirements specification: Reaching millions in a matter of seconds*. Retrieved 02 April, 2007, from http://www.ceasa-int.org/library/Handset_Requirements_Specification.pdf

The European Commission. (2009). *The CHORIST project: Integrating communications for enhanced environmental risk management and citizens safety*. Retrieved 07 November, 2009, from http://www.chorist.eu/index.php?page=1&sel=1

The European Telecommunications Standards Institute. (2003). *Requirements for communication of ctizens with authorities/organizations in case of distress (emergency call handling)*. Retrieved 10 May, 2007, from http://etsi.org/WebSite/homepage.aspx

The European Telecommunications Standards Institute. (2006a). *Analysis of the short message service and cell broadcast service for emergency messaging applications: Emergency messaging, SMS and CBS*. Retrieved 10 May, 2007, from http://etsi.org/WebSite/homepage.aspx

The European Telecommunications Standards Institute. (2006b). *Emergency communications (EMTEL): Requirements for communications from authorities/organizations to individuals, groups or the general public during emergencies.* Retrieved 10 May, 2007, from http://etsi.org/WebSite/homepage.aspx

The European Telecommunications Standards Institute. (2010). *Study for requirements for a public warning system (PWS) service.* Retrieved 10 Feb, 2010, from http://webstats.3gpp.org/ftp/Specs/html-info/22968.htm

The Federal Communications Commission. (2005). *Review of the emergency alert system.* Retrieved 13 April, 2008, from http://www.fcc.gov/eb/Orders/2005/FCC-05-191A1.html

The International Telecommunications Union. (2007). *Compendium of ITU'S work on emergency telecommunications.* Geneva, Switzerland: The United Nations Agency for Information and Communication Technologies.

The Minister for Police and Emergency Services. (2005). *First calls made as part of early warning trial.* Retrieved 04 June, 2007, from http://www.legislation.vic.gov.au/domino/Web_Notes/newmedia.nsf/35504bc71d3adebcca256cfc0082c2b8/4ae0fe91bdeb3e8aca25704d000729b0!OpenDocument

The United States Department of Homeland Security. (2008). *National emergency communications plan.* Retrieved 06 October, 2009, from http://www.dhs.gov/xlibrary/assets/national_emergency_communications_plan.pdf

The Victorian Bushfires Royal Commission. (2009). *Victorian bushfires royal commission interim report.*

The Victorian Department of Treasury and Finance. (2009). *Request for information (RFI) for: Location based identification of active mobile handsets for emergency notification purposes.* (RFI Number: SS-06-2009). Retrieved 19 November, 2009, from https://www.tenders.vic.gov.au/tenders/tender/display/tender-details.do?id=87&action=display-tender-details&returnUrl=%2Ftender%2Fsearch%2Ftender-search.do%3Faction%3Dadvanced-tender-search-closed-tender

Thoroughvision Pty Ltd v. Sky Channel Pty Ltd. (2005). FCA 1527.

Time Magazine. (2010). *How prisoners harass their victims using Facebook.* Retrieved October 15th, 2009, from http://www.time.com/time/business/article/0,8599,1964916,00.html#ixzz0gb2oD8Ge

Timmons, S. (2003). Nurses resisting information technology. *Nursing Inquiry, 10*(4), 257–269. doi:10.1046/j.1440-1800.2003.00177.x

Timpka, T., Nordqvist, C., & Lindqvist, K. (2009). Infrastructural requirements for local implementation of safety policies: The discordance between top-down and bottom-up systems of action. *BMC Health Services Research, 9*(1), 45. doi:10.1186/1472-6963-9-45

TISN. (2003). *Fact sheet: What is critical infrastructure? Trusted Information Sharing Network.* Canberra: TISN.

TISN. (2004b). *Critical infrastructure protection national strategy.* Trusted Information Sharing Network (TISN). Retrieved from http://www.tisn.gov.au/agd /WWW/rwpattach.nsf /VAP/ (930C12A91 01F61D4349 3D44C70E84EAA)~National+CIP+Strategy+2.1+final. PDF/$file/National +CIP +Strategy+ 2.1+final.PDF

TISN. (2006). *Critical infrastructure protection: Whose responsibility is it?* Trusted Information Sharing Network (TISN). Retrieved from http://www.tisn.gov.au/

Togt, R., Beinat, E., Zlatanova, S., & Scholten, H. (2005). Location interoperability services for medical emergency operations during disasters. In P. v. Oosterom, S. Zlatanova & E. M. Fendel (Eds.), *Geo-information for disaster management* (pp. 1127-1141). Berlin/ Heidelberg, Germany: Springer

Toigo, J. W. (1996). *Disaster recovery planning: For computers and communication resources.* John Wiley & Sons, Inc.

Toigo, J. W. (2002). *Disaster recovery planning: Preparing for the unthinkable* (3rd ed.). Prentice Hall.

Tsalgatidou, A., Veijalainen, J., Markkula, J., Katasonov, A., & Hadjiefthymiades, S. (2003). *Mobile e-commerce and location-based services: Technology and requirements.* Paper presented at the The 9th Scandinavian Research Conference on Geographical Information Sciences, Espoo, Finland.

Turban, E., King, D., Lee, J., Liang, T. P., & Turban, D. (2010). *Electronic commerce 2010: A managerial perspective* (6th ed.). Boston, MA: Pearson.

Turban, E., Leidner, D., McClean, E., & Wetherbe, J. (2006). *Information Technology for management–transforming organisations in the digital economy* (5th ed.). USA: John Wiley & Sons Inc.

Turel, O., Yuan, Y., & Connelly, C. E. (2008). In justice we trust: Predicting user acceptance of e-customer services. *Journal of Management Information Systems, 24*(4), 123–151. doi:10.2753/MIS0742-1222240405

Turner, M. J., Oltsik, J., & McKnight, J. (2008). *ISO, ITIL and COBIT triple play fosters optimal security management execution.* SC Magazine Awards 2009 - USA. Retrieved February 1, 2009 from http://www.scmagazineus.com/ISO-ITIL-and-COBIT-triple-play-fosters-optimal-security-management-execution/article/108620/

Turnitin. (2009). *Answers to common legal questions about Turnitin.* Retrieved February, 2010, from http://www.turnitin.com/ resources/documentation /turnitin/ sales/ Turnitin_FAQ_Legal.pdf

Turow, J., Feldman, L., & Metlzer, K. (2005). *Open to exploitation: American shoppers online and offline.* A Report from the Annenberg Public Policy Centre of the University of Pennsylvania.

Tyler, T. R., & Lind, E. A. (1992). A relational model of authority in group. *Advances in Experimental Social Psychology, 25*, 115–192. doi:10.1016/S0065-2601(08)60283-X

Uhlirz, M. (2007). A market and user view on LBS. In Gartner, G., Cartwright, W., & Peterson, M. P. (Eds.), *Location based services and telecartography* (pp. 47–58). Berlin/ Heidelberg, Germany: Springer. doi:10.1007/978-3-540-36728-4_4

UNAIDS. (2009). *Papua New Guinea: Country progress report.* Retrieved July 12, 2009, from http://data.unaids.org/pub/Report/2008/papua_new_guinea_2008_country_progress_report_en.pdf

UNCTAD. (2007). *Information economy report 2007-2008 science and technology for development: The new paradigm of ICT.* Geneva, Switzerland: United Nations Publication.

United Nations News Centre. (2010). *Earthquakes the deadliest of all disasters during past decade.* Retrieved 29 January, 2010, from http://www.un.org/apps/news/printnews.asp?nid=33613

University of Waikato. (2005). *Waikato environment for data analysis* v3.5.3. Retrieved on October 8, 2006, from http://www.cs.waikato.ac.nz /ml/ weka/

Verbowski, C. (2006). System administration: Drowning in management complexity. In *LISA 2006: Proceedings of the 20th Large Installation System Administration Conference.* Washington, DC: USENIX. Retrieved on February 2, 2010, from http://www.usenix.org/media/events /lisa06/ tech/mp3/ verbowski_mgt_complexity.mp3

VeriGuide. (2010). *Homepage information.* Retrieved May, 2010, from http://www.veriguide.org

Victoria Park Racing and Recreation Grounds Company Ltd v. Taylor. (1937). 58 CLR 479.

Victorian State Parliamentary Offices. (2003). *Watching brief on the war on terrorism: Submission by the state Of Victoria to the joint standing committee on foreign Affairs, defence and trade hearing on Australia's counter terrorism capabilities.* Retrieved 18 January, 2009, from http://www.aph.gov.au/House/committee/jfadt/terrorism/subs/sub13.pdf

Vijayan, J. (2009). *Social networking sites leaking personal information to third parties.* Retrieved November 10th, 2009, from http://www.networkworld.com/news/2009/092409-social-networking-sites-leaking-personal.html

Vogelsmeier, A. A., Halbesleben, J. R. B., & Scott-Cawiezell, J. R. (2008). Technology implementation and workarounds in the nursing home. *Journal of the American Medical Informatics Association, 15*(1), 114–119. doi:10.1197/jamia.M2378

Von Solms, B. (2005). Information security governance: COBIT or ISO 17799 or both? *Computers & Security, 24*(2), 99–104. doi:10.1016/j.cose.2005.02.002

Wagner, S., & Sanders, G. (2001). Considerations in ethical decision making. [Kluwer Academic Publishers, The Netherlands.]. *Journal of Business Ethics, 29*, 161–167. doi:10.1023/A:1006415514200

Wang, H., Lee, M. K. O., & Wang, C. (1998). Consumer privacy concerns about Internet marketing. *Communications of the ACM, 41*(3), 63–70. doi:10.1145/272287.272299

Wang, S. S., & Hong, J. (2010). Discourse behind the forbidden realm: Internet surveillance and its implications on China's blogosphere. [Elsevier.]. *Telematics and Informatics, 27*(1), 67–78. doi:10.1016/j.tele.2009.03.004

Wang, C., & Wulf, W. A. (1997). Towards a framework for security management. *NIST NISSC Conference Proceedings*. Retrieved from http://csrc.nist.gov/nissc/1997/proceedings/522.pdf

Ward, K. J. (1999). The cyber-ethnographic and the emergence of the virtually new community. *Journal of Information Technology, 14*, 95–105. doi:10.1080/026839699344773

Warschauer, M. (2002). Reconceptualizing the digital divide. *First Monday, 7*(7).

Wasko, M. M., & Faraj, S. (2000). It is what one does: Why people participate and help others in electronic communities of practice. *The Journal of Strategic Information Systems, 9*, 155–173. doi:10.1016/S0963-8687(00)00045-7

Weber, J. M., Malhotra, D., & Murnighan, J. K. (2005). Normal acts of irrational trust, motivated attributions, and the process of trust development. In Staw, B. M., & Kramer, R. M. (Eds.), *Research in organizational behavior* (pp. 75–102). New York, NY: Elsevier.

Weill, P., & Ross, J. W. (2004). *IT governance: How top performers manage IT decision rights for superior results*. Boston, MA: Harvard Business School Press.

Wellheiser, J., & Scott, J. (2002). *An ounce of prevention: Integrated disaster planning for archives, libraries, and record centers*, 2nd ed. Scarecrow Press. The Canadian Archives Foundation. Lenexa, KS: ARMA International.

Wellman, B., & Gulia, M. (1999). Net surfers don't ride alone. In Wellman, B. (Ed.), *Networks in the global village* (pp. 331–366). Boulder, CO: Westview Press.

Wen, H. J., Schwieger, D., & Gershuny, P. (2007). Internet usage monitoring in the workplace: Its legal challenges and implementation strategies. *Information Systems Management, 24*, 185–196. doi:10.1080/10580530701221072

West Australian Newspapers Ltd. (2009). *Submission to the Senate Standing Committee on Environment, Communications and the Arts*. Retrieved May 14, 2009, from http://www.aph.gov.au/senate/committee/eca_ctte/sports_news/submissions.htm

Westbrook, J. I., Ampt, A., Kearney, L., & Rob, M. I. (2008). All in a day's work: An observational study to quantify how and with whom doctors on hospital wards spend their time. *Electronic Medical Journal of Australia, 188*(9), 506–508.

Westbrook, J. I., Braithwaite, J., Georgiou, A., Ampt, A., Creswick, N., & Coiera, E. (2007). Multimethod evaluation of information and communication technologies in health in the context of wicked problems and sociotechnical theory. *Journal of the American Medical Informatics Association, 14*(6), 746–755. doi:10.1197/jamia.M2462

Whitehead, M. (2007). A typology of actions to tackle social inequalities in health. *Journal of Epidemiology and Community Health, 61*, 473–478. doi:10.1136/jech.2005.037242

Whitney, L. (2009). *Employers grappling with social network use*. Retrieved November 20th, 2009, from http://news.cnet.com/8301-10797_3-10360849-235.html

Whittaker, S., Isaacs, E., & O'day, V. (1997). Widening the net: Workshop report on the theory and practice of physical and network communities. *SIGCHI Bulletin, 18*(1), 27-32.

Williams, P. A. H. (2008). When trust defies common security sense. *Health Informatics Journal, 14*(3), 211–221. doi:10.1177/1081180X08092831

Williams, F. (2008, June 5). Blast disrupts gas supply to miners. Herald Sun, (p. 78).

Williamson, O. E. (1993). Calculativeness, trust, and economic organization. *The Journal of Law & Economics, 36*, 453–486. doi:10.1086/467284

Wilson, P. (1983). *Second-hand knowledge: An inquiry into cognitive authority*. Westport, CT: Greenwood Press.

Wilson, J. (2007). MySpace, your space, or our space? *New Frontiers in Electronic Evidence. Oregon Law Review, 86*, 1201.

Wilson, B., & Ryder, M. (1996). Dynamic learning communities: An alternative to designed instruction. In M. Simonson (Ed.) *Proceedings of selected research and development presentations* (pp. 800-809). Washington, D. C.: Association for Educational Communications and Technology. Retrieved on January 20, 2010, from http://carbon.ucdenver.edu/~mryder/dlc.html

Wimberley, P., & Walden, D., Wiggins, Miller, R., & Stacy, A. (2005). HIPAA and nursing education: How to teach in a paranoid health care environment. *The Journal of Nursing Education, 44*(11), 489–492.

Wire, C. M. S. (2010). *Social media is good and bad for business*. Retrieved January 10th, 2010, from http://www.cmswire.com/cms/document-management/smb-tech-rollup-social-media-is-good-and-bad-for-business-with-security-top-of-mind-006711.php

Wolak, J., Finkelhor, D., & Mitchell, K. J. (2004). Internet-initiated sex crimes against minors: Implications for prevention based on findings from a national study. *The Journal of Adolescent Health, 35*(5), 424–433. doi:10.1016/j.jadohealth.2004.05.006

Worchel, P. (1979). Trust and distrust. In Austin, W. G., & Worchel, P. (Eds.), *Social psychology of intergroup relations* (pp. 174–187). Monterey, CA: Broks/Cole.

World Health Organisation. (2005). *The know do gap*. Geneva: Proceedings from Gap Knowledge Translation in Global Health.

World Health Organisation. (2009) *Choosing the channels of communication*. Retrieved July 1, 2009, from http://www.wpro.who.int/internet/resources.ashx/TFI/choosing+the+channels+of+communication.pdf

Wu, J. J., & Tsang, A. S. L. (2008). Factors affecting members trust belief and behaviour intention in virtual communities. *Behaviour & Information Technology, 27*(2), 115–125. doi:10.1080/01449290600961910

Xue, N., & Shen, L. (2003). Chinese word segmentation as lmr tagging. In *Proceedings of Second SIGHAN Workshop on Chinese Language Processing*, (pp. 176–179).

Yan, Z. (2009). Limited knowledge and limited resources: Children's and adolescents' understanding of the Internet. *Journal of Applied Developmental Psychology, 30*, 103–115. doi:10.1016/j.appdev.2008.10.012

Zajac, J. D. (2010). Medical identity fraud in the United States: Could it happen here? *The Medical Journal of Australia, 192*(3), 19.

Zand, D. E. (1972). Trust and managerial problem solving. *Administrative Science Quarterly, 17*(2), 229–239. doi:10.2307/2393957

Zucker, L. G. (1986). Production of trust: Institutional sources of economic structure. In Staw, B. M., & Cummings, L. L. (Eds.), *Research in organizational behavior* (pp. 53–111). Greenwich, CT: JAI Press.

Zweig, D., & Webster, J. (2002). Where is the line between benign and invasive? An examination of psychological barriers to the acceptance of awareness monitoring system. *Journal of Organizational Behavior, 23*(5), 605–633. doi:10.1002/job.157

About the Contributors

Marian Quigley, PhD, BA, HDTS (Art & Craft) is an Adjunct Research Fellow in the Faculty of Information Technology, Monash University, an Animation Curator for *australianscreen online*, and a freelance writer, editor, and artist. Marian has over thirty years of teaching experience in secondary and tertiary institutions teaching Art, English, Creative Writing, Communications, Media Studies and Information Ethics and has also supervised a number of postgraduate and honours students. Prior to her retirement in 2006, she was a senior lecturer, postgraduate coordinator and director of research in the Berwick School of Information Technology, Monash University. Marian's major research interests are the social effects of information and communication technologies and animation. She has published three books: *Encyclopedia of Information Ethics and Security* (IGI Global, Hershey, PA, USA, 2007); *Women* Do *Animate: Interviews with 10 Australian Women Animators* (Insight Publications, Mentone, Australia, 2005) and *Information Security and Ethics: Social and Organizational Issues* (IRM Press, Hershey, PA, USA & London, UK, 2005), as well as numerous book chapters, journal articles and conference papers.

* * *

Suchit Ahuja is a recent Master of Science graduate from the Department of Computer & Information Technology at Purdue University, West Lafayette, Indiana, USA. During his graduate study, Ahuja focused primarily on Information Technology Management areas including information security management and business/IT alignment, with secondary focus on IT governance, risk and compliance. In addition, his research interests include topics related to health Information Technology such as health Information System design & development, e-healthcare & mobile healthcare systems and health information security & patient privacy. He has also been employed with Purdue University as an Applications Analyst at the Office of the Vice President for Research.

Anas Aloudat is a PhD candidate in the School of Information Systems and Technology, at the Faculty of Informatics, at the University of Wollongong. His thesis is investigating the utilization of nationwide location-based services for emergency management within Australia from social and behavioural perspectives. Mr. Aloudat holds a Master of Science in Computing from the University of Technology, Sydney. He is presently a sessional lecturer/tutor and research assistant at the University of Wollongong. He is a member of the IEEE Society on Social Implications of Technology, a member of the Civil Emergency Alert Services Association, a member of the Disaster Preparedness and Emergency Response Association and has been a member of the Research Network for a Secure Australia since 2006.

Michael J. Chapple, PhD is Senior Advisor to the Executive Vice President and concurrent Assistant Professor of Computer Applications at the University of Notre Dame. Dr. Chapple specializes in information security issues and has 15 years of experience in the public and private sectors. He is a technical editor for Information Security Magazine and has written a dozen books, including Information Security Illuminated, SQL Server 2008 for Dummies, and the CISSP Prep Guide. Dr. Chapple earned both his bachelor's and doctoral degrees from Notre Dame in computer science & engineering. He also holds a MS in computer science from the University of Idaho and an MBA from Auburn University.

Chi Hong Cheong is working as a research assistant under the VeriGuide project. In particular, he works on the document analysis research and development of the VeriGuide project, which includes citation extraction, citation analysis, and inter-document relation discovery. He received his BSc (first-class honours) and MPhil degrees from the Chinese University of Hong Kong (CUHK) in 2004 and 2006, respectively. He is also currently a PhD student at the same university. His research interests are database systems, computer and network security, and text mining.

Prajesh Chhanabhai is undertaking research at the University of Otago in the area of Health Informatics. His research focus is on empowering the health consumer with a specific interest in enabling this in the developing world. In the same notion, he has an interest in m-health, social network sites and generation Y, and how these relate to health information sharing and health information security.

Regina Connolly is a Senior Lecturer in Management Information Systems at Dublin City University Business School, Dublin, Ireland and is programme director of the MSc in electronic commerce. In her undergraduate degree, she received the Kellogg Award for outstanding dissertation and her MSc degree was awarded with distinction. She was conferred with her PhD in Information Systems from Trinity College Dublin. Her research interests include electronic commerce, online trust and privacy issues, website service quality, e-government, and strategic information systems. She has served on the expert e-commerce advisory group for Dublin Chamber of Commerce, which has advised National Government on e-commerce strategic planning.

Charles R. Crowell, PhD is a professor in the Department of Psychology and also serves as Director of the Computer Applications Program at Notre Dame. Professor Crowell's work investigates a spectrum of psychological phenomena ranging from the basic mechanisms underlying human behaviour to the ways in which humans interact with and are influenced by technology. He also maintains an ongoing interest in the societal and ethical impacts of various modern technologies such as humanoid robots, virtual worlds, and electronically-mediated communication.

Nickolas Falkner is a lecturer in the School of Computer Science at the University of Adelaide. After over 10 years spent in network and systems administration, he returned to university to pursue further study and received a PhD in the discovery and classification of information in large systems from the University of Adelaide. His teaching areas include computer networks, ethics in Information Technology and puzzle-based learning. In recent years, he has increased the profile of ethical issues in the computer networks course, including discussions of the role of professional responsibility and the adoption of hybrid ethical solutions to achieve an ethical workplace. His research interests include wireless sensor networks, automated network configuration, data fusion, and data stream management. He is active in educational research, with a focus on increasing student participation, retention, and enthusiasm.

Juanita Fernando, PhD, is with the Faculty of Medicine, Nursing & Health Sciences at Monash University. Dr Fernando chairs the Health Sub-Committee of the Australian Privacy Foundation, is a Councillor with the Australasian College of Health Informatics and a member of the Australian Health Informatics Education Council and the Health Informatics Society. Her postgraduate teaching has covered a range of subjects from contemporary issues in health informatics to electronic health records, health Information Systems management, and research methods. Dr. Fernando's research concerns clinical informatics with a particular emphasis on information security and e-health tools and their contribution to best-practice work-flow methodologies in the health sector.

James (Jim) Goldman is Professor and Head of the Purdue Malware Lab in the Department of Computer & Information Technology at Purdue University where he founded the Telecommunications and Networking Technology (Network Engineering Technology) program. Jim has over 20 years of experience in telecommunications strategy, network engineering, and project management of regional, national, and global networking & security projects. Jim is a CISSP (Certified Information Systems Security Professional) with advanced training in computer forensics and is detailed to the FBI Cyber Crime Task Force. He has passed the certification exam for ISO27001 (Information Security Management System) Lead Auditor. He is an internationally published author with market leading textbooks in data communications and networking. An award-winning teacher, Jim is the recipient of Purdue's Murphy Award for Outstanding Undergraduate Teaching and was honored as a University Faculty Scholar and enrollee in Purdue's Book of Great Teachers. He received the INITA (Indiana IT Association) CyberStar Award in 2001 for Outstanding Indiana IT Educator. INITA CyberStar award was the predecessor to TechPoint's MIRA award. He is co-founder and President of InfoComm Systems, Inc., a network engineering and security consulting firm located in the Purdue Research Park. InfoComm's clients include Fortune 100 companies, hospitals, electrical utilities, and state and local governments. Among Jim's areas of research and publication are municipal telecommunications strategy, Information Technology economics and investment strategy, information security management, network security investment strategy, steganography and application of high performance computing to information security and cyber forensic problems including malware and botnet analysis.

Dennis C. Guster is a Professor of Computer Information Systems and Director of the Business Computing Research Laboratory at St. Cloud State University, MN, USA. His interests include network design, network performance analysis and computer network security. Dr. Guster has 25+ years of teaching experience in higher education and has served as a consultant and provided industry training to organizations such as Compaq, NASA, DISA, USAF, Motorola, and ATT. He has published numerous works in computer networking/security and has undertaken various sponsored research projects.

Alec Holt is the Director of the Health Informatics programme at the University of Otago, Dunedin, New Zealand. He has a global interest in ICT for developing countries (ICTD) and is linked with the Global Alliance for Information and Communication Technologies and Development (GAID) - Department of Economic and Social Affairs (UNDESA) - United Nations.

Bill Hutchinson was formally the Foundation IBM Chair in Information Security, Director of SECAU (Security Research Centre) and was coordinator of the Information Operations and Security programmes at Edith Cowan University, Western Australia. Bill was the co-founder of the Journal of Information Warfare. He has 30 years experience in Information Systems, management and security in government, the oil and finance industries, and academia. Bill has had numerous papers on information warfare, deception, system theory, and environmental security published. He is the co-author of *Information Warfare: Corporate Attack and Defence in a Digital World* and is an honorary professor at Edith Cowan University and Deakin University.

Irwin King is the Principal Investigator, Chief Technologist, and Co-founder of the VeriGuide project at the Chinese University of Hong Kong (CUHK). He is an Associate Editor of the IEEE Transactions on Neural Networks (TNN) and IEEE Computational Intelligence Magazine (CIM). His research interests include machine learning, Web intelligence & social computing, and multimedia processing. In these research areas, he has over 200 technical publications in journals and conferences with over 20 book chapters and edited volumes. He is also a member of the Board of Governors of INNS and a Vice-President and Governing Board Member of APNNA. He received his BSc degree in Engineering and Applied Science from California Institute of Technology, Pasadena and his MSc and PhD degree in Computer Science from the University of Southern California, Los Angeles.

Tak Pang Lau is working as the Project Leader of the VeriGuide project. He received his BSc and MPhil degrees from the Chinese University of Hong Kong (CUHK) in 2004 and 2006, respectively. In addition to documenting similarity comparison and its application in plagiarism prevention and detection, he is also interested in and working on enriching the VeriGuide system with various document analytic features, such as readability analysis, structural extraction, and inter-document relation discovery.

Olivia F. Lee is an Assistant Professor of Marketing at St. Cloud State University, MN, USA. She has worked as an operation manager at two university hospitals, and as a senior e-business market analyst in a business-to-business company prior to her academic career. Her research work focuses on technology practice in business environment, service organization and business resilience strategy. She has published her work in *Psychology and Marketing*, *Healthcare Marketing Quarterly*, *Journal of Information Technology Management*, *International Journal of Organization Analysis* and *Review of Business Research*.

Shona Leitch is a Senior Lecturer and Postgraduate Course Director in the School of Information Systems, Deakin University, Australia. Dr. Leitch completed her BSc (Hons) Psychology in 1998 and her PhD in 2008 in Educational Systems Analysis and Design. Dr. Leitch has worked in tertiary education since 2000, firstly in indigenous education, then Information Technology, and finally, Information Systems. Her current research interests include ethics, Web 2.0 technologies, and their applications to different environments and human and ethical security issues. Dr. Leitch has published over 30 conference papers, journal papers and book chapters and received research funding for her work into using Web 2.0 technologies in a tertiary teaching environment.

Lori N. K. Leonard is a Collins Endowed Professor and an Associate Professor of Management Information Systems at the University of Tulsa. Dr. Leonard received her PhD from the University of

Arkansas and is a member of the Association for Information Systems and the Decision Sciences Institute. Her research interests include electronic commerce, ethics in computing, C2C commerce, and online trust. Her publications have appeared in *Journal of the Association for Information Systems*, *Journal of Computer Information Systems*, *Journal of End User Computing*, *Information & Management*, *Electronic Markets*, *Journal of Organizational Computing and Electronic Commerce*, *Journal of Electronic Commerce in Organizations*, *Journal of Business Ethics*, as well as in other journals and proceedings of various conferences.

Tracy S. Manly is an Associate Professor of Accounting and the ONEOK Professor of Business in the Collins College of Business at The University of Tulsa. Her research interests are in ethics, accounting education, and taxation. Her work has been published in the *Journal of the American Taxation Association, Issues in Accounting Education, Advances in Taxation, Tax Notes Today, the Journal of Business, Finance & Accounting, and Global Perspectives on Accounting Education* among other journals. Manly was named the 2008 Oklahoma Society of Certified Public Accountants Outstanding Educator and was awarded the Innovation in Teaching and Learning Award at the Oklahoma Higher Education Teaching and Learning Conference.

Cliona McParland is currently a PhD student at Dublin City University Business School under the supervision of Dr. Regina Connolly, Senior Lecturer in Management Information Systems. Her PhD is in the area of technology-related privacy concerns with a particular emphasis on the analysis of dataveillance behavioural outcomes in the computer-mediated work environment. Her research interests include information privacy concerns, e-commerce, dataveillance and e-commerce risk and security management.

Katina Michael (MIEE'04, SMIEEE'06) holds a Doctor of Philosophy in Information and Communication Technology (ICT) from the Faculty of Informatics at the University of Wollongong, NSW, Australia ('03); a Master of Transnational Crime Prevention from the Faculty of Law at the University of Wollongong ('09) and a Bachelor of Information Technology from the School of Mathematical and Computing Science, NSW, Australia at the University of Technology, Sydney ('96). She is presently an Associate Professor at the University of Wollongong in the School of Information Systems and Technology ('02-'10) in Australia, and has previously been employed as a Senior Network Engineer at Nortel Networks ('96-'01). She has also worked as a Systems Analyst at Andersen Consulting and OTIS Elevator Company. Michael has published several edited books, but more recently co-authored a 500 page reference volume: *Innovative Automatic Identification and Location Based Services: from Bar Codes to Chip Implants* (Hershey, PA: IGI, 2009). She has published over 85 peer reviewed papers. Michael researches predominantly in the area of emerging technologies, and has secondary interests in technologies used for national security and their corresponding social implications.

Eun G. Park is Associate Professor in the School of Information Studies at McGill University, Montreal, Quebec, Canada. She holds a PhD from the University of California at Los Angeles, an MLS from the University of Illinois at Urbana-Champaign, and an MBA from the University of Pittsburgh. Her research interests include digital archives, digital preservation, metadata, authenticity and authentication, electronic records management, and social aspects of Information Technology. She teaches courses on metadata, electronic records systems, digital preservation, and records management. She has been awarded major grants from the Social Science and Humanities Research Council (SSHRC), SSHRC International Opportunity Fund, and Fonds de recherche sur la société et la culture (FQRSC). Eun is leading research teams regarding building digital archives of photos and films in the contexts of AIDS and HIV, InterPARES (International Research on Permanent Authentic Records in Electronic Systems) Project, and others.

Graeme Pye is a Lecturer with the School of Information Systems, Deakin University, Australia. He has successfully completed a PhD in critical infrastructure security and system modelling that involved developing a method utilising system security analysis and modelling at the School of Information Systems, Deakin University, Australia. Graeme is now continuing with further research as an early career researcher at the School of Information Systems and is continuing to focus on investigating the security aspects of Australian critical infrastructure and the relationships between associated infrastructures. He is also interested in information warfare and benchmarking information security in business.

Aaron Striegel (PhD) is currently an associate professor in the Department of Computer Science & Engineering at the University of Notre Dame. He received his PhD in December 2002 in Computer Engineering at Iowa State University under the direction of Dr. G. Manimaran. His research interests include networking (bandwidth conservation, QoS), computer security, Grid computing, and real-time systems. During his tenure as a student at Iowa State, he worked for various companies in research and development, including Sun Microsystems, Architecture Technology Corporation, and Emerson Process. He has received research and equipment funding from NSF, DARPA, Sun Microsystems, Hewlett Packard, Architecture Technology Corporation, and Intel.

Matthew Warren is the Head of School and a Professor in the School of Information Systems, Deakin University, Australia. Professor Warren has gained international recognition for his scholarly work in the areas of information security, risk analysis, e-business, information warfare and critical infrastructure protection. He has authored/co-authored over 225 books, book chapters, journal papers and conference papers. Professor Warren has received over $Australian 3,000,000 of research funding awards from national and international funding bodies including the Australian Research Council (ARC), the Engineering and Physical Sciences Research Council (EPSRC) in the UK, the South African Research Foundation and the European Union. Professor Warren is the former Chair of IFIP TC 11 Working Group 11.1 – Security Management and a former Director of the Australian Institute of Computer Ethics.

Mary Wyburn is a senior lecturer, Business Law Discipline, in the Faculty of Economics & Business at Sydney University. Her research interests are in the area of intellectual property law, in particular copyright, as well as in insolvency law. Mary was a member of the University of Sydney Human Research Ethics Committee in 2005 and 2006 and her teaching includes the regulatory environment and ethics of marketing. Before she became an academic, Mary practised as a solicitor in a commercial law firm and later as a legal officer with the Australian Copyright Council. She has acted as a consultant to copyright industry organisations including those in the music and publishing fields.

Qing Zou is a PhD student of the School of Information Studies at McGill University, Canada. He has been the Systems Librarian at Lakehead University Library, Thunder Bay, Canada since he received his MLIS from McGill University in 2005. His research interests include digital archives, integrated library systems, institutional repositories, metadata, knowledge organization systems, ontology, and social aspects of information science.

Index

Symbols

(RAIH) redundant array of inexpensive hosts
244, 245

A

academic environment 172, 191
academic quality 172, 191
activity analysis 265
AIDS 120, 121, 123, 125
application layer 255
application proxy firewalls 260, 261
Aristotelian moral virtues 39
Aristotle 39
Australian Communications and Media Authority (ACMA) 80, 137, 141, 142
Australian Competition and Consumer Commission (ACCC) 79, 80
Australian Computer Society (ACM) 198, 211
Australian Football League (AFL) 69
automated plagiarism detection system 172,
174, 175, 183, 191, 192, 195
automated system 174
automatic plagiarism detection system 175,
177, 179, 180, 181, 183, 191, 195

B

backup site 236, 238, 253
balanced scorecard (BSC) 277, 278, 280, 283,
284, 285, 286, 287, 288, 289, 290, 291,
294, 295, 296, 297, 298, 300, 301, 303,
309
Balanced Scorecard Institute (BSCI) 280
bastion host 260

Bebo 48, 62
biometric implementations 101
Bird Flu 116
blogs 4, 16
breakthrough technologies 129
Bulletin Board Systems (BBS) 4
bushfire 214, 220, 223, 225, 229
Business Software Alliance (BSA) 198, 199

C

Campus-wide E-mail System (CWEM) 189
Capability Maturity Model Integration (CMMI)
278
Centre for Learning Enhancement And Research (CLEAR) 187
Children's Online Privacy Protection Act
(COPPA) 278
client computer 238
Commonwealth Scientific and Industrial Research Organisation (CSIRO) 225, 227
communication networks 216, 230
communications technology 69
communication techniques 111
communication technologies 111, 112, 113,
115, 116, 122, 124, 127
communication tools 3, 4
Community Information Warning System
(CIWS) 138
computer infrastructure 231
computer mediated communication (CMC) 49
Computer-Mediated Surveillance 171
computer security 254, 255
computer threat 204

control objectives for Information Technology (COBIT) 277, 278, 280, 281, 282, 283, 284, 285, 286, 287, 290, 291, 292, 293, 294, 295, 296, 297, 298, 299, 300, 301, 303, 305, 306, 307, 308, 309
convenience versus security 204
convergence of communications 113
copyright 66, 69, 70, 71, 72, 73, 74, 75, 76, 77, 78, 79, 80, 81, 82, 83, 84
copyright issues 172, 179, 180, 187, 188, 191
copyright law 66, 69, 71, 72, 78, 79, 81, 83
copyright legislation 69, 72, 73, 77, 79
copyright material 66, 71, 72, 73, 76, 77, 78, 84
Council of Australian Governments (COAG) 140, 142, 143, 151
counter-litigation 179
Cricket Australia (CA) 70
critical infrastructures 214, 215, 216, 219, 221, 222, 226
critical infrastructure systems 214, 215, 216, 219, 220, 221, 222, 223, 228
customer relationship management (CRM) 264
cyberbullying 29, 36
cyber criminals 55
cyberspace 3, 19, 20, 22
cyberstalking 29

D

data acquisition 180
data collection 158
data management 196, 231
Dataveillance 171
decentralisation 201
decision tree 267, 270, 271, 272, 273
demilitarized zone (DMZ) 257, 258, 260, 264, 270, 271
developing countries 111, 112, 113, 116, 117, 118, 119, 120, 121, 124, 125, 128
digital bridge 117
digital certificates 99, 109
digital communications 66, 67, 81
digital communications marketplace 81
digital communications technologies 66, 67
Digital Divide 111, 112, 113, 114, 117, 118, 122, 123, 125, 126, 127, 128

digital era 231
Digital Health 128
digital libraries 179, 188
digital media 66, 71, 80, 82, 83
digital signatures 99, 109
disaster planning 233, 252
disaster recovery (DR) 231, 232, 233, 237, 245, 248, 250
disciplinary committee 174, 175, 177, 178, 179, 180, 182, 183, 188
distributive justice 28, 37, 40, 162, 168
domain name service (DNS) 238, 239, 240, 244, 248
dual firewall 260
dynamic host configuration protocol (DHCP) 239, 240

E

Early Warning Network (EWN) 139
economic well-being 216, 230
e-health 87, 88, 89, 90, 91, 92, 93, 94, 95, 96, 97, 98, 99, 100, 101, 102, 103, 104, 105, 106
e-health budgets 98
e-health systems 89, 90, 95, 96, 97, 98, 99, 101, 103, 104
Electronic Panopticism 171
electronic performance monitoring (EPM) 162
electronic systems 196
embezzlement 207
Emergency Management Australia (EMA) 130, 133, 135
emergency management (EM) 129, 130, 131, 132, 133, 134, 135, 136, 138, 141, 143, 148, 151
emergency management training 134
emergency service organization (ESO) 137, 142
employee morale 156, 160
environmental change 218
Environment, Communications and the Arts (ECA) 66, 67, 68, 69, 70, 72, 75, 76, 77, 78, 79, 80, 81, 82
equipment failure 231
ethical behaviour 199, 211
ethical code 196, 211

ethical considerations 129, 130, 143
ethical dilemma 225, 226
ethical framework 198, 204, 210, 211
ethical imperative 214
ethical issues 66, 78, 82, 172, 180, 181, 182, 189, 191
ethical vacuum 196
European University Information Systems (EU-NIS) 299, 307

F

Facebook 4, 13, 14, 16, 28, 30, 35, 41, 42, 44, 46, 47, 48, 49, 50, 51, 53, 54, 55, 56, 57, 58, 59, 60, 61, 62, 63, 64
Family Educational Rights and Privacy Act (FERPA) 278
fantasy communities 5
Firewall ACL Creation Tool (FACT) 267, 271, 272, 273
Firewall Audit Support Tool (FAST) 266, 267, 268, 269, 270, 273
firewall deployment 257
firewall devices 254, 262
firewall rule 255, 258, 259, 264, 266, 271, 273, 274, 276
firewall rulebase 254, 255, 258, 259, 261, 262, 263, 264, 265, 266, 267, 274, 276
firewall rulebase management 254, 255, 261, 263
firewalls 240, 244, 247, 248, 254, 255, 260, 261, 262, 265, 266, 267, 275
firewall technology 260, 275
Flicker 4
free information 201
front-end module 184, 190

G

global economy 235
global eco-systems 218
global orientation 240
governance, risk management, and compliance (GRC) 279, 305
graceful degradation 253
Gramm Leach Bliley Act (GLBA) 278
gross national income (GNI) 112

H

hacker community 200, 201
hacker ethics 201
hackers 175, 180, 183, 189
hazards 129, 130, 131, 133, 134, 135, 144, 154
health identifier (HI) 93, 106
health information 111, 112, 114, 116, 119, 120, 121, 122, 124, 125, 126
Health Insurance Portability and Accountability Act (HIPAA) 278
hierarchy of privacy 167
HIV 121, 123, 125
HIV/AIDS 121, 123, 125
hybrid ethical approach 196

I

ICT company 211
identification (ID) 100
inadequate design 231
Information Classification Matrix (ICM) 288, 290, 298, 299
information communication technology (ICT) 111, 117, 125, 126, 197, 198, 207, 208, 209, 211, 220
Information Security Management (ISM) 277, 278, 279, 280, 281, 282, 283, 284, 286, 287, 295, 297, 298, 299, 303, 304, 305, 309
information security management systems (ISMS) 277, 278
information security strategies 277, 278, 279, 280, 286, 294, 295, 301, 305
information technology (IT) 87, 88, 89, 92, 94, 95, 98-104, 107, 108, 175, 183, 221, 231, 232, 235, 237, 239, 240, 241, 243, 244, 247-251, 278-309
Information Technology Services Centre (ITSC) 187, 189
Infosec Assessment Methodology (IAM) 298, 299, 307
infringement 66, 69, 71, 73, 74, 75, 76, 77, 79, 81
inside jokes 30, 31, 34
instant messaging (IM) 4

Integrated Public Number Database (IPND) 130, 140, 141, 142, 151, 154
intellectual property 69, 70, 71, 73, 84
interactional justice 162
interest communities 5
Internet phones 4
Internet Relay Chat (IRC) 4
intranet 254, 257, 258
invisible supervisor 160
IP address 256, 258, 259, 260
IT department 175, 183
IT devices 88, 89, 99
IT Infrastructure Library (ITIL) 278, 308, 309
IT security structure 240
IT solutions 235
IT support staff 87, 92, 101, 102, 103, 104

K

Key Goal Indicators (KGIs) 294, 296, 301, 302, 303, 305, 306
Key Performance Indicators (KPIs) 291, 294, 296, 301, 302, 303, 305, 306

L

learning environments 29, 30
LinkedIn 28, 30, 33, 34, 48, 52
local area network (LAN) 238, 244, 247, 249, 253
location-based services (LBS) 135, 136, 137, 142, 143, 144, 145, 152, 154

M

maximum security effectiveness 254
Measure and Evaluate (ME) 290, 295, 301, 304
meritocratic advancement 201
messenger programs 4
mobile location information (MoLI) 142
mobile technology 117, 118, 123, 129, 130
modern computer network 254, 255
modern computer systems 196
modern day computer security 254
monitoring technologies 156, 157, 160, 161, 162, 163, 164, 166

moral luck 207
MySpace 28, 29, 30, 41, 43, 44, 48, 50, 60, 61, 62, 63

N

NASH system 100
National Authentication Service for Health (NASH) 99, 100, 101, 104, 109
national emergency warning system (NEWS) 130, 140, 141, 142
National Health System (NHS) 91, 106
National Rugby League (NRL) 75, 76
national security 129, 134, 141, 143, 144, 146, 147, 154
National Security Agency (NSA) 298, 299, 307
natural disasters 231
natural hospital environment (NHE) 89, 90, 91, 92, 94, 95, 96, 97, 98, 99, 100, 101, 102, 103, 104, 110
natural resources 218, 227
negligence 211
Nessus Attack Scripting Language (NASL) 273
network 233, 236, 237, 238, 239, 240, 242, 243, 245, 246, 247, 249, 253
network address translation (NAT) 260
network components 254
Network File System (NFS) 232, 239, 253
network firewall 254
networking 214, 221
network layer 255, 256
network time protocol (NTP) 239
network time server 239
network traffic 180, 183

O

Office of the Privacy Commissioner (OPC) 141
online resources 179, 189
online spaces 3
optimal rule ordering (ORO) 262
organisational productivity 156
originality report 186, 188
orphaned firewall rules 254, 261, 262, 263, 266

P

packet filtering firewalls 260, 261
patient care 87, 88, 89, 90, 92, 93, 94, 95, 96,
        97, 98, 99, 100, 101, 103, 104, 110
personal computers (PCs) 112, 234, 247
personal information 46, 50, 51, 53, 54, 55, 56,
        60, 63
personal privacy 157, 162
personal security 58
Pervasive Computing Environment 171
pervasive technologies 156
philosophy 37
phishing 54, 55, 60
physical layer 255
PKI implementations 100, 103
plagiarism 172, 173, 174, 175, 176, 177, 178,
        179, 180, 181, 182, 183, 184, 185, 186,
        187, 188, 189, 190, 191, 192, 193, 194,
        195,
plagiarism case 178, 179, 182, 183, 191, 192
PlayStation 5
policy maker 174, 175, 182
principle of least privilege 259
privacy and security (P&S) 88, 89, 90, 94, 97,
        98, 101, 102, 104
privacy concerns 156, 157, 159, 161, 167, 169
private communication 99, 109
procedural justice 162, 168
public health 226
public key infrastructure (PKI) 99, 100, 101,
        103, 104, 109
public relations 37

R

really simple syndication (RSS) 4
record and information management (RIM)
        233, 251
redundant array of inexpensive disks (RAID)
        234, 244, 253
relationship communities 5
rights theory 28, 37, 39
right to improve 206
rulebase 254, 255, 258, 259, 261, 262, 263,
        264, 265, 266, 267, 268, 269, 270, 272,
        273, 274, 276

rule review 264, 265

S

Sarbanes-Oxley (SOX) 278
SARs (Severe Acute Respiratory Syndrome)
        116, 146
screened subnet 257, 260
Second Life 4, 16
security attacks 231
security breaches 231
security concerns 200
security threats 254
server computer 238
Service Level Agreements (SLAs) 137
service oriented architecture approach (SOA)
        232
short message service (SMS) 118, 123, 137,
        138, 139, 147, 149, 151, 153, 154
single host computer 234
Skype 4
social computing 1
social cues 4, 5, 10
social interaction 46
social networking 27, 28, 29, 30, 31, 32, 33,
        34, 35, 36, 37, 39, 40, 41, 42, 43, 44, 46,
        49, 53, 55, 61, 62, 63, 254
social networking site (SNS) 27, 28, 29, 32,
        33, 35, 37, 40, 41, 42, 47, 48, 49, 50, 51,
        52, 53, 54, 55, 56, 57, 58, 60, 65, 67
social networks 3, 28, 30, 31, 32, 34, 37, 38,
        39, 41, 42, 43
social organizations 2
social vacuum 4
socioeconomic status 112
stakeholders 37, 39
standard emergency warning signal (SEWS)
        138
standardized mobile service area (SMSA) 142
stateful inspection firewalls 260
state of emergency 132, 134
student-oriented 175, 176, 177, 187
surveillance 156, 157, 158, 159, 160, 162, 163,
        164, 165, 166, 167, 168, 169, 171
Systems Security Engineering Capability Matu-
        rity Model (SSE-CMM) 277, 278, 280,
        281, 284, 285, 286, 294, 297, 298, 300,
        303, 304, 305, 308, 309

T

teacher-oriented 175, 176
text-based systems 4
text messages 154
transaction communities 5
transport layer 255, 256
triple-homed firewall deployment 257
Trojan Horse 65
Twitter 4

U

underserved populations 112, 123
unfair scoring 174
unique health identifier (UHI) 92, 99, 110
unlimited access 201
unmanned aerial vehicles (UAVs) 134
unregulated behaviour 158
utilitarianism 28, 37, 38, 40, 45, 208, 210, 212

V

veil of ignorance 38, 44
VeriGuide 172, 175, 183, 184, 185, 186, 187,
        188, 189, 190, 191, 193, 195
Victorian bushfires 129, 140, 152
Victorian Racing Club (VRC) 75
video conferencing 4
virtual communities 1, 2, 3, 4, 5, 6, 8, 9, 10,
        11, 12, 13, 14, 15, 16, 17, 18, 19, 20, 21,
        22, 23, 24, 26
virtualization 231, 232, 233, 234, 235, 236,
        237, 238, 242, 243, 245, 247, 248, 249,
        250, 251, 252
virtual machines 239, 242, 243, 251, 252, 253

virtual operating systems 235
virtual private networks (VPNs) 232, 245, 253
virtual spaces 3
virtue ethics 28, 37, 39

W

water supply infrastructure 214, 224, 225
Web 1.0 47, 65
Web 2.0 46, 47, 51, 62, 63, 64, 65, 115, 119,
        124, 125
well-educated speakers 36
wide area network (WAN) 233, 234, 237, 245,
        246, 247, 249, 253
Wii 5
wikis 4, 16
work environment 157, 160, 161, 166
workplace environment 156, 159, 163, 164,
        166
workplace surveillance 156, 157, 161, 162,
        163, 166, 171
World Health Organisation (WHO) 119, 120
world wide web (WWW) 238, 251

X

Xbox 5

Y

YouTube 4, 28

Z

zones of control 255